The Analysis of Communication Content

The Analysis of Communication Content

Developments in Scientific Theories and Computer Techniques

Edited by

GEORGE GERBNER
OLE R. HOLSTI
KLAUS KRIPPENDORFF
WILLIAM J. PAISLEY
PHILIP J. STONE

JOHN WILEY & SONS, INC. *New York · London · Sydney · Toronto*

Copyright © 1969 by John Wiley & Sons, Inc.

All Rights reserved. No part of this book may be reproduced by any means, nor transmitted, nor translated into a machine language without the written permission of the publisher.

Library of Congress Catalog Card Number: 74-78476

SBN 471 29660 0

Printed in the United States of America

Contributing Authors

F. EARLE BARCUS
School of Public Communications
Boston University

CASIMIR BORKOWSKI
Knowledge Availability Systems Center
University of Pittsburgh

BARRY S. BROOK
Music
Queens College
City University of New York

JAMES DEESE
Psychology
The Johns Hopkins University

PAUL EKMAN
School of Medicine
University of California

WALLACE V. FRIESEN
University of California

GEORGE GERBNER
The Annenberg School of Communications
University of Pennsylvania

DONALD H. GOLDHAMER
Social Psychology
University of Chicago

CALVIN S. HALL
Institute of Dream Research and
University of California
Santa Cruz

NORMAN I. HARWAY
  Medical Center
  University of Rochester
DAVID G. HAYS
  Linguistic Research
  The Rand Corporation
OLE R. HOLSTI
  Political Science
  University of British Columbia
HOWARD P. IKER
  Medical Center
  University of Rochester
KENNETH JANDA
  Political Science
  Northwestern University
KLAUS KRIPPENDORFF
  The Annenberg School of Communications
  University of Pennsylvania
JULIUS LAFFAL
  Psychology
  Connecticut Valley Hospital and Yale University
JOHN E. MUELLER
  Political Science
  University of Rochester
J. ZVI NAMENWIRTH
  Department of Sociology and Anthropology
  University of Connecticut
DANIEL M. OGILVIE
  Social Relations
  Harvard University
WILLIAM J. PAISLEY
  Institute for Communication Research
  Stanford University
GEORGE PSATHAS
  Sociology
  Boston University
JOSEPH RABEN
  English
  Queens College
  City University of New York

ANATOL RAPOPORT
  Mental Health Research Institute
  University of Michigan
KARLENE H. ROBERTS
  Graduate School of Business
  Stanford University
GERARD SALTON
  Computer Science
  Cornell University
SALLY YEATES SEDELOW
  English and Information Science
  University of North Carolina, Chapel Hill
WALTER A. SEDELOW, JR.
  Library Science, Sociology, and Information Science
  University of North Carolina, Chapel Hill
EDWIN S. SHNEIDMAN
  Center for Studies of Suicide Prevention
  National Institute of Mental Health
JOHN A. STARKWEATHER
  Medical Psychology
  University of California, San Francisco
PHILIP J. STONE
  Center for Advanced Study in the Behavioral Sciences
  Palo Alto, California and Department of Social Relations,
  Harvard University
THOMAS G. TAUSSIG
  University of California
EUGENE WEBB
  Graduate School of Business
  Stanford University

Preface

Content analysis of communications is a research activity and field of inquiry of general interest and wide applicability. It may be helpful in any search for fuller or more specialized types of significance than can be obtained by other methods alone.

This book is in four parts. They deal with (1) theories and concepts of analysis, (2) problems of inference from content data, (3) methods of recording and notation, and (4) computer techniques. They bring together for the first time a variety of approaches to the scientific analysis of many types and modes of communication which include the affective and persuasive as well as the informational, the pictorial and musical as well as the verbal, the unintentional as well as the consciously planned, the personally conveyed as well as the technologically mediated, and the individual or interpersonal as well as the collective and publicly shared. Their disciplinary sources, subject matter examples, and scope of practical interest include the arts and humanities, the social sciences, linguistics, and the information sciences.

The chapters have been written with two types of reader in mind: (1) researchers specializing in content analysis and (2) scholars in any field who wish to review the "state of the art" and assess its applicability to their special interests. To assist these scholars this preface includes a brief account of authors by field and indicates the main disciplines and subjects from which their contributions are drawn.

The other objectives of these preliminary comments are to place content analysis in perspective as a specialized research activity in the study of communications, to trace the development of this book, and to acknowledge the help and cooperation of many persons and institutions.

THE FIELD OF CONTENT ANALYSIS

The study of communication focuses on interaction through messages. Messages are the crucial links of the communication chain. They can span time and distance to connect communicating parties in patterns that record and evoke significance.

But not all significance can be evoked by inspection nor is all significance accessible to casual observation. The purpose of any analysis is to illuminate or to make possible inferences about something that is not otherwise apparent. In the analysis of messages this particular "something" is a type of significance or "content" that becomes available to an analyst who uses particular methods for specific purposes.

Man's search for hidden or subtle significance in the symbolic context that shapes his own consciousness is probably as ancient as human consciousness itself. Religious, academic, political, and other professional specialization in that search is a time-honored practice in such diverse fields as philosophy, rhetoric, criticism, cryptography, the inquisitorial and other censorious pursuit of heretical or rebellious tendencies, and the analysis of dreams, symbols, myths, and word associations. With the rise of new communications media and mass publics, the search for significance beyond that "meeting the eye" was extended to technologically based and mass-produced message systems which now permeate so much of our imagery and imagination.

The analysis of message content, therefore, is not only a task of specialists working under the label of communication research, although theirs may be the main responsibility for theoretical and methodological development. The activity itself is relevant to all those concerned with symbolic output in art, music, literature, history, psychiatry, psychology, sociology, anthropology, and the mass media.

The framers of modern constitutions and the rulers of modern states revealed keen awareness of the strategic importance of communication channels, structures, and controls. Political scientists and communication researchers, concerned with the allocation of attention and power, pioneered in the development of theories of public information and political symbolism. Other social scientists developed theories of intrapersonal, interpersonal, and intergroup communication which also required the analysis of message content.

The "art" and the "science" of such analysis are ably described in Klaus Krippendorff's "Introduction to Part I" of this volume. I point out here that the more systematic and objective approaches do not replace the need for intuition, judgment, and insight. Conjecture gives direction to research, and interpretation gives bite to its findings. Scientific procedures can be used to test alternative contentions and to explicate their forms to permit automatic processing by computer. Reliable and valid analytical procedures are needed to make it possible to base ultimate interpretation and judgment on significance that is representative of the phenomena under investigation, generalizable within specified limits and under specified conditions, and explicitly relevant to purposes, proposals, or theories to be developed or tested. The traditional reliance on intuition and personal judgment alone could not satisfy these criteria.

The need for systematic and objective determination of various types of communication significance led to the rise of content analysis as a distinct field of communication research. The first major summary of research in the field (Berelson, 1952) revealed that despite widespread activity no major theoretical orientations had emerged. Methodological developments, although becoming more sophisticated, were also limited by the lack of technical ability to handle large amounts of data of great complexity. It was under these circumstances that the Committee on Linguistics and Psychology of the Social Science Research Council called the first conference on content analysis in 1955 at Allerton House, University of Illinois.

THE ALLERTON HOUSE CONFERENCE

The Allerton House conference resulted in the publication of *Trends in Content Analysis* (Pool, 1959). The conference converged on problems of inference from verbal material to its antecedent conditions, on internal contingencies between symbols, and on the need for developing analytical methods relevant to both "representational" and "instrumental" (e.g. intentionally or unintentionally manipulative) communications. The conference report also noted the historical differences between the approaches of linguists and content analysts and concluded that "the fruitful interchange between content analysis and linguistics is only beginning" (Pool, 1959:233).

Within ten years after the Allerton House conference a series of major developments appeared to have created conditions favorable to rapid progress. Research in linguistics, in the relation of language and thought, and on models of the cognitive process produced new theories relevant to content analysis. Cybernetic logic and computer-based techniques made possible the processing of huge quantities of complex data, provided new means for transforming information in a preprogrammed manner, and required clarification and rigorous explication of previously intuitive analytical procedures. Barcus (1959) completed a comprehensive survey of the field. A handbook of new techniques (North et al., 1963) related content analysis to the study of international crises. Stone and his associates (1966) published a review of research strategies and developed the first general set of computer programs for automatic content analysis. Krippendorff (1967) coupled a critical examination of analytical theories with a proposal for a general framework and an information calculus for message analysis. Ole R. Holsti (1968) provided a new survey of content analysis studies. All of these activities revealed burgeoning research in many fields and significant—though often unrelated—theoretical and methodological advances. The time seemed ripe for consolidation and reassessment.

THE ANNENBERG SCHOOL CONFERENCE

The editors of the present volume met at The Annenberg School of Communications, University of Pennsylvania, Philadelphia, in the spring of 1966. Others who participated in this initial session and gave valuable assistance throughout were Lee Benson, History, and Henry Teune, Political Science, of the University of Pennsylvania, F. Earle Barcus, Communication, Boston University, Richard Fagen, Political Science, Stanford University, and Edwin B. Parker, Communication, Stanford University. It was decided to enlist the collaboration of scholars whose current work would be most relevant to a review and assessment and to commission studies reflecting recent progress and pointing to next steps. The planning group undertook to solicit contributions from a wide range of disciplines in the humanities and social sciences and to place them in a framework of theoretical relevance to the main tasks of content analysis. The major goals set by the planning session were the following:

1. To bring together recent diverse theoretical and methodological contributions.
2. To bridge the gap between theories and new technologies.
3. To share outstanding work among scholars and students—potential users of content analysis—from many disciplines.
4. To elicit additional contributions by an exchange of ideas and a review of the work of the principal contributors.

The planning group felt that these objectives, and particularly the goals of discussion and review, could best be reached by calling a general conference of interested scholars and inviting, for the first time, wide participation from many fields. At this point the encouragement and support of three organizations (as well as, of course, the host institution) became instrumental to further progress. The International Business Machines Corporation gave generous help both in staff assistance and the funding of commissioned papers. The grant support of the American Council of

Learned Societies and the National Science Foundation assured the financing of the conference. The call was issued in the spring of 1967 to a national conference on content analysis which proposed to

assemble leading theorists, researchers, and active or potential users of advanced theory and technique. Principals and participants will come from the arts and humanities, the biological and social sciences, linguistics, mathematics and other information and computer-oriented sciences. They will review recent progress, explore applications to a variety of research problems, and point to next steps in the scientific study of message content.

The conference took place at The Annenberg School of Communications on November 16–18, 1967. It attracted more than 400 scholars from about 85 educational and scientific institutions in the United States and Canada. The commissioned papers were read and discussed in panels that focused attention on the issues reflected in the organization of this book. After the conference the contributions were revised in light of the discussions. The editors also undertook to include in the book pertinent portions of the conference discussions, to elicit additional contributions intended to fill some of the gaps, and to write introductions to their respective parts. The general editing took place in the summer of 1968. The result is not a record of "proceedings" but instead the outcome of a three-year effort to summarize major recent developments in content analysis and to strengthen the foundation for future progress.

APPROACHES AND APPLICATIONS

The contributions came from several disciplines and represent many approaches and applications. As already mentioned, the book is not organized along disciplinary lines or by fields of application. The editors felt that their primary task was to focus on issues and developments of critical relevance to further progress in the field of content analysis itself. The papers (which now constitute chapters in this book) were commissioned, edited, and grouped with that end in mind. The introductions to each part indicate the relevance of the contributions to issues in the development of content analysis. Nevertheless, these chapters contain much material relevant to other interests of users and potential users of content analysis techniques. The following is a brief account of each part, which notes the authors' field of specialization and the disciplinary or subject-matter applicability of their contributions.

Part I centers on theories and analytical constructs. Its editor, *Klaus Krippendorff,* a specialist in communication theory, introduces the reader to the tasks of the analyst and develops the view that "content" is largely defined by analytical situations and purposes. Krippendorff's definition of content analysis is "the use of replicable and valid methods for making specific inferences from text to other states or properties of its source." Notice that the term "text" is used in its most general meaning to stand for texture or pattern in any communicative mode and the term "source" is also generalized to denote any system to which inferences may be made from "text." *Anatol Rapoport,* mathematician, philosopher, and system theorist, develops the notion that dynamic properties of large corpuses of verbal output may be studied statistically as if they had a "life of their own." *James Deese,* psychologist, discusses cognitive principles of semantic organization. *David G. Hays,* linguist, describes characteristics of knowledge as the linguistic foundations for a theory of content analysis. In his own chapter Klaus Krippendorff contends that three basic formal models of the relation between text and content account for most efforts to analyze messages.

Part II deals with the problem of inference from content data. Its editor, political scientist *Ole R. Holsti,* traces in his introduction the continuities and shifts of interest in various aspects of inference from the 1955 Allerton House conference to the 1967 Annenberg School conference. Holsti also provides cogent introductions to the issues of quantification, norms, standard categories, the role of computers, and their relevance to inference in content analysis. *William J. Paisley,* communication researcher and coeditor, discusses the analysis of style as "deviation from encoding norms," with reference to literary, political, and other types of discourse. *George Gerbner,* communication researcher and coeditor, suggests standard category classes based on a theory of inference from mass-mediated public message systems. *Calvin S. Hall,* psychologist, reports on the formulation of categories, units, and norms used in the analysis of dream protocols. *Julius Laffal,* psychologist, describes a conceptual dictionary developed for the automatic analysis of the language content of individual speakers. *Joseph Raben,* professor of English, challenges the ingenuity of analysts to trace the history of literary affinities and affiliations submerged in vast quantities of poetic and prose context. *John E. Mueller,* political scientist, reviews problems and achievements in analyzing diplomatic documents in international relations. *Philip J. Stone,* social researcher specializing in computer analysis, and coeditor of this book, reports on attempts to develop "disambiguation rules" for computer identification of different senses of high-frequency English words. *J. Zvi Namenwirth,* sociologist, demonstrates how inferences from a trend analysis of a particular value concept in American political party platforms might contribute to a theory of social dynamics. *Daniel M. Ogilvie,* social psychologist, reviews research (based on case studies and folktales) that traces a type of fantasy theme called "ascensionism" or "Icarus complex." *Edwin Shneidman,* clinical psychologist and chief of the Center for Studies of Suicide Prevention, National Institute of Mental Health, suggests a method for analyzing certain aspects of the "logics" of individual "cognitive styles" and applies it to a suicide note, a political discourse, and psychological test protocols.

In Part III the focus shifts to ways of recording and notation of "text" in different modes—nonverbal as well as verbal. Editor William J. Paisley introduces the reader to problems inherent in the extension of methods founded on verbal analysis into the domains of musical, vocal, and visual content. *Barry S. Brook,* musicologist, presents a code for the computer analysis of musical style. *Paul Ekman,* social psychologist, and his associates describe a unique technique for the automated analysis of pictorial records, with applications to the study of behavior in psychiatry, anthropology, programmed instruction, and other fields. *John A. Starkweather,* medical psychologist, discusses methods for the measurement and analysis of nonlinguistic vocal qualities in human speech. *Eugene Webb,* social psychologist, and *Karlene H. Roberts,* industrial psychologist, examine some unconventional uses of content analysis and illustrate one of them with lovesong lyrics of the American musical stage.

Part IV directs attention to computer techniques. Editor Philip J. Stone introduces this part with a brief account of the interactions of The Annenberg School conference and closes it with a condensed record of one of the conference's lively sessions. John A. Starkweather's "overview" sorts out the different computer-aided approaches to content recognition represented in this volume as well as in the literature. *Donald H. Goldhamer,* social psychologist, describes the General Inquirer computer program (developed by Stone and his associates) and draws on recent linguistic theory for guidance in overcoming some problems in computer "reading" of text. Ole R. Holsti describes a computer-based analogue of "evaluative assertion analysis" for studying attitudes and beliefs of political elites, particularly in foreign-policy decision making. *Howard P. Iker* and *Norman I. Harway,* psychologists, report research on a computer program designed to reveal word clusters and changing associations in verbal data (such a therapeutic interviews) without having to provide a priori categories. *Kenneth Janda,* political scientist, describes a microfilm and computer system used in a comparative study of political parties around the world. *George Psathas,* sociologist, presents a program for the analysis of two-person verbal interactions. *Gerard Salton,* information scientist, relates content analysis to information retrieval. *Sally Y. Sedelow,* professor of English and information science, and *Walter A. Sedelow, Jr.,* historian and information scientist, report their work on the computer analysis of literary themes and styles. John A. Starkweather contributes a program for conversation with the computer, applicable to instruction, interviewing, diagnosis, or therapy. *Casimir Borkowski,* linguist and information scientist, presents a technique for the automatic assignment of certain expressions to specified "sublanguages" for the analysis and retrieval of specialized types of information.

Wide as it is, the spectrum of approaches and applications reflected in this book by no means exhausts the fields and workers active in content analysis, the issues that need special attention, or the sources of further development. One key problem is specialized education in content analysis. *F. Earle Barcus,* communication researcher, conducted a survey on this subject. The findings are summarized in the Appendix.

OTHER CONTRIBUTIONS

I am grateful not only to fellow editors, contributors, and colleagues, whose names have been mentioned above, but to an even larger number of persons whose assistance and cooperation have been instrumental to the conference and the publication of this volume. Lee Benson and Philip and Betty Jacob of the University of Pennsylvania provided stimulation and encouragement. Edmund A. Bowles, IBM's emissary to the humanities, Thomas J. Condon of the American Council of Learned Societies, and Charles R. Wright of the National Science Foundation believed this project worthy not only of financial support but also of their personal participation. Bernard Wishy gave effective collaboration in preparing for the conference and Philip Schuman helped in its coordination. Initiative and assistance beyond the call of duty were provided, in various staff capacities, by Mrs. Kiki Faye, Barry Hampe, Mrs. Sultana Krippendorf, John Massi, Mrs. Eleanor Moloney, Miss Judith Sorrentino, Miss Amy Stanley, James R. Taylor, Albert S. Tedesco, and Mrs. Joyce Wattenberger. John A. Sullivan, as Wiley representative at The Annenberg School conference, expressed his interest by personal involvement as well as publishing advice, and Mr. Malcolm Easterlin served as Wiley editor with patient and cheerful competence.

At the conclusion of The Annenberg School conference Klaus Krippendorff intended a compliment when he thanked me for "arranging things so well and leaving the thinking to us." This, then, puts both credit and blame where they belong in this truly collective endeavor.

Ardmore, Pennsylvania   *George Gerbner*
July, 1969

Contents

The Analysis of Communication Content

1 Theories and Analytical Constructs

Klaus Krippendorff, Editor

INTRODUCTION TO PART I

KLAUS KRIPPENDORFF

The Annenberg School of Communications
University of Pennsylvania

There is no doubt that a large part of human behavior is symbolic. To organize his natural and social environment, man has relied on messages, and the body of these messages has never been in full accordance with the ideal of objective representation. Symbolic configurations of higher forms of organization not only control and structure individual behavior but also may have a life of their own. The study of how such symbols are exchanged in complex webs of social interactions and of how messages are transmitted in self-modifying networks of communication is expected to yield significant insights into human social behavior on all levels of inquiry. Content analysis is involved in inquiries of this kind.

The body of literature on content analysis has been growing steadily since the beginning of this century. Berelson and Lazarsfeld (1948) and Barcus (1959) have shown its exponential growth, a growth that is characteristic of most institutions that use information accumulatively. On the surface, these quantitative developments seem to indicate a healthy state of affairs. But works of a methodological or theoretical nature, papers that attempt to elaborate critical issues, or proposals that give direction to this kind of inquiry are distressingly hard to find.

What accounts for this disparity in content analysis literature is not so obvious. Perhaps it is the result of the inherent complexity of the subject matter, or it could originate from the absence of abstract theoretical concerns. But in view of the increasing investment being made in the design of computer techniques for analysis, theoretical frameworks that lend themselves to algorithmic representations and solutions to methodological problems become the critical prerequisites for further progress. The contributions to this section of the book should be read with future developments in mind.

In this introduction, I must clarify a few issues that may facilitate an understanding of the process of analyzing message content. These issues, in part, have emerged from discussions during the Annenberg conference. The chapters in this section discuss theoretical frameworks and constructs for content analysis taking the approach of general systems theory, linguistics, psychology, and communication theory, respectively.

WHAT CONTENT ANALYSIS IS NOT

The one issue that permeated most of the discussion was the nature of content: how it can be conceptualized, and why it poses unique analytical problems. The fact that no consensus could be reached is not surprising. I think, however, that there was considerable agreement on what content analysis is not.

Let me describe a highly simplified communication situation and try to phrase the arguments in its terms. It may be said that a source *encodes* some *content* into a transmittable linguistic form—a signal—which is *decoded* in turn by a receiver. The decoding process then results in some symbol that resembles or *represents* the content that the source intended to convey. This situation is depicted in Figure 1. Now, it is tempting to suggest that the scientific analyst of message content *is* such a receiver whose job is simply to reverse the encoding process and use rigorous quantitative techniques in order to get at the initial event of the sequence of transformations. However, such a conception of the content analyst's task is too restrictive in the following respects.

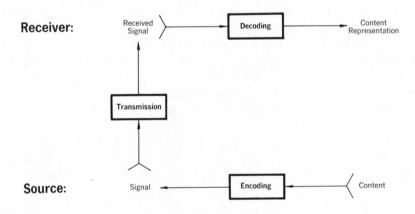

Figure 1 Simplified communication situation.

A. Content analysis is not limited to the analysis of verbal data. Although newspapers, political speeches, and letters have been a major preoccupation until rather recently, painting, facial expressions, intonations in speech, music, and other nonlinguistic forms of communication can be subjected to the same kind of analysis. This is being done even though "content" is not always conventionally attributed to these forms.

B. Content analysts are rarely interested in what messages are *intended* to mean. Hidden attitudes, the identity of authors, statistical trends of symbolic forms, and the like have fascinated a number of analysts while conscious intentions appear merely as a more specialized target of inquiry.

C. The referents of "source" may range from individual authors to a whole culture and from small institutions (for example, a television station) to complex organizational forms on a national or international may have to include inter-individual structures and, as far as the complexity level. Thus, *encoding* cannot refer to intra-individual processes alone. It of the process is concerned, it may well exceed the conceptual capacities of analytically unequipped human analysts.

D. Although content analysis often involves counting and sometimes casts results in tabular forms, quantitative procedures neither guarantee objectivity nor are they necessarily *appropriate* in all situations. In fact, qualitative procedures can be equally rigorous, and computer processing of natural language data often requires essentially nonstatistical analytical procedures.

E. Since messages can be viewed from an indefinitely large number of legitimate perspectives, unqualified references to *THE content* of documents or, simply, of text as the object of content analysis are unacceptable. Content evolves in the process of analyzing messages in a particular *situation* and for a particular investigative *purpose* from which it cannot easily be separated.

Unfortunately, there is no generally accepted agreement on a positive notion of "content." The above negations neither define the term nor do they delineate the scope of content analysis. They do suggest, however, that some of the traditional ways of conceptualizing "content" have been too narrow to account for the content analysts' aims and do not lend themselves to methodologically acceptable frameworks for the semantic analysis of text.

THE ART AND THE SCIENCE OF ANALYZING MESSAGES

A second issue that came into focus during the conference was the status of fully explicated analytical procedures. In this regard it is perhaps instructive to recall Irving Janis' excellent description of what content analysis meant twenty-five years ago. According to him, the term referred

> . . . to any technique (a) for the *classification* of the *sign-vehicles* (b) which relies solely upon the judgments (which, theoretically, may range from perceptual discrimination to sheer guesses) of an analyst or group of analysts as to which sign-vehicles fall into which category, (c) on the basis of *explicitly formulated rules,* (d) provided that the analyst's judgments are regarded as the reports of a *scientific* observer (Janis, 1965: 55).

It is important to notice that this definition required that the judges' intuitions be constrained by explicit coding instructions, while the critical process of semantic interpretation was left entirely implicit. The judges could rely freely, for instance, on their familiarity with the language, their expertise in the subject matter, and their ability to gain interesting insights. Traditional content analysis may be said to have presented a technique for reliably *intuiting content* rather than analyzing it. However, when modern content analysts take the word "analysis" in its literal sense and use, for example, computers for compatible interpretation of text, no part of the procedure can be delegated to the inexplicable process of intuition. The verbal definitions of categories that were sufficient for human judges have to be operationalized in detail, translated into the terms of an algorithmic language, and thoroughly tested. The explication of intuitively obvious semantic interpretations and judgments constitutes the most formidable obstacle in computer applications. Naturally, the latter are appealing because of their efficiency and unambiguous results. Although the computerization of content analysis by no means can be considered a final goal, the explication of analytical procedures is a fundamental prerequisite of science.

There can be no doubt that much of our current concern with messages cannot fully eliminate the judgments of qualified analysts. But to use human judges exclusively in the way traditional content analysis has done is nothing but a way of evading the problem of explicating precisely those processes on which the very conclusiveness of the technique depends. For it is actually only the explicit component of an analysis that can be subjected to methodological examination. Inquiries into its intuitive component, no matter how important, belong to a different domain. The use of computer technology has made modern content analysts painfully aware of the difference between controlled conjectures and explicit analytical techniques.

In the discussion, Anatol Rapoport addressed himself to this point, suggesting a distinction between the art and the science of analyzing messages:

I look upon content analysis as a sort of diagnostic technique. Just as medical diagnosis is partly an art and partly a science and is most effective when the art and the science are combined, so I look upon content analysis as a combination of an art and a science.

Dr. Hays, yesterday, said in his opening remarks that "the best content analyst is a good conversationalist. . . . content analysis is an essential part of good conversation." I agree with that from the art point of view. That is, the good conversatialist understands what you say and also what you don't say. He can ferret out the very kernel of your meaning and can make you understand his. As a good conversationalist he practices an art.

But there is also a science of content analysis. This science is practiced, for example, by programming a computer for analytical purposes. Just as you see through the microscope that which you would not see with the naked eye, so can the computer process data and call attention to certain properties that would not have been discoverable otherwise.

What to pay attention to, what to conjecture about and how to process the data is a matter of art. What to conclude is not a matter of art because there are very definite procedures for deciding when a conclusion is probably justified and when it is not. For many content analysts, particularly in the psychoanalytic domain, the singling out of a stimulating conjecture is often sufficient to spin a theory. I think that challenging conjectures are extremely valuable but they should not be treated as if they were conclusions. They have to be put to the test. Such tests involve rigorous examination of the analytical procedures and are always designed to disconfirm the conjectures. Only when the conjectures pass these hard tests can they acquire the status of respectable evidence.

THE MESSAGE ANALYTIC SITUATION

In my own work on the methodology of content analysis (Krippendorff, 1967) I have found it convenient to define "content," if at all, only in reference to the situation in which messages are analyzed. Let me give a general description of what I consider a typical message analytic situation.

1a. In the environment of an analyst there always exists *a real system* which is singled out for attention. This real system may be called the source. No matter how the analyst chooses to delineate the boundaries of a source, he is usually confronted with many interacting components among which information is exchanged. There is no logical limit to the kind of source[1] that an analyst may be confronted with: for example, international systems, political organizations, mass media institutions, con-

---

[1] Notice that I use "source" to denote any system that is identifiable by its variables and of which some information about its structure is available to the analyst. A source in this sense includes the case in which two human communicators or social organizations interact through the exchange of signals or messages. Such situations are often described in terms of "source" or "sender," "transmitter" and "receiver." Thus, the term "source" has a generic meaning and is not limited to single communications agents that are identified by their signal sending activity. It is entirely general.

versational exchanges within small groups, systems of linguistic references, and cognitive interactions. These sources may thus be composed of neurons, physical objects, linguistic items, human individuals, social groups, or nations.

1b. The source is only *partly observable* to the analyst. Large segments of it remain, to a significant degree, inaccessible to direct observation: diplomatic documents represent only a small aspect of international behavior; the mass media make available only the "front" of a vast entertainment industry; psychotherapeutic interviews tap only a small fraction of a patient's personal history; and markings on stone often are the only remains of an extinct but once complex civilization. This partial observability is not just a problem of sampling. What is exhibited to the analyst is itself a property of the source.

1c. Transmission of data from the source to the analyst is *one-way* only, that is, the analyst cannot manipulate the source and is restricted to study it *unobtrusively.* The war-time propaganda analyst can neither request information from an enemy country nor is the monitored domestic propaganda typically directed toward him. The analyst of historical documents can neither check on the situation therein described, nor can the deceased author be aware of or able to react to how he is being studied through the medium of his writings. Even the recorded responses to interview questions become similarly detached from and independent of the interaction situation in which they were generated. The analyst's results have no effect on the behavior of the source.

2a. The analyst's efforts are motivated by his interest in acquiring *knowledge* of some properties of the source, knowledge of some states or events that are not *directly accessible* to him: the work of historians being most obviously concerned with this indirect kind of knowledge. But, similarly, political analysts may be interested in knowing about the cultural revolution in China without participating in it; students of the mass media may wish to quantitatively assess hidden gatekeeping mechanisms; or psychologists may be concerned with certain latent attitudes or the psychopathologies of presidential candidates without having the opportunity of a direct confrontation.

2b. The analytical problem is to inferentially link available observations, the raw data, or, in short, text,[2] to specific events, behavior, or

---

[2] In the restricted sense, "text" refers to linguistic expressions in written form. The data of content analysis are not limited by this understanding of the term; but they always exhibit some organization, pattern, or some "texture" on which semantic interpretations depend critically. I, therefore, propose a more general notion of "text." Accordingly, the term may refer to a variety of data the "texture" of which becomes apparent through its identifiable and distinguishable constituents.

phenomena associated with the source. Just as the reader of a letter may wish to understand what it is about, so does the analyst attempt to regard text as *messages about specific states* or properties of its source: stories obtained during a Thematic Apperception Test may be utilized to infer a subject's motivation, personality, and cognitive structure; domestic propaganda may constitute the basis for inferring whether a secret weapon exists; public speeches honoring a head of state may be processed to reveal the power structure within a governing elite; and stylistic features in literary works may provide the clues to the authorship of unsigned documents.

3. A scientist must account for procedures of data transformation so that their reliability and validity can be examined independently of their particular results. Unlike intuitive interpretations of text, scientific analyses of message content thus require that the analytical procedures be explicit, performed on unambiguous notations, or cast in the terms of a formalized language. This requirement has two technical corollaries, indicated below.

3a. Prior to explicit analysis, available raw text must be formalized, that is, it must be translated into unambiguous analytical terms on which conclusions may ultimately rest. Processes of formalizing text are variously referred to as data making, coding, or *recording.* Traditional content analyses have preferred semantical and attitudinal categories or category schemes as a way of formalizing verbal data. Some recent computer programs, such as the General Inquirer (Stone et al, 1966), represent input text as a finite string of selected word stems, but more elaborate descriptive devices for text are not uncommon.

3b. Since the intended inferences are made to unobserved states or properties of a source not manifest in the recorded text, a formalized language or some appropriate notations must be available to the analyst. This notational system must be able to represent the source either in whole or as far as the analyst's inferential interest is concerned. Within such *notational constructs* for a source, recorded text may become explicitly meaningful to a scientist: psychodiagnosis presupposes a technical jargon by which psychopathologies are defined unambiguously; anthropologists who regard the remains of an ancient culture as messages about its social structure need an adequate language in which the "content" of these messages may be formulated; and political analysts of diplomatic documents may have to employ elaborate system constructs within which intentions, consequences, change of power structure, and the like find adequate representation. The analyst's notational constructs may involve nothing more complex than a relation between a set of indices and a set of names, as is the case in problems of authorship identification; or, they may require a complex syntax to describe the possible events within an international system.

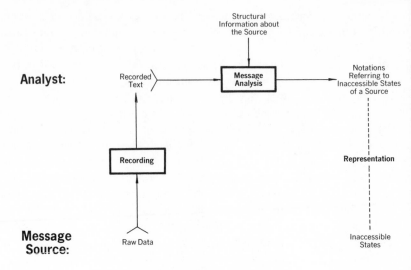

Figure 2   Message analytic situation.

A graphic presentation of the described message analytic situation appears in Figure 2.

The above framework has several important implications. First, it suggests a distinction between direct observations and indirect evidence. If messages are regarded as *informative about* something, then their "content" may profitably be considered as constituting *indirect evidence.* Content, then, cannot be analyzed in the same way that direct observations are analyzed, but it may be *inferred* by more or less rigorous procedures. Second, messages do not exist in isolation. However, they may become informative to *some analyst* to whom they convey information about states or properties of a clearly designated source. Rather than introducing an element of subjectivity into an analysis it suggests realistic references for analytical results. Third, as Anatol Rapoport pointed out, the manner in which a source is delineated, which aspect of text is recorded, and how it is processed are matters of art. However, the conclusiveness of the inferential process and the factuality of the inferred content belong to the domain of a science of content analysis. The latter presupposes explicit notational constructs of the source. Fourth, just as any observation can potentially assume message characteristics for the receiver to whom it becomes informative, so may formalized data be processed in such a way that valid information about unobserved components of a source is gained, regardless of whether data were generated for this purpose. The framework is thus sufficiently general to account for a large variety of situations in which some kind of content inferences are made by scientific analysts.

In view of this discussion I propose a differentiation between traditional content analysis and a more general notion of analyzing messages. In traditional content analysis the processes of interpreting text semantically are incorporated in human judges who systematically intuit the content of messages. Explicit techniques are merely used as aids to identify, to sort, or to count the constituent units of text, or the judges' semantic responses to them. In scientific approaches to content analysis, emphasis is placed on explicit techniques for regarding a text as being informative about some specific aspects of its source. *Content analysis* may therefore be redefined as *the use of replicable and valid methods for making specific inferences from text to other states or properties of its source.*[3]

It is the structure of a source, not the analyst, that should provide the objective references for content analytic methods. On the other hand, it is the analyst, not the source, who should impose his purpose on how a source is delineated and how messages are analyzed.

ANALYTICAL CONSTRUCTS

Much effort in the social sciences is devoted to testing hypotheses about discernable patterns in data. Confirmed hypotheses may inductively lead

---

[3] This definition deviates in several respects from previous definitions of content analysis of which the one attributed to Berelson is by far the most popular: "Content analysis is a research technique for the objective, systematic, and quantitative description of the manifest content of communications" (Berelson and Lazarsfeld, 1948:5). By leaving the crucial term "content" undefined, the definition fails to delineate the empirical domain of the technique. References to "objectivity," "system," and "quantification" merely stipulate that the technique conform to scientific standards and be valid.

Among the most recent definitions is the one proposed by Ole Holsti and Philip (Stone et al., 1966:5). Here content analysis becomes a technique that facilitates rather than accounts for the making of inferences from text. According to Stone, it is that part of a scientific inquiry in which the constitutent elements of texts are identified and measured. While providing the *raison d'être,* subsequent inferences are extraneous to the content analysis process (1966:16).

In the above the necessity of explicating the inferences from text to its possible "contents," which probably offers the most crucial distinction between treating data as observations, and treating data as messages about particular unobserved phenomena, is not recognized. In contrast to this, the significance of content inferences has been emphasized by Alexander George (1959a), Charles Osgood (1959a:36), George Gerbner (1958a:86), and Klaus Krippendorff (1967) and was a prime focus of the Philadelphia conference.

to theories which, in turn, may be used deductively to generate further hypotheses that can again be tested in the presence of data. These processes of inquiry are relatively well understood.

In content analysis, however, hypothetico-deductive theories play another role as well. They are crucial in *justifying* particular content inferences from text. That does not mean that content analysis does not intend to lend evidential support to theories in the social sciences but, instead, that content analysis is, to a significant degree, a consumer of established theories of symbolic behavior.

The crucial role of theories in content analysis may best be understood by differentiating between two types of justification that Feigl (1952) termed validation and vindication. In this context, *validation* is a mode of justification according to which the acceptability of a particular analytical procedure is established by showing it to be derivable from general principles or theories that are accepted quite independent of the procedure to be justified. On the other hand, *vindication* may render an analytical method acceptable on the grounds that it leads to accurate predictions (to a degree better than chance) regardless of the details of that method. The rules of induction and deduction are essential to validation while the relation between means and particular ends provide the basis for vindication.

In traditional content analysis, the research designer is often unaware of how much knowledge about a source actually goes into the search for productive categories. It is again the use of computers that forced the analyst not only to become extremely explicit in his design of the inferential procedures but also to find adequate justifications for the analytical constructs employed in it.

For example, the General Inquirer accepts text as input and produces— the intermediate steps ignored—statistical indices of some sort that can be interpreted, for instance, as indicative of the author's intention to commit suicide (Stone and Hunt, 1963). The relative success of these inferences vindicate the analytical procedure. However, it is also possible to validate the procedure in whole or in parts thereof. Its tagging procedure, for example, maps word-stems into a small number of tags that have analytical significance and lend themselves to statistical characterizations. This procedure can be considered as the operationalization of a kind of semantic theory that could either be put to test in experimental situations involving human subjects or, more efficiently, be deduced from a more general theory if it were available.

Unfortunately, established theories of symbolic behavior that are general enough to validate specific analytical constructs for content inference are rare. And much of content analysis is either justified on entirely intuitive grounds or by vindicative arguments. This state of affairs was observed long ago by Harold Lasswell who observed that:

. . . there is as yet no good theory of symbolic communication by which to predict how given values, attitudes, or ideologies will be expressed in manifest symbols. The extant theories tend to deal with values, attitudes, and ideologies as the ultimate units, not with the symbolic atoms of which they are composed. There is almost no theory of language which predicts the specific words one will emit in the course of expressing the content of this thought. Theories in philosophy or in the sociology of knowledge sometimes enable us to predict ideas that will be expressed by persons with certain other ideas or social characteristics. But little thought has been given to predicting the specific words in which these ideas will be cloaked. The content analyst, therefore, does not know what to expect (Lasswell, 1952: 49).

In effect, this state of knowledge still exists as far as the availability of suitable theories is concerned. Several disciplines, however, have attended to some of these questions. Each has followed its own approach, according to objectives that are not always comparable and with varying degrees of success. It seems that more is known about the formal structures of theories of symbolic behavior than about their actual content. The four contributions to this section of the book make suggestions that lend themselves to concrete content analytical constructs or examine their possible analytical power.

In Chapter 1, Anatol Rapoport discusses how a large body of verbal data might be described as a system and what this may offer to content analysis. In essence, general systems theory is a mathematical approach to complex behavior with particular emphasis on interactions among entities. Some of the crucial questions raised are: (1) whether a verbal corpus can, in fact, be described as a system; (2) on what entities such a system will have to be constructed; (3) what it means to say that a corpus "behaves," "evolves," etc.; and (4) how laws of interaction can be conceptualized in such situations. If these questions can be answered in favor of systems theory, then a large array of mathematical techniques promptly become available to content analysts, which in turn promise to facilitate the construction of powerful analytical tools.

Chapter 2 takes an entirely different view. Traditional content analysis, it will be recalled, gave primacy to a category representation of semantic units in text. Recent advances in psycholinguistics seem to indicate that this is only one of many common forms. This is the context in which James Deese's article should be understood. It presents an inquiry into that cognitive apparatus of the speaker of a language which may account for the semantic relations between words and objects or between linguistic and nonlinguistic events. To facilitate the design of computer software,

Deese characterizes these semantic relations as mappings of concepts representing segments of a language (including words) into cognitive structures. His chapter suggests and describes a number of basic types of semantic interpretations which the designer of general content analysis procedures may wish to operationalize. A clarification of and formal distinction between types of semantic structures not only orients further empirical research but it may also facilitate the translation of knowledge in the social sciences (particularly psycholinguistics) into valid analytical constructs. For the content analyst, I see the possible transfer of validity as the most important contribution of this line of research.

Proposals for the study of relations between linguistic expressions and real world phenomena or imaginary objects have not found fertile ground in modern linguistics where advances are made mainly in the area of grammar. David Hays' article (Chapter 3) disregards this diciplinary confinement and offers an outline of what a theory may have to look like that would link natural language utterances to properties of its source. With interest in the analysis of political documents and intellectual roots in both sociology and linguistics, Hays discusses the linguistic prerequisites of such a theory. The key to his approach lies in his notion that in any linguistic exchange communicators utilize a substantial amount of non-linguistic background knowledge. Informal conversations and official exchanges of diplomatic documents are alike in that messages are not only interpreted in the terms of this background knowledge but also add to it continuously. Although the proposed theory is developed from an account of what a human being does when engaged in conversation, it is aimed at a computer-aided analysis of documents in psychology, sociology, and political science.

Chapter 4 does not propose a particular theory of symbolic behavior from which analytical constructs may be derived. Instead, it presents an inquiry into the constructs that are used. Choices among content analysis procedures always imply assumptions regarding the structure of a source and crucially affect the kind of content that a text presumably conveys to an analyst. While the appropriateness of such choices can only be assessed in reference to a particular message analytic situation, it is possible to evaluate the inferential power of analytical constructs quite independently of such situatioṇs. In spite of the divergent "investigative styles" of content analysts, it seems that three formally distinguished classes of analytical constructs or three basic models of messages account for much of the current investigative efforts. Chapter 4 examines the nature and limitations of association models, discourse models, and communication models of messages.

SOME COMPARATIVE DISTINCTIONS

The contributions in this and other sections of the book can be compared on a variety of dimensions. For example, both Deese and Hays consider semantic processes to which a large number of individuals presumably conform. Their crucial differences lie, however, in the way they consider information to be processed. Deese's contribution is intended to lead to computer dictionairies that would map a large number of independent segments of text, including words, into a semantic structure that has psychological significance. A content analysis that used such constructs would presumably produce a semantic reduction of text yielding message characteristics that are uniform across many individuals and a very large number of different situations.

On the other hand, the analytical construct of a conversationalist that Hays implies in his theory would demand that situation- and individual-specific knowledge be prime factors in determining the possible contents of a document. Consequently, the inferences drawn from a text could not be divorced from a particular individual and from a particular situation. Moreover, the interpretation might change as information entered. Thus, while Deese offers constructs for semantic interpretation made by a statistically generalized individual, Hays proposes to design his program as adaptive to particular analytic circumstances.

There is also a place and a need to consider symbolic processes on a large scale. This, it should be pointed out, is not just a matter of the volume of text being considered but one of appropriate analytical constructs. Counting recurring characteristics in a single document is procedurally indistinguishable from counting the same characteristics in a year's supply of radio programming. However, a large corpus of text may have dynamic properties of its own that are not manifest in an unordered collection of letters, for example, regardless of their number. Rapoport must be given credit for having pointed up the problem and the possibility of studying, as a system, something that has been completely neglected by content analysts: large corpuses of verbal output. Macro analysis of this kind clearly contrasts with most content analysts' orientation toward inferences of psychological significance.

Somewhere in between the two extremes lies another area, which content analysts have not yet penetrated with methodological rigor. This is the area of communication among individuals on the one hand, and, on the other, communication among organized social entities. Symbolic behavior is essentially an intersubjective activity and the self-modifying character of communication processes tends to develop social networks among individuals that may assume superindividual properties. To make inferences from the observed exchange of messages to the behavior of such communication networks requires analytical constructs of a high order of complexity. The fact that communicators engage in such processes rather skillfully suggests that models of such situations may one day be feasible. Chapter 4 considers some formal prerequisites for constructs of this kind.

Among the problems frequently raised during the discussion was the significance of statistical constructs in content analysis. Perhaps this concern was motivated by the old conflict between quantitative and qualitative content analysis which has created two schools without resolving the issue. Chapter 4 suggests that such issues should not be resolved by fiat, but instead by examining the adequacy of a procedure with regard to a particular source. It seems that statistical type analytical constructs are more appropriate when the source is relatively unconscious about the messages it produces while a more conscious communication calls for more algebraic or logical type constructs that can be dealt with in equally rigorous terms. This distinction between situations in which these two types of constructs are more appropriate or less appropriate does not coincide with the macro-micro distinction mentioned earlier. Statistical constructs may be appropriate to handle emotional expressions as well as the large-scale evolutionary processes of verbal corpuses. But it is in the intermediary area of communication that logical type constructs are called for.

These introductory comments cannot reproduce the spirit of the discussions. Many issues were raised and few could be or were resolved. Common to all chapters of this section, and perhaps indicative of some progress in content analysis, is the concern with theories or proposals for theories that may validate rather than vindicate content analytic constructs.

1   A System-Theoretic View of Content Analysis

Anatol Rapoport

Mental Health Research Institute
University of Michigan

My interest in content analysis stems from an impression that both its general orientation and its techniques can be valuable adjuncts to the use of system theory in the study of large social systems. Accordingly, I shall describe in general terms the outlook that underlies this approach, the difficulties encountered in developing it, and the way in which, in my opinion, the further development of content analysis may help in the overcoming of these difficulties.

THE CONCEPT OF A SYSTEM

There are two ways of viewing a system. The biologist has the advantage in that the kind of objects he deals with are very definitely systems in the sense that they are organized entities. The organism is a system *par excellence* because it acts as a whole in an organized fashion. Thus, intuitively, one might define a system as a portion of the world that resembles an organism in certain crucial characteristics. From the biologist's point of view, one would have to define a system in those terms that are most like the properties of an organism. To a biologist, a system is a generalization of the concept of the living organism and, as such, it describes a portion of the world that has a recognizable structure; it has recognizable patterns of behavior and it undergoes long-term secular changes that, on the grand scale, are called evolution. These three aspects, then, are the aspects of the system that a biologist is interested in—structure, function (or behavior), and evolution.

The mathematician, on the other hand, must have a more precise definition. His conception is farther removed from the intuitive notion of what an organism is like. But it has the advantage of being more tractable to precise analytic methods. From the mathematical point of view, a system is a portion of the world that, at a given moment of time, can be described by the instantaneous values of a set of variables. Some of these variables

17

may represent observables, most easily exemplified by physically measurable quantities (for example, positions, velocities, temperatures, densities, and electric charges). Some of the variables may represent inferred nonobservable quantities, such as probabilities. The set of instantaneous values of the variables constitute a *state* of the system. Theories of systems may be static and dynamic. A static theory singles out those states in which the system can persist, the so-called *equilibria* or *steady states* in the system. In particular, if the variables that comprise the state of the system remain constant in time, obviously the system persists in that state.

A static theory, accordingly, is concerned with the "structure" of the system, that is, with the description of the relations, among the variables, not with their changes in the course of time. A dynamic theory, on the other hand, studies the *behavior* of the system, meaning the progression of the system from state to state. In particular, if the system is not in one of its steady states or equilibria, it will move through some sequence of states, perhaps toward an equilibrium, perhaps away from it, or from one equilibrium to another. If the structure of the system and/or its equilibria themselves change in time, especially if they undergo long-term systematic changes, we are dealing with the *evolution* of the system, and the corresponding dynamic theory is an evolutionary one.

The task of a general system theory is to deduce the equilibrium states and/or the short-term and long-term changes that classes of systems undergo; in other words, to deduce or to postulate "laws" that govern the existence, the behavior, or the evolution of classes of systems. These laws involve interdependencies among the variables or the responses of the system (in terms of the changes in its state) to inputs impinging on it from the environment. In fact, it is the operation of such laws that makes the portion of the world under consideration a system. If these laws are not operating or cannot be discovered, no theoretical advantage is derived from calling the portion of the world singled out for attention a "system."

SYSTEMS OF RECOGNIZABLE EVENTS
AND OF BEHAVIORAL ELEMENTS

An important question is whether the notion of system can be extended to portions of the world which are of interest only if they are described by other than physical variables. The fact that there are such portions of the world is evident. As an example, consider a living organism. To be sure, certain aspects of such entities can be described in terms of traditional physical variables. Organisms have shapes, masses, temperatures; they obey mechanical laws of structure and motion; and they embody chemical processes and the like. However, if we confined our attention to these aspects and the variables associated with them, we would not be describing a system in the sense defined. For even though the laws of interaction of these variables (for instance, mechanics, thermodynamics, and electrostatics) are known, the number of component parts is so vast that we could not specify even a single "state" of such a system, let alone deduce the progression of states strictly from the operation of these "known" laws, or derive the evolution of classes of organisms. On the other hand, if we turn our attention to other less precisely defined variables, at times we can learn a great deal about the states and about forms of behavior. In the case of a living organism like a cat or a human being, we can define elements of behavior in gross, intuitively understood terms and, through these, we can make some sense out of what we observe. Thus we can say of a cat that it will, under certain conditions, vocalize, eat, play with a ball of string, chase small animals, mate, and nurse its young. These are elements of gross behavior. They are all but impossible to describe precisely in purely physicalist terms but, nonetheless, are easily recognizable and thus restore the hope that we may be able to describe a living organism as a system with the elements of behavior as its "states."

The "laws of interaction" involving the newly singled-out variables cannot be deduced from known (physical or chemical) laws. This is true not because it is, in principle, impossible but because it is practically an almost unthinkable task. We therefore face the necessity of discovering "from scratch" laws of interactions of states described by patterns of behavior (if such laws exist), that is, by observing regularities in the changes of the system. In other words, in the realm of behavioral sciences, if we choose to study behaving entities as systems, we are forced to a relatively primitive level of cognition—the "barefoot" empirical level—on which the physical sciences also started their history but which they have long since outgrown.

Even the purely empirical program, however, is easier stated than carried out, because "elements of behavior" are not nearly as clearly defined as physical variables. This makes problems of experimental control formidable. In fact the entire purely behaviorist approach to the study of living organisms is jeopardized by the immense difficulty of deciding what is and what is not relevant in defining an element of behavior and in tracing the "causal chains" with which we usually associate any process subject to "laws."

The outlook for extending the system point of view to other than physical systems seems somewhat brighter when we turn our attention to large collections of living organisms, for example, biological populations and large social aggregates such as cities, nations, and the like. The reason is that in aggregates consisting of large numbers of similar individuals, or of a few large classes of individuals, we can again single out well defined observables, for example, *proportions* of individuals comprising the several constituent classes of a population. Thus, a biological population consisting of several species (or higher taxonomic types), a so-called *ecosystem,* can be characterized by the proportions of the several types.

Mathematical genetics is essentially a system theory of populations, where the observable states are the distributions of the phenotypes in the population. However, if these were taken as "the" states of the system, it would be very difficult to construct a good theory. The Copernicus of genetics, Gregor Mendel (1924), in effect proposed a different set of states: the distribution of *genotypes* in the population. These states cannot be directly observed (at least, not with the naked eye) but can only be postulated or inferred. Mathematical genetics is essentially a system theory whose axioms are the laws of transition from one genotype distribution to another (assuming either random or specifically biased mating patterns).

Mendel's theory was a simple static one. He derived just the equilibrium states for the genotype distributions. Later this theory was mathematically formalized and extended by the British mathematician, G. H. Hardy (1908). Given the phenotypes associated with respective genotypes, one can deduce the directly observable states of the population (the phenotype distribution) from the postulated genotype distribution.

This theory is powerful because it begins with simple, mathematically tractable assumptions. Thus the implications of the simple model can be easily worked out. A gradual approach to a realistic model can be accomplished by adding more determinants of structural changes. For example, Mendel's model does not exhibit evolution even if the dynamic aspects of the genotype distributions are examined. The only changes in these distributions are those that drive the system toward its steady states. However, when specific evolutionary determinants are added (for instance, mutation pressure, selection pressure, immigration, and emigration), inferences can be made about the gross secular changes of the system; that is, the evolutionary theory becomes an extension of the static one. This extension was actually brought about by the mathematical biologists of the 1930's and 1940's such as J. B. S. Haldane (1954), R. A. Fischer (1930), and Sewell Wright (1932).

In short, a portion of the world can be described as a system if certain variables can be singled out in a way that allows an unambivalent determination of their values and if the interactions among the variables is theoretically tractable; that is, the laws of interaction can be postulated from which deductions can be made, which deductions permit the prediction of the system's evolution (an evolutionary theory), its behavior (a dynamic theory), or at least of the conditions that stabilize the system in some state (a static theory). "Behavior," it should be noted, is always defined in mathematical system theory as a succession of states, and "evolution" is defined as a succession of equilibria.

Two other types of phenomena must be mentioned briefly in connection with system theory applied to nonphysical systems. One is language statistics, and the other is economics. Language statistics is concerned with the statistical distributions of linguistic elements in a large sample of spoken or written outputs (corpuses). Economics deals with patterns of production, consumption, accumulation, and exchange of "goods." Both are examples of phenomena in which well-defined numerical variables can be singled out and where at least something is known about the interdependence of these variables, which permits us to carry out systematic investigations aimed toward a system theory of these phenomena. Notice that these variables, like the elements of behavior mentioned above, are definitely not physical ones. In language statistics they are, primarily, frequencies of occurrence, which are dimensionless numbers; in economics they are usually prices, interest rates, volumes of production and consumption, rates of exchange, and the like. Some of the economic variables involve material units, but the physical aspects of these units are generally irrelevant. For example, a ton of steel, an ounce of gold, or a barrel of oil are, formally speaking, units of mass or volume. In economics, however, the physical aspects of mass and volume are of little or no importance. Nor are the chemical properties of steel, gold, or oil, as a rule, relevant in economics. It has been observed that we can study the physical or chemical properties of a dollar bill forever without getting the slightest notion about the significance of this object in the economic system of the United States or in the world market.

INDICES AS BASES FOR SYSTEM CONSTRUCTS

A variable whose significance in an investigation does not depend on the physical entities or events from which it is derived is called an *index*. (At least I propose this definition.) The definition points up an important difference between the use of mathematical methods in the physical and behavioral sciences. Physical quantities are typically bound up with units and dimensions (space and time coordinates, mass and charge units, for instance). Indices are frequently dimensionless numbers (probabilities, frequencies, ratios). These numbers are usually obtained not by measurements but by counting. Of course, measurements are also reducible to counting, but the range of things counted in physical measurements is restricted to material particles, space and time intervals, and the like.

In the behavioral sciences, the entities that are counted to yield indices can be anything. The only thing that is demanded of such entities is that they be clearly *recognizable*. Thus the experimental psychologists, using quantitative methods, counts the numbers or frequencies of bar presses produced by rats or the number of syllables recognized by a human subject in a memory task. The economist counts the numbers of dollars changing hands in transactions, or numbers of transactions, provided that these are clearly identified. The language statistician counts the frequencies of occurrence of certain relatively well-defined linguistic entities, (for example, phonemes and morphemes in a corpus). The quantitatively oriented sociologist counts numbers of people in certain well-defined categories. In every instance, "well defined" does not necessarily mean formally and rigorously defined but rather unambiguously recognizable. The criterion of definition is thus a pragmatic or operational criterion. It may be difficult or impossible to define a "bar pressing" formally, but it is easy to recognize it so as to make a bar pressing a countable unit.

The question of what to count in constructing an index is an essential question of methodology in the behavioral sciences. In selecting the entities to be counted, the behavioral scientist is guided largely by intuition. This is where "art" rather than science plays the prominent role. It is clear, however, that if indices derived from counting are to serve as tools of research, the criteria of usefulness of indices must be scientific criteria. What are these?

We have already mentioned one—the entities counted must be unambiguously recognizable. If they are, we assign to them the status of "objective reality." By definition, objective reality is what several independent observers agree upon. The key term in this definition is "independent" not "several." Thus millions of observers may agree on the existence of a causal relation between events A and B, but this agreement may be no more than a reflection of a prevailing superstition. These observers have not arrived at their view independently. On the other hand, the testimony of only two witnesses is often sufficient to establish the occurrence of an a priori improbable event, provided that the witnesses can be shown to have made completely independent observations. For example, if the last sentence were reported verbatim by two witnesses who have not been in contact with each other, we could safely assume that the sentence was, indeed, spoken. The two conditions (independence of observation and a priori improbability of the event) would have been fulfilled.

The other criterion of the suitability of an index is much more difficult to establish. It concerns the relevance of the criterion for constructing a system. Once a set of objective indices has been singled out, a set of instantaneous values can be used to define a state of the system. The important theoretical question is now whether something interesting can be said about the states. Are the variables selected so that given changes in some bring about consistent changes in the others? If so, can some theoretical sense be made of these changes? For example, can they be shown to be "adjustments" in the process of the system's "seeking" some equilibrium state, or do they exhibit gross secular trends, suggesting the evolution of the system? Are the changes perhaps self-enhancing (auto-catalytic)? Surely questions of this sort are relevant, for example, in economics. This is because portions of economics are relatively well formulated as system theories, and this gives the observations on changes in state some theoretical leverage. It is precisely the answers to such questions that constitute theories of supply and demand, of business cycles, of inflations and deflations, and the like. As long as we discuss these purely methodological matters, we are less interested in the accuracy of such theories than in whether they fit into a well organized and nontrivial intellectual scheme.

The aims of content analysis can also be examined from the point of view just described. Frequently the end product of content analysis is an index, or a set of indices, which is supposed to represent objectively some attitudinal level characterizing the "author" (often a collectivity of authors) of a verbal output. It is assumed that the index thus developed, in fact, represents what it is supposed to represent, and also that what is represented is, in some way, relevant to the behavior of a system. Suppose, for example, that the author of such an output is a human individual (say a mental patient) and that we seek an objective index of his mental state from the analysis of his verbal output. It is easy to construct indices by counting unambiguously recognizable verbal events. It is a different matter to decide whether the indices thus derived represent anything significantly relevant to the subject's mental states. Or suppose that the "author" is the "elite press" of a country. Again, we can derive any number of indices by counting the frequencies of certain words, phrases, and allusions that appear in the massive outputs of these media. The more important (and, of course, much more difficult) task is to decide whether these indices are indicative of something beyond themselves.

Where do we seek answers to such questions? One way suggests itself naturally. If an index is indicative of something beyond itself, it must be correlated with something else. The most natural candidate is another index. Hence a search for correlations between indices is or ought to be an integral part of content analysis viewed as a tool of a system theory. The other index may be of the same sort or of a different sort. It is tempting to choose an index of a different sort with a view of establishing a correlation between the features of a verbal output and nonverbal events.

For example, if from the content analysis of the elite press or a similar source we establish an index that supposedly represents the level of hostility or of tension between two nations, we naturally wish to know whether this is actually what the index represents, and we are led to seek correlations of the index with, say, indices of political events. I shall discuss this approach in more detail later.

STATISTICAL APPROACHES TO THE STUDY OF LANGUAGE

Language is itself an object of study of prime importance. Although content analysis is not primarily concerned with purely linguistic (that is, syntactical) features of communication, it seems to be deeply rooted in a statistical approach to phenomena most closely associated with language. Moreover, the statistical study of language is vastly facilitated by the tremendous volume of verbal data that new and powerful data-processing machinery is able to process. And content analysis has greatly profited from these possibilities.

As is now widely recognized, language is a phenomenon that can be studied on several different levels of abstraction. The lowest of these levels, pertinent to linguistics proper, is the syntactical level, the subject matter of structural linguistics. The problems of that discipline are those of identifying relevant units of spoken language and the ways in which they are related to each other in utterances. These units are phonemes, morphemes, words, phrases, and sentences. The regularities that emerge in studying sequences of these units constitute generalized grammar. The next level—the semantic—is concerned with establishing relations between certain linguistic units and the world. For example, it is held that the smallest language unit which has such a relation is the morpheme. A perennial problem of semantics is to decide when two or more units (words, phrases, sentences) have the same or similar referents in the outside world. Finally, on the pragmatic level, the fundamental problem is to establish relations between linguistic and nonlinguistic behavior of language users.

Statistical linguistics has been concerned with the distribution of structural units in large samples of verbal output. If these distributions are to be assigned the status of "objective reality," they must exhibit some sort of stability. Certainly, such stability can be observed if one takes large enough samples, simply in consequence of the operation of the law of large numbers. From this point of view, therefore, the so-called "laws" of statistical linguistics are no more than a consequence of the characteristics of all large aggregates, and there is nothing specific about them that sheds light on language. The relevance of language statistics to linguistics becomes apparent only if the statistical distributions are, in some way, descriptive of some aspects specifically characteristic of language or language behavior.

Attempts to establish such relevance have been made. One approach is the well-known method of using language statistics to resolve questions of disputed authorship. Presumably the parameters of distributions of structural units are characteristic of authors, styles, periods, and the like, and comparative studies provide evidence of probable authorship of texts. Another approach was the attempt to relate language statistics to information theory. This was undertaken by Benoit Mandelbrot (1953). Mandelbrot derived the well-known Zipf's law (Zipf, 1949) of word-frequency distributions by postulating a trend toward maximizing the average information (in Shannon's sense) conveyed by a word under the restraint of holding the average "cost" of a word constant (cost being related to length). What made Mandelbrot's theory attractive was that the law he derived theoretically was a slight generalization of Zipf's empirical law, and it yielded an even better fit to observed frequency distributions. Moreover, the parameters of the new law were given an interpretation related to certain characteristics of the corpus (for example, richness of vocabulary) which could be estimated independently. A rationale for Zipf's law was offered also by H. Simon (1955) on the grounds of entirely different considerations. The equilibrium distributions were derived by Simon from postulates related to the tendencies of the producer of a corpus to adhere to the gross statistical characteristics of his language as a whole (in Saussure's [1931] terms, *la langue*), on the one hand, and to his own language habits (in Saussure's terms, *la parole*), on the other. Thus the parameters of the distributions derived by Simon (which have a different mathematical form from those of either Zipf or Mandelbrot but similar gross characteristics) lead to different interpretations of the significance of language statistics.

Other approaches, using the concepts of *la langue* and *la parole* (that is, respectively, the characteristics of the language as a whole and of its manifest samples), were proposed by other authors, notably G. Herdan (1960). In short, an interpretation of statistical linguistics on the lowest (syntactic) level of analysis already has some language-related content.

The early formulations of content analysis were direct extensions of the method of statistical linguistics to the semantic level. Frequency counts of words selected with the view of discovering the preoccupation of the author involves the referents of the words. There is little doubt that such preoccupations can be discovered from obvious but perhaps superficial manifestations. However, on the whole, little purpose is served by such investigations, since they would hardly be likely to reveal more than was known already. Of obvious interest is the question of whether frequency counts of words can tell us more about what is behind the corpus than what we already know. Using the example of an earlier system theory, can we postulate a semantic "genotype distribution" which underlies the directly observed "phenotype distribution" and provides a key to understanding the changes occurring in the latter? To answer this question we must single out data that presumably reveal more than do frequencies of selected words. This is where the "art" of content analysis takes precedence over the science. As already stated, the "art" component of a science (in particular, of a science to be formulated as a system theory) concerns the selection of things to pay attention to. If a science is to be formulated as a system theory, this involves the selection of system variables whose values will define the system states. The science comes in at the stage of finding, guessing, or postulating the system *laws* that govern the relations of the variables to each other, the progressions of the system through sequences of states, and possibly of the way that the states of the system are related to those of other systems.

THE NATURAL HISTORY STAGE OF CONTENT ANALYSIS

The literature on content analysis is full of attempts to attack important social problems such as those posed by the presumed causal relationship between violence on the television screen and crime in the streets, the effects of political propaganda on the possibility of war, or attitude changes in response to educational material.

Research motivated by concretely perceived life problems is directed toward attempts to explain "events." Of obvious interest are "dramatic" events especially those that we would like to foresee, to control, or to prevent. For example, economics as an applied science is understandably concerned with crises, inflations, and similar dislocations of economic systems. Hence the economists interested in practical applications seeks to single out observable or inferrable indices that could serve as warning signals, and especially indices that can be manipulated (for example, by legislation) and that have a demonstrable causal relation to the events in question. Similarly, a pragmatically oriented psychiatrist (for instance, one assigned to an army unit) would be primarily interested in psychic trauma that would prevent the soldiers from performing their assigned tasks, and thus he would want a "psychiatric theory" in which diagnostic indices would be singled out in a way calculated to enable him to foresee such events. There is no question that much of content analysis in the field of international relations is motivated by a hope that indices might be found in the verbal outputs of diplomatic exchanges or in the elite media which could be used in "diagnostic" procedures.

However, this "direct" assault on problems of obvious practical interest by the tools of content analysis has serious drawbacks. Let us examine them. Let us see, for example, what would have been the case if the investigations of the physical sciences were similarly motivated. The most dramatic events of our physical environment are floods, earthquakes, volcanic eruptions, and droughts. If physical investigations had been directed from the start toward the study of these unquestionably significant phenomena, there is little likelihood that a serviceable physical science would have developed. The "causes" of these phenomena are simply too complex to yield to analysis in terms of clearly observed warning signals. And even if such indices were obtained, it is doubtful whether they would have been of much use in controlling natural cataclysms (although the opportunities for escape may have been enhanced).

As it turned out, physical science, and the control of environment that it conferred on man, got its impetus from observations of *regularly* occurring (hence undramatic) events—for example, the periodic motions of heavenly bodies. To be sure, knowledge of these events was of practical significance (for example, in marking of the seasons and in navigation). Nevertheless, the most important product of early scientific practice was the inculcation of the habit of systematic observation and consequently of focusing attention on events that are easiest to describe systematically—the regularly occurring events. It was this habit that gave rise to science and nurtured its growth. Fortunately (from the point of view of the development of science), the most regularly occurring events (movements of heavenly bodies and alternation of seasons) had practical significance in the lives of the early agricultural communities. The practical significance provided the motivation for observation; the regularity made the systematic descriptions of the events feasible.

In the development of the biological sciences, the story was repeated. Motivations for studying living things and life phenomena were provided by the necessities of hunting and of animal husbandry and by the problem of disease. Regularities were manifest in the possibility of classifying animals and plants and in simple correlations between crude medical interventions and their aftermaths. These regularities were not nearly as simple and obvious as those observed in the inanimate world. Consequently, the biological sciences matured later and were ridden with superstitions longer than the physical sciences. Long after astrology was banished from the scope of respectable science, medicine was pervaded with metaphysical speculations that had little or no bearing on the subject matter with which medicine was presumably concerned.

In the realm of behavioral sciences, it is generally recognized that the situation is even more complex. Perhaps it is unfair to say that the behavioral *sciences* are ridden with superstitions, if only because we *define* the criteria of science in such a way as to make scientific knowledge incompatible with superstition. It is not to be denied, however, that many formulations about human behavior in which abstract concepts play an important part, and which therefore in an earlier age might have been considered as a part of science, have almost the same relation to actuality as the fantastic formulations of eighteenth-century medical theories had to physiological processes.

I think that an important impetus to superstition is given by premature theoretical attacks on pressing problems. By a "premature theoretical attack," I mean an explicit formulation of causal chains that one is impatient to establish in the solution of the problem. What usually happens is that the problem attacked is too broad to permit a direct straightforward solution. But because the problem is obvious and pressing, it permits a *verbally simple formulation*. Thus it is important in many instances to foretell the future. In many instances it is possible to do so by noting correlations between specific signs and events that follow (for example, portents of weather, symptoms of onsetting diseases). Because the problem of foretelling the future is ubiquitous and often pressing, it is easily formulated in general instead of in specific terms: "How can we foretell the future?" The propensity for wishful thinking and for *selecting* events that corroborate preconceived notions has led to the proliferation of pseudosciences— astrology, phrenology, and the like. Similarly, the problem of preventing and combating disease can be easily formulated in terms so broad that attention is drawn away from relevant systematic investigations and toward deceptive metaphysical speculations about the nature of health and disease, away from actually relevant events. Science, as we know it, although motivated by broad and pressing problems, progressed by systematic investigations of areas that naturally lent themselves to such investigations. It is interesting that quite often this necessitated a deliberate turning away from the "practical" problems, in order to pursue lines suggested by the need to expand an area of knowledge so as to make it more logically coherent. The result was the emergence of the so-called "mature" sciences, well-knit bodies of reliable knowledge and systematic thought which, as we now know, have often provided solutions to problems quite different from those originally posed but often of equal or even far greater importance.

In the widely accepted view, a science "matures" in passing from the descriptive stage to a "hypothesis-testing" stage. But not all hypotheses can be tested with equal ease. The classical method of testing hypotheses (developed in the natural, especially the physical sciences) is by the controlled experiment. This method was transplanted into experimental psychology. As is well known, however, the experimental method is a less powerful tool in psychology than in the physical sciences, for several reasons. One is the indeterminacy of results under apparently similar conditions. Another is the limited range of events that can be studied experimentally. Another, perhaps the most important, is the absence of system laws of sufficient generality to suggest a well-directed experimental program which would yield results that could be welded into a unified theory. In the social sciences, the range of events amenable to experimental manipulation is even narrower, and the empirically oriented social scientist is confined to programs of more or less systematic observations, choosing for his variables events that can be easily identified and counted. These events are not necessarily relevant to fruitful theory building.

As a result, there has developed in psychology and in the social sciences a method of research that has come to dominate these fields and that contributes to the danger of stagnation. I am referring to the formalism of "hypothesis-testing" by establishing correlations. The validity of the results is not in question. The techniques of observation and statistical evaluation have become sufficiently sophisticated to establish their statistical significance. Nor do the investigators often fall into the trap of concluding causal relations from correlations alone. Indeed, techniques have been developed for testing the direction of causality, if such exists, between correlated indices. The disturbing question, which I am certainly not the first to raise, is whether a compilation of correlations is likely to contribute much more than a catalogue, whereas the need is that of a theory.

In this connection the concluding statement of Gerald Marsden, in his review of content analysis studies in therapeutic interviews, is revealing:

> Despite the burgeoning of content analysis studies of therapeutic interviews in the past two decades . . . , one is struck by the relative infrequency with which any of these systems has resulted in more than an initial thrust at a given research problem. System after system has been developed and presented in one or two demonstration studies, only to lie buried in the literature, unused even by its author. Moreover, few variables or notions about therapeutic interviews have received anything approaching programmatic or extensive content analysis investigation. This has resulted in redundancy; systems were developed with apparent unawareness that other approaches to the same problem, or efforts to apply the same approach to other problems, had already been reported (Marsden, 1965).

Redundancy is, perhaps, the least unfortunate by-product of ad hoc isolated studies. In fact, it might be said that redundancy has its uses: it tends to counteract the paucity of replications in the behavioral sciences, which makes it so difficult to decide just what results have been reasonably established. Lack of direction, however, is a very serious shortcoming.

In my opinion, this chronic weakness of the behavioral sciences, which is to some extent felt in content analysis, stems in large measure from impatience to establish an application potential. Of course, the very considerable successes of applied content analysis are not to be discounted; and there is every reason to encourage the development of this method as a diagnostic tool (for example, in the studies of international crises, of biases in mass media, of the outputs of mental patients, and the like).

However, in pointing to the current stage of content analysis in the natural history of the behavioral sciences, I hope that I have not given the impression that I am advocating a retreat to a more primitive level of investigation, since content analysis already is being used extensively in the context of hypothesis-testing, presumably a more advanced stage. What I am advocating is not free-wheeling descriptions of the contents of verbal outputs but rather systematic descriptions, where "systematic" is to be understood literally, that is, in the sense of being system-oriented. This involves much thought in the selection of variables and their quantification—in other words, the selection of semantic units applicable to a wide variety of contexts, analogous to the structural units of classical linguistics.

TOWARD SYSTEMATIC DESCRIPTIONS OF VERBAL CORPUSES

In content analysis, to my way of thinking, the systems of interest are large corpuses of verbal output. The question then arises: Can a large corpus, in fact, be described as a system? Can it be said that a verbal corpus behaves? Does it make sense to speak of the "response" of such a system as if it were a living organism? Could something equivalent to evolution be observed in these corpuses?

At first thought, this seems to be impossible, since a corpus is something that has "happened," not something that persists in time, the way a physical system does. With just one additional assumption, however, we can get around this difficulty. We can imagine that successive similar verbal outputs from the same source represent a manifestation of the "system" at successive moments of time. Fortunately for the system approach, this assumption can be defended. I am referring to the striking stability of large verbal outputs of individuals speaking or writing on the same topic, especially in the political sphere—a sad reflection, perhaps, on the rigidity of the corpus producers, but hardly disputable in the face of evidence.

In a somewhat analogous way, successive generations of termites produce termite cities of practically identical structure. The actual production is a dynamic process, and a stochastic one at that, involving thousands of organisms whose individual motions certainly undergo statistical fluctuations. Yet the end product exhibits a remarkable structural constancy in each successive manifestation.

In observing the process of its generation, a corpus may easily be said to behave. In a dialogue, for example, or in situations of surface contact between two cultures, behavior becomes manifest in the interaction between two or more corpuses. The evolution of language, the evolution of a style, or the evolution of an idea provide examples of long-term secular changes. Thus it is not too far fetched to say that verbal corpuses behave and evolve and have their own invariancy, which makes them susceptible for a system theory approach.

However, these answers are not so obvious because a verbal corpus has no definite underlying physical laws that could be discovered. It is true that a verbal corpus is produced by living organisms that, in time, are part of the physical world and therefore probably obey physical laws. In principle, one can say that a chain exists from the underlying physical events to the meaning of a word and to the socially channeled verbal output. In practice, it is impossible to trace the chain from the beginning to the end. It is therefore necessary to find more abstract ways of describing large-scale verbal output; not in terms of measurements but by other means of quantification (counting, for example). A corpus, then, would be systematically described in terms of frequency or temporal distributions of its semantic units.

One of the central problems of content analysis is therefore to isolate the elements that compose the system and describe them in whatever form of quantification seems appropriate. Since the laws of the physical base of verbal output are too far removed to be considered, it would be futile to search for them. Content analysts have the problem of postulating the laws of interaction within a corpus *de novo*. If these laws are formulated in tractable mathematical terms then they constitute a mathematical model of a corpus from which, in turn, consequences can be deduced that can be subjected to empirical verification. This is the general strategy that would have to be followed in developing a systems theory of large verbal outputs. However, the crucial problem of isolating system components that are identifiable and lend themselves to system laws that appear sufficiently invariant so as to have predictive consequences is far from being solved in content analysis. Let us examine a few ways of describing a large verbal output and study their relevance to the system-theoretic view that I am proposing.

In considering the literature of content analysis I was favorably impressed by the approach of North, Brody, and Holsti (1964). I think they are on the right track, although only subsequent developments will decide this question.

These investigators seem to have made a fortunate choice of material: public speeches by political leaders in times of international crisis. I suppose that the exchange of diplomatic correspondence in crisis periods can be considered to constitute a more general body of data of similar sort.

I do not quite agree with the rationale given for the choice of such material. I feel that the authors have a stronger case than they actually present.

North, Brody, and Holsti write:

> Foreign policy decisions are conceptualized as a search for satisfactory alternatives from among the range of those perceived by those who must make choices. A feasible approach to the "behavior" of nation-states, therefore, is to concentrate on attributes of those relatively few individuals in any given government who make foreign policy determinations and commit their nations to a course in international activity.

Implied in this statement is, apparently, a justification for using the verbal output of individuals as data in explaining the behavior of nation-states, on the grounds that the perceptions of these individuals will influence their decisions; and their decisions, in turn, will commit nations to courses of action. These assumptions, however, may be unnecessary. The perceptions of events that comprise international relations need not be those of individuals. They are more likely to be cultural perceptions reflected in the pronouncements of the spokesmen for the culture (who may have become spokesmen precisely because their perceptions are faithful reflections of the predominant cultural perceptions). By "culture" I do not mean culture in the anthropological sense but in a social sense (exemplified by the conventional wisdom of political elites). Thus, while it is conceivable that international relations are given an impetus in one direction or another by the peculiar perceptions of a Hitler, a Stalin, a Mao, or a Johnson, the question of the extent to which such impulses are determinants of large-scale system behavior is an open one, which need not be raised in the context of content analysis. In fact, the same authors quote Thomas Kuhn to illustrate the limits of predictability of even physical events:

> . . . suppose we tell a physicist that at precisely noon on March 13, 1980, we will release a feather from a plane flying due east over the Statue of Liberty at ten thousand feet and six hundred miles per hour. Not a scientist on earth would risk a dime, much less his reputation, predicting where and when (within a hundred yards) the feather would land (Kuhn, 1962).

If prediction of specific events is at this time unthinkable as a task of the science of international relations, there is no point in invoking the perceptions of individuals as determinants (via their individual decisions) of such events. In fact, the very concept of "decision on the basis of scanning perceived alternatives and a choice of acceptable ones among them" can be seriously questioned in the context of international relations; but I shall not raise that issue here.

If, however, verbal outputs of individual decision makers are taken to be representative samples of *cultural* perceptions (for instance, of political elites), the case for content analysis as a tool of research in international relations become stronger, since it need not depend on the vulnerable assumption of the importance of individual perceptions and decisions.

What impressed me especially favorably in the method of content analysis developed by the Stanford group was the way the units of analysis were chosen and coded. They define a *theme* as a statement that can be coded in terms of (1) the perceiver, (2) the perceiver when other than the author of the document, (3) the agent, (4) the action, (5) the referent, (6) auxiliary verbs, and (7) the target. Plainly speaking, a theme is identified by stating who does what, how, to whom, according to whom. This, of course, is not the only semantic paradigm of assertions, any more than subject-verb-object is the only grammatical paradigm of a sentence. Nevertheless it makes sense to concentrate the analysis on *some* paradigm, and in the context of the chosen area (statements of political leaders at times of international crisis), this seems to be a very good choice. (In other contexts—for example, the therapeutic—other paradigms are probably more pertinent.)

Having chosen the "semantic dimensions" (that is, the qualitatively distinguished variables), the next step is the assignment of values to variables. This is done by means of biographical and geographic dictionaries and an evaluative dictionary. The former identifies the perceivers, the actors, the targets of action, and the like. The latter attaches intensities to actions along dimensions previously proposed by the designers of the semantic differential: *value* (good—bad), *potency* (strong—weak), and *activity* (active—passive) scales. The verbal output (that is, the material analyzed) can now be *coded* as a sequence of values of variables. The rest is statistical analysis, which can be pursued to any desired depth. One can read off distributions of a great variety of variables and compute the statistics of such distributions. The sum total of these constitutes a "profile" of a corpus. The profiles of different corpuses from similar or contrasting sources can be compared (for example, those produced in the Cuban crisis, which dissipated, with those produced in the 1914 crisis, which exploded) and the temporal changes in corpuses can be traced. Criteria can be developed for a taxonomy of corpuses. In short, the method suggests a basis for a "natural history" of large verbal outputs. I think such a natural history is needed if a system-theoretic approach to content analysis is to make progress.

If, then, successively produced corpuses are merely manifestations on the time axis of an underlying dynamic system, we can very well speak of the responses of that system to inputs and of its long-term evolutionary changes. The inputs can, of course, be perceptions of events or of corpuses produced by other agents.

Recent content analysis studies in international relations reflect just that point of view. One of them, which I heard reported recently by Dina Zinnes, dealt with the diplomatic exchanges during the summer of 1914, with special emphasis on inferred interactions between indices of hostility in these exchanges. The study was quite in the spirit of Lewis F. Richardson's attempted analysis of arms races (Richardson, 1960).

There are, however, instructive differences between the recent study and the older one. Richardson started with a definitive mathematical model of an arms race. It was a quite simple-minded model involving two linear differential equations in which were embedded both positive and negative feedback factors of interaction. Richardson's indices were armament budgets and interbloc trade volumes. He assumed that an index of hostility is compounded from armament budgets and trade volumes (the latter with negative sign), and that the other's hostility is an enhancing factor while one's own current armament level is an inhibiting factor in the rate of growth of one's own hostility. (If this should seem strange, the model is easily reinterpreted in a way that exhibits the stimulus to armaments as the algebraic difference between the other's and one's own armament levels.)

Since armament budgets and trade volumes are observables, Richardson's model is, in principle, testable. It was actually tested and gave "good agreement" with the observed growth of the armament budgets of the Great Powers in the years preceding 1914. However, the significance of the agreement is an open question. For one thing, it is extremely difficult to conceive the rate of growth of armament budgets as a continuous variable, inasmuch as budgets are fixed annually. The use of difference instead of differential equations does not help, because the period studied comprised only five years. Since only four intervals were involved in the *changes* in the armament budgets of the rival blocs, the test of the model consisted essentially of fitting only four points to a straight line with two free parameters which, of course, fixed two of the points on the line. The other two points fell squarely on the line, but this "agreement" hardly constitutes a dramatic confirmation of Richardson's arms-race theory.

An even more unfortunate circumstance (again from the point of view of theory construction, not necessarily from the point of view of human welfare) is the paucity of bona fide arms races. The Entente-Central Powers race is a rare classic. Subsequently, Richardson studied the arms race of 1933 to 1939 (Germany versus the USSR) and that of 1948 to 1953 (the United States versus the USSR). Richardson died in 1953 while that race was still going on. The results were less clear than in the first study, part of the difficulty being that of finding a meaningful economic unit after the demise of the gold standard.

Subsequent research revealed that very few wars between the Peloponnesian war in the fifth century B.C. and the First World War were associated with conspicuous arms races. This paucity of data makes the choice of arms races a poor one in the context of designing theories of large interacting social systems (in particular, of war-waging states), important as this area of inquiry may be.

In my opinion, content analysis provides an excellent opportunity to put such theories of interaction to work in an area where there is a richness of data, and where the continuous nature of the variables (demanded in the application of the more powerful mathematical tools) can be better approximated. For example, in another study Richardson attempted to construct a dynamic theory of war moods, immediately preceding, at the outbreak, in the course of, and in the aftermath of a war. His approach is quite analogous to the genotype distribution approach to population genetics in that he distinguishes between "covert" (genotypic) moods and "overt" (phenotypic) moods. The data he used to fit his equations were extremely scanty: for instance, a few speeches and a by-election in Britain in 1917. Techniques of content analysis would have provided him with as much data as was required to test his mathematical theories, especially if the theories had been guided by a preliminary purely descriptive treatment of the data.

In advocating concentration on the descriptive approach, I am merely pointing out that attempts to construct mathematically definitive models of interaction, although methodologically highly respectable, may be premature in the context of the behavioral sciences. We do not know what the "laws of interaction" may be, nor how to isolate classes of situations where the same laws apply; and it is unlikely that we can guess the mathematical form of such laws from a priori considerations. It is important to get good structural descriptions of systems that represent corpuses of verbal output as a sound preparation for genuine mathematico-hypothetical theory construction. In the context of content analysis, this would mean a description of a corpus in terms of its "semantic structure." The exact meaning of this term cannot be specified in advance. One of the tasks of the theory would be to work out the operational meaning of this intuitively suggested concept. Once we begin to "see" corpuses as systems, hypotheses to be tested will very likely suggest themselves. The important thing is to have hypotheses suggested by the system properties rather than chosen on an ad hoc basis. The latter approach permits us, perhaps, to answer specific questions of interest but contributes little to the broadening and deepening of a content-analytic theory of verbal outputs.

CONCLUSIONS

I have argued for a system-theory approach to large corpuses of verbal output as a fruitful tool for content analysis. Since such corpuses have no immediate physical base and are composed of an extremely large number of elements, the search for system laws that are mathematically tractable is probably greatly facilitated not by premature attempts at hypothesis testing but by a more conservative statistical characterization of their content. By this I do not mean to exclude the consideration of a few documents that are generated by one or more independent individuals. But it is reasonable to suspect that the reproduction of the great quantities of verbal forms that circulate within social organizations or cultures follows a more stable pattern and thus lends itself more readily to reliable knowledge about the behavior and the evolution of verbal corpuses.

Just as all living organisms live in certain specialized environments to which they adapt and which completely determine their lives, so do human beings live, to a significant extent, in an ocean of words. The difference is that the human environment is, to a large extent, man made. We secrete words into the environment around us just as we secrete carbon dioxide and, in doing so, we create an invisible semantic environment of words which is part of our existence in quite as important ways as the physical environment. The content of verbal output does not merely passively reflect the complex social, political, and economic reality of the human race; it interacts with it as well. As our semantic environment incorporates the verbal outputs secreted into it, it becomes both enriched and polluted, and these changes are largely responsible for the course of human history. It behooves us to study this process.

The study of how a semantic environment impinges on man's existence, how it determines the kind of social organizations that can grow, and how it specifies individual behavior involves the most difficult level of analysis. If we focus on this environment in order to derive social laws of human behavior, I am afraid that we will get into insuperable difficulties simply because we do not know enough about this verbal output. Therefore, we must study this corpus for its own sake (at least, for some time) without reference to the symbol user. In other words, I suggest that the purely statistical aspects of a verbal corpus are not to be ignored even though their practical use is not immediately apparent. We must sharpen our methodology on tractable problems before we can hope to undertake those of great human significance.

I am quite aware of the danger of this point of view and the numerous objections that have to be considered rather carefully. In regard to the use of intensity measures derived from frequencies or other "obvious" indices, one recalls the sardonic comments of Noam Chomsky in his review of Skinner's *Verbal Behavior* (Chomsky, 1959). Chomsky takes Skinner to task for suggesting that promptness of response, repetition, voice volume, and the like are natural indices of the intensity of motivation. Chomsky cites the hypothetical case of two women, each receiving a luxurious bouquet. The first woman, instantly after seeing the flowers, shouts "Beautiful! Beautiful! Beautiful! Beautiful!" at the top of her voice, thus giving evidence, according to Skinner's criteria, of a strong motivation to produce the response. The second woman, upon opening the box, says nothing for ten seconds, then whispers, barely audibly, "Beautiful . . . ." Presumably she exhibits a "weak motivation to respond."

Similar objections can be raised against the description of corpuses mainly in terms of statistical distributions. It is possible to question the relevance of the statistical approach to the really significant features of language. Such questions have been raised with reference to statistical linguistics. It has been argued (I believe with justification) that the study of the statistics of "strings" of linguistic units (for example, with reference to conditional distributions) sheds practically no light on grammar. To put it another way, even though a grammar of a language may determine the statistics of a large population of strings, it cannot itself be derived from these statistics. There are other such examples. It is extremely doubtful whether the laws of falling bodies, for example, could have ever been derived from a statistical analysis of the trajectories. Nor is it likely that the "real meaning" of chess can be derived from a most far-reaching study of statistical distribution of the moves.

All of these criticisms revolve around the same warning. In examining the immediately observable, the easily measurable, and the unambiguously countable we may be missing the real underlying meaning of the phenomena that we wish to understand. This warning is certainly always in order. However, pending the discovery of some profound characteristics of communication that may reveal the irrelevance of what content analysis has undertaken to study, I think there is little else content analysis can do except plod on. I suggest, however, that as the indices singled out for attention reflect more closely the psychological states of the speakers and writers (such as the "themes" singled out by the Stanford group in comparison with specific words) *and, at the same time, the solid ground of objective analysis is held,* the relevance of the method to the behavior of large scale systems should increase.

To illustrate this point I call attention to the spectrum of psychological theories. At one extreme there are the psychophysical theories founded on carefully controlled replicable experiments, rooted in physical laws, and supported by unquestionably objective evidence of physically measurable data. At the other extreme are the imaginative metaphorical speculations of psychoanalysis. In between are theories of various "grades of hardness" in experimental, social, and clinical psychology. I submit that the objectivity (or reliability, or respectability) of these theories is related roughly inversely to their relevance to the proper subject matter of psychology: the human psyche. The same spectrum is seen in linguistics. Structural linguistics is "hard" but far removed from what human communication is "really" about. Literary cricitism is "soft" and often irresponsible, but it tries to come to grips with some very important things that people are trying to say.

In my opinion, behavioral science need not always be impaled on the horns of this dilemma—whether to sacrifice significance for reliability of knowledge or vice versa. That this is often the choice comes, I think, from the circumstance that it becomes progressively harder to "do science" as the subject matter becomes more elusive; and also from the fact that people of different temperament and with different interests are attracted into the one or the other mode of investigation.

The continuity of knowledge could be preserved if "hard" methods were introduced into "soft" areas very gradually, consolidating each strip of "conquered territory"; and also if the hardheads and the softheads listened more to each other. It seems to me that content analysis lends itself very well as a field of inquiry in which this consolidation can be achieved.

2 Conceptual Categories in the Study of Content

James Deese

Psychology
The Johns Hopkins University

Content analysis is essentially a practical enterprise. It is simply a collection of techniques for providing interpretations of texts and similar products. In the social sciences, practical scientific activity often makes a greater contribution to theoretical studies than the other way around. I suspect that this may characterize the relation between content analysis and theoretical semantic studies. Nevertheless, psychological studies in semantics have something to offer to content analysis. The object of this chapter is to present a particular psychological semantic theory in the context of content analysis, in the hope that those responsible for devising techniques in content analysis may find my views useful.

The primary objective in any content analysis is to provide some interpretation of a cultural product of possible symbolic significance. When the cultural product is linguistic, the usual form of the interpretation is a paraphrase. The paraphrase resulting from content analysis usually has two characteristics: (1) it produces propositions capable of being subjected to statistical treatment; and (2) it generally reflects some special purpose. The various interpretations of text that arise out of content analysis are highly selected and altered accounts of what is in the original. Content analysis does not try to discover all of the possible themes in some product, but only some portion of them—that portion being determined by the psychological or social aims of the analysis and by the necessity for statistical treatment. These characteristics of content analysis forever set it off from any semantic component of general linguistic theory or from any psychological interpretation of semantic processes. Nevertheless, both of these may inform content analysis and, in the *General Inquirer* (Stone et al., 1966), we have already seen some of the fruits of the application of general linguistic theory.

Because content analysis is not a straightforward application of various paraphrasing and/or coding devices to some document or cultural product, some special problems arise. The most important of these is whether the message we have extracted by content analysis is a possible interpretation of the original product from the point of view of the author, or if it is an interpretation that only a specialized audience (that is, the person or persons doing the content analysis) could give. Most schemes for content analysis take, as their point of departure, the view that the purpose of the analysis is to determine some underlying themes in the message intended by the author of some work, or at least one that perhaps, in an unconscious way, reflects the personalities and motives of the producer. However, specific outcomes of content analysis often exhibit the message of the analytic audience rather than the message of the producer. This is often the case, I think, in particular kinds of literary analysis in certain psychoanalytic interpretations, and it even contaminates formal and scientifically oriented content analysis.

We recognize that such is the danger (if it is a danger) that arises out of the selective nature of any content analysis. The varieties of interpretation or even, in some formal sense, paraphrase of any given message are endless. Although we must suppose that we rather quickly exhaust the information in some message (say a poem) placed there by the author (either intentionally or unconsciously), we never can exhaust our own reactions to it, and those reactions are, of course, varieties of interpretation. Nor does the explicit and formal character of content analysis (as compared with literary analysis) save it from an ambiguity of interpretation in this respect. However, it is at least possible that the application of psychological notions of semantic productivity and semantic change may provide some guidelines both for limits in interpretation and extension of present methods.

Psychological semantics starts with the notion of meaning. We must give an account of this notion before presenting specific ideas about semantic structures and their application to linguistic coding and linguistic change. The concept of meaning describes a relation between some more or less arbitrary symbols, interrelated with each other in a complex and partially structured way, and human experience. The relationship depends on a third term: human cognition. The forms of human cognition determine the nature of the relationship between symbols and experience, and they determine the way in which any interpretation (including content analysis) works. The linguist can ignore cognition, since he is only concerned with the interrelations among the symbols (whether considered only grammatically or considered grammatically and semantically).

Therefore, the psychological structure of meaning is a set of relations between (1) some aspects of a particular language, (2) ideas in the minds of people who use the language, and (3) objects and events in the perceptual-physical world. Common sense epistemology leads us to expect some orderly relation between the perceived world and ideas in the head, and these ideas correspond to some aspect of language. Thus, the relation between language and the world is, psychologically, an indirect one. The way in which the world is characterized by language is as much a correlate of cognitive structures as of the world. I say correlate rather than cause because the relation between ideas, reality, and language is mutually interactive.

The three-part relationship implies that any treatment of the structure of language and the relation between language and the world is mentalistic. Modern linguistic theory (Chomsky, 1965) is avowedly mentalistic, but only in a limited way. Linguistic theory, insofar as psychological processes are concerned, is limited by the fact that it is only liguistic. Linguistic theory brings to bear on language a conceptual apparatus that has no relations whatever to cognitive function generally. It is purely and solely linguistic. This is no handicap in the study of language as such, but in any enterprise dedicated to recovering some of the psychological properties inherent in language, it is limiting. I hope that the views given here will serve as a supplement to linguistic theory rather than as a contradiction to it. My chief goal is to provide some notion of the psychological structures responsible for certain relations between words and the world, and these call on structures that are not linguistic in the ordinary or in the technical sense. They are not linguistic in that they serve other functions, such as the organization of visual perception.

The notion of paraphrase arises because, in any language, there are alternative ways of expressing the same idea. Furthermore, there are accepted relations between questions and answers, between successive statements in a dialogue, and the like, some of which transcend purely linguistic relations. These relations demand that a specific process, such as paraphrase, be determined by a more general process of interpretation. Finally, linguistic analysis itself depends on an interpretation that draws upon the implicitly understood notion of underlying ideas or deep structures behind linguistic segments. We may regard linguistic analysis, in part, as the decomposition of some linguistic segment into some underlying components. We need not take the view that these components are somehow "real" or psychologically fundamental units. They may be devices of linguistic convenience. In fact, one can make a very strong methodological argument to the effect that all such analyses are simply conveniences. Any analysis, including content analysis, is a kind of interpretation, and it must arise from the same source that gives rise to other classes of linguistic interpretation. This means that it is determined not by theories of psychological processes but by the needs of a particular analysis. Psychological theory, however, may inform such analyses.

The relations between linguistic and nonlinguistic events (the world, in Wittgenstein's sense) are said to be semantic or meaningful. Meaningful and semantic relations, however, also exist within a language itself, and these may parallel certain other intralinguistic relations, such as those between elements of a propositional logic or grammatical system. Also, nonlinguistic interpretations can be placed upon linguistic and nonlinguistic events alike. Aesthetic reactions and certain aspects of nonlinguistic symbolism (iconography) are examples of such interpretations. Recognition and appreciation of musical sequences provide the most interesting examples because they are so abstract.

Psychologically, any interpretation may be said to signal a state of understanding in the individual who does the interpreting. I have made this proposition central to a cognitive linguistic theory to be presented elsewhere. Here I shall simply baldly state it, since the question of the psychological nature of understanding has little bearing on content analysis. However, we must accept the notion that interpretation is not identical with understanding; it is one manifestation of it. A clear separation of these two psychological notions makes it possible for us to dispense with the idea that any psychological reaction to an extended sequence of linguistic material consists of a more or less continuous interpretation placed on that sequence. It does not. It consists of a somewhat continuous state of understanding. Understanding signals the potential for interpretation, but not the ability, as many students discover to their dismay at examination time. A distinction between understanding and interpretation does have significance for content analysis, as I shall point out shortly.

A brief comment on the nature of the sentence is necessary, since the sentence occupies a fundamental role in modern linguistic theory—one that is not paralleled in earlier theories or in semantic psychological theories. However, both from psychological and practical considerations, content analysis need not be constrained by any linguistic role given the sentence. There is actually no compelling reason, while looking for meaningful, fundamental structures, to give any priority to the sentence or its representation at some more abstract level. The problem of meaning requires that we investigate, at any level, the potential for understanding This is another way of saying that meaningful interpretations may be placed on linguistic segments at any level, although they are more easily placed at some levels rather than others.

When we investigate the meaning of sentences and phrases, we invoke some view of the nature of grammar. No content analysis can ignore grammar, though I know of no effort at content analysis that uses modern grammatical theory in its most extended and fundamental aspects. We necessarily invoke some view of grammar when we investigate the meanings of separate elements (such as words) since, in doing so, we must draw upon general grammatical structure in order to intuit the elements— to abstract them from their context. This abstraction depends on an appreciation of the nature of sentences and grammatical phrases. The meanings of particular words, however, can be explicated without reference to a well-developed theory of grammer. This perhaps is saying nothing more than that dictionaries, no matter how uninformed by linguistic theory they may be, are useful. Dictionaries imply, by their very existence, that individual elements, such as words, can be associated with meanings of various sort, and that these meanings can be described independently of particular sentences or sentence structure in general. What is not always apparent is that dictionaries provide only a possible or potential interpretation of any given linguistic element. There are as many kinds of dictionaries available as there are varieties of interpretation. The varieties of dictionaries lead us directly to our problem, which is to characterize the types of psychological structures responsible for the linguistic interpretation of such segments of the language as individual words.

There is no compelling linguistic or psychological theory that requires dictionaries to take any particular form. However, any dictionary exemplifies some psychological and linguistic notions. There is certainly no necessary reason why we must have access to dictionaries by means of an alphabetical listing of the leftmost letter of the individual words. Most dictionaries are so organized because of the conventions of reading in a particular language—conventions that are utterly arbitrary form the linguistic point of view. The forms of definition also appear to be arbitrary from a psychological point of view, but they are not. They exemplify various cognitive processes at work. A casual inspection of any dictionary reveals that entries vary. Sometimes they have something of the form described by a particular semantic theory, but more generally they are mixed bags. They are mixed bags, I think, for an important psychological reason: semantic interpretations depend on not one but a variety of cognitive structures.

A few dictionaries are built on logical or theoretical principles. Some of the dictionaries described in the *General Inquirer* fall into this category. So does Roget's *Thesaurus*. That dictionary is sufficiently interesting in the present context to warrant a comment. It is essentially a concept dictionary. In it, all the words that express the same concept (or, in an alternative description, share the same semantic markers) are brought together. There are in Roget's *Thesaurus* six general classes (semantic markers at the highest level): (1) abstract relations, (2) space and motion, (3) matter, (4) intellect, (5) volition, and (6) moral powers. These, in turn, form subclasses. There are, for example, three subclasses for matter, and nine subclasses for volition. Under each of these, there are a number of subordinate classes. Each of these finally exists in some fundamental binary state. For example, *will* is contrasted with *necessity*, *activity* with *inactivity*. Under each of these fundamental oppositional states, there are a number of entries which, in particular linguistic contexts, may be used to express the meaning of that concept. Roget's *Thesaurus* is only one of many schemes for the universal classification of the categories of human thought. It exhibits most of the faults of all of the others.

Roget's classification is only partly convincing. However, for the most part, it does not matter. Most users of the *Thesaurus* use the alphabet listing simply to find synonyms and closely related words. Any form of a good synonym dictionary would do just as well. Roget's scheme ought to be more useful, however. The trouble is partly with Roget's nineteenth-century English prejudices, but more, I think, with the limitations imposed by his decision to force all concepts into the single mold provided by his classification scheme. Not all concepts have a structure that can be described by a branching-tree structure (nor, for those that do, do we always find binary branches at the terminals). In the system devised by Roget, the word infancy is used to describe a concept in class I (abstract relations) because it refers to time. A pragmatic system would also have it entered as a class III (matter) word, because it refers to a condition of vitality. However, for his concepts (though not, of course, for the vocabulary expressing the concepts), Roget and most of his successors have avoided cross entries.

Roget's binary opposition plan is often forced (indeed, he cannot always find a simple opposite). We may agree to Roget's *gravity* versus *levity*, and to *life* versus *death*. Since we know about complementary colors, we may even agree to *blueness* versus *orange* and *redness* versus *greenness*. However, why *gray* versus *brown*? Would everyone agree that *water* is to be contrasted with *air*? Many of Roget's pairs are unconvincing. They are unconvincing because he describes, by a binary relation, words, the human conception for which cannot be forced into a binary oppositional mold. Roget's scheme fails, not because there are not conceptual branching trees, not because people do not think in binary relations, but because the variety of human concepts exemplified in human languages is simply too great. There are other conceptual schemes that have different abstract structures, and not all concepts are determined by all categories.

It is my purpose, in the remainder of this chapter, to describe some of the categorical types that describe human concepts as those concepts are exemplified in language. The list is not an exhaustive one. There is, so far as I know, no general theory that would place any kind of bounds on the number of various kinds of structures in human thinking.

There are structural types that are rare in human thinking. Many of these can be used only with the aid of auxiliary computing devices (such as pencil and paper), and they are properly categorical types used by systems larger than the individual human mind. The general point can be made with those described here. It is that an interpretation can occur only when some experience or intellectual content is referred to a particular categorical structure. The idea is very close to Kant's use of the notion of the categories of understanding. My list is certainly smaller than that supplied by a computer scientist or someone else interested in abstract logical structures. On the other hand, it describes a device—the human mind—much clumsier and more inefficient (if more flexible) than any artificial intelligence.

Understanding signals the potential for assimilation of information to underlying structures. Those structures are not necessarily linguistic but, when they are, they make possible syntactic and semantic interpretation. Semantic interpretation can be described as a process of mapping concepts representing segments of the language, including words, into underlying structures. In conjunction with linguistic structures, this interpretation may give rise to some linguistic output, such as a paraphrase or an answer. Without further explanation, I shall present the list of structure types.

1. *Class Structures.* Class structures are exemplified by Roget's classification system or, alternatively, by the structure employed by Linnaeus in his system of biological classification. Abstractly, a categorical structure can be represented as an hierarchically ordered branching tree in which each node represents some set of attributes or markers which characterize all concepts below that node. The attributes marked on the node may or may not be linguistically represented encoded at the level of words or morphemes, but if they are so represented they need not be by attribute names. Roget attempts to place an appropriate word from ordinary English at each node (sometimes missing the mark widely). In the Linnean system, words denoting things (animal and plant names) are rearranged so that certain features of those things obey the hierarchical ordered principle, but the attributes themselves do not encode the attributes themselves.

Ordinary folk do not think of most of the words employed by Roget to mark his concept tree as being in a class structure, nor do they think of animals as being arranged in a Linnean structure in any consistent way. A much stronger tendency in folk taxonomy is to group animals into farm animals, wild animals, and the like (see Henley, 1968). This tendency reveals more of a grouping structure than a class structure.

The greatest use of such class structures in human thought is in the relationships of subordination and superordination. The complete Linnean system, in order to be used by a human being, must be committed to memory by rote and, even then, only constant use will keep it viable. However, people readily use the relationship of subordination and superordination. In fact, any concept in the world can be thought of as belonging in some subordination or superordination relation. Some words more readily evoke such structures than others, and they evoke them in a deeper, more immediate, and sensible way. I do not wish to describe data in this chapter; therefore, suffice it to say that some associative data (Deese, 1965) and some of the judgmental and definitional data obtained by Willner and Reitz (1966) reveal the varieties of interpretive structures possible. Definitions of words supplied by ordinary people will commonly consist of a general class name ("a dictionary is a kind of book") together with some differentiating attributes. Such a definition reveals a mixed structure, but only a single application of the operation of subordination.

2. Grouping. A group structure results when a set of concepts shares some set of attributes in common. However, the attributes do not always intrude themselves into human thinking. People think of things that are grouped together simply as being "similar." The similarity operation in thinking is ambiguous, since things are sometimes thought of as being similar when some abstract dimensionalized space better describes the concept structure. That is because such concepts can be conceived of either as existing in a three-dimensional spatial model or as being defined by three-dimensionalized attributes. The operation, or grouping, like the superordination-subordination operation, can be almost universally applied. Almost anything can be said to be similar to anything else (though the attributes in certain instances must be excepted). Any judgment of similarity may be defended or explicated by pointing to a set of attributes that the concepts judged to be similar have in common. It is possible to pair words randomly and come up with some reasonable way in which the concepts represented by the words are similar (Johnson, 1968). However, an immediate judgment of similarity, implied by some metaphor or simile, may be unrelated to the results of a search for underlying attributes. In short, the explication of a judgment of similarity, even by the person responsible for the judgment, may be false.

Often concepts that are grouped may have names, in which case application of the subordination-superordination relation is possible. However, the possible existence of that relation should not obscure the basic operation of grouping. If a grouping occurs, more than one attribute must define the grouping. This is because similarity is a judgment that can only occur when more than one attribute is required in making the judgment. Some concepts may be related through a single attribute. In that case, they may well comprise a scale of some sort. But since they cannot be said to be similar in varying degrees, they do not exhibit a grouping relation.

3. Dimensional Ordering or Scaling. Certain concepts can be thought of as being ordered or measured on some scale. They express some more or less fixed value on a quantitative scale. The scale itself may have any one of the five abstract properties. These are (1) intensity, (2) numerosity, (3) probability, (4) position or length, and (5) time. The last two properties have directional aspects and, for that reason, may be conceptually a bit different from the other three. Each has a metaphorical extension, and these extensions are of great importance in semantic use.

There is considerable psychological literature on scaling. This literature is mainly concerned with the permissibility of applying various arithmetic operations to judgments, and it nearly always misses an important point. Whatever the merits—the reliability and interindividual agreement—of any scaling operation, as a cognitive act it must be judged only as an intellectual process. Undoubtedly most of such judgments are metaphoric extensions of experience with ordinary material things and space. They may be sophisticated judgments only to the extent that our ordinary experience permits sophisticated use of those arithmetic operations.

4. Spatial Representation and Models. Certain relations can be projected onto a spatial representation. Maps are familiar two-dimensional representations of real, two-dimensional (or three-dimensional) experience. Ordinary maps are generally more abstract than we give them credit for being. It is surprising that they are so readily interpreted even by the untutored. Furthermore, maps of a high degree of abstraction are a cultural universal. Some primitive maps are so abstract that they have not been immediately recognized by Europeans for what they are. The Marshall Islanders, for example, possessed a complicated lattice system for portraying the location of islands in the sea together with the prevailing direction of wind and waves (Lyon, 1928).

Maps exist in the head, of course, as is testified to by Tolman's memorable phase, "cognitive maps." Maps in the head, furthermore, are not to be limited to portraying isomorphic distance relations. They can be generalized graphs. In addition, there are models. As a matter of convenience, I shall use the word maps to refer to two-dimensional representations and two-dimensional projections, and I shall use the term model to refer to any three-dimensional representation. We have already noted that representation in the head of spatial position and time may be restricted to a single dimension. However, such representations have a kind of direction (they define vectors). Because they have direction, they imply some co-ordinates. These coordinates are usually those of ordinary space (or space and time), and they often take the individual as a point of reference or origin.

Finally, some spatial representations are quite explicit, while others may be revealed only by taking the implications from other relations revealed in human thinking. The distinction between explicit and implicit spatial representation is complicated by psychological investigation which makes the implicit representation explicit. Color space is an example. The laws of color perception lead to the representation of the relations between all colors in the form of a three-dimensional figure. That figure, the result of psychophysical and purely psychological research, is so well known now that, for many people, it becomes an explicit representation of color space or, at least, that portion of the figure concerned with hue and saturation does. Various studies of color names and other cognitive and linguistic aspects of color show us that the color solid is more than psychophysical, it is cognitive. Yet it is clearly a cultural phenomenon localized to Western culture and its contacts. The cognition of the color solid does not exist in other cultures. There is some evidence to suggest that a two-dimensional bipolar representation, or even a single-dimensional bipolar representation, is culturally more common (see Conklin, 1955).

Various physical systems are, for those instructed in that branch of physics, explicit. Another implicit system is the three-dimensional representation of emotional expression. It is less firmly defined than the color solid, but I think it does reflect ordinary usage as well as psychological theory. All such models are limited to an upper bound of three dimensions. This is because they are all ultimately metaphorical extensions of experience in ordinary three-dimensional space. More abstract conceptions (as, for example, N-dimensional space or non-Euclidean space) have no direct representation in cognition and human languages. They are limited to their logical or mathematical operations and other, less direct structural representations in human thought.

5. *Abstract Relations.* Certain cognitive operations, similar to those implicit in scaling and in map and model construction, may have no physical representation. Other operations, exemplified by various logical relations, sometimes have physical representations in scales, maps, and models but, more often, they are viewed as abstract. The fact that the cognitive operations are not always as abstract as they are portrayed as being is substantiated by a large experimental literature concerned with the study of the way in which people use such relations, a literature that extends from the classical work of Woodworth and Sells on the atmosphere effect

in syllogistic reasoning to the recent concern of social psychologists with the logical structure of balance theory.

These relations may well be similar to models. Some are extensions and perhaps abstractions of social relations. For example, a common linguistic device is one that indicates possession or ownership. Such a device may be generalized in certain languages (generally, the Indo-European languages) to denote a relationship of dependence or modification. The use of the preposition *of* is an example. Unlike temporal and spatial prepositions (for instance, *before* and *under*), *of* has no properties than can be conveniently displayed in a pictorial representation or map.

There are many different possible abstract systems, most of which are too complicated for unaided human use. However, I suggest that to the extent that they are genuinely represented in human understanding, they may not be so abstract as their logical descriptions may imply. Consider, for example, the common use of Venn diagrams to explicate set theory or the logic of classes.

6. Binary Attribute Structure. The existential property of any analytic attribute is that it exists in a binary state. Each attribute may be defined only by reference to one or the other of its alternative states. The attributes themselves have only a contrastive or oppositional relation.

The independence of attributive pairs and the productiveness of the illustrated by certain pairs of common English adjectives. *Hot* can only be defined by reference to *cold,* and it is completely independent of other contrasting pairs, such as *tall-short* or *good-bad.* In other words (no matter what is implied by the semantic differential), *hot* things are neither less nor more likely to be *good, bad, active,* or *passive.*

The independence of attributive pairs and the productiveness of the oppositional device are readily attested to by the presence (in English and related languages) of the attributive negative. The attributive negative must be interpreted as the opposite of, not the complement of, the state that it modifies, and this implication must be regarded as part of the structure of attributive description. Something that is *not good* is generally interpreted as something that is *bad,* and an *unheated* room is, in its most obvious ordinary meaning, a *cold* room, though logical analysis would say that it is simply a room for which no heating device exists—irrespective of temperature.

Thus, the negative in English is ambiguous in interpretation. The complementary negative signals the complement of that it modifies or the opposite. The negation of color name in English signifies the complement. Something that is not *red* is not necessarily *green, blue,* or any other color. Color names in English do not exist in attributive pairs, but are part of a spatial model. Hence the complementary negative, not the attributive negative, applies to them.

The opposition negative is, of course, productive. In English there are many prefixes (for example, *un, im, in,* and *non*) and at least one suffix (*less*) that have been, at various times, productive, and most of which are still productive. These affixes signal the opposite and, when they are attached to a word or morpheme denoting one state of an attribute, they have a clear and unambiguous interpretation. The oppositional device shows us that the two states of any attribute are independent of all other attributes, since otherwise the device would not have any determinate interpretation. The productive device, of course, exists along side of the separate forms (*big, little*). These we must learn as attributive pairs without formal markers.

The negation, then, has two interpretations: a true negation or the complement and a false negation or the opposite. The fact that we can readily interpret the same phase either way (it is possible, for example, to consider the phrase *not bad* as implying the complement) shows us that semantic interpretations are not to be tied to any linguistic representations in a single and invariant way. Semantic interpretations consist of the application of denotata to cognitive structures and, within certain limits, denotata may be combined with various structures to produce different interpretations.

Certain attributes when named in English may be modified intensively. This modification represents the application of the scaling operation to the attributive structure. It is revealed in the general case by the existence of the comparative and superlative and in particular cases by the existence of such words as *huge,* which generally refer to a position more extreme than one of the primary attribute terms (*big-little*), where the position is defined by the application of scaling to the binary attribute. Not all attributes can be scaled (*inside-outside,* for example), and some of the words in English that denote relative positions on intensive scales are ambiguous as to attribute. *Grand* and *great* are ambiguous with respect to the attributes of size and value. Again, ambiguity reveals two or more underlying interpretations. Notice in this case, however, that the two interpretations simply provide different content to the same semantic structure.

The words that indicate intensive modification or scaling of an attribute are not likely to take one of the productive affixes. That is, they are not part of the antonymy structure itself, but of the scale having the direction indicated by the attribute named. As is the case with certain attribute pairs, such words are high in frequency of use. While not fixed in size, the class of these words is generally a small one. Like the contrasts that are made from historically independent forms, their meanings must be learned arbitrarily, and thus there cannot be many of them in any given language.

The categorical types produce psychologically distinct operations, and their distinctiveness arises both from their subjective expressions and their behavioral effects. Within certain limits the applicability of one or another of the categorical types is not determined by the objective content of the concept in question. The categories differ in appropriateness and difficulty for a given content. However, with few restrictions, all categories may be applied to all conceptual material. Some of the great labor and significant human achievement in scientific theories represent difficult or psychologically inappropriate application of particular categories to particular content.

Certain conceptual structures may be represented analytically in a way that is so difficult for human thought as to be almost unthinkable. Something like this, I think, has occurred with kinship systems. Descent, in a kinship system, is usually recognized to exist in one of three forms: unilateral descent, bilateral descent, and what Murdock calls double descent. In unilateral descent, ancestral line is traced only from one side, either in matrilineal or patrilineal form. In bilateral descent, ancestral line is traced from both sides. From the tree, other familial relations will be determined. In fact, however, the way people think of kin relations is confused and mixed. People are quite capable of thinking first one way and then another, as different kinds of models are applied to the problem of familial relations, and they do. It is only for certain ceremonial, legal, or linguistic purposes that kin relationships may be said to take a particular form. A form that is the "kinship system" of a particular society is not limited by that society's ceremonial or linguistic conventions; it is limited by the conceptual structures to be applied. To be sure, certain concepts may be encoded into a given language in a simple way, while others may require a circumlocution for their expression in that same language. Most of us have no trouble with the concept *uncle*. We can detect its implication of laterality (perhaps even through an imaged spatial representation), of sex and generation. Furthermore, although English has no simple way to express it, we can easily distinguish between our own uncle and our spouse's uncle (whom we may, for some purposes, call "my uncle"). We can even see that an uncle is a point in a descent tree (either as the apex in a tree going back in time, or the origin of a tree going forward in time). All of these notions are easily represented cognitively, and they can be expressed in ordinary English. However, we cannot see the term *uncle* in its fullest abstract familial representation as a particular node in a generation lattice with an independent dimension of sex and laterality. Such a conception must remain purely abstract and unrepresented in direct human thought because it is almost unimaginably complex. It is actually, however, the generalized "kinship system."

DeSoto (see, for example, DeSoto, 1961), in various places, has commented on the predisposition toward single ordering and the difficulties of thinking of branching tree relations. DeSoto argues that there is an intrinsic human preference for a single order over any form of partial ordering or multiple ordering. There is, he argues, a human tendency to arrange elements in a line. DeSoto's arguments are compelling. It is conceptually easier to locate concepts in line rather than in a branching tree. However, the branching tree is easily represented as structure, something that the *n*-dimensional lattice is not. The limitation we have in dealing with particular relations within a tree at only a small number of different levels is a difficulty in memory and accuracy. It is not a conceptual difficulty, as certain other purely abstract representations—such as the lattice—would be.

Another problem in any attempt to represent meanings in different ways, as content analysis does, is introduced by the possible confusion between the schematic structure of similarity relations and abstract representations. The similarity relations among concepts may be represented as a structure having metric properties in some space. Often such spatial representations of similarity are misleading.

There are several senses in which this kind of representation may be inappropriate. It may be inappropriate because it is a domain to which similarity analysis coupled with spatial representation simply does not apply. We do, for example, think of familiar objects (such as different makes and models of automobiles) as being more or less similar to another, but we do not imagine these objects as projected in a graphic or spatial arrangement. Psychological multidimensional scaling can represent similarity spatially, but such a representation does not portray how people think about the relations between the objects. The appropriate application of similarity judgments is not coextensive with the application of those relations in some multidimensional space, at least insofar as cognition is concerned.

Philosophic systems, scientific explanatory devices, and the arcana of religious mysticism make use of symbolism that presents abstract relations in some physical representation. Squares, triangles, and other spatial shapes may be used to represent relations that have no direct physical representation. Consider, for example, the well-known explication of meaning by Ogden and Richards by reference to a triangle. Often such abstract representations have their only real meaning in (or can reliably be interpreted by means of) the implication of the spatial position in the diagram. Content analysis has not sufficiently explored this kind of representation of communications of various sorts, nor has there been sufficient investigation of the psychological characteristics of such representation.

A brief comment on scaling or ordering is useful in this context. Almost any conceivable concept may be envisioned as either the name for something that can be quantified or ordered or as a position on a scale of some sort. "Probability" is the name of such a concept, and "probable," "unlikely," and "possible" are names in ordinary English for at least ordered positions on that concept, as Howe (1966) shows. Almost every sensory modality has one attribute that is described as intensive and thus scalable. Because sensory modalities have other attributes as well, intensity can be represented, after some scaling operations, in a space. This rather technical usage on the part of psychologists has a kind of counterpart in the common and apparently metaphorical use of "high" and "low" to express position on certain intensive attributes (and pitch in the case of hearing). Therefore, it would seem that sensory intensities are cognitively represented by directed lines in space.

English has many phrases that contain metaphorical extensions of spatial relations. Consider the phrases, "a high intensity light," "you are nearly right," "low grade ore," "far out music," "close friend," and "distant relative." These all express some ordered or scaled relation by means of modifiers which, in their literal senses, are taken to be descriptive of some positional relations in a space. Notice that the coordinates of the space very often take as the origin the position of the person. Such representations should be cultural universals according to the theory presented here. Both Maori and Malay (more or less unrelated languages) use terms denoting height to refer to exalted or important people, as do European terms. In addition, Maori uses words denoting height to indicate the state of being thrilled or excited (which also has a counterpart in English). There is neither Maori nor Malay evidence of confusion between forms denoting high and those denoting strong or intense. In Maori, forms meaning strong are also used to mean stiff, hard, persistent, violent, and bold. In Malay, strong has surprisingly similar associations. The strong-force-intensity association of English, if present at all in Maori or Malay, is too subtle to be revealed by ordinary bilingual dictionaries.

The adverbial modifiers, which serve to scale or order adjectives or verbs, are well described in ordinary English handbooks, and they have been thoroughly studied in the psychological laboratory by Cliff (1959) and Howe (1966) those studies imply that these adverbs (*very, probably, often*, etc.) are multiplicative in their effects. That is, they are genuine modifiers; they move the meaning of the word they modify along some quantitative dimension without themselves adding substantive meaning. The scaling operation itself is independent of whatever it scales.

The main point I wish to make by alluding to these results is that categorical structures place the ultimate limits upon the interpretations human beings find possible to make. In fact, my view is that human experience is far more limited in its interpretive abilities than are computers. I may, for example, talk and think about n-dimensional factor structures (where n is greater than three), but I have no way of representing these structures to myself in any adequate manner that permits me to make geometric operations upon the factor space in a direct way (as opposed to the mechanical application of some computational device). I may represent a diagram of two or even three dimensions, and I can think in an abstract way about n dimensions, but I cannot represent n greater than three dimensions in my own experience. As a result, my thinking about factor analysis as applied to psychological testing is more likely to reveal the application of a grouping structure. I abandon geometric representation when factors exceed three and, instead, group tests in some quasi-intuitive way based on their factor loading. This approach is a common one among factor analysts.

Understanding signifies the potential for interpretation. Interpretation occurs when some categorical structure is applied to some content. Interpretation is responsible for linguistic outputs of various sorts—paraphrases, definitions, answers to questions, and the like. The particular output will depend on the demands of the situation as well as the interpretation, of course, but the categorical structure revealed in the output will depend only on the structure of the human mind.

Certain categorical structures cannot be applied to certain contents. Nevertheless, there is wide freedom in the adjustment of the world of experience to cognitive categories. I have already alluded to the spatial representation of color in Western culture, a representation that renders impossible true opposites in English color names. However, color as such may have a much simpler representation. There is some evidence that many primitive cultures represent colors in a pair of binary attributes, attributes that roughly correspond to light versus dark colors, and long versus short wavelength colors. European languages apply a spatial representation to the structure of human emotions. This makes possible a kind of rough correspondence between the color space and the emotion space (since they are both three-dimensional models). I need hardly remind you of the association between *red* and *anger, yellow* and *cowardice, green* and *envy,* and *blue* and *depression,* for example. These associations have a limited cultural distribution. It is perfectly feasible to force thinking about human emotions into a grouping structure, and there is strong evidence for such thinking in other cultures. Although the particular association of colors and emotions referred to is culture-bound, the potential for such associations in the generality is not.

A categorical structure dictionary does not exist. The beginnings of one exist in the appendix of Deese, *The Structure of Associations* (1965), but the brief dictionary presented there is limited by its dependence on one type of information (free associations) and by its attempt to force all lexical elements into one of two classes. Furthermore, it does not recognize that a limited grammar of categories is possible. For example, in English, the prefixes *un, im, non,* and the like always seem to signal the opposite, although the term *not* is ambiguously either a signal for the opposite or the complement. Thus, the use of the prefixes can be taken to indicate the presence of a binary opposition structure.

Casagrande and Hale (1967) have provided an analysis of a radically different language, Papago—an American Indian language, that uses a categorical scheme similar to that proposed here. These authors show that binary oppositional relations are coded in Papago as they are in English. This kind of coding may well be a linguistic universal. They also show that other categorical relations are morphologically encoded in this language. More importantly, their work reveals striking differences between Papago and English in the assignment of content to categories. For example, a Papago speaker will define the nose as (1) that which is between the eyes and the mouth, and (2) as the organ for breathing. Thus, Papago first assigns a spatial description and then a class description. An English speaker's definition will nearly always start with class inclusion ("the organ for breathing"). Even if a definition codes the spatial location feature, it will do so via a class membership structure ("a part of the face"). These differences in assignment of contents to categories may well be an important mark of stylistic differences between cultures.

In formal intellectual processes, English speakers rely heavily on class membership. If I had to describe, as a kind of statistical average, the typical form of formal definitions given by ordinary folk, I would describe them as consisting of (1) a supraordinate term, and (2) a single attribute. Thus an *orange* is "an edible fruit" and psychology is "the science of behavior." However, in linguistic contexts it is intuitively clear (though an explication may be difficult) that other structures dominate. It is my impression that things and concepts (*oranges* and *psychology,* for example) tend to be dominated by a grouping structure in ordinary thought. Therefore an orange may be used to stand for some bundle of attributes— attributes that describe things similar to oranges—but the exact collection of attributes is indefinite because the grouping does not specify them. Here the grouping schema dominates. This is why, I think, Laffal (1965) and others, including myself, have found associative data so rich in interpreting linguistic material. Associations yield almost directly the grouping schemata to which particular lexical elements may be assigned.

A categorical dictionary must, as should any good dictionary, give some idea of the kind of context in which any given lexical item would belong to a particular category. A purely mechanical (context free) categorical dictionary would be of limited value in exhibiting how people may interpret particular linguistic segments. The information for such a dictionary must come from the way in which people react to a variety of contrived linguistic situations. Free association tests, definitions of the sort asked for in traditional vocabulary tests, word usage tests, rating scales of various sorts, requests for analogies, interpretations of analogies, requests for categorization, and the like are all examples of the situations needed. These devices are familiar to psychologists, and some information exists based on all of them. Writing a cognitive dictionary really only requires a concerted effort to obtain the appropriate normative information and the means to code that information into dictionary form.

3 Linguistic Foundations for a Theory of Content Analysis

David G. Hays

Linguistic Research
The Rand Corporation

The analysis of content is a central topic in all of the sciences dealing with man. The capacity for speech is man's most striking characteristic, and language is bound up with rational thought, the emotions, and all of the distinctively human parts of man's internal life. Much of culture, and almost all of social organization, would be unthinkable without man's faculty of speech. Arguments about the relative primacy of language and thought are bootless because the two are biologically the same; the proper business of psychology is not to determine whether thought is possible without language but, instead, to determine how the two are jointly possible.

The study of content is also a central issue in linguistics. In fact, the deepest schism in this field is surely the one that divides traditionally American linguistic theory, which aims at characterization, from all the rest, which aims at correlation of content with expression. Now, it is true that certain rapprochements have been attempted in the last few years. Indeed, many American theoreticians are now attending to questions of content-expression correlation: "The grammar [of a language] as a whole can . . . be regarded as . . . a device for pairing phonetically represented signals with semantic interpretations" (Chomsky, 1964:9). Whether the mode of expression be phonetic or written is unimportant, and even if semantic interpretations cannot be identified with content they are close to it. The social scientist must welcome the new movement because its tendency is to make linguistics useful to him. This new tendency gives me my theme.

For the sake of concreteness, let us keep in mind some of the typical streams of material whose content a social scientist might wish to analyze.

1. *A sequence of editorials.* The staff of a newspaper, experiencing an epoch, produces a series of essays, recapitulating some of the day's events, placing them with respect to historical trends, theory, and dogma.

57

It expresses opinions about the true nature of situations that are necessarily not fully comprehended, and opinions about the responses called for.

2. *International exchanges of an official character.* This kind of correspondence might well be compared with a sequence of newspaper editorials, except that there are two or more parties involved, each pursuing a policy of its own.

3. *Personal documents.* These may be letters, diaries, or written materials of other kinds. Except for the particularity of content, these materials could be compared with newspaper editorials or governmental notes.

4. *Interview transcripts.* Usually there are two parties. One of the parties is naïve, and the other is sophisticated. The purpose of the interview may be, for example, therapeutic or diagnostic.

5. *Social interaction.* Two or more persons participate, discussing a fixed task or whatever topics they deem suitable.

No matter what the situation is, material with content to be analyzed is the product of human actors. The analyst's object is, in some sense, to understand them. The understanding of one person in particular is to be attained, if at all, only by cross-comparison of the specific facts known about him with a general scheme. In the cases of interest to us, what he says, and the situation in which he says it, furnish the data; the general framework must come from sociology, psychology, political science—and linguistics.

Until recently, the formulation of psychological and sociological theories of content was of limited interest. Technically, the job was almost hopeless, since neither mathematics nor technology furnished models of appropriate kinds; a theory that explained comprehension by putting a picture inside the hearer's head was patently no theory at all, since it had no laws for the conversion of one picture into another—or for any process. Strategically, it was not crucial to provide theories of content because linguistics was not prepared to do its part.

The situation is now changing, as we shall see. Therefore, it behooves workers in social science to attend to linguistics and to construct content analysis theories. The interest of this kind of research is naturally increased manyfold by the availability of the computer, which makes it possible to apply a theory to appropriate quantities of textual materials, so that the theories developed can, in practice, be tested. (For my views about the use of computers in linguistics, see Hays,1967a.)

CONVERSATION AND CONTENT ANALYSIS

The best content analyst is a good conversationalist. In fact, content analysis is an essential part of good conversation. When the going is easy, the analysis is not conscious. In difficult cases, as when governments are exchanging notes during a crisis, each communication received is carefully analyzed by professionals before any attempt is made to devise a response.

In any exchange, each participant possesses substantial background knowledge. He brings some part of this to bear on communications received; the supposition that he can apply all that he knows in any instance is an idealization of a high order. Each participant also knows, in particular, what the other participants have been saying. This information is presumably fresher and more readily available; in many instances, the conversationalist may be able to put the new message against the background of virtually everything that has come to him in the exchange. Next, the conversationalist is himself a participant; he has at hand (1) his own previous statements, (2) the things he wanted to say but has not yet had occasion to say, and (3) the things he could have said but chose (for one reason or another) to keep to himself.

Given a new message with this much background, the alert conversationalist draws inferences of many kinds. At one level, he notes the consistency of the new message with what he knows, and also with what he assumes his interlocutors to know on the basis of prior experience. Inconsistencies can be attributed to error, to change of policy, to tactics of misdirection, and to other factors. The conversationalist also makes inferences about attitudes toward himself, toward other participants, and toward objects of mutual interest. If the conversationalist is well equipped with theory, he may make inferences about such states as anxiety, needs, and so on. Finally, given his background knowledge, the new message and the inferences he draws from it, and his own policies, the conversationalist constructs a reply. The burden that all this imposes is shown by the degree to which we become engrossed in conversations, by the intensity of concentration that a psychiatrist or psychologist must devote to his clients, and by the existence of large numbers of specialists on Soviet, Chinese, and many other governments. To ask so much of social scientists would be vanity or folly, if it were not for the possibility that automatic computers will eventually relieve them of the burdensome details.

From the perspective we have been taking, the contribution of linguistics is hidden. As we shall see, its contribution is small but crucial.

EXPRESSION AND CONTENT

The contribution of linguistics is, in fact, to explicate the relationship between overt expression and content; linguistics should furnish a partial model of the conversationalist (see Hays, 1967a, Chapter 13; and Lamb,

1965). A message in natural language has just two natural forms: spoken and written. Spoken language is produced by articulatory mechanisms and is recaptured by the ear and the auditory systems of the brain. Between the two, there is an acoustic signal. For many years, linguists and engineers have been attempting to simulate speaking and hearing. Although they have achieved some successes in both of these domains, they have failed in such degree as to show beyond doubt that neither the production mechanism nor the recognition mechanism is simple. We can therefore no longer suppose, if we were ever tempted to do so, that—for example—background knowledge is stored in the brain in the form of acoustic signals. Whatever is stored must certainly be put through a complicated encoding to make the articulatory apparatus work, and must be isolated from the recognition apparatus by another complex recoding.

A similar analysis of the relationships between written language and knowledge could be made. Now, content analysts do not generally attempt to begin their work with acoustic recordings, nor (if they propose to make the analysis automatic) do they begin with written materials. They sometimes do, however, begin with texts punched on Hollerith cards or recorded or magnetic tape, and go immediately to procedures based on psychological, sociological, or political hypotheses. According to contemporary linguistic theory, a content analyst taking this tack is surely misguided. The remarkably complicated relationships between content and acoustic signals are simplified very little, by passing from acoustic signal to binary encoding of words in their normal spellings.

Although they differ with respect to details, all schools of linguistics concur in recognizing that human speech consists of small units bound together by diverse mechanisms. These units, which we can conveniently call morphemes, contribute in a direct way to expression of content. By and large, if two messages differ considerably in morphemic composition they are expressions of different content. But content is certainly not expressed completely by the choice of certain morphemes in any language. Complexities must be expressed, and syntactic devices are available in every language to facilitate expression. The difference between "the dog chased the cat" and "the cat chased the dog" is plain enough, yet these two sentences have the same morphemic composition. Furthermore, perhaps because of the necessity of building up great complexes, every natural language seems to provide more than one form of expression for any content. "The dog chased the cat" has (almost) the same content as "the cat was chased by the dog." The same content seems to be most of what is expressed by "the dog's tendency to chase the cat." True content analysis is therefore not best taken as a direct psychological analysis of expression forms; syntactic analysis must intervene.

At least metaphorically, and perhaps concretely, this amounts to syntactic transduction. The input to the transducer is a binary encoding of text in normal orthography (a linguist would suggest a modest preliminary step, isolating such features as capitalization, to simplify the logic of syntactic transduction). The output is a formula in notation specified by grammatical theory. Formulas of this class are superior to text in normal orthography, as input to content analysis systems, for two reasons. First, these formulas make grammatical relations explicit and tend to bring together at one place the representation of a conceptually simple characteristic that is represented in part at several places in a natural sentence. For example, "the dog chased the cat" and "the cat was chased by the dog" differ in several ways, but the corresponding formulas differ only in that one is marked "active," the other "passive." Second, these formulas are canonical forms in the sense that they reduce diversity. For example, "the cat which the dog chased" corresponds to a formula composed in part of the formula for "the dog chased the cat."

Now, it is by no means obvious that the stages of linguistic analysis, as seen in the abstract, need be reified, yet one is tempted to do just that. The brain might then be supposed to have some portion devoted to the reduction of acoustic signals to canonical forms, and another portion where syntactic rules are applied to convert canonical phonological forms into canonical syntactic forms. One can, in this fashion, take several additional steps; the next is semantical.

Although the study of semantics has not been pursued as successfully as the study of syntax, linguists are beginning to develop evidence for another stage of rule application and reduction to canonical form. For instance, there is the fact that a word can have two meanings but the same syntactic properties. There is the fact that many idioms are syntactically normal, but have meanings as composites that cannot be deduced in the standard way from the meanings of their parts. There is also the fact that vocabularies are organized in ways known to the speakers who use them that are not reflected in morphemic composition. Componential analysis seems to be a way of bringing such vocabulary organization to light (see, for example, papers in Hammel, 1965). Kinship and color terms, regardless of morphemic composition, seem to be systematically organized. Content, then, would be more directly reflected by the presence of certain components than by the presence of certain morphemes.

Everyone knows about idioms, and everyone knows that many words have multiple meanings. An equally obvious fact, once it is noticed, is that grammatical constructions have multiple meanings as well. To make sense of that statement, we may have to clarify our understanding of having meaning. The fact is well illustrated (Fillmore, 1966) by three sentences: "the door opened," "the janitor opened the door," and "the key opened the door." Does the verb *open* change meaning? Whether one answers that question with a "yes" or a "no," one feels that the issue remains unsettled. Grammatically, "door" is the subject of the first sentence, "janitor" is the subject of the second, and "key" is the subject of the third. If we conjure up images to suit the three sentences, the action of opening is the same in all three. What changes is the relationship between the entity named by the grammatical subject and the common event. Herein lies another reason for passing to canonical semantical forms before applying psychological theory in the analysis of content; in a semantic formula, these three relationships—and others—can be distinguished by primitive notation.

More obscure than questions of semantics are those of reference. In any reasonable discourse, certain entities, objects, events, or abstractions are mentioned repeatedly. In any narrative, some characters play central roles. If it is not possible to recognize, each time a character is mentioned, that he is the same one mentioned previously as performing or suffering certain actions, possessing certain properties, and so on, but that he is different from others, there is no hope of making sense of the whole story. Perhaps the establishment of referentiality is beyond semantic analysis of received messages, or perhaps it is a part of that analysis; or, perhaps, the metaphor of successive transductions between clear-cut stages is overdrawn.

Philosophical and linguistic semanticists tend to think of language as standing in some more or less direct relationship to the world as known to physical science. Psychologists may respect this view as appropriate to the tasks of philosophers, but its omission of everything that might be called cognitive makes it unsuitable to their purposes. Cognitive processing would then constitute another section in the model of the conversationalist, and certainly one beyond the reach of pure linguistics. Perceptual and motor sections, if needed at all, must be built by psychologists.

If we insist upon reification, each of these sections of the model is a transducer, each a different segment of the brain. At least, this is true for the linguistic stages. The acoustic signal is transduced into a phonological canonical form; that form is transduced into a syntactic canonical form; and so on. Only the first form, the acoustic signal, is presently observable. All of the other forms are hypothetical, and so are the transductions. Until about 1960, American linguists at least were flatly unwilling to accept such hypothetical forms. They insisted on remaining close to the form of observable speech. Before that time, many linguists in Europe and some in America had speculated about the value to linguistics of hypothetical forms remote from speech, but it has been the influence of Chomsky that converted large numbers of American linguists to the acceptance of grand theory. The plain fact is that much about language cannot be explained without grand theory, and what could not be explained is precisely what must be explained if content analysis is to work.

Whereas the business of linguistics seems to be the explication of several transductions, the business of psychology seems to be something else. The hypothetical forms yielded by the last linguistic transduction can be taken, for the present, as the forms on which cognitive processes work. Although the input and output of a linguistic process are of different kinds, according to our speculation, the input and output of a cognitive process are of the same kind—the kind called content.

The content of a text is to be represented by a formula; the content of a man's whole life could be represented by a formula of the same class, and so could a culture—with certain exceptions. Most knowledge is stored in formulas of this class, although some knowledge can presumably be stored in other forms: knowing how to hammer a nail is one thing, knowing a poem well enough to recite it is another, but knowing the role of the papacy in world history is something else again. Only knowledge of the third kind is being considered here.

Knowledge, as we are defining it, is the basis of thought, the raw material and end product of cognition. Knowledge is the innermost limit of linguistic transduction; linguistics is called to account for the conversion of what is heard into an increment to knowledge, and the conversion of some fragment of knowledge into what is uttered. Philosophers, psychologists, cultural anthropologists, and linguists all have a right to speak on the characteristics of knowledge: what class of formulas is appropriate to the data they jointly gather? Serious consideration of what content analysis ought to be must begin with the characteristics of knowledge.

KNOWLEDGE

Knowledge, we speculate (as in Hays, 1967b; but notice that we are reworking ground where many philosophers have preceded us), has to do with actions, things, and properties. Let us call a small composite, made up of an action and a few things implicated in it, an event statement. One part of knowledge is a collection of event statements, which we shall call an encyclopedia. We suppose that some statements enter an individual's private encyclopedia as the consequence of his direct observation, others from reading and listening, and others by his taking thought—that is, by derivation in some manner from the knowledge he acquires by looking and listening.

The statements in an encyclopedia are linked together in several ways.

The most direct manner is by temporal and causal linkages between actions.

Another mode of linkage between events is through the things that participate in many events. Both things and actions are characterized by their properties. Thus, further linkages exist between two events which, although they involve different actions and different things, involve actions or things with the same properties. Things and actions—and properties— have names. Events involving different things with the same name are linked, but if thinking follows such links it is likely to become confused.

Properties have properties. For example, being animate is one property and being human is another, but it is true of these two properties that every human thing is animate. The property of being male is a permanent property, whereas the property of being 27 inches tall is temporary for a human being.

Some of the entities a person knows about are individual and concrete. Others are general. For example, one may know that his wife, a definite individual, read the newspaper this morning; one knows of human beings in general that they are capable of reading, and of newspapers that they are objects that can be read. The presence of these general statements in an encyclopedia can be used in accounting for acceptance or rejection of new statements. The sentences that one hears or reads are often ambiguous. If one's interlocutor says, "My wife read the newspaper this morning," one can check the acceptability of this sentence (that is, of the statement it represents) by looking for a known generalization of it. The interlocutor's wife is human, and a newspaper is a printed document. The generalization is that *human things read printed documents,* which is known to be true. The generalized human thing that reads has perhaps the additional property of being not blind; in that case, one could conclude that the interlocutor's wife is not blind.

Part of a person's knowledge is procedural, consisting of rules for drawing conclusions or doing overt actions. Some rules of cognitive procedure must be innate, differentiating man from the beasts; whatever they are, these are the true laws of thought. Other procedures are plainly learned, some in school and some outside. Another part of a person's knowledge is affective. Probably the simplest workable scheme for introducing affect is to define two properties, one positive and one negative. Since thought moves from thing to thing and event to event, affect would tend to radiate.

Purposes are also part of knowledge, but two varieties can be distinguished. One is a complex of event statements taken by the person to describe not his present situation but one he intends to bring about. The other is a procedure taken by the person to be in partial control of his own behavior. Anyone with a purpose of the first variety is presumably on the lookout for procedural purposes to move him toward his goal.

To deal effectively with others of his own kind, a person must know (that is, have in his encyclopedia) that they too possess knowledge, including their own procedures and goals. He must be able to sort out what he and his interlocutor both know, what he alone knows, and what his interlocutor alone knows. In part, such knowledge can take the form of event statements, in which the event is knowing, the agent is the interlocutor, and the object is an event statement.

We speculate, then, that every person has a store of knowledge, not in the form of sentences, but in the form of a network of things, actions, and properties. Understanding a message consists of transducing it into a form comparable to that of the stored network, and making tests against what is known. In some cases, the new statements thus obtained are added to the network of permanent knowledge. To produce a sentence, a person focuses his attention on certain statements and, from them, transduces a message.

CONTENT ANALYSIS

Content analysis is the determination of characteristics of a source from the natural-language utterances it emits. The characteristics should be important, with respect to our theories or our practical concerns, and they should be correct. For reasons of economy, we could wish for analytic procedures requiring only a small amount of text to determine many characteristics; looking another way at the same principle, we should prefer a theory that more completely accounted for the source's utterances, given its characteristics. Judged by these criteria, theories that account only for the frequencies of certain words or classes of words, or for the association of certain combinations of words are weak (that is, poor) theories. The thesis of this chapter is that the analysis of content will achieve its greatest successes by operating with a model of the conversationalist.

For example, let us take the case of a sequence of editorials. The analyst would begin by constructing an encyclopedia corresponding to the editorial writer's initial knowledge of a given situation; much of the encyclopedia would be common knowledge in the editorial writer's culture, and part would be a picture of the editorial reader. The analyst would provide for addition to the encyclopedia as the editorial writer witnessed the events unfolding. Then, given two or more conflicting hypotheses about the editorial writer's purposes and strategies, the analyst would attempt to account for the editorials actually produced. The analyst's theory would have to explain such phenomena as differential attention, techniques of argument, and many things more.

The analysis of diplomatic exchanges would require a similar model, except that an encyclopedia would have to be constructed for each participating country, each would have its own strategy, and so on. Each government, on receipt of a message, would apply its own model to test whether the purposes of its own prior messages had been fulfilled. It would then, perhaps, alter its estimates of the other country's response mechanism and reconsider the attainability of its own purposes, revising them or not.

If the analyst's material consists of personal documents, he will have to have psychological theories of greater precision and detail than ever before in order to explain their content. Or consider the case of interviewing. An appropriate goal for the content analyst is the construction of a computer system that would act as diagnostic interviewer. The system would have as one component an encyclopedia of what any client would be expected to know. Its objective would be to enlarge that encyclopedia, but specifically in areas of theoretical significance. The system would have to be equipped to make diagnostic inferences and test them by putting additional questions. In the area of social interaction, a proper goal is to explain the attitudes of participants to each other and toward the task in hand by inference from their discussions. Plainly, this calls for a strong theory of attitude formation and change.

PROSPECTS

I have not attempted, here, to set forth a theory of content analysis; instead, I have concentrated on the linguistic prerequisites. I have tried to argue that the proper representation of content for psychological, sociological, or political analysis is very different from the representation given by ordinary speech. I have also argued that the method of assigning properties to words and counting appearances of properties is insufficient; the content of a message should be analyzed in terms of what has gone before, in terms of the relationship between the message and what the sender or receiver already knows.

The action program I am calling for is a difficult one. It will certainly require several years to carry out. It calls for contributions from linguists, content analysts in several fields of social and behavioral science, and computer programmers.

Linguists are asked to furnish transducers. The fundamental necessity is a sound theory; thereafter, descriptions of concrete languages are needed, and computer programs for doing the transductions. Linguistic theory has advanced a long way in ten years, and is now flourishing; content analysis based on theory already published could be exciting, but the work of the next few years is likely to improve our theory of the abstract form of human knowledge substantially. Description of natural languages—that is, the writing of dictionaries and grammars—is proceeding. The situation will be much better when large centers are charged with the preparation and maintenance of descriptions, in accordance with sound theory and in forms suitable for computer input. Computer programs have been written in experimental versions, generally operating slowly because the experimenter is too impatient to make them operate fast (Kuno, 1966; Zwicky et al., 1965; and Kay, 1967). Nevertheless, the content analyst can use them for his experiments, knowing that faster versions can be written later.

Content analysts are asked to write encyclopedias, including models of the subject's purposes, procedures, and models of those to whom he speaks or writes. Happily, these models are presumably what the psychologist, sociologist, political scientist, and historian all want. A theory of content analysis, stripped of its linguistic components, is viewed to be one of the proper objects of behavioral science—in no sense a bastard or stepchild. True, a theory with the requisite degree of explicitness and detail does not exist, and probably could not be managed without the computer. However, we do have computers, and I claim that they are wasted if they serve behavioral science only for statistical (or word-matching) operations. Rightly viewed, content analysis is a core problem in the study of man, and to work at solving it could alter the social and behavioral sciences in fundamental ways.

4 Models of Messages: Three Prototypes

Klaus Krippendorff

The Annenberg School of Communications
University of Pennsylvania

In this chapter I suggest three basic models of analytical constructs that seem to underly much current research on the content of messages. Traditional content analysts preferred to intuit systematically the content of verbal data and thus avoided the explication of the process by which content is derived from text. The search for adequate models of such processes is not merely a matter of intellectual curiosity. For example, when algorithms for automated analyses are sought, their availability is crucial and their theoretical and methodological implications must be understood. Here, I shall not attempt to give a detailed *formalization* of such models, nor can I treat their logical consequences in detail. Instead, I shall focus on the *principles* that go into their construction. These models are thus quite general and can be discussed without reference to particular communication situations: as prototypes. By isolating them, I hope to sharpen a few issues that seem to be critical for further developments in content analysis.

Message Analysis

One of the most distinctive features of messages is that they provide indirect (vicarious) information to a receiver, that is, information about events that take place at a distant location, about objects that have existed far in the past, and about ideas in other people's minds, for example. I maintain that the ability of a message receiver to regard sensory data as indirectly informative about a source is what content analysis must cope with *explicitly*.

In a particular message-analytic situation (as diagrammed in Figure 2 of the "Introduction to Part I") we always observe:

1. *A source,* that is, a "real" system that is in some way delineated or understood by the analyst.

2. *Text,* that is, data with an inherent structure that are presumably emitted by the source.

3. *The analyst* who wishes to gain knowledge about certain inaccessible features of the source.

4. A replicable and valid *inferential procedure* that transforms a representation of text into notations for inaccessible states or properties of a source:

$$\text{Recorded text} \rightarrow \begin{array}{l}\text{Notations} \\ \text{referring to} \\ \text{inaccessible} \\ \text{states}\end{array}$$

These observations suggest that *content analysis* be restricted to *the use of replicable and valid methods for making specific inferences from text to other states or properties of its source.* This definition excludes some of traditional content analysis insofar as the critical process of content inference is based entirely on human intuition and explicit techniques are merely aids to handle large quantities of data. Also it imposes a constraint on the many ways data can be transformed by admitting only those analytical processes that are justifiable in reference to a particular source.

Informational Prerequisites

Although it is important to delineate the framework within which I wish to confine myself, I am not so much interested in what content *is* or how it *ought* to be defined. These are normative questions. In my view, content evolves in the course of analyzing messages in a particular *situation* and for particular investigative *purposes*. It cannot easily be separated from these two variables. Therefore, I would like to turn the question around and ask what conception of "message content" is implied in a particular content analytic technique. Or, more generally stated, I want to examine what a message source looks like through the assumptions that content analysts tacitly make after having decided on a particular analytical construct.

The decisions that content analysts must justify provide clues to another way of looking at the same problem. W. Ross Ashby (1960) has shown that the making of appropriate selections (among notations for unobserved states as a consequence of available text) is intrinsically related to the quantity of *information available.* Indeed, many of the content analyst's problems arise from the fact that knowledge about a source is sparse and has to be used effectively. The design of adequate constructs for content analysis always relies on information about the structure of a source that is external to the text, and their analytical success is a function of the quantity of structural information available to the analyst (Krippendorff, 1967). These considerations lead to four important questions.

1. What is the structure of the information that enables an analyst to make content inferences about a source?

2. How can the needed information be acquired, and what are the criteria for assessing the validity of this information?

3. How can given information be operationalized, for example, how can structural information be represented in algorithmic form?

4. What evidence establishes the validity or the *success* of the message analytical process as a whole?

Clearly, the answer to question 1 is a prerequisite for serious consideration of all of the other questions. And the concern with structural information that goes into the design of explicit techniques involves questions of "procedural adequacy" as a *component of analytical success.*

However, in content analysis this success is also affected by solutions to another problem that I mention briefly: the raw data in content analysis—text—is not only complex both syntactically and semantically but it is essentially nonformalized. The formal transcription symbols in terms of which text is represented often captures only aspects of the text's virtual complexity. Therefore, the most obvious prerequisite for analytical success is that the recorded text accurately represent relevant features of the text. The same is required for the notations in terms of which content inferences are cast. They are expected to represent unambiguously features of a source that are of interest to the analyst.

To achieve this (which I call *observational adequacy*) is not an easy matter: what is recorded in content analysis is often neither relevant nor significant, and what is relevant and significant in the light of systematic theory is often difficult to transcribe. Since the level of knowledge about a source may change during the course of an analysis, the relevance of observations is not even determinable a priori. In addition, when content inferences refer to hypothetical rather than observational variables, their adequacy can only be assessed indirectly (construct validity) making the control of this component of analytical success correspondingly more difficult.

It is possible to satisfy the requirements of observational adequacy and still fail to make valid content inferences. There is yet another component of analytical success which stems from the appropriateness of an analytical procedure in reference to a particular source. This standard will be called *procedural adequacy.* Formally, stated procedural adequacy is achieved when the analytical construct is a homomorphic representation of significant characteristics of the source. But this is again easier demanded than accomplished. In concrete message-analytic situations it is often difficult to identify what is significant. Available knowledge about a source may not be complete nor easy to fully operationalize. Therefore, in order to specify analytical constructs in sufficient detail, structural information about a source is often supplemented by arbitrary assumptions.

Models of Messages

Evidently, procedural adequacy cannot be assessed in isolation from a particular message-analytic situation, that is, without regard to the structure of a source and to the investigative purpose of the analyst. But it is possible to consider in isolation the *formal characteristics of procedural constructs* that content analysts employ to render recorded text informative about its source. These considerations provide the bases for recognizing certain similarities among analytical techniques and for ascertaining their methodological implications. We can also regard these constructs as explicit manifestations of structural information about a source and continue to discuss the class of sources for which given techniques would be adequate procedurally. We are then concerned with their theoretical implications.

It should be pointed out that these topics raise questions about the nature of messages, that is, how indirect information is conveyed to an analyst. In essence, these questions belong to the domain of semantics. However, since the discipline has acquired so many different orientations, and since my concern is far more specialized to empirical inquiries, I shall refer to the formal characteristics of content analytical constructs by the more germane term *models of messages*. Models have the advantage of being amenable to mathematical treatment without reference to what they represent. Inquiries into models of messages may thus serve to put analytical constructs on a sound logical foundation, clarify their workings and, what is perhaps more important, relate them to relevant branches in mathematics, statistics, and logic. This chapter constitutes only the beginning of such an inquiry.

In the content analysis literature in which the attempt is made to treat available text as messages about properties of its source, essentially three models seem to account for most of the content inferences. Each model leads to a different way of regarding messages as informative; each has its own merits and limitations. I have labeled these models as follows.

1. *Association models* of messages, which realize contents in statistical correlations between observational variables.

2. *Discourse models* of messages, which consider contents as linguistic referents and realize them in denotations and connotations.

3. *Communication models* of messages, according to which contents become manifest in processes of control within dynamic systems of interaction.

ASSOCIATION MODELS

The General Nature of Such Models

The conceptually simplest of the three models of messages is based on the idea of statistical association between co-occurring events. It assumes that a source can be represented adequately within a *finite number of dimensions* that are logically or observationally distinct for the analyst, but statistically related as far as the source's manifest properties are concerned. Just as the members of a population may be characterized by a particular set of attributes, so are the possible states of a source depicted as consisting of a finite number of components.

Informativeness within such models of messages is consequently assessed by *statistical measures of association*. When the correlation between two sets of dimensions is high, then, in general, an observation on one set of dimensions yields information about the other set and can hence be considered a message about those other dimensions, or a symptom, or an index. The recognition of the message characteristics of some text presupposes that the analyst knows the correlation, among the variables particularly the *multivariate probability distribution* over the source's components.

An extremely simple and, by now, classical example of the use of association models for making specific inferences from text is John Dollard and Hobart Mowrer's study of the Discomfort Relief Quotient (Dollard and Mowrer, 1947). This quotient is computed from the frequencies with which two classes of words occur in recorded speech and was found to be indicative of a speaker's state of stress on the grounds that the extent of stress as observed and the value of the quotient correlated significantly. George Mahl and Gene Schulze (1964b) reviewed this research tradition recently and showed that a host of measures such as speech-disturbance ratios, verb-adjective ratios, and speech rates do have similar diagnostic value to psychologists interested in information about a speaker's concurrent emotional or psychopathological states.

Association models of messages are by no means confined to psychological endeavors. Solutions to the literary scholar's problem of identifying the author of unsigned documents may involve identical conceptions. For example, when stylistic indices can be found that vary little within and as much as possible across the works of suspected writers, authorship may be inferred. Whether such stylistic indices are computed on the basis of the authors' vocabulary (Yule, 1944), on certain function words (Mosteller and Wallace, 1964), or on other minor encoding habits (Paisley, 1964), their informativeness is rendered by demonstrating statistical associations.

In *mass media* research, association models are even more prominent. For example, measures of the *diversity of political symbols* occurring in the major newspapers of a country have been shown to be indicative of socioeconomic crises and feelings of uncertainty (Pool, 1951); journalistic assessments of *sensationalism* lead to measures that correlate highly with intuitive judgments regarding this concept (Tannenbaum and Lynch, 1960); similarly, attempts to infer the *readability* of a text resulted in the proposal of a set of indices (Flesch, 1951). The basic assumption of much of traditional content analysis has been that the relative *frequency* with which a certain reference is made within a text correlates with the *attention* or *importance* assigned by a writer to the object referred to. Unfortunately these statistical associations needed to validate the inferences are often assumed and are rarely tested for their significance.

The content inferences that association models of messages can account for thus involve the following items.

1. A set of elements, the *recording units* of text that can be enumerated or quantitatively assessed so as to be amenable to statistical procedures.

2. One or more *measuring operations, m_i*(text). Defined over the units of recorded text, the measurements are relatively invariant with respect to certain dimensions of the source's emissions. Each measuring operation is a mapping:

$$\text{Unitized text} \rightarrow m_i(\text{text})$$

3. A set of *operationally defined terms, df*(state), or variables that represent extratextual states or properties of the source. These terms constitute the possible contents among which selections are made.

4. Rules of content inference, that are defined on the observed probabilities of co-occurrences, make up the *association logic* of the model. These rules assign probabilities, P_m, over the set of terms, $df(\text{state}_j)$, that are conditional on the set $\{m_1(\text{text}), m_2(\text{text}), \ldots\}$ of measurements:

$$\{m_1(\text{text}), m_2(\text{text}), \ldots\} \rightarrow P_m[df(\text{state}_j).$$

Notice that the conditional probability, P_m, is a *frequency* interpretation

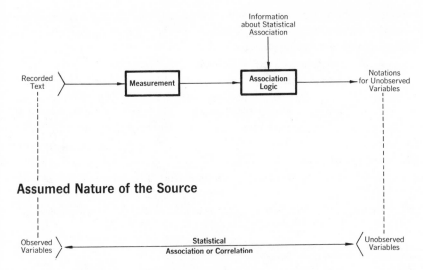

Figure 1 Association models of messages: procedures.

of probability and the rules of content inferences are not mappings. A text can be said to be informative about unobserved states of a source if the probability distribution significantly deviates from chance.[1]

Association models of messages thus require two procedurally independent components: a measurement component and what I call an association logic. The former reduces the irrelevant complexity in text so that the latter can provide the specific content inferences. This is shown in Figure 1.

More or less hidden, association models appear in a variety of essentially different *research designs*. Naturally, commitments to this prototype are most explicit in experimental approaches. For example, attempting to show the validity of his contingency analysis, Charles Osgood (1959a) set up a situation in which word association structures could be measured by a standard association test and correlated with the results of a contingency analysis of the subjects' verbalizations.

Trying to find an objective procedure for distinguishing real from simulated suicide notes, Philip J. Stone and Earl B. Hunt (1963) were aided

[1] Informativeness within association models can be given a more precise notion by means of Shannon's information theory. If C is the set of possible contents of interest to the analyst, and $H_m(C)$ is the partial conditional entropy in C, the particular measure m being known, the information I that m conveys about C is

$$I = H(C) - H_m(C)$$

by a computer program that enumerated the occurrence of specified classes of words within text. After inspection of the frequency tabulations, a decision criterion was developed. The above-chance frequency of success subsequently established its informativeness.

Earl Hunt's Concept Learner, on the other hand, is a computer program that discovers relevant associations automatically. Given two texts that are differentiated according to an outside criterion (for example, being for or against a legislative proposal), the Concept Learner develops a discriminate function that accounts for this differentiation. This discriminate function, which actually takes the form of a decision tree involving as many measures as necessary, can subsequently be used to render a third text informative about the outside criterion, for example, whether it supports or rejects the proposal (Hunt, Marin, and Stone, 1966:159).

Powers and Limitations

Researchers who employ association models as a basis for their inferences are bound to believe that the informativeness of a text about a source's states increases with the *number* of different *measurements* that are considered. This belief results from the nature of multivariate techniques, which suggest that the predictability of a phenomenon can only increase with the number of variables observed.[2]

The lesson of much content analysis has been that an increase in the number of measurements does not necessarily approximate procedural adequacy. As more and more measurements are considered as "predictors," the relative informativeness of each additional one becomes progressively less and always reaches a point of equilibrium at which the inferential power of association models is simply exhausted. Let me point to four fundamental limitations of association models of messages which are inherent in their assumptions about the nature of a source and that cannot be overcome by any increase in the number of measurements on text.

1. Association models treat the system under consideration as *ergodic sources.* This is because of the aggregate nature of statistical indices which are computed over the occurrences of specified units within text. Discontinuities in the frequencies of word use and verbal clarification of meanings and their consequences must escape the analysis when words or phrases are numerated without regard to their position within a text. Unique occurrences, on the other hand, do not significantly contribute to correlations

---

[2] In terms of information theory (see footnote 1), this results from the fact that whichever two measures m_1 and m_2 are given

$$H(C) - H_{m_1}(C) \leq H(C) - H_{m_1 m_2}(C)$$

sought and, although they may be informative according to some other model of messages, they disappear in this prototype. The use of the association model presupposes that the enumerated characteristics *permeate* the given text *statistically.*

2. Association models preclude considerations of *reference meanings.* No statistically significant correlation has yet been shown to exist between the types of objects in a speaker's or writer's environment and the type of words he chooses to use. For example, the frequent use of the term "peace" in a text neither indicates whether the writer finds himself in such a state nor whether he desires it. It does not even indicate whether he has ever experienced such a state or whether he knows what it means connotatively or denotatively. Unless experimental situations impose serious constraints on verbal responses, inferences about what a text refers to on the basis of association models become vacuous. Thus while such models undoubtedly may render data informative in some sense, they are incapable of dealing with linguistic references, denotations, or connotations. This fact cannot be emphasized strongly enough, since much use of language is understood as being representational.

3. Association models are incapable of making inferences about *syntactically expressed* contents. In other words, while co-occurrence and transition probabilities can be used to construct a kind of primitive grammar, association models are not powerful enough to consider sentential grammars. One of the most outstanding facts of language is that the number of sentences that a given language admits is practically unlimited and that each sentence is essentially a novel sentence.[3] A statistical treatment of sentences becomes meaningless, however, when repetitive occurrences are rare. Attempts to force syntactically complex linguistic expressions into a *finite nonrecursive* enumeration scheme—just to obtain some frequencies above one—discards much of the communicative capability of verbalizations.

4. Association models are inadequate when a source exhibits some intelligence and exercises some cognitive control over its products, that is, when the text is generated to reach a source's varying objectives. This inadequacy was first realized by George Mahl who was puzzled by the difficulty of inferring the emotional states of a speaker when linguistic assertions are *used instrumentally.* He argued, with association models in mind, that:

(o)ur culture places a premium on the concealment of many drives and affects, and at the same time our language training and communication habits emphasize the importance of lexical content. Since affects cannot be abolished by the censor-

[3] This has been the main argument of the transformational school in linguistics for a recursive description of grammar. See, particularly, Noam Chomsky (1957).

ship of their expression, and since the nonlexical attributes are not the central targets of cultural or personal control, it is to be expected that the nonlexical features are theoretically potential targets for consistent rewards and punshiments (and may thus) acquire instrumental functions. . . . To the extent that this is so, the value of the nonlexical attributes for the content analysis will decrease. In general, it would seem to be most advantageous for the content analyst interested in drives, motives, etc., to select those nonlexical attributes that are not likely to have been influenced consistently by rewards and punishments in the past. The nonlexical attributes meeting this criterion are those that are most likely to be most remote from awareness in both the speaker and the listener (Mahl, 1959: 101–103).

Although Mahl's argument refers to content inferences of emotional states only, it focuses on a general inability of association models. William Paisley's phrase "minor encoding habits" points in the same direction by suggesting that stylistic indices may reveal the identity of an author only as long as he is unable to control their variation (Paisley, 1964). The identification of psychopathologies is also conditional upon the inability of patients to manipulate the symptoms to his advantage.

This limitation may be converted to an analytical advantage when correlations are found that yield information about consciously concealed states. Stuttering, blushing, "freudian slips," and the like, may provide clues for such information, and interrogations in court usually search for such leakages in order to interpret the verbalizations of a witness.

It should be made clear that association models of messages—while probably most favored by content analysts—(1) reduce message sources to statistical aggregates with ergodic properties, (2) discard their possible linguistic ability, that is, their use of grammatical expressions of linguistic references, and (3) discount the possibility of cognitive manuevers and their conceivably instrumental use of messages. When a source cannot be so regarded, then association models of messages become procedurally inadequate.

DISCOURSE MODELS

The Domain of Such Models

I have argued that association models of messages are inadequate when there is reason to believe that the message characteristics of a given text are language-like; when a text can be assumed to refer to, rather than correlate with, unobserved states of a source; and when message contents are, in some significant sense, novel (as is usually the case in human communication). Now I shall argue for a more powerful model—one that treats messages as *discourse*.

First, let me discuss some features of discourse as I understand them.

1. Typical discourses such as a political speech, a set of private letters, a monograph, a news report, a fairy tale, or a scholarly treatise essentially describe extralinguistic phenomena, or are representative of events or ideas that are potentially to be found within a source. That is, some words occurring in the discourse are names and refer to, denote, or connote nonlinguistic objects or concepts. Some sentences are descriptions of observed or fictional events, and descriptions usually require more than one sentence.

2. Discourses may be thought of as generating their own parameters, delineating relevant issues, and defining the meanings of terms that represent unobserved phenomena. Insofar as this is the case, sentences of a discourse may not be taken in isolation.

3. Discourses are either the product of one person or are composed in such a way that they are essentially free of inconsistencies or contradiction in reference to their source. This does not mean that an analyst may not discover logical gaps or fallacies in the arguments but that the discourse may be said to be consistent with the speaker's or writer's point of view, the ideological orientation or idiosyncratic logic of the source.

The aim of discourse models of messages, then, is to account for a reader's ability to *understand what a discourse is about.* This ability is manifest in the ability to respond to questions about the source that are pertinent to the analyst and that draw on a linguistic interpretation of the text. This ability to answer questions from a text presupposes an adequate symbolic manipulation of what a text implicitly or explicitly conveys, and thus involves both *paraphrasing* such information in the analyst's unambiguous notations and *inferring* from this information whatever the analyst wants to know about the source.

Since the formal notations referring to the possible content of interest to the analyst, and the given text, are now taken to be representative, in order to avoid confusion, two borderline cases of content inferences should be mentioned. The simplest situation is one in which the text is already cast in the analyst's terms; in this case, paraphrasing becomes superfluous and inferences are reduced to *logical implications.*[4] However, the most difficult situation arises when the given text takes the form of a language foreign to the one in terms of which the analyst wishes to represent his results. Discourse models will then have to produce a *translation* in which the relevant referential content of the discourse is maintained and only irrelevant information is eliminated in the course of the process.

[4] It should be remarked that whenever traditional content analysis aims at describing the manifest content in the author's language, such a situation in fact exists. When such content analyses follow purely descriptive aims even logical implications are supposedly excluded.

Happily, practical situations of message analysis are more likely to be concerned with a text that is recorded in a form closely related to the analyst's output language (English, for example), and the major task of discourse models becomes merely one of *extracting* relevant information from a text and of making content inferences from such information.

Unlike association models, discourse models involve the consideration of linguistic meanings. Furthermore, the goals of discourse models overlap with the aims of linguistic theory. It is not too difficult to differentiate between a native speaker's linguistic ability and his familiarity with or possession of structural information about a source. Both contribute to his understanding of what a discourse is about, but only the former is within the scope of linguistic theory. It provides the syntax, semantics, and phonology of a language that will be discussed under the *grammar* component of discourse models. The other two components of this model, *kernelization* and *discourse logic,* represent the structural information about a source. The manner in which these components are procedurally related is illustrated in Figure 2, which includes terms that will become clear later. Let me outline some of the respective features of these components.

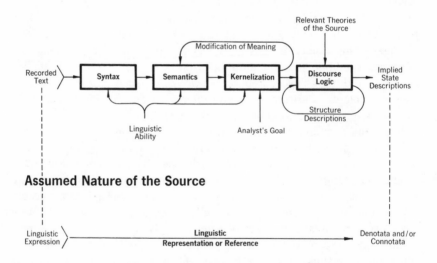

Figure 2   Discourse models of messages: procedures.

The Grammar Component

According to the transformational school of linguistics, the aim of a linguistic theory of language is to find adequate representations of the structural information that speakers employ in analyzing and generating verbalizations. The confinement to structural *information about a language* is crucial for linguists because the information that a language may represent knows virtually no limitation.

Jerry A. Fodor and his associates conceive of the grammar of a language, which represents a native speaker's linguistic ability, as having three parts: a syntax, a semantics, and a phonology (Fodor, Jenkins, and Saporta, 1967). When text is in written form, the *phonological* part becomes superfluous. The *syntactic* part is thought of as a device that either generates a set of representations of all and only the well-formed sentences of a language or assigns to each sentence proper a set of descriptions accounting for the possible ways the sentence could have been generated by that device. Jerold Katz and Jerry Fodor conceptualize the *semantics* of a language as consisting of a lexical dictionary and projection rules. The lexical dictionary provides an entry for each lexical item in a sentence and lists its possible meanings or senses, relevant semantic dimensions, and their use. The projection rules provide the basis for amalgamating syntactic descriptions and meanings to obtain the possible semantic descriptions or readings of a sentence (Katz and Fodor, 1964b). Accordingly, the function of the grammar of a language is to determine the number and kind of readings a native speaker would give to each sentence. For example, the sentence

Time flies like an arrow

may be found to be syntactically normal and to have three semantic readings: (1) there is a species called "time flies" that prefers arrows; (2) it is imperative to time the flies as quickly as possible; (3) time moves very swiftly. (Notice that the paraphrased content which I used to exhibit the different readings is not a product of a grammar, which would indicate only that "time flies," for example, is a legitimate noun phrase in English).

A grammar is thus considered as accounting for the process that can be depicted as follows:

$$s \rightarrow \begin{Bmatrix} d_1(s) \\ d_2(s) \\ \cdot \\ \cdot \\ \cdot \\ d_n(s) \end{Bmatrix}$$

where $d(s)$ is a semantic interpretation of the sentence s of a text. At this stage of linguistic theory, such grammars are still quite complex and not at all perfect. But their function within a discourse model becomes clear if we keep in mind (1) that information about the physical or social environment of a speaker is not incorporated in a grammar, and (2) that meanings are not considered above the sentence level. Consequently, the lexical dictionary characterizes the use of linguistic items *intralinguistically,* that is, it *lists* meanings or *intentional semantic interpretations,* and not the possible *referents* of those items. The projection rules select among those meanings to satisfy the particular sentential contexts within which the item occurred. Since there are numerous words that have meaning but no referent (for example, "maybe," "or," "hello," and "spirit"), and the converse does not exist, a consideration of intralinguistic uses of linguistic items precedes that of their possible referents. Likewise, semantic descriptions of sentences clearly precede characterizations of their contents.[5]

The Discourse Logic Component

Since the aim of message analysis is to obtain information from given text about some unobserved part of a source of interest to the analyst, grammar alone will not suffice. The extensionality of its output is uncertain. What discourse models have to account for is a reader's ability to understand the sentences of a discourse referentially. One test of this ability would involve pointing to the objects to which a text may refer. Since the nature of the message-analytic situation makes this virtually impossible, the only other test is for the reader to be able to draw inferences from the text which are both valid in reference to the source and relevant to the analyst's problem. To make valid and relevant inferences, it seems necessary that the reader have, in addition to his familiarity with the language, some basic knowledge about the subject matter of the discourse, that is, he must employ extralinguistic information.

The reader's understanding of the referential content of sentences may become manifest in his ability to infer, for example, from the two sentences

Mark Twain is the author of Huckleberry Finn
Samuel Clemens lived in Hannibal

[5] This point is reflected in László Antal's work. He argues that the sentence, "The sum of the angles of a triangle is 180 degrees," is meaningful to whoever is able to give a semantic description of the sentence just on the basis of the knowledge about the use of its constituent words and their relative syntactical positions. But for an understanding of what the sentence is about (that is, for a comprehension of its content), other than linguistic knowledge is required. Evidently, an English-speaking child may be able to describe the sentence semantically without understanding it. The ability to semantically describe a sentence is a prerequisite for its understanding. "The purpose of the sentence, and indeed that of language as a whole, is to convey content, and both form and meaning (syntax and semantics) are the means to achieve this end" (Antal, 1964:24).

that the author of Huckleberry Finn lived in Hannibal, which presupposes information about the identity of references. The information that justifies the inference from

Robert has a driver's license

that Robert is above 16 years of age (depending on the state), not blind, knows how to drive a car, and can identify traffic signs, for instance, represents knowledge about a set of properties that are antecedent to the one referred to in the sentence. From

Jim met his son Bill yesterday
Mary and Jim have been married for 25 years
Sam's mother Mary smokes a pipe

it is not difficult to infer that Bill and Sam are brothers, provided that some information about kinship relations is available. Similarly, even the obvious inference from "A is larger than B, B is larger than C" to "A is larger than C" presupposes information about the transitivity of the relation "is larger than." On the other hand, the relation "is father of" has quite different properties, which must be known in order to make content inferences that are adequate in reference to a particular source.

These examples show that the information that must be supplied by the reader in order to demonstrate his ability to understand the sentence of a discourse represent *structural features* of the source; such features appear in patterns or functions that may hold true for classes of the source's states. The component that accounts for a reader's ability to make adequate inferences from given sentences may be called *"discourse logic."* It can be considered the most distinctive feature of discourse models of messages. The discourse logic component suggests that a distinction be drawn between two kinds of sentences:

1. *State descriptions,* "st," or sentences that refer to particular states of the source.
2. *Structure descriptions,* "sr," or sentences that refer to relations among states or classes of states of the source.

The *rules of content inference* that are permissible within a discourse logic are then of the deductive type, for example,

$$(st_i, st_j, \ldots, sr_{ij} \ldots {}_k) \rightarrow st_k$$

The discourse logic of such models thus produces new state descriptions that are logically implied by the text. Whether the structure descriptions are exclusively extracted from the text or whether they are incorporated into the analytical process prior to the analysis, the content inferences are determined by this pool of knowledge.[6] A discourse logic evidently presupposes that the text is kernelized and put into a canonical form so that the collection of descriptions represents the relevant content of a connected discourse as a whole.

The Kernelization Component

Discourse logic essentially requires *a set* of statements in a canonical form, the elements of which are such that they can be taken out of context and used as a basis of valid inferences. A grammar, on the other hand, provides semantic characterizations for each sentence in isolation. If the input of the kernelization component is considered *a string* of concatenated sets of semantic descriptions for each sentence occurring in the text, then a context-dependent interpretation of content may be achieved. Therefore, the major aim becomes one of breaking a semantically interpreted text into *context-independent* units and of transforming these units into the *canonical form* of state or structure descriptions. Let me be more specific about this aim.

1. One of the important features of discourse, with implications for the construction of a grammar, is its ability explicitly to define or implicitly to modify the meanings of terms occurring in the same discourse. Such definitions or modifications may affect subsequent readings of a sentence in a way not normally considered when interpreted out of context. I cannot fully agree with Katz and Fodor when they assume that a grammar provides a set of alternative semantic interpretations of a sentence among which a speaker may merely select on the basis of his knowledge about the physical setting in which the sentence was uttered. At least as far as the expression of referential content is concerned, language is a very flexible device. Although it is easy to imagine a story, for instance, in which the sentence

Careless little dogs sleep quietly

is informative about some state of affairs, it is possible to find or construct a discourse within which the grammatically normal sentence

Colorless green ideas sleep furiously

becomes not only meaningful[7] but also has content. The grammar that

---

[6] This collection of state and structure descriptions is presumably what David Hays conceptualizes as the "encyclopedia" that a conversationalist consults in order to construct a reply to a received document (Hays, *infra,* Chapter 3).

[7] In a discussion of "grammatical meaning" Roman Jacobson reports that "Dell Hymes actually found an application for this sentence in a senseful poem written in 1957 and entitled 'Colorless Green Ideas Sleep Furiously' " (Jacobson, 1959:144).

Katz and Fodor suggest would be insensitive to linguistic environments which may specify the meanings of such a sentence's components and would not assign any semantic description to the latter sentence. It is only when such sentences are taken *without their linguistic environments* that they appear semantically odd. Almost every discourse can contain such sentences as

> *By "X" is meant "such and such"*
>
> *I want "X" to refer to "such and such"*
>
> *"X" is defined as "such and such"*

Sentences of this sort refer not to extralinguistic events but to the use of the linguistic item "X" within a discourse and establish a semantic convention. Let me refer to such sentences as meaning descriptions, "sm." Meaning descriptions often take up large portions of political, private, and scholarly discourses and effectively override established meanings.

Therefore, what I am advocating is an adaptive lexical dictionary, in which meaning descriptions can be incorporated after proper translation into respective canonical forms.

2. Much of normal discourse relies heavily on implicit rules for the use of otherwise semantically indefinite linguistic items. For example, pronominal forms are almost always used and perceived as having definite references that are understood in the context of other sentences. If statements are to be taken as elements in a set without loss of their contents (that is, if their semantic interpretations involving pronouns are isolated from their immediate linguistic environment), then pronouns must be replaced by the nouns for which they stand. Similarly, when a time sequence of events is implicitly referred to by the sequential order of their linguistic representations, a kernelization that loses those references may yield unwarranted inferences. Thus, although a language surely does not provide grammatical constructs above the sentence level (as Katz and Fodor correctly recognize), speakers do tend to use rather efficient referential constructs to disambiguate grammatically indefinite references. Rules based on such constructs clearly involve information outside the boundary of a sentence. The explication of these rules may be difficult, but their effective use is indispensable when a connected discourse is to be transformed into a set of state and/or structure descriptions without loss of the relevant content of the discourse as a whole.

3. The kernelization component must account for a speaker's ability to rephrase sentences or sets of sentences into a standard format. Semantic descriptions of both their operant and their transform are to remain equivalent (Chomsky, 1957; Harris, 1952). Some such transformations refer to kernelizations of a compound sentence, such as "he read an inter-

esting book" → "he read a book and the book was interesting"; others produce information equivalent transforms of a kernel sentence, for example, "he drove the car" → "the car was driven by him." But of particular importance are transformations that eliminate information that is irrelevant for the intended inferences. For example, an analyst who is interested only in interrelations among actors referred to in a text may want to reduce the information represented in two sentences

A British diplomat was forcibly detained by Red guards as he was getting out of his car. He was put on trial in the street and released after one hour of interrogation.

to "Red guards detained the British diplomat$_1$," and "the British diplomat$_1$ was put on trial by Red guards" or even further "(active) Chinese/vs./ (passive) British." The adequacy of such paraphrases obviously does not depend on linguistic considerations alone but, to a large extent, on information about the referential nature of the formalized language used by the analyst.

The function of the kernelization component may be shown, analogously to the above, by

$$
\begin{Bmatrix} d_1(s_1) \\ d_2(s_1) \\ \cdot \\ \cdot \\ \cdot \\ d_m(s_1) \end{Bmatrix} \cap \begin{Bmatrix} d_1(s_2) \\ d_2(s_2) \\ \cdot \\ \cdot \\ \cdot \\ d_n(s_2) \end{Bmatrix} \cap \cdots \cap \begin{Bmatrix} d_1(s_u) \\ d_2(s_u) \\ \cdot \\ \cdot \\ \cdot \\ d_z(s_u) \end{Bmatrix} \rightarrow \begin{Bmatrix} st_1, & st_2, & \ldots, & st_v \\ sr_1, & sr_2, & \ldots, & sr_w \\ sm_1, & sm_2, & \ldots, & sm_x \end{Bmatrix},
$$

where the left side of the arrow denotes its input, which takes the form of a concatenation, "∩," of the semantic descriptions of the sentences of the text, and the output is a set of state descriptions, structure descriptions, and meaning descriptions.

Powers and Limitations

The grammar that I have been referring to is, to my knowledge, the only form that has led to computable algorithms. Although its current stage of formalization is still too complex and computationally too expensive to show significant analytical advantages when compared with the linguistic efficiency of speakers, the progress thus far achieved is remarkable. But, since I am not primarily concerned with linguistics, let me illustrate some of the other components of discourse models, no matter how primitive their current manifestation may be.

In the few cases in which the output of *kernelizations* is actually written down, the transformation that accounts for it is achieved mostly by knowledgeable analysts and not by explicit processes. Although this step cannot be considered an explicit analysis, it nevertheless exhibits its significance whenever text is considered as having representational message characteristics. For example, Ole Holsti made use of a canonical statement format in which sentences representing actions and perceptions of actions by major national policy makers could be recorded. The seven possible constituents of such state descriptions are as follows.

The perceiver
The perceiver other than author of the document
The perceived
The action
The object acted upon (other than an actor-target)
The auxiliary verb modifier
The target and incorporated modifier (North et al., 1963:137)

If the relationships expressed by a sentence coincide with those implied in the definitions of these facets, then the assumed content of the statement can be paraphrased and represented in such a canonical form. Thus the terms of the analyst's formalized language determine the kind of information that can be utilized for subsequent content inferences.

In an ongoing international study of values in politics at the University of Pennsylvania, relevant portions of political speeches were rephrased to make the structure within which political values are expressed available for subsequent inferences (Krippendorff, 1966b). Similarly, Collette Piault (1965) used a notational system consisting of sets of attributes, relations, references, and two classes of objects in the terms of which interview data could be represented for further processing. But the kernelization in all cases was done cognitively, that is, by the intuition of an analyst.

With discourse logics, examples are fewer. When the content of a text is represented in some canonical form other than simple categories, most content analysts go immediately into enumerations, and thus approximate the limitations of association models. One good example of a discourse logic (primitive but, nevertheless, convincing) is incorporated in Osgood, Saporta, and Nunnally's (1956) "Evaluative Assertion Analysis." The canonical form of its state descriptions consists of two linguistic items referring to different objects and an expressed relation between them. The relation is regarded as associative or dissociative, and the affective evaluation of one object is known, by attribution or otherwise, while the evaluation of the second must be inferred. This inference is accounted for by the congruity principle of affective cognition. The algebraic operations of the discourse logic, which this principle suggests, are fairly simple and explicit. They purport to operationalize some psychological processes that are assumed to be universal to all individuals.

Although I regard discourses as representative of states and structures of a source, quite often they can be considered as *argumentative,* in the sense that conclusions are developed and are more or less explicitly accepted. Such discourses may reveal some aspects of the logic underlying the use of references and contents. Edwin Shneidman, who made use of this information, suggested that there are individual differences in thinking or cognitive maneuvers which may be manifested in the idiosyncracies of either deductive or inductive reasoning, in the form or the content of the (explicit or implied) premises, in logical gaps or unwarranted conclusions, and the like. Under the assumption that each individual employs an "idiologic" that is both consistent and acceptable to him, it is possible to infer the logical conditions under which idiosyncracies of reasoning and cognitive maneuvers appear rational. In doing this systematically, the analyst constructs a discourse logic or "contralogic," as he calls it, which "would be that theoretical logical system (which might be operating unconsciously in the mind of the speaker) which would serve to undo or rectify or make reasonable the apparent idiosyncracies of the speaker's logical positions. Its purpose is to permit (the analyst) to see what is required—what the speaker must implicitly believe—to logically 'explain' the speaker's own special logic" (Shneidman, 1963:183). Although Shneidman uses these logical constructs only as an intermediate step to infer psychological traits, the work shows the need for discourse logics when an analyst considers verbal material as having referential contents.

The scarcity of examples seems to suggest that a complete formalization of discourse models may well be too complex to be practicable. Models of the ability of a reader to handle cognitively information about the subject matter of a text require a considerable amount of theoretical comprehension before they can be put into algorithmic terms. This is true even if an analytical procedure is conceived to handle just one specific discourse. Nevertheless, I think this development of theory is a prerequisite for the design of computer programs that process the linguistic contents of volumes of verbal data automatically.

In my opinion, the best example of a discourse model of messages, which has been fully computerized, is described by Robert K. Lindsay (1963). It is too simple to be useful for practical analysis, but it clearly demonstrates how discourse models of messages have to be constructed algorithmically. Lindsay's program accepts only sentences in *Ogden's Basic English* and is aimed at representing and making inferences about kinship relations. Such sentences as

Joey was playing with his brother Bobby in their Aunt Jane's yard when their mother called them home

are first subjected to syntactic analysis from which syntactic characterizations of their sentential structure is obtained. A semantic analysis subsequently searches for all expressions that connote kinship relations. Sentences that are relevant, according to this criterion, are then kernelized and paraphrased to obtain state descriptions in canonical form of the type "Joey is brother of Bobby." The originally rich content of the discourse is thus reduced to the dimensions relevant for the intended inferences. The main objective of this work was to find an inferential memory that represented the discourse logic implicitly. Structural information about the source (the system of kin relations) was thereby assumed perfect. The discourse logic thereby constructed accounts for inferences from the additional sentence

Bobby's sister Judy married Edward

that Judy is Joey's sister, that Edward is Joey's brother-in-law, for instance, thus giving a clear demonstration of some *understanding* of what the discourse is about.

The program also demonstrates another feature of discourse models that contrasts with association models. From the above sentences, some uncertainty regarding Jane's exact position within the kinship network still remains. The reader is informed that Jane is either the sister of Joey's mother *or* she is the sister of Joey's father, but not both. As Lindsay points out, it would be inappropriate to assume "a connection such that a given stimulus will sometimes evoke one association, sometimes another on a probability basis. . . . (N)o reader would conclude half the time that Jane is the sister of Joey's mother and half the time that she is the sister of Joey's father, altering his decision from time to time" (Lindsay, 1963:231). While it is not unreasonable to consider logical interpretations of probabilities for discourse models, a *frequency interpretation of probability* as required in association models would be entirely inappropriate here.

Discourse models of messages, the structure of which I have just characterized, are meant to represent a reader's ability to understand what a discourse is about. Although such models render a text infinitely more informative about a source than association models can ever accomplish, even if their formalization were accomplished, they are still limited on several grounds. Let me mention only two basic sources of procedural inadequacy.

1. Discourse models cannot handle the kind of outside evidence that an informed reader may utilize in determining which statements are true, invalid, or indeterminate. The rejection by a reader of a statement that

appears contrary to experience has its analog in contradictions between statements of the discourse logic component. But to determine which of the contradictory statements has to be accepted or refuted requires information *about those statements,* such as the credibility of the source, which discourse models cannot handle. The same inability refers to attitudinal propositions and quotations. The sentence

Brown said, "Red guards tried a British diplomat"

for example, is about Brown making a certain noise. The fact that this noise can also be regarded as having content requires an additional level of discourse.

2. When a source aims at certain effects, statements may be primarily of an *instrumental* character rather than representative. In these situations, discourse models may yield entirely inadequate results. Arguing about the instrumental use of language, George Mahl enumerated the situations in which a child may utter "I am hungry." It may be used when it is unwilling to go to bed, when in need for attention, for instance, and perhaps also when hungry. To consider the statement as referring to an existing state of hunger *whenever* it is uttered may be entirely misleading (Mahl, 1959:94). The same situation exists for the analyst of war propaganda who wishes to infer whether referred to reprisal weapons in fact exist (George, 1959a:148). Lies are, after all, the most extreme form of instrumental communications. If they appear in a discourse, particularly when consistent with the remaining content, inferences from a discourse model of messages are bound to be fallacious.

COMMUNICATION MODELS

The Domain of Such Models

Communications exchanged in interpersonal conversations, political dialogues, and between social institutions, regardless of whether they are regarded as propaganda, official documents, ultimata, treatises, commands, expressions of compliance, and the like, differ from discourses as considered above in at least three fundamental ways.

1. These communications, while sometimes containing linguistic references, are to a significant degree composed of sentences that do not convey a representational kind of information about the states and the structure of a source. Questions, demands, requests, instructions, and greetings cannot be verified in the same way in which state descriptions or structure descriptions can be verified and do not constitute the same type of content for which discourse models account. Yet such linguistic forms are signifi-

cant for the understanding of interactions among language users. Although sentences of this type are not primarily representational, their content may become manifest to an analyst in the *interactions* among communicators.

2. Even when such communications have clear representational message characteristics, they may have to be viewed as instrumental to the achievement of the source's objectives. Purpose is basic to all sources to whom intelligence can be attributed and, in the case of human beings, instrumentality may enter all spheres of their overt behavior. Neither association models nor discourse models are powerful enough to consider purposive verbalizations. For example, a guest who may want to lead his host to the position of offering him a drink by saying "It's really hot today" may or may not have made a true statement. But the assertion may trigger a behavioral trajectory that terminates with, among other things, the guest's obtaining a drink. If these consequences provide an intelligent communicator with the criteria for making choices among instrumental verbalizations, then the analyst must search for the content of messages in terms of their possible *consequences*.[8]

3. Such communications often occur in situations comprising several communicators, each pursuing its own objectives. The recorded text, the data that communication models require, cannot be considered as a single consistent discourse but as representing a pattern of linguistic and nonlinguistic interactions between parties, *a chronology of exchanges* among purposive communicators. Each of these exchanges is generated by one party and *directed* to other parties. Being a response to previous exchanges, each of them is assigned *a point in time* relative to each other.[9]

[8] Such conceptions of content are quite uncommon in the tradition of Western philosophy of language. The only recent systematic approach that attempted a reconstruction of linguistic theory in this direction is John Austin's work on *How to Do Things with Words* (1962) in which behavioral consequences are associated with linguistic utterances.

[9] Notice that several studies have recorded the direction of exchanges. In his canonical recording format, Ole Holsti recognizes at least the producer of the statements and the perceiver of the situation to which they refer (North et al., 1963:137). Another way of recording interactions is suggested by Elihu Katz et al., (1967) who propose to analyze the nature of persuasive appeals that clients of a formal organization use in support of requests for services. The six-faceted canonical form includes the client's perceptions of his role in relation to that of the formal organization. Such ways of recording do not necessarily produce chronologies of interaction of the kind that communication models require, particularly when the verbalizations of only one party are considered and when the order of the exchanges is neglected so as to make the text amenable to statistical description. The latter is the case for data generated in the course of Robert Bales' *Interaction Process Analysis* (1950).

Thus the relevant context of sentences of the text has not only a linguistic dimension but includes the system of interactions and the changes in the parameter of such a system as well.

Perhaps we can appreciate the complexity of the source with which communication models of messages have to deal by considering an example of a chesslike game. In this hypothetical game, each player chooses his own objectives and has some advantage in not revealing them to the other player; rules are freely negotiable during the play and may, indeed, be violated; and each party may want to put only few of his pawns on the board and is free to talk about the position of the rest. All that the analyst obtains is the chronology of moves and verbal exchanges.[10] Discourse models would merely infer what pawns are being talked about. Association models would be quite inappropriate in such situations, since the most significant aspects of the game are not discernible in terms of statistical correlations. Communication models of messages, on the other hand, are expected to render the recorded verbalizations informative about the implicit and explicit rules that develop in the course of a play, about the pattern of compliance to these rules, about the objectives on which each player may settle interdependently, and about the nature of the cooperative or competitive relation that may emerge between them. Thus, the analyst who attempts to understand the system from the recorded exchanges with the aid of communication models of messages may at times have to outwit the players' intentions, predict the consequences of their moves, and describe the interlocking properties of the play which govern both the linguistic and nonlinguistic interactions. In other words, the analyst aims at inferring the structure of a dynamic system, its operating rules, and controls from the recorded linguistic exchanges between, and interactions among, potentially purposive communicators.

Analytical constructs of communication situations that could render such a chronology of exchanges informative about the parameters of a dynamic system or, more specifically, models of messages that identify the content of linguistic and nonverbal interactions with the product of control processes governing the interactions among purposive communicators are extremely complex and difficult to formalize. I cannot claim to have solved any of the problems associated with such models, nor do I believe that algorithmic solutions can be found within a short period of time except, perhaps, for the most reduced cases. My confidence in the *feasibility* of constructing communication models of messages lies in

[10] In a standard game of chess, verbalizations exchanged between experienced players are irrelevent to the game. Rules are not negotiable, and information about the state of the play is always perfect. Communication models of messages would hardly be appropriate.

the fact that intelligent communicators continually use communication conceptions when either generating messages that have certain intended or unintentional effects of analyzing received messages in these terms. Even when those messages are exchanged between social groups or nations, analysts have been able to make rather reliable speculations regarding the patterns about which such messages may be informative. Systematic attempts to extract military intelligence from domestic war propaganda (George, 1959a), the little published work of numerous foreign specialists who analyze diplomatic exchanges before adequate responses are formulated, and scholarly concerns with the possibilities of inferring whether the signatories of a disarmament agreement still conform to their commitments (Singer, 1963) provide, if not examples of success, at least signs of reasonable hope. I am therefore convinced that it may be possible to make progress in understanding communication models of messages if at least some of their formal prerequisites are clarified. I shall begin with the instrumental frame of reference.

Requisite Information Hierarchies

The last conference on content analysis twelve years ago introduced the issue of instrumental communications. Reporting on how far the discussion had gone, Ithiel de Sola Pool suggested four variables: the content (which was used almost interchangeably with our "text"), the author's internal states, his manipulative strategies, and the states of the universe. Much of content analysis was then concerned with making inferences from text to an author's internal states according to an association model. "Instrumental" was attributed by Pool to "that which is manipulated (and thus varied in its relation to the thing being indexed so as to achieve the author's objectives)." Relying on this association model, the assertion of the independence of manipulative strategies and internal states implies the absence of stable relationships between text and internal states, thus making the task of the content analyst extremely difficult (Pool, 1959b).

Many everyday instrumental acts refer to the manipulation of causal chains. Wishing to enter a house, a visitor may have several possible acts at his disposal; a particular choice among them always represents the outcome of complex cognitive processes. Only the behavior is observed: a particular button is pushed and entry to the house is granted if certain other conditions are satisfied. Although correlations between the objective (entering the house) and the observed instrumental act may be found, it makes little sense to *explain* instrumental behavior in terms of correlations.

I think the simplest framework accounting for instrumental acts is one that regards the action of an agent in reference to his attempt to keep some essential states (which may be subject to external disturbances) under control. At least the following may be distinguished:

(a) The agent's internal states to be controlled instrumentally.

(b) The voluntary strategies available.

(c) The perceivable environmental situations.

(d) The agent's knowledge about the changes in the internal states as a consequence of initiating certain strategies in given situations.

(e) The agent's objective, a subset of the internal states.

(f) A rationale (or principle of evaluation) for choosing among available strategies on the basis of the current essential state, the objective, and the predicted consequence.

Even if the situation corresponds to this simple framework (the alternatives are finite and enumerable, and the environment of the manipulating agent is a strictly causal one), the analyst must find not only a representation of the information the agent uses but also a representation of the information the agent possesses about the consequences of his strategies. Analytical constructs of instrumental behavior at once involve a *hierarchy of types of information* and their effective operationalization.

When the situation is such that the manipulating agent communicates verbally with other intelligent beings, his requisite knowledge increases tremendously in complexity. Even a rational child who, for example, considers lying to its parent will have to possess at least something equivalent to a discourse model that represents the parent's ability to understand its assertions. Also it must have knowledge about the parent's access to factual information about the subject matter, plus knowledge about the behavioral consequences conditional on their possessing the kind of information the child is intending to produce. The situation of a congressman who wishes to amend or to delete certain sentences from the *Congressional Record* is more complex. He probably has good reasons to take information about the English language for granted, but in order to assess the consequences of the sentences that are of concern to him, the politician may have to consult his images about the political system within which he sees himself interacting with his colleagues, with the administration, with pressure groups, and with the public. Considering each of these potential recipients' expertise with the subject matter, their beliefs and values, the congressman may have to estimate what message characteristics these sentences will have for them. Considering further their individual objectives and ability to express their consent or dissent to the proposal, he may have to ascertain how their responses might retard or enhance his own political future, for example. In short, the representative is considering a network of possible interdependencies among purposive political subsystems in his environment, each of which must be characterized by a hierarchy of types of knowledge. Even if the analyst wishes to make inferences only about the intentions of the child's statement or of the politician's amendment or deletion, he will have to have constructs that are at least as complex as the information the manipulating agent uses in making decisions among possible instrumental verbalizations.

One of the crucial formal prerequisites of communication models of messages involving purposive systems is therefore an adequate representation of information *about* information *about* information, etc. Such a hierarchical structure is already invoked when statements are contrasted with information about what the statements claim to represent. Both the instrumental use of lies and inferences from apparent inconsistencies (typical of much of political analysis of documents) presupposes the ability to manipulate such representational hierarchies of information. In human-interaction situations, such hierarchies can become extremely complicated. In the information about the opponent that the agent employs is typically embedded the opponent's information about the agent, which in turn contains the information he possesses about the agent's information about him, etc. Representational theory handles such hierarchical structures only very clumsily. A *recursive* formulation of "information about," to my knowledge, has not been developed. Such a formulation is probably one of the prerequisites for constructing adequate communication models of messages when communicators can be attributed with some intelligence.

The Form of the Content Inferences

Let us leave the recursive formulation of representational information as an open problem and examine the nature of the consequences with which communication models will have to deal. Particularly, let us examine the form of the inferential argument for which the analyst seeks structural information about a source.

Suppose the state description "It's really hot today" is made at a party. Its factual content is quite trivial, since it may be verified by immediate experiences of each participant. A unique motivation of the speaker is not immediately ascertainable from the statement alone, nor is it likely that a unique behavior will follow. But the statement may impose a particular constraint on the consequent interactions, leaving open a large class of appropriate illocutionary responses. While demanding some recognition of its receipt, the statement may stimulate an expression of disagreement among participants and may establish a situation in which, for instance, a host recognizes his chance to demonstrate his hospitality. The consequence of the statement is less likely to be one particular response than it is the exclusion of a certain class of otherwise possible responses, leaving a wide variety of choices to the participants. Thus content, according to this model of messages, might be said to become manifest in the *constraints* imposed on a situation *as a consequence* of linguistic and nonlinguistic exchanges.

The content of instructions may be similarly considered. Whether they appear as rules of thumb, as sales guidelines, or as national policies, their linguistic form can hardly be said to be descriptive of events or ideas. When instituted, they have a profound effect on the organization and coordination of behavior by excluding certain trajectories and leaving others open for individual and situation-specific interpretations. The content of explanatory frameworks also may be assessed in terms of the structure they impose on the possible observations; the content of collective symbols becomes manifest in the channeling of diverse individual activities in a certain direction; and the content of political values can be regarded as manifest in the kind of decisions they legitimize. Similarly, laws do not contain rules for good conduct; instead, their content is manifested negatively in that they specify the punishments that can be expected when criminal acts are exposed. Symbols, political values, and laws no doubt make up much of what is exchanged in a technologically advanced society. Such communications do not have referents, but they do impose constraints on the subsequent behavior.

In their discussions of the instrumental use of language, Mahl (1959) and Pool (1959b) give the impression that the antecedent "intent" of purposive verbalizations differs from their descriptive contents only by being latent and nonconventionalized. I think, however, that a conceptualization of messages as informative about the direction of control of interactions by virtue of the constraints they impose on the possible consequences differs from discourse models of messages in a more fundamental way.

The inferences that discourse models provide are usually *positive* in the sense that a given linguistic item refers to, connotes, or denotes a particular object or class of objects, and sentences describe particular states or structures in their terms. In contrast to this, communication models always regard content inferences *negatively:* the instrumental communicator within such a system of interactions will have to choose assertions that restrict the consequent acts in such a way that the remaining free variation conforms to his objectives. The observer of a dynamic system which involves symbolic behavior will have to consider all conceivable alternative trajectories, and try to ascertain why, when a large number of them do not occur after certain linguistic expressions are introduced, the particular trajectory that is observed is one of those that was not excluded. Similarly, the message analyst attempts to make inferences from the recorded interchanges to the nature of the constraints that either exist and thus govern the system of interactions, or to the communicational binds that linguistic utterances and nonverbal acts impose on a situation. He may have to tolerate the fact that he cannot determine exactly which behavior will in fact occur, exactly which internal states may have initiated the consequent constraint, and exactly which rules of interaction actually govern the situation. A variety of interaction models must be considered simultaneously.

As Gregory Bateson remarked, the classical example of this negative form of inferences is the theory of evolution under natural selection. The theory suggests which organisms cannot be viable in a particular environment but is unable to say which ones will actually emerge. He states that:

> The negative form of these explanations is precisely comparable to the form of logical proof by *reductio ad absurdum*. In this species of proof, a sufficient set of mutually exclusive alternative propositions is enumerated, e.g. "P" and "not P," and the process of proof proceeds by demonstrating that all but one of this set are untenable or "absurd." It follows that the surviving member of the set must be tenable within the terms of the logical system. This is a form of proof which the non-mathematician sometimes finds unconvincing and, no doubt, the theory of natural selection sometimes seems unconvincing to non-mathematical persons for similar reasons—whatever those reasons may be (Bateson, 1967).

But there is a second determinant of the form of content inferences that deviates even further from traditional arguments. In the biological sphere, evolution by natural selection is a unidirectional process: there is no feedback to parent generations. Instrumental communications, and consequently the control processes they establish within a system of interaction, are critically linked to *conceivable feedback* loops and presuppose a *circular form of content inferences* with which other models of messages are not concerned.

The child who does not mind lying may consider giving a description of the events that not only structures its parent's perception but subsequently prevents the parent from imposing undesired restrictions on the child. But often the child is not sophisticated enough and considers only one such inferential loop while the parent may project further to consider subsequent feedback loops and to estimate the degree to which the statement may be trusted. Similarly, the congressman who subsumes his speech under political objectives is bound to make his inferences along the circular flow of consequent events. At each stage he may want to consider the extent to which his speech imposes a constraint on the situation, what

other constraints exist, and how the series of consequent constraints ultimately control his own variety of possible acts.

Although descriptive statements may indeed impose constraints on subsequent behavior as a secondary phenomenon, a large class of linguistic
forms pertain primarily or exclusively to such constraints. This is particularly true for demands, claims, treaties, and the like. Demands may be
"verified" by compliance, and the content of demands thus becomes manifest in the system of interactions among at least two communicators. In
particular situations, the assertion of demands implicitly or explicitly informs the recipient about rewards and punishment consequent to his choice
of a particular behavior, and may force compliance by making these conceivable consequences credible. The communication of demands cannot
therefore reasonably be made unless it leads to a projection into future
behavior of at least two interaction loops:

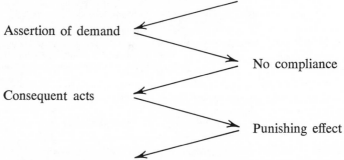

In order to understand and describe the structure of communication
situations in which linguistic exchanges determine the parameters of the
interaction, the task of the analyst becomes one of inferring from the
chronology of exchanges the circular form of *mutually imposed* and *interlocking* constraints. The latter are often called interaction *binds* (Watzlawick, et al., 1967). The form of content inference that communication
models of messages are intended to facilitate may therefore be said to
be:

1. *Negative,* that is, it entails the ascertaining of the constraints imposed
on a variety of possible consequences rather than the isolation of a particular trajectory,

2. *Circular,* that is, it is based on inferring the contents of linguistic
exchanges along the possible chains of events each ultimately closing at
its respective origins rather than on inferring in one direction only and
involves

3. Analytical *constructs of control* with some order of prediction for

rendering the recorded text informative about the interaction parameters of the source.

These circular inferences, which theoretically could go on *ad infinitum,* may find their definite limitation in the hierarchy of information that each party possesses about the information each other party possesses, etc. Once this information is exhausted in this circular extrapolation from past inter-actions, very little can be said beyond it. But practical limitations are more likely to set the limit on the understanding of the system of interac-tions: with each inferential loop the variety of possible trajectories that an analyst may wish to consider spirals to increasingly unmanageable proportions.

Some Manifestations of Constraints

This peculiar nature of the content inferences that communication models provide profoundly affects their possible validation. Although there is no operational test for the procedural adequacy of discourse models (Chomsky, 1957), their performance can be at least checked against the ability of knowledgeable speakers of a language to understand what a discourse is about. Intersubjective agreement almost belongs to the very definition of "language." The dynamic relations among communicators that develop in the course of verbal exchanges are, on the other hand, rarely so institutionalized and their assessment requires considerable in-sights as far as the analyst is concerned.

I mentioned that the recorded text can be regarded as a chronology of exchanges between communicators which are patterned according to time, place of origin, and destination and may contain references across these exchanges as well. As Ross Ashby (1958) and Charles McClelland (1964) suggest, the analyst who attempts to understand the source's sys-tem of interaction will have to infer from this record the existing and consequent constraints accounting for and imposed upon the nature of the source. Difficulties arise because this chronology represents only a single trajectory of interactional behavior and provides no obvious evi-dence of the trajectories that were excluded in the course of the underlying process. Even when the chronology covers a long period of time, the number of possible trajectories is often so large that they cannot be "acted out" *systematically.* Even when the interaction situation is relatively stable (that is, relations are invariant), inferences about the existence of con-straints still remain difficult. For example, even if all citizens confined their behavior to what is prescribed by law, it would neither be possible to ascertain the explicitly prescribed limits from the observed behavior nor whether the law is in fact effective. Similarly, a naïve observer would have difficulties inferring the effective rules from observing only the chess players' moves. In both cases, linguistic and nonlinguistic behavior may have to be consulted in conjunction.

I see essentially three ways of obtaining *evidence* for the existence of symbolically induced constraints. The least reliable inferences may be made from explicit compliances to demands, from pledges, or from commitments, whatever form they may take. Layman Allen (1963), for example, showed how many possibilities are left open to the signatories of a segment of the nuclear test ban treaty. And the analysis of political values in decision making, which is proposed by Philip E. Jacob and James J. Flink (1962), is a similar attempt to ascertain constraints on alternatives that are accepted within a source for whatever reasons. But treaties may be made with the implicit understanding that they can be broken and political values may be asserted without making decisions accordingly. Thus, if taken alone, the validity of this form of evidence is highly questionable.

The second way of obtaining evidence for the existence of constraints is found in the communicator's account of his insights about the excluded alternatives. Private diaries by political decision makers often provide such information. For example, when choices among possible actions are justified in the light of the undesirable consequences associated with some of them, the severity of situational constraints reveals itself quite clearly. The expressed insights of our thirsty guest at the party may similarly provide clues as to the nature of the existing constraints. He may reason like this: "I will lose my status as a guest if I am caught grabbing a whiskey bottle; I will be thought rude if I assert that I am thirsty; I cannot afford to insult the host by asking why he didn't serve drinks, etc." The assertion of a statement which "survives" this negative reasoning will not reveal very much about the structure of the situation. Perhaps interview techniques could tab this evidence, but when communicators generate their verbalizations instrumentally, the analyst rarely can rely on it.

The third form of evidence may be found in the consequences of violating a constraint no matter how it was introduced. This again exhibits the control aspect with which communication models are essentially concerned. It suggests that the seriousness of promises could be inferred from the consequences of not sticking to them; that the power of demands becomes evident in what follows from failures to comply; and that the reality of commitments appears in the condemnation of deviations. In the extreme, the assessment of the content of law would require a study of the crimes that are identified and punished according to the text. This would reveal which paragraphs are merely paper within a legal system and which paragraphs effectively limit the possible behaviors of citizens. When less institutionalized forms of interaction are analyzed, the identification of instances of violation and condemnation is not always an easy matter. Even the identification of provocative and conciliatory moves involves a considerable amount of information about the structure of control processes within the source without which communication models do not yield adequate content inferences.

The Components of Communication Models

I hope it is quite clear from my discussion that the analytical constructs of control processes involving higher orders of prediction from verbal interactions are very little understood and demand considerable investigative attention before rigorous message analytic procedures can be designed. There is no single form of evidence for the existence of controls affected by the linguistic and nonlinguistic exchanges. The analyst must utilize all of them simultaneously and, particularly, must consider apparent inconsistencies, violations, and justifications in order to develop suitable constructs of control processes which in turn will help him to assess the variety-limiting consequences of social exhanges. Current attempts to obtain evidence about control relations that emerge between nations, social organizations, or individuals are either extremely reduced (to nonverbal interaction) or remain on the level of *post hoc* explanations. Perhaps the work of the Palo Alto group, which recently presented a perceptive analysis of the interactions depicted in Albee's *Who's Afraid of Virginia Woolf* (Watzlawick et al., 1967) could provide a starting point.

Although I cannot point to any noteworthy formalization of communication models of messages (see Figure 3), they all involve extracting from a chronology of linguistic and nonlinguistic exchanges the following material.

(a) Information about the identity of the *basic communicators* of the source and their respective boundaries.

(b) Information about the *states of each component* of the source, including the communicators' possible perceptions of the situation, their communication and behavioral strategies, evaluative frameworks, and objectives.

(c) Information about the *transmission facilities,* time delays, channels, and stable relations between the communicators.

(d) Information about the existing constraints that have evolved in the course of previous interactions, that is, the system's basic operating rules and parameters, the definition of the situation and of the communicators' roles, shared or not.

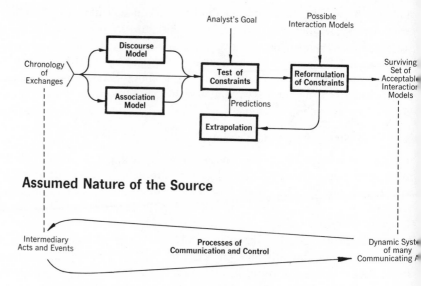

Figure 3   Communication models of messages: procedures.

(e)   Information about the *mechanisms of control* and the regulating power of the exchanged verbalization which structure those mechanisms.

(f)   Information about the hierarchical structure and quantity of *knowledge available* to the communicators about the possible dynamic interdependencies between the source's components.

Since the mathematical problems of communication models of messages are in no way close to being solved, it is difficult to discuss the components that go into their construction in sufficient detail. However, it is possible to conclude this section on communication models with a few hypotheses about them. It is quite clear that some of the information that needs to be extracted from the chronology presupposes both association models and discourse models of messages. These models may have to be constructed separately for each of the source's communicators. The constraints that are extrapolated from the large number of initially empty formal skeletons of possible interactions then have to be tested iteratively against the bulk of valid inferences supplied by these models of messages. Across these formal structures the test eliminates those that prove to be not powerful enough. Within each formal skeleton, information obtained from the chronology specifies the parameters and thus affects the kind of constraints that are extrapolated from it. What survives after repetitive scanning of the chronology is a set of acceptable interaction models. This set may be said to constitute the analyst's understanding of a communication situation.

Whether the outcome of such content analyses is indeed predictive may depend not only on the structural information available from the source and the power of the interaction model in terms of which such information may be organized, but also on whether enough invariant constraints are manifest in a particular communication situation. By definition, randomness cannot be accounted for, and it seems that human communication, no matter how restricted by conventions, personalities, and the laws of self-modifying interaction patterns, allows a considerable amount of freedom of choice. The message content that communication models supply will have to consider this uncertainty.

CONCLUSIONS

Let me summarize my points. I think it is important to abandon conceptually the idea of analyzing *the* content of *a* message. Content may be *inferred* by an analyst in reference to some source against whose behavior content inferences may be validated.

By defining *content analysis* as *the use of replicable and valid methods for making specific inferences from text to other states or properties of its source,* I wish to emphasize that it is *the analyst* to whom a text may become informative about unobserved states, events, or phenomena of the source; furthermore, analytical constructs for making the inferences *should be explicit* so that detailed examination is possible, independent of the particular situation in which they are applied; and, finally, inferential procedures must be *justifiable* in reference to a particular source whether by validation or vindication.

The choice of a particular analytical construct for the analysis of messages implies certain assumptions about the nature of the source. This raises the important question of the procedural adequacy of such constructs in particular situations. But regardless of whether these questions are answered affirmatively, three prototypes of analytical constructs or basic models of messages seem to be distinguishable. I referred to them *as association models, discourse models,* and *communication models of messages.* Their crucial differences appear (a) in the assumptions made about the structure of the source, (b) in the kind of information relevant for designing the required analytical procedures, (c) in the structure that is initially imposed upon the input data when recording them, (d) in the message characteristics that the data acquire in the course of the analytical process (that is, the inferred content), and (e) in the kind of evidence required for verifying the content inferences made. Let me summarize these differences in Figure 4 without reviewing them in detail.

With this differentiation I do not wish to imply that such models provide

	Association Models	Discourse Models	Communication Models
Semantic relation of messages	Statistical dependencies: association, correlation, causal or not	Linguistic reference: denotation or connotation	Controls or interactional consequences
Assumed structure of the source	Finite state, ergodic, and stochastic source with multivariate events	A language together with an object system (of ideas or events) to which it refers	Linguistic and non-linguistic exchanges among potentially intelligent and purposive communicators within a system of interactions
Information relevant for analytical procedure	Multivariate probabilities of co-occurrences or transitions between observable events	Nature of linguistic processes of analysis and understanding of what linguistic forms are about	Nature of control mechanisms implicit in communication networks and consequent to verbal and nonverbal exchanges
Structure of the recorded text	A set of constituent elements (recording units) without regard for their order	A string of linguistic items with special attention to their order of occurrence	A (space, time) pattern of exchanges of strings of linguistic items and nonlinguistic events
Form of the inferred content	Frequency-probabilistic characterizations of state descriptions of potentially observable components	State descriptions of unobserved events implied by what the text refers to	Representations of effective constraints imposed on the interaction among communicators
Evidence required for verification	Observational confirmation of stochastic "predictions"	Judgments regarding the validity of inferred state descriptions made by native speakers of a language who are familiar with the source	Information about the purpose of demands and pattern of compliance, insights into the reasoning about available alternatives, manifest violations of constraints

Figure 4   A comparison of models of messages.

mutually exclusive alternatives for an analysis. Communication models often presuppose and incorporate the information provided by both discourse models and association models. If it is compatible with an analyst's inferential aim, then, the statistical operations of association models may well be applied subsequent to the algebraic operations of a discourse logic. However, the analytical functions of these models, their logical possibilities, and their limitations should be understood.

If one prefers semiotic terminology such as that of Charles Pierce (Burks, 1949), then one would probably have to say that association models consider a text as a set of *"indices,"* discourse models regard a text as a pattern of *"symbols,"* while the view of communication models would have to remain unlabeled although subsumable under the *pragmatic* branch of the theory of signs. But this apparent congruency with semiotic terminology is only a superficial one and may become misleading when specific investigative techniques are discussed. If one shares the semioticists' search for the *relations* according to which symbols are interpreted, then one would have to say that association models are concerned with *correlational* dependencies, causal or not; discourse models deal with systems of linguistic *references,* denotations or connotations; and communication models consider *controls* or interactional *consequences.* But these are only convenient labels.

I do think that the concern with models of messages is more productive for the study of social communication than the semiotic approach has been. This is because the former aims at representing *partial theories of a source,* that is, its symbolic processes, with which the latter has not been able to deal. Let me give just one example of the confusion that results from such global labels as "symbol" and its "interpretation." At a recent conference, Jurgen Ruesch and Samuel Eisenstadt got into an interesting argument about whether a system of symbols, in order to be effective within a society, require homogeneous or heterogeneous interpretations. Ruesch exemplified his point by referring to traffic signs, the heterogeneous interpretation of which would result in disastrous accidents. Eisenstadt, on the other hand, referred to "The Rock of Israel," which is known to connote quite a number of things to different citizens of Israel without making the symbol less powerful in regard to the national identity it promotes (Thayer, 1967:473–476). It seems that because the intent to survive the traffic hazards is shared by a population of drivers with approximately equal power to influence the situation, the interpretation of traffic signals can be reduced to discourse models. When a political, symbol is chosen to organize and channel a large variety of different activities, each guided by potentially different objectives, such reduction may not be appropriate. In each case the term "interpretation" has to denote quite different processes although all may involve inferences about what the "symbol" relates to.

I have mentioned only briefly the *possibility* of *computerizing* these models. Let me make only a few additional comments on this problem. Regarding association models, I see no serious obstacles. Computer programs for statistical procedures are easily available, although not all of them accept verbal data as inputs. In this respect, the pioneering work of Philip Stone et al. (1963; 1966) should be mentioned.

Regarding discourse models, the situation does not look as favorable. Programs providing semantic characterizations of natural language sentences currently require an undue amount of time, and their results are not always useful. In order to derive more practical algorithms, it is probably advisable to accept goals that are less ambitious than those considered by linguists. But even if the obstacles to such semantic characterizations were removed, I suspect that it is unrealistic to expect general algorithms for the analysis of all conceivable discourses. The information that would have to go into such a discourse logic would have to represent all a speaker knows about the world. But I do believe that it is possible to develop discourse logics for limited domains or specialized subject matters, the structure of which is known or not too involved. Kinship relations is but a primitive example of certain list structures into which other discourses may be mapped as well. Available simulation languages may set limitations for such content inferences. I see the formalization of specialized discourse logics and compatible kernelization procedures as the most important step toward inferring a text's referential content.

The problems of computerizing communication models of messages are, I think, extremely difficult to solve. Clearly, their formalization presupposes both adequate association models and adequate discourse models. But I wonder whether the currently available software is capable of representing systems of linguistic and nonlinguistic exchanges *among* intelligent communicators. Perhaps this kind of message analysis is better accomplished by human analysts who can specify the constraints of a situation more easily by using computers merely as aids for conceptualization. An attempt to formalize even a limited communication model of messages would be a great step forward. Whether this is possible at all, I am unable to judge.

Finally, much of our concern with the content of messages is to discover the nonobvious, to infer what is hidden, to gain information about what cannot be seen, and to make messages out of signals that remain signals for others. It always requires an *analytical sophistication* that is greater than that possessed by the source. If analysts reduce the power of their analytical facilities for the sake of efficiency, or in compliance with narrow scientific standards, then their inferences may become quite misleading. It is almost always possible for an intelligent source to outwit an analyst with a reduced repertoire of models of messages by relying on a way of concealing or conveying significant information that is more powerful than his models can handle. It is for this reason that I call for a thorough examination of the adequacy of available analytical constructs of messages in the light of known or conceivable sources of information.

II   Aspects of Inference from Content Data

Ole R. Holsti, Editor

INTRODUCTION TO PART II

OLE R. HOLSTI

Political Science
University of British Columbia

The problem of inference lies at the heart of all systematic inquiry, including that conducted by means of content analysis. The purpose of any inquiry is to make valid inferences from data, and every aspect of the research process (from its design through coding and statistical analysis) is ultimately guided by the goal of improving the quality of inference.

Two consequences necessarily follow from this view. First, grouping the following chapters together under the heading "inference" is not intended to imply that they are unique in this respect; indeed, the reader may find other chapters that are more germane to his special interests. Second, all of the many aspects of research related to inference from content data cannot be covered in equal depth in these studies; some topics receive consideration in several of them, others are mentioned only in passing, if at all.

In order to place the following chapters into broader perspective, it is useful to recall briefly the issues that dominated the discussions at the 1955 Allerton content analysis conference, the proceedings of which have been published under the title *Trends in Content Analysis* (Pool, 1959a). This seems especially appropriate because inference was the central concern of that conference. Discussion centered on three identifiable clusters of problems. The first of these was the "what" and "how" of measurement—units, the qualitative-quantitative debate, and the utility and limitations of frequency, contingency, and intensity measures. The 1955 conferees also devoted some attention to the question of theories and models of the communication applicable to content analysis. The relative merits

109

of the "representational" and "instrumental" models of communication for making inferences about the motives, values, beliefs, and attitudes of sources were considered at some length. Finally, the problem of standard categories for content analysts was discussed, especially with reference to measurement of tensions and valence of assertions.

Against this baseline, we can consider several questions. Which of the issues relating to inference that concerned content analysts in 1955 continued to engage their attention at the Annenberg conference? Which were of less interest? What new issues and approaches to them have emerged during the 12 years between the 1955 and 1967 conferences?

Figure 1, a summary and comparison of topics that received major treatment at the two conferences, reveals a continuing interest in certain problems. This is notably the case with models of encoding and decoding relevant to content analysis and the question of standard categories. Systems of enumeration and units of analysis (subjects of considerable discussion in 1955) received less consideration at the latter conference. On the other hand, several of the chapters that follow focus on norms and illustrate the role of computers as an aid to inference in content analysis, problems not discussed 12 years earlier.

We can also compare our contributions with those of the earlier conference according to purpose, using the more or less traditional categories of inferences about the characteristics, antecedents (the encoding process), and effects (the decoding process) of communication. In summarizing the 1955 papers, Pool (1959b:191) wrote that "on the whole our emphasis has been on inferences about the sources . . . of messages." This is also

Aspects of Inference	1955 Allerton Conference	1967 Annenberg School Conference									
		Gerbner	Hall	Laffal	Mueller	Namenwirth	Ogilvie	Paisley	Raben	Shneidman	Stone
Models of encoding/decoding	+	+		+	+	+	+	+		+	
Systems of enumeration	+	+	+		+						
Standard categories	+	+	+	+			+				+
Norms		+	+					+		+	+
Role of computers				+		+	+	+	+		+
Units of analysis		+								+	+
Causal inference						+					

Figure 1 The 1955 Allerton and 1967 Annenberg conference papers compared according to aspects of inference (the plus sign indicates topics discussed at some length or for which the paper is of special interest).

true of the present articles. Although they represent different disciplines and their research questions are as diverse as discovering the unique elements of an individual's pattern of logic and identifying attributes of patrilineal and matrilineal societies, Hall, Laffal, Mueller, Ogilvie, Paisley, and Shneidman are concerned almost exclusively with making inferences about sources from the messages that they produce.

Namenwirth and Raben discuss content analysis as a method of generating data for the purpose of making inferences about communication sources, but their research is also concerned with the *effects* of communication. Indeed, the purpose of Namenwirth's study is to discover whether political ideas, as expressed in American party platforms, cause or reflect social change. Similarly, Raben's discussion of content analysis in literary studies is concerned with the antecedents of poetry, the broader social context within which poetry is written, as well as the form and style of previous poets. But the same techniques may also be used to trace the effect of communication, as Raben demonstrates in examples of the Miltonian influence in Shelley's poetry.

The chapters by Gerbner and Stone are less easily classified. Gerbner's proposal for analysis of "public message systems" is less concerned with the causes and effects of communication than with the need to identify salient elements of the cultural context within which encoding and decoding take place. But his questions and categories almost inescapably lead to the consideration of other problems: What is the role of the public media in shaping, maintaining, and modifying public beliefs about what is, what is important, what is right, and what is related to what? Why do systems— and even subsystems, for example, different generations or racial groups in contemporary America—differ in their beliefs about these elements of existence?

Finally, Stone's "disambiguation" project has such broad applicability for all computer-based content analyses that it cannot be classified according to any single type of research. A dictionary of word senses with rules for distinguishing between them clearly will be useful to all content analysts using computers, whatever the purposes of their research.

Let us now examine, in more detail, some of the problems relating to inference on which the following chapters shed light.

MODELS OF ENCODING OR DECODING

Models of communication processes relevant to content analysis are discussed fully in another section of this volume,[1] but several of the chap-

---

[1] See the chapters by James Deese, David Hays, Klaus Krippendorff, and Anatol Rapoport, *infra*.

ters that follow also address themselves to this issue. The debate between advocates of "representational" and "instrumental" models of communication (which occupied a central position at the 1955 conference) is not taken up explicitly in the present chapters, but some of its chief questions remain. The representational and instrumental positions are perhaps most clearly illustrated here in the articles by Laffal and Shneidman. Laffal's discussion of the role of words in cognitive structures implies that inferences about cognitive orientations may be based directly on the lexical attributes of text. Shneidman's technique of logical analysis, on the other hand, appears to be based on assumptions of the instrumental model; that is, that the analyst must "read between the lines" of his text in order to make inferences. This is perhaps best illustrated in his example of a patient who announces "I am Switzerland." The interpretation that the patient desires his freedom clearly depends on more than lexical attributes of the sentence.

Paisley's discussion of style is a cogent reminder, with implications that go well beyond the boundaries of stylistic research, that verbal behavior may reflect factors other than merely those of the author's personal attributes. The thesis that he develops with respect to studies of style and sources of norms bears some resemblance to Alexander George's (1959b) explication of the instrumental model. Questions about the applicability of the representational model also appear to be the basis of Mueller's critique of some recent content-analytic studies of international politics.

Namenwirth's chapter also has relevance for models of encoding. His findings suggest that the use of political symbols is the result rather than the cause of social change.

SYSTEMS OF ENUMERATION

Discussions of measurement during the 1950's tended to focus on several issues, one of which was the relative merits, with respect to the quality of inferences, of qualitative and quantitative content analysis. At times the controversy could be reduced to two viewpoints: "If you can't count it, it doesn't count" versus "If you can count it, that ain't it." This issue has almost disappeared from the recent literature. For example, three recent reviews of the field (Barcus, 1959; Stone et al., 1966; and Holsti, 1968a, 1969) agree that a rigid distinction between these forms of measurement poses a dichotomy that is useful neither for limiting the scope of content analysis nor for evaluating a specific piece of research. None of the articles that follow deal with the qualitative-quantitative debate. The viewpoint that the analyst should use a combination of all methods that aid the process of inference seems to dominate the field today. This is clearly illustrated in Gerbner's chapter. Each of the four main questions in his program for analysis of public message systems calls for a different system of enumeration: *frequency analysis* (what is?); *scaling for intensity* (what is important?); *nonfrequency* or what is sometimes called qualitative analysis (what is right?); and *contingency analysis* (what is related to what?).

The lack of interest in the quantitative-qualitative distinction need not, however, indicate a consensus on systems of enumeration.

In reviewing the work of the previous content-analysis conference, Pool concluded that frequency counts are at least as useful for measuring intensity or importance as any available alternative. Despite the diverse disciplines and theoretical concerns represented in the present chapters, the assumption that frequency measures provide a useful basis of inference from content data appears to underlie most of them. It is basic to Stone's work toward developing rules of disambiguation for his computer dictionaries, because frequencies of word meanings set the initial framework within which the routines are written. This is also the case in Laffal's preparation of a computer dictionary of 114 variables. Ogilvie and Namenwirth are concerned with much more limited areas of verbal behavior— Icarian imagery in the folk tales of primitive societies and economic concerns of political parties in the United States during the past century and a quarter—but the frequency with which content attributes appear is the initial basis of enumeration. The same is true in much of Raben's literary research, in Paisley's identification of "minor encoding habits" and other attributes of style, and in Shneidman's logical content analysis.

Mueller, however, calls into question the assumption—and often it remains just that—that frequency may be taken as a valid index of importance. In this respect his critique of some studies relating to foreign policy decision-making could, without stretching the meaning of his chapter, also be extended to Namenwirth's chapter. The possibilities and limitations of inferences drawn from frequency measures is far from a closed issue, and can only be settled by evidence derived from multiple measures on the same body of data,[2] not merely by convention or convenience. Only in this way can we discover the classes of communicators, content variables, and types of documents in which we can have confidence on inferences drawn from frequency counts.

The widespread interest in contingency analysis at the 1955 conference is also evident in several of the present contributions. In testing between alternative explanations of Daniel Paul Schreber's delusions, Laffal illus-

---

[2] For rare examples of systematic evidence on this point, see George (1959a), which gives some interesting findings on the relative merits of frequency and nonfrequency measures for purposes of making inferences from propaganda, and Schneider and Dornbusch (1958, Appendix C).

trates an application of this technique for the purposes of making inferences. Hall also reports that contingency analysis has proved a useful
method of resynthesizing content elements after they have been isolated
in the initial stages of analysis. Contingency analysis, in a somewhat different sense, appears in Stone's disambiguation project. Rules for assigning
the proper word sense are based largely on the contingency of the word
to be defined with other words.

Finally, measurement of intensity (also of interest at the 1955 conference mainly because of Charles E. Osgood's technique of "evaluative assertion analysis") has engaged the interests of relatively few content analysts. Of the chapters that follow, only Gerbner's discusses this
type of measurement.

STANDARD CATEGORIES

One of the questions frequently discussed among content analysts is
that of *standard categories* to facilitate comparative and cumulative research findings. There are few areas of content analysis in which such
categories have emerged, however, and Pool's assessment of a decade
ago is still reasonably accurate:

> It is questionable, however, how ready we are to establish standard measures . . .
> in content analysis. Such a measure is convenient when a considerable number of
> researchers are working on the same variable, and when someone succeeds in work-
> ing out good categories for that variable. It is doubtful that either of those criteria
> can be met in most areas of content analysis (Pool, 1959b:213).

There are several reasons for the limited progress. Many areas of social
inquiry have not achieved sufficient consensus on theory to inform the
selection and operational definition of categories. But this is not the sole
explanation. The premium on "originality" in research and the concomitant reluctance of analysts to adopt the categories of others—tendencies clearly not limited to content-analytic research—is a factor of
no little importance. Perhaps this observation can best be illustrated in
studies of psychotherapeutic interviews. The volume of investigations, as
well as the quality and ingenuity of many studies, is impressive. But even
allowing for diversity stemming from theoretical differences, the proliferation of research has not been matched by efforts to replicate and integrate
methods and findings. The author of a recent review of the literature
draws the following conclusion.

> System after system has been developed and presented in one or two demonstration
> studies, only to lie buried in the literature, unused even by its author. Moreover,

few variables or notions about therapeutic interviews have received anything approaching programmatic or extensive content-analysis investigation. This has resulted in redundancy; systems were developed with apparent unawareness that other approaches to the same problem, or efforts to apply the same approach to other problems, had already been reported (Marsden, 1965:315).

A similar assessment can be applied to many other areas of social and humanistic research.

A third barrier to development of standard categories is a practical one. Even researchers who might have been inclined to adopt categories developed by others have found that these categories were not defined precisely enough to permit replication. Moreover, the laboriousness of coding tended to discourage analyzing the data twice—once with one's own categories, and a second time with those found useful in another study. There are, however, some indications that developments in computer-based content analysis are eliminating some of these problems, a point that I shall discuss in more detail later.

Finally, whatever the merits of standard categories, they are not an end in themselves. As has been true in the past, many of the most interesting and significant content-analysis studies will continue to depend on categories developed specifically for the data and problem at hand.

Only a few of the chapters that follow (notably those by Gerbner and Hall) deal explicitly with the issue of standard categories, but several other chapters are also relevant to the question. For example, they illustrate both deductive and inductive approaches to developing categories. In Ogilvie's study of the Icarus complex in three individuals and 44 primitive societies, in Namenwirth's analysis of party-platform during a century and a quarter of American history, in Laffal's test of alternative explanations of Daniel Paul Schreber's delusions, and in Shneidman's method of studying systems of logic, selection and operational definition of categories were guided by prior theories.

At times, as Hall and Paisley point out, there is no alternative to developing categories inductively, an observation that appears to be supported by some authorship studies. The Mosteller and Wallace (1964) analysis of the *Federalist Papers,* in which many types of categories were tried in order to find some that worked, is perhaps the most convincing example of this type of research. In contrast, Morton's (1963) study of the Pauline Epistles, which began with categories assumed to be universal "fingerprints of the mind," is subject to serious question on several counts. Illustrating the inductive approach to categories are the chapters by Hall, Stone, Laffal (in his analysis of children's stories), Raben, and Paisley. In each instance the data base itself provided the initial criterion for category decisions.

There may be some value in distinguishing these alternative approaches to category construction, but we should not leave the issue with the suggestion that they are mutually exclusive. It is commonplace to state that there should be continual moving back and forth between data and theory, and that out of this process will emerge more useful categories. This point is illustrated in the work of Stone and his colleagues. Although Stone's project on disambiguation clearly represents the inductive approach to categories, he reports that his work is already raising questions of a theoretical nature about the *Harvard Psychosociological Dictionary,* which has its roots in several well-defined theories.

To what extent do the present articles contribute to or foreshadow progress toward development of standard categories? There is perhaps some reason for optimism, especially if we view these contributions as only partial reports of the work in which their authors are engaged. Laffal's chapter illustrates the use of a general set of categories for psycholinguistic research described in greater detail in an earlier publication (Laffal, 1965). The same is true of the chapters by Hall, Shneidman, and Gerbner whose categories are more extensively reported elsewhere (Hall and Van de Castle, 1966a; Shneidman, 1966; and the works cited in Gerbner's chapter, *infra*). The disambiguation project undertaken by Stone and his colleagues is an ambitious effort to improve the validity of the *Harvard Psychosociological Dictionary,* which has already been used in a number of studies (Stone et al., 1966). The categories used by Namenwirth and Ogilvie can also be viewed as candidates for standard categories in the study of Icarianism and economic values. Whether any of these gains wide acceptance by others studying similar problems is, of course, a question that can only be answered in the future. But it appears that there are at least some areas in which there is somewhat greater cause for optimism than was the case at the 1955 conference.

NORMS

Norms are used here in the empirical rather than the prescriptive sense; that is, our interest is in the modal range of communication behavior for various classes of communicators under specified conditions.

The role of norms in inference is that they provide a benchmark against which the analyst can compare his findings. This is a specific application of the general rule that meaningful analysis requires at least one formal comparison. Consider some typical problems that have been investigated by content analysis:

Does newspaper X provide good coverage of international news?

Do textbooks in nation Y reveal high need for achievement?

Does patient Z's verbal behavior indicate progress in psychotherapy?

Valid inferences from documents produced by newspaper X, nation Y, and patient Z require a valid external criterion for comparison—for example, norms for metropolitan dailies in general, textbooks from various nations, and patients who have undergone successful therapy. Stated somewhat differently, valid inferences depend on the quality of both the analyst's data and the criterion (or norm) being used for comparison.

Hall cites two interesting examples in which analysts, apparently unaware of existing norms, were led to faulty inferences. The first study revealed that the content of dreams in a New Guinea tribe contained more misfortunes than good fortunes. Because members of this tribe hold a pessimistic view of life, the authors concluded that dream content faithfully reflected their waking-life attitudes. But, as Hall points out, misfortunes exceed good fortunes in dreams of people throughout the world, including those whose attitudes toward life are optimistic. In the other study, dreams of the elderly were found to contain many themes of diminished resources to cope with problems. But inferences relating this content characteristic to age were ill-founded because the same thing is encountered in the dreams of the young.

Although Paisley's chapter focuses directly on stylistics in the arts, he directs our attention to an issue of relevance in virtually all content-analytic research: What norms are relevant to the problem at hand? He identifies eight types of norms that may account for variations in style, and he develops a case for considering each of them as a potential source of variance in the production of messages. The quality of inferences is then proportional to our ability to gain control over sources of variance that are extraneous to our hypotheses.

Mueller's critique of recent content-analytic studies of international politics can be viewed as a more specific application of Paisley's theme. Although Mueller also raises questions about such problems as the adequacy of archival materials, he focuses on the problem of gaining control over sources of variance other than those predicated by the hypotheses under analysis. Specifically, he calls attention to the potential impact of channel, stimulus, and context on messages.

The present chapters illustrate concern for norms of several types. Stone's work is at the level of all-language norms; the enterprise hinges on first discovering the distribution of word meanings (that is, norms) among communicators in general, and then working out the decision rules for identifying the proper meaning of each word. For this task Stone, and his colleagues are working from a broad empirical base—one-half million words of text produced by a wide range of different subjects.

Most of our contributions are concerned with specified classes of communicators: primitive societies (Ogilvie); American political parties

(Namenwirth); children in various age groups (Laffal); and dreamers categorized according to age, sex, and many other attributes (Hall).

Finally, two chapters focus on identifying individual norms. Shneidman's research stems from the conviction that there is no universal norm for logic—only a series of individual styles of logic. He illustrates his technique of content analysis with data from the Kennedy-Nixon television debates during the 1960 presidential campaigns. Paisley uses the same data to illustrate quite a different feature about individual norms—the relative potencies of major and minor encoding habits for discriminating between sources.

At this point the importance of standard categories becomes clearer. Establishing norms may not be easy even for groups whose membership is very limited. For example, Mosteller and Wallace (1964), in their study of the authorship of twelve *Federalist Papers,* were in effect faced with identifying stylistic norms for two classes of sources, each with a membership of one—James Madison and Alexander Hamilton. Yet the task proved more difficult than they had anticipated. Most social scientists and humanists are interested in larger classes of communicators. Moreover, their interests may not be confined to content attributes that are as easily defined as those used in the anlysis of the *Federalist Papers*—word frequencies. In such cases, the establishment of norms is often an undertaking that exceeds the time and resources of any single investigator. But even when many analysts are working in a single area of inquiry, results are not cumulative unless they are using identical categories and, therefore, the abstraction of norms from them may be difficult if not impossible.

THE ROLE OF COMPUTERS

Probably the most important development in content analysis since the 1955 conference has been the development of a wide variety of computer-based techniques. Paisley and Raben properly remind us that there are areas of continuing interest to humanists and social scientists which continue to be better handled by more traditional methods of textual analysis. Yet without overlooking this important point, it would be hard to overestimate the potential significance of computers for improving the quality of inference. Several of the following chapters provide ample evidence in support of this observation.

We can consider the role of the computer in improving the quality of inference in several ways. Perhaps the most obvious of these is that because computers improve the reliability of coding they enhance the quality of inference. This point is especially relevant to those who, like Stone, Laffal, and Ogilvie, are working with long word lists which must be coded into a large number of categories. Evidence from the RADIR studies of political symbols conducted by Harold D. Lasswell and his colleagues indicates that when the number of categories is large, even if they are defined rigidly and exhaustively—that is, every member of a category is listed—reliability may prove disappointingly low. This problem is virtually eliminated in computer-based content analyses.

One of the limitations of computers—that their tolerance for ambiguity is zero—can also contribute to the quality of inference by forcing greater clarity in the explication of theory. Not the least problem in the social sciences and humanities is that they have suffered in varying degrees from vague concepts. "Icarianism" and "wealth-other" are potentially of this type, but when they are defined explicitly and exhaustively (as in the studies reported by Ogilvie and Namenwirth), we have little difficulty in understanding what they mean. This is not to say that the reader must accept their definitions, but if he does not, at least the areas of disagreement are out in the open rather than hidden within a verbal thicket.

Both the initial impetus and the ultimate feasibility of Stone's ambitious work on disambiguation stem from the introduction of computers into content analysis. When reasonably well-trained persons are engaged in reading and coding text, homographs generally present few difficulties because the context provides sufficient clues for making reliable decisions. Computers, however, are unable to distinguish which of several possible word meanings is the proper one. In the first generation of computer programs, investigators usually made a priori guesses about which meaning would occur most frequently, and the only method for eliminating inevitable errors was to retrieve each theme and eliminate faulty codes by hand.

The task that Stone and his colleagues have set for themselves is thus a product of the computer age in content analysis; it seems equally clear, however, that the availability of computers is virtually a necessary condition for its completion. The data bank upon which the project is based, the ability to retrieve and categorize all words and their context, and extensive testing of decision rules for disambiguation are all manageable because of computers.

The ability of computers to process reliably enormous quantities of documentary data is also an obvious point that requires little elaboration here. This characteristic is not unrelated to the quality of inferences, a point that is illustrated by Ogilvie's chapter. The fact that his conclusions are drawn from a broad empirical base—more than a third of a million words of folk tales were analyzed—can be attributed partly to the speed and economy with which such analyses can be done by computer. Moreover, he was able to make extensive use of data borrowed from another scholar who had collected them for quite different purposes. Although such exchanges of data were possible before they were stored on IBM cards, they were relatively rare,[3] partly because data coded for one purpose were seldom useful to those whose theoretical interests differed.

The role of the computer is equally clear in Raben's research agenda. The identification of similarities in poetic style across time spans of several centuries would have seemed a hopelessly ambitious venture before computers could be harnessed to the task of searching for and matching content attributes in millions of words of text. Literary research of this type will also depend on the ability of scholars to establish central data banks of text on IBM cards.

Finally, there are indications that recent developments in computer-based content analysis may facilitate development of standard categories. Earlier we identified some of the practical barriers to replicative content-analysis research. Computer-based research at least offers a potential remedy for the problem because the sharing of dictionaries is facilitated. Equally important, costs of reanalyzing data on IBM cards can be measured in added dollars spent on machine time rather than in the more valuable currency of the analyst's time in completing his study. Unambiguous, easily shared, and conveniently used categories do not, of course, insure wide acceptance. But it seems safe to predict that *if* progress is made toward development of standard categories (and, thus, of norms), it will come about largely as a result of computer-based research.

Let me conclude with some general issues relating to the role of computers in inferences from content data. Too often the question is dominated by enthusiasts ready to tackle any problem with computers (but with much less concern for the purpose of their research) and by critics (for example, Barzun, 1965) whose definition of "trivial" includes any study in which computers may play a role. Neither group will find much support in the present chapters.

Paisley and Raben, who discuss subjects within the domain of the humanities, are as explicit in defining the limitations of computers as they are in demonstrating ways in which they may serve the broader goals of the humanistic tradition. It is hard to improve on Paisley's disarmingly simple prescription that man and machine should divide their tasks to maximize the unique capabilities of each. The work of Stone and his colleagues, including that reported in their chapter in this volume, demonstrates to the uncritical enthusiasts the painstaking efforts that are necessary to develop and refine a tool such as the General Inquirer. This work

---

[3] An exception is illustrated in Laffal's use of children's stories gathered by two other scholars. But this example does not render less valid the point that data sharing is more common when the data are in machine-readable form.

also demonstrates to the hypercritical that judgment and sensitivity to potential sources of error (as in the pre-disambiguation General Inquirer dictionaries) are not automatically sacrificed when the computer and print-out replace the pencil and lined pad. The Namenwirth and Ogilvie studies indicate that research of a wide scope—either across time or place—can be undertaken without a concomitant sacrifice of precision. Such studies are not, of course, impossible to design and execute by manual techniques. But we should not casually dismiss the lesson of the RADIR studies of political symbols of the early 1950's. The enormous labors associated with analyzing millions of words of text proved a deterrent to other studies of a similar scope until content analysis by computers was feasible.[4]

These, then, are some of the issues related to inference from content data for which the following chapters have relevance. To conclude by asserting that they have not neatly resolved all the problems of inference[5] is not merely another way of sneaking the overworked phrase that "further research is needed" into the discussion. Instead, it is to state once again the point made earlier that inference is a part of all inquiry and that it is inextricably related to every step in the research process. Thus, problems of inference can no more be resolved once and for all than can the search for knowledge.

[4] The need for machine assistance on this type of research was foreseen by the authors of the RADIR studies. See Lasswell, Lerner, and Pool (1952).
[5] As Namenwirth points out in his chapter, these papers have considered aspects of inductive inference but not those of deductive reasoning.

5 Toward "Cultural Indicators": the Analysis of Mass Mediated Public Message Systems

George Gerbner

The Annenberg School of Communications
University of Pennsylvania

The systematic analysis of message content is a traditional area of study in communication research and related fields. Recent developments led to a revival of interest in the area. But none of the new frameworks and approaches presented considers the analysis of message systems addressed to heterogeneous and anonymous publics, such as mass communications, a source of theoretical development not necessarily generated in other areas of interest. The purpose of this chapter is to suggest an approach that justifies such development and that can also lead to results of practical policy significance, such as a scheme of social accounting for trends in the composition and structure of mass-mediated public message systems. The approach is based on a conception of these message systems as the common culture through which communities cultivate shared and public notions about facts, values, and contingencies of human existence. The approach is not inconsistent with Krippendorff's theoretical formulations. It derives support from Rapoport's notions of system analysis. It has some affinity with Hays' description of knowledge. And it shares the focus of this section on types of inference and standard categories (or category classes).

THE NEED FOR INDICATORS

The "Cultural Revolution" is not only a Chinese slogan. It is also a fact of social life whenever a particular political-industrial order permeates the sphere of public message production. A change in the social bases and economic goals of message mass production leads, sooner or later, to a transformation of the common symbolic environment that gives public meaning and sense of direction to human activity. The need is for a theory that can lead to the development of "cultural indicators" taking the pulse of the nature and tempo of that transformation.

Our theoretical point of departure, then, is that changes in the mass production and rapid distribution of messages across previous barriers of time, space, and social grouping bring about systematic variations in public message content whose full significance rests in the cultivation of collective consciousness about elements of existence. (Notice, at the outset, that the terms "common," "shared," "public," or "collective" cultivation do not necessarily mean consensus. On the contrary, the public recognition of subcultural, class, generational, and ideological differences and even conflicts among scattered groups of people require some common awareness and cultivation of the issues, styles, and points of divergence that make public contention and contest possible. The struggles for power and privilege, for participation in the conduct of affairs, for the redistribution of resources, and for all forms of social recognition and justice are shifting more and more from the older arenas to the newer spheres of public attention and control in mass-produced communications.)

Selective habits of participation in one's cultural environment limit each of us to risky, and often faulty, extrapolation about the cultural experience of heterogeneous communities. Informed policy making and the valid interpretation of social response increasingly require general and comparative indicators of the prevailing climate of the man-made symbolic environment. But knowledge of a message system, over and above that which we select for our own information or entertainment, and which has significance for a collectivity such as an entire cultural community, cannot be given in the lifetime experience of any single person.

What *can* be given is a representative abstraction from the collectively experienced total texture of messages, relevant to certain investigative purposes. Sampling is not the major problem, and neither is the efficient processing of large quantities of data, although these are important procedural considerations. Nor is great theoretical challenge involved in the analysis of mass-media messages for specific critical, control, evaluative, or policy purposes. The outstanding problems are (1) the development of a generalized scheme applicable to the investigation of the broadest terms of collective cultivation in different cultural communities, and (2) making these terms salient to elements of existence represented in public message systems. Philosophers, historians, anthropologists and others have, of course, addressed themselves to such problems before. But the rise of the institutionalized and corporately managed cultivation of collective consciousness by mass media has given a new urgency and social policy significance to the inquiry.

CULTIVATION OF PUBLIC CONSCIOUSNESS
THROUGH MASS COMMUNICATION

A word on "cultivation." I use the term to indicate that my primary concern in this discussion is not with information, education, persuasion, and the like, or with any kind of direct communication "effects." I am concerned with the collective context within which, and in response to which, different individual and group selections and interpretations of messages take place. In that sense, a message (or message system) cultivates consciousness of the terms required for its meaningful perception. Whether I accept its "meaning" or not, like it or not, or agree or disagree, is another problem. First I must attend to and grasp what it is about. Just how that occurs, how items of information are integrated into given frameworks of cognition, is also another problem. My interest here centers on the fact that any attention and understanding cultivates the terms upon which it is achieved. And to the considerable extent to which these terms are common to large groups, the cultivation of shared terms provides the basis for public interaction.

"Public" is another word of special significance here. It means both a quality of information and "an amorphous social structure whose members share a community-of-interest which has been produced by impersonal communication and contact" (*A Dictionary of the Social Sciences,* 1964, p. 558). As a quality of information, the awareness that a certain item of knowledge is publicly held (that is, not only known to many but *commonly known that it is known to many*) makes collective thought and action possible. Such knowledge gives individuals their awareness of collective strength (or weakness) and a feeling of social identification or alienation. As an "amorphous social structure, etc." a public is a basic unit of and requirement for self-government among diverse and scattered groups. The creation of both the consciousness and the social structure called public is the result of the "public-making" activity appropriately named publication. "Public opinion" is actually the outcome of some sort of eliciting and sharing private views through their publication—as in the publication of polls.

Publication, as a general social process, is the creation and cultivation of shared ways of selecting and viewing events and aspects of life. Mass production and distribution of message systems transforms selected private perspectives into broad public perspectives, and brings mass publics into existence. These publics are maintained through continued publication. They are supplied with selections of information and entertainment, fact and fiction, news and fantasy or "escape" materials which are considered important or interesting or entertaining and profitable (or all of these) in terms of the perspectives to be cultivated.

Publication is thus the basis of community consciousness and self-government among large groups of people too numerous or too dispersed to interact face-to-face or in any other personally mediated fashion. The truly revolutionary significance of modern mass communication is its "public-making" ability. That is the ability to form historically new bases for collective thought and action quickly, continuously, and pervasively across previous boundaries of time, space, and culture.

The terms of broadest social interaction are those available in the most widely shared message systems of a culture. Increasingly these are mass-produced message systems. That is why mass media have been called the "agenda-setters" of modern society. Whether one is widely conversant or unaware of large portions of them, supportive or critical of them, or even alienated from or rebellious of them, the terms of the culture shape the course of the response.

The approach I am suggesting is, therefore, concerned with the overall patterns and boundary conditions within which the processes of individual cognition, message utilization, and social interaction occur. The approach is directed toward answering the most general questions about the broadest terms of collective concept-formation given in mass-produced public message systems: What perspectives and what choices do they make available to entire communities over time, across cultures, and in different societies? With what kinds and proportions of properties and qualities are these choices weighted? What are the underlying structures of association in large message systems that are not apparent in their separate component units?

THE NEED FOR "CULTURAL INDICATORS"

We need to know what general terms of collective cultivation about existence, priorities, values, and relationships are given in collectively shared public message systems before we can reliably interpret facts of individual and social response. For example, it means little to know that "John believes in Santa Claus" until we also know in what culture, at what point in time, and in the context of what public message systems cultivating the reinforcement or inhibition of such beliefs. Similarly, interpretations of public opinion (that is, responses to questions elicited in specific cultural contexts), and of many social and cultural policy matters, require the background knowledge of general "cultural indicators" similar to the economic indicators compiled to guide economic policy and the social indicators proposed to inform social policy making.

What distinguishes the analysis of public, mass-mediated message systems as a social scientific enterprise from other types of observation, commentary, or criticism is the attempt to deal comprehensively, systematically, and generally rather than specifically and selectively or *ad hoc* with problems of collective cultural life. This approach makes no prior assumptions about such conventionally demarcated functions as "information" and "entertainment," or "high culture" and "low culture." Style of expression, quality of representation, artistic excellence, or the quality of individual experience associated with selective exposure to and participation in mass-cultural activity are not considered critical variables for this purpose. What is informative, entertaining (or both), good, bad, or indifferent by any standard of quality are selective judgments applied to messages quite independently from the social functions they actually perform in the context of large message systems touching the collective life of a whole community. Conventional and formal judgments applied to selected communications may be irrelevant to general questions about the presentation of what *is,* what is *important,* what is *right,* and what is *related* to what in mass-produced composite message systems.

NONRELEVANCE OF SOME CONVENTIONAL DISTINCTIONS

Just as we make no a priori assumptions about the significance of style, quality, and subjective experience associated with different types of message systems, we do not recognize the validity of conventional distinctions of function attached to "nonfictional" versus "fictional" modes of presentation. "Fact" may be stranger than fiction, and the veracity of "fiction" may be greater than that of the presumably factual. Regardless of verisimilitude, credibility, or what is actually "believed" in a presentation, message systems cultivate the terms on which they present subjects or aspects of life. There is no reason for assuming that the cultivation of these terms depends, in any significant way, on the mode of presentation, on agreement or disagreement with or belief or disbelief in the presentations involved, or on whether these presentations are presumably factual or imaginary. This does not mean, of course, that we do not normally attach greater credibility to a news story, a presumably factual report, a trusted source, or a familiar account than to a fairy tale or to what we regard as false or inimical. What it does mean is that in the general process of image-formation and cultivation, "fact" and "fable" play equally significant and interrelated roles.

There is, however, an important difference between the ways "fiction" and "nonfiction" deal with life. Reportage, exposition, explanation, argument—whether based on fact, fancy, opinion, or all of these—ordinarily deal with specific aspects of life or thought extracted from total situations. What gives shape, focus, and purpose to the "nonfictional" mode of presentation is that it is analytical; it implicitly organizes the universe into classes of subjects and topics, and it devotes primary attention to one or more of these subjects and topics.

The usual purpose of the fictional and dramatic modes of presentation is to present situations rather than fragments of knowledge as such. The focus is on people in action; subjects and topics enter as they become significant to the situations.

From the point of view of the analysis of elements of existence, values, and relationships inherent in large message systems, fiction and drama thus offer special opportunities. Here an aspect of life, an area of knowledge, or the operation of a social enterprise appears imaginatively recreated in its significant associations with total human situations. The requirements that make the treatment of specific subjects secondary to the requirements of telling a "good story" might make the treatment of those subjects more revealing of the underlying assumptions cultivated in the story-telling process.

I must stress again that the characteristics of a message system are not necessarily the characteristics of individual units composing the system. The purpose of the study of a system *as system* is to reveal features, processes, and relationships expressed in the whole, not in its parts. Unlike most literary or dramatic criticism (or, in fact, most personal cultural participation and judgment), this approach to message-system analysis focuses on the record of institutional behavior in the cultural field, and on the dynamics of message-production and image-cultivation in a community but not necessarily in selective personal experience and response.

The systems with which we deal contain images and motion as well as words. This places great demands on methods of recording and notation, and challenges the ingenuity of the scientific analyst. Because of the necessity to abstract propositional forms from statements made in a variety of modes, methods of analysis must rely on explicitly formulated rules and procedures. But there is no reason to assume that the system-theoretic notions developed in Rapoport's chapter in this book are not as applicable to these as to other "large corpuses of verbal data." Rapoport's description of man's "ocean of words" provides a vivid rationale for the study of the process in which mass-produced messages play a key part:

Just as all living organisms live in certain specialized environments to which they adapt and which completely determines their lives so do human beings live to a significant extent in an ocean of words. The difference lies in the fact that the human environment is to a large extent man made. We secrete words into the environment around us just as we secrete carbon dioxide and in doing so, we create an invisible semantic environment of words which is part of our existence in quite as important ways as the physical environment. The content of verbal output does not merely passively reflect the complex social, political, and economic reality of the human race; it interacts with it as well. As our semantic environment incorporates the verbal outputs secreted into it, it becomes both enriched and polluted, and these changes are in large measure responsible for the course of human history. It behooves us to study this process (Rapoport, Chapter 1, *supra.*)

TERMS OF THE ANALYSIS

The approach needed is that capable of abstracting and analyzing the most general terms of cultivation given in mass-produced public message systems. Generality is necessary to encompass many specific classes of statements and diverse investigative purposes within comparable terms of the same framework. But this kind of generality implies a high level of abstraction and selection which, in turn, arises from a conception of salience to some general investigative purpose. As I have already stated, the present purpose is not governed by direct interest in sources as senders or in interpreters as receivers of messages. It is, however, governed by interest in the cultivation of consciousness of elements of existence inferred from public message systems. Our task is to combine generality with salience to the composition and structure of knowledge given in large-scale message systems addressed to collective social entities.

We begin by defining such knowledge as propositions expressed in the images, actions, and language of the most widely shared (that is, mass-produced and rapidly distributed) message systems of a culture. Elements of existence refer to the assumptions, contexts, points of view, and relationships represented in these message systems and made explicit in the analysis.

A summary of the questions, measures, and terms of general analysis of public message systems appears in Figure 1. The questions relate to the cultivation of collective notions about (1) "what is" (that is, what exists as an item of public knowledge), (2) "what is important" (that is, how the items are ordered), (3) "what is right" (or wrong, or endowed with any qualities, or presented from any point of view), and (4) "what is related to what" (by proximity or other connection). The corresponding terms of analytical measures are those of (1) attention, (2) emphasis, and (3) tendency (the first three describing the composition of the system—that is, what elements compose it and how they are distributed in it) and (4) structure (that is, how they are put together or related to one another). A brief discussion of each of these terms follows.

1. *Attention* is the result of selection of phenomena to be attended. A measure of attention is an indication of the presence and frequency

Questions	Definitions	Measures and Terms of Analysis	Brief Explanations of Questions
1. WHAT IS?	Public assumptions about existence	Distribution, frequency of *attention*	What things (or kinds of things) does this message system call to the attention of a community?
2. WHAT IS IMPORTANT?	Context of priorities	Ordering, scaling, for *emphasis*	In what context or order of importance are these things arranged?
3. WHAT IS RIGHT, ETC.?	Point of view, affective qualities	Measures of differential *tendency*	In what light or from what point of view are these things presented?
4. WHAT IS RELATED TO WHAT?	Proximal or logical associations	Contingencies, clustering; *structure*	In what structure of associations with one another are these things presented?

Figure 1   Questions and terms of public message system analysis.

of subject elements (topics and themes, for instance) in a message system. The significance of attention as an aspect of the process of message-production and image-formation is that it stems from (and, in turn, cultivates) assumptions about existence; it provides common conceptions about what "is" (or, at least, what is sufficiently common and public knowledge to form a basis for social interaction).

2. *Emphasis* is that aspect of the composition of message systems which establishes a context of priorities of importance or relevance. The context of emphases sets up a field of differential appeal in which certain things stand out. Emphasis "structures the agenda" of public conception and discourse cultivated in message systems. Measures of emphasis may be based on such indications of size, intensity, or stress as the headlining of topics in news items or the featuring of certain topics or themes as the major points of stories.

3. *Tendency.* The position of a system (as of an individual) in time, space, and in the overall structure of social relations enters into the approach, point of view, or direction from which it deals with aspects of existence. The directionality of presentation—the explicit or contextual judgment of qualities of phenomena expressed in the presentation—is called tendency.

The broadest overall dimension of judgment is a summary evaluation of the goodness or badness, rightness or wrongness of things. A measure of the favorable-unfavorable associations expressed in the comparative study of message systems may be called *critical tendency;* it is based primarily on whether a subject or topic appears in a supportive or critical context.

But judgment is, of course, multidimensional. *Differential* tendency can be used to describe a measure indicating directionality of judgment in several different dimensions.

4. *Structure* is that aspect of context which reveals relationships among components. These may be simply proximal, which we may call *clustering* or they may be causal or other logical relationships. In this approach we are primarily interested in explicating the "logic" implicit in the proximal structuring or clustering rather than in forms of reasoning; the former is more likely to be a property of large systems and thus not easily available to scrutiny. For example, the reasoning employed in the assertion that "John loves Mary and will marry her" (whether expressed in a sentence, a story, or a series of visual images) is apparent in that single statement. But if we compare two large message systems and find that the proximal occurrences of the words or concepts of "love" and "marry" are significantly more frequent in one than in the other, we have discovered an element of comparative linkage or structure, and a kind of "logic," that would not be revealed by inspecting propositions separately.

The above terms of analysis are suggested as standard category *classes.* The specific categories, and other methods of analysis, require considerable elaboration which cannot be attempted here. This approach to message-system analysis is itself a part of a larger framework for an institutional approach to mass communications research described elsewhere (Gerbner, 1966a; 1967a). And although many studies cited in this volume and in the literature fit one or more of the general terms sketched above, the only investigation using all of them has been limited to a comparative study of the portrayal of education in the press and mass fiction of ten countries (Gerbner, 1964a).

The reader interested in a specific example of attention analysis may find it in a study of convention press coverage (Gerbner, 1967b). Analyses of trends in attention may be found in a study of "Psychology, Psychiatry and Mental Illness in the Mass Media: A Study of Trends, 1900–1959" (Gerbner, 1961a); or of "Education About Education by Mass Media" (Gerbner, 1966b). Studies focusing on emphasis include a comparative investigation of U.N. press coverage (Gerbner, 1961b). Differential tendencies were investigated in the study of ideological perspectives in the French press (Gerbner, 1964b), and in a comparative study of characterizations in mass fiction and drama (Gerbner, 1966c). The analysis of message system structure was attempted in the comparative portrayal of education study cited above.

I know of no comprehensive and comparative studies of the kind that might yield the cultural indicators needed for a realistic assessment of the much-debated condition of man in modern "mass cultures." One reason might be the paucity of explicit formulations of the theoretical significance and types of inference that might be derived from the analysis of mass-mediated public message systems. Another might be the lack of general terms salient to such analysis. The intention of this chapter has been to try to narrow these gaps.

6 Studying "Style" as Deviation from Encoding Norms

William J. Paisley

Institute for Communication Research
Stanford University

These thoughts are collected under a title that may provoke two questions: Why study style at all? Why study style as if it were "only" deviation in encoding behavior?

WHY STUDY STYLE AT ALL?

To confuse the issue, two usages of style are current. Style often refers to the *characteristic* form and content of works created in a certain period, in a certain place, by certain men—for example, Renaissance, Florentine, the School of Leonardo. Style also refers to an *individual*'s uniqueness, wherever he is, in whatever period. Distinguishing between style as a time-place-group characteristic and style as individual uniqueness, the first question then becomes two questions: Why study the ways in which an entire group expresses itself differently from other groups? Why study the ways in which an individual expresses himself differently from the group whose models are his point of departure?

Of several good answers to the first question, I prefer: to open a window onto the purposes and values that the group holds. If we compare, for instance, the idealization of Hellenic sculpture with the unflattering realism of early Roman sculpture, we can guess which group established the first bureaucracy in the Mediterranean world. From the megaliths of Stonehenge to the spires of Chartres to the beams of Eiffel's tower, a group expresses its purposes and values in its artifacts.

If an individual's purposes and values are as interesting and important

* The Annenberg Conference originally commissioned a study on this topic by the author. Although it was impossible to prepare a paper in time for the conference, Professor Holsti graciously consented to include the work in this volume. An earlier version of this chapter was presented at the University of Wisconsin–Milwaukee symposium, "Communication Theory and the Arts," in April 1967.

133

as those of the group, then we have an answer to the second part of the first question. Microcosmically, each individual acts out the group's struggle to establish, interpret, and perpetuate itself. Each expressive behavior, well analyzed, is another window opened on the event. From Sigmund Freud's *The Psychopathology of Everyday Life* (1938) to Erving Goffman's *The Presentation of Self in Everyday Life* (1959), important works have reminded us that the individual whose "style" is being analyzed need not be an artist and that behaviors exhibiting his "style" need not be elaborate or even conscious expressions of the purposes and values we wish to infer.

If I emphasize analyses of style that support inference, I do not mean to slight simple descriptions of content and form. My own work is primarily descriptive. The inferential and descriptive goals are complementary. Inference is a link to the human condition—an assessment of motives, causes, or effects. Descriptive analysis provides hard data without which inference remains speculation.

WHY STUDY STYLE AS DEVIATION IN ENCODING BEHAVIOR?

Now it is time to confront the concept of encoding behavior. By encoding behavior, I mean any activity in which a person selects elements from a symbol system and arranges them in a pattern spread over time, or space, or both. Most but not all encoding behavior is further characterized by purposefulness in creating one pattern instead of others, by a belief in the coherence of the pattern, and by the expectation that the pattern will be perceived and used in some way (appreciation is a form of use) by other people or by the encoder himself at a later time.

The symbol system can be all the words in a writer's vocabulary. It can be the composer's resources of pitches, tempi, timbres, and so on. It can be the painter's palette, or the dancer's repertory of movement and attitude, or the construction materials available to an architect. As we see in contemporary sculpture, it can be any collection of artifacts from the popular culture. In *The Silent Language,* the anthropologist E. T. Hall (1959) argues that time and space are symbol systems that we use as frames for our other expressions. There are more symbol systems than we can enumerate and, among the most interesting of them, are the speech and gesture of ordinary people in ordinary situations—the theme of Freud and Goffman.

But, if by encoding behavior I mean some symbol-arranging activity such as writing, then why not just call it writing? Because encoding behavior as a concept reminds us of two important facts:

1. *Encoding* is a process of selecting from what is available. Availability should be qualified in terms of the potential and the probable. Every

writer has a potential vocabulary at least as large as all words found in all dictionaries plus all the neologisms his imagination can furnish. By comparison, his utilized vocabulary is quite small and, within that vocabulary, probabilities of use are very disparate. In extemporaneous speech, 50 most-used words make up half of all his utterances. His 500th most-used word is likely to occur only once in a string of 10,000 words.

If we say encoding rather than writing, we may remember that we are looking at a process of selection, and that what was available to be selected, potentially and probabilistically, is of great interest.

2. *Behavior* is an activity, abstracted for analysis from a sequence of activities that may have significant continuity for the person being observed. Encoding behavior occurs within a context of other behaviors—some ongoing others finished but lingering in their effects, others not yet begun but anticipated in thoughts and feelings. What is affecting in Pagliacci's determination to clown is the off-stage tragedy from which he has no time to recover. Anticipation of personal tragedy to follow is evident in suicide notes analyzed by Charles Osgood and Evelyn Walker (1959b).

When we say encoding behavior, perhaps it will remind us that *we* have chosen to abstract for analysis one activity that is woven into the fabric of a person's daily routine. We may not know what the writer was doing before he sat down to write, but we know that behavior dissolves into behavior, and feeling into feeling.

Behavior should also imply a family of similar behaviors engaged in by other people and by the person himself at other times. The family of behaviors should suggest norms—uniformities in the way the activity is usually done. That is, the writer cannot approach his activity as if he were the first person on earth to assemble words in a pattern. He may not be able to verbalize the norms that bear upon his task, but he recognizes them and his writing shows it. Norms are distinguishable in his language, in the form he has adopted, in his historical period, in the position he adopts relative to his subject matter and to the reader, and so on.

Norms interest us because the writer's eye and ear will not allow him to follow them slavishly. He will deviate from the norms to achieve effects. When we know the norm, we are more likely to notice his deviation and to apprehend his purpose in deviating.

Two Premises on Which the Encoding Behavior Approach Depends

The student of style is unlikely to accept an encoding behavior approach unless he agrees with the following positions.

1. *Analyzing* style and *appreciating* style are separate activities. One *analyzes* patterns of use and nonuse, conjunction and disjunction, emphasis

and understatement, and so on. One *appreciates* how effectively or satisfyingly the creator has dealt with his chosen form and content. Informed appreciation begins with a completed analysis of some kind, as supporting evidence for one's impression that the work *does* possess certain attributes.

2. The *procedure* of analysis should be so straightforward that, if another person were to conduct it independently and without knowledge of prior results, he would necessarily arrive at the same conclusion. This is science's reliability criterion of interobserver agreement. If two people can independently arrive at the same conclusion, applying the same analysis procedure to the same data, then we have some confidence that the procedure is free of hidden assumptions and private meanings, that the analyst is not merely case-making.

Some humanists may object to the scientific criterion of reliability. Certainly J. M. Robertson would have felt unfairly constrained by it, in his preparation of *The Shakespeare Canon* (1922–1930), when (in the words of E. K. Chambers, 1930) he ran "like a hound through the undergrowth, catching a scent of Marlowe here, and whimpering there at a suspicion of Kyd or Peele." If, however, the student of style can say, "Do the analysis yourself, following these steps, and see if you reach the same conclusion," then we can discuss reasonably the issue of whether *these* indicators are indeed the best ones on which to base an interpretation.

Attributes of the Encoding Behavior Approach

The encoding behavior approach to stylistics has the following attributes that distinguish it from traditional stylistics.

1. Style Has an Explicit Operational Definition. No longer the essence of a work that is nowhere isolatable, style is now defined as "an individual's deviations from norms for the situations in which he is encoding, these deviations being in the statistical properties of those structural features for which there exists some degree of choice in his code" (Osgood, 1960). I would amend this definition to cover less, and more. Less, in that almost any work presents us with more analyzable elements, each with its associated norm(s), than our analysis can possibly encompass; the definition should acknowledge some selection of elements or "features." More, in that the person brings his *own* norms to the situation (for instance, a regional norm, a family norm), and these norms interact with the situational norm to predict his encoding behavior. Deviations should therefore be reckoned from the composite of all norms that bear upon the particular act of encoding. Below, I shall discuss these relationships more formally.

2. Specific Content Elements Must Be Named as the Indicators of Style in a Particular Analysis. Taking literary text as an example, the range of analyzable content elements extends from individual letter-choices to the most encompassing form-selection (such as the decision to write a set of short stories instead of a novel). In between fall many content elements: the word, the phrase, the clause, the sentence, the paragraph, and the section or chapter.

Neither end of this range is the most profitable level of analysis. Letter-choices would be trivial indicators of style even if they were not constrained by the combination of vocabulary and orthography. This does not mean that authorship differences cannot be found at that level; I (Paisley, 1966) found statistically reliable authorship differences in letter use in analyses of *Iliad* translations (I'll mention later my purpose in studying translations), but these were undoubtedly downward reflections of vocabulary differences. Similarly, the most encompassing form-selections are made from a small set of much-used forms. The fact that a writer's corpus consists mainly of short stories is not a powerful stylistic insight; too many other writers share that form.

But in the range from words to paragraphs we find content elements that *are* powerful indicators of style. And some elements—these or others—must be specified and adhered to as the foci of the analysis. If the analysis concerns vocabulary differences, then the operational definition of *that aspect* of style is a set of deviations from vocabulary norms, and the content element is the word.

3. The Choice of Content Element Is Determined by the Goal of the Analysis. If this seems too obvious a point, there is a lesson to be learned in the history of authorship attribution studies. For many years this goal was approached via the wrong content elements, wrong in that they did not lead to the most powerful discrimination between possible authors of disputed works. Even George Udny Yule (1944), otherwise an infallible student of style, was (in retrospect) misguided in his choice of common nouns as content elements for attributing the authorship of the *Imitatio Christi* to Thomas à Kempis. The attribution is undoubtedly correct, but Yule's labor was needlessly increased by his choice of relatively rare words that are constrained almost as much by the topic of a text as by an author's vocabulary. He had to scan large amounts of text to create stable frequencies of these nouns, and—as he observes a bit sadly (p. 266)—just one often-repeated metaphor, an uncharacteristic whimsy of the author, can send a rare noun almost to the head of the frequency list.

Within the past five years we have learned the most efficient content elements for attributing authorship, although (as I noted in an earlier paper, 1964) the 19th-century connoisseur, Giovanni Morelli, struck upon the principle intuitively, used it to identify misattributed Renaissance art throughout Europe, and passed it on to his pupil, Bernard Berenson. This is the element I call the "minor encoding habit." Both inconspicuous and ubiquitous, it is too much in the background of a work to be noticed by an imitator or to be varied consciously for effect by the author himself. In painting, Morelli observed, it may be the rendering of fingernails or earlobes. In music, as I found (Paisley, 1964), it can be simple pitch transitions.

The best demonstration to date of the discrimination achieved by "minor encoding habits" is the study of the *Federalist* papers by Frederick Mosteller and David Wallace (1963). Specifying the most common function words (articles, conjunctions, and prepositions) as their content elements, they found odds of millions to one in support of their attribution of the disputed papers to Madison rather than Hamilton.

Some misunderstanding followed the talk of "minor encoding habits," especially when I extended the principle to the study of extemporaneous speech in the 1960 Kennedy-Nixon debates (Paisley, 1967). Although very strong authorship patterns were once again found, the question was raised, "What does this analysis tell us about the unique styles that carried both men so far in American politics?" The answer, of course, is that it tells us nothing at all. The content elements chosen were appropriate for an authorship study, but the point of greatest *idiosyncrasy* is quite unlikely to be the source of greatest *effect* in political speech making. Idiosyncrasy is greatest at a "thoughtless" level of encoding; persuasive effect is undoubtedly greatest at the level of conscious and adroit selection of words and phrases.

Therefore, again, the choice of content element is determined by the goal of the analysis. Content elements appropriate for authorship attribution are out of place in a study of the author's purposes and values. Elements appropriate for a study of purposes and values can tell us little about the sources of effect.

4. The Analysis Procedure Must Be Unambiguous and Repeatable. The encoding behavior approach implies a quantitative analysis. A fair test of content element specification is the analyst's ability to count one when he sees one. Combined with a system for sampling text, or indeed encompassing it all, a precise specification of content elements leads to an analysis procedure that is unambiguous and repeatable.

It is difficult to develop unambiguous procedures. There are always borderline elements to be classified, and even with computers we are dismayed by the sheer volume of text to be digested. But Louis Milic (1964, p. 59), for one, suggests that it might be good discipline: "Any scholar knows that he would rather guess than count and the literature is in consequence riddled with inaccurate and imprecise quantity statements for which exact quantities could have been easily substituted." Even if we draw back at the "easily," we too would prefer that a number be trustworthy, if it appears at all in a study of style.

5. The Analysis Must Be Comparative. In traditional stylistics it is possible to discuss a work in isolation. It begins, it develops, it ends. Things that happen in the middle have their genesis in things that happen at the beginning. Point leads to point. The creator's skill and style can be discussed impressionistically without reference to models.

In the encoding behavior approach, isolated analyses lead to trivial descriptions of what elements are present in what quantities. For example, "I" may occur 18 times per 1000 words in a certain text. Perhaps "we" occurs only 11 times per 1000 words. Are we ready to make an inference about the writer's egotism? What if we check the norms and find that "I" is expected to occur 25 times, "we" only 7 times? The writer is less self-centered and more group-centered than we thought.

To answer the question, "Why study style as deviation in encoding behavior?", I have tried to describe some of the attributes of the encoding behavior approach, since the answer must lie there. In general, the encoding behavior approach forces us to be explicit, and to seek agreement, about what is being analyzed, and how, and in comparison with what external norms or points of reference. It shifts the definition of style from an ineffable quality to a bounded set of content elements—with the understanding that the elements selected for a particular analysis do not "exhaust" the style of a work.

The encoding behavior approach also strips from the term style its connotations of good form, balance, internal consistency, and so on. Style becomes a neutral term, operationally defined only as a set of deviations from encoding norms. Thus defined, style is present in every work to the same extent. We cannot say that a work "lacks style."

DECISION-POINTS IN THE ANALYSIS OF ENCODING BEHAVIOR

After listing attributes of the encoding behavior approach, it may be useful now to outline procedural decision-points.

1. What Are the Goals of the Study? First, will the study yield a simple description, an "appreciation," or an inference? Hopefully the goal is not stated, "I want to study X's style," because this translates to, "I want to study the sum of X's deviations from norms bearing upon particular acts of encoding." To what end?

2. What Exactly Is the Corpus Under Analysis? The size and range of the corpus is entirely the analyst's prerogative. Perhaps it includes all the work of several men; perhaps it is a single poem. It is important only that the "data base" match the stated scope of the analysis. Otherwise, when a man's collected works lie open on the desk, it is tempting to fire at targets of opportunity, to run objective analyses on subjectively chosen excerpts, thus hiding one's case-making in the prior step of selecting the corpus.

As these analyses become increasingly a task for the computer, explicit statements of the corpus will be a natural by-product of the preparation of machine-readable materials.

3. What Content Elements Shall Be Chosen, in Keeping with the Goals of the Analysis? If the goal of the analysis is simple description, then the analyst is bound by a cartographer's obligation not to omit significant features from his map. His chosen content elements would probably begin with words, progressing to sentence construction, punctuation, paragraph organization, and so on.

If the goal of the analysis is inference, then the choice of content elements will be governed by the logic of any connection between indicators in the work and states of mind, intentions, effects, and the like. This is a validity problem, and content elements should be chosen provisionally, then tested against external criteria. A good example of this process is reported by Osgood and Walker (1959b) in their study of the "style" of genuine versus phony suicide notes. Several content elements on which they hoped to base the discrimination failed them; others passed the test.

4. How Shall the "Data Base" Be Sampled? One possible decision at this point is that it shall not be sampled at all, that every unit in it shall be included in the analysis. More often, such a census is neither possible nor necessary to establish stable patterns. This decision depends both on the size of the corpus and on the complexity of the content element(s) being accounted for. If it is to be a sampling rather than a census, there should be a simple, objective, repeatable procedure for choosing the subset of content to be analyzed.

5. What Norms Are Relevant? After several allusions to the principle of multiple impinging norms, it is appropriate to consider what these norms may be (as illustrated also in Figure 1):

(*a*)   *The "all-language" norm.* For English or any other symbol system, there is a grand norm that might be estimated by comprehensive

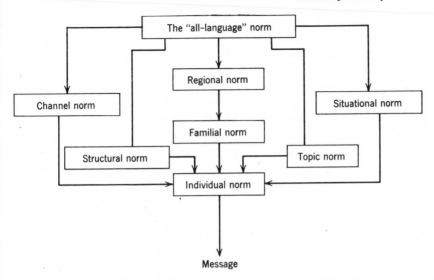

Figure 1 Some of the norms bearing on an act of encoding.

sampling of variations. The language changes too quickly for us ever to estimate the grand norm. However, it serves as a hypothetical point of reference for *all* variation. The norm created by a large sample of diverse texts is a useful approximation to the grand norm. A good example is the norms for present-day American English created by W. N. Francis (1964) from an eclectic sample of one million words.

(*b*) *The channel norm.* By channel, I mean to encompass both sense modality and medium. English, for instance, is both heard and seen. Within each of these modalities, there are several media. *Written* English in a note to oneself, in a personal letter, in the newspaper, and in a scientific article may be more similar than any one is to *spoken* English.

(*c*) *The structural norm.* Within the set of encoding acts directed toward any channel, there will be differences specific to the structure of each act. Does the writer believe he is producing prose or verse? Does the speaker believe he is presenting a speech or making an offhand comment?

(*d*) *The topic norm.* Of greatest significance when words are the chosen content elements, the topic norm simply reminds us of the necessity of using different symbols, and common symbols in different proportions, when treating different topics. No less a student of style than T. C. Mendenhall (1887) confounded topic (and structure) with authorship differences when he attempted to compare Bacon's *Civil and Moral Essays* with Shakespeare's plays.

(*e*)   *The situational norm.* Whatever the channel, whatever the structure or package, whatever the topic, the encoder finds himself in one of many unique situations. Does he face a friendly or hostile audience? Is his reader an adult or a child? At the moment of encoding, is he by himself or in the company of others? Is the situation relaxed or stressful? Does he feel in command of the material he is encoding? These components of the situation could be separated into norms pertaining to the audience, the encoding environment, the encoder's emotional state, and so on. Or, compositely, they represent the sum of special circumstances that the encoder is conscious of, beyond those of the channel, the structure or package, and the topic.

(*f*)   *The regional norm.* This might also be called a dialectical norm. It is the local realization of the all-language norm. It is primarily the norm of the community in which the encoder learned to make himself understood.

(*g*)   *The familial norm.* At least in the case of language, intensive shaping of encoding behavior occurs in the family. Beyond regional norms, or even in opposition to them, the encoder's childhood family is a second source of norms that he will bring to the situation with him.

(*h*)   *The individual norm.* Partly derived from regional and familial norms, partly a result of his schooling and unique experiences, the individual's own norm is a strong theme on which channel, structure, topic, and situation will play variations. Like every other norm cited here, the individual's own norm is not expected ever to appear in pure form. Every encoding act involves a unique set of constraints that draw the individual away from his norm. Nevertheless, such a norm is ascertainable from large samples of his encoding behavior and could be validated in other, independent samples.

Figure 1 shows that each of these sources of variation is expected to leave its imprint on the message. Operationally this means that, if the message were compared with appropriate controls (and, in every case, samples were large enough to represent stable encoding patterns), the specific effect of each source of variation could be isolated. In practice, such a feat of control is still beyond us, but it is crucial to an explication of style in terms of norms and deviations that such isolation of effects be possible in principle.

If comparisons must be made in the absence of these norms, the alternative is an implicit control on as many sources of variation as possible in a set of comparison texts. For example, in the Kennedy-Nixon debates, both men were *speaking* to television cameras and to a group of questioners present in the studio (same channel). Their remarks were in the

Table 1.   *Frequences per 2500 of selected "major en-coding habits" in the Kennedy-Nixon debates.*

	Kennedy				Nixon			
Debate	1	2	3	4	1	2	3	4
Word								
country(ies)	2	7	0	10	5	5	1	5
federal	13	1	1	0	9	1	0	0
program(s)	13	3	5	0	12	4	0	3
dollar(s)	11	3	9	0	2	3	0	5
debt	3	0	1	0	2	0	0	0
treaty	0	0	14	0	0	3	1	0
attack	0	0	4	2	0	2	9	1
war	1	0	8	3	2	3	12	1
Soviet	0	3	3	8	0	1	2	11
China	0	1	5	3	0	1	0	1
Cuba	0	6	2	1	0	10	0	3
Formosa	0	0	8	2	0	0	8	2
Berlin	0	0	4	3	0	0	4	0

form of *answers to questions* (same structure). Both responded to a *single set of questions* (same topics). Both, we may assume, realized that the context was that of a *debate between two Presidential candidates* (same situation). What was left uncontrolled is the set of individual norms and the familial and regional norms that stand behind them. This is as it should be: individual variation was the focus of the analysis.

Tables 1 and 2, presenting data from the Kennedy-Nixon debates, show that norms *interact* with the level of content element chosen. In Table 1, selected "major encoding habits" are clearly affected by the topic of each debate—domestic policy, foreign policy, and the like. For example, both men peak on "federal" and "program" in the first debate, on "Cuba" in the second debate, on "war" and "Formosa" in the third debate, and on "Soviet" in the fourth debate.

In contrast, many "minor encoding habits" in Table 2 follow the individual norm rather than the topic norm. This is true of some of the most common words in the language, such as "of." Parenthetically, it is interesting that "I" and "we" follow the *topic* norm: both men are I-oriented in the first and third debates and we-oriented in the second and fourth debates.

A more elaborate set of controls—in lieu of norms—was used in an-

Table 2. *Frequencies per 2500 of "minor encoding habits" in the Kennedy-Nixon Debates—all words occurring at the rate of 1/100 or greater in either man's total sample*

	Kennedy				Nixon			
Debate	1	2	3	4	1	2	3	4
Word								
a	52	40	44	34	32	40	45	40
and	74	58	59	56	46	59	57	57
for	32	23	16	14	39	23	13	28
have[a]	18	25	19	20	38	33	28	39
he	4	13	26	9	23	18	25	34
I	68	50	74	54	70	44	65	51
in	71	76	50	66	57	66	52	51
is	32	22	25	21	31	36	31	25
it	37	37	23	21	35	31	38	20
of[a]	78	86	82	83	54	73	66	61
that[a]	71	72	71	62	109	80	108	83
the[a]	211	182	180	185	197	153	145	144
this[a]	7	16	11	10	19	26	32	31
to	62	66	67	72	74	70	82	80
we	23	61	30	70	30	70	43	76

[a] Notice the strong mean differences between Kennedy and Nixon in these cases.

other study mentioned above, a study of letter distributions. I reasoned that letter distributions in English were subject to the influence of four major factors: authorship (style), topic, structure (prose and verse), and time of composition (on a scale of centuries). Therefore, I selected English translations of the *Bible* and the *Iliad* with controlled variation of author (actually, translator), topic, structure, and century of composition. The analysis was designed so that only one factor was free to vary in each comparison (for instance, in testing the time-of-composition factor, the same *Bible* excerpt was found in 14th-, 16th-, and 20th-century versions, with as much replication as possible over authors in each century to avoid contaminating the time-of-composition difference with an authorship difference).

If these five decisions are complementary, then the analysis procedure is predetermined and mechanical, whether performed by hand or by computer. An unusually subtle or complex content element might create a "know one when you see one" problem, requiring tests of the reliability of the analysis procedure. Otherwise, at this point the encoding behavior approach parallels any other systematic approach, marshalling its findings to fulfill the goals of the study.

ADDENDUM ON METHOD: WHAT THE COMPUTER CAN DO

Twenty years ago the title, *The Computer and Literary Style* (Jacob Leed, ed., 1966), could have reminded us only of the writing machine that Gulliver found at the Academy of Lagado. Ten years ago we would have understood what role the computer was to play, but we would have despaired that text is long, the computer's memory short. Today the computer has grown into a central role. Vast random-access storage is commonplace, and the trillion-bit memory is coming. Character-recognition devices are transferring the printed page to computer memory with increasing reliability, and millions of words of text are rendered in machine-readable form every week as an artifact of computer typesetting. On-line interaction with the computer from a console with cathode-ray-tube display permits previously unimagined review of sources and collation of texts.

Thus far, the computer has best shown its power in authorship-attribution studies. We have already touched on the Mosteller-Wallace demonstration that Madison must have written the disputed *Federalist* papers. Other examples are Milic's (1966) test of the proper attribution of Swift's *Letter of Advice to a Young Poet,* O'Donnell's (1966) test of Stephen Crane's *The O'Ruddy,* and (more controversially) the Reverend Morton's (1966) studies of Greek prose, including the Pauline epistles.

The computer's prominent role in authorship studies does not follow from unique compatibility between computer procedures and methods appropriate to such studies. The computer can assist *any* rigorous, quantitative study of style. Authorship studies won a headstart on the computer because the analyst in these instances was prepared to specify the *content elements* to be examined, the *texts* to be sampled, and the *statistical procedures* to establish discrimination.

In contrast to such specificity, other computer-based studies of style are too diffuse and open-ended. This is true regardless of the competence of the analyst—for instance, John Carroll's (1960) "Vectors of Prose Style" encompasses *68* style variables, each measured in 150 passages. Such "fishing" is characteristic of pioneering studies, but the power of the computer is not thus fully exploited.

In dividing labor between man and machine, we should remember which tasks each does poorly. The machine has no sense of completeness, elegance, or parsimony in the statement of a problem. The man has a record of poor reliability in counting, noticing, comparing [see Frederick

Mosteller's (1964, p. 7) reminiscence of graduate-student days when Frederick Williams and he attempted to settle the *Federalist* dispute via manual word counts, leading to "the discovery of an important empirical principle—people cannot count, at least not very high"]. If the man will state an interesting, well-explicated, well-bounded problem, then he can expect the machine to:

1. Count occurrences of any content element that can be specified unambiguously.
2. Order the counted elements—that is, compile a concordance.
3. Refer to any list external to the text and tag text elements with information from the list—for instance, find all the prepositions in a text and label them as such.
4. Count joint occurrences of elements within sentences, elements within paragraphs, and so on.
5. "Map" patterns of element occurrence throughout a text [see the Sedelows' (1964, p. 215) MAPTEXT, "used to look for patterns of rhythm, of texture, and of form"].
6. Discover syntactical dependencies, to a presently limited extent— that is, parse sentences.

Without exception, these are tasks that the analyst is pleased to delegate, notwithstanding his discovery that the computer must know exactly what it has been called upon to do, whereas in his own work he gets by on notions.

Computer processing and the encoding behavior approach to individual differences, both upstarts in the hallowed precincts of literary and artistic criticism, are similar in their insistence on explicit procedure. The scholar should not perceive the new ground rules as a threat to his prerogative in realms of intuition and insight. All his observations are based on *some* data; there is no reason to fear the effects on his scholarship of richer, more reliable and more sharply focused data.

7 Content Analysis of Dreams: Categories, Units, and Norms

CALVIN S. HALL,
Institute of Dream Research and University of California,
Santa Cruz

My experience with content analysis is limited to its application in the analysis of dreams, although recently one of my students, Richard Lind, and I have been engaged in the content analysis of literary works, specifically those of Franz Kafka. Even this new interest stemmed from dreams, however, since Kafka recorded a number of his dreams, and our foray into literature began by correlating the contents of Kafka's dreams with his writings and with biographical material. Because my concern with content analysis grew out of very practical considerations in trying to quantify a specific and fairly unique type of material, what I have to say may be so circumscribed as to have little or no generalizability to other areas in which content analysis is employed. On the other hand, discussions of content analysis which are not grounded in investigatory activity often seem to be suspended in conceptual space and are hard to bring down to empirical earth. There is a danger that we may come to regard content analysis as a thing in itself rather than as a means to an end. Therefore, it is necessary to remind ourselves that content analysis is a tool that should be shaped to the material in hand. It is by means of empirical diggings coupled with occasional conceptual soarings that a general set of principles—if there are any—eventually will be discovered.

Before I discuss norms and categories I must make a few observations concerning the past and present status of research on dreams. Prior to 1900, dreams hardly existed for science in spite of a long cultural and even intellectual tradition regarding their significance, a tradition that still flourishes among many peoples of the world (von Grunebaum and Caillois, 1966). Western science and Western society assigned dreams to the *demi monde* of superstition and occultism. In 1900, Freud attempted to make dreams scientifically respectable but, looking back on his efforts, all that he seems to have accomplished was to encapsulate them in psychoanalysis. No matter how great the impact of this movement may have been on psychotherapy and intellectual currents of the 20th century, it was denied the good science seal of approval. It was not until 1953, when Aserinsky and Kleitman (1953) discovered a correlation between dreaming and rapid eye movements during sleep, that the study of dreams became a respectable scientific enterprise that merited the attention of reputable scientists and received generous financial support from public and private agencies.

The majority of investigations since 1953 have been concerned with dreaming as process, specifically with eye movements, brain waves, and other objective indicators of dreaming and their correlation with such variables as age, sex, phylogeny, psychopathology, time of night, personality measures and, most of all, with physiological, neurological, and biochemical conditions. What people dream about—the subject matter of dreams—although by no means neglected has not enjoyed the widespread popularity of physiologically oriented studies. This imbalance between process and content results, in part, from the continuing influence of Freud, which has proved to be a deterrent to the scientific study of dream contents. For according to Freud and his followers, the dream as recalled—its manifest content—is presumed to have little or no meaning in its own right. It is merely the husk that must be winnowed by free association to get at the kernel—the latent content—which contains the meat and matter of the dream. Psychologists, although disavowing much of Freudian psychology, have been reluctant to transgress this psychoanalytic pronouncement and treat the reported dream as a psychological datum in its own right. Instead, they have devised projective tests that are not as potentially powerful for illuminating personality as dreams are.

No other application of content analysis, to my knowledge, has encountered a similar situation. For, in addition to the animosity that any type of content analysis calls forth from those who prefer to gain knowledge by intuition and impression, the content analysis of dream protocols is regarded in many quarters as being trivial if not meaningless. Let those who subscribe to the doctrine of latent content apply content analysis to free associations, which are also verbal material. What little has been done along this line suggests how fruitful the method of content analysis can be.

CATEGORIES

Types of Dreams

The formulation of categories to be used for content analysis presents options and decisions. As a general rule, the choices made by an investigator will, or should be, determined by his research objectives. If he is clear about his objectives, the formulation of appropriate categories will follow as a matter of course. In practice, it is not that simple. Objectives cannot always be specified in advance, particularly in an area that only recently has been opened for investigation. Useful categories cannot be established until one knows what categories are possible. This knowledge can only be acquired through extensive familiarity with the material.

In dream research, the formulation of categories often begins at that point when the investigator thinks he can detect differences among protocols. Then he derives categories that he hopes will objectify and quantify his impressions. For example, Rechtschaffen, Verdone, and Wheaton (1963) collected dreams from subjects during different stages of sleep. It was their impression that dreams reported from awakenings when the eyes were not moving were more likely to involve thinking about something, whereas dreams reported from awakenings when the eyes were moving were more likely to be perceptions of something. When they established criteria for distinguishing between the two types of dreams—thinking versus perceiving—and counted the number of each type obtained from the two stages of sleep, their original impression was confirmed. These types of dreams, having been identified, are now available for use by other investigators.

The classification of dreams by types is not of recent origin. People have always distinguished between good and bad dreams, true and false ones, big and little dreams, and so forth. Freud identified five types of dreams: wish dreams, anxiety dreams, punishment dreams, traumatic dreams, and neutral dreams. Anyone who has extensive familiarity with dreams tends to think of dreams in terms of types.

One difficulty with classifying the dream as a whole is that many dreams do not fit into neat compartments but overlap several classes. A dream may contain both thinking and perceiving, or it may be both pleasant and unpleasant. Wish, anxiety, and punishment are not uncommonly found in the same dream. Still, in our experience, these very broad categories that characterize the dream as a whole do have their uses.

One problem that arises in connection with distinguishing types of dreams is who shall do the categorizing—the dreamer himself or another person. It can make a big difference. In one of our studies, dreamers were asked to characterize their dreams as bizarre or not bizarre. There were many discrepancies between their characterizations and judgments made by independent observers. What appeared to an outsider to be a very bizarre dream was often regarded by the dreamer as a perfectly natural sequence of events during the dreaming itself. This problem should not be confused with the question of interjudge consistency.

Thematic Analysis

Dreams may also be classified in terms of their predominant themes. Themes may be formulated either in purely empirical terms, or they may be derived from a theory of personality. An empirical thematic analysis consists of characterizing what the dream is about in a condensed statement, such as: dreamer finds a lot of money, dreamer misses a train, dreamer is attacked by a wild animal, dreamer loses a tooth, and dreamer has sexual relations. This type of analysis has been used in investigating typical dreams. The same drawback applies to classifying dreams by themes as to classifying them by types, namely, that many dreams contain more than one theme. In such cases, a dream may be "scored" for as many themes as it contains, or a dream with multiple themes may be discarded.

Deriving thematic categories from a theory of personality is much more complicated than purely empirical formulations. First and foremost, one must be thoroughly conversant with the theory in order to derive categories that reflect the theory accurately. Second, but no less important, one should be thoroughly familiar with dreams in order to adapt theoretical categories to the specific contents of dreams. It is possible that dreams have little or no relevance for some theories, and a great deal for others. It is my impression that dreams are immensely useful for testing propositions derived from Freud's and Jung's theories of personality. Very likely this is true because these theorists made considerable use of dreams in developing their theories. The existential-phenomenological theorist, Medard Boss, has also paid attention to dreams. On the other hand, dreams have been ignored in self and behavioristic theories. Consequently, it may be futile to try to find support for them by the content analysis of dreams. Theoretically, relevant data cannot be extracted from dreams if they are not there to be extracted.

Even if the theory is one that is congenial with the subject matter of dreams, there is still the problem of translating the theory—or that aspect of it that one wishes to test—into scorable manifestations in dreams. If an investigator decides, for example, to establish a scale for scoring anima figures in dreams, what criteria shall he adopt? The best criteria are those that the theorist himself has set forth. Unfortunately, one will not find anywhere in Jung's extensive writings a list of criteria for identifying anima figures. My student, Stan Smith, who was interested in this problem, read through a number of Jung's books and noted every instance in which Jung "pointed" to an anima figure in dreams. He then derived a set of categories for encompassing all of the specific instances that he had collected. Each category was liberally exemplified by quotations from

Jung. By employing this laborious procedure, Smith could be fairly confident that his categories reflected Jung's concept of the anima.

If a theorist has not set forth criteria for a given concept it is necessary for the investigator to do so. This is a hazardous undertaking because there is always the danger that the theory will be misrepresented. Many theory-oriented studies have foundered on the reef of irrelevance.

Elements

A dream report may be broken down into elements for the purpose of content analysis. What are these elements? The basic ones are the individual words used by the dreamer in describing the remembered dream. The investigator may, if he chooses, let each different word constitute its own category, as Kenneth Colby (1958) did, or he may subsume these lexical units under a number of headings as was done by Benjamin Colby et al. (1963). Most dream analysts prefer, however, to work with selected groups of elements. Van de Castle and I (Hall and Van de Castle, 1966a) have devised a system for classifying dream characters, settings, objects, actions, emotions, and modifiers. For example, characters who are mentioned in the dream report are classified by sex, age, relationship to the dreamer, and a number of other features. Actions are subdivided into physical, verbal, locomotion, expressive, cognitive, visual, and several others. Such scales have proved to be useful in comparing subjects differing in age, sex, ethnic background, and pathology, and subjects exposed to differential experimental treatment (for example, Hall and Domhoff, 1963; Smith and Hall, 1964; Hall and Van de Castle, 1966b; Hall, 1966).

One common objection that is raised against the decomposing of a dream into its elements is that the sense or coherence or structure of the whole dream is reduced to a heap of meaningless fragments. Our studies belie this criticism. Elements may have significance in their own right. For example, Van de Castle (1966) found that the incidence of animals in dreams varied with age and culture. Domhoff and I (1963) discovered that males dream more about other males, whereas females dream equally about the two sexes. This difference is independent of age and cultural background.

Moreover, after a dream has been decomposed, it can be resynthesized. Two methods for performing a resynthesis of dreams have been used. One is the method of contingency analysis, which Charles Osgood (1959a) described at the 1955 conference on content analysis. By this method, one can determine what elements in a dream cluster together to a degree greater than would be expected by chance. I applied contingency analysis to a long series of dreams obtained from a young man in order to show that certain elements which are associated either directly or symbolically with anal functioning hung together. Such items as tunnel, pressure, explosion, brown, dirty, water, and empty occurred in the same dream more frequently than would be expected by chance. Van de Castle showed that when an animal appears in a dream, aggression and anxiety also occur in the dream. Contingency analysis is a very powerful quantitative technique and deserves to be more widely employed in content analysis studies.

Another method of synthesizing the elements of dreams consists of combining them to form incidents or interactions. For example, our system for analyzing aggressive interactions involves combining characters with aggressive acts. Let us say that the dreamer, a man, is physically attacked by another man who is a stranger to him. This is coded as 1MSA 7 > D. 1 stands for an individual, M for male, S for stranger, and A for adult. 7 in our aggressive scale stands for a physical aggression, and D is the Dreamer. The arrow indicates that the 1MSA is the aggressor and the dreamer is the victim. Additional elements may be included in order to enlarge the scope of the incident. These may consist of an analysis of what brought on the attack, how the dreamer reacted to the aggression, and what the final outcome was.

The combining of elements in this manner results in the identification of larger themes just as thematic analysis does. However, in my opinion, it is superior to thematic analysis. First, it is difficult to characterize a theme by a purely impressionistic, intuitive, or qualitative approach. One is forced to be analytical whether one is aware of it or not. Since this is the case, why not use an explicit, formalized, and systematic procedure of analysis and synthesis? Second, it is much more difficult to get agreement among judges for thematic categories than for classes of elements. Since interjudge reliability is the chief snag of content analysis, anything that improves reliability without attenuating validity or significance is greatly to be desired.

Individual Versus General Categories

An individual category is one that applies to the dreams of a particular individual. Dorothy Eggan (1952) employed such categories in analyzing the themes in the dreams of a Hopi Indian. I also used individual categories in an investigation of the dreams of an "anal" character. A general category is one that applies to the dreams of a number of individuals. Each type of category has its uses. Individual categories enable the investigator to study unique features of a dream series and to observe changes in the incidence of the category over a period of time. General categories permit one to make comparisons among individuals and groups of individuals.

UNITS

A decision required of the content analyst is how the material with which he is working shall be divided into scorable or codable units. Discussion of this question will be limited to experiences with dreams. In my opinion, there is no single best way of unitizing dream protocols. The choice of a unit depends on the objectives of the investigation.

When one classifies dreams by types or by *single* themes, the dream report is the unit. The fact that dream reports differ in length does not have to be considered in making these classifications. There are other problems, however. A single report may contain what appears to be either two or more separate dreams or two or more different scenes of the same dream. Such cases may be handled in one of two ways: by discarding these reports which, in any event, are few in number, or by asking the dreamer to distinguish reports that contain two or more dreams from those that consist of two or more scenes of the same dream. The subject is usually able to make this discrimination without difficulty. A report that consists of several scenes is then treated as one unit, and a report that contains two or more dreams is treated as two or more units.

In the analysis of elements and incidents, the length of the dream report must be taken into account, since the longer it is the greater is the probability that an element or incident will appear in it. The correlation between number of words and number of characters, for example, is not perfect, but it is high enough to be significant. The influence of report length can be eliminated by any one of a number of procedures.

When the contents of dreams obtained from two groups (for example, males versus females) are being compared, reports can be matched for length. This is the procedure that Van de Castle and I (1966a) used when norms were derived for the contents of male and female college student dreams. When the reports of one group differ markedly in length from those of another group, so that matching is out of the question, the procedure can be followed of dividing the number of words in a report by the frequency of an element or an incident. For example, total wordage of a report can be divided by the total number of characters in order to obtain a quotient, words per character. This procedure had to be used when dreams collected at home were compared with dreams in the laboratory, since the latter were longer, on the average, than the former.

When subclasses of a given category are being compared, the effect of report length can be eliminated by converting each frequency of a subclass into a proportion of the total frequency of the category. Our aggression category, for instance, contains eight subclasses of aggression. When we wished to compare aggression in children's dreams with aggression in adult dreams, the frequencies in the eight subclasses for each age group were changed into proportions. The investigator should first determine whether there is any significant correlation between dream length and the obtained proportions. It may be, for example, that long dreams contain a higher proportion of a certain category than short dreams do. In this case, the procedure is inapplicable.

Social interactions between the dreamer and other characters require a special kind of treatment. The number of aggressions in which a dreamer is involved with a subclass of characters depends, to some extent, on the number of characters of that subclass who are mentioned in the dream report. As a rule, for example, a male dreamer is involved in more aggressions with male characters than with female characters. In a typical male series, however, there are twice as many male characters as female characters. Consequently, the probability of having an aggression with a male character is double that of having an aggression with a female character. In order to control for this differential probability, the number of aggressions with males is divided by the number of male characters, and the number of aggressions with females is divided by the number of female characters. The unit in this case is the character.

Another procedure that eliminates unequal number of characters is to derive an index from the comparison of two kinds of social interactions with different subclasses of characters. It is equally possible for a dreamer to have an aggressive or a friendly encounter with a given character. If the character is taken as the unit, it can be determined how many aggressions and how many friendly interactions occur between the dreamer and a given subclass of characters. For example, a dreamer may have twenty aggressive and ten friendly interactions with male characters which yields a ratio of two to one. This ratio can be directly compared with one for aggressive and friendly encounters with female characters. In practice, proportions are preferable to ratios. A proportion is obtained by dividing the number of aggressions with a given class of characters by the number of aggressions plus the number of friendly interactions with that class of characters. A proportion greater than .5 indicates that there are more aggressions than friendly encounters, and a proportion less than .5 indicates that there are fewer aggressions than friendly encounters.

One of the most ambitious attempts to unitize dream reports was made by Campbell Perry (1964). The scoring unit that he devised is defined as something happening to a specific agent in a particular location. A dream is broken down into these AHL units, and each unit is scored for whatever variables the investigator is interested in.

Other dream investigators have used the word as a unit.

It may be concluded that as much thought and ingenuity is required to select appropriate units as to derive appropriate and relevant categories. There are as many pitfalls to be avoided in the one as in the other.

NORMS

The establishing of norms entails a lot of tedious work that most of us are unwilling to undertake. As a consequence, few adequate norms are available for the large majority of variables in which psychologists and other social scientists are interested. The lack is bewailed, but few of us are willing to make the effort to correct it. Some play the ostrich game and hope that by burying their heads the whole problem will vanish. The problem does not vanish, of course, but the meaningfulness of conclusions drawn from unnormed data does evaporate. Two recent dream studies illustrate the sad effects of an ostrich policy toward norms. In one of the studies (Barad et al., 1961), dreams collected from old people were analyzed and it was found that the theme of diminished resources was quite common. Diminished resources means that these old people were not able to deal effectively with problems that appeared in their dreams. If the investigators had analyzed the dreams of younger people, they would have found approximately the same incidence of ineffectual coping. Diminished resources is the norm in dreams, no matter what the age, sex, or cultural background of the dreamer may be. In another study (Meggitt, 1962), dreams commonly reported as being of great significance by a New Guinea tribe were found to contain many more misfortunes than good fortune. The investigator observed that, in this respect, their dreams reflected their waking life attitude, since these people take a rather pessimistic view of the world. Misfortunes, however, far exceed good fortune in the dreams of people throughout the world, and are not peculiar to any one ethnic group.

There are some special problems in connection with determining norms for the contents of dreams. First, there is the question of how the dreams are collected. If a number of people are asked to report a single dream, the dreams obtained will differ appreciably from those obtained by asking each of a number of persons to report a series of from ten to twenty dreams. The reason for the difference is that when a person is asked to tell only one dream he ordinarily selects an unusual and highly dramatic one that has stuck in his memory. Since it is often not feasible to collect a series of dreams, norms should be established for single dreams as well as for dream series. The norms for single dreams should not be used for dream series or vice versa.

Recently, it has become possible to collect dreams under laboratory conditions by awakening subjects during periods of rapid eye movements. Laboratory dreams differ in many respects from dreams collected at home under natural conditions (Hall and Van de Castle, 1966b). Consequently, the norms for laboratory dreams will differ from those for home dreams. Moreover, dreams that are reported when subjects are awakened during periods when the eyes are not moving differ from those 'that are obtained when the eyes are moving. There is even some evidence that the contents of dreams change in systematic ways throughout the night, and that they also change during successive nights of sleeping in the laboratory. Since there is no way of determining what the total dream life of a person is, it is impossible to define a representative sample of dreams. Consequently, it is necessary to establish norms for home dreams, laboratory dreams when the eyes are moving, laboratory dreams when the eyes are not moving, and possibly for dreams reported at different times of awakening during the night and for dreams collected during successive nights in the laboratory.

The problem of norms becomes especially crucial when an investigator wishes to determine whether an experimental variable introduced prior to or during sleep influences what subjects dream about. A violent Western film is shown to subjects just before they go to sleep, and during the night they are awakened to report dreams. Has the film affected the subject matter of their dreams? It does not suffice to point out that the dreams contain a lot of aggression, because aggression is a common theme in dreams. The investigator often employs a control group which is not shown the film or which is shown an unexciting film, and compares their dreams with those of the experimental group.

I prefer to use a different methodology, however, which consists of establishing norms for the individual dreamer so that he can serve as his own control. The following experiment (Hall, 1967) illustrates this methodology. The question to be answered by the experiment was whether a stimulus that was presented subliminally during a rapid eye movement period would be incorporated in the dream that was reported when the person was awakened. For example, the experimenter thought about and pantomined a prize fight in one room while the subject was asleep in another room. In the dream that was reported when the subject was subsequently awakened, he told about watching a prize fight. One could not wish for a more direct representation of the stimulus material. Yet its appearance in the dream may have been purely coincidental rather than produced by the stimulus presentation. What is the probability of a person dreaming about a boxing match? According to norms established by the analysis of hundreds of dreams reported by males roughly comparable to the subject in question, prize fights are rare—about 1 in 500 dreams.

It is known, however, that dreams (particularly those that are reported in the laboratory) reflect the waking interests and concerns of the dreamer. If he is interested in skiing, he dreams about skiing; if he is interested in sports cars, he dreams about sports cars. Perhaps, then, the subject was interested in prize fighting, and the incidence of this topic in his dreams would be much larger than the group norm. In order to control for this factor, it was necessary to obtain a number of dreams from the person and figure his rate for dreaming about prize fights when no stimulus was presented. The rate was actually zero.

In another study, a set of dreams that were obtained from the 17 American climbers, who took part in the Mt. Everest Expedition, were content-analyzed. They reported many more overt sex dreams than a norm group of nonclimbers. This is not surprising, since the climbers were isolated from heterosexual contacts for a number of months. The comparison of climbers' dreams with those of nonclimbers may not be warranted, however. It is possible that some of the mountain climbers may be highly sexed, and that even when heterosexual outlets are available to them, they still have more sex dreams than nonclimbers. The comparison that should be made is between the dreams of individual climbers during the expedition and their dreams at home. It should be done climber by climber, rather than as a group, because there were large differences among the men in the number of sex dreams reported.

The content analysis of long dream series has been one of our major interests. These are dreams that have been recorded by a person for a number of years. One such series, which was analyzed (Smith and Hall, 1964), was begun when the dreamer (a woman) was 25 years old, and was terminated a few days before she died in her 78th year. The aim of the study was to determine whether her dreams became more regressive as she grew older. There was a lot of dreaming about the past in her later years, which corroborates the common conception that old people do regress, but when her dreams as a young woman were examined virtually the same rate of regression was present.

In the light of these findings and others that might be cited, it would be wise for the dream analyst to consider the appropriateness of group versus individual norms.

CONCLUSION

Indigenous to the methodology of content analysis are a number of complex problems for which few ready-made solutions exist at the present time. Three of these problems—categories, units, and norms—and some ways of dealing with them have been discussed in this paper with reference to the area of dream research. The applicability of these procedures to other areas of inquiry in which content analysis is indicated remains an open question. About the only conclusion that can be safely drawn is that prudence, alertness, ingenuity, and flexibility are required of the content analyst who would avoid the many reefs on which his research may founder.

8 Contextual Similarities as a Basis for Inference

Julius Laffal

Psychology
Connecticut Valley Hospital and Yale University

There are two psychologically interesting types of inference to be made about speakers from their language content: (1) an inference in which one infers the significance of a word in the psychological structure of an individual or a group, and (2) an inference in which one infers something about the psychological structure of a speaker or group of speakers from the words they use. In the first case, the contexts surrounding the key items are the basis of inference; in the second case, inferences are made from the total content of the speakers' texts. To make these inferences from texts implies a theory about the relationship between the language of speakers and their psychological structure, and a practical method of applying the theory in textual analysis. This chapter outlines such a theory, concerning the role of words in the cognitive structure of the individual; it describes a cognitive-conceptual dictionary of English words and a computer program for applying the dictionary in content analyses; and it presents several studies of inference from language. One of the studies deals with the psychological significance of key words in the language of a single speaker; the others show how cognitive orientations of children may be inferred by analysis of their language content.

THE ROLE OF WORDS IN COGNITIVE STRUCTURE

Linguists going back to Von Humboldt (Ullmann, 1962) have tried to establish that the world view of a culture is largely determined by the language of the culture. The idea has gained recent prominence in the United States as a result of the writing of Benjamin Lee Whorf (1956). Such linguistic propositions about language and culture refer in general terms to language and culture at large. For the psychologist, the crucial question is: What are the processes *within the individual* that make it

159

possible to speak of a relationship between language ꞏnd experience, or between language and culture?

Regarding this question, it is significant that two of the great psychological innovators of our century, Sigmund Freud and John B. Watson, were in essential, if unwitting, agreement about the nature of language in the psychological economy of the individual.

Language figured importantly in Freud's thinking about a central proposition in psychoanalytic theory: the existence of an unconscious. In an early work, *On Aphasia* (Freud, 1891), he attempted to clarify aphasic phenomena by postulating a dual cognitive process in which the individual could have a "presentation of the thing" and a "presentation of the word." In his later writing (Freud, 1915) he spoke of an unconscious idea as being made up of the presentation of the thing, and of a conscious idea as being made up of the presentation of the thing plus the presentation of the word belonging to it. What Freud meant by presentation of the thing and presentation of the word may, interestingly enough, be elucidated by some quotations from John B. Watson who believed that he was controverting Freud's views. Watson (1924, pp. 209, 210) stated:

> The Freudians, as you know, claim that the childhood memories are lost because childhood is an age where free, spontaneous actions bringing "pleasure" come under the ban of the social; society punishes and a painful repression into the "unconscious" takes place . . . The unsatisfactory ground for this assumption is now apparent. *The child had never verbalized these acts.*
>
> Bodily habits form normally, both habits of avoidance and of approach, and habits of manipulation; but the bodily habits *lack verbal correlates because the infant puts them on at a later age.*
>
> I believe the whole of Freud's "unconscious" can be adequately cared for along the lines I have indicated.

A careful examination of Freud's writings on language (Laffal, 1964a, 1967a) suggests strongly that Freud's presentation of the thing is equivalent to the bodily habits and events described by Watson, and that Freud's presentation of the word is what Watson calls a verbal correlate. Freud believed that stimulation of sensory organs entails consciousness, and also that verbalizations give rise to consciousness because of their auditory-motor aspects. Memories may therefore become conscious if they are associated either with sensory images or with verbalizations.

What Freud meant by presentation of the thing and presentation of the word, and what Watson meant by bodily habit and verbal correlate can be clarified by an example. On being offered a dish that I have never eaten before and which does not look familiar, I make implicit habitual preparations for eating. In this sense I have a presentation of the thing without yet having the verbal correlate or word presentation for the experience of eating this particular food. The fact that the food and the setting stimulate visual, olfactory, and other sensory responses accounts, in Freud's view, for the conscious awareness of the experience.

Later, I may recall the experience by remembering the word, *papaya,* or by remembering sensory qualities of the experience. If neither the word nor the sensory quality can be recalled, the fact that there was an experience about eating may linger vaguely in memory. This is the kind of minimal recall that uses such statements as, "There was something about that place, I can't remember just what." If someone says, "Papaya," the experience is then immediately present, and I have a full sense of awareness where previously there was only a troubling sense of something indefinite. The presentation of the thing in Freud's terms, or the bodily habits in Watson's terms, exists in the form of internal adaptations or patterns that define an experience grossly. The experience itself is given specific attributes and is brought more fully into awareness by recall of the word or of the sensory events.

The implication of these ideas is that, in large measure, what becomes conscious is what the individual has words for. When a word is attached to an experience, there is an increase in cognitive and referential precision which may, in some instances, amount to becoming "aware" of what was previously only vague and undefined. Language thus raises to the level of consciousness inner processes otherwise out of, or only dimly in, awareness, while serving as a means of sharing the fact of such processes with others. Once the tokens of language become selectively related to bodily states and experiences, language itself becomes a means of evoking such states and of being conscious of them. Although language plays this central role in consciousness, it also is the link between the individual's experience and the cultural world view.

The manner in which language operates as a determiner of experience and of cognitions within the individual's psychological structure is also suggested by recent findings on organization of verbal material in recall (Bousfield, 1953; Tulving, 1962; Cofer, 1966; and Deese, 1965) and by the mediational theory of Osgood, Suci, and Tannenbaum (1957). Words are associated with implicit mediational responses or sets. These sets have certain organizing and defining properties, and it is possible to describe them as "concepts" or "areas of meaning." The individual's response to verbalizations entails these experiential concepts and, presumably, as concepts themselves structure the individual's orientation to experience. If analysis of language can address itself to these conceptual-experiential entities rather than to specific word meanings, the possibility arises of discovering and dealing with fundamental cognitive orientations of individual speakers and groups.

A CATEGORY DICTIONARY AND CONTENT ANALYSIS PROGRAM

Efforts to define universals of language content assume that the universals approximate major experiential or cognitive processes within the individual, which are represented or evoked each time he uses or hears a relevant word. Conceptual dictionaries are collections of the words of a language organized in such a manner as to reflect the kinds of content represented in the words. These dictionaries differ from the ordinary dictionary, which arranges words alphabetically and whose major purpose is to define words, but they have some affinity with the thesaurus and the synonym dictionary.

One such modern attempt is a conceptual scheme of the French language devised by Hallig and Wartburg (1963). These authors believe that the meaning of a word is made up of several components, of which one is a logical universal, or general conception. In addition, there are secondary meanings (which they exclude from their analysis) involving subjective associations, feeling tones, and transient connections. They believe that while the meaning of a word may change with particular circumstances, the logical universal is a durable conceptual presentation, implicit in the word, which does not change.

Their plan of concepts begins with the postulation of three superordinate domains: the Universe, Man, and Man and the Universe. There follow such subdivisions as Heaven and Atmosphere, Earth, Plants, Animals; Man as a Physical Being, Spirit and Intellect, Man as a Social Being, the Social Organization; the *A Priori,* Science and Technique. Within each of these subdivisions there are further branches. Hallig and Wartburg assert that in classifying words they assume the standpoint of the gifted average individual observing the world with a prescientific, naïve realism, and that their groupings of words reflect the conceptual cognitive groupings which occur intuitively to such a naïve observer. Nevertheless, their scheme is highly logical and tightly organized into a hierarchical structure.

The stress upon a logical system is undoubtedly related to these authors' interest in a conceptual structure applicable to language as a whole, rather than to any particular speaker's language. Although some of the students of Hallig and Wartburg have studied the language of individual writers (Fermin, 1954; Keller, 1953), this has been primarily to elucidate the conceptual framework of a period in the growth of a language rather than for the purpose of understanding the writer as a person. An interest in the broader aspects of language, as against its pertinence to individual speakers, tends to push a conceptual scheme toward categories relevant especially to the social group and social conditions rather than to the individual's experience.

A contrasting approach may be seen in one conceptual scheme produced by a literary scholar, Caroline Spurgeon (1958), in a study of Shakespeare's imagery. Spurgeon classified all the images from Shakespeare's plays and from the writing of his contemporaries, Christoper Marlowe and Francis Bacon, according to their themes or subject matter. The major groupings of themes which she found were: Nature (including vegetation, weather, planets, and geography); Animals; Domestic themes (including home, human relations, life, and death); Body, (including food, drink, and illness); Daily life (including war, travel, commerce, and government); Learning (including religion, law, and science); and, finally, Arts and Imagination. The typical linguistic approach to a conceptual scheme of language is to define a system beforehand and then to place words within the system. Spurgeon, however, simply bundled images by similarity of reference, without concerning herself with superordinate ideas and logical structure, except in subsequent organization of what she had found.

In the work being reported here a conceptual dictionary of the English language was developed following a method similar to Spurgeon's. Words from many texts were grouped together if they seemed to have a common element of reference, and a series of concepts emerged from these groupings. Two simple criteria were employed to limit and define the word groupings: (1) that the groupings contain, within a broad range, approximately equal numbers of separate word tokens, and (2) that the groupings be readily discriminable from each other by judges. In practice, this meant that rubrics such as "Nature" and "Man," which draw huge numbers of tokens, and rubrics such as "right" and "left" or "heterosexual" and "homosexual" (as opposed to "sexual"), which draw very few word tokens, were rejected. The development of the dictionary and the category system is described in detail elsewhere (Laffal, 1965), and will not be discussed here. To see how the bundling of words might work, we need only take a page or two of text, and group the words wherever they seem to have a similar or related meaning. We will discover a group of words such as *up, top, high, roof, peak, summit, above,* and others that have in common a reference to upward direction; and words like *anger, hatred, rage, fury, contempt, hostility;* and words referring to heat and fire, like *burn, boil, conflagration, flame, ignite, blaze, combustion,* and *char;* and, again, words like *grass, bush, plant, flower, tree,* and other references to vegetation. At the outset the bundles of words are small and numerous, because we wish to stick to synonyms and words very similar in meaning. But we soon notice that two or more groups of words are, at some points, very close to each other in the kinds of things they are referring to, and that it is possible to merge these groups under a broader embracing idea. What we end up with, finally, is a moderate number of conceptual domains, each made up of words having some element of meaning in common. Words often share a meaning with several conceptual domains, so that in our final system of concepts, numerous words will appear in more than one conceptual group.

The present system classifies most of the common words of English into one or two of 114 possible categories.[1] Unlike linguistic schemes, there is no hierarchical structure. Each category entails only itself and does not necessarily entail any other category. The dictionary is part of a 7094/7040 DCS computer program, which will produce a profile show-

[1] There are two additional noncontent categories (a NO-SCORE category, and a HAND-SCORE category) for words that are not categorized, such as the article *the,* and for words such as pronouns that receive the classification of their noun referents.

ABSURD	EAT	OUT
AGREE 1 (SYMPATHY)	END	PLACE
AGREE 2 (AGREEMENT)	ESSENTIAL	PLAY
AGREE 3 (SIMILARITY)	FALSE	POSSESS
ALL 1 (WHOLE)	FAR	REASON 1 (COGNITION)
ALL 2 (MUCH)	FAST	REASON 2 (EDUCATION)
ALL 3 (FREQUENT)	FEATURE (BODY)	REASON 3 (SCIENCE)
ANIMAL	FEMALE	SACRED
ART	FORWARD	SEA
ASTRONOMY 1 (SPACE)	FUNCTION (BODY)	SEE
ASTRONOMY 2 (WEATHER)	GO	SELF-REFERENCE
BACK	GOOD	SEPARATE
BAD	GROUP	SEX
BEGIN	HAPPENING	SHARP 1 (SHARP)
BIG	HEAR	SHARP 2 (EMPHASIS)
BLURRED	HELP	SLOW
CALM	HILL	SOME
CHANGE	HOLLOW 1 (DWELLINGS)	STRUCTURE
CLEAN	HOLLOW 2 (OBJECTS)	SUBMISSION 1 (WEAK)
CLOTHING	HOT	SUBMISSION 2 (INFE-
COLD	HOUSEHOLD	RIOR)
COLOR	ILLNESS	TIME 1 (PAST)
COMMERCE	IN	TIME 2 (PRESENT)
CONFINE	INDIVIDUAL	TIME 3 (FUTURE)
CONFLICT 1 (HARM)	JOIN	TIME 4 (GENERAL TIME)
CONFLICT 2 (HATE)	LANGUAGE 1 (SPEAK)	TRANSPORTATION
CONFLICT 3 (DISAGREE)	LANGUAGE 2 (WRITE)	TRIVIAL 1 (UNIMPOR-
CRIME	LAW	TANCE)
CURE	LITTLE	TRIVIAL 2 (DE-EMPHASIS)
DEAD	LIVING	TRUE
DIFFICULT	MALE	UNREAL
DIRTY	MATERIAL	UP
DOMINANCE 1 (STRONG)	MEASUREMENT	UPSET
DOMINANCE 2 (LEAD)	MECHANISM	VEGETATION
DOWN	MONEY	WANT 1 (NEED)
DRINK	NEAR	WANT 2 (ABSENCE)
DURABLE	NEGATION	WORK
EARTH	NUMBER	YOUNG
EASY	OPEN	

Figure 1 Alphabetic listing of categories by heading word.

DOWN: This category is to be understood in conjunction with UP. In general, words that have some reference to "downness" or "upness" are scored under one of these categories. Words in which there is an implicit reference to up and down are scored in whichever category is appropriate and may be scored both categories. Thus, a word like *suspend* is scored DOWN, as having the implicit notion of *hang down; elevator* is scored UP and DOWN, since both of these notions are implied. Ordinarily one extreme, UP or DOWN, will be clearly dominant. "This is the *bottom* (DOWN) of the barrel."

DRINK: All words referring to the activity of drinking and to potables, as well as to containers where the drink reference is clear, are scored here. "He was addicted to the *bottle* (DRINK, HOLLOW 2)." SEA will often be a second scoring. "They had *soda* (DRINK, SEA) at the party."

DURABLE: The types of words scored here are:
   (a) Words referring to continuity, persistence, a continuing stretch of time, stability, changelessness, continuous recurrence, endurance, eternity, and long-lastingness. An additional TIME scoring is often appropriate. "He *still* (DURABLE, TIME 4) lives here."
   (b) Words referring to the usual, customary, or habitual. "I'm *used to* (DURABLE) doing it this way."

EARTH: All references to terra firma are scored here. Aspects of the terrain other than waterways are scored under EARTH. References to valleys, mountains, hills, land, fields, countryside, gardens, clods, stones, and rocks are scored here. Size of the reference to terra firma is not important. Thus, *continent* and *plot* (of land) are both scored here, as references to the solid part of our geography. "The *ground* (EARTH) is soft."

Figure 2   Description of several categories.

ing the frequency of occurrence of the 114 categories in any language sample. Texts to be analyzed are prepared by some simple editing procedures for card punching, involving mainly the elimination of common suffixes.[2] If it is desired to deal only with words relevant to a limited number of the 114 categories, the program will do so, outputting listings of such words, location of each word in the text, and counts for each category. The program is capable of handling an unlimited number of batches of up to 15 separate speakers (or texts) at one time, with virtually no limit on the amount of text in each batch. Computer processing time for 20,000 words is about 20 minutes.

Figure 1 shows the categories by heading word. The categories have been described with many examples in Laffal (1965). The range of meanings covered in a category is suggested by the descriptions of a few of the categories in Figure 2.

[2] Within the near future, the program will be able to analyze a text with no prior editing of the text.

APPLICATIONS

A thorny problem in automatic content analysis is that of ambiguity of word meanings (see Chapter 11 by Philip J. Stone, *infra*). The conceptual dictionary, described above, takes into account all of the common meanings of a word, and sequences them by judged order of frequency in the language. In the computer analysis, ambiguous words—defined as those for which there is more than one dictionary entry—are dealt with by making certain options available to the researcher. He may apply to an ambiguous text word none, the first, the first two, the first three, the first four, or all of the different sets of categories given to the word in its various meanings. Some ambiguous words will have only two significant different meanings, while others may have ten or twelve. Depending on the researcher's choice, he may risk being overinclusive in order to be sure that he has captured the actual meaning of ambiguous words, or he may risk losing the actual meaning of some ambiguous words by limiting the number of meanings allowed to enter into the analysis.

To illustrate how the analysis of total language content has been applied, I will describe several studies. In these studies, the various language samples are broken down into profiles, showing frequency of occurrence of references to each of the 114 contents. These profiles are then compared to each other by correlation, to show how similar or dissimilar the contents of the speech samples are. I will begin by mentioning one finding (Laffal, 1967b) which, I believe, has considerable importance in understanding the nature of communication in small groups. The finding is that when people enter into a conversation with each other about some subject, their language content becomes very similar. When they switch to discussion of another subject, again the speakers become similar to each other in their content, but significantly different from their own content in the previous discussion. This phenomenon has been observed both in the two-person conversation and in the three-person conversation. There is thus, literally, a sharing and a joining of contents when people converse with each other, to the extent even that individual differences in content largely disappear. This is a phenomenon of conversation, which may also have implications for the psychotherapeutic situation, where usually the therapist says very little.

The total content analysis of conversations shows language to be a flexible instrument, in which the contents change markedly when the subject matter changes. This may surprise some readers, since language is notoriously redundant and as few as 300 words make up more than 60 percent of total vocabulary usage in ordinary writing. If the fact of redundancy is examined closely, however, it will become evident that 15 or 20 words (mainly "little" words like the articles *the, an, a;* the conjunction *and;* the verbs *was, is, had;* some prepositions like *to, with, in, for, at,* and *on;* and the pronouns *that, it, I, he,* and *you*) make up about 30 percent of word usage. These are words that generally are not given category scores in the present system; or that, in the case of pronouns, ordinarily take the meaning of their referents. Thus, while a limited number of words may recur with high frequency in separate samples, the significant content of the samples will differ considerably.

Let us examine an application of the total content analysis to a study of symbolic significance of key words in the writing of a famous psychiatric patient. I have described this study elsewhere (Laffal, 1960; 1965), but discuss it here again because it demonstrates how one may make inferences regarding the meaning of a word in the psychological economy of an individual.

Daniel Paul Schreber was a doctor of jurisprudence and a prominent judge in Germany at the end of the last century. After becoming psychotic he published an account of his delusions. He believed that God sought to unman him and transform him miraculously into a woman for the purpose of creating new human beings. On the basis of Schreber's memoirs, without having known him personally, Freud undertook to trace the etiology of Schreber's delusions, and formulated what has become a widely held theory of paranoia in which homosexuality and projection are the key syndromes (Freud, 1911). Macalpine and Hunter, English psychoanalysts, who published an English translation of Schreber's autobiography (Schreber, 1955) disagreed with Freud's homosexual interpretation of Schreber's delusions, and maintained that a wish for ambisexuality and self-contained procreative powers was at the root of Schreber's illness (Macalpine and Hunter, 1955). They contested Freud's account of the symbolism of the sun as father in Schreber's delusions, and argued that the sun had feminine connotations as well for Schreber. A theoretical issue bearing on the symbolism of the sun in Schreber's writing was thus clearly posed. Freud, on one side, argued that the sun was a father symbol for Schreber, and Macalpine and Hunter, on the other side, argued that the sun represented a combination of female and male qualities for the patient.[3]

If Schreber used the same concepts in writing of the sun as he did in writing of father figures, this could be taken as evidence that his associations to the two were alike and that, in effect, they meant the same thing to him, as Freud asserted. If, however, Schreber wrote about the

---

[3] The Icarus complex, discussed by Ogilvie in this volume (Chapter 13), has unmistakable connections with Schreber's fantasies, although it is beyond the scope of the present paper to discuss the similarities.

sun in the manner that he wrote about women, this could be considered as evidence for the Macalpine and Hunter view that the sun had important feminine aspects for him. The problem posed was to compare the contexts of the word *sun* and various other key words in Schreber's autobiography in order to determine their relative similarity to each other in the patient's language, and hence in his cognitive orientation toward them.

Unfortunately, the third chapter of Schreber's autobiography, which dealt intimately with members of his family, was deleted from the work by official censorship, so that there are practically no references to Schreber's father in the book. This makes a direct comparison of language related to father with language related to the sun impossible. Nevertheless, there are some indirect ways of approaching the problem. It is clear that Freud believed God was the central father figure for Schreber. Macalpine and Hunter do not accept this view and, consistently with their position about the sun, assert that Freud ignored the female significance of God also. Certain predictions arise from these differences of view.

If Freud's contention that the sun and God were father symbols for Schreber is correct, there ought to be a similarity in the way Schreber wrote about both of these, and both ought to be more similar to the way Schreber wrote about male figures than to the way he wrote about female figures.

If the Macalpine and Hunter view is correct, there ought also to be a strong similarity between the way Schreber wrote about the sun and God, but how he wrote of them ought to be similar to the way he wrote of females.

Freud maintained, in addition, that Dr. Flechsig (Schreber's physician) was the subject of the patient's homosexual longings. In this sense, both God and Dr. Flechsig stood as dominant male figures in relation to Schreber. If Freud is correct, there ought to be a strong relationship in the way Schreber wrote about Flechsig and about God, and both of these ought to be more strongly related to the way Schreber wrote about males than to the way he wrote about females. Macalpine and Hunter are not specific in interpreting the symbolism of Dr. Flechsig in Schreber's psychology, but they appear to suggest also some element of identity with God.

In the analysis of this material (done by hand scoring rather than computer), contexts from Schreber's autobiography,[4] which contained only one of the words *sun, God,* or *Flechsig,* or a male or female reference, were marked for transcription. A context was defined as a sequence beginning three lines before a line containing the key word and ending three

---

[4] As translated by Macalpine and Hunter (Schreber, 1955).

lines after a line containing the key word. A roughly equivalent number of such contexts was taken out for each key word, and the total contextual material for each key word was divided in two in order to provide reliability data. The words in the contexts of the key words were categorized, and the profiles showing frequency of occurrence of the various categories then became the basis for comparison of key words. These profiles were correlated with each other in order to determine which pairs of profiles were more alike. Table 1 shows the average correlations of the profiles

Table 1 *Average correlations of key words in Schreber's memoirs, ranked from highest to lowest (Laffal, 1960, p. 477)*

Context Profiles Correlated	Average Correlation
male—Flechsig	.636
God—Flechsig	.558
male—female	.531
female—sun	.517
female—Flechsig	.479
sun—Flechsig	.454
male—sun	.427
male—God	.422
female—God	.338
sun—God	.290

ranked by size of correlation. Significance tests for the differences between correlations were derived by obtaining empirical distributions by computer, of comparable numbers.

The findings, briefly, were that the contexts of *God* in Schreber's autobiography were more like the contexts of *male* than of *female* (at the .15 level of significance) thus supporting Freud's view; similarly, the contexts of *Flechsig* and *male* were more similar than those of *Flechsig* and *female* (at the .04 level of significance). With respect to the symbolism of the sun, contexts of *female* and of *sun* were more highly related than those of *male* and *sun,* although not significantly so. This last result supports the Macalpine and Hunter view that the feminine connotation of the sun is at least as strong as its masculine connotation in the autobiography. An interesting outcome was that the correlation between profiles of God and sun was rather low, calling into question the assumption by Freud as well as by Macalpine and Hunter that the sun and God symbolized the same thing for Schreber.

The Schreber study shows how the application of total content analysis may lead to inferences regarding the significance of key words in the psychological structure of an individual. The next studies to be described draw inferences regarding the experiential orientation and the cognitive development of children from total content analyses of their stories and their word associations.

A book by Pitcher and Prelinger (1963) presents stories told by boys and girls from ages 2 to 5, taken down in shorthand by one of the authors. These were a group of economically privileged children attending a nursery and kindergarten of a private school. Most of the children were of superior or high average intelligence. When the occasion presented itself and the child was for the moment playing alone, the teacher (E. Pitcher) asked, "Tell me a story. What could your story be about." For the older children, where the author visited a school, she took each child aside in a separate room and had him tell a story. Only those stories were rejected which were a retelling of a familiar fairy tale or television show.

The stories in the Pitcher-Prelinger book were edited and transcribed onto IBM cards and were analyzed by computer to obtain profiles showing the distribution of the content of each sex-age group.[5] In order to sharpen the subsequent analysis, all categories showing a frequency of less than 1 percent of the total responses within each profile were eliminated. Also eliminated was the one category (ANIMAL) which showed a uniform high frequency (over 7 percent of the total) for each profile. These extremely low- and extremely high-frequency categories are eliminated because they contribute only to raising all correlations between profiles and do not contribute to discriminating between profiles. However, the fact that the ANIMAL category was universally high already tells us that this category is a significant content for all the children in the study. The 8 profiles, now consisting of 52 categories each, were then correlated and factor analyzed.

The factors are shown in Table 2. Several things stand out. The first factor is a "female" factor. The girls in all age groups load very highly on it. When we look in detail at the categories that contribute most heavily to this factor, we find that YOUNG, FEMALE, and HELP are the three outstanding contributors. In the category system, FEMALE and HELP are the two scorings which apply to the word *mother* and its variants. These findings suggest that the girls of the study had, as central themes in their fantasy, ideas relating to mothers (feminine helpers) and children.

[5] Ambiguous words in the text were assigned the first (most common) meaning in the computer dictionary.

Table 2. *Rotated factor loadings, correlations of free speech of boys and girls, ages 2 to 5*

Sex	Age	Factors				
		I	II	III	IV	h²
Boys	2	32	−40	31	−79	98
Girls	2	89	−17	21	−31	96
Boys	3	47	−70	17	−47	96
Girls	3	85	−35	17	−27	95
Boys	4	24	−85	37	−24	97
Girls	4	67	−29	58	−25	93
Boys	5	36	−42	75	−30	96
Girls	5	87	−26	33	−10	94
Percent total variance		40	23	17	15	95

The second factor is more clearly relevant to boys, with ages 3 and 4 showing predominance. The most significant categories here are GO, MALE, and TRANSPORTATION. Thus, the boys in the group, particularly those in the 3- and 4-year bracket, had prominently in their fantasies, references to maleness, physical movement, and vehicles of transportation.

The third factor applies primarily to girls, age 4, and boys, age 5. Primary categories are MALE, GO, and BODY FEATURE. The BODY FEATURE and MALE categories would be consistent with a psychoanalytic view that, at this age, both boys and girls are in the oedipal period and are becoming preoccupied with sexuality, and particularly with the relationship to father.

The fourth factor seems most clearly applicable to boys, age 2, although to a lesser degree it is characteristic of boys, age 3, suggesting a decay process with age. Here, the outstanding categories are CONFLICT 1 (HARM), GO, and YOUNG. Like the other boys, the two-year-olds were also occupied with physical movement. Like the girls, they were occupied with ideas about children; but violent aggression was their most prominent concern and distinguishes them most clearly from other groups.

If comparable data were available from older children, the further development of category predilections could be traced, and the manner in which these category preferences relate to cognitive development might be established. Some additional data, not strictly comparable with this story-telling material, come from the word association lists published by Palermo and Jenkins (1966). These authors administered an oral word association test with 100 stimulus words to 50 boys and 50 girls in each of the grades one through four, from three Minneapolis public schools. They describe the children as having been drawn from middle and upper socio-economic-class families. Thus, the sample is socioeconomically similar to the Pitcher-Prelinger subjects, although geographically different.

Each of the responses to the 100 stimulus words was categorized by hand scoring. Words with questionable meaning were discussed by two scorers and categorized by agreement. A profile of responses for each grade-sex group was derived by lumping all responses to the 100 stimulus words together. As in the previous study, categories showing fewer than 1 percent of the total responses for each profile were eliminated from the further analysis, as was the category, EAT, which showed a consistently high frequency of more than 5 percent of the total responses for each profile. The 8 profiles, now consisting of 45 categories, were correlated, and the matrix of correlations was factor-analyzed. The factor analysis is shown in Table 3.

Table 3. *Rotated factor loadings, correlations of word associations of boys and girls, grades 1 to 4*

		Factors				
Sex	Grade	I	II	III	IV	h^2
Male	1	49	−86	07	16	100
Female	1	47	−87	03	−13	100
Male	2	79	−55	25	02	99
Female	2	78	−59	17	−02	99
Male	3	81	−56	08	04	98
Female	3	84	−53	02	−02	99
Male	4	90	−42	01	06	99
Female	4	89	−43	03	−04	98
Percent total variance		58	39	1	1	99

Unlike the story-telling results, the word-association factor analysis reveals no sex factor. This is not surprising in word association, since the studies that have shown sex differences in such a task (Palermo and Jenkins, 1965) appear to find the differences primarily in low-frequency responses. The fact that there were no content differences between the sexes in the present analysis, suggests that actual content in word association may be quite the same even where word responses differ.

Two factors appear to account almost completely for the variance in the matrix of correlations. The first factor is one that increases with age, while the second factor follows an opposite trend. When the three categories that contribute most importantly to each of the two factors are examined, some interesting material emerges. The first factor is positively loaded with the categories COLOR and SLOW, and negatively loaded (indicating a disproportionately low number of responses) with the category CLOTHING. Rather low down on the list of other categories contributing to the first factor is the ANIMAL category. The second factor is heavily loaded with GO and ANIMAL, while EASY contributes negatively.

In the previous study it was seen that the category ANIMAL was universally high in the free speech of the younger children, and the category GO was particularly significant for boys of all ages and for girls of age 4. The word-association data seem to indicate that increasingly through age 9 (fourth grade), there is a reduction of these animal and physical movement categories which predominated in the free speech at earlier ages.

The categories COLOR, SLOW, and EASY are of special interest, since an examination of the actual responses reveals, surprisingly, a certain element in common. COLOR and SLOW contribute heavily to the first factor, and EASY contributes heavily to the second by its relative low frequency. It turns out that the stimulus list makes possible a large number of opposite or contrast responses which fall into these categories, and that the older children simply give such responses more often than do the younger children. Thus, for the older children, *slow* as a response is given much more frequently to the stimuli *quickly* and *faster,* and the response *sit* is given more frequently to the stimulus *stand.* In the case of color responses, many of them are of the contrast type. Thus, the older children more frequently give *white* as the response to *black; black* as a response to *white;* and *dark* as a response to *light.* The same situation applies in the case of the category EASY. Here, the older children respond with *smooth* and *soft* to the stimulus *rough;* give *soft* in response to the stimuli *hard* and *loud;* and give *light* in response to the stimulus *heavy,* all with much higher frequency than the younger group.

Carroll, Kjeldergaard, and Carton (1962) have shown that a large component of what is referred to as commonality of response to the Kent-Rosanoff word association stimuli is based on responses to a relatively small subset of stimuli which tend to evoke opposites, and that groups of individuals who have high or low opposite scores tend to respond differentially to many other stimulus words. The present finding suggests that there is a marked increase in opposite responding from six to nine years of age, and that increasing commonality of responses in older children may in part be attributable to the development of this contrast response.

These studies on the conceptual categories in the language of children also reveal how unfortunately little we know as yet about the development of concepts. Therefore, any conceptual scheme for the analysis of total language content must, at present, certainly confuse what is early in development and what is late, what is a more simple experiential building block, and what is already a complicated conceptual structure built on more fundamental ideas. Ultimately, any conceptual organization of language must rely on the evidence of developmental and experimental studies. The total content analysis, described here, offers a tool for studying cognitions of individuals and groups, while contributing to such evidence.

SUMMARY

Language played an important part in Freud's thinking about conscious and unconscious processes. He believed that experiences to which words were attached were conscious experiences and that, without associated words, experiences remained unconscious. John B. Watson described language and consciousness in essentially these same terms. The role of language in consciousness may be viewed as the microcosm of the language-culture problem discussed by linguists. Words operate as determiners of consciousness and as organizers of experiences, not so much by their quality as specific tokens as by some mediational or cognitive-conceptual property. It is to these cognitive-conceptual aspects of meaning that language content analysis addresses itself. In this chapter, a conceptual dictionary is described, which has been developed primarily for the analysis of the language content of individual speakers. The dictionary is part of a 7094/7040 DCS computer program capable of automatic decoding of the total content of any English language sample. The output shows the frequency of occurrence of each of 114 possible categories in the sample. Several applications of the analysis are described. In one application, inferences are drawn regarding the symbolic significance of key words in the autobiography of the famous psychiatric patient, Daniel Paul Schreber. In two other studies, inferences regarding dominant cognitive orientations and the conceptual development of children are derived from analysis of the content of their story telling and of their word associations.

9 Content Analysis and the Study of Poetry

Joseph Raben

English
Queens College

This chapter, on possible inferences from the content analysis of poetry, should alert us to the recognition of a reciprocal relationship: critics and historians of literature may learn from the content analysts a new and potentially valuable approach to their subject matter, but an awareness of what this method, as presently construed, cannot tell us when applied to literary art may broaden the definition of content and spur us to find new ways of measuring it. Such an extension is appropriate now, partly because the field is new and therefore pliable enough to mold, and partly because attempts are already being made to transfer the techniques evolved for psychosociological investigations to what (for want of a better term) we call "creative" writing. Not only must these techniques be greatly refined before they can be properly used in this new application but such refinement may also increase their utility in their original sphere.

Two problems can represent the directions in which content analysis requires broadening, particularly if it is to serve the needs of literary critics. The first is that of form, the relationship between an idea and the pattern of words into which it is cast. The second problem derives from the fact that no poet who sits down to compose poetry can be oblivious of all the books, and particularly of the poetry, he has read before. The very need that drives him to struggle with verse has made him sensitive to the felicities and the deficiencies of his predecessors and contemporaries. In some way and to some degree, he must react to this matrix that shapes his art. It is these two elements—form as a part of meaning and the relation of each document to its verbal milieu—that heretofore have been inadequately explored by the practitioners of content analysis.

The first of these elements—the quality of the relationship between form and content—is easily demonstrated. To consider one example of many, Shakespeare's customary employment of blank verse shows him to be completely conventional in at least this aspect of his art: Marlowe, Kyd, Jonson, and all his other contemporaries wrote their dramas in such

175

unrhymed iambic pentameter. But the same verse form in the poetry of John Milton, a half century later, is a symbol of his rebellion against both the political and poetic conventions that surrounded him. Milton, a defeated rebel in the stronghold of his conquerors, blind, impoverished, and ignored by the Restoration poets who had found favor with the new king, refused to write in the rhymed couplets established by D'Avenant and Dryden as the fashionable pattern in which heroic verse could be composed. In a special preface to *Paradise Lost,* he announced that he was rejecting rhyme, which he had used in earlier poems, and going back to the measure of Homer and Virgil, avoiding what he called "The Invention of a Barbarous Age"; he hoped that his poem would be an example "of ancient liberty recovered to Heroic Poem from the troublesome and modern bondage of Rimeing."

We can note, as another example, the disappearance of the sonnet after Milton's death until it was resurrected, around the time of the French Revolution, by Wordsworth, Coleridge, and Shelley. These young radicals sought to bring the spirit of Milton's republicanism back to life in an England suffering a strong conservative, monarchistic reaction against Jacobinism and against Napoleon. Appropriately, they experimented with the blank verse technique derived from *Paradise Lost,* and also tried their hands at the sonnet. Wordsworth says specifically that he had not thought of this form until his discovery of Milton's accomplishment with it. Thus the mold into which a thought is poured can be, itself, an important aspect of the final shape which that thought assumes. Of course, we must also examine the content and many other aspects of a poem to confirm the initial judgment based on the recognition of form. In Wordsworth's hands, to continue with one poet, the sonnet often contains diction and phrasing reminiscent of Milton. In a poem beginning "Scorn not the sonnet," he tells his contemporary critics how composing in this form has soothed poets from Petrarch to Spenser; he concludes:

> When a damp
> Fell round the path of Milton, in his hand
> The Thing became a trumpet; whence he blew
> Soul-animating strains,—alas, too few!

Appropriately, therefore, another of his poems on the moral decline of England, opening "Milton! Thou should'st be living at this hour," is also in the sonnet form.

What is true of rhyme and of a special form like the sonnet is true in varying degrees of the other formal aspects of poetic style. The emotional value of rhythm, the patterns created by varying line lengths, the larger patterns woven from these in rhyme schemes and stanzas, the accumulative impact of repeated stanza forms—all these are part of the meaning of the poem, at least equal to the sum of the definitions of the words. In no other verbal communication, therefore, is precise word choice of greater importance, for here not only the semantic quality but the aural as well must be measured. In most of the poetry known in Western civilization, some nonsemantic value—length of vowel, pattern of stress, initial or final sound—is an element in a pattern that complements the pure sense. When the balance between sense and sound is disrupted, what remains is no longer poetry, since a restatement in prose has omitted one of the essential aspects. The absolute interdependence of these two elements of poetry is succinctly expressed in Frost's famous dictum: "Poetry is what gets lost in translation."

It is clear, therefore, that content analysis of literary art cannot proceed by the simple substitution of generic terms for specific terms. Like the conventional literary historian, the content analyst must recognize the emotional and intellectual impact of form, and must find means of taking it into account. And if the computer is to serve us in finding deeper truths about verbal art, it must do more rather than less with those qualities that historically have been the concern of literary critics and historians. As for the material I have just discussed, no computer is necessary to determine whether a poem is a sonnet. But when we are dealing with large quantities of rhymed poetry, we should notice the words that are emphasized by the repetition of their stressed syllables. In the following stanza from Richard Wilbur, observe how a high proportion of the meaning is carried by the rhyme words:

> How shall the wine be drunk, or the woman known?
> I take this world for better or for worse,
> But seeing rose carafes conceive the sun
> My thirst conceives a fierier universe:
> And then I toast the birds in the burning trees
> That chant their holy lucid drunkenness;
> I swallowed all the phosphorus of the seas
> Before I fell into this low distress.

If position in a line of verse can lend an emphasis beyond that created by a high order of recurrence, may not the same be true of a sentence of prose? Does a word or phrase in the middle of a sentence tend to make less of an impression than one at the beginning or end? Do sentences at the beginning or end of paragraphs similarly create more impact than they would if placed less conspicuously? Does the repetition of sounds until they form a pattern create an effect (perhaps subliminal) that embraces the meaning or even generates a whole complementary stratum of meaning?

In the study of poetry the problem of position is complicated by the fact that it is not merely where the eye recognizes a metrical unit, but also where the ear hears it, that determines the phrasing and the emphasis. If we entrust such an analysis to a computer, we must, of course, teach it to recognize all the ways we have for spelling the same sound in English, a language which often seems to have evolved a method to disguise rather than reveal pronunciation, and which is so inconsistent that it probably is too unreliable to serve for automatic transliteration. And once we go back in time, we compound the problem further, since not only do vowels (the basis of rhyme) shift with remarkable frequency but the tolerances of rhyme change from age to age and from poet to poet. Yet there are reports of programs being created for automatic phonemicization of several poorly spelled languages, including English. Whether these prove satisfactory or we need to rely on manual preediting, the study of rhyme as an aspect of meaning, at least in recent poems, cannot be ignored.

In the quotation just given from Wilbur, there appears a slant rhyme: *known/sun.* In three of the other five stanzas of this poem, there is a similar approximation of identity: *end/wind, wave/love, resignations/patience.* Can the computer also be programmed to recognize such rhymes? Often they are of special significance to the meaning of a poem, part of a subtle technique, evolved in the last century or so, of suggesting a tentative, approximate, or imperfect idea by expressing it in rhymes that are slightly out of correspondence. Emily Dickinson, for example, raised this to a high art. In her poem beginning

> After great pain, a formal feeling comes—
> The Nerves sit ceremonious, like Tombs—

she mildly shocks us both by the unexpected simile and by her failure to complete the rhyme as we expect her to. Sense and sound reinforce each other. Then the two lines that complete the quatrain are conventionally rhymed:

> The stiff Heart questions was it He, that bore,
> And Yesterday, or Centuries before?

Immediately there is a contrast in tone: here is completeness, a suggestion of tranquility in the poet's identification of her pain with that of Christ, the acceptance of all human pain as the prelude to heavenly peace. Surely, all this is not expressed only by the pattern of the rhymes, but they reinforce the sense of the poem. In each of its three stanzas, the identical tension and release is repeated: *round* is paired with *Ought,* then *grown* with *stone;* finally *Lead* with *outlived,* and *Snow* with *go.* The art which determined to express itself by such means requires human readers to respond with no less concern for every detail.

The computer analysis of prose will fall behind rather than excel human analysis if it does not consider these aspects of meaning. For the utilization of sound patterns to reinforce and even partly to generate meaning is not limited to verse. Let us consider a paragraph from a short story by Joseph Conrad, "The Secret Sharer." Perhaps because English was not his mother tongue and he mastered it only in his maturity, Conrad seems to have developed a fine ear for the aural potentialities of the language, as even a brief quotation reveals:

> There must have been some glare in the air to interfere with one's sight, because it was only just before the sun left us that my roaming eyes made out beyond the highest ridge of the principal islet of the group something which did away with the solemnity of perfect solitude. The tide of darkness flowed on swiftly; and with tropical suddenness a swarm of stars came out above the shadowy earth, while I lingered yet, my hand resting lightly on my ship's rail as if on the shoulder of a trusted friend. But, with all that multitude of celestial bodies staring down at one, the comfort of quiet communion with her was gone for good. And there were also disturbing sounds by this time—voices, footsteps forward; the steward flitted along the main deck, a busily ministering spirit; a hand-bell tinkled urgently under the poop-deck. . . .

Among the more readily discernible techniques of poetry employed here are rhyme, alliteration, consonance, and assonance. Notice not only the obvious "glare in the air," in which the intellectual link between the two words is reinforced by their resemblance, but also "interfere," which is subtly joined to them by a slant rhyme. In the phrase "principal islet of the group," the first and last words are suggestively linked by the vocal coloring of the *p*'s and *r*'s; when this same combination occurs a few words later in "the *sol*emnity of *per*fect *sol*itude," we hear not only the association of the two nouns reflected in the repetition of their initial syllables but also their link to the little islets created by the *p-r* combination in the adjective. A similar pattern of sounds occurs in "the *c*omfort of *q*uiet *c*ommunion"; here the *k*-sound is visually disguised in one word as *q*. But there is no obscurity in the identification of "my *sh*ip's *r*ail" as the "*sh*oulder of a *tr*usted *fr*iend." If we place two phrases in parallel,

> The *t*ide of   dark*ness* flowed on   *sw*iftly
> and wi*th*   *t*ropical sud*denness*   a *sw*arm of stars

we observe a pattern of approximate duplication of sounds and rhythms that emphasizes how swiftly the stars do appear at sunset near the equator: the darkness does come like a rapid tide. It is not the number of times that Conrad states the idea but the care with which he allows an extra-semantic element to communicate it that requires our scrutiny. Here is a challenge to tax the utmost ingenuity of those dedicated to computer analysis of literature.

For the present, it is the other problem of the content analysis of poetry, that of literary context, to which the computer seems closer to providing a solution. If anything, the machine promises to exceed the capacities of even the most precise and comprehensive human reader in accumulating data for critical evaluation. In the past, literary history has been written mostly in either mechanically objective terms or as a collection of highly subjective judgments. Thus the student of literature may be informed of the dates on which certain works were published or of the known biographical facts concerning the author. He may, on the other hand, be asked to accept all the subjective evaluations of the historian as though they also were fact. Clearly neither of these approaches—alone or in combination—will produce history. In literature, as in any other series of events, history is the complex of interactions between contemporaries and between generations. Each creator of literature is at the intersection of an almost infinite complex of affiliations, not only with the artists he knows but with others whom he knows only indirectly through their work. A true history of literature would trace at least the major lines of such affiliation.

In its customary operation, literary history has, in general, been missing the factual basis of particular data which could be accumulated and sifted to produce a record of its evolution. The raw materials have always been available, but in such huge quantities that no single reader could aspire to encompass any significant portion of them, and—given the range of responses to literature—experiments in group activity have been understandably few and imperfect. Whenever the production of literature has been treated as a series of relatively isolated events, it has inevitably suffered from a lack of dimension, an absence of any clear description of creativity as an intellectual process of infinite complexity.

One phenomenon, however, has been generally recognized: eras of poetry may follow each other, but they usually do not evolve from their immediate predecessors. Ordinarily, each generation of writers reacts against its artistic parents and seeks elsewhere the models for its emulation. We have always known this as a general truth. We note, among many other instances that could be added, how the poets of England in the sixteenth century turned to French and Italian models, how those of the seventeenth and eighteenth centuries sought exemplars in Latin poetry, how in the nineteenth century there was a strong revival of the traditional English ballad form after it had long been almost dead as a vital force, and how in the twentieth century the rhythms of English poetry seem generally attributable to those of Hebrew as reproduced in the King James Bible. But poets do not respond to a general school of poetry; they select particular models and strive to emulate and, if possible, excel them. Thus the study of the relations between, for example, the English Renaissance poets and their Italian models would necessitate a close comparison between each poem of one group with all of its possible antecedents in the other group. The bulk of the material that must be analyzed to establish the precise nature of such affiliations has harshly restricted the number of such studies. We are only recently, for instance, beginning to measure the important role of Dante and other Italian poets in the work of England's chief epic poet, John Milton.

The computer's ability to aid in revealing these intellectual affiliations between great creative minds rests on the hypothesis that the prime evidence is the basic unit of literature—the word. The machine can readily demonstrate that many (perhaps all) poets, when they emulate others in form, also tend to emulate them in diction. This phenomenon may be accounted for to some degree by the limits of language, by the inevitability that certain common terms will be associated in parallel contexts. But, as has already been stressed, poets do not habitually choose the common terms; their choice is dictated by semantic considerations, and by the demands of rhyme, alliteration, and assonance, which are as much a part of poetry as the dictionary meanings. Therefore, when we find Milton writing of the four elements in chaos which are

> Levied to side with warring *winds,* and *poise*
> Their lighter *wings,*
> > (*Paradise Lost,* II, 905–906)

and then pick up Shelley and read an invocation of the four elements, ending with

> ye swift whirl*winds,* who on *poised wings*
> Hung mute and moveless o'er yon abyss,
> > (*Prometheus Unbound,* I, 66–67)

we must recognize a force greater than coincidence or even common subject matter dictating similar expression. There is no necessity for Shelley's having chosen to describe one of the four elements with the words *whirlwinds, poised,* and *wings* other than his desire to charge his words with additional connotation by relating them to the masterpiece of his classic predecessor.

This tendency to echo distinctive phrases from earlier works may characterize poetry more than other art; it is certainly more significant than most literary historians have acknowledged. But recognition of that tendency is the goal toward which the history of literature must move, since the possibility of our appreciating the totality of a poetic experience requires that we respond to those elements that are intended to strike sympathetic overtones by evoking memories of earlier emotional commitment to other poems.

It is this phenomenon of intellectual affinity exhibited in shared diction which seems, of all aspects of literary style, to be most readily susceptible at present to computer analysis. It requires the least preediting and the smallest contamination of the data by subjective and culturally biased attitudes. If all we do to a word is remove an inflectional ending, we are still dealing with that word, not a synonym for it, or its part of speech, or a numerical equivalent, or a category into which we or a machine have determined it should go. Any correspondences between two or more texts which are recognized on the basis of their shared diction should be obvious to all who see them. And the greater the quantity of shared significant diction, the more meaningful, presumably, is the link it represents. Literary concern ordinarily lies beyond this prime level of meaning; it may lie with recognizing affinities between an artist's creation and his biography, or his involvement in the social and political turmoil of his time, or his attempt to escape from that turmoil. But if we keep our focus on his words, we may be led to corroborating evidence of his attempts to organize them into patterns that are intended to reflect the matrix of already extant poetry within which he is composing.

The importance of shared diction can be demonstrated by introducing some further parallels between Milton's major poem, *Paradise Lost,* and Shelley's comparable work, *Prometheus Unbound.* Such an analysis can do much to reverse some of the customary evaluations of both men. Milton has often been thought of as being puritanical, sober, and deeply religious. Shelley is generally regarded as licentious, irresponsible, and atheistic. To find a major affinity between them, even if only imagined by Shelley, would enlighten us on several topics. By noting what parts of Milton's poetry Shelley was most attracted to, we would provide ourselves with a scale to measure what Shelley himself considered important in poetry. Furthermore, we may accept one poet's judgments about another as having at least as much validity as those of other critics; if, for example, Shelley tells us that Milton, in the most significant portions of his poetry, can be interpreted as advocating rebellion, particularly against God, we are forced to reexamine the critical judgment that establishes him as an advocate of stability.

Some understanding of the relationship between the two men and some projection of a computer application to the problem of measuring it can be evolved from the close examination of numerous passages from their major poems. A multitude of such creative reconstructions of passages from Milton (and from other poets) suggests that, at least for Shelley, this is a major part of the creative faculty. Like Milton himself, who constantly evoked echoes of all his sources—in the Bible, in the rabbinical and patristic commentary, in the pagan classics, and in Renaissance literature—Shelley chose to deepen the experience of his reader by coupling the overtones of his major predecessors. His realization that he was perhaps oversubtle led him to address *Prometheus Unbound* to "the highly refined imagination of the more select classes of poetical readers." Milton, more succinctly and candidly, had called them the "fit audience though few."

The illustration just given, of the "whirlwinds on poised wings," is of the sort that we are now learning to retrieve by computer. Our present capability is limited to identifying passages containing a larger number of words in common, and we have no means yet of recognizing patterns of meter or of sounds. When we have refined the computer to the high demands made by such poets, we may be able to probe literature on levels presently barred to us. At present, in order to suit this work to the limits of the machine, we must concentrate on passages where a relatively high number of significant words occurs in relatively close proximity, usually within the same sentence. These parameters exclude the two brief passages just quoted, but this loss has been balanced by an accumulation of other data on the multidimensional associations between these two minds.

An illustration of the way in which the computer can aid us in tracking a major motif through a poet's work is Shelley's constant return to a single passage in *Paradise Lost.* Near the end of Book One, the rebellious angels in hell stand dumbly on the shore of the burning lake they had been plunged into by the edict of God. Now they are about to reassemble to consider how best to continue the war against heaven. Satan, their general,

> Then straight commands that at the warlike sound
> Of Trumpets loud and Clarions be upreared
> His mighty *Standard;* that proud honour claimed
> Azazel as his right, a Cherub tall:
> Who forthwith from the glittering staff *unfurled*
> Th' imperial ensign; which, full high advanced,
> Shone like a *meteor streaming* to the wind,
> With gems and golden lustre rich *emblazed,*
> Seraphic arms and trophies; all the while
> Sonorous metal blowing martial sounds;
> At which the universal host up-sent

A shout that tore Hell's concave, and beyond
Frighted the reign of Chaos and old Night.
(11. 531–543; italics added)

Shelley distinctly echoed these lines in at least four important poems, and other poems derive distinctive diction from immediately contiguous lines. This persistence in drawing repeatedly on a single source indicates its hold on his imagination, the penetration into his memory, exercised by these few lines. The chief explanation for this tenacity is Shelley's association of Satan with the general spirit of revolution. Reversing Milton's announced ethical polarity, he made God the tyrant of the world and his adversary the advocate of freedom. When, therefore, he wished to project an image of liberty bursting forth and breaking the bonds of oppression, he drew his language from passages like the one describing Satan's challenge to the established order.

In 1819, the upsurge of the democratic spirit that Shelley dreamed of occurred in Spain: a constitution was proclaimed and the Inquisition abolished. In an enthusiastic response, he composed an "Ode to Liberty," expressing the hope that this was but the first of many revolutions. In one strophe he calls upon "king-deluded Germany" to follow the lead of Spain. Invoking the spirit of a Teutonic chief who fought the Romans, he thus equates him with the rebel in Milton's poem:

> Tomb of Arminius! render up thy dead
> Till, like a *standard* from a watch-tower's *staff*,
> His soul may *stream* over the tyrant's head . . . .
> (11. 196–98)

And, later that year, when the Neapolitans also revolted, Shelley encouraged them with another ode. In this poem, he could utilize the convenient symbol of Vesuvius and the volcanic islands off the adjacent coast, which he associated with Typhoeus, the mythological rebel against Jupiter imprisoned under a volcano:

> From that Typhaean mount, Inarime,
> There *streamed* a sunbright vapour, like the *standard*
> Of some aethereal host . . . .
> ("Ode to Naples," 11. 45–47)

These lines are followed by Shelley's declaration that prophetic cries of liberty are rising all around, a clear derivation, even though it engendered no verbal parallels, from Milton's shouting devils in hell.

Within a few days of the "Ode to Naples," Shelley composed a more playful poem, apparently concerned with the creative spirit of poetry, which he called "The Witch of Atlas." The armies of this spirit seem to be the generally rebellious elements, as is evidenced by their verbal links to Satan's cohorts:

> And then she called out of the hollow turrets
> Of those high clouds, white, golden and vermilion,
> The armies of her ministering spirits—
> In mighty legions, million after million,
> They came, each troop *emblazoning* its merits
> On *meteor* flags; and many a proud pavilion
> Of the intertexture of the atmosphere
> They pitched upon the plain of the calm mere.
> They framed the imperial tent of their great Queen
> Of woven exhalations, underlaid
> With lambent lightning-fire, as may be seen
> A dome of thin and open ivory inlaid
> With crimson silk—

Again, there are distinct verbal links, while the image, if not the words, of the phrase "exhalation, underlaid with lambent lightning-fire" associates rebellion with the volcano, as Satan is found in *Paradise Lost* among the subterranean fires.

By 1821, the Greeks had joined the movement for national liberation, and Shelley composed a dramatic poem, "Hellas," to celebrate their expected triumph. In one of the choruses, he equates creation with liberty:

> In the great morning of the world,
> The Spirit of God with might *unfurled*
> The flag of Freedom over Chaos,
> And all its banded anarchs fled,
> Like vultures frighted from Imaus,
> Before an earthquake's tread—

In this passage, we find only one word from the source passage, but it constitutes a link with chthonic eruption, and also there is a distinct echo of another passage in *Paradise Lost* where Satan is described as "a vulture, on Imaus bred." We note here both the aural generation of Shelley's words *fled* and *tread* from Milton's *bred,* and the transference of ugly characteristics from the spirit of liberty to its oppressors.

Such a minute sampling as has just been given must represent a much larger number of similar verbal correspondences. The computer alone cannot produce literary interpretations; some knowledge of the circumstances in which the poem was composed would seem to be necessary in tracking a recurrent motif. But, conversely, the recognition of the motif often illuminates the poem, as when, in "The Witch of Atlas," the elements of poetic creativity are described in terms intended to suggest their identity with the rebellious angels. Although the introduction of the computer has a long way to go to complete the expulsion of impressionistic criticism, it has demonstrated its ability to do better and faster what human minds have struggled to do in the way of collecting the objective facts for a history of intellectual, creative interaction. In the end, it may be the machine, by enhancing our perceptions of the writer's intention, that enlarges the study of literature to the dimensions of the truly humane.

In this chapter, I have restricted myself to illustrations from my own area of competence and special interest. But the qualities I have described do not exist only in *belles lettres*. The operations of the human brain are presumably alike—in kind if not in degree—in any creative activity, the composing of diplomatic correspondence and political acceptance speeches as well as poetry. When I say that the study of literature requires us to expand our definitions of content analysis, I do not mean for literature only: no study of the meaning of verbal communication is satisfactory if it limits itself to the narrowest concept of meaning. There is universal significance in the choice of one word over its synonyms, of one combination of sounds, of one syntactic structure. Until today, we could not attempt to study the meaning of all these aspects of communication. With the computer to aid us, there can be no excuse for not adding these new dimensions to our knowledge and understanding.

10 The Use of Content Analysis in International Relations

John E. Mueller

Political Science
University of Rochester

As the science of linguistics inexorably develops increasingly sophisticated procedures for ordering and analyzing the content of communication, there will be more and more demands for sociological and psychological theories to put the linguistic developments into broader context. This chapter reflects some of the grosser areas of concern that confront theorists as they attempt to apply linguistic developments to diplomatic documents in the area of international relations—although some of the comments may be applicable to other areas of interest as well.

As an analytic convenience, the communication scrutinized by the content analyst can be viewed as a *response* by a certain type of person in written *form* to a *stimulus* in a specific *context*. This formulation suggests the four overlapping areas of concern that will be discussed here.

FORM

Students of international relations, whether they apply content-analytic techniques or the more traditional historical ones to the situation, must deal almost exclusively with available communications in written form. Occasionally the participants are available for interviews afterward or agree to have their oral communications transcribed at the time but, even in these cases, they are aware that what they are saying is for the record and that it may come back to haunt them at a later date.

There are, of course, the inevitable problems (especially in this increasingly telephonic age) connected with the erratic and selective availability of relevant documents. The 1914 crisis era is extraordinarily attractive because events conspired to cause the early and rather thorough publication of great volumes of diplomatic documents from this period. Even in this case, however, there are signs that there has been a tendentious selectivity in the release of the French documents while important Serbian documents are still unavailable. Additionally, even private documents are not always honest reflections of the author's state of mind; as one former State Department official, Roger Hilsman (1967:xvi), has recently noted, "Statesmen today are so terribly conscious that historians will soon be along to pore over their documents and judge their actions that they are tempted to write the documents with this fact in mind."

Furthermore, a great deal of human communication is simply not transmitted in verbal—much less written—form. Actions, whether the raised eyebrow or the atomic explosion, can speak both louder and softer than words. (Tacit communication is extensively analyzed in Schelling, 1963, 1966.) Actions can also speak differently: words and actions are so frequently at variance that we have a word to describe this state of being—hypocrisy. When actions are gross enough—mobilization, the withdrawal of ambassadors, armed attack—they can readily be taken into account by the analyst, and documentary and action data can be used to reinforce each other in a broader theory of conduct, a route chosen by some investigators (for example, North et al., 1964).

More important perhaps, it is frequently true that what is being *communicated* is not being *said*—especially in diplomacy where this knack has been raised to a high art. Euphemism, tone, analogy, and Aesopian language with its more sophisticated developments are used to cloud the issue (see George, 1959a). Sometimes the subject that is being talked about is so well understood by the communicators that it need never be directly mentioned: in the records of the Japanese cabinet debates about surrender in August 1945, the atomic bomb is barely mentioned, yet commentators are reluctant to conclude that its existence had no bearing on the final decision. For this reason it would seem to be a mistake to conclude, as one study has, that because the German decision makers in 1914 did not constantly comment on the numbers of rifles in the French army, they were less than fully conscious of the military capabilities of their opponents (Zinnes et al., 1961).

A final concern involves the difference between written and unwritten (verbal) communication. The very fact that a communication is put in writing rather than transmitted orally is a meaningful step, one fully appreciated by diplomatic analysts. A written communication tends to be more formal, more serious, and less remediable than a verbal one, and its author expects to be held more fully accountable for what he has said.[1] The fact that a series of messages have appeared in print may be far more important than any variations of intensity noticeable among the written

---

[1] Consider, for example, the import of the query, "Will you put that in writing?"

communications. Thus, analysts of documents generated by the disputants in the Sino-Soviet debate may find that the polemical shrillness varies from time to time, but the major increase of hostility was registered when the dispute broke out in print. Documentary analysis in this case taps only a truncated portion of the hostility scale.

Content analysis in international relations, then, can only give a part of the picture. As is true with the analysis of roll calls in legislatures, the material analyzed reflects only partially and imperfectly the material of the political arena. And theory based on the method, therefore, can only be partial.

CONTEXT

Unlike the typical experimenter or survey researcher, the content analyst of diplomatic documents deals with data generated under comparatively "natural" circumstances. On the other hand, he is unable to control the context in which the communication analyzed is generated.[2] Nevertheless the content of the communication is determined to a considerable degree by the circumstances under which it is uttered.

Communications intended for private ears can be expected to differ from those intended for public ones, although some analyses of the 1914 documents reportedly suggest that the difference may not always be great.[3] Private documents may vary among themselves according to their intended receiver: diaries, for example, presumably are more intimate than letters to acquaintances. General Douglas MacArthur's privately expressed estimates of the probability of success of the Inchon landing in 1950 varied—depending on the audience—from near certainty to 5000 to 1 against him (Higgins, 1960: 45ff.). There may be important differences even among public documents, depending on the context. It has often been observed that speeches by statesmen to congregations of their own countrymen tend to differ from those delivered to foreigners, just as the views of American politicians on civil rights tend to be different when they are voiced in Mississippi rather than in Michigan. Even when the audience is constant, communications can differ if the contextual format alters slightly: observers have noted that formally prepared statements by the precise and purposeful Robert S. McNamara show considerable discrepancies from his informal, extemporaneous statements uttered before the same Senate committees (Brodie, 1966:11).

[2] For a similar comparison, see Mitchell (1967).
[3] There is also impressionistic evidence that former Secretary of State John Foster Dulles' "public assessments of various characteristics of the Soviet regime were identical with his private beliefs." See Holsti (1962, 1967b).

The contextual conditions can demand a certain patterning of communications behavior, forcing the speakers into roles.[4] Generals defending budget requests can be expected to stress the unpreparedness of the present military force,[5] while the Japanese method for conducting committee meetings can demand frequent statements of positions that bear little relation to the resolutions finally taken (see Wohlstetter, 1962:345). As conditions alter, entire concepts can change meaning: one analyst notes that the pressure of time in the 1914 crisis took on a different meaning as the crisis developed (Holsti, 1965d:368).

STIMULUS

As part of the context, the actual stimulus that generates the response to be analyzed is of major importance and must be carefully included in any comprehensive content analytic theory imposed on international documents. Survey analysts and experimenters, characteristically, are able to control the stimulus, while content analysts in this area can only compare reactions to stimuli that happen to be similar. The danger, in part, is that the stimulus will differ significantly from instance to instance.

In the political dialogue on American policy in Vietnam, Secretary of State Rusk frequently looked like a relative hawk within the administration while Secretary McNamara tended to look like a relative dove. This difference seems to stem in part from the fact that Rusk's public pronouncements were stimulated by the questions of the doves on the Senate Foreign Relations Committee, while McNamara's statements were stimulated by the queries of the hawks on the House Armed Services Committee. Thus Rusk often seemed to be urging a tougher policy while McNamara seemed to choose a softer one when, in fact, the two men might not differ at all if the stimuli were constant. Even seasoned political speechmakers like General DeGaulle seem to have been stimulated at times by enthusiastic audiences into making pronouncements that, in more sober moments, might be considered inopportune.

It is also possible that the subject will be inspired to disclose his feelings only when the stimulus is appropriate. Suppose, for example, that one compares documents generated in a crisis with those generated in a non-

---

[4] Sometimes the patterning of communication behavior demanded by the context can render communication impossible. There seems to be no way the passenger in the rear seat of an automobile can get a front-seat passenger to roll an open window half way up. The front-seat passenger invariably seems to assume that the request is simply a polite way of asking that the window be closed all the way.

[5] A point that seems to be less than fully appreciated in Zinnes et al., (1961:470–71).

crisis situation and finds a great deal of hatred expressed in the crisis. It may be concluded that crisis stimulates hate, but another possible conclusion is that crisis simply stimulates one to express the hatred felt constantly at all times. Either conclusion is interesting, of course, but the implications are substantially different. The stimulation to express one's feelings seems to vary even among noncrisis situations. In one study it is found that Soviet official expressions of affect for the United States were strongly positive during Soviet-American negotiations at Camp David, while during the period in which the test-ban treaty was signed, the Soviets were not stimulated to express very much affect—either positive or negative—toward the United States (Holsti, 1965c:122; 1966a:351).

RESPONSE

A common assumption in both content analysis and survey research is that the subject, under certain circumstances, will say what he thinks. The problem here is partly that some people never say what they think, but also that people, even under constant conditions of context and stimulus, differ considerably in the manner in which they divulge what is on their minds. The style of some is articulate and sophisticated, while others, like former U. S. Ambassador to the United Nations Arthur Goldberg, prefer to substitute redundancy for eloquence. Some are direct and sincere, while others, especially in the diplomatic corps, speak with forked tongues. The talk of some is filled with florid irrelevancies, while the talk of others is clipped and to the point. Some, like the Chinese Communists, continually pitch their remarks at a shrill scream while others are characteristically restrained—and because of it more effective when they have something shrill to say. Some let themselves go in their communications, while others, like good Bolsheviks (and Yankees), live under a code which stresses that personal feelings must be controlled (see Brodie, 1966:143). Furthermore, the style of speech for an individual can vary greatly, depending on the context (see Frye, 1963).

The problems stressed in this discussion of context, stimulus, and response bear most heavily on the dilemma of aggregation. When each of the three variables are controlled—in a comparison of newspapers' editorial reactions to a single event, for example—one is presumably relatively safe. But to gain statistical power, aggregation and its inevitable blurring of distinctions often must be resorted to. Can Kaiser Wilhelm's paranoic concern about the abstract British threat to Germany, as expressed in his private marginalia, be justly aggregated as a perception of hostility with an Austrian prime minister's formal denunciation of Serbian terror? Only a continual process of breaking down and restructuring aggregates can indicate whether more has been gained than lost in the aggregation.

THE ANALYSIS OF DIPLOMATIC DOCUMENTS

In international relations, a number of studies of international diplomatic documents using content analysis have emerged over the past several years.[6] Most of them were conducted at Stanford University under the general direction of Robert C. North. The technique has been applied most extensively to the documents from the crisis of 1914.[7] As noted above, documentation from this period is extraordinarily extensive although, even here, there exist biases and deletions that could be significant.

The documents were first analyzed to derive a frequency distribution for perceptions by the international decision makers of "significance of conflict," "capability," "coalition," and "hostility," (Zinnes et al., 1961). Perceptions of hostility greatly outweighed perceptions of capability. Therefore, it is concluded that there was a great deal of hostility in the system which tended to overbalance concern with the objective realities of opposing force which, in turn, suggests "that rational considerations may exert limited influence on the decision to wage war." However, there are other interpretations of these data. A perception of capability is defined as

. . . a statement concerning the power of another state or a coalition of states, or a statement with regard to the changing power of either a state or a coalition of states. These statements generally appear in the data in the form of amounts of material.

Thus, capability perceptions appear to be largely notations of a quantitative sort of an opponent's military strength. It is possible that these perceptions are not very common in such a crisis period simply because they are already known and are in the backs of the minds of the decision makers. For example, as noted above, German intelligence on the number of French rifles is not likely to be a prime subject of conversation, since

---

[6] Notice that this survey is devoted to content-analytic studies that use international diplomatic documents. Of course, analyses of other sorts of documents, especially newspapers, frequently have considerable relevance to international relations. Among the studies that might be mentioned in this regard are Angell et al. (1964); Coddington (1965); Galtung and Ruge (1965); Ohlström (1966); Namenwirth and Brewer (1966); Foster (1935); Rosi (1964); and Wright and Nelson (1939).

[7] See especially Zinnes et al. (1961); North et al. (1964); Holsti (1965d, 1965e); Holsti and North (1965b, 1966b); Holsti et al. (1968b); Zinnes (1962); and North (1967).

that number would already be fairly well known and taken into consideration in the military plans. Futhermore, it is not clear in the abstract what these numbers really mean. Standards of phraseology or habits of speech may determine certain ratios and tempos of perception frequencies quite apart from the objective situation. Perhaps leaders in crisis always speak this way whether they go to war or not. Although a type of perception may be uttered more *frequently* in a certain period, it does not follow that emotions behind such explicit perceptions are necessarily more *important* to the perceiver.[8]

As was recognized in the cited article, what is needed to help clarify, if not solve, the problem is some comparative data from another similar body of documents analyzed in the same way. A study was begun at Stanford on the Bosnian crisis of 1908 in which the same states went through a strikingly similar period of tension, but without going to war. This study, however, was never completed. If an examination of the Bosnian crisis showed a similar hostility-capability ratio, the basic thesis might need some redevelopment. The low number of significance statements found tends to weaken the case for the thesis. The data presumably indicate that the leaders in 1914 were not expecting a large, significant war. Thus the deterrent threat might be considered to be ineffective not because it engendered overwhelming hostility, but because it was too feeble to impress the decision makers sufficiently with the dangers of a war.

In this study, then, a series of numbers come out of a single grossly aggregated body of data gathered during a crisis, and propositions about crisis behavior are made. But there is nothing to compare the numbers with except our intuitive notions about what sorts of patterns should emerge. Later studies have analyzed the 1914 documents in different ways by using content-analytic techniques of greater sophistication—or, at any rate, greater complexity. However, they have not sought to retest the basic thesis of the first study, but seem to be content to accept it as proved.

These studies have attempted to reduce the problem of gross aggregation by dissecting the crisis itself either by looking at trends as the crisis deepened or by comparing the reactions of the decision makers toward the actions and attitudes of allies, on the one hand, and enemies, on the

[8] See, especially, George (1959b). An analogous problem is found in a study by Holsti (1965d). It is argued there, for example, that decision makers will perceive "their own range of alternatives to be more restricted than those of their adversaries." In investigating this assertion it is found that decision makers, in 1914, tended to perceive themselves more frequently as having only one possible course of action while perceiving their opponents more frequently to have more than one course of action. These data, however, only gauge the relative *frequency* of certain kinds of perception; they say nothing about the *content* and therefore the *range* of the alternatives noted in the various perceptions.

other. Although comparison of the 1914 crisis with other historical events (usually the Cuban missile crisis) is sometimes found in these studies,[9] the other events have never been content-analyzed in the same way, and therefore the comparisons are based on intuition and traditional historical techniques, not content analysis.[10] Conclusions from 1914 must retain the status of those derived from a case study. To an extent, this is unfortunate: to learn that the proposition "if x perceives itself the object of hostility, then x will express hostility" (Zinnes, 1962) holds true for the decision makers in 1914 is but a small advance over historical speculation. Some comparison is possible *within* the crisis documents, of course. Some of the studies compare perceptions just before the war began with perceptions earlier in the crisis period. Thus, for the same communicators in similar context, the stimulus of intense crisis can be compared with relatively mild crisis, but not with noncrisis.

Since the 1914 data are split apart and aggregated in various ways, one can observe the emergence of some of the difficulties noted earlier. Germany, rather persistently, seems to overemote, for example. Part of this may result from the inclusion of the Kaiser's colorful marginalia in the analysis, while comparable impromptu notations are not available from other decision makers.

Some of the conclusions in these studies about the final German decision to go to war might have been altered if a distiction had been made in some of the coding categories to separate responses to stimuli seen to be "real" from responses to stimuli of a more ephemeral nature. Specifically, perceptions of "hostility" or "injury" might have been subdivided to differentiate the "they-hate-us" perceptions from the "they-are-attacking-us" perceptions. The studies frequently insist that the Germans saw so much threat and "hostility" in the air and were "under such severe stress that any action is preferable to the burden of sustained tension" (Holsti, North, and Brody, 1968b:137). Although it is true that the Germans—especially the Kaiser—were impressed because Germany was unloved in the world, many of the hostile perceptions must have resulted from the Germans' belief that they were about to be attacked themselves. In fact, they apparently thought that they *had* already been attacked by the Russians and were convinced that a French attack was underway, noting several supposed instances of border violations by France (Kautsky, 1924:504–532). Furthermore, the Schlieffen plan to which they were committed directed that in any two front war a quick knockout blow

[9] The content-analytic comparisons between 1914 and 1962 found in Holsti et al. (1965a) seem quite inappropriate.
[10] A promising beginning has been made, however, in comparing the 1914 conclusions with experimental data on crisis behavior (Zinnes, 1966). See also Hermann and Hermann (1967).

at France was to be delivered followed by an offensive at the slower mobilizing Russians. And, in the military thinking of the time, it was entirely axiomatic that the power that moved first had a major advantage.[11]

Whatever the limitations of these studies of the 1914 case, they have frequently generated insights into the analysis of that period, while testing and suggesting hypotheses about crisis behavior. Often it is the quantitative rather than the qualitative nature of the findings that is of interest. Few historians would be surprised to learn that the decision makers of 1914 more frequently saw only one course of action open to them, whereas they envisioned their opponents as having several courses of action available (Holsti, 1965d); it is the extreme numerical imbalance of these perceptions that is striking.

Too often, it seems, the laboriously gained quantitative power of the

[11] See Brodie (1959:Ch 2). It is also argued, largely on qualitative grounds, in the early article (Zinnes, et al. 1961:473) that "both Austria and Germany possessed evidence of their own inadequate capabilities" and in a later study by North et al. (1963:172) that ". . . German leaders had at their disposal persuasive evidence of the weakness of Germany and Austria-Hungary relative to the capabilities of Great Britain, France, and Russia." Objectively, it is easy to state, after the fact, that Germany was *not* relatively weak. For Germany almost won the war in 1914 and, after an unexpectedly long period of bloodshed, it almost won again in 1918. In 1915, things looked so good for Germany that Bulgaria joined the Central Powers in the belief that theirs was the winning side. Thus, any "persuasive evidence" the leaders may have had of the inadequacy of German capabilities should properly have been skeptically weighed. Moreover, much of the evidence cited comes in the form of special pleadings by von Moltke for a larger force—a perennial demand of military commanders (Zinnes et al., 1961:470–471). And it must be remembered that this "evidence" came surrounded by information on carefully wrought and optimistic plans of military conquest in a general atmosphere in which the seemingly painless Franco-Prussian War was taken as the norm. In addition, conflicting evidence was received. Judging from a careful count of Russian railway mileage, the German General Staff concluded, probably accurately, that Russia would not be "ready" for war until 1916 (Tuchman, 1962:43).

But what is needed for the analysis is not only the possession of "persuasive evidence" by the leaders about relative weakness but also their own perceptions under crisis of their supposed weakness. Holsti and North assert that ". . . top German decision-makers were fully cognizant of Germany's inability successfully to wage a general European war in 1914" (Holsti, 1965b:161; Holsti, 1965d:371). To be sure, misperception, misconstruction, and miscalculation abounded in those tragic days, and it appears clear from his marginalia that Kaiser Wilhelm was reacting in a manner that can only be described as paranoid. It is also true that the German documents do reveal a concern with the devastating potentialities in the developing situation. However, this concern is belated and was admitted to be "fleeting" in the original article (Zinnes et al., 1961:471)—as the frequencies of the "significance of a conflict" perception in the content data show. And although the Germans went to war with a reasonable awareness that they might lose, these feelings were also mixed with a certain confidence: on June 1st, Moltke said, "We are ready, and the sooner the better for us" (Tuchman, 1962:44).

data is submerged in homogenizing indexes or factor analyses with the results being reported blandly in terms of tendency statements or dichotomous proclamations that statistical significance has or has not been obtained. Historians and propaganda analysts have already pored over the documents using a form of content analysis of their own, and usually have a reasonable idea of what is going on. The contribution of quantitative content analysis in this area is less likely to be the emergence of astonishing new interpretations of historical events than the refinement of earlier qualitative speculations by adding a quantitative tone to them. To pin a number on an "obvious" qualitative finding is no small achievement.

Published content analyses of more recent international events have involved a comparison of documents uttered by the same decision-making sets—Chinese and Soviet publicists—at points in time that differ in the amount of international conflict that seems to prevail (Holsti, 1965c, 1966a; Zaninovich, 1962; and Holsti et al., 1965a). The documents are all public ones and thus form a less rich set (but more homogeneous in terms of "context") than the one available for the 1914 analyses. In the terms used above, the Sino-Soviet studies more or less seek to control the respondents and the context while the stimulus varies. The few studies thus far published are promising and, although questions of interpretation can be raised,[12] they have been cautiously presented as illustrations rather than finished products; thus, comment would seem to be somewhat premature. The value and feasibility of the application of the General Inquirer in its semantic differential form to these international documents might

---

[12] The principal hypothesis thus far tested with these data is, in its operational form, "Chinese and Soviet attitudes toward the United States will tend to be similar in periods of high interbloc conflict, whereas during periods of decreasing tensions, attitudes toward American policy will diverge" (Holsti, 1965c, 1966a). Accordingly, Soviet and Chinese attitudes toward the United States are compared in several periods in the cold war. Unfortunately the periods selected to represent "low interbloc conflict"—Soviet-American negotiations at Camp David, the settlement of the missile crisis, the signing of the test-ban treaty—are all times in which the Soviets consciously increased tensions within the bloc by rejecting the Chinese and turning to the United States for closer ties. Thus it was not a case of *general* interbloc relaxation causing intrabloc diversity, but one in which one bloc partner sought to reduce interbloc tension despite the knowledge that such a move would increase intrabloc frictions. To find the Soviet Union saying nice things about the United States in these periods while the Chinese kept up their anti-American line is to be expected. A more fitting strategy would be similar to one adopted by Zaninovich (1962) in an earlier study, one that was highly imaginative and promising but that apparently was never followed up. He compared Sino-Soviet perceptions in a month of low general tension (January, 1960) with those in a month of high tension (May, 1960).

better be assessed by linguists and communication theorists. An outsider might be led to wonder, however, what it all means when he finds that the United States in the first days of the Cuban missile crisis was almost as likely to regard its own actions in a negative light as in a positive one; that, as the level of American actions decreased in violence or potential violence, the Soviet Union was inclined to find the United States both decreasingly active and decreasingly passive; and that throughout the crisis the Chinese viewed their own actions, equally with those of the Cubans, in overwhelmingly negative terms (Holsti et al., 1965a).

As for the contribution of content analysis to international relations theory, it seems clear that the method has proved itself worthy, at least in certain areas—especially the area of crisis behavior. Although sometimes the cost in time, tedium, and money may seem excessive, the method's promise encourages the observer to anticipate the inexorable linguistic developments hopefully.

11 Improved Quality of Content Analysis Categories: Computerized-Disambiguation Rules for High-Frequency English Words[1]

Philip J. Stone

Center for Advanced Study in the Behavioral Sciences
With Marshall Smith, Dexter Dunphy, Edward Kelly,
Ken Chang, and Tom Speer, Harvard University

THE PROBLEM

This chapter reports work on a language-analysis problem that we believe to be fundamental to the development of many computer applications. The problem is perhaps most clearly recognized in computer-aided content analysis because of our particular concerns and extensive experience in applying available techniques. Although mechanical translation projects might have taken a lead, they have been occupied with other issues.

Often, the user of a content analysis category, developed by a previous investigator, is satisfied with the theoretical merits of the category, but he is critical of the selection of entries that make up the category. This is particularly true for entries that are homographs (that is, a written word is constant, but its meaning varies widely depending on the context). For example, a user might complain that the word "kind" should not have been included in the General Inquirer's[2] Harvard Third Dictionary category "SIGN-ACCEPT." While the word occasionally means benevolent, it actually has other meanings more than 80 percent of the time.

[1] The support of this research by the National Science Foundation (GS-178, GS-1253) is gratefully acknowledged. We thank Louise Woodhead, Susan Brander, Daniel Ogilvie and Robert F. Bales for their participation and work in coordinating this project. The quality of this project had depended on the careful work performed by a number of undergraduates, some of whom (including Stephen Bates, Peter Stumpp, and Douglas Tonn) have stayed with the project for most of its duration. Their patience and willingness to explore has been most appreciated.

[2] Readers unfamiliar with computer-aided content analysis systems are referred to the section on computational techniques in this book. A description of the current General Inquirer category assignment procedures is briefly outlined in the chapter by Goldhamer in this volume.

If we were to content analyze the sentence, "There are three major kinds of Communists today," we might agree that "kind" could be tagged as "SIGN-COGNITIVE-DIFFERENTIATION," but the tag SIGN-AC-CEPT is quite irrelevant! The difficulty is compounded by the fact that "kind" is a high-frequency word, perhaps often causing the SIGN-AC-CEPT tag tallies to be so erroneous as to be useless or actually misleading.

Instead of having content analysis categories consist of words, we need to have them consist of word senses. The tagging of the word "kind" then would depend on which meaning is being used. Higher-order content-analysis categories for measuring themes could then, in turn, be built on the co-occurrence of word senses rather than words.

Three years ago, we decided to work on the problem of developing routines for having the computer identify word senses. Rather than build these routines for a theoretical framework represented by a particular content analysis set of categories, we constructed a set of low-inference procedures that could be used in building many different kinds of content analysis dictionaries. We did not intend to undertake building procedures for all of the words in the English language, nor did we hope to identify all of the shades of meaning that future content analysts may want to distinguish. Instead, we decided to attempt to develop procedures for distinguishing between the senses of high-frequency words occurring in everyday English. At the suggestion of psycholinguist Herbert Rubenstein, this came to be known as the "disambiguation project."

In offering routines for the higher-frequency word senses, it should be understood that the user can add routines for lower-frequency words that happen to occur in the text he is studying. He can also add word senses that might not have been included in our procedures. Hopefully, our contribution would usually get rid of at least 80 percent of the mistagging that now occurs because of word ambiguity. In fact, our preliminary results indicate even better success.

While the disambiguation project was primarily undertaken to improve content analysis procedures, we have been aware that disambiguation is also crucial for many of the functions that computers will perform someday as public utilities. A typewriter keyboard connected to a computer will probably become standard equipment in the future school classroom, business office, and home. The computer will be offering services of teacher, personal accountant, psychotherapist, order clerk, librarian, travel agent, private secretary, manuscript editor, emergency medical advisor, and test examiner, plus many services unknown today. There will be both general services for the public and special services for the doctor, lawyer, merchant, chief, and many other occupations. The computer must be able to interact with all of these people in an open-ended manner by using at least rudimentary English. It is therefore important that the computer be able to recognize English word senses rather than English words.

We hoped that disambiguation might take place independently of complete syntactic analysis. For some content analysis applications, an elaborate syntatic analysis is important. For example, Ole Holsti discusses, in this volume, how his research on the statements of political elites requires keeping track of who is perceived as doing what to whom. However, most content analysis applications to date have not needed extensive syntactic analyses, but have just relied on counting the frequencies with which different concepts occur. The recent successes of Kuno (1965) and others indicate that the computer will perhaps one day be able to provide syntactic analysis capabilities that can satisfy content analysis needs. But rather than wait for these developments we speculated whether it would be possible to focus on disambiguation now and consider syntactic analysis later.

It could be argued that disambiguation cannot take place independently of a complete linguistic analysis. Is not syntactic recognition part and parcel of the same cognitive processes that perform the disambiguation? Do not both need to be unraveled together in order for either to be solved? When our project first began, some persons carried the point further and argued that a complete syntactic analysis must take place *prior* to any attempts at disambiguation. Considerable efforts at this stage went into demonstrating these different points of view.

A further argument could be made that disambiguating a particular word requires more information than is contained in the single sentences—that, for instance, we need to know what general topic is being discussed. Although a number of examples of this can be cited, the more realistic questions for us are the following ones:

1. How often, in fact, is disambiguation dependent on extra-sentence information?
2. What kinds of extra-sentence information are most often needed?
3. How difficult is it for the computer to obtain and keep files on this information?

These logical issues were further compounded by the fact that our computer dictionaries do not include all the words that appear in the text. There are too many low-frequency words to make such inclusion feasible. In particular, the names of common objects and proper names are frequently omitted. Just the names of the different kitchen accessories together with the names of food items would fill a good-sized dictionary. While a young child has learned most of these words, the computer must treat them like blank spots in the sentence. Some inferences about these blanks often can be made from the context. For example, the presence of an article and the transitivity of the verb may indicate whether the noun is count or noncount, animate or inanimate. Yet, the presence of these blank spots puts the computer at an important disadvantage, even relative to a child.

An initial step, then, was to turn to psycholinguistics and ask, "How do people do disambiguation?" More precisely: "How would people do it if there were blank spots in the text (such as, for example, occurs in 'Cloze' procedures)?" Unfortunately, psycholinguistics has been concerned with a variety of other problems and has not given this much attention.

Similarly, we expected that computational linguistics, which is broader than the more specific problems of mechanical translation, might provide useful guidelines. Although the publications of Hays (1967a), Garvin (1963), Salton (1965b), and others show many advances, we again found little that helped with our specific problem.

A STRATEGY

We knew that it would be an impossible task to spin out disambiguation rules from thin air. We needed a data base for examining how language is used. By late 1964, about 6 million words of text had been keypunched for different General Inquirer studies. A sample of about one-half million words (510,976, to be exact) was drawn from 56 of the different available sources. The sources were divided into 9 types, the amount of material included in each approximately representing the importance of that area in our past research. These areas included conversational materials, personal documents, dream reports, responses to survey research questions, TATs, literary sources, editorials, speeches, and folktales. This half-million word sample was then processed through a key-word-in-context (KWIC) procedure. As might be imagined, this required several hours of computer sorting and resulted in an alphabetical printout several feet thick.

An example of the printout is shown in Figure 1, in this case, the word "bit." The key-word-in-context listing shows that the meaning of "somewhat" (as in "a bit frightening") is much more frequent than the meaning of piece (as in "a bit of gold"). References to the act of biting occur occasionally ("the animal bit him on the wrist"). The senses of the word "bit" as it is used in carpentry, information theory, or the horse's bit do not occur in the listing and thus perhaps could be ignored in a general purpose set of disambiguating procedures. If needed for a particular content analysis study, these specialized meanings could be easily added.

The availability of the key-word-in-context listing changes the situation for a person attempting to write disambiguation rules. Rather than guess

Figure 1 Sample of key word in context: bit.

how the word "bit" is used, he has information on how many times in a sample of a half-million words the word is used in a particular way. He can avoid word meanings occurring too rarely to be of importance and can locate those contextual cues that are in:portant in identifying the different senses of a word.

One of the surprising results of the KWIC procedure is that the few words provided on either side of a key word usually provide enough context to identify the correct word sense. Not only is extra-sentence information not needed, but also it is usually unnecessary to have the complete sentence available, let alone an unraveling of its syntactic structure.

The main source of exceptions to this is that the pronoun referents are often not clear apart from a larger context. For example, the use of "it" will occasionally make the printed KWIC line ambiguous, unless we are somehow told what "it" is. However, even for such an extremely ambiguous word as "play," the KWIC procedure provides enough context to correctly identify more than 95 percent of the 176 occurrences in our sample. For most words, the KWIC procedures provide enough context to identify the word sense of each occurrence.

From this experience with the KWIC procedure, we concluded that diambiguation does not require prior or concurrent complete syntactic analysis, nor does it require extensive files of extra-sentence information. Indeed, if disambiguation could be completed prior to syntactic analysis, it should greatly simplify the task of unraveling syntactic structure. Many English words, such as "judge," "play," and "run," are used both as nouns and as verbs. The identification of word senses tells us whether it is the noun or verb sense that occurs. We decided, therefore, to attempt disambiguation by itself.

Many word senses are determined by being next to or near another specific word. Thus the word "turn," for example, takes on particular meanings if it is preceded by "take," "in," or followed by "loose," "table," "down," "up," "on," or "out." We refer to these dependencies on specific other words as idioms. They correspond to Webster's definition of idiom: "an expression in the usage of a language that is peculiar to itself, either in grammatical construction or in having a meaning which cannot be derived as a whole from conjoined meaning of its elements." For our diambiguation purposes, "United States" is an idiom, since it has a unique meaning that is not the sum of the two constituent words.

Our procedure for disambiguating idioms is the "word test." The computer is told to search ahead or backward in the text for a particular word or string of words. Included with these directions are parameters indicating how far forward or backward the search should go. For example, if the idiom were "rock the boat," the directions might be either of the following:

1. Upon finding the word "rock," look ahead so many words for the word "boat."
2. Upon finding the word "boat," look backward so many words for the word "rock."

The word test can thus be entered after the dictionary look-up procedure has found the word "rock" or "boat," depending on the investigator's preference. In fact, it saves computer time if the word test is triggered by the less frequently occurring word. That way, the test is made less often.

By allowing for intervening words, a number of idiom forms can be handled. In addition, the procedures are designed so that the investigator need not concern himself with what regular suffixes are on either word unless he wants to. In this way, one test (for instance, allowing for three intervening words between "rock" and "boat") would handle all of these occurrences:

rocked his boat
rocking the boats
rocks the boat
rocked the ever-loving boat

Further technical details on how the word test is programmed are presented in the Appendix to this chapter.

The word test is the most frequently used procedure for disambiguating. In testing the several hundred ambiguous words for which we have already written disambiguating procedures, it is the word test that turns out to be doing the disambiguating about 70 percent of the time.

However, a second kind of test is needed for problems such as the following one. The idiom "turn in" can mean to surrender. It can also mean to go to bed. The two senses can be disambiguated if, as one additional test, we add a check for whether a pronoun occurs between "turn" and "in" as in "he turned him in." Rather than have a separate word test check for each possible pronoun, we need to have the ability to test whether any one of a class of words has occurred. In this case, we would want to check for the occurrence of pronouns.

A class of words used in this way is called a "marker." Markers are assigned to words by looking up each word in the text in a dictionary. After a marker has been assigned, the presence or absence of a marker can be tested in the course of disambiguating other words. The second disambiguation procedure is thus called a "marker test"; its technical details are outlined in the Appendix.

We have found a whole series of marker categories to be useful in disambiguation. In some cases, a marker is a syntactically oriented list of words, such as the markers "pronouns" or "determiners." Other markers are more semantic in their emphasis, as the markers "body parts," "emotions," "collective animate groups," or "human animate groups." We view the separation between syntactic and semantic properties as fuzzy at best, and the longer we work with these kinds of problems, the fuzzier it seems to get. For our purposes, marker categories are selected solely because they are useful in disambiguation.

Most of the important marker categories, such as "pronouns" or "determiners," consist of relatively short lists of words. Some categories that might have been useful had to be discarded because they would be composed of too many words. For example, it might be useful to have a marker category containing reference to all things that can be put to functional use (that is, the concept of "tool" in the widest sense), but this would be a very large category indeed. Fortunately, we find that it is the markers composed of short lists of words that are most needed in disambiguation.

Our present list of markers is shown in Figure 2. We have settled on this list of markers after considerable experimentation and experience in their use. A few markers may eventually be dropped because they are not used often enough to be justified. For the most part, however, we think that Figure 2 represents our final list of markers.

IDENTIFICATION OF WORD SENSES

The development of disambiguation rules can be divided into two parts: (1) the identification of word senses to be disambiguated, and (2) the writing of rules to disambiguate these senses.

The identification of word senses from the KWIC listing is usually a fairly straightforward matter, but sometimes problems arise. Some words have widely different, nonoverlapping meanings that are easy to distinguish. For example, "board" means either a piece of lumber or an administrative body, two quite different things. On the other hand, the meanings of "liberty," for example, range all the way from philosophical ideas concerning political systems or religious ethics to a soldier's week-end "liberty" from camp. One could argue that substantially different meanings of "liberty" are being used with each of the contexts—social, political, religious, and pragmatic—in which it occurs. If such a spectrum of meanings exists, where should the lines be drawn? Here we must rely mainly on the judgment of the person writing the rules. If the occurrences within part of the spectrum are infrequent, he is more likely to clump them together as being one sense than if there are many occurrences with different shades of meaning. If the only disambiguation rules he can find are unusually tortuous and inefficient, it is likely that he is attempting to read in distinctions that are not clearly evident from the context available, and that some further clumping may be more realistic.

As a guideline for when to distinguish word senses, we have compiled some general principles in the form of questions, indicating where a distinction that is important for many content analysis purposes is at stake and disambiguation should be attempted.

1. Is the word being used in an interpersonal or an impersonal sense? For example, the clock "works" is an impersonal use of the term, while for Jones to "work" for the ABC Corporation implies an interpersonal network.

2. Is dominance or submission, acceptance or rejection implied? For example, "work for" implies submission while "work with" implies equality and acceptance.

3. Is the word being used in a psychological or nonpsychological sense? Examples: "She melted in his arms" versus "The ice melted"; "She felt angry" versus "She felt the texture of the fabric."

4. Is the word used in a denotative or in an abstract sense? Examples: "They poured concrete into the form" versus "He is in good form."

5. Is action, cognition, or communication implied? Examples: "He ordered them from the florist"; "He ordered the ideas in his mind"; "He ordered the flowers when they arrived."

6. If a transitive action, is it being done to people or to things? Examples: "He ordered the men into the building" versus "He ordered the flowers into a symmetrical pattern."

7. Does it refer to a state of nature or is it man-made? If a process, does it occur naturally or must it be initiated by humans?

In addition we have been careful to distinguish accompanying syntactic shifts in senses of a word. Noun-verb distinctions are usually made in identifying word senses. Modifiers are separately identified when they have a somewhat different meaning from their noun or verb usage.

For our purposes, the success in identifying word senses is the usefulness of these senses in content analysis dictionary construction. During the summer of 1967, Dexter Dunphy and Philip Stone attempted to use the more than 1000 words already examined to start construction of the *Harvard Fourth Psychosociological Dictionary,* a continuation of the general-purpose content analysis dictionary efforts described in Stone et al., *The*

Determiners	(det)	Includes the following 6 subcategories:
Articles	(art)	a, an, the
Demonstratives	(dem)	Two subcategories
	(D1)	This, these
	(D2)	That, those
Genitives	(gen)	my, our, your, his, her, their, its . . .
Numbers	(numb)	Two subcategories:
	(card)	one, two, three . . .
	(ord)	first, second, third
Negative	(neg)	no, not, never, neither, nor
Prearticle	(pre)	both, each, either, all, any, enough, another, half, few, fewer, many, several, often . . .

Subcategories may be combined by writing the code combination:

(artdemgen) (artnumb), etc.

Likewise, "all determiners *except* genitives" may be indicated by writing:

(det - gen), etc.

Prepositions	(prep)	in, at, over, around, about, through, to, from, away, out, toward, down, up . . .
Pronouns	(pron)	Two subcategories:
Definite	(def)	Four subcategories:
nominatives	(def 1)	he, she, we, they, you
objectives	(def 2)	him, her, us, you
reflexives	(def 3)	myself, herself, themselves
other	(def 4)	one, someone, who, anyone, none, somebody, everybody, etc.
Indefinite	(indef)	it, itself, everything, anything, something, nothing, etc.
First Word of Sentence	(B)	The first word in a sentence.
Punctuation/conjunction	(PC)	Two subcategories:
Punctuation	(per)	period, exclamation point, question mark
Conjunction	(conj)	Two subcategories:
	(conj 1)	and, but, or
	(conj 2)	that, because, if, when, since, etc.
Interrogatives	(int)	interrogative words; who, what, where, when, how, why, etc.
Root word	(-)	The word as it occurs in the root form.
"ing" ending	(ing)	All words ending in "ing" except king, wing, ring, sing, etc., i.e., "ing" forms of verbs.
"ed" ending	(ed)	All words ending in "ed" except sled, reed, seed, etc., i.e., "ed" forms of verbs.
"s" ending	(s)	
Special verbs	(verb)	Eight subcategories:
Being verbs	(be)	be, being, is, am, was, were, etc.
Linking verbs	(link)	seem, feel, look, sound, see, means, appear . . .

Figure 2   List of markers used by disambiguation project.

Becoming verbs	(Vb)	become, remain . . .
Have	(hav)	have, has, had, having, etc.
Modals	(mod)	can, may, shall, will, must
Go verbs	(go)	go, going, gone, went, etc.
Do verbs	(do)	do, did, does, etc.
To	(to)	"to" as an infinitive
SEMANTIC		
Animate	(ani)	All self-propelling live objects—dog, cat, animal, etc. No pronouns or human nouns; only "lower" animals.
Human	(hu)	All human nouns: officer, man, teacher, parent, etc. Three subcategories:
Male	(male)	male humans
Female	(fem)	female humans
Kinship	(kin)	brother, sister, uncle, etc.
Collective	(coll)	All collective animate groups: mob, crowd, flock, herd, group, etc.
Abstract noun	(abs)	Three subcategories:
Abstract	(abs 1)	liberty, truth, honesty—abstract concepts, "isms," and "nesses."
Time	(time)	morning, o'clock, day, night, etc.
Distance	(dist)	mile, yard, foot, etc.
Social Place	(place)	house, factory, yard, street; this includes nonspecific places, such as the above, but *not* geographic, proper name locations such as Chicago, Africa, etc.
Body Part	(body)	head, heart, leg, liver, etc.
Political	(polit)	government, delegate, legislative, etc.
Economic	(econ)	spending, budget, fiscal, deficit, etc.
Frequency	(freq)	occasional, seldom, often, etc.
Color	(color)	orange, red, blue, green, yellow, etc.
Communication	(com)	newspaper, message, book, phone, print, pencil, etc. Any device used for communicative purposes.
Emotions	(emot)	anger, fury, distress, happy, etc.
Sensations	(sens)	touch, feel, hear, etc.

Figure 2   (*Continued*)

General Inquirer (1966). We found that having word senses available greatly changed our perspectives on what were useful, or even feasible, content analysis categories. For example, a category like "CONTROL-VERBS" is considerably changed in the effectiveness of its coverage by being able to include the appropriate word senses of such common words as "run" ("he runs his home town") or "handle" ("he knows how to handle the problem").

Generally, we found that the word senses that had been distinguished usually matched our needs or occasionally made somewhat finer distinctions than we needed. Despite the fact that we have had as many as fourteen people at a time working on the project, a good correspondence seems to have been achieved between the semantic distinctions made and the requirements of the kinds of content analysis dictionary building in which we are currently involved.

SOME EXAMPLES OF DISAMBIGUATION PROCEDURES

Let us consider several examples of disambiguated words to examine our procedures for recording word senses and disambiguation rules. By paying attention to the sequencing of disambiguation rules, fewer rules need be written and both computer storage space and computer processing time demands are reduced.

After the disambiguation procedures for a word are finished, the results are keypunched on cards. Figures 3 to 6 were produced from this keypunched information. A special IBM 1401 program controls the layout, produces subtotals and totals, and makes appropriate cross-checks. Summary figures on different aspects of these disambiguations are tabulated and printed at the end of the run. One product of our project will be to have, in this format, a volume for all the words disambiguated.

Our first example (Figure 3) is the word "matter" with 151 occurrences in the half-million KWIC sample, if we include the "s" and "ed" suffix occurrences along with occurrences of the root word. The different senses are identified in the top half of the figure. There are six senses with 3 of the 151 KWIC lines not found to be adequate context for identifying the word sense.

The rules for disambiguating these six senses are given in the lower half of Figure 3. Each test begins with a "P," "F," or "O," indicating whether the search is to be of the previous text, the following text, or the word being disambiguated. If "P" or "F" is specified, a number follows indicating how far away the search is to be carried. A test specification follows, preceded by a plus or a minus sign indicating whether it is the presence or the absence of the characteristic that is being tested. If the test word is in parentheses, it refers to a marker; otherwise, a word test is being performed. If nothing immediately follows, the column to the right labeled "sense" indicates the sense that should be assigned using the sense numbers given on the top half of the page. If a series of hypens follow, the satisfaction of the test is to be a condition for entering the next test to the right of the hyphens. If a test fails, the computer tests the rule below it, with control going back to the left when a new numbered rule occurs.

WORD SENSES

OVERALL FREQUENCIES	ROOT	--S	ED	ING	TOTAL
	127	23	1		151
1. NOUN — A SUBJECT, THING, AFFAIR, CONCERN, OR SET OF CERCUMSTANCES, UN-DERSTOOD TO REFER TO A PARTICULAR OCCASION BUT NO FURTHER PAR-TICULARIZATION.	42	20			62
2. NOUN IDIOM — -NO MATTER- - REGARDLESS OF.	35				35
3. IDIOM NOUN — -A MATTER OF...- - A -CASE-, A -CASE IN POINT- OF A THING, AFFAIR, SUBJECT, ETC., EMPHASISING THE QUALIFICATION -OF-.	22				22
4. VERB — TO BE OF SIGNIFICANCE.	13	3	1		17
5. IDIOM NOUN — (BE) THE MATTER (WITH) - AMISS WITH.	10				1C
6. IDIOM NOUN — -FOR THAT MATTER- - AS FAR AS THAT IS CONCERNED.	2				2
7. AMBIGUOUS — AMBIGUOUS.	3				3

SENSE	ROOT	--S	ED	ING	TOTAL
2	35				35
3	22				22
4	13				13
5	8				8
5	2				2
4		2			2
6				1	1
1	42	21			63

MISTAG   1

RULES
```
1.   P 1 + NO
2.   P 1 + A-------------------F 1 + OF
3.   P 4 + (MCDC)
4.   P 1 + THE----------------P 2 + (BE)
                             -F 1 + WITH
5.   P 3 + IT----------------O + (S)
                             -O + (ED)
6.   P 2 + FOR THAT
7.   OTHERWISE
```

RULE TOTALS ARE OFF   (OLS04)   COMPUTED SUM IS 148   BALANCE FAILURE   1

Figure 3

The information to the right of the rules in parentheses indicates what errors would be made using the rules of the KWIC sample. The number of errors and the sense numbers that would have been erroneously assigned are indicated.

As soon as tests are satisfied, testing stops and the sense indicated is assigned. Thus it makes sense to order the rules so that, on the average, as few tests are made as possible. The numbers in the five right-hand columns indicate how many cases are handled by the rule. Those rules handling the most cases are thus usually placed first.

In the rules for the word "matter," the tests for frequently occurring idioms are given first, thus allowing the computer to make these identifications quickly and not proceed further. The first rule looks to the preceding word to see if it is "no." The second rule first looks to the preceding word to see if it is "a," and, if so, looks to the following word to see if it is "of." Together, the first two rules take care of one-third of the occurrences of "matter" in the KWIC sample.

The third rule attempts to get at the verb sense of "matter" as in "it matters to me." The preceding four words are examined to see if any of them are modals (can, may, shall, will, must, etc.) or "do" words (do, does, etc.). If any of these are found, the word is classified as sense four.

The fourth rule tests for two idiomatic ways of using "matter" to mean "something amiss," namely, "be the matter" and "the matter with." The immediately preceding word is tested for "the." If "the" is found, then the second preceding word is tested for a "being" marker. If this fails, a test is made to see if the immediately following word is "with." If this also fails, we proceed to the fifth rule.

The fifth rule asks whether the previous word was "it" and, if so, whether the word "matter" has an "ed" or an "s" suffix. If these are satisfied, again sense four is assigned.

The sixth rule tests the phrase "for that matter." Notice that one word test can be applied to the string of words, "for that."

Finally, if all these six rules fail, the control branches to the "otherwise" condition and sense one is assigned. The comment in parentheses on the line labeled "mistag" indicates that this would result in one error with the KWIC sample, assigning sense one where sense four should have been assigned.

Observe that the disambiguation of sense one, which is probably the most difficult to identify, has been handled by delegating it to the "otherwise" position. Since 62 out of the 151 cases are sense one, about 40 percent of the occurrences will have to be processed through all six rules. Nevertheless, this strategy was probably the most efficient that could be discovered for disambiguating "matter" (in terms of number of rules needed and average computer time to disambiguate).

Additional comments on the bottom allow for noting any errors. The total number of mistags is reported with the label "balance failure." In addition, if cross-checks do not match, this is recorded. In this case, no attempt was made to write rules for the three ambiguous cases, so a message is printed, reporting that the rules only account for a computed sum of 148 cases, while there were altogether 151 cases in the sense listings.

Although many words can be disambiguated without recourse to markers, some words are notable exceptions. An example of the extensive use of markers is the word "stop" (Figure 4). Here six different kinds of markers are used. Notice that one set of rules for "stop" is quite effective at handling both the root word and the different suffix variants.

While a third of the occurrences of "stop" are identified as sense one by the "otherwise" condition, another 20 percent of the occurrences are classified as sense one by the second and third rules. The user should realize that he is not free to remove the second and third rules and assume that these sense-one occurrences will drop to the "otherwise" condition. Many of these occurrences might then be picked up and misclassified by any one of rules four to nine. Again, we emphasize that what has been constructed has been a system of rules rather than just a randomly ordered list. The ordering of the rules often contains considerable disambiguation power in itself, and must not be tampered with without checking the KWIC listings to see what the effect would be.

Notice that the set of rules developed for the word "stop" would make three errors in classifying the occurrences appearing in the KWIC listing. In this case, the person creating the rules, Mr. Pinney, was able to handle 182 out of 185 KWIC occurrences with ten rules, deciding that the other three cases were not worth additional rules. For our purposes, there is a time when it is more practical to cease and desist!

As final illustrations here, we present two very high frequency words: "think" and "like."

The multiple meanings of "think" have long been a particularly vexing problem for a number of General Inquirer content analysis applications. For example, a "think-involvement" index was dominant in Ramallo's (1966) study of field volunteers, an index that was complicated by the multiple uses of the word "think" itself. In view of these past struggles, it is a point of mild chagrin to find (Figure 5) that four rules can handle 1575 instances of this word with only one categorization error!

The word "like" (Figure 6) is an instance where the disambiguation of the suffix forms is quite different from the root, and they should be

WORD SENSES

OVERALL FREQUENCIES	ROOT	--S	ED	ING	TOTAL
	109	12	54	10	185
1. VERB — TO COME TO A STAND, CEASE MOVING, HALT, PAUSE...	55	7	35	3	100
2. VERB — TO CEASE FROM, DESIST, LEAVE OFF, DISCONTINUE	30	4	7	1	42
3. VERB — TO RESTRAIN, HINDER, PREVENT	23	1	10	6	40
4. VERB — TO BLOCK, OBSTRUCT, (-STOPPED UP DRAIN-)			2		2
5. NOUN — PLACE WHERE BUS, TRAIN, ETC. HALTS AND EXCHANGES PASSENGERS	1				1

RULES

		SENSE	ROOT	--S	ED	ING	TOTAL
1.	F 1 + (ING)	2	30	4	7	1	42
2.	F 1 + (PER)	1	12	1	9		22
3.	F 1 + AND	1	6	1	6		13
4.	F 1 + (PRCN)	3	9		4	2	14
5.	F 1 + (ARTDEM)	3	9			1	15
6.	F 1 + (GEN)	3	5				5
7.	P 1 + (EE)	4			3		3
8.	F 1 + UP	5			2		2
9.	P 1 + BUS	1	1				1
10.	OTHERWISE		37	5	20	6	68

(03S03)

BALANCE FAILURE 3   MISTAG 3

Figure 4

ENTRY WORD... THINK   IDENTIFICATION   679   DISAMBIGUATION GUIDE   PAGE   3

WORD SENSES

OVERALL FREQUENCIES	ROOT	--S	ED	ING	TOTAL
	1286	74		215	1575

1. VERB   TO HOLD AS AN OPINION, TO BELIEVE, SUPPOSE - --I THINK (THAT) HE IS WRONG--

| | 1109 | 58 | | 17 | 1184 |

2. VERB   TO MEDITATE, PONDER, COGITATE, EXAMINE, CONSIDER - --HE SAT THERE, JUST THINKING.--

| | 37 | 9 | | 161 | 207 |

3. VERB   TO CONCEIVE, IMAGINE, BRING TO CONSCIOUSNESS - --THINK OF AN EXAMPLE

| | 140 | 7 | | 37 | 184 |

RULES

		SENSE	ROOT	--S	ED	ING	TOTAL
1.	F 1 + ABOUT	2	37	8		57	102
2.	F 1 + OF	3	140	7		37	184
3.	F 1 + THAT	1	145	5		17	167
	(01S02) MISTAG						
4.	O + (ING)	2	964	54		104	104
5.	OTHERWISE	1				104	1018

BALANCE FAILURE   1

Figure 5

215

ENTRY WORD... LIKE   IDENTIFICATION   844   DISAMBIGUATION GUIDE   PAGE   4

WORD SENSES	OVERALL FREQUENCIES	ROOT	--S	ED	ING	TOTAL
		162	12	18	4	196
1. ADJECTIVE-ADVERB	HAVING THE SAME CHARACTERISTICS AS, SIMILAR TO, RESEMBLING, ANALOGOUS TO, IN OR AFTER THE MANNER OF, FOR EXAMPLE, JUST AS, AS, SUCH AS.	100				100
2. VERB	TO DERIVE PLEASURE FROM, TO FIND AGREEABLE OR CONGENIAL, TO FEEL ATTRACTED TO SOMEONE OR SOMETHING.	62	12	18	1	93
3. NOUN	THE ATTRACTION TO, PLEASURE IN, OR ENJOYMENT OF SOMETHING OR SOMEONE, FANCY OR INCLINATION.				3	3

RULES		SENSE	ROOT	--S	ED	ING	TOTAL
1. 0 + (-)------------(P 2 + DOMOD)) (01S01)	MISTAG	2	42				42
-P 1 + (DEF) (01S01)	MISTAG	2	16				16
-P 1 + LOOK		1	26				26
-P 1 + SOMETHING		1	6				6
-E 1 + (TO)		2	6				6
-OTHERWISE		1	66				66
2. P 1 + (DEF)		2	7	8			15
3. 0 + (ING)------------P 1 + (DET)		3				3	3
-OTHERWISE		2				1	1
4. OTHERWISE		2	5	10			15

BALANCE FAILURE   2

Figure 6

handled separately. With this separation, surprisingly few tests need to be made to categorize the word. In a sample of words to disambiguate "like," only two errors are made.

THE VALIDITY OF THE PROCEDURES

One haunting question in our work has been whether the rules we have developed are idiosyncratic to our KWIC sample. Will they really work on a new sample of text?

We have seen that in the examples of "stop," "like," and "think" the person creating the rules consciously allowed for a few errors to be made. In fact, these errors are very small in number when all words are considered. On our first 400 ambiguous words, covering about 49,900 KWIC occurrences, a total of 884 such conscious errors were allowed (or less than 2 percent). If in our past content analysis work using words rather than word senses, we have been misclassifying these ambiguous words 25 percent of the time[3], we have, indeed, eliminated better than 90 percent of the error resulting from word ambiguity—that is, if the error rate holds up as well on a new sample.

As yet, the disambiguation rules have not been put on a computer and used to content analyze text. There are, however, other sources of evidence as to how well our procedures will hold up on a new sample.

In several cases, our project member decided not to use all of the listing in the KWIC sample, but instead had the computer pick out a subsample and list it separately. In these cases, the KWIC listing was much longer than needed to develop rules to the point of being cumbersome to use. Rather than use all 1656 occurrences of "like" appearing in the KWIC sample, a subsample of 196 occurrences was used to identify the word senses and to develop the rules. Another example of where this was done is the word "that."

As a validity check, we selected another subsample of the root word "like." Since our original sample had 162 occurrences of the root word, we made our new sample the same size, and used the rules Mr. Speer had developed from the original sample to classify the new sample. First, the other sense distributions were surprisingly similar: 101 occurrences were found to be sense 1; 61 were found to be sense 2. The rules correctly classified 158 out of 162 occurrences. In fact, two of the four errors were instances of marginal English! The different rules for the word "like"

[3] A conservative estimate; remember that in the case of the word "kind" our error rate was 80 percent.

also had very similar disambiguating power in handling the new sample. The following shows that similar numbers of cases were handled by each rule in both samples.

Rule	First Trial	Second Trial
1	42 (1 error)	36 (2 errors)
2	16 (1 error)	21
3	26	26
4	6	8
5	6	3
6	66	68 (2 errors)
	162	162

In the case of the word "that," our original set of rules allowed for 23 errors in an original KWIC subsample of 250 occurrences (an unusually large percent), but this is not surprising considering the difficulty of the word. In a new subsample, the same rules were found to lead to 26 errors. Preliminary results such as these give us some confidence that our procedures will have considerable validity when applied to new text.

A DICTIONARY OF WORD SENSES

It should be evident from this description that our disambiguation procedures fit together as a logical package. Although new disambiguations may be added, the investigator is not free to remove semantic markers or delete rules without risking extensive consequences. Therefore, we have decided to put our disambiguation procedures, including semantic marker lists, into the General Inquirer as a package, and to provide a base dictionary of word senses, rather than words, which the investigator can classify as he sees fit. Instead of having the word "STOP" in the dictionary, the dictionary will have "STOP1," "STOP2," "STOP3," "STOP4," and "STOP5" as entries. The investigator can either assign tags to these entries, have the computer ignore their occurrences, or have the computer note their occurrences on what we call a "leftover list." If he decides to add a word sense that is not already included but occurs in his data (for instance, "STOP6" for "whistle stop" in analyzing the texts of Sinclair Lewis), this is also possible. To do this, he would have to go to the diambiguation part of the Inquirer and insert the additional test at the appropriate place in the disambiguation of the word "stop" in his own copy of the program.

CONCLUSIONS

Although we do not expect all of our disambiguation rules to hold true on new text as well as "like" or "that," we have considerable confidence in the outcome of our project and in the utility of these labors for future computer applications (including content analysis) that involve processing every day English. Our project has explored the alternative that disambiguation could take place prior to the analysis of syntactic structure, and we have found this to be a workable strategy. Indeed, we now think that future work on analysis of syntactic structures may be aided and simplified by being able to use word senses as initial data rather than words.

This chapter has attempted to trace the logic and development of our disambiguation project at Harvard. We have attempted to show how some of our initial gambles seem to be working out, and we have provided a glimpse of a few examples from the more than 1000 words that have already been examined. The last word on disambiguation will probably never be written, but during the coming year we hope to attain our initial goals. The task has taken longer than we originally anticipated; we hope that the results are worth the effort.

TECHNICAL APPENDIX

Let us comment briefly on the procedures for implementing the "word test" and the "marker test" (also known as a "tag test") routines in the General Inquirer system. At present the Inquirer is being maintained and improved for the IBM 7094 by Donald Goldhamer of the University of Chicago, and the IBM 360 OS by Philip Miller of Washington University, St. Louis. On the IBM 7094, the programming is in FAP or MAP while on the IBM 360, PL/I has been heavily used. In using the IBM 7094, core-memory size has always presented serious constraints on the size of the core-memory resident content analysis dictionary. This limitation is often greatly reduced in the case of the IBM 360, especially those installations with both fast access core memory and a large (one or two million byte) intermediate speed access core memory. If the program and the few very high frequency words of the dictionary can be stored in fast memory and the rest of the dictionary stored in intermediate speed memory, it becomes possible to use very large dictionaries in content analyzing text while keeping the costs quite low.

A number of the more recent options offered in both the IBM 7094 and IBM 360 versions are described by Donald Goldhamer in his chapter in this volume. Suffix chopping is now done in a series of stages, with dictionary lookup occurring after each stage and a marker assigned to the word for each suffix that is removed. A number of different contextual features, including word position in the sentence and document identification information, can be consulted in assigning tags.

For users who have a larger IBM 360 system, a number of further luxuries are now implemented (or eventually will be implemented) upon the release of more advanced versions of OS. The number of tags is increased from a maximum of 256 to 256^2 (that is, two bytes). Extra space is available for contextual test routines without having to impinge on the number of words included in the dictionary. The different phases of content analysis will again be integrated on one machine, drawing for each phase on as much of a partitioned machine as needed, rather than using two different computers. Tag assignments throughout the different phases of processing will be kept associated with the text word that caused their assignment, instead of being kept in an isolated string for each sentence.

In order to satisfy the needs of the word test routine, the text tagging procedure has now been made a multistage operation. In the first stage, suffix removal and dictionary lookup occurs. Thus, when the computer begins the second stage, it knows what the roots are of each word, and is able to make the word test, when directed, on the word root rather than the inflected word forms.

The first stage leaves each word of the sentence marked with a number, the number being the address of where the dictionary entry of that word is located in the computer. In the second stage, the computer may use this number to get quickly back to the dictionary entry. In addition, however, when the second stage begins, words in the sentence may be referenced not only by their alphanumeric characters but also by their much shorter dictionary address numbers.

The storage space required for word tests is considerably reduced if the number is used to identify test words rather than the actual alphabetic letters composing the word. The word tests are keypunched in the form indicated in the Goldhamer chapter, *infra,* with the test words spelled out. The conversion to the number form is automatically made by the computer when the word test instructions are compiled for storage in the computer memory. If a test word does not happen to be included already in the dictionary, the computer automatically adds a dummy dictionary entry for that word so that it can assign an address number.

The marker test procedure presents some more difficult problems that can be managed with strategies of different degrees of complexity and elaboration. The assignment of markers begins with the second stage. As markers are assigned to successive words across the sentence, it is a relatively simple matter to have the computer consult those markers that have already been assigned to previous words before assigning a marker to the word under consideration. If, however, the marker test involves searching further down the sentence, the marker test must be delayed until these assignments are made. The computer sets flags by these words and continues down the rest of the sentence. After the second stage is completed, it checks to see if any flags have been set.

Usually, at this point, the computer can go back to the flagged words, check the specified part of the sentence environment for the markers specified in the marker test, and make the assignments or branches based on the completion of the test. In some cases, however, a stalemate may arise. The disambiguation of word A in a sentence may require a marker test of word B, and the disambiguation of word B may require a marker test of word A. At present, upon finding such a stalemate, the computer skips over the marker test specified for the first of the words occurring in the sentence and goes on to make any further word tests or marker tests that may be part of its disambiguation procedure.

Hopefully, this bail-out strategy will result in a minimum of classification errors. The analysis could be carried a step further before resorting to a bail-out procedure, such as examining the remaining disambiguation tests of the other word to see if any of them result in assignment of the marker. If none of them assign the marker, then the marker test of the first word would have failed in any case and the next test can be safely entered. Such strategies, at this point, are being deferred until they prove necessary.

12 Some Long- and Short-term Trends in One American Political Value: A Computer Analysis of Concern With Wealth in 62 Party Platforms[1]

J. Zvi Namenwirth

Department of Sociology and Anthropology
University of Connecticut

Content analysis of American party platforms is a convenient way to assess changing magnitudes in a variety of political and social values. The information produced shares a "small talk" quality with much content analysis research and the bulk of historical inquiry: people like to know what others do, think, feel, and want. Furthermore, the distance of time imbues historical findings with an aura of mystery that, in turn, seems embedded in a yearning for descriptive knowledge of the past.

I, for one, have little patience with descriptive studies, particularly those in the area of values. My interest is abstract and theoretical. It is centered on a perennial issue in philosophy and social theory: Do changes in values cause changes in the social environment, or do they merely reflect social changes brought about by the internal dynamics of the social process? Where so many thoughtful men have held conflicting points of view, there is little reason to expect that the truth is either simple or unambiguous. Indeed, there is little reason to expect that the causal relationships between values and social change are the same for all times, all values, or all social processes.

Pondering these issues, Harold Lasswell and I came to believe that for social change to cause value change, the act must precede the thought,

[1] The research for this study was supported by an NSF grant to the Yale Political Data Program. I gratefully acknowledge the advice and assistance of my research staff at Yale, and especially thank Mary Frank Gaston for computations; Kathleen A. Dilzer for editorial work and secretarial help; and John R. Hall for data analysis, but even more for a great many innovative ideas, both substantive and methodological. I thank M. Harvey Brenner for his useful suggestions concerning time trend analysis, and Harold D. Lasswell for his stimulating ideas and value formulations that have been so essential to the approach of this chapter. Although the praise is shared by all, the final responsibility for the study is mine alone.

223

while for value change to affect the social order, the reverse must be true (see Namenwirth and Lasswell, forthcoming). Let me elaborate.

Aggregate social processes often cause social change. For instance, population growth (a favorite example in this line of argument) will change the per-capita distribution of social goods and it will often do so differentially for the different age groupings, the sexes, the various income strata, and other pertinent political groupings. The principles and mechanisms of the precipitant causes are rarely understood or even perceived by contemporaries. Nonetheless, the resulting social changes may produce severe dislocations in the distribution of social goods in terms of existing expectancies. These dislocations then cause changes in the various conceptions of what the ideal production, allocation, and distribution should be.

On the other hand, for value change to cause social change it must redirect the allocation of social goods and therefore steer the political mechanisms which control these allocations. But in order to redirect the production and distribution of goods, the decision process must gain control of the material as well as the social environment. Thus it follows that the increasing knowledge of the dynamics of things material and social and the subsequent mastery over these environments would make social change increasingly sensitive to changes in the value structure of society. At the same time, however, an increasing ability to gauge social preferences would tend to restrict leaders in their freedom to manipulate the social system. Therefore the net effect of these interactions between value change and social processes is not immediately clear.

These conceptualizations stress the mediating role of the political process in the nexus between value and social change. They explain the selection of party platforms for the study of value change and its social causes and consequences,[2] while predicating many other features of the analysis. Before advancing with this analysis, let me first define some of the basic concepts and describe the ways in which they were measured.

The distinction between goods and values is basic to the whole enterprise. Goods are the available resources of a society at any one time, and these resources are not restricted to material and economic resources per se, but include the whole range of scarce desirables such as friendship, recognition, health, or power. The aggregate sum of resources (their production, allocation and distribution, and especially the inequality of this distribution across pertinent social groupings) constitutes the social struc-

---

[2] For a more systematic justification of this conceptualization and the choice of party platforms, see Namenwirth and Lasswell (forthcoming).

ture of a society at one point in time. Social change, therefore, connotes a change in this structure of goods and its attributes over a period of time.

Values, on the other hand, are goal states, conceptions about the desirable (rather than actual) level of goods and their production, allocation, and the like in some future society. Value change implies changes in these conceptions of goal states and their hierarchical organization. Lasswell distinguishes between eight classes of values: power, rectitude, respect, affection, wealth, well-being, enlightenment, and skill (see Lasswell and Kaplan, 1950). My associates and I compiled, over the past few years, the *Value Dictionary,* which contains at present 76 categories, most of them subcategories of these eight classes of values. From these, I selected for this chapter the *Wealth* value, which was defined as "services of goods and persons accruing to the individual in any way whatever."

The *Wealth-other* category, my present value index, is a residual category, excluding the subcategories *Wealth-participants* and *Wealth-transaction,* and including a great variety of words such as affluence, capital, currency, factory, livestock, steel, and unemployment—195 words in all. Consequently, the residual category is poorly defined, but this lack of precision (if not validity) of the category is offset by a gain in reliability—a not uncommon dilemma in content analysis. To measure value change, I counted words, but as this is a favorite pastime in content analysis, I need not dwell on it here.

To measure social change in material goods, I used social indicators collected by various agencies of the United States Government and recorded in *Historical Statistics of the United States.*[3]

Finally, a common and untested assumption of the trade predicates the entire study. The assumption maintains that differential occurrence of the category *Wealth-other* from document to document presents a precise measure of differential concern with the category, while this concern in turn is an appropriate measure of the relative priority of the value in the total value scheme of each and all documents.

LONG-TERM TRENDS

Using standard General Inquirer procedures (Stone et al., 1966), I computed the percentage frequencies of the category *Wealth-other* for

---

[3] (U.S. Bureau of the Census, 1960:1965). Data for more recent years were obtained from the World Almanac (1965) and the National Industrial Conference Board's Economic Almanac (1964).

the platforms of the two major parties for each presidential election from 1844 to 1964 (62 platforms in all).[4] Figure 1 shows these frequencies.

A number of regularities are immediately evident. First, later platforms tend to devote more attention to the category than earlier platforms. Second, this linear tendency is interrupted by a number of peaks and valleys, the major positive deviations occurring in 1896 and in 1936. Finally, both parties' platforms tend to follow these patterns in a similar fashion, although the average Democratic concern exceeds that of the Republicans'. The magnitude of such general trends is so overbearing that many smaller and less pronounced regularities become overshadowed. For this reason, it is advisable to decompose the *Wealth-other* frequencies into long-term trends and campaign-to-campaign deviations from those trends.

Two linear regressions of the *Wealth-other* categories over time represent the long-term trends while making the fewest possible assumptions about those trends. Figure 2 supports the earlier observation that, on the average, concern with *Wealth-other* increases over time. Furthermore, the rate of increase (slope) is greater for the Democratic platforms than for those of the Republicans.[5] Thus, Democratic concern begins to exceed Republican concern about 1860, and it does so at an increasing rate. For the entire period of 1844 to 1964, the Republican party platforms lagged an average of about eight years behind the Democratic platforms.[6] Nevertheless, the two trends are, of course, highly correlated.

The estimation of long-term trends of these data by simple linear regressions has a number of theoretical and empirical limitations. At some point in time, the increase in *Wealth-other* concern must reach an upper limit determined by the semantic and grammatic structure of language. It would be impossible to write a political document containing only words classified

---

[4] With the exception of the 1964 platforms, I used the text compiled by Kirk H. Porter and Donald B. Johnson (1961). My source for the 1964 Democratic platform was the pamphlet. *One Nation, One People* (Democratic Platform Committee, 1964). The 1964 Republican platform was used as printed by the *New York Times* (July 12, 1964:56; July 13, 1964:20). Prior to 1856 there was no Republican party. The three earliest "Republican" platforms were actually Whig platforms, and this political equivalency is not beyond dispute. This point has been argued in Namenwirth and Lasswell (forthcoming).

[5] Similar findings hold true for other values with linear trends. When the trend is positive (for example, in the cases of concern with *Wellbeing-somatic* and the residual *Skill* category), the Democratic slope is greater than the Republican; when the trend is negative (for instance, in the *Rectitude-scope* and *Respect-indulgence* categories), the Republican concern decreases at a greater rate than does that of the Democratic platforms.

[6] The lag was calculated by taking the difference between the year the Democratic linear regression reached its average level and the year the Rebublican linear regression reached that same level.

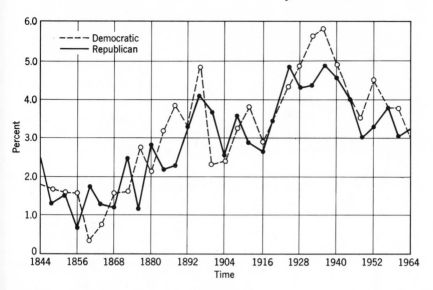

Figure 1 Percentage frequencies of *wealth-other* concern in Democratic- and Republican-party platforms (1844 to 1964).

as *Wealth-other*. For similar reasons, there must also be a lower limit to these linear trends. Therefore, linear change is possible only within a limited time range. Inspection of the actual observations indicates gross and systematic deviations from the linear trends. For all of these reasons, the long-term trends were also determined by using a procedure of moving averages.[7] Figure 3 shows this approach to *Wealth-other* nonlinear trends. While not contradicting any of the observations made concerning the linear trends, the trends, described by moving averages, present additional information.

The upward trend in concern with *Wealth-other* is not continuous, but shows two peaks followed by a decline. The peaks occur in the last decade of the nineteenth century and around 1932—both periods of severe economic dislocation. Furthermore, since the height of the depression of the 1930's, the average concern with the category has steadily declined.[8] Finally, the most striking feature of these long-term trends of the two parties is their similarity. Indeed, the correlation between these two trends is

[7] The five-entry moving average used here takes the mean of *Wealth-other* concern in the first through the fifth election years, the second through the sixth years, and so on.

[8] (Smith, et al., 1966:373). Using two different dictionaries, Smith et al. find a decrease in references to economic matters over time since 1928.

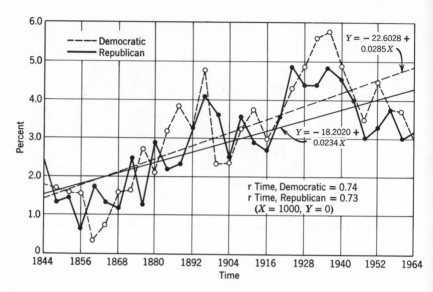

Figure 2 Linear regressions of time and *wealth-other* concern in Democratic- and Republican-party platforms (1844 to 1964).

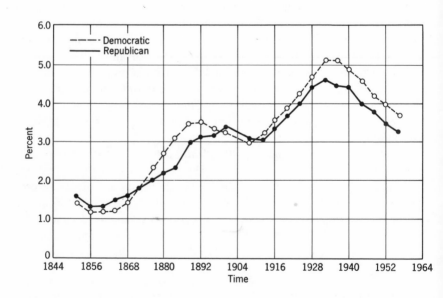

Figure 3 Twenty-year moving averages of *wealth-other* concern in Democratic- and Republican-party platforms (1852 to 1956).

.98, approaching identity. However, it is one thing to describe this relationship and quite another to account for its magnitude.

Let me distinguish briefly between three somewhat different theories. The idealist theory would argue that immanent cultural processes produce value changes that will be reflected in the components of the society (in this case, the political parties and their platforms). The similarity in the changes in value concern in the two parties is therefore a reflection of the changes in societal values, which result from some immanent process of spiritual growth and decay. A utilitarian theory would argue that for parties to maximize their appeal to the electorate, they must closely respond to changing value preferences of this electorate. (Notice that for such a utilitarian theory, the changing value preference of the electorate is a given, rather than a matter to be explained.) Finally, a materialist theory would argue the priority of social change (without necessarily explaining such social change), so that in this case the similarity in changing concerns is caused by one underlying process of social change.

Certain of these positions cannot be accepted or rejected by using empirical data; they are nondisprovable. However, we can notice the close correspondence between long-term trends of moving averages and one economic indicator.

Figure 4 depicts the long-term trend of the social indicator (percentage unemployed of the total labor force from 1912 to 1956) along with the trends of both party platforms' concern with *Wealth-other* for that same period.[9] In the long run, a change in the social indicator is correlated with changes in the Democratic platforms .94, and with changes in Republican platforms .91.[10] From these trends, however, it is not obvious whether long-term changes in the economic performance of American society pre-

[9] It was necessary to use moving averages rather than linear regressions to estimate these trends since unemployment data are unavailable for the years before 1900 and, since that time, the relationships are better described by parabolas than by linear regressions. The unemployment five-entry moving average was determined by averaging unemployment for five four-year periods ending in election years—moving by dropping the first four years and adding an additional four-year period, for example, 1901–1920 = first average; 1905–1924 = second average; and so on.
[10] Correlations of *Wealth-other* trends with other economic indicators were much smaller than those with unemployment.

Economic Indicator

		Wholesale Price Rate	Business Failure Rate
Wealth-other Trend	Democratic	− .26	.08
	Republican	− .43	.33

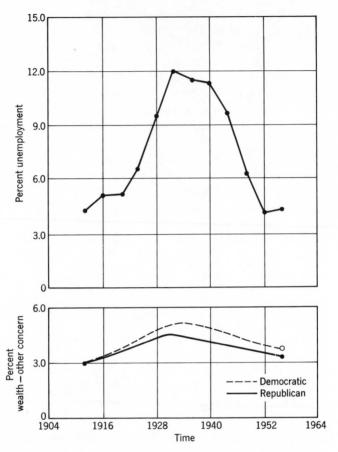

Figure 4 Twenty-year moving averages of unemployment and Democratic and Republican *wealth-other* concern (1912 to 1956).

cede, coincide with, or follow long-term changes in party platform concern with *Wealth-other*. To shed further light on this important issue, we compared the long-term trends in the party platforms' concern with *Wealth-other* with the long-term trends in unemployment for the year preceding the election, the year of the election, and the year following the election (see Table 1). In spite of the small number of observations, some generalization does seem warranted. First, value change does not precede economic performance, as can be seen in the smaller correlations in the third column of Table 1. Second, in the case of the Democratic platforms, the long-term trend of unemployment in years preceding the elections predicts long-term trends in *Wealth-other* concern somewhat better (it explains 10% more of the variance) than do long-term trends of unemployment in election years themselves. Inspection of scatter diagrams (see Figures 5–7) is illuminating.

The improved fit of the unemployment trend for the years preceding the election with the *Wealth-other* trend usually results from the reduced

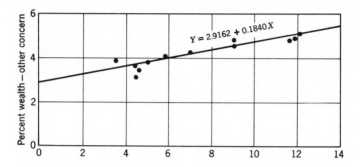

Figure 5 Percent unemployment—year preceding election.

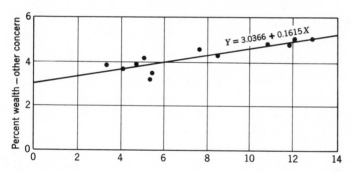

Figure 6 Percent unemployment—year of election.

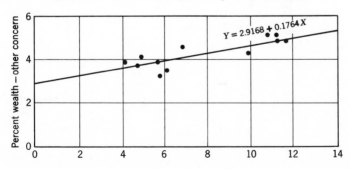

Figure 7 Percent unemployment—year following election. Linear regressions of unemployment with the Democratic *wealth-other* moving average.

spread about the regression line in low-unemployment periods. Although, from Table 1, the relationship for the Republican platform trends would seem to be of a different order, it is actually the same, as Figures 8–10 and Table 2 indicate. This is not apparent in the correlation coefficient because the relationship between long-term unemployment and *Wealth-*

Table 1. *Correlations of Long-term trends in unemployment with Wealth-other concern (N = 12)*

		Unemployment Rate		
		Year Preceding Election	Year of Election	Year Following Election
Wealth-other Scores	Democratic	.93	.88	.81
	Republican	.90	.90	.88

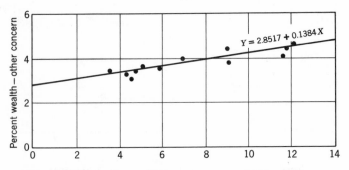

Figure 8 Percent unemployment—year preceding election.

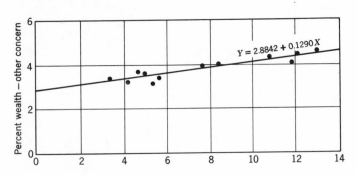

Figure 9 Percent unemployment—year of election.

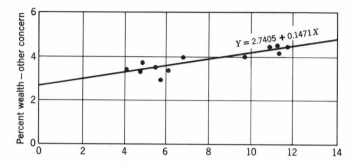

Figure 10 Percent unemployment—year following election. Linear regressions of unemployment with the Republican *wealth-other* moving average.

other trends is more curvilinear in the Republican than in the Democratic case.

For both Democratic and Republican trends, in periods of low unemployment there is an increasing spread about the regression line from years preceding, and years of, to years following the elections. Why would this be the case? It would seem that in times of economic prosperity, unemployment in the year of the election is less noticeable, the concern with the economy is less urgent, and the estimation of the economic situation is rather insecure (because the year is far from completed). Consequently, the perceptions of the state of the economy are determined more by the completed year preceding the election. On the other hand, in times of high unemployment, concern with wealth and the economy in general is so urgent and the failing state of the economy so obvious that the unemployment rates of the years preceding the elections and the election

Table 2. *Sums of Wealth-other residuals (absolute values) for periods of low unemployment**

		Unemployment		
		Year Preceding Election	Year of Election	Year Following Election
Wealth-other Scores	Democratic	1.3170	1.8629	1.9032
	Republican.	0.9774	1.2503	1.2943

* Periods & low unemployment are defined as those years in which the employment rate falls below the median for all the years under consideration.

years themselves equally well predict the trend of concern with *Wealth-other*.

The fact that the relationship between long-term unemployment data and concern with *Wealth-other* is more curvilinear in the Republican than in the Democratic case warrants one further remark. This difference between the two parties indicates that, in the long run, during periods of high unemployment, the increase in unemployment has a smaller effect on *Wealth-other* concern in Republican than in Democratic party platforms. In other words, in times of high unemployment, the Republican party is less sensitive to changes in unemployment than is the Democratic party. At any rate, to explain all these covariations the discussion has relied on a theory that long-term changes in economic performance cause long-term changes in value concern with *Wealth-other*.

SHORT-TERM CHANGES

Having discussed some internal and external dynamics of long-term trends, I shall now examine the deviations from these long-term trends. The long-term trend indicates the expected level of concern for a particular party and a particular time. Deviations (residuals) from this standard therefore indicate short-term movements which must be attributed to special circumstances of the political process, that is, the internal dynamics of particular elections: ahistorical issues, personality conflicts, and the like.

Plotting the Democratic and Republican residuals from the long-term linear trends,[11] Figure 11 further illustrates the shortcoming of the linear regression as an estimate of the long-term trend: the deviations are generally negative in the early and late periods and positive in the middle period, indicating that residuals from a linear regression are still affected by a long-term historical trend. For this reason, I prefer to use deviations from the moving averages (as described by Figure 12) for the analysis of residuals.[12]

Although at first the observations look somewhat random, closer inspection reveals a most interesting change over time in the nature of the relationship between Democratic and Republican campaign-to-campaign deviations. Whereas, in the earlier periods, the residuals are either negatively correlated or completely unrelated, in later periods they seem to be positively correlated.

[11] $R_i = Y_i - \hat{Y}$ where R_i = residual for a particular year, Y_i = *Wealth-other* concern for that year, and $\hat{Y} = a + bx_i$.

[12] $R_i = Y_i - Y_{i-2}$ to $_{i+2}$, where R_i = residual for a particular year, Y_i = *Wealth-other* concern for that year, and Y_{i-2} to $_{i+2}$ = moving average whose middle entry is *Wealth-other* concern in year i.

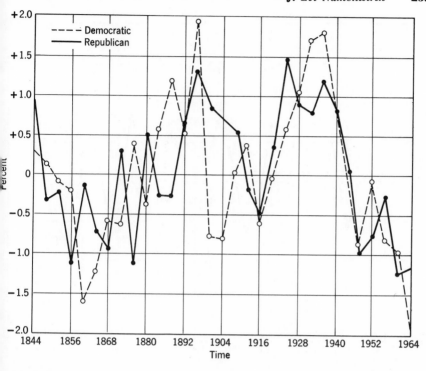

Figure 11   Democratic and Republican *wealth-other* residuals from linear regressions of raw scores.

   To demonstrate this change in the relationship, I correlated the residuals of the two parties for the first ten election years, then for the second through the eleventh year, and so on, producing a ten-entry moving correlation (shown in Figure 13). Although each of these correlations uses only ten entries, the trend from correlation to correlation is consistent enough to permit some further generalizations. Until about 1892 there appears a strong negative correlation between the two parties: if one party increases its concern with *Wealth-other,* the other party is likely to have decreased its concern with the category. If a common external variable is at all responsible for the pattern of these deviations, we must assume that each of the parties responded to that variable in an opposite manner. A more plausible explanation of this finding is that, in the absence of information about the values of the electorate and changes thereof, the Democratic and Republican parties depended on reacting to each other in their competition for the electorate, so that concern with the value *Wealth-other* was closely related to the dynamics of interparty conflict. This interparty conflict, as a main determinant of short-term fluctua-

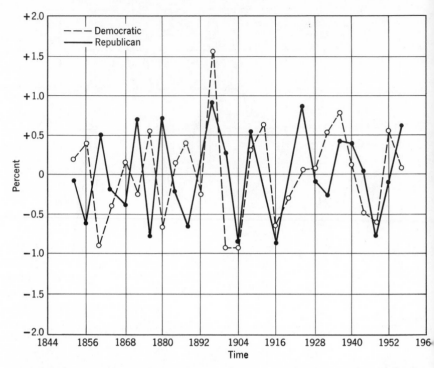

Figure 12   Democratic and Republican *wealth-other* residuals from moving averages.

tion in value pronouncements, was further intensified by the deep political and regional cleavages of the latter half of the nineteenth century: Slavery, the Civil War and Reconstruction. Political parties are unlikely to respond in similar fashion to electoral *Wealth-other* concern when they are so deeply divided on so many other issues. Once these overbearing domestic issues had been settled, the residuals became more positively correlated, for the campaign-to-campaign responses became more dependent on common external factors.

To demonstrate the relation of campaign-to-campaign deviations to these external factors in the late period, I correlated the residuals with a number of social indicators. Using election results as a political indicator,[13] I found that the correlation between the percentage of the popular

---

[13] Since this study deals only with the platforms of the two major parties, I calculated percentage share of the vote by using total votes cast for the two major parties as the base; for example, Democratic percentage = number of votes for Democratic candidate divided by the total number of votes cast for both the Democratic and Republican candidates. Correlations obtained by using election data computed by other methods (percentage of total electoral vote) were not so large.

vote for the Democratic candidate and Democratic *Wealth-other* residuals is .41, while the same correlation for Republican data is .16. The immediate interpretation would be that for the Democrats to talk about *Wealth-other* in excess of the expectation for the election year leads to a moderate increase in their percentage of the vote, while for the Republicans, such a response has little or no effect on election outcome. If indeed, this relationship were true, a utilitarian theory could explain the increasing long-term differentiation in concern with *Wealth-other* between the two parties. However, the short-term relationships between residual *Wealth-other* concern and Democratic share of the vote are largely spurious.

Let me explain. In the later period, during times of high unemployment, there was a greater likelihood that Democrats would win the presidency. The correlation of unemployment rate residuals with Democratic percent of the vote is .50, and with Republican percent of the vote, —.50. Furthermore, election-year unemployment residuals correlate with Democratic *Wealth-other* residuals .56, and only .01 with those of the Republicans. Figure 14 represents these triadic relationships in a causal model according

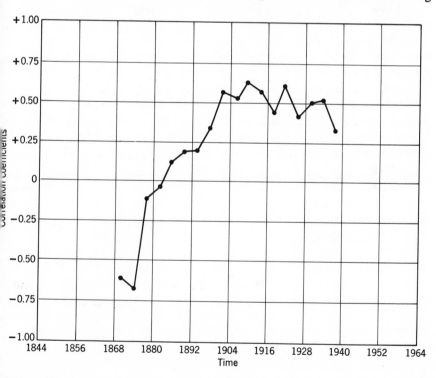

Figure 13 Ten-entry moving correlation of Democratic and Republican *wealth-other* residuals.

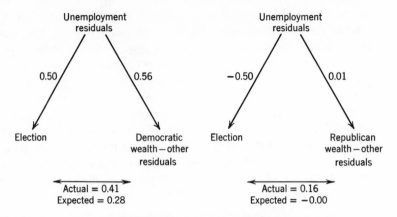

Figure 14 A causal model.

to Blalock.[14] In the case of both platforms, the conclusion seems clear: variation in unemployment causes for both parties a change in election results and, in the case of the Democrats, a campaign-to-campaign fluctuation in the concern with *Wealth-other*.

Causal analysis, using contemporaneous covariation, cannot settle the temporal priority of one variable over another. To bolster the causal conclusions, I examined the relationship while lagging and leading unemployment data. The results of this analysis are shown in Table 3.

This table indicates that for the Democratic platforms, change in unemployment precedes rather than follows short-term change in concern with *Wealth-other*. However, this time lag must be very small indeed, since unemployment in an election year is more strongly associated with

[14] (Blalock, 1960:337–343). Also see *Causal Inferences in Nonexperimental Research* (1961).

Table 3. *Correlations of unemployment rate residuals with Wealth-other residuals*

		Unemployment		
		Year Preceding Election	Year of Election	Year Following Election
Wealth-other Residuals	Democratic	.46	.56	.27
	Republican	−.05	.01	−.19

Table 4. *Correlations of economic indicator first-order differences with Wealth-other residuals*

		First-Order Differences		
		Wholesale Price Index	Consumer Price Index	Business Failure Rate
Wealth-other Residuals	Democratic	− .56	− .44	.35
	Republican	− .45	− .20	.30

Wealth-other residuals than is unemployment in the years preceding elections. Republican platforms, on the other hand, are completely insensitive to short-term changes in unemployment. Considering the fact that the Democrats are more dependent on the good will of the workers than are the Republicans, their greater sensitivity to unemployment is not surprising.

The question therefore arises: Are the Republican party platforms more sensitive to economic changes directly affecting their constituencies (for example, business failure rates and indices of inflation)?[15] As Table 4 indicates, both parties are sensitive to the selected indices. Considering the small differences in these correlations, overinterpretation is an obvious danger. Nonetheless, there is a clear trend: the Democrats are more sensitive than the Republicans in all cases. Also, the differences between Republicans and Democrats are somewhat larger in regard to the unemployment indicator than in regard to the indicators of inflation and business fortune and risk. Consequently, the analysis of short-term trends provides information about both the internal and external dynamics of these changes—which are, in most cases, at variance with the dynamics of long-term trends.

DISCUSSION

This chapter is a clear example of inference based on content analysis, and let us face the problem of inference without further delay. Inference

[15] In order to isolate short-term changes in these indicators, I used first-order differences (for example, election-year business failure rate minus the business failure rate for the year preceding the election). I felt that, in the case of inflation and business failure, the relative change from year to year would be a more pertinent indicator of the perceived state of the economy.

is but an elegant and fashionable term for after-the-fact induction.[16] Fishing is the more derogatory term, the sole difference being that in the case of inference, the fisherman not only counts his catch but also tries to account for it. To put it on a somewhat more formal basis, the rules of induction are either unknown, unspecified, or adapted to the findings at hand. It is this circular element in much induction that is especially bothersome in content analysis. It also explains the curious asymmetry of our procedures. It is relatively simple to infer from content the causal predispositions of the communicator—attitudes, values, drives, and so on—but by knowing the causal factors, it is hardly possible to predict the ensuing communications. What is clearly needed is a causal theory of communication, of symbol construction, and of language behavior.

My own inquiry is subject to the above limitations. However, analysis of *Wealth-other* concerns in party platforms does produce some interesting similarities and differences between the Democratic and Republican value articulations. In the long run, both parties move closely together, although the Democrats increase their concern at a greater rate than do the Republicans. Consequently, the discrepancy in these value articulations has tended to increase in the past 120 years. Still, in these long-term movements, the parties respond in a similar manner to the overall changes in the economic environment.

The short-term, campaign-to-campaign changes are quite another story. First, the relationship of value articulations between the two parties changes over time. Whereas in the earlier period (1844–1896) the parties move in opposite directions from campaign to campaign, in the later period (1896–1964) they tend to move in similar directions. Second, while the Democratic party responds immediately to short-term changes in the economy, the Republican party does not respond at all to unemployment and only weakly to other indicators of the economic cycle.

The present analysis confirms many well-known historical generalizations. It demonstrates that since the middle of the last century, the Democratic party has become the progressive party, while the Republicans have increasingly lagged behind. It confirms the greater sensitivity of the Demo-

---

[16] Unfortunately, the concept of inference is often used rather loosely in content analysis. Whereas, when speaking of inference, the content analyst refers to the problems of induction and inductive reasoning, the more frequent connotation of inference is one of deductive reasoning. The real issue, however, is of different order. Many scholars in the humanist tradition contend that inducing lawlike regularities from linguistic data creates a special class of problems over and above the already formidable problems of induction in general. The arguments for this contention seem to me to be spurious. See Namenwirth and Lasswell (forthcoming). For a recent discussion of problems and controversies in induction, see Kyburg and Nagel, eds. (1963).

cratic party to the fate of the economy, to the plight of the working man, as well as to the changing fortunes of the well-to-do. Since 1860, the Democrats have consistently shown greater concern for wealth than the Republicans; they seem to be more in tune with the materialism so characteristic of our industrialized society. The Republican party, on the other hand, is either not sensitive at all, or far less sensitive than the Democratic party to economic change, particularly in regard to short-term changes. This indifference to changing social circumstances can well be explained in terms of political philosophy: it is the earmark of conservatism. Conservative value articulations remain directed toward the preservation of past conceptions of historical reality and ideological reconstructions.

The preceding interpretations stand in need of further confirmation. After all, these observations are based on the internal and external dynamics of only one value subcategory. The projected analysis of all the other categories in the *Value Dictionary* may well lead to further specification, modification, if not outright rejection of the present interpretations. This is especially true in regard to propositions about the major theoretical issue. Yet in respect to certain wealth values, the conclusion is obvious. In the total scheme of values, social changes cause rather than follow the changing priority in wealth values, at least since the beginning of this century. Whether the same is true for all values (and if so, whether it is true to a similar extent) is an empirical question that Harold Lasswell and I hope to answer. The present exercise has been useful in sharpening the tools of analysis, measurement procedures as well as conceptual instruments for this more encompassing endeavor.

13 Individual and Cultural Patterns of Fantasized Flight

Daniel M. Ogilvie

Social Relations
Harvard University

In 1955, Henry Murray wrote a case study titled "American Icarus" in which he reintroduced a personality dimension labeled ascensionism. The concept "ascensionism" is explained in the following passage:

> This is the name I have given to the wish to overcome gravity, to stand erect, to grow tall, to dance on tiptoe, to walk on water, to leap or swing in the air, to climb, to rise, to fly, to float down gradually from on high and land without injury, not to speak of rising from the dead and ascending to heaven. There are also emotional and ideational forms of ascensionism—passionate enthusiasm, rapid elevations of confidence, flights of imagination, exultation, inflation of spirits, ecstatic mystical upreachings, poetical and religious—which are likely to be expressed in the imagery of physical ascensionism. The upward thrust of desire may also manifest itself in the cathection of tall pillars and towers, of high peaks and mountains, of birds—high-flying hawks and eagles—and of heavenly bodies, especially the sun. In its most mundane and secular form, ascensionism consists of a craving for upward social mobility, for a rapid and spectacular rise of prestige (Murray, 1955:631).

To a large degree, according to the above description, everyone is in one or more respects ascensionistic. Every child wishes to stand and grow tall. It is not rare to witness a youngster climb a couch or a tree. Status concerns and interest in upward social mobility, at least in our society, is common. In a sense, then, ascensionism characterizes us all. It is as though a chunk of our physical and social behaviors has been isolated and named and possibly nothing more.

However, this dimension takes on special proportions when it is considered in the light of the case of Grope, the hero of Murray's conceptualization. This college student, who was no standout among his classmates, characterized himself as a "small frog in a big puddle." But this had not always been the case. In grammar school and, to a lesser degree,

243

in high school, he had experienced enviable success scholastically, physically, and socially. Illness during the sixth grade and halitosis in grades eight through ten were blamed for his physical (athletic) and social setbacks. However, his late adolescent passivity and low need for achievement were combined with a still active need for recognition and excitance (enjoyment of novelty, excitement, thrills, spectacles, and the like), and this package of needs forewarns us that Grope had not given up on himself as a possible hero. "I am just biding my time and waiting for the day when my soul will ignite and this inner fire will send me hurtling (two rungs at a time) up the ladder of success." Here ascensionism is clear, but it becomes even more prominent when Grope's fantasy life is considered.

What terrestial prominence Grope had lost during the course of adolescence was regained many times over in fantasy. Murray writes, "It is when weighed in the scales of imaginary activities that Grope stands out as an unduplicated wonder . . . Having rejected most opportunities to participate in real endeavors, he had little to interfere with his enjoyment of countless private shows of his excelling fitness for irreal endeavors, mostly of heroic scope" (Murray, 1955:616). Taking up a substantial portion of his daytime fantasies and nightly dreams were images of himself and others rising in the air, flying, or even more dramatically, shooting through space and landing on Mars. These images of self-propelled or assisted flights were not new additions to Grope's imaginary repertoire. As early as age 8, Grope dreamed that he rode through the sky on the rump of a maid whose breasts had touched off an "interior excitement" the day before. Fantasies of urinating on women from the sky were also prominent at an early age.

In the context of this description of Grope's fantasy life, ascensionism is more than just a wish to stand erect, to dance on tiptoe, more than enthusiasm. It is a dimension that is predominant and psychologically salient in Grope. It is not an arbitrary chunk of conceptual possibilities. For Murray, it is one of six interrelated components of Grope's covert personality. Two of these components—(1) cynosural narcissism ("a craving for unsolicited attention and admiration, a desire to attract and enchant all eyes") and (2) falling ("an undesired or accidental descension of something") and/or precipitation ("a consciously or unconsciously desired calamitous descension")—are combined with ascensionism to form an "integrate," the Icarus Complex. The three remaining covert components of Grope's personality are urethral erotism (a fixation at the urethral-phallic stage, the "apperception of sex in urinary terms"); craving for immortality (the yearning for perpetual existence); and depreciation and enthrallment of women ("a conception of women as objects to be utilized for narcissistic gain"). This last component is coupled with some degree of homosexuality and "suffusing" femininity. Urethral erotism is viewed as vital to the formation of this complex, whereas craving for immortality and depreciation and enthrallment of women are viewed more as offsprings of it.

To give a complete description of Murray's original conceptualization of the Icarus Complex would entail a full description of his case study, including the supporting evidence from which his argument was drawn. All that can be accomplished by the above brief summary of covert components of Grope's personality is a spotty transmission of the flavor of the case study and an introduction to the elements that are viewed as crucial to this personality integrate.

The most intriguing aspect of this case description is its apparent generalizability. Grope is both an individual with a unique style, a unique set of values, needs, experiences, hopes, fears, and frustrations *and* a member of a class or personality "type." Grope does not stand alone as the only individual who has fantasies of flight. His history of enuresis does not make him the world's champion bedwetter.

Although the Icarus Complex has not received the universal acclaim that has been showered on the Oedipus Complex, Murray's description of the complex has stimulated several unpublished studies. Joseph Lord (1952) documented a positive relationship between enuresis and the inclusion of ascensionistic-descensionistic themes in responses to projective devices in young boys. James Ciarlo (1964) found a higher incidence of "generalized ascensionism" (climbing, jumping, making model airplanes) in childhood play of potential pilots than he did in the descriptions of early play patterns of young men not interested in flight as a career. Two additional studies have partially documented a relationship between Icarianism and gang delinquency (Ogilvie, 1962; Hartman, 1964). Finally, Guptill (1965) records support for his hypothesis that sports parachutists maintain the complete array of Icarian components in fantasy productions, whereas experienced pilots suppress all components except for ascensionism.

To a substantial degree, the studies cited above were not related in an integrated way. This has left us with something less than a solid core of knowledge about the development of flight fantasies; why they linger in the imaginations of some individuals, vanish from the minds of others, and never appear in any form for still others. Nonetheless, these studies have left us with an orientation by tentatively documenting Icarianism as a male phenomenon and, furthermore, documenting the relationships between the development and maintenance of Icarian fantasies and female dominance and/or fear of women and/or feminine identification.

THREE CASE STUDIES

In an attempt to clarify and systematize some of the knowledge already gained and hopefully to add to that knowledge, I undertook three case studies of individuals who, in one way or another, manifested exaggerated Icarian characteristics. This effort to understand the psychodynamics of Icarianism through individual case studies reveals a conviction that a useful way to gain leverage on a problem of personality development is through concentrated investigations of individuals. After individuals have been studied and ideas have been generated, the next step (from my point of view) is to systematically investigate variations of the same phenomenon by using a broader data base. It is the latter step of the simplified two-step procedure that will receive emphasis in this chapter (the study of folktales) but that discussion must be prefaced by a brief presentation of findings from individual case studies.

The three individuals who provided me with a major proportion of ideas for this investigation were a student (studied directly), an artist, and a murderer (both studied through secondary sources). The student, Tonka, was a college undergraduate who, over the course of several months was involved in interviews, wrote a lengthy autobiography, and completed a battery of tests including TAT compositions and Rorschach responses. Tonka's outstanding Icarian endeavor began at the age of 7 when he initiated a project of constructing an instrument out of a battery, wire, and an old fan that, when strapped to his back, would carry him into space. Despite two years of intermittent labor, lack of mechanical knowledge plus a weak battery led to the ultimate failure of this otherwise gallant effort.

The artist is Marc Chagall, who was included in this study because of a strong tendency to paint vivid figures floating above the ground, often burning and/or surrounded by water. In addition to providing us with his paintings (the source of our initial attraction to Chagall), he also has written an autobiography, *My Life,* in which he captures and sensitively describes his early thoughts, experiences, and fantasies. In this autobiography our initial impressions of a possible Icarian are confirmed when cathection to fire and heat, the apperception of sex in urinary terms, narcism, the desire for immortality, bisexuality, and descension appear with remarkable clarity.

Finally, the murderer was Perry Smith, the self-admitted and subsequently executed killer of the Clutter family; the pathetic hero of Truman Capote's "nonfiction novel" *In Cold Blood.* Our attraction to Perry as an Icarian was his repeated fantasy of being enfolded, lifted from the ground, and carried away to paradise by a huge, yellow, parrot-faced bird.

On a most general level and, consequently, an unsatisfactory level, the results of the case studies of these three individuals suggest that fantasies of flight are developed and maintained as pregenital expressions of sexuality. In each of the three cases we can trace the course of development that led to psychological fixations of a pregenital nature. To be completely fair to one's audience—not to mention fairness to one's own argument—every piece of evidence that led to the above conclusion should be presented. Unfortunately, this cannot be done in a short amount of space. Therefore, just a few examples of the sorts of information on which this conclusion is based will have to suffice.

Marc Chagall

At the age of five or six, according to his autobiography, Chagall began to study with a rabbi tutor whom Chagall called (appropriately) the "little bedbug." "We didn't send for him. He came of his own accord, the way a marriage broker comes or an old man carries away corpses." At the end of each week of studying, on Friday, this rabbi took Marc to the baths and made him stretch out nude on the bench. "Birch rods in hand, he examined my body closely, as if I were the Bible." Although Chagall gives no indication of whether he enjoyed these inspections, we might suppose that these examinations had a stimulating and arousing effect on the young boy.

One Saturday, instead of going bathing in the river (an activity he enjoyed), Chagall's mother sent him to study the Bible with his rabbi. "However, I knew at that hour the rabbi and his wife, completely undressed, slept silently in honor of the Sabbath. Well then, let's wait till he puts on his pants!" Chagall knocked on the door and opened it quickly. He was immediately attacked by the rabbi's dog—"a reddish-brown mongrel, old and bad-tempered, with sharp teeth." The dog was "mad" and Chagall reports that it took twelve bullets to kill the animal. Young Chagall was sent to Petersberg for medical attention and was given four days to live. "Charming. Everyone takes care of me. Each day brings me closer to death. I'm a hero."

Gradually, Chagall recovered and was able to return home. When he entered his house he found it full of women, grave men, and noise. Suddenly there was the piercing wail of a newborn infant. "Mama, half naked, pale, with a faint pink flush on her cheeks is in bed. My younger brother had just been born." As if to reinforce the already solid association between sexuality, biting, blood and death, Chagall witnessed the next scene:

. An old man, murmuring the prayer, cuts with a sharp knife the little bit of skin below the newborn babe's belly. He sucks the blood with his lips and stifles the babe's cries and moans with his beard.

Pathetically Chagall concludes by writing, "I am sad. Silently, beside the others, I munch pastry, herring, honey-cake."

For Chagall, genital sexual maturity had been blocked by fears of genital mutilation. Symbolically, this is expressed in many of his paintings in which he depicts males with mangled (or absent) arms and legs. In other sketches and paintings, he leaves out the genital area of his figures completely.

In primary school, when others masturbated, Chagall was confused; he claims he did not understand. "I don't know why, but at that time I began to stammer." When his professors asked him to recite in class, he could not, "And yet I knew my lesson." Now both weapons were gone. Genital erotism was stifled and, since sexuality was an oral phenomenon for him (the dog made certain of that), even speaking became, at times, impossible. When he was instructed to demonstrate his knowledge, he could not. "I felt as if a reddish dog had run up and was barking over my prostrate body. My mouth was full of dust. My teeth hardly looked white at all."

From that point on, erotic feelings were expressed in terms of rivers (urethral erotism) floating bodies, and rising objects. This primitive, diffuse, decentralized expression of sexuality was "necessitated" by an unsurmountable fear of and confusion about more direct forms of sexual expression. For example, Chagall spent much of his adolescence paying "assiduous attention to girls." He claimed to know very little about the art of making love but the sight of girls tormented him. During this period he spent much time on roofs and loved to watch fires. At others times he writes, "You don't know how happy I am—and I don't know why—lying feet under the bed (his mother's bed) or on a roof, in some sort of hiding place. Under the bed—the boots. I lose myself deep in thought. I fly above the world."

Perry Smith

Our second reconstruction of possible reasons for an inability to successfully reach a stage of genital maturity comes from the biographical materials gathered on Perry Smith by Truman Capote. A series of incidents that stood out in Perry's mind occurred when he was between the ages of three and five. Ailments had forced his parents, Tex and Flo, to retire from their main occupation of participating in rodeos throughout the Southwest. They settled in Nevada where Tex involved himself in picking berries and making "bootleg hooch." It was at this time that Flo began to "entertain" sailors.

When he (Tex) came home a fight ensued, and my father, after a violent struggle, threw the sailors out and proceeded to beat my mother. I was frightfully scared, in fact all of us children were terrified. Crying. I was scared because I thought my father was going to hurt me, also because he was beating my mother. I really didn't understand why he was beating her but I felt she must have done something dreadfully wrong.

Later, in Capote's report, he cites Perry's discussion of the time he and his brother and sisters watched a Negro hired hand having intercourse with his mother. When Tex returned home he evidently "suspected what was happening" and a memorable fight—the final battle—took place between Flo and Tex. Weapons included horsewhips, scalding water, and kerosene lamps. The fight led to the parents' separation, and Flo took the children to San Francisco. This also marked the beginning of Perry's tour of orphanages and detention homes.

It was during Perry's stay in a Catholic orphanage that the parrot first entered his fantasies and became a frequent and welcome visitor in his dreams. A persistent problem for Perry at that time (and a problem that continued until his death) was bedwetting. To the nuns running the orphanage, this was an unnecessary habit that had to be discontinued. Their method of cure consisted of beating Perry with belts or a flashlight everytime a wet bed was discovered. Other forms of treatment for Perry's incontinence included submersion in cold water (Perry attributes his catching pneumonia to this method), and placement of an ointment on his penis that "burned something terrible."

The above experiences influenced Perry's development in a variety of ways, but the emotional consequences of these experiences stand out as all-important. These experiences led to severe sexual repression, on the one hand, and an irreversible unconscious association of sex with aggression, on the other. Beatings, to him, had sexual implications. His mother was beaten for sexual misbehavior. He was beaten by nuns for his own brand of uncontrolled sexual expression (urethral erotism). Hence Perry could not achieve a level of mature sexual expression. In fact, he had "no respect for people who cannot control themselves sexually." He frequently argued with Dick (his accomplice) about his "disgusting" sexual involvement with women.

Perry never gave the slightest hint of progressing past the urethral-phallic stage of psychosexual development and, aside from finding some sexual outlet through aggression, total satisfaction for him was expressed in terms of being a passive recipient of nurturance and care, of being lifted by the huge parrot to a place that provided an inexhaustible supply of food. In his dreams and fantasies he searched for that unrecoverable state of infantile bliss. His unconscious theory of sexual expression was that of a narcissistic body (his own) being passively erected to a height where he attained a sense of "unassailable power."

Tonka

Briefly, and with no detail, Tonka, our student who at an early age tried to construct a flying machine, did not experience a trauma equivalent to Chagall's nor did he receive the consistent maltreatment and neglect experienced by Perry Smith. Instead, a general anxiety about sexual involvement began quite early with an eroticized relationship between himself and his mother. This relationship was made even more intense by the absence of his father during much of the first three years of Tonka's life. Fantasies of being destroyed, of never being able to separate himself from a seductive but aggressive mother (and never being certain that such separation would be advisable), seemed to have retarded (or, at least, slowed) normal emotional maturation. His attempt to fly is viewed as a desire to make a sudden break from his mother ànd at the same time, ironically, be reunited with her. In Tonka's case, fantasies of active and dramatic voyages into the sky faded when forced passivity (a severe illness) initiated the attention and narcissistic gratification that he craved.

Again, the conclusion drawn from these case studies about the underlying meaning of fantasized flight is that it symbolizes an undifferentiated eroticized feeling (much like the feeling an infant must experience when he is lifted into his mother's arms) that is the infantile equivalent of genital erotism. Possibly a better way to state the case is that feelings associated with genital sexuality are replaced by remnants of earlier "safer" feelings associated with a sense of security. The fantasy is indicative of a regression to, or an ability to progress from, a narcissistic (pregenital) stage of psychosexual development.

ANALYSIS OF FOLKTALES

Now let us discuss our efforts to translate ideas, suggestions, and insights gathered from research on Icarianism into a systematic exploration of folktales from a wide variety of societies. Folktales have been chosen as a reasonable focus for the continuation of this study because, like dreams and fantasies, they are thought to contain psychologically meaningful themes that, when looked at carefully, reveal underlying patterns of needs, thoughts, frustrations, and desires. An obvious difference between individual fantasies and societal folktales is that the former is produced for the benefit of one mind and the latter is produced for the enjoyment of many. Therefore, the likelihood is small that a series of folktales will tell us much about specific individuals within a society, and we might expect to find less sharply delineated themes in folktales than we find in dreams. Yet, our research is based on the assumption that folktales contain culturally important themes and, for some societies, *a* relevant theme may be the Icarian theme. That is, just as there are individual differences with respect to the expression of a theme, there may be cultural differences with respect to the expression of the same theme. In a similar vein, an exploration of other themes that covary with the expression (or lack of expression) of Icarian themes in folktales may correspond in some respects with the covariation of themes we have seen in the study of individuals. In other words, we have documented and temporarily are proponents of a particular point of view concerning the dynamics of Icarianism on the level of personality development of individual people. A careful description of the interrelation of Icarian themes with other themes on a cultural level may reinforce some of our notions. At the same time, we have attempted to make our descriptive procedures broad enough to allow for the emergence of new insights and fresh perspectives into the operation of this seemingly unique and at least partially universal package of themes.

Most of the folktales used in this study were selected by William Davis in conjunction with an investigation of the relationships between use of alcohol and thematic content of folktales (Kalin, 1967; McClelland, 1966). This sample of folktales was supplemented by parts of a sample collected by Benjamin Colby as part of his efforts to construct an instrument to measure between-culture differences (Colby, 1966a, 1966b, 1967). A total of 626 folktales from 44 primitive societies were used in this study. On the average, there were 14 folktales for each of the 44 societies. An effort was made to select societies that are representative of the five major cultural areas of the world. Although the ideal of equal representation was not realized, Figure 1 indicates that partial equalization was obtained.

Since the grand total number of words in all folktales exceeded 355,000, the analysis was facilitated by (and could not have been accomplished without) the use of a computer system of content analysis called The General Inquirer (Stone et al., 1966). For our purposes it is sufficient to describe this system as a computer searching and matching operation. The computer reads the first word of a document (in this case, the first word of a folktale), searches for that word in a dictionary that is stored in the computer, and if that word is located in the dictionary, attaches the meaning to it that is prescribed by the dictionary specification. When the first word has been located and defined, or not located and consequently not defined, the second word is read in and the search operation is continued; and so on, to the end of the document. After the document has been "processed," the investigator has a number of options available to him; the simplest of which is instructing the computer to

Africa	Insular Pacific	Eurasia	North America	South America
Ashanta	Buka	Ainu	Arapaho	Araucano
Basuto	Dusun	Baiga	Creek	Carib
Ganda	Ifaluk	Chenchu	Hupa	Cuna
Kikuyu	Ifugao	Chukchee	Jicarilla	Jivaro
Lamba	Fiji	Khasis	Kaska	Taulipang
Lango	Maori	Lakher	Naskapi	Toba
Nama	Ulithi	Lepcha	Ojibwa	Tucuna
Thonga		Palaung	Omaha	
Tiv		Tanala	Paiute	
			Teton	
			Zuni	
			Papago	
$n = 9$	$n = 7$	$n = 9$	$n = 12$	$n = 7$

Figure 1   Cross-cultural distribution and names of societies used in Icarus study.

total the number of times a specific definition has been applied to words in a document.

The "dictionary in a computer" is not Webster's. Like *Webster's Dictionary*, a content analysis dictionary contains words and their meanings but, unlike *Webster's Dictionary*, the meanings attached to words are variables that, for one reason or another, are important to the investigator and the number of these variables (or definitions) is finite. For example, the dictionary developed for this investigation, the Icarus Dictionary (Ogilvie, 1967), contains only 74 possible definitions and these definitions were attached to approximately 2500 words. These definitions are given in Figure 2. (The variables are printed in small letters under the various subheadings that are intended as a device to systematize an otherwise curious list of categories.)

The definitions included in Figure 2 were derived from a variety of sources. Some of the variables came from Murray's article, "American Icarus." Others were included as a result of the theoretical and empirical efforts of Lord, Ciarlo, Hartman, and Guptill. Other concepts that emerged from the case studies of Chagall, Smith, and Tonka were also translated into content analysis categories. Each category (variable) defines a series of words which in some cases denote and in other cases connote that particular concept. For example, the category "ascend act" includes verbs that imply the act of physical rising. Flap, flutter, climb, leap, rise, and (the idiom) "go up" are examples. By contrast, "descend act" defines words such as dive, plunge, slide, topple and (the idiom) "climb down."

PEOPLE
self
selves
other
kin male
nonkin male
kin female
nonkin female
kin neuter
CREATURES
animals, fish, and insects
birds
ELEMENTS
atmosphere
fire and heat (denotative)
fire and heat (connotative)
cold
water (denotative)
water (connotative)
TIME
time (long)
time (short)

MOVEMENTS AND ACTIONS
instrumental activity
leave
return
move swift
move slow
move (general)
stay
ASCEND
ascend act
high natural object
high artifact
high mythical object
height (denotative)
height (connotative)
DESCEND
descend act
low natural object
low artifact
low mythical object
depth (denotative)
depth (connotative)
RESTRAIN
restrain (denotative)
restrain (connotative)

ORAL
ingest
hunger
oral supply
oral (connotative)
oral bodypart
ANAL
anal imagery
anal bodypart
clean
SEX
sex (denotative)
sex (connotative)
sex bodypart
AGGRESSION
aggressive act (physical)
aggressive act (nonphysical)
aggression (general)
aggressive implement
EMOTIONS
positive affect
sadness
fear
anger

COGNITIVE PROCESSES
thought
communicate
sensation
END STATES
success
failure
peace
strength
weakness
death (denotative)
death (connotative)
OTHER TAGS
affiliation
religion
pomp
narcissistic artifacts
release
change

Figure 2 Tag categories of the second Icarus Dictionary.

253

Obviously, the development of a content analysis dictionary to be utilized in such an investigation is of critical importance. Again, space prohibits an adequate discussion of all the issues, considerations, and problems that must be confronted, explored, and solved during the course of dictionary construction. A satisfactory dictionary cannot be developed in a week or two weeks; instead, the major portion of a year or more may be consumed before an investigator (or, more certainly, his colleagues) is satisfied with his variables and the words that are defined by them.

Icarianism in Folktales

Armed with the folktales and a method for their analysis, the first step of this research was undertaken. As mentioned above, Murray first named and isolated the Icarus Complex as an integrate of the following themes: flying, falling, fire, water, immortality, and narcism. Although the expression of one of these themes does not invariably lead to the expression of them all, a positive relationship among the themes had been demonstrated through case studies. The first questions to be asked in this investigation are: "Do these same themes tend to cluster in folktales?" "Does the appearance of one of these themes predict with any degree of certainty the appearance of the others?"

Before processing the folktale materials on the computer to determine the existence of a cluster of Icarian related themes, the collection of folktales from each society was divided in half. Since the average number of folktales for each society was 10, this division reduced the average to 5. The first half of each collection of folktales from the 44 societies was then processed by The General Inquirer using the Icarus Dictionary. Percentage scores for each variable for all documents for each society were punched on summary IBM cards. (Percentage scores were tabulated instead of raw scores because the length of folktales varied to such a degree that a comparison of raw frequency scores would be difficult to interpret.) These summary cards were used as input to the Data-Text System (Couch, 1966), which computed correlations between the 74 variables and factor analyzed the resulting matrix.

It should be made clear that the factors were computed solely for the purpose of discovering whether a cluster of Icarian themes emerged. At this point no attempt has been made to interpret the "factor space" that resulted from these computations. Instead, attention was paid to uncovering numerical support for the possibility of a cluster of Icarian variables. When the analysis of the first half of the folktales was completed, the second half was then processed and the correlation matrix that resulted from this analysis was factor analyzed. The results of these separate analyses (and subsequently the analysis of the entire corpus of data) revealed a factor (always Factor II) that included variables clustered at one end of the factor that correspond closely to the cluster of themes that, together, led to Murray's original conception of Icarianism. (These results are shown in Table 1.) That is, ascensionism and descensionism, rising and falling, water and heat, have clustered with a high degree of stability. The variables "time (long)" and "Stay" were included in the dictionary as possible measures of a concern with immortality. They, too, appear in this cluster. The variable that is missing from this cluster is narcism. It is not known whether its absence should be attributed to extremely weak measures of its expression or to a "real" lack of relationship.

Icarianism and Societal Residence Patterns

The realization of a stable cluster of Icarian related themes led to the next step in this investigation. First, we were interested in the possibility that some societies incorporate Icarian related words in their folktales more often than other societies. If so, we could rank-order these societies according to their relative concern with Icarian themes and compare Icarian societies with non-Icarian societies (relatively speaking) on other dimensions. In some of the research cited at the beginning of this chapter,

Table 1. *Factor analysis of tags applied to folktales*

First Half		Second Half		Total Sample	
Variable	Loading	Variable	Loading	Variable	Loading
Ascend Act	−60	Connot Hgt	−54	Descend Act	−73
Hi Nat Obj	−60	Denot Depth	−51	Denot Depth	−71
Descend Act	−53	Ascend Act	−48	Ascend Act	−66
Atmosphere	−42	Hi Nat Obj	−47	Hi Nat Obj	−66
Connot Depth	−40	Stay	−42	Connot Hgt	−56
Sensation	−39	Descend Act	−40	Denot Hgt	−53
Time Long	−37	Water	−33	Connot Depth	−48
Water	−33	Sensation	−31	Sensation	−44
Denot Hgt	−32	Denot Heat	−29	Denot Heat	−43
Denot Heat	−32			Water	−43
Denot Depth	−30				
Failure	+37	Pos Affect	+36	Denot Sex	+33
Denot Death	+40	Denot Sex	+37	Failure	+36
Affiliation	+41	Failure	+38	Aff Act nPhy	+37
Leave	+47	Inst Thought	+41	Denot Death	+40
Denot Sex	+46	Communicate	+42	Communicate	+50
Connot Sex	+47	Agg Act nPhy	+44	Affiliation	+59
Agg Act nPhy	+63	Affiliation	+48		
		Denot Death	+54		

authors suggested (and had various sorts of information to support their suggestion) that family structures, in which mothers are more dominant than fathers, are more conducive to the development of Icarian fantasies than are family structures in which males are clearly the dominant force. To further explore this possibility, the percentage scores for each society on all of the variables that formed the Icarian cluster were totaled and the societies were then aligned on the basis of their scores. The resulting distribution of scores revealed 17 societies that were "high" in terms of their tendency to include Icarian themes in their folktales, and an equal number of societies that were isolated at the "low" end of the continuum, by virtue of a relative absence of Icarian concern.

(A separate analysis of the topographical features did not explain the "high-low" distribution of these societies. That is, high Icarian societies did not receive that distinction by virtue of any tendency to live in mountainous regions. If a relationship between topographical features and the use of Icarian words had been demonstrated, the relationship could have been explained solely on the basis of high Icarian societies using words and phrases suggested by the features of the land occupied by the societies.)

The variables that did demonstrate considerable relationship between the "high" and "low" groupings of societies were the ratings compiled by Murdock (1962), indicating the preferred "profiles of marital residence" of each of these societies. These ratings demonstrated that societies ranked low on the inclusion of Icarian themes were likely (14 of the 17 cases in that category) to come from societies that place decision-making powers in the hand of husbands or patrilineal kinsmen. On the other hand, societies that sanction joint decisions by both husband and wife, or societies in which females are given the larger share of decision-making responsibilities, are likely (again, in 14 of 17 societies) to score high on our index of Icarianism.

The major finding from this analysis of residential patterns can be stated in the following manner: paternal dominance is negatively related to the expression of Icarian fantasies. This negative relationship between male control and Icarianism is open to a variety of interpretations. One interpretation is that strong paternal control facilitates progression from pregenital to later stages of emotional maturation. The absence of such control makes this process more difficult.

Covariation of Themes

Finally, we come to the question of what (if anything) is expressed in folktales from low Icarian societies that is either not expressed or expressed in a different form in folktales from high Icarian societies. In order to exaggerate the thematic differences that might exist between high and low societies, the 9 highest societies were compared with the 9 lowest societies. This further reduced the sample from 34 to 18. An investigation of the variables that differentiated between the 9 highest and 9 lowest societies (aside from the Icarian variables) pointed to the importance of the following content analysis categories: without exception, low Icarian societies obtained higher counts on "denotative sex," "aggressive act (non-physical)," and "communication." Another variable "affiliation" also distinguished between these groupings with the exception of one society in the low Icarian group that fell into the high Icarian range of scores.

Let us take a closer look at the variables that differentiated between these societies. The themes that received marked emphasis in low Icarian societies form a cluster that is readily interpretable. The most striking correspondence among these 4 categories is their inclusion of words that are used almost exclusively in *interpersonal* contexts. The variable "denotative sex" is composed of words that refer directly to sexual processes or sexual acts. Copulate, ejaculate, embrace, fornicate, love, and hug are examples of such words. "Aggressive act (nonphysical)" consists of words that are used to convey direct verbal attacks. Some examples are abuse, argue, bicker, blame, chide, jeer, nag, reprimand, and telloff. "Communication" includes words that most generally are used in contexts of interpersonal verbal contact. Among these words are: ask, discuss, inform, inquire, remind, reply, said, talk, and told. Finally, "affiliation" includes words that are used in contexts of social phrases (for example, thank you), affection (friend), and assistance (helping and kind). Hence, be it copulating, arguing, commenting, or helping—all of these concepts convey overt interpersonal involvement. Affect is expressed directly; communication occurs readily.

But this is not the case in folktales from high Icarian societies. Instead, societies that include an abundance of fire, water, height, depth, rising and falling imagery in their folktales, also receive high counts on the variables, "sensation" and "time (long)." Twenty-seven of the 41 words defined by "sensation" denote the use of visual capacities (for example, gaze, look, perceive, stare, and watch). The remaining 14 words denote use of other human sensing devices of smelling, hearing, and touching. "Time (long)," as the title suggests, is a category that includes words that convey the notion of waiting, slowness, or a period of long duration. Await, eternal, gradually, linger, slow, and year are among such words.

In certain respects, these findings seem to be consistent with the results of our exploration of individual case studies. If we consider the not unpopular notion that successful navigation to and through the genital stage of sexual development brings with it a concomitant development of ego functions related to verbal communication of needs, interpersonal mastery and a gradually maturing recognition and expression of emotional states then we may not be surprised at the positive relationship between variables related to interpersonal transactions and low Icarian scores. For individua Icarians, it has been argued that emotional states remain diffuse and relatively undefined and undifferentiated. Emotions that are normally channeled into interpersonal relations are, instead, expressed through symbols of fire, water, rising and falling. Congruent with this "spatialization" o relatively undifferentiated emotional states is an underlying desire to re main young—to live forever. This desire stems from a regressive puf to return to a stage of infant dependency; to a time when "the service was good" (as Tonka put it), when needs were attended to, when the frightful thought of emotional independence was not an issue.

The last finding from the analysis of folktales to be discussed is ir relationship to a variable, "change," that had successfully remained hidder until near the end of the study. This category had originally been included in the Icarus Dictionary as a potential measure of identity confusion That is, abundance of "change" imagery (people changing into creatures males turning into females, females becoming males, and the like) migh be interpreted as indicative of underlying sex role confusion. But on the basis of total frequencies across any of the groupings made earlier "change" had not discriminated between high and low Icarian societies However, the variable "change" became prominent when sentences including words denoting females were retrieved by feeding the appropriate instructions to the computer. Totals of other themes that surrounded the mention of females revealed a difference between high and low Icarian societies in their use of words defined by "change." Folktales from high Icarian societies included words related to change in conjunction with references to females much more frequently than did folktales from the low group. A documentation of this difference is one thing; to understand it is another. The best way to understand it is to retrieve and read the sentences causing the difference. Fifty-eight sentences from the 9 high Icarian societies and 18 sentences from the low Icarian societies matched our retrieval specifications. An inspection of these sentences showed that the majority of sentences from high Icarian societies (41 of the 58 sen tences) could be classified under the heading of "women changing their form." Examples are:

(A)   I looked up and saw her actually turn into a bear.
(B)   Instead of divorcing her man, she pretended she was dead.
(C)   The two old women and the girl just changed into mice.
(D)   She became a porcupine.

Seven of the 18 sentences from the low Icarian folktales were classified under this heading.

The sentences that exemplify the changing women imagery do not lead to an "identity confusion" interpretation as much as they suggest the interpretation that women cannot be trusted; they are changeable and must be watched. In relationship to our study of Tonka the correspondence between changeable mothers and the ambivalence they engender is clear. It should be noted that 22 of the sentences retrieved from high Icarian societies that were classified as "women changing their form" were from 3 of the 4 high Icarian societies that give males the dominant voice in major decision-making matters. Hence, these results suggest that low Icarian societies are either patrilocal or virolocal (with males in command) unless these marital resident profiles are combined with folktale imagery depicting changing women in which case we are likely to be dealing with a high Icarian society.

CONCLUSION

To conclude, the analysis of folktales has demonstrated a certain correspondence between the manifestation of Icarianism on a cultural level and the manifestation of the Complex on an individual level. It would be difficult to state, however, that a one-to-one relationship existed between the two levels (whatever that might mean in this context). Instead, a rather appealing complementary relationship was uncovered with case studies leading to the specification of new variables that were utilized in research with folktales. In turn, the analysis of folktales has tended to broaden our perspective on Icarianism and has forced us to consider more carefully a range of personality variables more encompassing than sexuality.

We realize, and have no intention of denying, that our interpretations are open to question. We feel strongly, however, that our method of approach to understanding Icarianism is appropriate considering the field's rather incomplete knowledge of the dynamics of personality. We are strongly committed to a descriptive approach to research as an initial step in gaining leverage on a problem posed by a conceptually confusing issue in human development. Techniques that permit patterns and relationships to emerge must be utilized as the first step toward a greater understanding, and it is this step that leads to more refined measures and focused designs.

14 Logical Content Analysis: An Explication of Styles of Concludifying

Edwin S. Shneidman

Center for Studies of Suicide Prevention
National Institute of Mental Health

" . . . everybody conceives himself
to be proficient in the art of
reasoning. . . . "
Charles Sanders Peirce

" . . . we cannot call a man
illogical for acting on the
basis of what he feels to be
true."
Kenneth D. Burke

"Everything we do seems to be
reasonable . . . at the time we
are doing it."
Donald Snygg and Arthur Combs

The purpose of this chapter is to suggest a method of analyzing certain aspects of an individual's cognitive styles and to relate these analyses to relevant aspects of his general personality functioning.

As a beginning, we assume that thought is a common characteristic of all humans (excluding neonates and unconscious persons). Each person does something that we call thinking, reasoning, cerebrating, deducing, inducing, syllogizing, coming to conclusions, inferring, and the like.

The most general term for these processes is "concludifying" (that is, coming to conclusions). It includes all of the mentational processes— cognitive maneuvers, logical gambits, sequences of associations, modes of induction, making deductive inferences—by which an individual can arrive at a firm or tentative conclusion.

Our second assumption is that individuals think in various *ways,* that is, that each individual has, along with his culturally common ways of thinking, some patterns of thinking that he may share with some other individuals and some that are unique to him. There is no one way of thinking, but there are many patterns of thinking.

It has been asserted that there are modes of thinking that are peculiar to cultures (Whorf, 1956; Sapir, 1956; and Nakamura, 1960); we believe that, within each culture, there are also individual idiosyncratic patterns of thinking which, in their totality, are then characteristic of (presently unrecognized) groups of individuals within that culture. We recognize that two or more persons might reach different conclusions for reasons other than their different logical patterns—for example, by beginning with different premises or by difference selections and distortions of the evidence—but, in the present context, the focus of our interest is on the forms of thought (and the consequences created by nuances of difference in these forms) rather than on the premises or the contents of thought.

Each individual has, along with culturally common ways of concludifying, some ways of thinking that he shares with others in his particular culture and some that are absolutely idiosyncratic for him. Thus, ways of thinking (like other aspects of personality functioning) can be viewed in terms of the characteristics that are universal, ubiquitous, and unique. There is not one way of thinking, but there are many ways. In this chapter, we are not concerned with "correct" thinking or argument. People do not make mistakes in their apparent logic; there are good reasons for their seeming to be unreasonable. Thus, we are interested primarily in the processes of concludifying in which an individual thinker engages. By illuminating the characteristics of an individual's cognitive processes, we might then infer the psychological "reasons" (as well as his personality characteristics) which, for him, are consistent with his ways of reasoning. Notice that we are little concerned with the notion of "error" in reasoning. "Error" has generally implied a departure from a particular (theoretical) standard of thinking, usually that attributed to Aristotle when he was thinking about thinking. "Reasoning," to quote William James, "is always for a subjective interest." The "marriage" between an individual's patterns of thinking and other aspects of that individual's personality is binding whether "in sickness or in health." We are interested in how people *do* think, not in how they *ought* to think.

Our third assumption is that if one knew the idiosyncratic characteristics of an individual's cognitive processes, he would then be in a position to infer other facts about that individual, especially what that individual's view of causality and order are, as well as certain personality characteristics which are consistent with that individual's modes of reasoning. And, by virtue of this knowledge, he would be in a position to enhance (or to frustrate) communication with that individual.

In this approach to the logics of communication, there are four major categories of analysis: Idio-logic, Contra-logic, Psycho-logic, and Pedago-logic.

IDIO-LOGIC

In this system, Idio-logic involves the individual's styles of thinking, referring to all those things that might be said—given the text of some original verbatim material (such as a political speech, a suicide note, or a psychological test protocol) by that person—about the syllogistic structure, the idiosyncrasies of either induction or deduction, the forms of the explicit or implied premises, and the gaps in reasoning or unwarranted conclusions, for example—indeed, anything that a logically oriented investigator who understood this approach could wring from a manuscript if he put his mind to it. These Idio-logical attributes are made up of two kinds of items: (1) *Aspects of Reasoning,* which include all categories that would traditionally be subsumed under "logical fallacies" (but that we do not view as fallacies but simply as idiosyncrasies), which relate essentially to the individual's inductive and deductive gambits and tactics; and (2) *Cognitive Maneuvers,* which describe the style of the development of thought, dealing especially with the flow of argumentation and with the cognitive interstices between the specific Aspects of Reasoning.

As indicated in Table 1, the Aspects of Reasoning are divided into these categories: (a) idiosyncrasies of relevance (for example, irrelevant premises, *argumentum ad populum,* false cause); (b) idiosyncrasies of meaning (for example, equivocation, indirect context, and the like); (c) enthymematic idiosyncrasies (for instance, contestable suppressed premises, suppressed conclusion); (d) idiosyncrasies of logical structure (isolated predicate and isolated term); and (e) idiosyncrasies of logical interrelations (for example, contradiction and truth-type confusion).

The Cognitive Maneuvers (Table 2) are divided into absolute statements (for example, to allege, to deny); qualified statements (to modify, to accept conditionally, and the like); initiating a new notion (for instance, to branch out, to interrupt, to digress); and continuing a previous notion (for example, to elaborate by phrase, to agree, to repeat).

Together, these Aspects of Reasoning and Cognitive Maneuvers represent an attempt to explicate all the idiosyncrasies of concludifying that an individual might manifest in his flow of thought. It seemed obvious that this general approach could be exemplified in an analysis of aberrant or "error-filled" materials. Studies of suicidal individuals and of psychiatric

Table 1. *Aspects of Reasoning*

	Kennedy (%)	Nixon (%)
I. IDIOSYNCRASIES OF RELEVANCE Those features of the argumentative style invoking the intrusion of conceptual elements extraneous to the argument.		
A. *Irrelevant Premise.* Premise is irrelevant to the conclusion it is purportedly instrumental in establishing.	8.7	4.9
B. *Irrelevant Conclusion.* Conclusion is irrelevant to the major body of premises which purportedly establish it.	7.4	2.6
C. *Argumentum ad Baculum.* Appeal to force or fear in one or more premises where the conclusion in question does not involve these concepts.	1.7	.6
D. *Argumentum ad Hominen.* Appeal to real or alleged attributes of the person or agency from which a given assertion issued in attempting to establish the truth or falsity of that assertion.	.9	3.8
E. *Argumentum ad Misericordiam.* Appeal to pity for oneself or for an individual involved in the conclusion where such a sentiment is extraneous to the concepts incorporated in the conclusion.	.9	.4
F. *Argumentum ad Populum.* Appeal to already present attitudes of one's audience where such attitudes are extraneous to the concepts incorporated in the conclusion.	3.4	12.0
G. *Argumentum ad Verecundium.* Appeal to authority whose assertions corroborate or establish the conclusion where no premises are asserted to the effect that the authority is dependable or sound.	1.7	.0
H. *False or Undeveloped Cause.* Falsely judging or implying a causal relationship to hold between two events.	1.3	3.7
J. *Complex Question.* A premise or conclusion of an argument contains a qualifying clause or phrase, the appropriateness or adequacy of which has not been established.	.0	1.9
K. *Derogation.* A premise or conclusion contains an implicit derogation of an individual or group, where the concepts expressing derogation are neither relevant nor substantiated.	.9	4.9
II. IDIOSYNCRASIES OF MEANING		
A. *Equivocation.* The use of a word or phrase which can be taken in either of two different senses.	6.6	2.2
B. *Amphiboly.* An unusual or clumsy grammatical structure obscuring the content of the assertion incorporating it.	4.8	3.0
C.1 *Complete Opposition.* The phrasing indicates an opposition or disjointedness of elements which are in fact opposed and disjointed.	2.6	.7

Table 1. *Aspects of Reasoning (Continued)*

	Kennedy (%)	Nixon (%)
C.2 *Incomplete Opposition.* The phrasing indicates an opposition or disjointedness of elements which are in fact not opposed or disjointed.	—	—
D. *Indirect Context.* Indirect phrasing is used rather than direct phrasing in contexts where the latter is appropriate.	—	—
E. *Mixed Modes.* An instance in which the context contains two or more of the following modes within the same context: descriptive, normative, or emotive-personal.	—	—

III. ENTHYMEMATIC IDIOSYNCRASIES
Argument contains suppressed premise or conclusion.

	Kennedy (%)	Nixon (%)
A. *Contestable Suppressed Premise.* A suppressed premise, necessary for rectifying initial validity of argument, is contestable.	5.2	3.7
B. *False Suppressed Premise.* A suppressed premise necessary for rectifying initial invalidity of argument is false, either logically or empirically.	2.6	3.0
C. *Plausible Suppressed Premise.* A suppressed premise necessary for rectifying initial invalidity of argument is plausible-but-not-obvious.	3.8	2.2
D. *Suppressed Conclusion.* The conclusion, while determined by the context of discussion, is never explicitly asserted, so that the point allegedly established by the argument is not brought clearly into focus.	.4	.7

IV. IDIOSYNCRASIES OF LOGICAL STRUCTURE

	Kennedy (%)	Nixon (%)
Isolated Predicate. A predicate occurs in a premise which occurs neither in the remaining premises nor in the conclusion, the function of such occurrence being to bind or relate the isolated predicate to other predicates, and *Isolated Term:* A predicate occurs in the conclusion which does not occur in the premise.	42.0	41.6

V. IDIOSYNCRASIES OF LOGICAL INTERRELATIONS

	Kennedy (%)	Nixon (%)
A.1 *Truth-Type Confusion.* A confusion between unquestionable assertions on the one hand—logically true assertions and definitions—with empirical assertions on the other hand.	2.2	6.4
A.2 *Logical-Type Confusion.* Confusion between general and specific or between abstract and concrete.	—	—
B. *Contradiction.* Making conflicting or contradictory assertions.	.9	.7
C. *Identification of a Conditional Assertion with Its Antecedent.* Treating an assertion of the form "If A, then B" as equivalent to A.	.0	1.5
D. *Illicit Distribution of Negation.* Treating an assertion	.9	.0

Table 1.   *Aspects of Reasoning (Continued)*

	Kennedy (%)	Nixon (%)
of the form "It is false that if A, then B" as equivalent to "If A, then it is false that B."		
E. *Illicit Derivation of Normative from Descriptive.* To derive a normative statement from a descriptive, statement that is, a statement of the form, "It is necessary that X," "One should do X," "X ought to be," from ordinary descriptive statements, that is, statements containing no words expressing imperativeness.	2.2	.7
Total	100	100

patients (Shneidman, 1961a) supported this contention. The fact that this approach was also applicable to the study of well-functioning individuals was demonstrated by a logical analysis of the Kennedy-Nixon "great Debates" of 1960 (Shneidman, 1963), if not by an analysis of a small group of Harvard undergraduates (Shneidman, in press).

. The numerals, listed on Tables 1 and 2 are the percentages taken from a detailed analysis of the first two (of the four) 1960 Kennedy-Nixon debate sessions. In this context, they only demonstrate that the distributions of the Aspects of Reasoning and the Cognitive Maneuvers of these two specific individuals were sufficiently different to distinguish them from each other, and further, to identify the separate logical styles of each. It was evident that Kennedy and Nixon were concludifying in very different ways; that is, independent of the *content* of their thoughts or the issues they were discussing, each would *process* the issue through his mind in ways quite different from the other. Given any issue, each would tend to cerebrate it in his own way and, perforce, come to *somewhat* different conclusions.

By way of illustration, consider the following genuine suicide note, written by a 23 year old Caucasian Protestant female just before her self-inflicted gun-shot death—where the notations above the content of the note refer to the headings in Table 1 and 2:

Dear Folks:
    II-D   II-D   I-F   II-c1   I-F, II-D
I know this won't seem the right thing to you but from where I stand it seems
II-D   I-F, I-J   39   II-A, II-B, I-J
like the best solution, considering what is inevitably in store for the future.
      46   10   II-c1
You know I am in debt. Probably not deeply compared to a lot of people but

Table 2. *Cognitive Maneuvers*

		Kennedy (%)	Nixon (%)
1a.	To switch from a normative to a descriptive mode.	.3	.6
1b.	To switch from a normative to an emotive or personal mode.	.3	.1
2a.	To switch from a descriptive to a normative mode.	.1	1.0
2b.	To switch from a descriptive to an emotive or personal mode.	6.6	5.2
3a.	To switch from an emotive or personal mode to a descriptive one.	4.6	3.0
3b.	To switch from an emotive or personal mode to a normative one.	.4	.6
5.	To enlarge or elaborate the preceding, relevantly or irrelevantly.	7.9	6.0
7.	To use an example, relevantly or irrelevantly.	2.3	2.7
8.	To deduce or purport to deduce from the preceding.	2.8	3.4
9.	To change emphasis, with continuity or warrant, or without continuity or warrant.	2.2	1.5
10.	To make a distinction between two preceding notions, a preceding notion and a new notion, or between two new notions, with or without warrant, justification, relevance.	4.1	5.9
11.	To branch out.	4.3	2.9
12.1.	To synthesize or summarize.	4.1	3.0
14.	To obscure or equivocate by phrasing or context.	6.9	4.6
16.	To smuggle a debatable point into a context which is semantically alien to it.	5.8	8.4
17.	To paraphrase or otherwise render as equivalent statements which, in general, are not to be taken as syntactically identical, with or without warrant.	1.7	2.4
21.	To give a premise or assumption for a statement explicit or implicit in the preceding.	5.0	5.8
25.	To be irrelevant.	7.3	9.6
26.	To repeat or rephrase.	1.7	1.2
28.	To allege but not substantiate.	4.4	6.3
31.	To deny or reject with or without warrant.	2.8	2.7
35.	To agree with the whole but take issue with a part, implicitly or explicitly.	1.0	1.3
37.	To shift focus from subject to audience.	.0	.0
39.	To accept conditionally.	2.9	1.6
41.	To render another's assertion stronger or weaker by paraphrase.	.3	2.0
42.	To digress.	.4	1.3
42.1.	To initiate discontinuities.	4.3	2.0
43.	To resolve discontinuities.	.0	.0
44.	To perpetuate or aggravate discontinuities.	1.5	.4
46.	To go toward greater specificity.	4.8	5.8
47.	To go toward greater generality.	1.4	.7
48.	To transfer or attempt to transfer authority or responsibility.	1.5	.9
50.	To attack.	3.4	3.8
53.	To introduce a new notion.	.0	.0
54.	Others (of less than 1% each)	2.9	2.9
	Total percentage	100	100
	Total number of units	725	678

I-E   10

at least they have certain abilities, a skill or trade, or talents with which to make a
I-E   I-F
financial recovery. Yes, I am still working but only "by the grace of the gods."

You know how I feel about working where there are a lot of girls I never could
II-D
stand their cattiness and I couldn't hope to be lucky enough again to find work
47
where I had my own office & still have someone to rely on like Betty. And above all,
7
most jobs don't pay as well as this one for comparable work. I get so tired, at typing

for instance, that I couldn't hold a straight typist position. I wish I had the social
I-F   I-H
position & "know how" to keep this job. That way I wouldn't worry myself into such
46
a dither that I make stupid errors. Sometimes they're just from trying too hard to

turn out a perfect copy to please someone. With 3 separate offices served by one

board its pretty hard to locate people for their calls. And when I do find them they
I-H, II-B
don't want to take them—for which I really can't blame them as some of them are
II-c2
ascenine. But when the calls come in on the bd I have to dispatch them one way
II-D
or another & the fellows don't seem to realize that.
I-A
Some girls can talk about their work to their girlfriends and make it sound
II-c1   II-D   42
humorous but I guess it sounds like complaining the way I talk. And when I mention

anything to Betty, either in fun or in an effort to correct a situation, it gets all
42.1
over the office like wildfire. Now, when I sit there paying attention to the board or
9, II-c2
my work the fellows think I'm purposely unfriendly. But just what is there to talk
I-H
about when you get tired of the same old questions & comments on the weather,

"how are you," "working hard or hardly working?" & you know better than to say

very much about things they're interested in or concerned about. I've usually tried
I-K
to either kid the person concerned about whatever it is or just shut up about it

because if one goes about telling the other persons business that can cause trouble.
II-c2
However, the kidding, or even a friendly interest, sometimes, can hurt. So where

are you? Might just as say very little and appear uncooperative or whatever they

think.

12.1   II-A, I-J, I-H

Due to these & many, many more frustrations from the board & other causes

I-D

I have become much more nervous than I was. You know what the medicine I

was taking did to me so far as my being extremely keyed up, irritable, etc. was

concerned. Now I feel just about as depressed as I was keyed up then. I couldn't

I-H

even talk coherently at times, and now I'm too concerned about my financial affairs

42   I-F

to know what it is safe to say. How I wish I could make "small talk" or "party

I-F   II-c2

chatter" like some girls do. But I can't compete with most of them for many reasons

& after trying to enter into social activities with kids in my age range, especially the

●   28

past year, I find that I can't compete with most of them. Even if I had all the

42.1

clothes to look the part I still wouldn't be able to act the part. Sorry I'm such a

disappointment to you folks.

I-H   I-A

I-A I'm saying these things so you'll understand why it's so futile for me to even

47

hope for a better job. And as long as I go on living there will be "working condi-

I-A, I-D

tions" when there are so many other better places for the money. I don't mean to

sound unappreciative of all you folks have done all thru the years to keep us kids

10   I-F, 7, I-J

well & healthy. It's just that I can't see the sense in putting money into a losing

12.1

game. I know I'm a psycho somatic—that's just it.

II-A

One reason for doing this now is that Bill will be back & wants his .22.

9

But the primary reason is one I think you already know—Mike. I love him more

I-D   II-c2

than anyone knows & it may sound silly to you but I can't go on without him.

5

What is there thats worth living for without him?

An analysis of the Idio-logic of this suicide note indicates that there were 47 instances of 13 different aspects of reasoning and 27 instances of 15 different cognitive maneuvers. The aspects of reasoning which appeared most frequently were I-F, Argumentum ad Populum, 8 instances;

II-A, Equivocation, 5; and 2-D, Indirect Context, 9. For purposes of illustration within this chapter, I shall use but two of the aspects of reasoning: I-F, Argumentum ad Populum, and II-D, Indirect Context.
A brief explication of Argumentum ad Populum (I-F) is as follows.

Definition. Argumentum ad Populum is an appeal to affective dispositions and attributes of one's audience, where such dispositions and attitudes are extraneous to the concepts incorporated in the conclusion. The speaker attempts to influence his audience to accept his conclusion or position by citing certain real or alleged states which, while not part of the objective content of his conclusion, are consonant with and elicit certain "folk beliefs," attitudes, or appraisals held by his audience and, by their very familiarity, function to blunt any more critical or objective assessment of the speaker's conclusion or position.

Example. "I think that in common decency and common honesty, so long as the Senator from Utah knows what the obvious error is which has been deleted, he should tell the Senate" (*Congressional Record*, McCarthy, 1954/15849/2.9).

Discussion. The phrase, "in common decency and honesty," is used here as an emotional appeal to the body of Senators present—an appeal that is extraneous to the issue of whether the Senator from Utah has provided adequate grounds for his behavior.

Indirect Context—Aspect of Reasoning II-D—is defined as follows.

Definition. The speaker uses contexts of the form "I think that . . . ," "It seems that . . . ," "It looks like . . . ," etc.—indirect contexts—as premises in an argument where the conclusion is in "direct" form, that is, is not relativized to appearances or beliefs, but is absolute. The speaker tends to relativize premises to himself (or to some other agency), while drawing conclusions which are not relativized. He weakens his premises to induce their acceptance and purports to derive a stronger conclusion than logically follows. He conceives of statements of the form, say, "I think that P" as logically equivalent to statements of the form "P" and uses the relativized statements in places where the non-relativized or "direct" form is logically required or contextually more appropriate.

Discussion. The preface, "I think that . . . " relativizes the above assertion to the speaker. For instance, if we take the "direct" part of the above, that is, the part starting with "in common decency . . . ," then the appropriateness, plausibility, or truth of this latter assertion could be discussed by sociologists, legal philosophers, legal scholars, ministers, etc., while the entire quoted assertion McCarthy makes, framed in indirect discourse, could be discussed only by a lie detection expert or McCarthy's closest confidants.

The final construction of the individual's Idio-logic is essentially an exercise in English exposition. One gives the greatest emphasis to the aspects of reasoning which appear most often, or seem to be "most important" in that subject's style of thinking.

One additional example: a very brief suicide note, "I love everybody but my darling wife has killed me." Its implied conclusion—in light of the deed that followed it—is: Therefore, I kill myself. In this short note one can detect two Idiosyncrasies of Reasoning: Equivocation (II-A) and False Suppressed Premise (III-B). The definition of Equivocation is: A word or phrase is used which can be taken in either of two different senses in a given context; or else in repeated use of a word or phrase, the sense of that word or phrase changes; the speaker does not fix the meaning of his terms; he leaves the interpretation open; he does not give necessary elaboration to fix unambiguously the meaning, or else he shifts from one meaning to another.

In terms of that suicide note, the implied conclusion (Therefore, I kill myself) is suppressed in the actual suicide note, but the note is taken as giving grounds, rationale, premises, warrant, etc., for the writer's taking his own life. The equivocation occurs with the word, "kill," which in the premises has the sense of "violated," "betrayed," etc.—that is, "killed" in the figurative sense—while "kill" in the conclusion is lethally literal in its meaning.

The definition of False Suppressed Premise is: A suppressed premise, necessary for rectifying initial invalidity of an argument, is false. The speaker tends to omit explicit mention of positions or assumptions which are central to his exposition and which, moreover, are almost totally idiosyncratic to him, being neither shared by others nor independently defendable. In the case of the brief suicide note, the false suppressed premises is: For any person X and for any person Y, if X loves Y and Y kills X, then X kills X.

The following are examples—using actual suicide notes—of some of the Cognitive Maneuvers:

(a) To allege but not substantiate (to make an assertion, which is nonobvious yet contextually important, whose context contains no premise which would tend to establish it): "I cannot live any longer, I do not wish to live any longer. Death is better than living. Sometimes it is the best."

(b) To deny or reject with or without warrant: ". . . and mother, I wish that you hadn't called me a liar, and said I was just like George, *as I am not.*"

(c) To move toward greater generality: ". . . and about William, I want to dismiss every idea about him. I don't like him any more than a companion; for a while I thought I did, but no more—in fact, I am quite tired of him, as you know. *I get tired of everyone after a while.*"

(d) To transfer authority or responsibility. (The speaker shifts to another person the responsibility for defending a position or handling a difficulty when it would appear incumbent upon the speaker to defend the position or eliminate the difficulty: "You alone know the answer. Your inhuman acts are the answer. Just search your mind and soul.")

(e) To cite a premise belatedly: "Do not hesitate to tell any of our friends that I took this step of my own free will; I am not ashamed of it. *There is no reason why I should continue to suffer with no hope of recovery.*"

(f) To repeat or rephrase: "I cannot live any longer. I do not wish to live any longer."

CONTRA-LOGIC

From the tabulations of an individual's Idio-logic, his Contra-logic—which represents his private epistemological and metaphysical view of the universe—may then be inferred. Under the assumption that there is a rationale behind each individual's reasoning, this procedure permits us to assert (or to estimate) what that rationale is, and thereby, to understand his reasons for his reasoning as he does. Contra-logic is our reconstruction of an individual's private, usually unarticulated notions of causality and purpose, which would make his Idio-logic seem errorless to him. The Contra-logic serves to nullify or contravene or "explain" that individual's Idio-logic and makes it sensible—for him. It answers the question: What must that person's beliefs about the nature of the universe be in order for him to manifest the styles of thinking that he does, that is, what are his underlying (and unverbalized) epistemological and metaphysical systems which are consistent with his ways of moving cognitively in the world? In the same sense that every person has an idio-logical structure which can be explicated, there is for each individual a complimentary contra-logical position which can be inferred.

An example will serve to clarify the concept of Contra-logic: A patient in a disturbed mental hospital ward—an example cited by Von Domarus (1944) and repeated by Arieti (1955)—unexpectedly says, "I am Switzerland." The reconstructed syllogism reads: I want to leave this locked ward—I love freedom; Switzerland loves freedom; (therefore) I am Switzerland. His Idio-logic is one of reasoning in terms of attributes of the predicate, but his style of reasoning would make "sense" to us (and does make sense to him) if it were the case (or if one supplied the implicit premise) that there were only one member to a class, that is, that Switzerland is the only entity that loves freedom. That is the Contra-logic which explains this Idio-logic, for in that case, it would follow without logical error that anyone who then loved freedom would, of necessity, have to be Switzerland. (The psychological concomitants of such a state are mentioned under Psycho-logic, below.)

Some other examples of Contra-logics, using a variety of kinds of individuals (a suicide, a Jekyll-and-Hyde homosexual, a chess champion, some noted political figures, etc.) are published in previous discussions of this method (Shneidman, 1957, 1961a, 1961b and 1963).

Let us continue our analysis of the suicide note from the 23-year old girl. The Contra-logic of Argumentum ad Populum is as follows.

Definition. It follows that one believes that: The acceptability or truth of a conclusion or position is not, and should not be, strictly a function of so-called "objective considerations," for any conclusion or position can be adequately assessed only in light of what the "going beliefs" and attitudes of the society are. Thus, the eliciting of these beliefs and attitudes by means of folk homilies, idioms, shibboleths, and the like is appropriate to assessment of the conclusion, that is, a conclusion is not independent of the whole nexus of societal beliefs, rather it is to be judged only in light of them, hence their elicitation is always appropriate. Truth is conventional and relative to society; it is not absolute or "extrasocietal." Concurrence of other men's views with the speaker's views is more important than concurrence of the speaker's views with the objective world.

The Contra-Logic of Indirect Context is as follows.

Definition. It follows that one believes that statements of the form "I think that P" are logically equivalent to statements of the form "P"; that is, indirect statements are logically on a par with direct statements. All knowledge is relative—relative to man, society, etc.—that is, to the perceiver or the asserter. There is no world or reality distant from our perceptions. There is no objective truth independent of, or in any way transcending, what any given man conjectures, surmises, and believes. A statement of the form "P" is to be understood as elliptical for "I think that P," that is, everything is indexed to the speaker.

We again examine the note from the suicidal girl, this time to see what can be said about her Contra-logic. Keeping in mind her use of Argumentum ad Populum and Indirect Context, the following might be said about her underlying idiosyncratic epistomological and metaphysical view of the universe:

There is no objective truth; what seems to be true for the observer is to be taken as true in fact (Indirect Context, II-D). Validation of one's beliefs is obtained by concurrence of those beliefs with prevalent societal beliefs and attitudes, that is, one is correct in one's beliefs if others agree with them (Argumentum ad Populum, I-F). Everything that one asserts is already implicit in one's beliefs; if someone disagrees with you, it is because his beliefs are different from your own (not because he may be reasoning differently) and there is nothing to negotiate (Complex Question, I-J). Everything is relative to underlying assumptions (Cognitive Maneuver 39, To Accept Conditionally).

PSYCHO-LOGIC

The concept of Psycho-logic refers to those overt and covert aspects of personality that are related to—reflective of, are of a piece with, grow out of, create, or participate with—the individual's styles of thinking. The Psycho-logic answers the question: What kind of person would he have to be (in relation to his mentational psychological traits) in order for him to have the view of the world that he does (Contra-logic) as manifested in his ways of thinking (Idio-logic)? The fact that an individual's ways of thinking and aspects of his personality (Psycho-logic) are synchronous should come as no surprise to any student of human nature.

What aspects of personality are included under the Psycho-logic? In the present context we can be interested only in those psychological aspects that are reflective of the individual's ways of thinking, that is, reflections of his mentational functionings. No claims as to the manifestations of characteristics in other-than-mentational areas of activity (such as physical, sexual, or social areas) can be made. Furthermore, it should be stated that only with the most severe reservations can one generalize from an individual's mentational behaviors in any one specific situation to his entire logical armamentarium.

To return to our "Switzerland" example of the man who (Idio-logically) reasoned in terms of attributes of the predicate, and who (Contra-logically) assumed that there was only one member to a class: that type of reasoning (Psycho-logically) reflects a mental state in which the focus of attention is narrowed (in this case, to one attribute of a class) and/or the freedom to widen or broaden the boundaries of the focus of attention is rather rigidly fixed. In such a state one might expect to see some of the following characteristics or symptoms: intense concentration or conflict; withdrawal from others; oblivion to ordinary stimuli; hypesthesia—even catatonic behavior.

Keeping in mind the restrictions indicated above, a set of Mentational Psychological Traits—that is, those psychological traits which can easily be related to patterns of thinking—is proposed. These traits are indicated in Figure 1.

To return again to our 23-year-old, suicidal girl, a summary of the Pscyho-logic for this girl might read: The subject is relativistic and fearful of commitment (Indirect Context, II-D); she is needful of approval from others and attempts to elicit that approval whenever possible (Argumentum ad Populum, I-F); she tends to be distrustful and, if opposed, is untractable and rigid (Complex Questions, I-J).

PEDAGO-LOGIC

The Pedago-logic (relating to the process of education or instruction or pedagogy) can be viewed as a possible practical application of this method. If the Idio-logic explicates an individual's styles of thinking, and the Contra-logic describes his underlying philosophy of the universe, and the Psycho-logic details his personality traits related to thinking, then the Pedago-logic is a prescription that permits us to modify the process of communication or instruction for that person so as to maximize his opportunities for learning. To use an analogy: everyone who moves at all can be said to locomote, but individuals locomote in many various ways. In this sense, the Pedagologic provides a way of "limping along" with the individual; it is a custom-fitted prosthetic device intended to facilitate his potential for locomotion. In the usual learning situation, there are at least two major aspects present: the substantive (what is being taught), and the process (the way in which the "what" is presented—the teacher's way or the textbook's way). Most of us adjust to the way of the text or the teacher, but our grasp of content would be even greater if the content were presented *our* way, in a textbook custom-made to reflect our styles of cognizing. A good military aide soon learns to tailor the briefings for his General to fit the General's ways of thinking; a master coach adapts his teachings to the styles of his star players, so that he can maximize their potentials for performance. The Pedago-logic is a prescription for maximizing (or minimizing) communication.

The "thrust" of the concept of the Pedago-logic is perhaps illustrated best by using an example involving individuals of limited intellectual capacity. We—Peter Tripodes and I—made a few visits to a state hospital for the mentally retarded where we recorded our conversations with a small number of below-normal young adults. We routinely asked questions intended to elicit some sort of concludifying responses, such as "Why do you think so?" in relation to such topics of interest as privileges, visiting hours, dances, work, and release from hospital. We then analyzed the kinds of Idio-logics displayed by our subjects. Our thought—based

A. *Scope* (or *Range*). Wide-ranged diverse, broad-scoped versus narrow-ranged, focused, specialized. Generally, the compass of foci of concern: large, medium, small.

A.1 Global, holistic, totality; molar, large units versus molecular, detailed, atomistic.

A.2 Combinatory, extrapolating, seeing implications versus concrete, unimaginative.

B. *Discreetness*. Dichotomous, binary, either-or versus continuous, neutralistic, both-and, n'chotomous.

C. *Flexibility*. Flexible, adaptable, mobile versus fixed, inflexible, firm, rigid.

D. *Certainty*. Dogmatic certainty, affirmation versus uncertainty, indecision, doubt, equivocation.

E. *Autism*. Good reality orientation, nonautistic versus poor reality orientation, projection of standards, autistic. Generally: realistic (certain), realistic (possible, probable), unrealistic (impossible).

F. *Creativity*. Creative, original; novel, new, versus conforming, commonplace, banal.

G. *Bias*. Objective, unprejudiced versus prejudiced, infusion of affect, subjective. Also: reductive (derogatory), neutral, elevative (laudatory).

H. *Consistency*. Consistent, reliable, predictable versus variable, unreliable, inconsistent, unpredictable, fluctuating.

I. *Accord*. Builds on past achievement, extends accepted positions, accepts present authorities, constructive versus contrary, iconoclastic, perverse, negative, naysayer, destructive.

J. *Organization*. Systematic, organized, methodical versus unsystematic, disorganized, unmethodical, loose, scattered, disjointed.

K. *Directiveness*. Goal-directed, planful, purposeful versus lacking in direction, planless, purposelessness. Generally: compulsive persistence, appropriate persistence, impersistence (abandoning goal).

L. *Activity*. Aggressive, involved, adventurous, assertive, taking initiative versus passive, acquiescent, receptive, detached, timid, letting happen (lethargic), not taking initiative. Generally: proactive (taking initiative), reactive, inactive (apathy).

M. *Spontaneity*. Spontaneous, uninhibited versus constructed inhibited, controlled.

N. *Precision*. Definite, precise, clear-cut versus indefinite, vague, amorphous.

O. *Pursuit*. Tenacious, perseverating, single-minded versus changeable, labile, easily diverted.

P. *Orientation*. Action or fact-oriented, practical, unreflective, extrinsic reward-oriented versus mentation-oriented, contemplative, theoretical, philosophic, intrinsic reward-oriented.

Q. *Awareness*. Awareness of own cognitive activity versus unawareness of own cognitive activity.

Figure 1 Mentational Psychological Traits.

on the notion that there are different ways to conceptualize (and thus to teach) *subtraction*—was to construct a few (three or four) simple textbooks teaching subtraction in the logical styles "consistent" with the three or four main types of logical styles we found among these subjects. Our hypothesis was that learning (measured, for instance, by rate, level of difficulty, and retention) by use of these "tailor-made" texts would be superior to learning from any one set (including their present set) of textbooks, simply because in the latter case some of the students would have to try to adapt to a style of presentation not peculiarly their own.

Although we did not have the opportunity to complete this study, the thoughts that stimulated its initiation may help to clarify the concept of resonating to another's logical styles. This same principle ought to apply, with even greater usefulness perhaps, in the school situation, or with military, industrial, or governmental personnel, especially in briefing leaders at the topmost levels. [Conversely, if one were meeting an opponent in a debate or at a bargaining table or in an international arena, it would behoove one to know that individual's logical styles (as well as one's own) in order more effectively to counter and to out-maneuver him—to beat him with his own game].

A summary of the Pedago-logic of the 23 year old girl's suicide note might include the following: The subject will either agree with you immediately or disagree with you forever, requiring a feeling of commonality in underlying beliefs in order to communicate with you (Indirect Context, II-D). This feeling of commonality might be elicited by your suggesting that your own beliefs are commonly held by others (Argumentum ad Populum, I-F). In the absence of such a feeling of commonality, she will tend to be oblivious to anything you might say thereafter (Complex Question, I-J). A summary of the analysis of her logics is given in Figure 2.

Returning, finally, to our I-am-Switzerland friend, one might concentrate on widening his intellective blinders, for example to show him (if it were possible) that there were countries other than Switzerland that loved freedom (Denmark and Israel, for instance) and that there were other-than-countries, that is, people who loved freedom (for instance, Jefferson, Lincoln, Paine, and LaFayette)—to break through, at the least, the narrow notion of Switzerland = freedom, and freedom = Switzerland. On the other hand, his very rigidity and inflexibility might militate against his listening effectively to any argument not isomorphic with his own fixed beliefs. It is interesting to contemplate his reaction to your responding to his "I am Switzerland" with "I am Switzerland too," to which, if you possessed (and held) the keys to his locked ward he might then say, "No, you are really Germany." Using this kind of language, you might

Aspect of Reasoning	Idio-logic	Contra-logic	Psycho-logic	Pedago-logic
Indirect Context (II-D)	Relativizes assertions to own or other's perceptions; concerned with the appearance of events rather than the events themselves.	There is no world or reality distinct from perceptions. There is no objective truth; there is only conjecture, surmisal, belief, etc.	Relativistic; fearful of commitment, feels divorced from reality, alienated from others.	This individual will see no objective grounds for your assertions, but will regard them as idiosyncratic to your point of view or attitude.
Argumentum ad Populum (I-F)	Appeals to affective dispositions and attitudes by the use of idiomatic expressions.	Truth is conventional and relative to society; societal attitudes are important determinants of truth and appropriateness.	Insecure; needy of approval; opportunistic.	This individual will tend to be responsive to the emotional content in metaphors, slogans, idioms, etc., and any other devices which connote widespread acceptance of your position.
Complex Question (I-J)	Uses phrasings that "beg" some critical points at issue by assuming that these points have already been established.	A position or conclusion cannot be negotiated or established by argument or proof, but is already incorporated in all one's assertions.	Distrustful, rigid, intractable, refractory. Tends to be fatalistic and tenacious.	In communicating with this individual, be fully explicit in making your point or she will tend to ignore it, having made up her mind beforehand.

Figure 2

then reply: "All right then, let's negotiate. At least, let's draw up a non-aggression pact." But, obviously, the most meaningful as well as the most direct response to his saying "I am Switzerland" would be to say—with seeming irrelevance but with piercing perspicacity: "I know that you want your freedom from this locked ward, and we'll see what we can do, you and I." Then you would be talking his logic and he would know that someone had truly understood him.

SUMMARY

As with any aspect of human personality, it is useful to consider man's mentational styles, following Kluckhohn and Murray (1953), in the tripartite terms of (a) which are common to all men—universal; (b) which are present in some men—ubiquitous; and (c) which are present in only one man—unique. In this chapter we have indicated our belief that what is *universal* about mentational styles is that every human (perhaps, other than neonates and decorticated nonneonates) engages in some forms of concludifying; what is *ubiquitous* about mentation is that there is a finite number of general patterns (combinations or styles) of logical behaviors (which can be conceptualized in terms of the relative frequencies and clusterings of Idiosyncrasies of Reasoning and Cognitive Maneuvers); and what is *unique* are the special nuances of patterning or styles of thought that specially characterize any particular individual's logical style.

All of this is conceptualized in terms of a four-part scheme:

(a) Idio-logic—which explicates the details of a man's logical styles.

(b) Contra-logic—which attempts to explain why his reasoning seems reasonable to him (by citing what appear to be his underlying philosophies of causal relations which would "explain" his logical style).

(c) Psycho-logic—which surmises which traits of human personality might well be found with (or are consistent with) the idiosyncratic logical styles and the underlying epistemology of that individual.

(d) Pedago-logic—which extrapolates from the other three conceptions and suggests what logical styles might be employed (by a teacher or mentor or aide) with an individual so as to communicate and teach (or, conversely, to frustrate and thwart) that individual most effectively.

The general approach is one of attempting, without prejudgment, to understand the net results of an individual's ways of thinking by examining, in terms of logical, epistemological, and selected psychological dimensions, what manner of mind it was from which those results had come.

III The Recording and Notation of Data

William J. Paisley, Editor

INTRODUCTION TO PART III

WILLIAM J. PAISLEY

Institute for Communication Research
Stanford University

Content analysis was born (or reborn) in this century in the field of journalism research. It has now attained some maturity in fields ranging from cultural anthropology to psychiatry. Content analyses of considerable sophistication were being performed in some fields as early as 25 years ago. Recent development of content analysis in these fields emphasizes computerized procedures (in place of tedious manual analysis) and more direct derivation of categories from behavioral theory (in place of *ad hoc* categorization).

Content analysis has flourished wherever two conditions are met: (1) verbal text provides abundant data, and (2) there is a preexisting theory of the relationship of text indicators to phenomena beyond text—for instance, behaviors, attitudes, and motives. *One frontier of content analysis is its extension to fields where one or both of these conditions cannot be met.*

Three chapters in Part III deal with the content analyses of *nonverbal* materials. The fourth chapter considers content analysis as a means of *forming* theory rather than testing it. To a greater extent than in other parts of this volume, these four chapters use the future tense to predict what content analysis *will* accomplish, once problems of conceptualization and data management have been cleared away.

THE TREATMENT OF NONVERBAL DATA

Content analysis in the social sciences and humanities has grown on a foundation of words. The word is a comfortable unit of analysis; we

283

can analyze individual words or combine them in phrases, sentences, or paragraphs. The computer accepts the word as input without transformation.

In terms of content analysis difficulty, there are two classes of nonverbal data. Music, as discussed in Chapter 15, resembles verbal text in its natural "building blocks"—notes, phrases, themes. All that is needed to make music fully content analyzable is a notational system that transforms pitch, duration, dynamics, and the like into the computer's character set. Barry S. Brook's "Plaine and Easie Code" accomplishes this transformation. It has proved itself both in stylistic analysis and in classification for information storage and retrieval.

Music and verbal text are so similar in their syntax that a notational system like the "Plaine and Easie Code" clears away all obstacles to the computerized content analysis of music, using procedures developed for verbal text. No such solution appears in the content analysis of *visual* records, as discussed in Chapter 16 by Ekman, Friesen, and Taussig. That is, the computer's ability to process visual content *directly* is limited to the simplest visual records, such as line drawings and black-and-white photographs.

Visual records differ from music on the attribute of unitization. We can dismantle verbal text and music down to letters and pitches, in many cases even counting and comparing the units in isolation from each other, but visual records are seldom divided into small natural units. Instead, we must create visual units arbitrarily, as by gridding a frame into very small squares. In other words, a painting or a photograph cannot be dismantled for storage in the computer, except in the sense that tiny squares scanned across its surface can be *digitized* with (for example) 0 representing white, 10 black, and 5 an intermediate gray. It is in this way that pictures of the Moon are transmitted back from lunar rockets. X-rays, aerial reconnaissance photographs, and bubble-chamber tracks are similarly processed by computer.

Digitizing scanned points is an often-proposed (perhaps inevitable) solution to the problem of storing and analyzing visual records in the computer. However, it is clear that storing the Mona Lisa in the form of millions of digitized points is qualitatively different from storing the letters of Hamlet or the pitches of La Mer.

We can assume that hardware advances will allow any visual record to be digitized for computer storage on point-by-point dimensions of hue, value, chroma, texture, and the like, but the next obstacle (that of making sense of these artificial units as stored) seems almost insurmountable. Progress in *pattern recognition* is painfully slow, even when research and development concerns only the simplest patterns, such as letters and numbers. There is, therefore, a real and enduring contrast between visual content, on the one hand, and verbal text and music, on the other. Content analysis of verbal text and music can take as data either the *content itself* or *dictated attributes* of the content—that is, statements about the content made by human observers or judges (for instance, an abstract, paraphrase, or even bibliographic summary of essential characteristics of the content). Content analysis of visual records depends, for the present and foreseeable future, on *dictated attributes only*. The computer itself *does not content analyze;* it only stores, in an optimally convenient manner, attributes of content as dictated by a human content analyst.

The Ekman, Friesen, and Taussig VID-R and SCAN provide an optimally convenient system for assessing visual records of great length that have been coded by a human content analyst. In effect, their system links the part of the human that works best (the pattern recognizer) with the part of the computer that works best (the iterater, the counter, the rememberer), and much thought and careful planning is given to the interface of the interdependent parts.

VOCAL INFORMATION THAT IS NOT VERBAL

A similar pattern-recognition problem arises in the analysis of vocal information other than words. Starkweather, in Chapter 17, discusses background for an on-line procedure to follow changes in (for example) emotional expression in voice signals from which recognizable semantic content (in the verbal sense) has been removed through filtering and integrating. That is, the pattern of words in an utterance is blurred beyond recognition by filtering out certain speech frequencies and by integrating impulses over brief periods of time. The signal that remains is data to be digitized for computer analysis. Such signals, Starkweather reports, "have been shown to be a sensitive measure of the identity of different speakers, of clinically perceptible variations in a speaker's mood of talking, of daily changes in mood as indicated by self-report and by observers' ratings, and of variations in voice which accompany emotional events."

CONTENT ANALYSIS IN THE CONTEXT OF
MULTIPLE OPERATIONISM

Multiple operationism is a scientific strategy that seeks *convergence* of findings derived from *different* research methods. It is assumed that, although research techniques have *un*correlated defects and biases limiting individual validity, multiple techniques brought to focus on the same problem should yield a *core* of valid findings that are correlated. For example, one could index political unrest in a Latin American nation by measuring gold outflow, incidents of domestic noncriminal violence, votes received by protest parties, slogans and posters appearing on walls, public rallies, and appearance of underground newspapers. Each of these measures is only a facet of political unrest (which resists definition in a single measure), but collectively, perhaps with the addition of others, they "triangulate" the central concept.

Content analysis has a special role in the multiple-operation approach. Unstructured content, perhaps collected unobtrusively, can be prepared for data analysis via the traditional procedures of content analysis, then combined with data from prestructured observation. Since biases and other sources of error differ in prestructured observation and content analysis, we can hope that these complementary approaches will agree on more valid findings that either alone can yield.

Webb and Roberts (Chapter 18) state the case, entertainingly as well as eloquently, for content analysis as the troubleshooter or test pilot of new areas of inquiry in social science. The data may be verbal (as is true of their own reported research) or nonverbal (as in a study of militaristic and nationalistic themes in German postage stamps). What unifies their many suggested applications of content analysis is a versatility and adroitness in choosing content analysis as *the most appropriate* procedure for opening up a new area of inquiry, defining a complex concept, and charting trends. Always content analysis is to be supported by other systems of measurement; always the data obtained from multiple methods are to be combined for the sake of construct validation. Such a position is refreshingly at variance with a traditional, heavy-handed insistence on content analysis alone for certain applications, and other measurement systems, used singly, for other applications.

The unity of Part III on the recording and notation of data thus comes from a theme of *extension*. Brook, Ekman *et al.,* and Starkweather extend content analysis beyond its foundation in verbal text, into domains of music, visual content, and nonverbal vocal information. Webb and Roberts extend content analysis by relating the procedure to other measurement systems, within a context of multiple operationism, and by prescribing new and versatile roles for it.

15 Style and Content Analysis in Music: The Simplified "Plaine and Easie Code"

Barry S. Brook

Music
City University of New York

The term "content analysis" is largely unknown in musicology, although some musicologists have been grappling with techniques of systematic and objective quantification under the name of "style analysis." I shall not attempt to differentiate between musical "style" and "content" analysis—if, indeed, any differentiation is possible—except to state that I believe that valid "style analysis" is possible in the arts only after what we are here calling "content analysis" takes place. Ideally, perhaps, good style analysis is the application of educated intuition and hypothesis to a thoroughgoing and objective analysis of content.

Unfortunately, the term "style analysis" has been used in music for a multitude of sinfully subjective descriptions and unsubstantiated conclusions. A famous instance of this can be found in the history of the authentification of the Haydn cello concerto in D major. For many years, no holograph or other primary source was known for this piece. When a set of individual manuscript parts was discovered bearing the name of Anton Kraft, first cellist of the Esterhazy orchestra, several historians soon found "internal stylistic evidence" to prove that the concerto could not, "obviously," be by Haydn, nor should it ever have been considered as such in the first place. The piece was even performed and recorded under the name of Kraft or Haydn-Kraft. When, finally, Haydn's own signed and dated autograph score was discovered (Nowak, 1954), corroborating "internal stylistic evidence" was produced, it seemed, overnight; and, although this time the conclusion in favor of Haydn's authorship was valid, the analysis itself was not.

Ignorance of what style is remains extensive today. I am fond of pointing this out whenever possible. One way I have done so is by means of a continuing experiment performed on musically literate audiences. It works this way: at the outset of a lecture, say on Classicism-Romanticism and the turbulent preromantic *Sturm und Drang* period in literature and

287

music, a group of five carefully selected but untitled excerpts is played. The audience, made up of graduate students in music and their professors, is asked to mark down their educated multiple choice guesses regarding: (1) the composer (six choices: Haydn, Mozart, Beethoven, Schumann, Schubert, and Mendelssohn); and (2) the approximate date (also six possible answers, between 1760 and 1850, in 15-year intervals). An immediate tabulation of the results invariably proves amusing and embarrassing—embarrassing especially to my professorial colleagues, who do as badly as the students. Answers are well scattered, ranging from Haydn to Schumann and up to the very romantic year, 1840. All five works are, in fact, by Haydn and all are dated 1770. Audiences are consistently taken in by the obvious emotional intensity of the excerpts while ignoring the many less apparent but more fundamental characteristics, such as harmonic language, harmonic rhythm, and phrase structure, which place the works precisely around 1770—squarely in the midst of what we music historians call the classical period.[1]

After performing this and similar experiments a number of times and continuing to grapple with the problem of understanding and defining musical styles, I came across a provocative article with what I then thought was the rather mystifying title "Identifying the Unknown Communicator in Painting, Literature and Music: The Significance of Minor Encoding Habits" (Paisley, 1964). Paisley refers to Bernard Berenson's famous "pebbles at the foot of a painting" which helped him identify the painters or forgers of the many canvases he expertized. Neither painter nor forger is consciously concerned with "minor encoding habits" (that is, painting the pebbles), hence his true self emerges. Paisley also reviews the well-known Mosteller and Wallace experiments in identifying, by a similar approach, the author of the anonymous portions of the Federalist Papers. He then applies the same principle to music and succeeded in doing what musicologists have long sought unsuccessfully to accomplish: he accurately identified, on internal evidence alone, the specific composers of a large body of brief "anonymous" musical themes. And he did it by a computer-assisted statistical analysis of each theme's melodic content, more specifically, by the sequence of intervallic relationships. Although the experiment's logic and statistical controls cannot be faulted, some of my musicological colleagues still refuse to believe that it can actually work. None, by the way, have attempted to refute it. Fortunately, more and more scholars have become convinced that objective content analysis in music is not only feasible but is essential, if real progress is to be made in defining musical styles and understanding how stylistic evolution occurs.

[1] This lecture demonstrated that the classic-romantic dualism, long accepted in art and literature history for this period, existed throughout the so-called classical era in music as well.

Other investigators who, like Paisley, are not primarily concerned with music, but more generally with information, perception, and communication, have provided powerful impetus to new statistical musical investigations. Among the most important is Abraham Moles (1958, 1965), who has long been involved· with theoretical aspects of experimental music in Paris including *musique concrète* and *l'objet sonore*. His book was recently translated into English by Joel E. Cohen, himself the author of a valuable study on *Information Theory and Music* (Cohen, 1962). In Germany, physicist Wilhelm Fucks of the Technische Universität in Aachen and his collaborators, Joseph Lauter and Walter Reckziegel, have performed a series of sophisticated statistical investigations into language and music structure. These analyses and "correlograms" of a large sampling of musical works from the Middle Ages to the present have been extensively reported since 1957 (Fucks, 1957; 1962, 1964, 1965).

In 1957, the American musicologist and aesthetician, Leonard B. Meyer of the University of Chicago, wrote a pathfinding article exploring the striking parallels he found between "Meaning in Music and Information Theory." "Among these," he writes, "were the importance of uncertainty in musical communication, the probabilistic nature of musical style, and the operation in musical experience of . . . the Markoff process. In particular, it would seem that the psycho-stylistic conditions which give rise to musical meaning whether affective or intellectual, are the same as those which communicate information." Since musical styles, whether of individuals, mediums, cultures or eras, are "internalized probability systems," Meyer continues, "out of such internalized probability systems arise the expectations—the tendencies—upon which musical meaning is built . . . In short, the probability relationships embodied in a particular musical style together with the various modes of mental behavior involved in the perception and understanding of the materials of the style constitute the *norms* of the style" (Meyer, 1957).

Professor Meyer concludes his study with a series of valuable cautions to statistical researchers in style analysis; I recommend them unreservedly. His delineation of the problems involved remains painfully valid today, especially in view of the number of investigations in this sphere undertaken within the last two or three years—a number that is growing at an astonishing rate.[2]

Musical data for analysis is available in two principal forms: acoustical (that is, the sound itself) and symbolic (the notation used to represent

[2] See *Writings on the Use of Computers in Music,* compiled by Gary Berlind in collaboration with Barry S. Brook, Lejaren A. Hiller, Jr., Jan P. LaRue, and George Logemann, Institute for Computer Research in the Humanities, New York University, 1965. Updated annually in *Computers and the Humanities,* Queens College, N.Y.

the sound). Much progress has been made in the measurement of the physical properties of sound events, in the field of sound synthesis, in psycho-acoustics and, recently, in music as performed (see Bengtsson, 1967). The revolution in the field of sound analysis, brought about by the oscilloscope, may soon be equalled by the capability that exists today to digitalize sound completely, to store it as a table of numbers, and to recreate it without perceptible loss or change.

Our concern here, however, is with music as annotated. The composer's written score, no matter how imperfect, is still the simplest way to arrive at an understanding of his intellectual intention. Notice that even aurally transmitted music, such as folk music and jazz, is still as a rule transcribed into written notation before analysis takes place. Conventionally, the composer has employed a sophisticated notational system that has taken two millenia to develop. Nevertheless, for pre-1800 music, it is often only the skeletal blueprint of his conception or, at best, an approximation that must be realized in live performances. (This is one reason why some contemporary composers are fascinated by the possibilities of today's electronic devices, which permit them to be their own performer and to build their pieces, inch by inch, on multichannel tape.) A welcome by-product of one of the most advanced computer-assisted analytical investigations undertaken in music to date has been precisely the help it affords in clarifying the composer's unspecified intentions. The Princeton study of the Masses of Josquin Desprez, led by Arthur Mendel and Lewis Lockwood, and based on IML-MIR retrieval programs written by Michael Kassler and Tobias Robison, has been getting promising results working with the difficult problem of *musica ficta,* the practice of employing unspecified accidentals in renaissance music (see Lockwood, in press).

Even dealing only with the composers' written symbols presents problems not shared by other disciplines. A single note, for example, represents

many rather imperfectly defined variables such as pitch, duration, timbre, and dynamics. Its position on the five-line staff defines its fundamental *pitch* or number of vibrations (technically, of course, this is true only if a sort of "Greenwich mean" pitch has been preestablished for it and a system of tuning has been decided upon).

Duration is indicated in our example, partially by the fact that the notehead is filled in and has a stem, and partially by the meter and tempo indications for the piece as a whole; real precision is achieved only if a metronomic tempo indication is added. *Timbre* is defined by fundamental and overtone vibration strengths and is determined by the voice(s) or instrument(s) (or combination of them) used to produce the vibrating note which, in turn, is affected by a variety of acoustical considerations (size and resonance of the room, for instance). The note also possesses *dynamics,* or amplitude of vibration which, if indicated at all by the composer, is usually presented only in relative and vague terms. More complex aspects of a single tone, such as attack, decay, and release are usually taken for granted, and not notated at all except by electronic composers who build each sound from scratch.

To produce a *melody,* the composer provides us with a consecutive series of pitches; our one note now takes on contextual connotations. For example, in the following three illustrations, our note's musical significance, function, and information content vary greatly:

Similar differences in role and importance occur when the same quarter note is used in various vertical arrays to produce *harmonies,* for example:

In both sets of examples above, the quantity of information conveyed by our note (within, in this case, the tonal system) varies from very great to almost zero.

The single note may now be combined with other single notes, each with its own assortment of variables and each existing in its own time span; they may all be woven into different vertical and linear textures heard simultaneously (homophony and counterpoint); they may be combined to form a variety of logical tonal and atonal systems or, for that matter, may be related only stochastically; they may be built into phrases, sentences, and larger structures of all kinds and shapes; and the whole may be contained in a musical composition lasting anywhere from a few seconds to many hours. The fusion of this multitude of variables into a meaningful universe of discourse will constitute the piece's style.

The time factor provides complications for music analysis not found in, say, poetry or painting. On the other hand, both poetry and painting most usually deal with questions of concrete meaning, with which music, an abstract art, is usually not concerned. By having so many variables occurring simultaneously, the music analyst seems to have more in common with the physician in the intensive-care section of a modern hospital where the critically-ill patient is continuously and simultaneously being tested for temperature, blood pressure, pulse, and the like.

The coding of notated music for analysis may be accomplished at many levels depending largely on the number of variables to be studied. The main difficulty is that, unlike poetry, for example, numerous musical events, occurring concurrently, need to be recorded by a linear notation. The *Simplified Plaine and Easie Code* is one of a number of computer input languages developed by a swiftly growing number of scholars to serve a variety of musical research purposes. It was originally designed in 1964 for bibliographic purposes to provide representation of the musical incipit (first ten notes or so); it has since been expanded to include the linear representation of the total musical score. The original bibliographic specifications were as follows:

> It must be speedy, simple, absolutely accurate as to pitch and rhythm. It should be as closely related mnemonically to musical notation as possible, so that it appears natural and right, avoiding arbitrary symbols. It should require only a single line of typewriter characters without the need for back-spacing or for a second pass over the line. It should be usable by non-musicians with only a few minutes of instruction, It must be easily recognizable as music from the symbols alone and immediately retranslatable, without loss, into conventional notation. It must be applicable to all western music from Gregorian chant to serial music. It must be universally understandable and internationally acceptable. It must be so devised as to be readily transferable to electronic data-processing equipment for key transposition, fact-finding, tabulating and other research purposes (Brook and Gould, 1964).

The *Simplified Plaine and Easie Code System for Notating Music* (Brook, 1965), which did away with some of the complications of the earlier version, presents the data in two sections.

Part I, Preliminary Information. This part indicates the name of the piece, the number of the movement, instrument or voice, clef, tempo, key signature, and meter. These are given in ordinary language in the order in which they are usually encountered on the page and are unambiguously abbreviated where appropriate. For example, in Beethoven's Symphony No. 5, the Part I data might read:

III, cello, F-4 clef (All, bBEAm, 3/4)

This means: 3rd movement, cello part, F clef on the 4th line (tempo = Allegro; key signature = 3 flats in minor; meter = 3/4.) Some of this information automatically alters the apparent meaning of the second part; for example, the key signature affects certain pitches thoughout the piece.

Part 2, The Notes. This is the code itself, which provides a precise rendition of all musical data as it appears on the staff. It incorporates a number of notational short cuts that make it possible to write the music down by hand, by typewriter, or by key punch, faster than the writing of ordinary notation.

DURATION. Given in numbers, 1 2 3 4 5 6 7 8 9 0, for both notes and rests. The numbers precede pitch letters and *remain in effect, crossing bar lines, until a different duration number appears.*

1 = whole note or rest
2 = half note or rest
4 = quarter note or rest
8 = eighth
6 = 16th
3 = 32nd
5 = 64th
7 = 128th
9 = Breve
0 = Longa

Dotted notes are indicated by a period following the duration number: 2.C = dotted half note C.

Rests are indicated by a hyphen: 4C-2- = ♩ ♩ ⁻

Ties are indicated by *an* underline (or plus) sign: 2C___4C (or 2C + 4C) = ♩ ♩

Triplets and other unusual rhythmic groupings are enclosed in parentheses preceded by total duration number: 4(8CDE) = ♫♪

PITCH: Given in letters, A B C D E F G.

Accidentals immediately precede pitch letters:

Sharp # (or X)
Flat b (or Y)
Natural n (or Z)

Register (octave placement) is indicated by commas or apostrophes placed in front of duration and pitch symbols and *remaining in effect until a different register sign appears.*

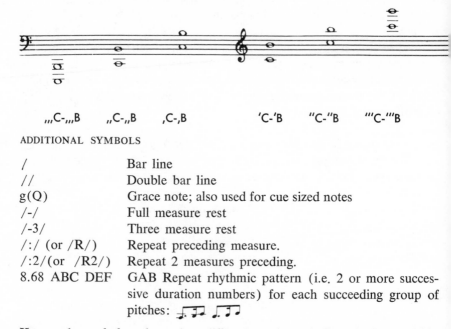

,,,C-,,,B   ,,C-,,B   ,C-,B   'C-'B   "C-"B   '''C-'''B

ADDITIONAL SYMBOLS

/	Bar line
//	Double bar line
g(Q)	Grace note; also used for cue sized notes
/-/	Full measure rest
/-3/	Three measure rest
/:/ (or /R/)	Repeat preceding measure.
/:2/(or /R2/)	Repeat 2 measures preceding.
8.68 ABC DEF	GAB Repeat rhythmic pattern (i.e. 2 or more successive duration numbers) for each succeeding group of pitches:

Keypunch symbols, where they differ, have been indicated above within parentheses. (Further supplementary symbols may be found in Brook and Gould, 1964 and Brook, 1965.)

If we now return to our previously mentioned example from Beethoven's Fifth Symphony, the opening cello line of the third movement will encode like this:

(Allegro, bBEA minor, 3/4)

,,4G / ,C   E G / '2C 4E / 2D ,4 #F / 2.G__ / G /

There is no ambiguity. Beethoven could have written the line of symbols instead of the notes without loss. Supplementary data such as slurs, dynamic marks, and staccato indications can readily be included when called for.

In this transference of conventional musical notation to a machine-readable, highly mnemonic, linear code, the musical data remain readily recognizable as such, usable, and classifiable by hand. This provides the researcher with an invaluable manipulating and proofreading potential not available with nonmnemonic codes.[3] The *Simplified Plaine and Easie Code* is now used for many bibliographic purposes including the preparation of thematic indexes, the lexicographic indexing, ordering and transposition of musical information; several foreign countries are using it to catalogue their holdings in early music. Jan LaRue of New York University is using it for his vast computerized union catalogues of 18th-century instrumental music. The code has been adapted by Murray Gould to deal specifically with Gregorian chant (Gould, 1967). It has been programmed by Richard Golden to drive a Cal-Comp plotter and is being prepared for use with other, more sophisticated printing devices such as the microfilm recorder. It has been expanded by Gould and George Logemann (in press) into a complete input process for the total representation of any traditional musical score.

For content analysis purposes, the implications of such developments and of the many other projects employing different premises and coding systems are fascinating. Thus far, although major breakthroughs are few, progress has been reported on many fronts. In addition to those previously mentioned, the following should be noted: Allan Forte's (1965, in press) studies of the structure of atonal music; Roland Jackson's (in press) investigations in harmonic analysis; Nanna Schiødt's (1967) analysis of melodic formulas in Byzantine Sticherarion melodies; Hana Malá's (1967) comparative analysis of Janáček choral works and Moravian folk songs in which style creating potential of a specific music element was studied; Eric Regener's (1967) system for music analysis; Jan LaRue's (1967) style analysis studies employing the time-line to link variables together; and Hans Peter Reinecke's (in press) analysis of musical structure.

Eventually, the optical scanner for music, by virtually eliminating the man hours now required for coding, key-boarding and proofreading, will make possible the creation of vast libraries of machine readable music.

---

[3] Whatever the input language, it is possible to proofread the coded data aurally with the help of a computer program that translates the coded pitches into sound vibrations.

The mettle of the musical content analyst will then really be put to the test. As Milton Babbitt stated:

> . . . those procedures which are normally termed 'substatistical': indexing, cataloguing and searching [must be followed by] those which are genuinely statistical: the formulation of attributive hypotheses in the interest of characterization and attribution, the testing of hypotheses, the sampling of compositions from a compositional population, the determining of correlations between dimensions of a work, between works, collections of works, scaling, sequential testing . . . (Babbitt, 1965:74).

Content analysis, or style analysis, is in its infancy in the field of musicology. We have much to learn from the techniques and procedures developed in other disciplines, and perhaps, especially because of music's abstract nature, something unique to offer in return. Our notational and recording systems have been developed to the point where the precise quantification with computer help of musical data is increasingly possible. Algorithms developed for use with these codes will be readily adaptable for operation, when needed, upon huge quantities of visually scanned input as well. The potential, or rather the availability, of machine help in the analytical control of many simultaneous variables—indispensable in musical content analysis—is exciting to contemplate. The fundamental problem remains: collecting and counting, no matter how speedy our machines or how sophisticated our programs, will be no more meaningful than they ever have been without the application of intelligent hypotheses and accurate analytical techniques to valid, scholarly objectives.

16 VID-R and SCAN: Tools and Methods for the Automated Analysis of Visual Records[1]

Paul Ekman
Wallace V. Friesen
and Thomas G. Taussig

University of California

The VID-R (Visual Information Display and Retrieval) system was designed for situations where permanent visual records of some phenomena are required, and where the analysis of such records must proceed on the basis of complex decisions made by a human observer. Let us outline some of the reasons why permanent records might be necessary and why analysis would depend on an observer's judgments rather than on some optical scanning procedure.

Permanent visual records, whether still photographs, motion picture film, or videotape, may be necessary if the phenomenon occurs rarely or is nonrecurrent. Permanent records are also necessary if the phenomenon is recurrent but generally inaccessible. A number of recurrent and available phenomena also may require permanent records. For example, when the investigator is uncertain about the unit of measurement and

[1] Paul Ekman and Wallace Friesen are associated with the Langley Porter Neuropsychiatric Institute, University of California Medical School, San Francisco. Thomas Taussig is affiliated with the University of California, Berkeley, and the Lawrence Radiation Laboratory. We express our appreciation to the persons who aided the development of this system: to Henry Jacobs who offered his experience in the video field to help us evaluate the latest equipment available and to introduce us to other knowledgeable persons in this field; to Jerome Russell for guiding us to creative persons working with computers, video, and interface equipment, and for offering his own knowledge of these fields to evaluate prospective contractors for the system; and, finally, to Charles Steinheimer, Field Representative for Sicular X-Ray, Donald Horstkorta, Regional Representative for Sony Corporation, and Jack Sanford, Senior Field Engineer for COHU Electronics, for sophisticated technical suggestions and guidance which allowed the development of an integrated system. Research and development of the equipment and methods were supported by a research grant (MH 11976-03) and a career development award (1-K3-MH-6092-02).

must apply different measurement techniques to the same record, repeated viewing is necessary. Or, the salient phenomena may be so rapid that they cannot be observed at real time but, instead, require slow motion observation. Or, many events occurring simultaneously may not be measurable in one viewing or pass but, instead, require multiple viewing of the phenomena.

Some permanent records can be subjected to automated analysis through optical scanning procedures. But such processing or conversion of a record into digital data is not possible if the events to be measured are complex patterns that are either difficult to define without previous study or are so complex or varied that they are prohibitively expensive to program for an optical scanner. Another, and perhaps more common problem, which prevents the application of optical scanning, is that the record was obtained in an environment where scanning procedures would not be applicable because of the difficulty in discriminating the particular event from the background, or from other irrelevant events. Another obstacle, again a common one, is that the investigation is exploratory; the investigator has not determined *a priori* units of measurement, but will develop them from inspection.

In the behavioral sciences, visual records of human behavior are often not amenable to optical scanning but instead must be viewed to be analyzed. Too frequently, however, the investigator is seduced by the allure of capturing the phenomenon on his film and neglects consideration of how to convert that record into data until he is confronted with a nearly overwhelming mass of motion picture film or videotapes. Although permanent records have the virtue of slow motion and repeated viewing, they are, one soon discovers, nearly as complex as the original phenomenon recorded; simply viewing them once will not often immediately reveal the proper units of analysis; if the phenomenon was baffling when it occurred, it will remain baffling when it is viewed on film. Moreover, it takes at least as much time to view a permanent record once as the phenomena originally required, and records are not data. While records may be the raw input for intriguing ideas and discovery, they must be converted into some digital form in order to be analyzed. It is no surprise, then, that rather large collections of motion picture films or videotapes of human interactions, stored in laboratories around the United States, not only have not been analyzed but may not even once have been viewed by the investigator. Imagine how long it would take you to look at the record of a complete psychoanalysis of 300 hours, if you watched it at real time only, including the time necessary for getting the film in and out of the projector, and making a few notes about what you observe in each reel!

Usually, when confronted with such a supply of records, the investigator inquires about hardware that might be available to help him wade through this mass. Unfortunately, he has not had much help. There are motion picture projectors that permit excellent viewing at slowed motion and real time and even reasonably accurate frame counts, but that do not allow viewing at faster than real time, have no capacity for fast search, and no automated retrieval. Editing equipment is excellent for fast search, although search cannot be done automatically, slow-motion viewing is not efficient, and image size is small. All motion picture devices suffer from the problems that rearrangement of phenomena for better inspection or specific analysis tasks, require cutting and splicing which is costly and time consuming, and there is no ability to store "on-line" with the visual record any indexing or measurements which could be used for retrieval of specific events for further analysis. Videotape recorders have fast search capacity, usually up to twenty times real time, but location of specific events means reliance on counters that are not indexed in enough detail for most purposes, and storage of indexing materials and measurements must be off-line.

Before describing the hardware system we have developed, let us first describe some of the functional specifications that would be desirable for any human viewing and analysis of permanent visual records:

1. *Viewing speeds.* The operator should be able to view his record at various slowed and accelerated speeds. Slow motion is necessary to insure reliable location and description of the event in some cases and, in others, even to see the event. Fast motion is useful both for rapid scanning to find an event, or for amplifying small slow movements that are difficult to perceive at real time.

2. *Digital addresses* for search and retrieval should ideally be stored for the smallest unit which a recording unit can differentiate (24 separate addresses per second with sound motion picture film, 30 per second for videotape). Search and retrieval should be possible by these addresses. The system should be capable of writing, storing, reading, and retrieving index information or measurement codes. Whether the index describes the activity shown in the record (for example, one person or dyadic interaction, basket weaving, or child training) or codes the observers' informal estimate of the value of a portion of the record, the ability to store such indexes and then retrieve the relevant portion of the visual record by means of them is crucial if the observer is to profit from the coding based on past viewing or the viewing of other observers. The ability to store measurements or codes and retrieve by means of them makes it possible to cull from the record all events coded in a particular way,

and view them again, either to check the reliability of the code, to recode if reliability turned out to be low, or finally to aid the coding of additional events.

3. *Search and retrieval.* The operator should be able to find automatically any event within his record, retrieving this event by requesting an address or by using an index or measurement code. Search should then be reasonably fast (at least 5 times real time) and exact in terms of stopping at the precise location requested. Such search and retrieval is necessary for a variety of reasons: to review previously measured phenomena; to compare events where initial observers coded them in some way; and to eliminate the necessity to view irrelevant events while waiting for the critical event.

4. *Temporal reorganization of the record.* Any series of events located in the record should be capable of being reorganized into a new record, in any predetermined sequence, for further viewing. This capacity allows the operator to sift from a record particular incidents or specific types of events, and gather them onto a single record for more rapid access. The production of such a reorganized selected record should, of course, be automated, based on operator instructions supplied in terms of code indexes, time code addresses, or coded descriptive measurements.

5. *Access to a visual library.* The observer should have rapid access to a visual example which defines the meaning or the boundaries of any of the investigator's codes or measurement procedures. Often the coding of human behavior involves the development of classes of behavior or units that are difficult to describe verbally or to remember when described verbally. A visual dictionary or library, with visual examples of the criterion for each type of event or code, can be the most economical way to define a measurement procedure. If the operator has immediate access to any entry in the library, he can retrieve that entry and visually compare the library definition with the event he is attempting to code.

VID-R was designed to accept either 16mm film or videotape as the original recording medium, although the analysis is performed on a videotape version of the record. We felt it important to design the system to accept either 16mm film or videotape as the original recording medium, for two reasons: (1) so that already existing film records and archives could be employed (and there are many large archives on film of phenomena which would be difficult or expensive to record), and (2) so that the high resolution possible with film records could be preserved if the other conditions of recording allowed full exploitation of this film potential. Actually, the choice of whether to record on film or videotape must be guided by a number of considerations. Although videotape as the original record sacrifices some of the resolution possible with film when lighting is bright, under the more usual conditions of lighting necessary to record the subject without his knowledge or without his continual cognizance of the lights, videotape may produce as good or better a record as film. Videotape can allow recording continuously for 1½ hours, while film is usually limited to 30 minutes. Because of lower costs, videotape can be used with multiple cameras; with two videotape records, either from different angles or one with a zoom, for less than the costs of one film record. And, of course, videotape can be erased or rerecorded; thus the camera can be left to capture unpredictable events and the waste time reused later. A final consideration is feedback to the investigator; with videotape, one can learn immediately whether the phenomenon being recorded is actually being recorded in a satisfactory way, but the use of film imposes at least one day's delay, while the film developer works, before you know whether you recorded what you think you did. Regardless of how the original record was obtained (film or tape), we think it must be transferred to tape in order to perform analysis in a way that meets the five demands we just outlined.

The components of the VID-R system are:

One film-to-television chain which allows the transfer of 16mm optical sound movies onto the video and audio channels of a videotape recorder.

Two Sony PV 120U videotape recorders with complete remote control of the functions; playback, record, fast forward, rewind, variable slowed-motion, stop motion, variable high-speed playback, and stop.

One video-disc recorder capable of recording at least 20 seconds of video information and playback at high-resolution slowed and stop motion.

Three high resolution television monitors.

One Teletype ASR 33, keyboard-printer with papertape punch and reader. This is the means of operator-system communication.

One Digital Equipment Corporation PDP-8 programmed data processor. This low-cost computer provides the logic for the operations to be described.

One video and audio interface to perform data transfers between the computer and recorders.

Three videotape recorder controllers capable of performing the instructions of the computer, to place the recorder into the proper motion to perform the task.

One or two high resolution Vidicon cameras for field recording.

The Film-to-Videotape Transfer

When 16mm film has served as the original medium for the research record, the film-to-television chain would be employed. Our chain uses an L-W Athena, 16mm Analyst sound projector modified for TV frame synchronization. This projector is capable of moving the film forward or reverse, at slowed motion of 1 to 12 frames per second, holding indefinitely on any single frame, or operating at the normal sound projection speed of 24 frames per second. This projector also has a frame counter that can be used to locate specific places on the film when only partial record transfers are required.

The COHU 8507 high resolution Vidicon camera, employed on the chain, is mounted on a motor-driven carriage to allow zooming. At one extremity of the Vidicon camera track, a one-to-one copy of the 16mm image is converted into a television signal. At the other extreme, the image is enlarged 6 times, and by up-down and side-to-side movement of the lens between the projector and camera, any portion of the filmed image may be focused on the Vidicon. Optics are not employed on either the projector or camera, but there is a single field lens in between projector and Vidicon, which can be adjusted for focus. The signal generated by the Vidicon camera may be displayed on the monitors and/or recorded onto videotape.

This film chain's unique features of slowed and stop motion projection and the capacity to zoom the image to six times normal size provide a flexibility for film analysis that will become more apparent as the applications of the system are elaborated. However, with the film chain alone, extensive editing of film can be made through this system. The control of finding and holding a position on the film and flexibility of projection speeds allows the investigator to produce tapes containing only salient events that he wishes to analyze, recorded at several speeds to aid his viewing.

Writing Digital Codes on the Videotape

As a video transfer is made of a film, the computer controls the recording function of the videotape recorder and generates sequential binary codes that are inserted outside the normal viewing portion of the picture on each video frame. In the data write mode, codes are loaded from the computer into a register and then shifted out and recorded serially in the horizontal scan of the video. Twelve bits of data per scan line are written on the videotape commencing after the horizontal synchronizing pulse. Information is recorded with a redundant code so that the information can be checked and corrected for error during later "reading."

Thus when numbering frames, 30 video frames per second are labeled with a discriminable code of 6 numerical digits, so as to allow the retrieval of any one of the 162,000 frames on a 90 minute reel of videotape. Locations of the beginning and end of visual behavior may therefore be established to the smallest measurable unit: the video frame.

Frame coding is not restricted to videotapes made during a film-to-television transfer. Videotape records made in the "field" and duplicate videotapes from a tape master may also be "numbered" during the recording of the video information. Furthermore, the process of generating sequential frame numbers may be interrupted. The computer is capable of "reading" the last locational code of the material presently recorded on a videotape and then will continue numbering all additional frames from that point of reference.

The computer and video interface equipment is not restricted to "writing" codes on any particular part of the video frame. The computer may instruct the interface so that code information continues to be inserted on each succeeding scan line of a video field until all information is recorded. Thus entire video fields may be used to record compiled locational indexes, digitally coded descriptions of the recorded behavior, or any other relevant information that can be coded digitally. The capacity of the computer-controlled-interface components to "write" and "read" binary codes recorded on the videotape is basic to the functional specifications described earlier. The components and procedures involved in meeting those specifications will now be described in some detail.

Viewing the Videotape Record

The operator can request, through the computer controller, all of the remotely controlled operations of the video-recorders. Normal playback, stop-motion, and variable slowed motion can be requested in either the forward or reverse mode. Fast forward and fast rewind can also be requested for search operations. An additional feature is that, through computer control of the speed of fast forward and rewind modes, a faster than real time playback can be requested. Finally, because the two video recorders and the video-disc recorder are all connected to the system, episodes on the videotape can be transferred to the disc for high resolution playback at slowed and stop motion speeds.

Frequently used sets of operations may also be requested by designating a "subroutine." For example, the following sequence can be repeated throughout the viewing of a record. The video-recorder is directed to search at fast forward speed for the beginning of a specified behavioral unit; this event is played back at normal viewing speed from beginning to end. The recorder returns to the beginning of the unit and repeats the playback at normal slowed or fast play speed with the simple designation of the speed. The recorder then can be directed to return to the beginning of the event to transfer to the video-disc if there is a need for higher quality slowed motion, or in careful scrutiny of single frames. When the operator is finished, he pushes the advance key and the recorder is moved to the next event on the tape. When a second video-recorder is used for comparative viewing, the computer-controller may be displaying events from one recorder while searching for another event on the second recorder, or as part of the "subroutine" may be making duplicate recordings between the display of events.

If there is a written record of the location of several incidents, the beginning and end frame numbers for a large group of units may be requested when the operator begins his coding operations. The computer would store the requested group and search, retrieve, and display each item in turn. This method, however, would make use of "off-line" records of the locations, codings and descriptions of incidents that have already been isolated. The VID-R system precludes the necessity for excessive "off-line" bookkeeping. Instead of requesting the display of a series of units by their previously located position in the tape, the operator may request the display of all incidents that have been described in a particular manner. The computer stores this request, refers to the summary index recorded at the beginning of the tape, locates and displays each incident meeting the description, and advances to the next event only after the operator has inserted additional codes or corrections and has otherwise completed his inspection. These locational procedures will be discussed in more detail.

High-Speed Search and Retrieval

Under the control of the computer, the videotape recorders are operated at the most economical speed to any requested position on the videotape record. When receiving a request to move the videotape to a particular location, the computer must "read" the position of the videotape from the frame locational code, compare this location with the one being requested, and determine the direction and speed of movement that is required. For long distances, the videotape recorder is switched into the high-speed forward or rewind mode and through the use of dead-reckoning techniques, moved to the approximate location. The recorder is switched to a slower speed and its exact location determined. As necessary, the computer returns the recorder to the high-speed mode, goes into the play mode, or reverses the direction of tape movement. When the requested position of the tape is approached the recorder is switched into the play mode and stopped at the exact position as desired. Using these techniques, the maximum time required to search from one end to the other of a ninety minute reel of videotape is approximately six minutes or 15 times real time. For short search distances the normal play speeds, slowed motion or controlled high-speed play modes are used to locate most economically the desired frame, so as to not overshoot the target location. During all locational operations, the video switching does not allow noise and irrelevant visual material to be displayed on the monitors, thus reducing confusions and distractions for the operator.

Temporal Reorganization of the Visual Record

Having determined the locations, coding, and descriptions of a set of events, the operator may wish to review visually all events given the same code. This can be done by requesting a high-speed search, then display, of each of these events. However, this system is also designed to allow the operator to describe the set of events by code or location and to request the automatic and continuous retrieval and rerecording of each occasion onto a second videotape. In this operation, each set of events where comparison is desired is clustered together. When played back, this "edited" videotape allows the operator to view all events given the same code without any interruptions from irrelevant material or search time. The production of an "edited" record from a single 90 minute videotape requires no operator functions after the selected sequences and their ordering have been requested. What has always been a tedious and expensive editing task with movie film (or could have been accomplished through tedious film-to-videotape transfers on the chain) can be completed automatically and at nominal expense. The advantage of this is that, for the first time, it is feasible to check reliability and validity of coding visually without frustrating interruptions and time delays.

Off-Line Records and Data Analysis

Since all communication in and out of the VID-R system is through the teletype, a typed or papertape record can be maintained of all located events, their codes, locations, and descriptions. Also, a videotape can be played back and the computer can direct a teletype record of any coded information. The duration of each event can be easily determined as well. When the computer is not needed for control of the rest of the system for a period of time, events can be collated by their location, mean durations, and frequencies; and the conditions under which particular events occur most frequently can be calculated by the computer. When the on-line operations of the computer are required for control functions, then the papertape can be read by an off-line system and even more complicated computations based on the codings, locations, and descriptions can be done. The unique capability of the VID-R system, in regard to off-line operations, is that records do not have to be kept in file but are collated from the videotapes only when needed.

The Visual Library

In the analysis of visually recorded information it is often desirable to define items in visual rather than verbal terms. If the operator who is coding a visual record has access to a library that contains visual examples of each item he is to locate or code, he can make a more precise judgment, through comparison of the library example with the record to be coded, than if he must translate a verbal description into visual terms that he then compares with the visual record. Three problems that have previously interfered with the use of such a library are overcome by the VID-R system: fast access to and retrieval from the library; compiling the library; updating or reorganizing the library.

In the VID-R system, the operator describes by means of a code relevant features of the visual event he is about to analyze. His coding descriptions are compared by the computer with the coding descriptions of the library entries; the computer then finds and displays on a monitor any library entries that have similar codes, and the operator can compare them with the event he is attempting to classify. If the computer finds no applicable entries in the library it informs the coder, and he can activate a subroutine that transfers the new event and its codes into the library, as a new entry defining a new class of phenomena.

The original library is compiled by transferring specific examples from other videotape records, with descriptive codes of each entry so that later retrieval is possible. When the events to be entered into the library have been determined, the operator can instruct the computer where to find them in the record, and the production of a library tape is then performed automatically. Adding additional entries to the library, as new events or classes of phenomena are encountered, is a simple matter, following the same procedures.

Up-dating the library, either by changing the specific examples in library definition, or by summarizing definitions into a broader definition, or by refining a single definition into two or more definitions, can be accomplished with precise location of the entry and precise insertions or deletions by computer control.

Although the use of the library procedure may sound complicated, its feasibility in time and expense is best seen by comparison with creating a library with film. If the library were built from film, there would be no computer-directed way of finding entries in the library, unless an off-line device were used. The creation of the library would be costly in time and materials, involving duplicate printing and compiling by splicing or optically printing the entries onto a reel. Even more terrible to contemplate is the cost of tearing such a library film apart to update, reorganize, or substitute examples.

APPLICATIONS OF VID-R

Now let us discuss some of the applications of VID-R. We shall illustrate the use of VID-R by describing, first, procedures we have developed for the analysis of nonverbal behavior shown by mental patients, then a technique for the complete analysis and classification of movements, and then a technique for the more selected analysis of specific types of movements. Finally, we shall briefly discuss how VID-R might be used to index film archives, and how it might be used in a completely different application: programmed learning.

Systematic Classification and Analysis of Nonverbal Behavior (SCAN)

We have developed the SCAN procedures for classifying all observable body and facial movements without reference to an *a priori* theory about classes or types of movements. The unit of movement, *the act,* is defined as either (1) the start and stop of motion in a given body area, or (2) the change of visual configuration in a continuous movement. SCAN is applied separately to the following body areas: head, hands-arms, shoulder-arms, feet-legs, knees-legs, and the face. These areas are divided in terms of possibilities for independent action, and are separated for analysis so that the coder can concentrate his visual attention with minimal distraction from other areas of the body. Let us explain SCAN in terms of the coder operations for one body area: the hands-arms.

The coder begins his work with a tape showing only this area of the body. During his first viewing, the coder locates the beginning and end frames of each visually distinctive movement. He instructs the computer to have the videotape recorder play back the record at real time. At the moment he observes movement in either hand, he presses a teletype key that reverses the recorder a few frames and plays back the approach to the movement at slowed motion. When he observes the first frame of movement he pushes the "start" key on the teletype. The computer reads the number of the frame that the operator has indicated, punches the number on papertape, and stores it in its core memory. The coder continues through the movement until the hand is motionless or the visual configuration of the movement changes and presses the "stop" key. The operator then describes the movement in terms of a code for the visual configurations of hand movements. The location of the end and the visual configuration code are also stored in the computer memory. At this point the computer moves the tape back to the beginning of the act and plays it back while recording it on a second videotape with information identifying it, for example, original identifying information codes and any code information. This second tape, which is on the second videotape recorder, will be referred to as the "working tape." The coder then proceeds to the next point at which either hand moves, and codes that movement, which is in turn transferred to the working tape. If this first step of coding has been done accurately, then the working tape should contain all hand movements shown on the original record.

Two verification steps usually follow. While reading begin and end locations from the working tape, the original record is played back at normal viewing speed. Each time the beginning and end of a movement is reached in the record the coder is notified audibly or by visual marker. Any movements that he has missed on the first viewing, or incorrectly located or coded, can be recorded at the end of the working tape.

The original locations and descriptions of the acts incorrectly identified on the first viewing are listed by the teletype, and erased from the working tape at the end of this verification phase. The second verification step is to look at the working tape and determine that each movement was recorded completely from beginning to end. This verification is usually done simultaneously with the next coding phase.

To continue our example of the coding of the hand movements in a single record, the coder puts the working tape on one recorder, and the library tape on the other. When the working tape approaches the first act, the act's description is transferred automatically to the computer, and the search of the library tape for examples of similar description is initiated automatically. This library search proceeds while the operator is viewing the first act to be coded. The coder compares the act with all similarly described acts in the library and, if any one of the library examples is like the new act, the new act is given the same categorical code number. If no movement on the library tape is like the new act, the new act is assigned a new categorical act code and rerecorded onto the proper location of the library tape with all codes, descriptions and locations. The library tape is returned to the beginning of the section and the coded information is added to the index. When this coding is completed, all codes, descriptions, and act locations are written at the beginning of the working tape and original tape.

The final verification step follows. A second working tape is made; all acts that were coded in the same manner are clustered together, adjacent clusters being determined by similarities in description. This tape is produced completely by the computer-controller system and allows the visual verification of the similarities of acts coded as the same, and of the distinctive features of acts coded as different.

After *all* body areas have been coded and verified in the manner just described for the hands, we would consider that we have *transformed* the behavioral record into *data* which can then be analyzed. For any area of the body, we know how many different types of acts occurred, the frequency of each type of act, the duration of each act, its exact temporal location and, if we like, the correlations between acts from different areas of the body. We can at any time visually retrieve any act from any body area for inspection. SCAN does not itself tell us the meaning of the nonverbal behavior; the SCAN output is the beginning point for our analysis of the data; SCAN transforms the film record into data which can then be studied. We have described elsewhere (Ekman, 1965; Ekman and Friesen, 1968) how we analyze SCAN output. Let us summarize briefly the methods we use so that you will not confuse the SCAN procedure with the methods for analyzing the SCAN output. Let me use, as an example, a hand-rub-hand act.

The SCAN output would tell us how frequently this occurred in a particular film, the duration of each such act, and its exact location. Our first method of analysis involves a search for the common characteristics (demographic or personality) of those individuals who frequently show this act; we would expect, for example, to find a higher frequency of this act in our records of interviews with agitated depressives than with nonagitated depressives or schizophrenics. Our second method of analysis is to determine any similarities in the setting when the hand-rub-hand act occurred. We have filmed psychiatric patients at the beginning, middle, and end of hospitalization; our expectation is that this act occurs more frequently at the beginning or middle of hospitalization than at the time of discharge. Our third method of analysis is a search for any other acts that typically accompany, precede, or follow this act, whenever it is shown. We might find that hand-rub-hand acts often occur when the patient breaks eye contact or turns away from the interviewer. Our fourth method of analysis is to check the verbal behavior emitted whenever this act occurs; some nonverbal acts illustrate the verbal behavior in one of six different ways (see Ekman and Friesen, 1967), but hand-rub-hand acts are not illustrators, and there is probably no relationship to any verbal content across people who show this act. Our fifth method of analysis is to show this act, isolated from its context, to a group of naive observers, asking them to describe their impressions of the person, and analyzing their descriptions for elements common to this act but not present in their descriptions of a different hand act. We would expect hand-rub-hand acts to convey the message of nervousness and self-soothing.

Analysis of Critical Incidents in Nonverbal Behavior

The use of VID-R in the study of nonverbal behavior is not limited to the type of grass-roots empiricism we have just described, in which every movement is isolated, classified, and counted. VID-R can also help in the study of selected incidents considered of critical importance for a theoretical reason. We are in the midst of such an application of VID-R in the study of hand-to-face movements. These movements are considered critical incidents for three reasons: (1) because the face is the site for sensory inputs, for breathing, eating, and making sounds, what the hand does to the face can reveal very personal psychological information relevant to the person's attempts to aid, interfere or otherwise deal with these activities; (2) because the face is the site for affect displays, when the hand touches the face it can show how the individual plans to cope with any particular emotion; and (3) because the face represents the self for many people, the hand touching the face can be interpreted in terms of what the individual is doing to the self, for example, attacking, supporting, and soothing. (A full description of the theoretical rationale of these self-adaptors appears in Ekman and Friesen, 1967.)

In considering hand-to-face acts, there are four variables to code: *location,* what part of the face is touched; *action,* what the hand does to the location; *hand part,* what part of the hand is involved in the action; and *duration,* how long it takes for the hand to get to the face, how long it is involved in the action, and how long it takes for the hand to leave the face and go elsewhere. Just considering the first three variables, a matrix could be generated consisting of at least 20 locations, 9 actions, and 7 hand parts. But do all of these occur in our records? Do they occur with sufficient frequency that we will be able to check any of our hypotheses about meaning? Here is where VID-R helps us.

The hand-to-face acts are scattered somewhere within the 120, 12-minute films of psychiatric patients that we have. Just to look at each act once, in order to develop a code, to determine how many cells in the action-location-part matrix should be considered, would take many days and, if we needed to look again or to have coders apply a scoring system, it would take just as long for them to find each occurrence, and to get each reel in and out of the projector. If we wanted to avoid such time investments, we would have to cut the films, splicing together onto a single reel(s) all hand-to-face acts; but this would be expensive in materials; with VID-R, we proceed as follows.

1. A videotape copy is made of each of the 120 films. The videotape is viewed on a monitor at 5-times real time, since hand-to-face acts are sufficiently salient to be noticeable even at fast time. Whenever the opera-

tor sees a hand-to-face act he activates a subroutine that slows the recorder down and backs it up; he then follows the procedures we described earlier, locating the precise beginning and end of the act and transferring the act onto a second videotape, with identifying information. Thus a working videotape would be compiled of all hand-to-face acts.

2. With such a working tape, or tapes, we could simply sit down and look at all occurrences in a relatively brief time. Or, we could have the operator apply an *a priori* code to all occurrences, storing the code digitally on the tape with each occurrence. VID-R could then produce a frequency distribution for the coding matrix and calculate operator reliability in using the code; after inspecting this information we could instruct VID-R to find and retrieve all hand-to-face acts with a given set of codes, so that we could visually check whether we are classifying as the same, acts which actually look alike.

Again it should be clear that VID-R is not analyzing data. It is collecting and organizing events that, when coded, are in a data form which can be analyzed. When the hand-to-face operations are complete we would have a listing of each type of hand-to-face act, the frequency for each patient, its durations, and its exact locations. To determine the meaning of hand-to-face acts, we would then apply to the VID-R output the five methods of analysis described above.

Indexing Film Archives

In our cross-cultural studies of nonverbal behavior we have been recently working with Dr. Carleton Gajdusek of the National Institute of Health, in the analysis of motion picture footage he and E. R. Sorenson have taken in New Guinea over the past ten years. Their films are a rich source of information about two very primitive groups of people, the Foré and the Kukukuku; most investigators would have difficulty recording this invaluable information which in a few years will, through culture contact, be gone. While these films contain a great deal of nonverbal behavior, they also show everything else possible about these cultures, since Gajdusek and Sorenson viewed as their purpose, at least in part, to record events that would be of interest to various scientific disciplines. They have effectively prepared their footage to preserve information about when and how it was taken (Sorenson, in press). But when one is talking about an archive of over 60,000 feet, there is a need not only for indexing but for the indexes to be search tags for rapid retrieval and visual display.

Let us say we are botanists, and we want not only to know how much footage they have on specific botanical phenomena but also to take a look at such footage and see whether it would be of sufficient pertinence for us to request a copy of those film sequences for further analysis in my laboratory. If their film were indexed (and Gajdusek and Sorenson have begun indexing), we might know where to look in the 60,000 feet of film; but finding each sequence would be enormously time consuming. VID-R could be of considerable help.

Let us suppose that a general index were devised which labeled botanical events, manufacturing, musical episodes, child rearing, child play, and adult conversation. The 60,000 feet of film would be copied onto video-tape, and the index stored on the videotapes. Now, as botanists, or any other investigators with specific interests, we may request through the index to view the events of potential interest; and VID-R uses the fast search to find and then display them to us.

Programmed Instruction

Often in programmed instructional materials there is a need to present information visually, as with drawings, photographs, films, or even printed material. VID-R offers the possibility of being able to store both single frame material and sequential moving visual events, indexed digitally on the tape, and thus retrieval by computer control at whatever point they might be necessary for presentation to the student. With videotape as the format, changing the entries can be accomplished with minimal costs. The main disadvantage of VID-R in this application is that search time could take up to 6 minutes; but this could be considerably reduced if material were stored in other than a random fashion, so that the need to search from one end of the tape to the other for the next step in a programmed learning sequence would be infrequent.

17 Measurement Methods for Vocal Information[1]

John A. Starkweather

Medical Psychology
University of California, San Francisco

Human voice signals carry information beyond that which can be transcribed into language symbols on the printed page. In addition to the information that is coded into linguistic content, the total communication in an interaction between speaker and listener often includes important vocal behavior as well as the information contained in verbal content and in nonverbal gestures and expression. Some people appear to be very sensitive to characteristics of a speaker's voice, and use them to make inferences about his personality and his emotional state at the moment. Most of us are able to identify close friends by voice alone and we can often tell the mood of those whom we know especially well. Also we can imagine situations in which it is important to assess a person's alertness, emotional state, or functioning ability under conditions where that person is remote from us and where our only contact is that of voice communication. It may also be important to establish the speaker's identity under such conditions, and we can imagine the usefulness of knowledge about whether a remote speaker is under coercion, under the effects of drugs, or perhaps has intentions other than those the words would normally imply. This chapter gives a very brief background of research on vocal behavior and describes some vocal data that fit the context of a pattern-recognition problem analogous to other areas of content analysis.

Extensive summaries and reviews of investigations that studied the transfer of vocal information have been published (Starkweather, 1961, 1964a; Kramer, 1963). Early studies made use of judges who provided data that often seemed ambiguous in showing more agreement between judges than in showing agreement with external criteria. A variety of means have been used to remove information related to verbal language content, and judges have then been able to relate the remaining material to emo-

[1] The work described here was supported in part by Contract NONR 3656(28), Office of Naval Research, and Contract DA-49-193-MD-2711, U.S. Army Medical Research and Development Command.

tional expression. They can often accomplish this with reasonably reliable agreement and sensitivity. The methods of removing verbal content have, on the one hand, involved electronic filtering to render content unintelligible and, on the other hand, the standardizing of content by imbedding a standard sentence in the middle of a context of different emotional tone and then playing only the standard portion to listeners. Many of these studies have compared the ability of judges having limited vocal information to that of judges working from verbal content alone as carried in a typewritten transcript. There are indications that vocal information can add to accuracy when the task is that of estimating the degree of a particular emotional state. However, when verbal content and vocal characteristics of speech are purposely arranged to be incongruent and nonmatching, judges have difficulty and disagree in their assessment of the emotional state of a speaker. Judges who demonstrate an ability to recognize an emotional state from vocal cues alone seem to depend on significant changes in pitch, rate, loudness, and other physical characteristics of the voice, but have no consistent way of describing these qualities that lie behind their judgment.

Objective measures of speech timing, rate, pitch, and frequency spectrum analysis have all been used to investigate the vocal communication channel and have, individually and in some combinations, been shown to be sensitive to personality and emotional expression in specific studies. In general, the investigators have used apparatus to measure available acoustical dimensions and have explored the relations between such measures and the characteristics of the speaker. They have not paid much heed to imitating the way in which vocal information is processed by a human listener. One technique that has been used a number of times for the purpose of removing verbal intelligibility and investigating the transmission of information about the speaker in the sound of his voice has been that of low-pass filtering of speech to remove sounds above approximately 600 cycles per second. A quotation from one study using this technique is ". . . that the use of a low-pass filter to obtain content-free speech may in effect produce a signal which has a more favorable signal-to-noise ratio for the communication of affect" (Alpert, Kurtzberg, and Friedhoff, 1963).

Although one's first thought of voice quality may be that of a likely importance of the high frequency structure of overtones, there is a consistent indication that the low frequencies of the voice are particularly important in terms of indicating variation of the speaker's emotional state. Since low frequencies are more likely to reflect a change in vocal-cord frequency rather than a change in the resonant cavities, questions have been raised with relevance to physiology, human development, and linguistics (Mahl, 1964a). Data are not available to indicate whether low frequency variations may result from generalized neuromuscular changes present throughout the body or from changes in the vocal apparatus alone. The insignificance of these same low frequencies for speech intelligibility leads also to the question of a possible inverse relationship between linguistic restraint, as is present for higher frequencies, and the ability to express emotion. It is, indeed, true that in English at least, pitch, loudness, and speech rate are not linguistically restrained, and are therefore free to indicate speaker identity and emotional state as they seem to do.

This emphasis on low frequencies is true for studies which play various portions of the voice spectrum to judges for interpretation, but it is not consistently true for studies which have investigated the predictive ability of direct acoustic measures of time-averaged voice spectra. If one has available a set of highly discriminating band-pass filters, it is possible to measure the average amount of sound energy which occurs in each portion of the audible frequency spectrum over successive periods of time where each period is sufficiently long to contain a sampling of verbal content. Such a technique has been used in order to allow the analysis of spontaneous speech where there is no possibility of controlling content and making it identical from one sample to another. The information contained in such data is undoubtedly different from that available to a listener, since it omits the variation in pitch which listeners call intonation but centers, instead, upon speakers' individual and average use of the frequency spectrum.

Time-averaged spectra of voice have been shown to be a sensitive measure of the identity of different speakers, of clinically perceptible variations in a speaker's mood of talking, of daily changes in mood as indicated by self-report and by observers' ratings, and of variations in voice which accompany emotional events.

One would expect that individual speakers would differ in their habitual use and emphasis on various portions of the frequency spectrum, and this is certainly the case. Time-average spectrum data can discriminate with a high degree of separation between different speakers, and can identify these speakers from new voice samples (Hargreaves and Starkweather, 1963). The data basic to this identification may bear little resemblance to that which is used by a human listener to identify voices among his acquaintances and, in spite of the distinctions that can be made between speakers, this same use of the spectrum varies for an individual as he expresses different feelings and moods. Change in the frequency distribution of voice energy can be viewed as a useful measure of changing emotional state in a variety of applied situations. Instead of describing our attempts at such applications, we shall describe vocal data for which new methods of discrimination and pattern recognition need to be developed.

Our goal has been to develop a method of following subtle changes in emotional expression as an on-line procedure and to do so regardless of the verbal content involved. Part of the averaging necessary to ignore phonemic differences in the verbal content is accomplished by integration over successive two-second periods of time. The audio signal from a human speaker is fed simultaneously to a matched set of one-third octave band filters. The filters have center frequencies from 80 to 5000 Hz, and are scanned and converted to digital form at 60 scans per second. Every two seconds the scanned and summed measurements produced from each filter are recorded on magnetic tape for further computer processing. Successive samples of such data may be presented in a three-dimensional figure. The coordinates are a dimension of increasing audio frequency, intensity as measured for the particular two-second period, and a time dimension that shows successive periods of such sampling. Although our full data contain some additional information about overall intensity sampled at a faster rate, this is a good representation on which to base a discussion of the recognition problems in these data. Such problems are similar to those found in other sources of data. The method is basically similar, for example, to one form of EEG analyzer (the Grey Walter) which operates on the basis of successive ten-second integration times.

Partly because of noise and nonlinearity problems in earlier analog apparatus, we have not until recently been able to present the data in a graphic way which allows a visual discrimination of voice samples, even though we found ways to discriminate samples by statistical procedures. The apparatus produces a set of numbers representing the average voice intensity spectrum for consecutive two seconds of elapsed time. One procedure has been to edit these data by computer, producing an average spectrum for each consecutive five seconds of the subject's speech, thereby normalizing the information with respect to pausing. In a study of depressed patients, a separate stepwise multiple regression procedure was used on each patient to develop regression weights from the five-second spectra to predict the mood ratings of each interview. Regression weights were computed from a portion of the data, taking the even-numbered interviews, and then the data from odd-numbered interviews were used to cross-validate the regression weights. The predictions of mood computed from this second set of data were then correlated with the ratings of mood which was the criterion information. The method has produced some practical results, and we have been careful to use fresh data on which to judge the prediction ability of regression weights already obtained. The method is statistically questionable, however, from a standpoint of using a regression procedure against an unchanging overall rating for the entire interview. In addition, we cannot claim to have complete independence of samples taken by sequential arbitrary divisions of the time scale. Under certain experimental situations, such as that implied by the problem of speaker identification, we have a classical problem of classification and a procedure of discriminant function analysis seems more applicable. The choice of such statistical methods and the respective power, limitations, and robustness of such methods has been considered in unusual detail by Mosteller and Wallace (1964), who use the disputed authorship of the Federalist Papers as a demonstration problem.

As methods for the recognition of meaning carried by vocal signals become further developed, they may play a role in complementing the results of analyses which concentrate on interpretation of verbal content. Some preliminary results of this kind, relating vocal and verbal information, have in fact been reported (Starkweather, 1967a). It is a modest start in this direction.

18 Unconventional Uses of Content Analysis in Social Science

Eugene Webb

Karlene H. Roberts

Graduate School of Business
Stanford University

Unconventionality is usually viewed as novelty, unorthodoxy, or bizarreness. Without fighting the sociologist's issue of how one defines the norm or the standard of conventionality—Is it a value notion or a simple term of statistical frequency?—we follow the tack that cleverness *per se* is not good, but innovation combined with rigor is good (Dunnette, 1966). The unconventional is a function of the zeitgeist—the technology, the theory and the predilections of an era. Papers presented at the Annenberg conference are marked by their unconventionality. They are not positioned at the drab middle of conventional wisdom; indeed, we value them because they are not.

Let us examine, first, the evolutionary notion of what makes for unconventionality in content analysis. Recently, Holsti (1969) demonstrated persuasively the metamorphosis from simple, nonexperimental description to the use of content analysis for hypothesis testing and theoretical inference. Marsden (1965) has written of three sequential models of content analysis: the classical model with its manifest content and quantitative method emphasis, a pragmatic model with an emphasis on coding categories descriptive of some condition of the communicator or the relationship between him and his communication, and the nonquantitative model, with its greater concern on such issues as content intensity. In other words, we might say that the conventional wisdom of content analysis has expanded from a labeling system for tagging descriptors into a procedure for defining variables. But one may also extend the use of content analysis—in a reasonable and still underexploited next step—to a search for the better definition of elaborate and theoretically awkward constructs.

319

Here one might study those pervasive but elusive constructs at the core of human behavior—such tangled and presumably real ideas as the concept of justice or the concept of love. It is at this point that unconventionality is most needed.[1]

Within social science the historical solution for the awkwardness of complex constructs has been avoidance: a retreat to the conventional approach of what has been called single operationalism ("Love is a warm puppy"). This simplistic approach is not always wrong. There may be cases in which it is true that one and only one sign detected in a content analysis is adequate to demonstrate a proposition.

One might achieve, for example, high validity in predicting the goodness of a cook by a single variable analysis of the range of spices in her kitchen. This is, of course, Marsden's pragmatic model of content analysis.[2]

A novelistic commentary on a single-operational content analysis is given below.

The obituaries were Poppa Hondorp's measure of human worth. "There's little they can add or subtract from you then," was his view. Poppa's eye had sharpened over the years so that he could weigh a two-and-a-half inch column of ex-alderman against three-and-a-quarter inches of inorganic chemist and know at a glance their comparative worth. When his son had one day suggested that the exigencies of the printer and makeup man might in part account for the amount of space accorded the deceased, Poppa Hondorp had shivered with . . . rage. . . . the obituaries were sacrosanct; *The Times* issued from an immaculate source (Stern 1960:24).

This example reflects long-term input of data and an evaluative scheme derived from the input. Poppa Hondorp might do as well as most biographers if there were a constant bias by printers and makeup men across the series (Campbell, 1958).

But we should like to argue for the use of content analysis as a way to develop an independent line of validation. If it is true that every measure is factorially complex and theoretically impure, then the conventional de-

---

[1] Addressing these concepts increases the level of nonobviousness. And, as nonobviousness increases, it may appear to an outsider (nonscientist) that either more novel or more foolish types of content analyses are undertaken. This is not a unique problem. We need only look on as a harried National Science Foundation defends a grant for the study of mother love in the rhesus monkey. To many of us, the rhesus seems as plausible a species in which to study love as any other, but Congressmen have not always shared that perception.

[2] In the study of social movements it is generally thought by theorists that a politically insurgent revolutionary movement must make visible appeals to a population. The appeal is as visible to a ruling regime as it is to the target audience. The content analysis of available materials should detect the presence or absence of cries made by insurgents to storm the barricades. Interpretation is something else, yet the cry is visible and one seldom needs multiple confirmations of it.

pendence on a single operational technique is inappropriate (Webb et al., 1966). It is proper to ask for the extension of content analysis to systematic inclusion in the testing of general behavioral principles. Multiple classes of data offer the greatest promise for strong inference and the greater integration of content analysis into the group of converging analyses is called for. If we argue for balancing the errors of other methods with content analysis, we must also ask to balance the limitations of content analysis with multiple data classes.

A precedent exists in the acceptance of multiple *samples* of materials to test an hypothesis or to describe a condition. M. L. Ray (1966a), in his statement of the applicability of content analysis to cross-cultural research, has observed how a series of different investigators used varied content sources to estimate the psychological values of Hitler's Germany. What is significant is that each investigator used one source and one source only.

McGranahan and Wayne (1948) content analyzed German plays; Sebald (1962) analyzed song books. Lewin (1947) looked at handbooks for youth organizations, White (1949) evaluated speeches, and Lasswell (1941) studied the press. In addition, Warchol (1967) recently made a content analysis of military and nationalistic illustrations on German stamps from the days of the Weimar Republic to the beginning of World War II.

Ray's review demonstrates the value of multiple confirmation within a single procedural class—content analysis. More powerful is the simultaneous convergence of materials from different classes of data. A notable case of this is the recent work by Sikorski, Roberts, and Paisley (1967). Content analysis served as a validating method. With questionnaire responses as one data source on what topics were concerning the public, these authors tested the validity of the survey data by going to a content analysis of letters to the editors of news magazines.

The extraordinary flexibility of content analysis presents a capacity for validity checks constrained only by the investigator's imagination. Imagination may sometimes be supplanted by hardware, but more often hardware development is essential to, or a product of, theoretical development.

Mitchell (1967), Holsti (1969), and Paisley (in press) have properly pointed to the importance of developing more sophisticated instrumentation for content analysis. The potential for greater data input and more discriminating analyses is obvious, and specific examples are provided by Chapters included in this volume. Our emphasis and cheering on of these developments derives from the belief that hardware improvement will allow one to find either new points to test theory—new outcroppings—or to see old material in better detail and texture.

Most scientists would recognize the wisdom of Hempel's comment that

"Concepts of science are the knots in a network of systematic interrelationships in which the laws and theoretical principles form the threads . . . threads converge upon, or issue from, a conceptual knot" (Hempel, 1966:94).

Just as theory may be a network of threads, only some of which are visible, partially visible also are the data points to test theory. The testing of theory can only be done at the available outcroppings, those points where theoretical predictions and available instrumentation meet.

Instrumentation gains are not limited to elaborate computer hardware. Haggard and Isaacs (1966) discovered micromomentary expressions— those facial expressions so quick as to be invisible—by slowing down movie film to four frames per second. Imagination and equipment joined to produce a new data source, a new point to test theory.

The computing hardware itself will permit us to rearrange the material of old content analyses in new searches for pattern. DeCharms and Moeller (1962) studied the relationship between achievement imagery and patent production. Employing a content analysis of children's readers from 1800 to 1950, and an index of patents granted during that period, they hypothesized a positive relationship and concluded that the hypothesis was probably too simple (Figure 1). With access to an on-line computer, their data were reanalyzed with a time lag correlation program. The processing took an elapsed time of two minutes at the console, one second of actual computer time, and cost 21 cents. Figure 2 shows the distribution of the time lagged correlations. The highest correlation exists if the patent production index is lagged 20 years. That is, take achievement level at one point in time and match it to patent production 20 years later. New hardware permits rapid analyses such as this, expanding the conventional technique of taking two variables head on in time, requiring a minimum amount of resources, and permitting a new sweep and new search over old content analysis data.

The DeCharms and Moeller work was an application of content analysis to test the validity of a general behavioral proposition. In a similar way, Joseph Matarazzo used content analysis in his study of the "speech duration effect." In the laboratory, Matarazzo and his associates (1963, 1964) were able to establish a reliable relationship between the length of response by an individual interviewed and the length of the interviewer's speech unit; the longer the question, the longer the answer. Going across samples of interviews, he replicated the finding in medical interviews, psychotherapeutic interviews, civil service and department store job interviews, and in "free" conversations between two persons. Most notably, in an opportunistic and unconventional exploitation of available data, Matarazzo studied tapes from space flights to see if the phenomenon held in exchanges

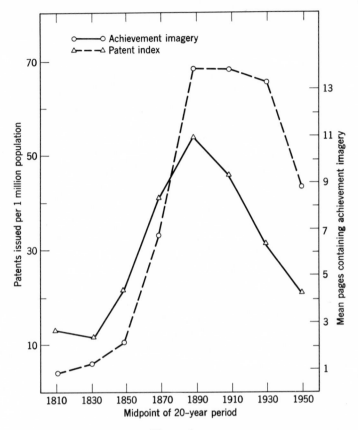

Figure 1

between astronauts and ground communicators. It did. Moreover, it held up at another outcrop, as a separate group of investigators found more evidence for the hypothesis with data from J. F. Kennedy press conferences (Ray and Webb, 1966b). There were a number of points at which the hypothesis could have been tested; the validity of Matarazzo's hypothesis is demonstrated by its capacity to resist rejection over a variety of different settings.

Another set of experiments used content analysis to test a general behavioral phenomenon—this time the hypothesis that value and need influence perception. It will be recalled that Bruner and Goodman (1947) started the "new look" in perception with their laboratory study of rich kids and poor kids judging the size of coins. Later, the brilliant but neglected experiment of Stayton and Weiner (1961) found the phenomenon to hold true when the direction of distortion was reversed. That is, they

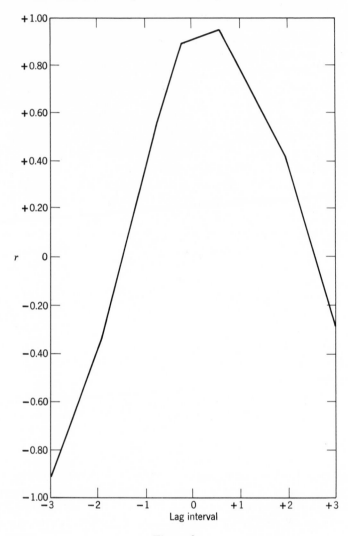

Figure 2

tested it in a situation where desirability was associated with smallness, not bigness. The object was a Volkswagen automobile and the subjects were scaled on their predisposition to own a Volkswagen. Those who particularly like Volkswagens saw the car as physically smaller than those who were indifferent to them.

Content analysis was employed in probing and expanding the test of this "new look" hypothesis. In a delightful set of studies developing content analysis as an independent line of validation, Solley and Haigh (1957) and Craddick (1961) found that children drew Santa Claus bigger before Christmas than after. Sechrest and Wallace (1964) rejected one rival hypothesis to the findings, a generalized euphoria, by sampling drawings of non-Christmas content. Only the Santa Claus was bigger before Christmas. In a flip-flop type of control, shifting both direction and content, Craddick (1962) showed that the mean size of children's drawings of witches decreased at Halloween. These four studies, paralleling the laboratory studies of preceptual distortion, illustrate the utility of content analysis for validating a general hypothesis.

Now, in the final part of our remarks, we should like to go back to the earlier mention of content analysis in the study of complex constructs.[3]

We propose to look at love, undertaking the venture with trepidation and offering no definitive statement, for surrounding the study of such constructs is a spongy circle of ambiguity, uncertainty, and bravura. Lacking an external validator, one must rely on the more tenuous steps of construct validity. We offer only suggestions of how content analysis might serve to edit among the large number of hypotheses in a subject matter in which everyone is expert and where there is a substantial amount of undigested knowledge.

In addition to many other fields, all disciplines within the behavioral sciences have examined love. No scholarly consensus has been reached on the topic and, among all of us, there is probably a substantial divergence on concepts of love.

One can read the social psychological literature on affiliation (Byrne et al., 1966) or ingratiation (Jones, 1964) as well as the sociological literature on the family—notably the controversy over whether people with similar or dissimilar interests get along better together (Kelly, 1941; Cattell, 1950; Cattell and Nesselroade, 1967). The experimental literature has contributed the ingenious work of Harlow (1958, 1960) on love among primates, as well as a gaggle of reinforcement-theory based investigations on the movement of the Norway rat. Anthropology provides the early statements of Margaret Mead on strange forms of love among the South Seas natives—as well as the recent sensitive writings of Oscar Lewis (1961, 1966). And then, of course, there is the clinical psychiatric experience: the classic psycho-analytic work of Fenichel (1945) and the more modern psychological analyses of affect by Tomkins (1962) and Schacter and Singer (1962).

[3] The section that follows has benefitted from the advice of a number of friends and relatives: J. H. Bryan, P. London, W. J. Paisley, D. F. Roberts, M. A. Webb, and K. E. Weick. Much of this counsel developed from a quasi-symposium at the 1967 meetings of the American Psychological Association. These people should share the blame or praise elicited by what follows.

The lyrics of popular love songs provide the content—centering on the distinctive and popular medium, the American musical stage. This exercise is limited to the first stage of construct validation, what Cronbach (1960) called seeing "what constructs might account for performance . . . an act of imagination based on observation." Songs are intuitively attractive as a data source on love (Johnstone and Katz, 1957; Horton, 1957; and Hayakawa, 1964). Most of us have noted the common experience of lovers fixing on "our song," an experience frequently grounded in inarticulateness. Donald Horton expressed it this way:

> In a culture in which skill in the verbal expression of profound feelings is not a general trait, and in which people become embarrassed and inarticulate when speaking of their love for each other, a conventional, public, impersonal love poetry may be a useful—indeed, a necessary—alternative (Horton, 1957:577).

Moreover, the popularity of these songs suggests that they are a love poetry viewed as acceptable or "right" by a large number of people. Without defending the universe of love songs as adequate for the study, the sheer success of such songs compels attention. The themes running through them are highly redundant, an implicit endorsement of these themes as proper public elements in expressing love.

Thus, with all temerity, let us examine the evidence from the love song literature as one source of data that may offer a better understanding of the concept of love.

As good scientists we might look first to overt behavior, not verbal statements of emotion. Liza Doolittle responded to Freddy's words:

Speak and the world is full of singing,
And I'm winging higher than the birds,
Touch and my heart begins to crumble
The heavens tumble, darling at thy . . .

Words, words, words,
I'm so sick of words.
I get words all day through, first from him, now from you,
Is that all you blighters can do?

Don't talk of stars, burning above,
If you're in love, show me.
Tell me no dreams filled with desire
If you're on fire, show me.
Here we are together in the middle of the night!
Don't talk of spring! Just hold me tight!

Anyone who's ever been in love will tell you that
This is no time for a chat!

Haven't your lips longed for my touch?
Don't say how much, show me, show me,
Don't talk of love lasting through time,
Give me no undying vow.
Show me now![4]

Or, from an earlier period, another song reflecting the behavior of love. In addition, these lyrics underline Donald Horton's point on the inarticulateness of love.

If I loved you,
Time and again I would try to say
All I want you to know.
If I loved you,
Words wouldn't come in an easy way,
Round in circles I'd go.
Longing to tell you
But afraid and shy,
I'd let my golden chances pass me by.[5]

Are people in love? They show it, of course, show it in their overt behavior and by emphasizing their similar characteristics. In Oklahoma we find an explicit statement of the signs of love in a song popular since it was first presented almost twenty years ago.

Don't throw bouquets at me,
Don't please my folks too much,
Don't laugh at my jokes too much,
People will say we're in love.

Don't sigh and gaze at me,
Your sighs are so like mine,
Your eyes musn't glow like mine,
People will say we're in love.[6]

A "critical incident" approach has been a popular route to the study of phenomena. Typically, this means a focus on the points at which a

[4] Copyright 1956 by Alan Jay Lerner and Frederick Loewe.
[5] Copyright 1945 by Williamson Music, Inc.
[6] Copyright 1943 by Williamson Music, Inc.

system (and that could be a pair of lovers) is out of equilibrium. Historians have searched for meaning by examining the points at which civilizations rise and fall. Political scientists and social psychologists have tried to learn of the forces promoting a stable society by looking at cases of instability: riots, insurrections, and political overthrow.

Then there is opportunistic field research, which takes advantage of naturally occurring critical events: the formation of a new volcano or a new nova, the effect of a president's assassination, and the behavior of people under the stress of natural disaster. Within clinical psychology, close observational studies have tried to locate the pivotal points at which a therapy succeeds or fails.

A critical incident strategy may be an equally profitable tack in the study of love. Love begins, and at critical points in the love (at the beginning, at times of conflict and reconciliation, and at the end) the character of the moods and psychological states are clearest. For example, a beginning:

> We've just been introduced,
> I do not know you well
> But when the music started
> Something drew me to your side.
>
> So many men and girls
> Are in each other's arms.
> It makes me think
> We might be similarly occupied.
>
> Shall we dance
> On a bright cloud of music?
> Shall we fly?
> Shall we dance?
>
> Shall we then say goodnight and
> Mean goodbye?
> Or perchance when the last little star has left the sky
> Shall we still be together
> With our arms around each other
> And shall you be my new romance?
> On the clear understanding that this kind of thing can happen
> Shall we dance? Shall we dance? Shall we dance?[7]

One step further down the road is a developing love. The lover savors the dimensionality of the experience and values so simple a thing as a name.

[7] Copyright 1951 by Richard Rodgers and Oscar Hammerstein II.

From *West Side Story,* Tony's response after meeting Maria:

Maria, I just kissed a girl named Maria.
And suddenly I found
How wonderful a sound can be.

Maria, say it loud and there's music playing.
Say it soft and it's almost like praying.
Maria, I'll never stop saying Maria.[8]

Tony's perception had changed and, throughout this love-song literature, one finds an emphasis on perception and what love does to the eye of the beholder. New worlds are seen, one has a heightened awareness of self, and the acceptance of a mundane world may be easier. We might notice that the accentuation in perception seen in love songs is a special case of accentuation derived from any emotional state. The earlier mentioned studies of Bruner and Goodman, Stayton and Weiner, Craddick, and Sechrest and Wallace all demonstrated that fear, anticipation, and expectation may sharpen perception.

Here, from three different shows, from three different lyricists, at three points in time, are expressions of that new perception:

I have often walked down this street before,
But the pavement always stayed beneath my feet before.
All at once am I
Several stories high,
Knowing I'm on the street where you live.
Are there lilac trees in the heart of town?
Can you hear a lark in any other part of town?
Does enchantment pour out of every door?
No, it's just on the street where you live.[9]

* * *

There were bells on the hill,
But I never heard them ringing,
No, I never heard them at all
'Till there was you.

There were birds in the sky,
But I never saw them winging,

[8] Copyright 1958 by Leonard Bernstein and Stephen Sondheim.
[9] Copyright 1956 by Alan Jay Lerner and Frederick Loewe.

No, I never saw them at all,
'Till there was you.[10]

* * *

I feel pretty. Oh so pretty.
I feel pretty and witty and bright,
And I pity any girl who isn't me tonight.
I feel charming. Oh so charming.
It's alarming how charming I feel,
And so pretty that I hardly can believe I'm real.[11]

She feels pretty, and exhilaration—if one accepts these songs—is an attribute of falling in love.

I'm as corny as Kansas in August,
I'm as normal as blueberry pie.
No more a smart little girl with no heart,
I have found me a wonderful guy.
I am in a conventional dither,
With a conventional star in my eye.
And you will note there's a lump in my throat
When I speak of that wonderful guy.[12]

Among these public love songs, there is a lack of explicitly erotic love, a content restriction of some moment. But one sanctioned form for the expression of physical love is cloaked with upbeat exuberance in, for example, a song like "June Is Bustin' Out All Over."

June is bustin' out all over,
The sheep aren't sleepin' anymore,
All the rams that chase the ewe sheep
Are determined there'll be new sheep,
And the ewe sheep aren't even keepin' score.
Because it's June . . . June . . . June.[13]

Thus far, the emphasis has been on the individual lover and his separate feeling. But love is two people and reciprocation as well. Brought together, being together, they attempt to share all.

Make of our hands one hand.
Make of our hearts one heart.

[10] Copyright 1957 by Meredith Willson.
[11] Copyright 1958 by Leonard Bernstein and Stephen Sondheim.
[12] Copyright 1949 by Richard Rodgers and Oscar Hammerstein II.
[13] Copyright 1945 by Williamson Music, Inc.

Make of our vows one last vow.
Only death will part us now.[14]

Some critical incidents are unpleasant: quarrels, conflicts, and parting. The idea of parting may be rejected and faults accepted—as in these lines from Carousel:

What's the use of wondrin'
If he's good or if he's bad,
Or if you like the way he wears his hat.
Oh, what's the use of wondrin, if he's good or if he's bad,
He's your feller and you love him,
That's all there is to that.

Common sense may tell you
That the endin' may be sad,
And now's the time to break and run away.
But what's the use of wondrin' if the endin' will be sad,
He's your feller and you love him,
There's nothin' more to say.[15]

Strife, as well as gentle moments, may show the form and shadow of love. When one of the lovers is angered, he may engage in the verbal sham of rejecting his dependence on the other.

There'll be spring every year without you,
England still will be here without you,
There'll be fruit on the tree
And a shore by the sea,
There'll be crumpets and tea without you.
Art and music will thrive without you,
Somehow Keats will survive without you,
And there still will be rain on that plain down in Spain,
Even that will remain without you.
I can do without you.[16]

We have searched these songs in an attempt to see how they have outlined the concept of love. The redundant themes of popular songs can help us with the elements of love by what they say of the exuberance in the discovery of love, the signs and pleasures of being in love, and—

[14] Copyright 1958 by Leonard Bernstein and Stephen Sondheim.
[15] Copyright 1945 by Williamson Music, Inc.
[16] Copyright 1956 by Alan Jay Lerner and Frederick Loewe.

sometimes unhappily—by what is lost or returned when love is gone. More detailed analyses might reduce the categories to everyone's satisfaction—or might detect the Dr. Johnson stone phenomenon. When Dr. Samuel Johnson first learned of the atomic theory of matter, he asked his tutor to kick a nearby stone. When the tutor did, Johnson said, "Whirling amalgam of atoms is it, it seems pretty solid to me."[17]

Or, in another medium, we return to the musical stage and Ezio Pinza:

> Who can explain it?
> Who can tell you why?
> Fools give you reasons,
> Wise men never try.[18]

[17] A later scholar stated the idea with more elegance. He wrote of two scientific tables, one the table presented to his eyes, the other consisting of "numerous electrical charges rushing about with great speed . . . their combined bulk amounts to less than a billionth of the bulk of the table itself. I need not tell you that modern physics has by delicate test and remorseless logic assured me that my second scientific table is the only one which is really there . . . On the other hand I need not tell you that modern physics will never succeed in exorcising that first table—strange compound of external nature, mental imagery and inherited prejudice—which lies visible to my eyes and tangible to my grasp." A. S. Eddington, *The Nature of the Physical World*, New York, Cambridge University Press, 1929. (Cited in C. G. Hempel, 1966:78.)

[18] Copyright 1949 by Richard Rodgers and Oscar Hammerstein II.

IV Computer Techniques in Content Analysis and Computational Linguistics

Philip J. Stone, Editor

INTRODUCTION TO PART IV

PHILIP J. STONE

Center for Advanced Study in the Behavioral Sciences,
Palo Alto, California, and Harvard University,
Cambridge, Massachusetts

The Annenberg conference was the first occasion for those concerned with different approaches to computer-aided content analysis to assemble and discuss their work. A number of introductions had to be performed because, in many cases, the participants had never met. Their purposes in being involved in computer-aided content analysis were as varied as the fields they represented: political science, psychiatry, sociology, English, and social psychology. Each had a complicated data-analysis problem. Each was trying to solve his problem in a way that seemed most reasonable. Yet, together, their approaches were very different.

The papers were delivered during the day in the Annenberg School main auditorium, with the glaring stage lights keeping the audience at a psychological if not real distance, and the large number of papers keeping the discussion to a minimum. It was at the discussion session held that evening in a much smaller room, after participants had time to enjoy a cocktail party and dinner at the University of Pennsylvania Faculty Club, that opinions began to flow freely and points of view came into sharper focus. The mood of the discussion session was active, yet mellow, and, I thought, characterized by good humor. Each participant had put years of his own time (and thousands of dollars of foundation money) into developing his approach. Each knew the inadequacies of his approach as well as anyone. This was not the time for an exposé, nor was there one to be had. On the other hand, this was not yet the time to lay plans for integrating the different approaches. Each approach still could use more development of its own.

From this confrontation, however, we have a record. Each of the participants had submitted a paper beforehand; the papers were revised after the meeting and are included here as Chapters of Part IV. A tape recording of the discussion, which I have attempted to transcribe and condense, appears at the end of this part.

Here, then, for the first time, is a resource where students and colleagues can compare different computer-aided content analysis approaches and come to an initial decision as to what kind of approach, if any, might be suited to their problems. In addition to having a presentation of the different approaches, the discussion section compares different approaches and deals with some of their major assumptions.

Although most of the participants were involved in social science research, we also invited a specialist in information retrieval. As the following chapters make evident, there is considerable overlap between the two fields, at least in the techniques that they use, if not in their purposes. Gerard Salton (Chapter 25) is the author of one of the most highly developed informational retrieval systems in existence today and is a well-known authority in the field.

Each of the participants has had the responsibility for developing a computer-aided content analysis approach, yet the participants differ in their technical backgrounds vis-à-vis the computer and the strategies they used to implement their systems. A few participants have done their own programming; others designed a system in detail and supervised the programming carefully. Still others sought assistance in designing their system, and delegated the programming tasks completely to others. These differences in approach are, to a certain extent, reflected in the styles of the chapters, although some of the most philosophical contributions (for example, Chapter 20 by Donald H. Goldhamer) are by persons most involved in the technicalities of systems design.

The articles, for the most part, present their approaches from the viewpoint of potential users, answering the kinds of questions that a user might ask. However, they differ greatly in their level of specificity. Each chapter assumes that the reader is aware, for instance, that it is possible for a machine to "read" actual text as it is punched on IBM cards or typed in from a computer console. Other chapters assume a little more technical knowledge about computers or assume some statistical knowledge, such as at least a rough familiarity with factor analysis.

For the reader without much background in this area, I suggest that he start with a chapter that provides illustrations of how data and directions are presented to a computer system. Chapter 21, by Ole R. Holsti, is probably the most appropriate in this regard.

Most of the systems described are implemented on a general-purpose computer. Two articles—Chapter 23 by Kenneth Janda and Chapter 27 by John A. Starkweather—assume some special equipment. For Janda, it is microfilm searching equipment, showing how large volumes of information can be quickly scanned for co-occurrence of information. For Starkweather, a special typewriter is tied directly to a "time shared" computer and used to obtain an immediate analysis of the text typed on it.

For the computer specialist, who wants detailed information of how the computer programs are designed, these chapters are only brief introductions to the different approaches. This book, obviously, is not the place for such specialized information. Since system designs are always being changed, he should write to the contributors for the latest information.

Our plan was to present the articles in alphabetical order. Inasmuch as part of John Starkweather's chapter offered some important distinctions for comparing different approaches, we asked him to divide his chapter, so that these distinctions might be presented at the beginning of Part IV, and the reader could have them in mind as he read through the remaining chapters. Casimir Borkowski did not present a paper at the Philadelphia meeting, but he participated in the formal and informal sessions. Afterward he sent a short article (Chapter 28) describing his approach to the study of sublanguages, suggesting that it might fit well with the other contributions. We think that his chapter is an important addition to Part IV. The reader should realize that the other contributors did not know that Borkowski's article would be included and, therefore, did not consider the issues that he raises.

As editor and chairman of the session, I thank the participants for their thoughtful care in preparing the chapters for this volume and for meeting deadlines both for the conference and for this book. As a person who has been actively involved in the field but who is not currently engaged in content analysis research, I hope my own biases have not interfered with a fair presentation of the different points of view.

19 Overview: Computer-Aided Approaches to Content Recognition[1]

John A. Starkweather

Medical Psychology
University of California
San Francisco

Content analysis involves attempts to score, categorize, and obtain useful objective data from written material or from transcripts of spoken communication. Although there are wide differences in the goals and approaches of individual investigators who are interested in content analysis, many of these workers have used the computer in recent years. The computer has, of course, been used for some time for statistical analysis of data. For many investigators, the computer has been a substitute for a great army of clerks in accomplishing the large-scale task of counting many thousands of words or phrases. More recently, the computer has been used to simulate one or both sides of interview situations, and this has required the development of more complex methods for the computer to deal with language content. As computers have become capable of interacting with human users in a conversational fashion, it has been necessary to develop recognition methods for the immediate handling of human responses.

One dimension on which we may arrange various computer approaches to content analysis is related to this quality of immediate response. We would place a need to analyze many different individuals (speakers or writers) and different situations at one extreme, and a need to deal with a particular point in an immediate conversation with a specific person at the other extreme. Three points on this dimension will be described.

CONTENT ANALYSIS USING GENERAL AND SPECIALIZED DICTIONARIES

In quantitative approaches to the content analysis of documents an investigator usually deals with standard units of writing or speech that

[1] The work described here was supported in part by Contract USDHEW-OE-6-10-131, U.S. Office of Education, and Contract NONR 3656(28), Office of Naval Research.

may be words or sentences. These units fall into categories such as words or phrases that suggest anxiety, words that suggest anger, and so on. We assume that, by studying the relative frequency in which such units occur, we may produce a new and useful description of a document or of a transcript of speech. A versatile computer program, which is useful in this kind of work, is the General Inquirer (Stone et al., 1962, 1966). This program expects incoming textual data to be arranged as sentences. It examines this text by making reference to a dictionary of word stems, using a dictionary that is variable and that may be developed with specific relevance and classifications useful for a particular area of investigation. Dictionaries for the General Inquirer, for example, have been developed to analyze political documents and psychiatric interviews. More general dictionaries are also used, and rules have been developed to code words which have multiple meanings. The sentence is used as a unit of measurement, and the incoming text is sometimes coded and preedited for the syntax position of words within sentences. In verbatim transcripts this may occasionally be difficult, since the unit of a sentence is not always well defined and syntax may be in disarray.

This approach, then, involves an attempt to produce a dictionary which, although it may be specialized in coverage, nevertheless attempts to handle the vocabulary usage of different speakers. It is very likely, therefore, to become quite large, with many thousands of words for use with text to be analyzed. Various aspects of this approach are discussed in the present volume in the chapters by Goldhamer (Chapter 20), Holsti (Chapter 21), Psathas (Chaper 24), and Stone (Chapter 29).

CONTENT ANALYSIS THROUGH DEVELOPMENT OF ASSOCIATED WORD GROUPS FOR A PARTICULAR SPEAKER

Quantitative methods developed for the study of verbatim transcripts of spoken material have tended to focus on word usage. The computer has been used as a clerical assistance to develop a form of specialized dictionary which applies only to the word usage of an individual person or to specific documents under study. Examples of this may be observed in the work of Harway and Iker (1964) and also Starkweather and Decker (1964). Both of these approaches have resulted in a statistical definition of word groups which were associated with each other in an individual speaker's usage. Such methods have been applied in a number of psychiatric case studies. As compared to the first form of content analysis described above, this approach tends to center on the word as a unit for measurement rather than the sentence. This avoids some problems encountered in handling unrehearsed spoken language rather than written language, but limits the linguistic complexity of the analysis. The method tends to use statistical procedures such as factor analysis or cluster analysis to develop a description of structure in the obtained data. Investigators have then been interested in the changes shown in such factors across time and for a change in speaking situation, as well as differences in such structure for different people. Chapter 22 by Iker and Harway, in this volume, discusses recent work using this approach. These authors argue that there is considerable advantage in avoiding the need for prior categories with which to classify verbal data.

Chapter 26, in the present volume, by Sally and Walter Sedelow describes a combination of manual and computer procedures which have been used to explore the categories found in existing general thesauri and a Dictionary of Synonyms. It may be that procedures developed for the statistical analysis of word associations will lead to an improvement of dictionaries used by systems which precategorize. The same will likely be true of a variety of techniques, such as those developed by Salton (Chapter 25), which are built for effective information retrieval by computer. A retrieval method which relies on prior indexing is described by Janda (Chapter 23).

CONTENT ANALYSIS BY RELIANCE ON THE CONTROL OF IMMEDIATE CONTEXT

When we become involved in the use of a computer for interaction between man and machine, it becomes necessary to find methods for immediate content analysis which can be specified and programmed as an entirely automatic process. The machine must have a means to recognize language responses by a subject and rapidly develop appropriate replies in return. We may look upon such activities as attempts to stimulate human information processing, and we may build machine methods to imitate human activity in as many respects as possible. On the other hand, we may simply use whatever machine methods seem pratical and appropriate in view of current machine capability and our present state of knowledge about conversational language. The results may or may not model what humans do, an issue that very much concerns Goldhamer in his contribution to this volume (Chapter 20).

An interest in simulation should lead one to review the work of Kenneth Colby (1966, 1967) and of Bellman, Friend, and Kurland (1966). Colby's program attempts to build up associations, or a belief structure, characteristic of a respondent dealing with an interactive system. Bellman and his colleagues describe the scoring of responses as having convergent versus divergent attributes with reference to the goals of an interview.

Their program models the interview as a multi-stage decision process having a branching structure of potential questions and replies.

Joseph Weizenbaum (1966, 1967) has been particularly interested in the credibility of a machine response to a subject who is interacting with it in a conversational fashion. In his work, we see a reliance upon immediate context and the development of rules of language processing which may apply only to a specific combin·.tion of attributes, not only for the indiviual subject being studied but also for a particular point in a conversation. I have developed similar concerns through attempts to use the computer conversationally (Starkweather 1965, 1967). David G. Hays, in Chapter 3 of the present volume states: "The best content analyst is a good conversationalist." This is true, however, only for certain goals of content analysis. Some workers who engage in complex retrospective analysis have goals of pattern recognition and classification that go beyond what one expects of a good conversationalist.

Conversational ability becomes possible if we are able to develop a form of content analysis that can deal with language fragments, fragments that are often incomplete or incorrect from a grammatical standpoint. Recognition of meaning in such fragments can lead to conversational responses which indicate "understanding" by the computer program. The program will be able to make responses that indicate appropriate and reasonable tracking between program expectations and person (user) expectations. Both conversational partners will remain in tune by moving together from one set of expectations to another. These expectations may be considered as the context that surrounds a particular point in the conversation, and they require miniature dictionaries to operate within such specific contexts. This is perhaps an extreme case of the multiple dictionaries mentioned by Psathas in Chapter 24. Chapter 27, by Starkweather, entitled "Pilot: A System for Programmed Inquiry, Learning, or Teaching" describes one approach to immediate and conversational content analysis.

20 Toward a More General Inquirer: Convergence of Structure and Context of Meaning

Donald H. Goldhamer

Social Psychology
University of Chicago

This chapter is concerned with a model for the development of computerized content analysis. This model has grown from an interest in reducing the large gap separating human "understanding" of langauge from the performance of existing content analysis programs. One program of this kind—the General Inquirer—will be described and then will serve as an example to illustrate three areas in which recent linguistic theory offers some modest guidance to the computerization of content analysis.

I shall include as "content analysis" only the approaches that seek to make *specific inferences* from a text to some characteristics of its source that are not directly observable.[1] We shall not be concerned here with approaches that consist of locating and counting words or of studying the co-occurrence of words without the interposition of an explicitly operationalized theory. Such processes are essentially information-retrieval and statistical operations and rely on the developing methodology of those disciplines. By this exclusion I do not mean to deny the contribution that these approaches can and have made to an understanding of textual materials.

The General Inquirer incorporates one of the approaches to the inference of content from text. Especially prominent in its approach is the role played by the investigator's theory—an explicit formulation of the relations between words or other observable elements of the text and the area of his substantive interests. This theory is represented in the General Inquirer program by a set of content categories, by a dictionary of word-category relations, and by theme-oriented summarizing procedures. As is true with other contemporary programs, the investigator is able to express his theory only in terms of the restricted elements directly

---

[1] For the rationale underlying this definition, see Klaus Krippendorff, "Models of Messages: Three Prototypes" Chapter 4, *infra.*

observable in the text. This contrasts with the ability of a human content analyst to apply immense implicit knowledge of the structure of the language and the context of the text's source as he identifies content categories in the text.

The emphasis of this chapter is on the logic and method of identifying specified categories of content in textual data. Only the relevant parts of the General Inquirer system will be considered.[2] The program described here is more advanced than that described in previous publications.

The following definitions of terms will help to describe our program:

Text is any written or transcribed verbal material—including irregular forms such as poetry or free associations.

Documents are sections of text which the investigator wishes to compare. The division of text into documents is a complex methodological problem of sampling or unitizing which we shall not consider here.

A *word,* for our purposes, is any string of letters and/or numbers (for example, happy, 1984, H_2O). Some punctuation, such as a hyphen or apostrophe, may be considered as part of a word.

STRATEGIES OF TEXT PROCESSING IN THE GENERAL INQUIRER

In approximate terms, the General Inquirer tagging program (hereafter called GIT) processes text one word at a time, accumulating and referencing information on a sentence and all words within it, and pausing at the end of each sentence to reexamine and summarize its content in the light of preceding sentences. All information about the sentence and its words is recorded and stored in the form of numerical tags. Tags may be assigned to specific words, to combinations of words, or to the entire sentence. GIT modifies only these tags; the words themselves are preserved unchanged, and become part of the program's output. This preservation of the original text is a great strength of GIT because it prevents the investigator from becoming blindly and irrevocably bound to his past assumptions.

As GIT reads words of text it searches its dictionary for each word and if a word is *not* found, it is examined for a variety of common

---

[2] To refresh the reader's memory, the General Inquirer is "a set of computer programs to (a) identify systematically, within text, instances of words and phrases that belong to categories specified by the investigator; (b) count occurrences and co-occurrences of these categories; (c) print and graph tabulations; (d) perform statistical tests; and (e) sort and regroup sentences according to whether they contain instances of a particular category or combination of categories" (Stone et al., 1966).

suffixes. If a suffix is found, it is noted and removed, and the dictionary is searched for the word in its shortened form. This allows us to use a compact dictionary referring to word roots rather than to every possible inflection of a word. (The procedures for removing suffixes need to be refined in their ability to distinguish true suffixes from word roots with similar terminal letters, for example, com*ing* versus *ring*.) Words that are not further reducible by this "chopping" procedure and are not found in the dictionary are placed on a list of "leftover" words.

If a word is found in the dictionary, GIT applies the investigator's definition of it as provided in the dictionary. The definition may consist of *tests* to be made and new *tags* to be assigned if the specified tests are successful. Tests may be made for a variety of *items*. Each test can specify a *direction* to search, a *range* (number of words) over which to search, and a *sequence* of any number of *items* to be sought. Several tests may be combined (by the logical operators *and, or,* and *not*) to form very complex sequences of conditions. The *items* that GIT can search for are: (1) the beginning of the sentence (distance from current word), (2) other words, (3) tags assigned to other words, and (4) sentence-level identification. We plan to extend this list to include tests of (5) current statistics on the sentence and document (length, . . .), (6) document-level identification, and (7) tags assigned to *previous* sentences.

Tests are powerful definitional tools. Tests of *words* allow the investigator to identify idiomatic phrases and conventional metaphoric expressions such as *United States, turn in, Our Father,* and *rock the boat.* For example, "boat" could be defined as:

$$\text{BOAT} = (\text{W}, -2, -4, \text{ROCK}, 12, = \text{ROCKBOAT}), 13$$

meaning "when the word BOAT is encountered in the text search the second, third, and fourth preceding words for the word ROCK; if the search is successful and ROCK is found, remove any categories assigned to ROCK and assign category 12 to the word BOAT, and continue with the definition supplied for the (pseudo) word ROCKBOAT; if the word ROCK is not found, assign category 13 to the word BOAT and go on to the next word."

Greater power lies in tests of *tags* assigned to other words and sentences, since themes, whole classes of words, and areas of meaning can thus be sought. Uses for this type of test are suggested by a search for all words reflecting "athletic sports" when one encounters "murder (the bum)," or a search for a pattern of frustration followed by aggression when testing a theory of motivation. For example, if category 22 is assigned to all words having to do with athletic sports, then "murder" could be defined as:

$$\text{MURDER} = (\text{T}, -10, +10, 22, = \text{DEFEAT}), = \text{KILL}$$

meaning "if category (tag) 22 is assigned to any of the preceding or following ten words then use the definition DEFEAT; otherwise use the definition KILL."

The greatest power is offered by tests of investigator-supplied information. Anything from the age of the speaker, to the time of day, to the political orientation of the intended audience can be keypunched along with the text and thereby taken into account when assigning content categories to a word or sentence. Thus, if the political party of the source is coded as the second column of sentence identification, the name Washington can be defined differently when a Republican is speaking than when a Democrat is speaking. If a Democrat is in the White House we could write:

$$\text{WASHINGTON} = (\text{I}, 2, 0, \text{R}, = \text{THEY}), = \text{WE}$$

Allowing the investigator to vary the direction, range, sequence of items, and the word that triggers a test provides flexibility for him to adjust the application of his theory: its level of abstraction, its closeness to the text, its systemacity, and its complexity and rigor.[3] Other variation in tests may be added as new needs arise. In particular, the consequences of a successful test (or combination of tests) needs to be refined, for currently the investigator is free only to add or remove tags of words that are directly involved in satisfying a test (that is, not intermediate or surrounding words). In the present GIT the investigator may make summary evaluations of the content of sentences at the end of each sentence (using independent "sentence summary" routines) during which he may remove, add, or modify any tags assigned to it.

SOME ISSUES IN COMPUTERIZING CONTENT ANALYSIS

We shall deal with three issues in the decoding of text. These issues identify areas for development, corresponding to areas of deficiency in

---

[3] Tests of words and tags that *follow* the word currently being processed are essential for efficiency, since a test of words should be initiated by its *least frequent* word, which is often not the last in its sequence (for example, "of *course*" but "*United* States"). Tests of tags often require searching the general environment in both directions. The logic of "forward" tests is quite complex because sought-for tags may not *yet* have been assigned to following words.

current computerized content analysis programs. The first issue relates to the availability and use of adequate information about the text and its context. Decoding text is so subtle a task that information about language and information about the contemporary world of the source are required in its performance. Such information must be generated by (or provided to) a program and it must be preserved and used in all stages of text processing. The second issue relates to a program's functional similarity to human language processing and its generality as a model of such processing. The third issue relates to the treatment of categories of meaning, in particular the interaction among the meanings of a whole text, of its component sentences, and of their component words and punctuation.

Since we draw upon linguistic theory, it is necessary to view linguistics in relation to content analysis before we elaborate on the above three issues. I do not propose to discuss the relevance of linguistic theory to content analysis; indeed, my contact with linguistic theory has been exclusively that of a content analyst seeking techniques and formulations that respond to deficiencies in his present repertoire. In this search I have not been disappointed, since linguists have concerns that parallel those of the content analyst. David Hays presents in this volume (Chapter 3) an enlightening introduction to these parallel concerns and calls attention to the trends in linguistics which have already produced those speculations upon which I draw in the present chapter. Hays' discussion of the processes involved in "understanding" as required by content analysis is especially recommended.

A recognition of some differences between content analysis and linguistic analysis is fundamental to our thinking. Content analysis is primarily concerned with understanding a body of text and with drawing inferences about the source from the text in accordance with some substantive theory. In the past, computerized content analysis has been restricted to word counting and closely related operations, although it has been clear that treatment of the overall, broad meaning of a text is a prerequisite for its satisfactory analysis. This conclusion has arisen from the failure of computerized content analysis to deal with aspects of natural language such as ambiguity, metaphor, and humor. We ascribe this failure to the fact that computerized content analysis has attempted to go directly from the text to the investigator's set of categories without taking into account the *mediation* of language—of broad meanings embedded in the language and culture as a whole. Human coders provide this broad language information "automatically" as a part of the process of "reading," and this may account for the lack of attention given to this process in computer applications.

The process of "understanding" text in the context of its *language* is the focus of linguistics. We are concerned with two types of linguistic relationships: (1) *syntactic* relationships which are formal, structural relationships among words or parts of words or punctuations; and (2) *semantic* relationships which are relationships of reference or shared meaning among words. Syntactics and semantics refer to relationships that are *part of a language itself,* derived from its grammatic rules. The boundary that we draw is between *linguistic* and *nonlinguistic* relationships of meaning among words. On the one hand, *linguistic* relationships are based on *reference* from one word to another *resulting from some rule of the language* (for example, from an adjective to a noun or a pronoun to a noun). We shall use the term *semantic* to refer only to linguistic relationships. Extralinguistic relationships, on the other hand, are based on *nonreferential* interdependence of words which arises not from rules of the language but rather from more abstract intersection of their meanings; we shall use the term *context* to refer to these extralinguistic relationships.[4]

We wish to exploit those linguistic theories which try to formally integrate semantics and syntactics (Weinreich, 1966; Fodor and Katz, 1964; Katz and Postal, 1964a; and Chomsky, 1965). At the same time we must go beyond the scope of linguistics to deal with *context* if our content analysis program is to distill text accurately. This is because ambiguity and metaphor, in which extralinguistic relationships are found, are frequent and pervasive in natural language.

Content analysis makes at least two further restrictions on our free use of linguistic theory. First, we may use linguistic analysis only to *mediate* between the text and the investigator's dictionary (his theory) because our program's output must reflect the *investigator's definitions and interests* rather than broader, but irrelevant, facets of the text's meaning. A second restriction is that we must be prepared to distill large volumes of text into a *few* relevant categories. As we describe some applications of linguis-

---

[4] To make the boundaries of semantics more clear, we refer to an article on semantic theory by Uriel Weinreich: "The goal of a semantic theory of a language, as [Weinreich] conceive[s] it is to explicate the way in which the *meaning of a sentence of specified structure is derivable from the fully specified meaning of its parts.* . . . The scope of accountability of the semantic theory cannot be less than that of the grammar. Consequently, the sentence is what we want to make our theory accountable for. Insofar as the rules of pronominalization, ellipsis, etc., involve references to extra-sentential environments, the scope of semantic theory has to be extended correspondingly. We do not, on the other hand, propose to hold the semantic theory accountable for resolving the ambiguity of *jack* ('1. lifting device; 2. metal toy for playing jacks') in the sentence *I realized we had no jack* by association with, say, *car* and break in an adjacent sentence (*On a deserted road that night our car broke down.*) Such phenomena are in principle uncoded and are beyond the scope of linguistics . . ." (Weinreich, 1966:417 and footnote 38).

tic theory to the present and future General Inquirer we shall keep these restrictions in mind.

Returning from our digression into linguistics, let us examine the three issues in decoding text that we introduced earlier.

Linguistic relationships, both syntactic and semantic, derive from *rules of the language*. They are therefore regular and general and can be sought systematically in any and all text in that language. Processing of linguistic relationships may be built into the rules of the program. On the other hand, contextual relationships derive from the *broad map of meanings* which are embedded in a *language and culture,* and which link particular words to particular concepts or other words in an almost completely arbitrary manner. They are, therefore, irregular and specific to the words which are actually present in the text. Processing of contextual relationships must be triggered only by key words specified by the investigator.

Linguistic and contextual relationships together cannot delimit which specific aspects of meaning are sought by the investigator; we also need guidance from theory. The primary function of the *dictionary* is to provide this theoretical guidance and this can be accomplished at three levels:

1. The initial impact of the theory via the dictionary is made through the investigator's *selection of content categories* from his culture's infinite set of categories of meaning. This specifies what meanings are to be reported (as output from our program); but it is a *static* influence and it does not incorporate the many areas of meaning which may be needed *in the intermediate process of decoding* the text.

2. A second level of influence is applied in the *text-to-categories mapping* which is the body of the dictionary. This influence is relatively dynamic but it results in a fixed strategy of identifying categories in the *empirical level* of the text itself.

3. The third (and the most dynamic and powerful) level of theoretical influence is applied through *summary* operations made across the *basic units* of processing. It is at this level that abstraction occurs, that themes and trends are detected, that *strategies* of identifying categories are adjusted, and that the investigator is allowed to take an overview, and to ask "What is going on in general?" as the text flows along.

All three of these levels of theoretical influence are needed to make the content analysis procedures valid to the theory.

We view the sentence as the reasonable unit for a program like the General Inquirer to process internally. However, severe limits are placed on the internal processing of contextual and semantic relationships when one is restricted to sentence-length units. Many referents of a sentence's words and most other words which provide context lie outside that sentence: pronouns refer usually to a noun found in a preceding sentence (for example, *Alice* is angry. I like *her* that way.), and, in another example, "yesterday's tragic events" refers to local and cultural knowledge which is not stated explicitly at all. At the start of a speech or monograph, a theme is often introduced which is never restated in full (for example, a sports columnist who mentions a particular baseball game and thereafter writes only of strikes, pitches, hits, runs). Somehow we must provide the computer with access to extrasentential and even extratextual information.

Recent work on GIT has emphasized the development of a special *linguistic and contextual* analysis of the text which is carried out prior to the investigator's *content analysis*. Initially we thought it would be possible to carry out a formal syntactic analysis of the sentence, but the algorithms which have been developed (Bobrow, 1963) for parsing and similar analyses cannot yield results suited to our needs. In general, these routines can only produce lists of *possible* syntactic interpretations. At best they assign a *probability* to each interpretation. They can thereby identify some potential sources of ambiguity but they offer little assistance in selecting the correct interpretation. For this step we need semantic and contextual information as well as syntactic interpretations.

Philip Stone's chapter in this volume (Chapter 11) describes disambiguation procedures aimed at the elimination of ambiguity of meaning for a large number of common homographs. For our present purposes we need note only that the process aims to identify and substitute unambiguous *word-senses* for many ambiguous *words* in the text. The investigator can then write his theoretical definitions using the unambiguous word-senses without reference to the original words.

The generality of the General Inquirer resides primarily in its capacity to apply any set of word-to-category definitions, using any set of categories on any type of text. As we discuss how these definitions are understood, remembered, and applied by GIT we shall not be concerned with the language and format of definitions, nor their translation (compilation) into lists of instructions, nor the *technical* aspects of the storage of those lists. We must, however, consider both the *logical structure* of these lists of definitions and the procedures for their *use,* since it is precisely here that semantic theory makes a special contribution and here that any program for content analysis will demonstrate its practical strength. My remaining concerns are thus with the organization of the dictionary and with the processes of combining content categories in meaningful ways.

Insofar as one is modeling human behavior by trying to replicate the results of human category assignment, one is concerned with the issues of the functional similarity between our computerized procedures and those followed by human coders. Rigidities and biases introduced into our model at this functional level could permanently limit its growth and our program's general usefulness. Functional compatibility is needed in two areas: (1) the program's *procedures* of decoding and categorizing text should be compatible with *processes* of human cognitive performance, and (2) the *logical structure* of the program's memory of meanings and relationships of meaning should be compatible with the performance of human semantic memory—for example, the ability of our program to replicate semantic processes of abstraction (requiring hierarchies of meaning) and to identify paraphrasings and synonyms (requiring linkage of words at each level of abstraction).

Discussion of this type of development and of the nature of human semantic memory is to be found in many disciplines: Reitman (1967) provides the perspective of the builders of computer simulation models. Quite a different but equally pertinent perspective is given by Polanyi (1967) in an epistemological discussion of "sense-giving and sense-reading of language." Polanyi's concept of tacit knowledge and its relation to focusing of attention seems to be a more thorough explication of the problem which Reitman describes as

. . . a search problem in game playing, pattern recognition, and problem solving programs. There are too many alternatives to evaluate, and humans notice things more quickly than we can account for in terms of our current conceptions of search strategies. In language translation it appears as a question of semantics: the human knows and is able to use more than we are prepared to encompass in our programs (Reitman, 1967:26).

Moreover, both perspectives suggest that human memory is not a "passive storehouse of information" but, instead, plays an *active* role in the retrieval of information.

Computer models of human long-term memory and mental association have been under development for more than a decade. Although none of these models approaches complete simulation of human-memory ability, and few embody "active" processes, one model (developed by Ross Quillian) contributed significantly to our thinking (Quillian, 1965, 1966). In its present form, his kind of model requires an extensive set of meaning categories and linkages and is presently impractical for general content analysis which requires a large vocabulary. Quillian's model would be applicable if we could restrict our vocabulary to a few words, or our definitions to a few semantic concepts (such as an investigator's set of content categories). Although restriction of the categories in our dictionary would not impede the process of categorizing text once it has been decoded or "understood," it would prevent our program from decoding any parts of text that are related in ways which could not be completely expressed by those concepts. This problem is not a technical problem but a logical one, which can be resolved only by the development of compact semantic taxonomies and abstract rules of semantic relationship; because one cannot base a large dictionary on an enumeration and mapping of a language's potentially infinite set of meaning categories. Such taxonomies and semantic rules should not be expected in the near future.

As with many complex systems, the whole is greater than the sum of its parts—the meaning of a body of text or of a sentence is more than the sum of the undifferentiated meanings of its component words. Current programs, including GIT, are inadequte in dealing with this complexity. In the present GIT, a content category is remembered (stored) either as belonging directly to a word, or conditionally to a word or phrase. We would like a program to retain all of the meaning which is given in the investigator's dictionary and to combine it systematically in accordance with the information which is obtained from linguistic analysis of the sentence. The accuracy (of meaning) with which dictionary and text are combined depends on the rules for such combination and their responsiveness to semantic distinctions. In semantic theory the process of combining categories of meaning is called construction. We are interested here in the form of constructions. Thus, for example, we might specify that the construction resulting from combining categories assigned to a noun and an adjective be of a different form than a construction resulting from a noun and a verb. *Rules* for combining categories of meaning are the special province of semantic theory. We notice that it is the *complexity* of the resultant *semantic structure of the sentence* which we seek to reflect in our program's output. Rules of construction could identify inconsistencies between words in number, gender and other areas of meaning, and could even specify the seriousness of the inconsistency. The cumulated inconsistencies of all the words in a sentence could provide a measure of the sentence's deviation from normal. Rules could indicate the degree of order and the number of levels of meaning in a sentence, as well as many other aspects of a sentence's semantic complexity. These sentence properties are not presently dealt with in computerized content analysis. However, they are *basic* guides to a hearer's interpretation of content, since they may indicate metaphoric and poetic use of language as well as *intentional* ambiguity and anomaly.

In addition to this refinement in procedures of combining categories we would work for some improvement in the *information* provided by the dictionary. At present this information consists only of the categories to be assigned to a word. I hope to see dictionaries extended to include:

1. *Syntactic as well as semantic information.* There seem to be solid linguistic arguments for the utility of integrating syntactics and semantics in this way.[5]

2. *Implicit, connotative meanings as well as explicit, denotative meanings of words.* We find that guidance in identification and interpretation of deviance also comes from the implicit meanings of words (for example, *male* implies *animate;* "pretty," when applied to a ship, implies "female" which in turn implies "lovingly handled"). Of course, many implicit meanings are more direct than these, and some treatment of them has been attempted in existing General Inquirer dictionaries (for instance, the category "overstate" in the Harvard III dictionary).

In conclusion, I have given an overview of some major issues that confront computerized content analysis. In most cases they reflect merely the distance between current achievement and our goal of relieving human coders of a bulky task which is subtle but habitual and hence boring. The progress made in the fields of linguistics and anthropology through the application of logic suggests that language is not so unlawful and illogical a morass as one would guess from its surface appearance. But perhaps decoding of language into categorized meanings *is* a task somewhat beyond the reach of logic. It is nonetheless sufficient to our goals if we are able to abstract the *regularities* of language in a manner compact enough to build into a computer program. For computers operate *systematically* on huge quantities of data regardless of whether we *understand* any *logic* in the procedures that they perform. We have not set out to develop a logical *predictive* theory of language use, but only to develop systematic procedures for the empirical distillation of a text.

[5] That is, by allowing syntactic form in entries of a semantic dictionary: see Weinreich (1966:446ff) with additional references. The reader is especially encouraged to refer to that literature for a discussion of this point.

21 A Computer Content-Analysis Program for Analysing Attitudes: The Measurement of Qualities and Performance[1]

Ole R. Holsti

Political Science
University of British Columbia

Perhaps more than any other research method available to social scientists and humanists, content analysis has been marked by a diversity of purpose, subject matter, and technique. It has been used for purposes as different as inferring enemy intention from wartime propaganda and settling questions of disputed authorship. Its subject matter has included not only the familiar products of the mass media but also ancient pottery fragments and psychoanalytic interviews. Content analysts have been armed with instruments of measurement as simple as the wooden ruler and as complex as multimillion-dollar computers. And, finally, they have dealt with measurement problems ranging from counting column inches on the front page of the local newspaper to assessing the degree of "need achievement" in the literary products of various cultures.[2]

Among the basic problems for which content analysis has been used is that of inferring authors' attitudes from the messages that they produce. Usually, attitudes have been classified into a category set consisting of pro, con, and neutral. Bases for classification of attitudes—that is, the "context units" which have been considered in judging whether an attitude is favorable, unfavorable, or neutral—have sometimes been the sentence or theme. Often, however, analysts have found that coding each small

[1] I am indebted to Philip J. Stone of Harvard University, who introduced computer content analysis to me, to Ann A. Enea and Horace Enea, who wrote the first version of the program described here, and to Kuan Lee, who programmed subsequent versions of it. Financial support from the Office of Naval Research (NONR 225 (82), Project NR 177 254) through the Stanford Studies in International Conflict and Integration, and from the Dean's Committee on Research at the University of British Columbia is gratefully acknowledged, as is a grant of computer time from the Stanford Computation Center.
[2] For extensive surveys of the content analysis literature, see Berelson (1952), Barcus (1959), Stone (1966), Holsti (1968a), and Holsti (1969).

unit of a document is too costly and, instead, they have relied on a single, overall judgment of attitudes expressed in the entire book, speech, editorial, or diary. Even such apparently simple coding operations have sometimes produced problems of reliability. For example, in their classic studies of elite newspapers, Lasswell and his colleagues (1952) were unable to reach better than 70 percent intercoder agreement on coding of this type.

Other research projects may require more precise and complex techniques of content analysis. In the first place, giving the entire document a single rating for each attitude object may result in the loss of certain nuances. It has been demonstrated that the choice of context units affects the results of content analysis; the larger the context unit that is coded, the less likely are neutral attitudes to be recorded (Geller et al., 1942). Moreover, it may sometimes be important to take into consideration not only the direction but also the intensity of expressed attitudes. Finally, some analysts may require a technique which distinguishes between various components of attitudes. For example, Parsons, Shils, and Olds (1952) point out that social objects may be significant as *complexes of qualities* or *complexes of performance*. In the former case, the object is considered in terms of its attributes, of *what it is,* whereas in the latter case the object is viewed in terms of *what it does.* Attitudes about qualities and performances may be (but need not be) congruent. A study of John Foster Dulles' attitudes revealed that when the Soviet Union was perceived to be acting most aggressively toward the West, his assessment of Soviet attributes was a negative one. That is, his views of Soviet qualities and performance were congruent. But when Dulles regarded Soviet policy as being more accommodating and less hostile, there was no corresponding reassessment of Soviet qualities (Finlay et al., 1967). Because the existence of discrepancies between components of attitudes is often of interest, a technique of content analysis capable of distinguishing between the subject's assessment of qualities and performance may sometimes be needed.

One method of content analysis which meets these requirements is "evaluative assertion analysis" (Osgood, 1959a). The first step in coding is the reduction of the entire text into simple assertions of two classes which correspond to assessments of "complexes of qualities" and "complexes of performance."

attitude object/connector/evaluative term
attitude object$_1$/connector/attitude object$_2$

Extensive rules for coding and scoring have been provided (Osgood et al., 1956). Because this method first reduces the sentence into its component parts and it specifies which elements of the sentence are to be scored, it can be used with a high degree of reliability. Coders can be trained rapidly, but the method is too laborious to be used for large volumes of data, and it is uneconomical if one's research design requires only gross measures of attitudes (for example, pro or con). As a result, relatively few studies using evaluative assertion analysis have appeared in the published literature.

The content analysis program described in this chapter represents the most recent in a series of efforts to provide a computer-based analogue to evaluative assertion analysis.[3] The substantive impetus for this effort has been an interest in the attitudes and beliefs of political elites and, more specifically, in those of foreign-policy decision makers. The problem of measuring attitudes is not, of course, of interest only to students of international relations, and the flexibility of the present program is such that it can be used with any variables, attitude objects, and class of documents. A schematic representation of the type of research design for which this program was developed is shown in Figure 1.

Not long after the "General Inquirer" was initially adapted for measuring attitudes in political documents, it became apparent that, partly because of the kinds of analyses for which these programs were to be used, three basic modifications would be highly desirable. First, the original programs were better suited to analyses in which inferences were based on word or "tag" frequencies than in those intended to measure the relationship between tags and attitude objects, or between two or more attitude objects. It was possible to undertake this type of analysis by means of a "sentence retrieval" program, but this required three separate computer operations, and the final output format was such that considerable time was required to construct summary tables after computer processing was completed. A second difficulty with the initial programs was their limited flexibility. Efforts to analyze data with dictionaries other than that for which it was originally prepared proved somewhat cumbersome. Hence the need for a program that could easily be used with any dictionary became increasingly evident. Finally, the problem of slow running time is one inherent in the COMIT programming language. Since the original versions of various General Inquirer programs appeared in the early 1960's, virtually all users have had their programs rewritten in languages that provide faster running time (Stone et al., 1966). The program described here is written in BALGOL for operation on IBM 7090 or 7094 computers.

In short, experience with these initial computer-content analysis programs was satisfactory in most respects, especially when measured against a baseline of manual content analysis. But it also became increasingly clear that a more flexible program, capable of producing direct quantitative

[3] Earlier efforts are described in Holsti (1964a) and Holsti (1967a).

ELEMENTS OF ANALYSIS	Data (Fig. 4)	Measurement of "Complexes of Qualities" (Figs. 5a–5b, 13)	Attitude Objects as Agents	Measurement of "Complexes of Performance" (Figs. 8a–8b)	Attitude Objects as Targets of Action	Measurement of "Complexes of Qualities" (Figs. 9a–9b)
RESEARCH DESIGN	Documents Selected for Analysis by Sampling Design	Determined by Selection of Dictionary	Determined by Selection of "Format Names" and "Proper Names"	Determined by Selection of Dictionary	Determined by Selection of "Format Names" and "Proper Names"	Determined by Selection of Dictionary
		(Figs. 2, 3, 12)	(Figs. 6, 7)	(Figs. 2, 3, 12)	(Figs. 6, 7)	(Figs. 2, 3, 12)

Author or Source

Qualities Attributed by Source ──→ Attitude Object A ──→ Actions as Interpreted by Source ──→ Attitude Obj. A, Attitude Obj. B, Attitude Obj. N

Qualities Attributed by Source ──→ Attitude Object B ──→ Actions as Interpreted by Source ──→ Attitude Obj. A, Attitude Obj. B, Attitude Obj. N

Qualities Attributed by Source ──→ Attitude Object N ──→ Actions as Interpreted by Source ──→ Attitude Obj. A, Attitude Obj. B, Attitude Obj. N

Figure 1 Design of measurements by computer content-analysis program.

output at lower machine and human cost, was highly desirable. The remainder of this chapter will describe the program in some detail under three headings: *dictionaries, data preparation,* and *data output.* The sequence in which various cards are assembled is specified in the conclusion.

DICTIONARIES

Each version of computer content analysis which has emerged from the General Inquirer system has, at its core, a dictionary in which entry words are defined with one or more "tags" representing categories in the investigator's theory. The dictionary provides the vital link between the theoretical formulation of the research problem and the mechanics of analysis. The necessity for developing rigorous rules concerning "tagging" of words, by forcing unstated assumptions into the open for critical scrutiny, is an important check on many theoretical aspects of the research.

Semantic Differential Dictionary

The dictionary based on the semantic differential which was developed for the earlier General Inquirer program remains the primary instrument in the present program (Holsti, 1964a; Stone et al., 1966). Dictionary entries are defined along three dimensions, each of which takes the form of a seven-point scale.

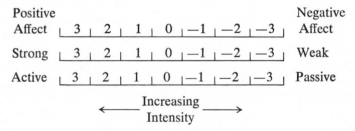

Any entry word may have as many as three definitions, each of which also carries an intensity rating (for example, penetration = negative 1, strong 3, active 2).

The three scales correspond to the *evaluative, potency,* and *activity* dimensions which have often been found to be primary in cognition irrespective of culture (see, for example, Osgood et al., 1957; Osgood 1962). The dictionary thus reflects the assumption that when political elites perceive themselves, other nations, events, or any attitude object, the most relevant discriminations are made in terms of these dimensions.

Like most derivatives of the General Inquirer system, this program produces a list of all words appearing in the text but not in the dictionary.

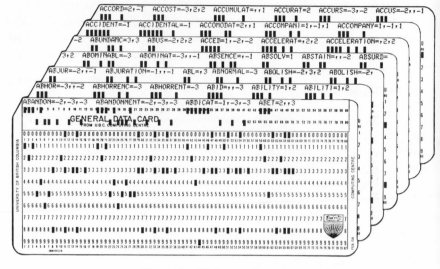

Figure 2   Dictionary format.

This "leftover list" makes it easy to determine the adequacy of the dictionary for any given sample of documents, and to identify those words which should be added to it. Several hundred words have been added to the original semantic differential dictionary of 3521 words.

Dictionary format for the program has been modified somewhat from that of earlier programs. Numbers and their positions are used to designate tag categories and intensity levels (Figure 2). The first position following the equal sign represents the affect dimension, the second is the potency dimension, and the third is the activity dimension. Numbers that appear in these positions refer to points within each scale. For example, the dictionary includes ACCOST = −3,2,2, indicating that the term is defined as *negative* (intensity 3), *strong* (intensity 2), and *active* (intensity 2). Extra commas are used to denote the absence of a tag—that is, the zero point on any of the scales. Thus, the double commas between 2 and 3 in the definition of ABET mean that it is scored zero along the potency dimension.

Entry words are listed in the dictionary in root form, with the frequently appearing endings *e, es, s, ed,* and *ing* removed. If a word in the text with any of these endings is not found in the dictionary, the computer will automatically remove the ending and look up the root word. Hence a single entry word (for example, *aid*) will pick up many forms of the word (for instance, *aids, aided,* and *aiding,* as well as *aid*).

Other Dictionaries

This program may be used with any dictionary adhering to the format specified in Figure 2. "Tags" for entry words are identified by a set of numbers ranging from +3 to −3 in three positions, defining a maximum of eighteen variables. These may be used to designate six points on each of three scales, as in the semantic differential dictionary, or they may be used to define eighteen separate variables. For example, a small supplementary dictionary for four variables—conflict, cooperation, economic development, and ideal values—has been prepared. It is punched in the format shown in Figure 3. Because the data tables can accommodate only eighteen tag categories, dictionaries with more variables must be divided into sets of eighteen or less and used in separate runs through the data. Thus, if the analyst should wish to use the Harvard Third Psychosociological Dictionary (Stone et al., 1966) with this program, he would need to divide it into four dictionaries of eighteen tags each and a fifth one with the remaining eleven categories.

DATA PREPARATION

To answer most questions about the author's attitudes, it is not enough to know that X, Y, or both X and Y occur in a sentence; it is usually

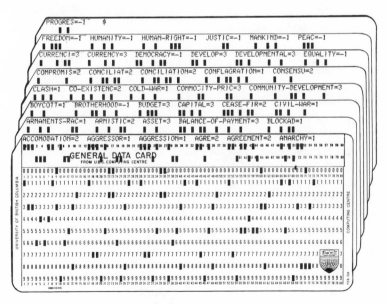

Figure 3 Dictionary format.

more important to know the perceived relationships between X and Y. Consider the following sentence:

> During the years since my last report, the wealthy nuclear powers have not provided enough vital economic aid to the many poor, underdeveloped, noncommitted nations.

Poor and *nuclear powers* both occur in the sentence, but we would surely be misled if we therefore inferred that the author of the document believed that these nations are poor. Nor does an analysis that informs us only that *noncommitted nations, aid,* and *nuclear powers* appear in this sentence tell us what the author believes about the relationship between these two groups of countries. The same information would be produced if the subject (nuclear powers) and object (noncommitted nations) in the sentence were reversed. Moreover, it would not enable us to distinguish between the sentence as it appears and the very different meaning it would have without the word *not.* Because such distinctions are crucial for the types of analyses described in Figure 1, some syntax coding is necessary.

The symbols for subscripting the text currently in use are:

The author of document (appears on ID card only)	/1
The perceiver when other than the author of the document	/2
The agent and modifiers	/3
The action and modifiers	/4
The direct object (when target is indirect object) and modifiers	/5
The target and modifiers	/7

The numerical codes indicate the agent-action-target (analogous to subject-verb-object) relationship, as well as linking all descriptive modifiers to the proper terms.[4] The subscript system described here is flexible and these numbers may be used to designate other types of relationships. But for reasons that will be made clearer when we examine the data output format, *this program will not operate on uncoded text.*

The entire theme may also be coded for certain essential information which cannot be effectively transmitted through word subscripting alone. Unlike the required syntax marks, data to be analyzed with this program may be (but need not be) theme-coded.

Three theme codes are currently being used:

The time element

C   Current
P   Past
F   Future

---

[4] More extensive coding rules are described in Holsti (1964b).

The mode of expression

D   Indicative
N   Normative
M   Comparative
V   Imperative
B   Probability
T   Interrogative
X   Aspiration

Conditional statements

A   Antecedent (if . . .)
S   Subsequent (then . . .)

These codes, which are preceded by a star, are inserted into the text as the first word of each theme. The entire text is punched on IBM cards in the format shown in Figure 4.

DATA OUTPUT

Table Format: "Complexes of Qualities"

As indicated in Figure 1, the data-output format in this program is designed to measure attitudes about both "complexes of qualities" and

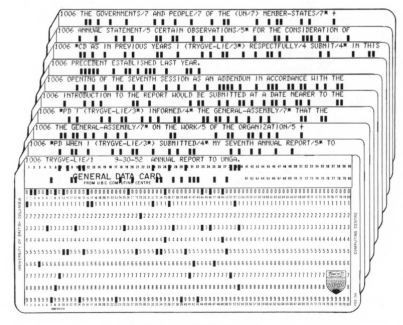

Figure 4 Data format.

"complexes of performance" from the content of communications. A's assertions about B's qualities may take a variety of forms. For example, each of the following assertions by A contain information, in the words coded with the same numbers as the code for B, about B's characteristics.

THE AGGRESSIVE/3 POLICIES/3 OF B/3 ENDANGER/4 THE PEACE/7. (Description of B as an agent of action.)

OUR/3 GOALS/3 ARE TO SUPPORT/4 OUR BRAVE/7 AND STURDY/7 ALLY/7 B/7. (Description of B as the target of action.)

B/3 IS/4 A STRUGGLING/3 UNDERDEVELOPED/3 NATION /3. (Predicate adjective and predicate noun.)

In each case, the numerical codes link attitude object B with the qualities attributed to it by the source. Questions may also be asked about what A says regarding B's performance toward A, B, C . . . N. Scores are based on words and phrases with the /4 syntax code in sentence in which B is the agent of action and A, B, C . . . N are the targets.

The tables produced by this program are intended to answer both types of questions exhaustively for any specified attitude objects, be they nations, institutions, groups, persons, concepts, programs, ideologies or whatever, which might appear in the data. The first pair of tables presents scores on the perceived qualities of attitude objects when they appear as agents in the sentence (Figures 5a and 5b). The top of the first table includes identification information for the document and a tally of the number of words it contains. Row headings identify the dictionary variables (or "tags") and column headings are the attitude objects designated by the investigator. Our example includes variables in the semantic differential dictionary and nine attitude objects—the United Nations, United States, USSR, West, East, nonaligned nations, U.N. member nations, Big Powers, and crisis—relevant to a study of the United Nations Secretary-General's attitudes. The initial figure in each cell represents a weighted (frequency $\times$ intensity) total for the designated relationship. Thus the 78.00 in the upper left-hand cell indicates a weighted score for the U.N. on the variable positive affect, and the number immediately underneath is the weighted score divided by the number of words in the text ($78.00/5877 = .013$).

The combination of frequencies and intensities resulting in a score of 78.00 is not revealed in Figure 5a. It might have been based on seventy-eight references scored "positive affect-intensity one" in the dictionary ($78 \times 1 = 78$), twenty references scored positive three and eighteen positive-one [$(20 \times 3) + (18 \times 1) = 78$] or any other combination of frequency and intensity totalling 78. A glance at the corresponding cell in

1009 HAMMARSKJOLD/1   1955   UNGAR REPORT   UNGA.

NUMBER OF WORDS IN TEXT- 5877

EVALUATIVE PERCEPTION ......AGENT

	U.N.	U.S.	USSR	WEST	EAST	N.A.	M.N.	BIGPOW	CRISIS	OTHER	TOTAL
POSITIVE AFFECT	78.000 .013	.000 .000	.000 .000	4.000 .001	.000 .000	17.000 .003	20.000 .003	.000 .000	3.000 .001	21.000 .004	143.000 .024
NEGATIVE AFFECT	1.000 .000	.000 .000	.000 .000	.000 .000	.000 .000	3.000 .001	7.000 .001	.000 .000	2.000 .000	20.000 .003	33.000 .006
STRONG	113.000 .019	.000 .000	.000 .000	3.000 .001	1.000 .000	15.000 .003	21.000 .004	.000 .000	.000 .000	57.000 .010	210.000 .036
WEAK	3.000 .001	.000 .000	.000 .000	.000 .000	.000 .000	.000 .000	.000 .000	.000 .000	.000 .000	10.000 .002	13.000 .002
ACTIVE	86.000 .015	.000 .000	.000 .000	2.000 .000	.000 .000	6.000 .001	9.000 .002	.000 .000	.000 .000	24.000 .004	127.000 .002
PASSIVE	25.000 .004	.000 .000	.000 .000	1.000 .000	.000 .000	.000 .000	2.000 .000	.000 .000	.000 .000	11.000 .002	39.000 .007

(a)

Figure 5a Evaluation of agent: intensity scores.

PREQUENCY TABLE	U.N.	U.S.	USSR	WEST	EAST	N.A.	M.N.	BIGPOW	CRISIS	OTHER	TOTAL
POSITIVE 1	26	0	0	2	0	5	2	0	0	9	44
POSITIVE 2	17	0	0	1	0	3	9	0	0	6	36
POSITIVE 3	6	0	0	0	0	2	0	0	1	0	9
NEGATIVE 1	1	0	0	0	0	3	2	0	0	4	10
NEGATIVE 2	0	0	0	0	0	0	1	0	1	5	7
NEGATIVE 3	0	0	0	0	0	0	1	0	0	2	3
STRONG . 1	20	0	0	1	1	4	1	0	0	10	37
STRONG . 2	39	0	0	1	0	4	7	0	0	16	67
STRONG . 3	5	0	0	0	0	1	2	0	0	5	13
WEAK ... 1	1	0	0	0	0	0	0	0	1	2	4
WEAK ... 2	1	0	0	0	0	0	0	0	0	4	5
WEAK ... 3	0	0	0	0	0	0	0	0	0	0	0
ACTIVE . 1	24	0	0	0	0	2	2	0	0	4	32
ACTIVE . 2	25	0	0	1	0	2	2	0	0	4	34
ACTIVE . 3	4	0	0	0	0	0	1	0	0	4	9
PASSIVE 1	9	0	0	1	0	0	2	0	0	1	13
PASSIVE 2	5	0	0	0	0	0	0	0	0	2	7
PASSIVE 3	2	0	0	0	0	0	0	0	0	2	4

(b)

Figure 5b Evaluation of agent: frequency scores.

the immediately following table (Figure 5*b*) reveals that the weighted score was based on forty-nine assertions about the United Nations as the agent, twenty-six of which were scored positive-one, seventeen as positive-two, and six as positive-three $[(26 \times 1) + (17 \times 2) + (6 \times 3) = 78]$. Because some statistical tests cannot be used with weighted data such as appear in Figure 5*a*, the frequency distributions provided in the table that follows are often useful for statistical purposes.

Any single pass through the data will accommodate analysis of up to twelve attitude objects. The next column—"others"—records scores for all other attitude objects which appear in the document. These will be identified in the "left-over list" which appears with each set of tables. Figures in the right-hand column—"total"—represent the total score for each row.

Column headings are controlled by two sets of cards. "Format Names" cards designate the titles at the head of each column and the order in which they are to appear. Each name or appropriate six-digit abbreviation should end on column 6 for proper alignment of the columns in the tables. The last card is punched with a dollar sign in column 15. The "Format Names" cards used to produce the tables in the example above appear in Figure 6.

A set of "Proper Names" cards (Figure 7) is used to identify the text words which are to be classified under each column heading. For example, in Figures 5*a* and 5*b* the column "United Nations" was defined by a series of terms designating persons and agencies associated with the U.N.[5] The United Nations appears in Column 1 of each table because it was placed first in the deck of "Format Names" cards; thus each of these terms was punched with = 1: ECOSOC = 1, FAO = 1, HAM-MARSKJOLD = 1, and so on. The same procedure is followed for all terms which are to be scored under each column heading.[6]

The second and third sets of tables produced for each document are similar in format to those described above, but they compute scores for perceived qualities of attitude objects in themes in which they appear as *direct objects* and *targets* of action. Consider again the example cited earlier:

DURING THE YEAR SINCE MY LAST REPORT, THE WEALTHY/3 NUCLEAR-POWERS/3 HAVE NOT/4 PRO-VIDED/4 ENOUGH/4 VITAL/5 ECONOMIC/5 AID/5 TO THE

---

[5] Figure 7 includes only a small sample (for purposes of illustration) of the "Proper Names" that were actually used to produce the tables in Figures 5*a*, 5*b*, 8*a*, 8*b*, 9*a*, and 9*b*.

[6] Notice that the punching of entries on "Proper Names" cards begins in column 2.

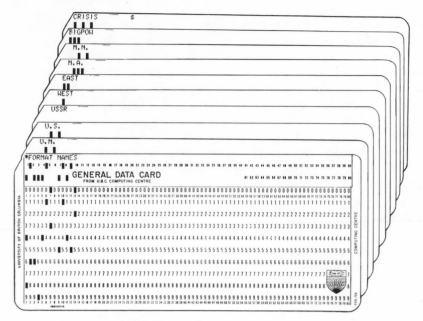

Figure 6 Format names cards.

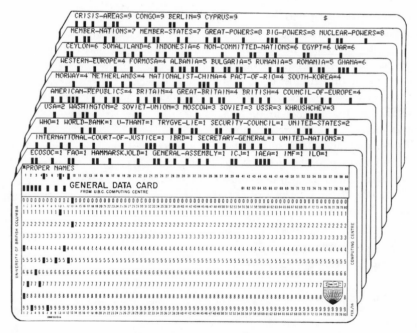

Figure 7 Proper names cards.

368

MANY/7 POOR/7, UNDERDEVELOPED/7, NON-COMMIT-TED-NATIONS/7.

The first pair of tables prints out scores for the subject of the sentence—nuclear powers—based on dictionary "tags" of the words used to describe it; the second pair of tables presents scores for the direct object based on the described attributes of foreign aid; and the third pair of tables indicates the author's attitudes toward the target of action, noncommitted nations. An example of the latter type of table is given in Figures 8*a* and 8*b*. Mechanics of scoring are the same as for the tables in Figures 5*a* and 5*b*.

TABLE FORMAT: "COMPLEXES OF PERFORMANCE"

To answer questions about complexes of performance, we need to determine how the source perceives A's (or B's . . . N's) actions toward A, B . . . N. This program produces a complete set of tables measuring the perceived relationship between every pair of attitude objects. Thus for each of the nine attitude objects for which Format Names and Proper Names cards were prepared in our example, the program computes and prints out a pair of tables scoring its actions in terms of the dictionary variables. In our illustrative document, the first pair of tables reveals the author's assessment of United Nations actions toward all targets (Figures 9*a* and 9*b*). A similar pair of tables is produced for the United States, USSR, West, East, nonaligned nations, U.N. member nations, big powers, and crisis areas. The basic table format and the method of computation are, with two important exceptions, identical to those described for earlier tables.

The first exception concerns the use of negatives. Clearly it is important to distinguish between two sentences such as "The nuclear powers have provided economic aid to the noncommitted nations," and "The nuclear powers have not provided economic aid to the noncommitted nations." When any action is modified by terms of negation—*no, never, not,* and the like—it is automatically given a reverse score. In the example above the term *provide* is tagged in the dictionary as "positive 1, strong 2, active 1." In the second sentence it is preceded by a negation, causing the program to score the action of the nuclear powers toward noncommitted nations as "negative 1, weak 2, passive 1."

A second feature of the tables for action relationships is that the mode of expression may result in a somewhat reduced intensity score. The mode of expression is indicated by a single letter code preceding each theme. The following codes and the intensity weights assigned to each are cur-

EVALUATIVE PERCEPTION .....TARGET

	U.N.	U.S.	USSR	WEST	EAST	N.A.	M.N.	BIGPOW	CRISIS	OTHER	TOTAL
POSITIVE AFFECT	34.000	.000	.000	.000	.000	6.000	4.000	.000	.000	47.000	91.000
	.006	.000	.000	.000	.000	.001	.000	.000	.000	.008	.015
NEGATIVE AFFECT	16.000	.000	.000	.000	.000	4.000	4.000	.000	.000	23.000	47.000
	.003	.000	.000	.000	.000	.001	.001	.000	.000	.004	.008
STRONG	56.000	.000	.000	.000	.000	17.000	8.000	.000	.000	66.000	147.000
	.010	.000	.000	.000	.000	.003	.001	.000	.000	.011	.025
WEAK	10.000	.000	.000	.000	.000	.000	.000	.000	.000	20.000	30.000
	.002	.000	.000	.000	.000	.000	.000	.000	.000	.003	.005
ACTIVE	36.000	.000	.000	.000	.000	9.000	4.000	.000	.000	43.000	92.000
	.006	.000	.000	.000	.000	.002	.001	.000	.000	.007	.016
PASSIVE	11.000	.000	.000	.000	.000	4.000	2.000	.000	.000	18.000	35.000
	.002	.000	.000	.000	.000	.001	.000	.000	.000	.003	.006

(a)

Figure 8a Evaluation of target: intensity scores.

370

FREQUENCY TABLE	U.N.	U.S.	USSR	WEST	EAST	N.A.	M.N.	BIGPOW	CRISIS	OTHER	TOTAL
POSITIVE 1	13	0	0	0	0	2	1	0	0	13	29
POSITIVE 2	6	0	0	0	0	2	0	0	0	11	19
POSITIVE 3	3	0	0	0	0	0	1	0	0	4	8
NEGATIVE 1	5	0	0	0	0	4	1	0	0	9	19
NEGATIVE 2	4	0	0	0	0	0	0	0	0	4	8
NEGATIVE 3	1	0	0	0	0	0	1	0	0	2	4
STRONG . 1	9	0	0	0	0	2	1	0	0	12	24
STRONG . 2	13	0	0	0	0	3	2	0	0	12	30
STRONG . 3	7	0	0	0	0	3	1	0	0	10	21
WEAK ... 1	2	0	0	0	0	0	0	0	0	4	6
WEAK ... 2	4	0	0	0	0	0	0	0	0	5	9
WEAK ... 3	0	0	0	0	0	0	0	0	0	2	2
ACTIVE . 1	6	0	0	0	0	3	1	0	0	13	23
ACTIVE . 2	12	0	0	0	0	3	0	0	0	12	27
ACTIVE . 3	2	0	0	0	0	0	1	0	0	2	5
PASSIVE 1	1	0	0	0	0	0	0	0	0	3	4
PASSIVE 2	5	0	0	0	0	2	1	0	0	3	11
PASSIVE 3	0	0	0	0	0	0	0	0	0	3	3

(b)

Figure 8b Evaluation of agent: frequency scores.

ACTION PERCEPTIONS

AGENT-- U.N.

	U.N.	U.S.	TARGET NATIONS USSR	WEST	EAST	N.A.	M.N.	BIGPOW	CRISIS	OTHER	TOTAL
POSITIVE AFFECT	9.900	.000	.000	.000	.000	6.000	1.500	.000	2.400	15.000	34.800
	.002	.000	.000	.000	.000	.001	.000	.000	.000	.003	.006
NEGATIVE AFFECT	.700	.000	.000	.000	.000	3.000	3.000	.000	.000	10.000	16.700
	.000	.000	.000	.000	.000	.001	.001	.000	.000	.002	.003
STRONG	25.400	.000	.000	.000	1.000	5.700	2.500	.000	5.300	44.900	84.800
	.004	.000	.000	.000	.000	.001	.000	.000	.001	.008	.014
WEAK	.000	.030	.000	.000	.000	1.000	9.000	.000	.000	.000	10.000
	.000	.000	.000	.000	.000	.000	.002	.000	.000	.000	.002
ACTIVE	18.700	.000	.000	.000	1.000	2.400	3.000	.000	4.200	29.000	58.300
	.003	.000	.000	.000	.000	.001	.001	.000	.001	.005	.010
PASSIVE	3.300	.000	.000	.000	1.000	6.000	9.000	.000	1.200	5.000	25.500
	.001	.000	.000	.000	.000	.001	.002	.000	.000	.001	.004

(a)

Figure 9a Evaluation of actions: intensity scores.

FREQUENCY TABLE	U.N.	U.S.	USSR	WEST	EAST	N.A.	M.N.	BIGPOW	CRISIS	OTHER	TOTAL
POSITIVE 1	4	0	0	0	0	1	2	0	1	4	12
POSITIVE 2	3	0	0	0	0	1	0	0	1	4	9
POSITIVE 3	1	0	0	0	0	1	0	0	1	1	4
NEGATIVE 1	1	0	0	0	0	1	3	0	0	2	7
NEGATIVE 2	0	0	0	0	0	1	0	0	0	1	2
NEGATIVE 3	0	0	0	0	0	0	0	0	0	2	2
STRONG . 1	6	0	0	0	1	1	3	0	1	6	18
STRONG . 2	6	0	0	0	0	1	0	0	2	13	22
STRONG . 3	3	0	0	0	0	1	0	0	1	7	12
WEAK ... 1	0	0	0	0	0	1	0	0	0	0	1
WEAK ... 2	0	0	0	0	0	0	0	0	0	0	0
WEAK ... 3	0	0	0	0	0	0	3	0	0	0	3
ACTIVE . 1	2	0	0	0	1	1	1	0	0	14	19
ACTIVE . 2	9	0	0	0	0	1	1	0	3	9	23
ACTIVE . 3	0	0	0	0	0	0	0	0	0	1	1
PASSIVE 1	3	0	0	0	1	2	0	0	1	1	8
PASSIVE 2	1	0	0	0	0	2	2	0	1	2	8
PASSIVE 3	0	0	0	0	0	0	2	0	0	0	2

(b)

Figure 9b Evaluation of actions: frequency scores.

rently being used:

Code	Mode of Expression	Weight
X	Aspiration	0.4
B	Probability	0.5
N	Normative	0.6
V	Imperative	0.7
D	Indicative	1.0
M	Comparative	1.0
T	Interrogative	1.0

Consider our previous example, which might also have appeared as:

The nuclear powers hope to provide economic aid to the noncommitted nations.

The nuclear powers may provide economic aid to the noncommitted nations.

When stated in these forms, the automatic intensity reduction feature of the program will multiply the score for action term—*provide* (positive 1, strong 2, active 1)—by the indicated weights. Hence, in the sentence above stating an aspiration, multiplication by 0.4 will result in a score of nuclear powers' action toward noncommitted nations of positive 0.4, strong 0.8, active 0.4.

The intensity reduction feature of the program is optional. The analyst who does not wish to employ theme codes may still use the program; in that case, all actions are scored at full dictionary value. The assigned weights for various modes of expression are, of course, arbitrary and may be easily changed. If the intensity reduction feature is used, two cards (Figure 10) are submitted with the data to identify the column on the data cards in which the theme code for modes of expression appears. The number in columns of the second card indicates that the various theme codes for mode of expression appear in column 8 of the data cards.

If codes for mode of expression are used, some apparent discrepancies between the tables providing weighted (intensity $\times$ frequency) and simple frequency scores will appear. In Figure 9a, United Nations actions toward crisis areas received a score for "strong" of 5.3, which is somewhat less than that indicated in the accompanying (Figure 9b) frequency table: $(1 \times 1) + (2 \times 2) + (1 \times 3) = 8$. This indicates that several of the action scores received less than a full value owing to their mode of expression.

Tables can be produced at any designated interval between or within documents. Each segment of text for which tables are to be produced

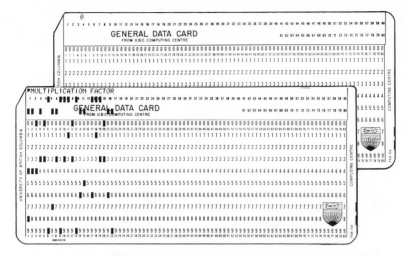

Figure 10 Multiplication factor cards.

is preceded by a "New Text" card. Scores will be computed for all subsequent text until a "Tag Tally" card is inserted, at which point the program prints out tables for the text between these two cards. This procedure is followed through to the end of the data, which is marked by a "Finished Card." The format of these cards is indicated in Figure 11.

TABLES WITH OTHER DICTIONARIES

If the analyst should wish to use variables other than those in the semantic differential dictionary, he may do so without recoding or in

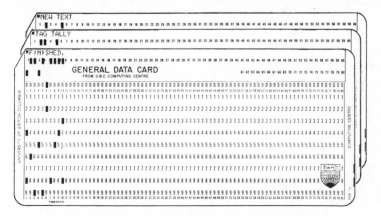

Figure 11 New text, tag tally, and finished cards.

Figure 12   Dimension names cards.

any other way changing his data. Once the data have been punched in the format described earlier, they may be reanalyzed as often and with as many different dictionaries as are necessary. Only two changes are required for reanalysis with a new dictionary. A deck of "Dimension Names" cards is submitted along with the dictionary entry words and tag definitions. As an example, we can consider the sample dictionary of four variables—conflict, cooperation, economic development, and ideal values—illustrated in Figure 3. The corresponding Dimension Names cards appear in Figure 12. Variable names are punched in columns 1–12 and a dollar sign is punched in column 15 of the final card. If the dictionary includes less than eighteen variables, as is the case in our example, blank cards are inserted to bring the total number of cards to eighteen.

Except for the variable names at the beginning of each row, tables produced with any dictionary are similar to those described earlier. Interpretation of the tables, however, will vary according to the nature of the dictionary. The simple frequency tables produced by this program can always be used, irrespective of the dictionary, but the weighted scores will be meaningful only with dictionaries in which tag definitions include intensity scores.

"Leftover List"

Preceding the tables for each document in a series of messages listing potential deficiencies in the data or dictionary. The appearance of single words on the list reveals that they are not listed in the dictionary. In Figure 13, *events, fore, concepts, static,* and so on are words that occurred in the text but are not in the dictionary. A rapid glance through this list reveals which words, if any, should be "tagged" and added to the dictionary for future passes through the data. Because mispunched or misspelled words will also appear on this "leftover" list, it can also provide a rapid check for the adequacy of keypunching.

The messages also reveal coding irregularities such as occurred in themes 2 and 8. The analyst can readily turn to these themes in his data to determine whether the problem is one that makes a substantive difference. Such irregularities do not stop the program from operating, nor do they prevent tables from being prepared.

The leftover list also discloses the attitude objects that appear in the document, but for which "Format Names" and "Proper Names" cards were not provided. A typical message is that reading "Nations assumed other," indicating that any references to unspecified nations were scored in the "others" column of the tables. This feature can be particularly useful for large-scale analyses in which the investigator may not be certain that given pass through the data has exhausted the information of theoretical interest to him. A glance through these messages reveals whether further runs incorporating attitude objects that appear as "others" with some frequency in the test are warranted. For example, if repeated messages about "interdependence" were to appear, as in the fourth line from the bottom of Figure 13, the analyst might decide to rerun all or parts of his data to pick up these references if he deemed them to be theoretically significant.

The sequence in which program dictionary, data, and other instruction cards is to be mentioned is indicated in Figure 14.

```
LEFTOVERS--

        EVENTS
        FORE
        CONCEPTS
UN IMPROPERLY TAGGED 7 IN THEME 1
        CERTAIN
NATIONS ASSUMED 'OTHER'
ORGANIZATION IMPROPERLY TAGGED 7 IN THEME 2
        STATIC
        MACHINERY
        IDEOLOGIES
        VIEW
        IDEOLOGIES
NATIONS ASSUMED 'OTHER'
        INSTRUMENT
NATIONS ASSUMED 'OTHER'
        SHOULD
RECONCILIATION ASSUMED 'OTHER'
NATIONS ASSUMED 'OTHER'
        SHOULD
        EXECUTIVE
        UNTAKEN
MEMBERS IMPROPERLY TAGGED 7 IN THEME 8
        FORESTALLING
        DIPLOMATIC
        POLITICAL
        SPIRIT
        OBJECTIVITY
        IMPLEMENTATION
        LATTER
CONCEPT ASSUMED 'OTHER'
        POINT
CONCEPT ASSUMED 'OTHER'
        IS
        INTERNATICNAL
INTERDEPENDENCE ASSUMED 'OTHER'
NATIONS ASSUMED 'OTHER'
CONCEPT ASSUMED 'OTHER'
        PHILOSOPHY
```

Figure 13   Leftover list.

CONCLUSION

At the outset we stated that the computer content-analysis program described in this chapter was intended to provide precise measurements of attitude with flexibility and speed. It is apparent that it does not meet all of these specifications equally well.

Assuming no coding or punching errors, this program does provide precise and reliable (but not, of course, necessarily valid) measures of attitudes. Moreover, the leftover list can be an invaluable tool for virtually eliminating both coding and punching errors.

The requirement of flexibility is also reasonably well achieved within the broad framework of analyses for which the program was developed.

It can operate with a variety of dictionaries and may be used to measure the author's views toward any attitude object. This does not mean, however, that the program will necessarily prove useful in all content analysis research involving attitude measurement. The analyst requiring only a rough index of attitude changes in a large volume of documentation will no doubt find the added cost of whatever precision is gained with this program superfluous and prohibitively expensive. Other research designs may require data in a format quite different from that provided here. Hence, as with any content analysis scheme, it is important for the analyst to determine whether the output of this program satisfies the requirements of his research design before coding and punching his text.

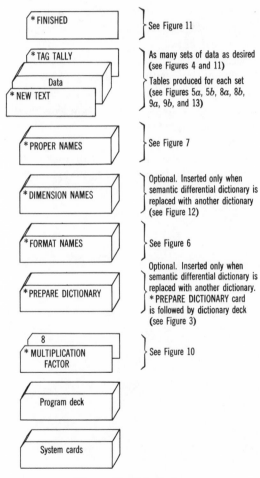

Figure 14 Job deck sequence.

Finally, the program achieves the goal of speed quite adequately if we consider only the costs of machine time. It is impossible to state precisely the running speed of this program, since it will vary depending on dictionary length, the number of tables to be produced, the number of objects for which attitudes are to be scored, and many other factors. A reasonable estimate might be based on a recent run in which the semantic differential dictionary was used to assess attitudes toward ten attitude objects. Sixteen documents totalling 92,000 words were processed in seventeen minutes, an average of more than 5300 words per minute. The program produced 13 pairs of tables (one for frequencies, one for frequency $\times$ intensity) for each document, for a total of 416 tables. In turn, each pair of tables listed scores for 180 cells (6 tags $\times$ 3 intensities $\times$ 10 attitude objects). These figures exclude scores computed for "others," attitude objects not included in the "Format Names."

The most serious drawback of the program is that the text must be coded manually before computer processing. The coding itself is easily learned; it can be accomplished with a high degree of reliability; and, because it requires syntactical rather than substantive judgments, it neither locks the analyst in to a single theoretical framework, nor does it "contaminate" the data for other types of analyses. Nevertheless, coding is time consuming—although far less so than many forms of manual content analysis—and it represents the highest cost factor in any research using this program. For this reason, the investigator contemplating its use should make certain that, in terms of his theoretical interests, its advantages outweigh the costs of coding.

22 A Computer Systems Approach Toward the Recognition and Analysis of Content[1]

Howard P. Iker
Norman I. Harway

University of Rochester Medical Center

The key question that we have been exploring for almost six years (Harway and Iker 1964, 1966; Iker and Harway 1965) is whether there exists a method for content analysis that will allow the user to discover what his data are about without having to furnish a priori categorizations within which to classify these data. Any other currently used content-analytic system of which we are aware requires, at least, that the user furnish a set of categories to which the various portions of the text are to be allocated. It is our purpose to demonstrate that there is an alternative to this approach.

Our original interest in the area was in the process of psychotherapy, in the changes in cognitive organization that occur as a result of treatment, and in the process of change. Psychotherapy, if we exclude for the moment certain of the behavioral therapies, involves the user of oral communication to modify, among other things, a person's perspective of himself and of his word. To the extent that this occurs, this change should be reflected in the individual's verbal behavior. Since the assumption is that the communications of the psychotherapist are influential in accomplishing this change, we are led to the question of the relationship between the substance and the structure of the oral communications among psychotherapist and patient, their change with time and with progress in treatment.

The basic assumption on which this system rests is that there exists sufficient meaning within the word and within the temporal associations among and between words to allow the elicitation of major content materials and categories. In short, it is the initial task of our approach to *generate* the kinds of informational categories with which many content-analytic systems begin.

[1] This research was supported in part by U.S. Public Health Service Grant MH-10444, National Institute of Mental Health. We acknowledge also the aid of Miss Janet Barber, Gerald Leibowitz, and Edward Ware.

381

Utilizing an associational approach as the foundation for our method, we take, as our unit of information, the word itself. Dividing an input document into segments of time, or segments of equal length, or equal numbers of sentences, and the like, it is possible to count the frequency with which each word occurs in each such segment. Using these data, intercorrelations among all words may be obtained; operationally, these intercorrelations represent the degree of co-occurrence (that is, association) between words as they are observed across successive units of the data base. This matrix of intercorrelations may then be factor analyzed to determine, in a systematic fashion, whether there are common factors that can account for the obtained associational matrix in an efficient and meaningful way.

In a factor-analytic approach toward this kind of data, it is necessary to reduce the number of different words that are examined. This criterion, a function of machine size, program running time, and factor interpretability, demands that the number of variables (words) analyzed be held to some reasonable minimum. It is the job of the system of programs that we have developed—WORDS—to allow this reduction and the subsequent statistical analyses that are necessary.

This chapter discusses the current implementation of the WORDS System, its goals and structure, the results and implications of some current research, and our plans for the future concerning changes in the system and directions for future research.

IMPLEMENTATION OF THE WORDS SYSTEM

Computing Facility

WORDS has been developed at the University of Rochester Computing Center on an IBM 7074 computer. The 7074, a second generation, medium-speed machine, has characteristics including extremely powerful input/output (I/O), and highly flexible scatter read/write commands. It is a fixed word length machine (five characters or ten digits with sign per machine word) with decimal arithmetic and hardware-supported floating point operations. The configuration at the University of Rochester operates with a 10K core and is supported by eight 729-IV tape drives and a 1301 disk file. Final output from the system must be to tape with all printing and punching done offline on an IBM 1401 configuration.

System Goals

Before beginning actual programming on WORDS, a set of system goals was developed. The considerations that dictated the choice of these goals were based on the several uses to which WORDS could be put. WORDS had to be capable of large-scale, repetitive, methodological investigations, since such program running times had to be as efficient as possible. WORDS had to be useful as a production device; as such, the ease of system use and good turnaround time were needed. Finally, WORDS would probably be used by other members of the University and therefore should not be difficult to learn.

With these considerations, as well as those dictated by the method itself, a set of generalized criteria were developed to help in directing the systems work and programming applications to follow.[2]

User Orientation. WORDS was designed to be as easy as possible to use and to learn. Despite this desire, the final results are far short of the mark as can be attested to by a 110-page user's manual. While the system is not inordinately difficult to use and does not require any extensive experience with computers or programming, its use clearly requires some amount of training. Considering the complexity of the total system itself, this requirement is not unreasonable; nevertheless, both we and the users would be happier if the method were easier to understand. Future implementations will result in a much more easily used system. This decrease in difficulty will come about for two reasons; the first is a direct result of our experience with the current system and knowledge of how we could make things easier even within the current system itself; the second reason stems from the greatly increased sophistication and flexibility of third-generation software which substitutes the operating system of the computer for much programming effort on the part of the developer.

Flexibility. WORDS is designed so that the user should have no great difficulty in manipulating his data as is necessary for production of appropriate output. Thus, WORDS has been written to allow the user to configure a run with as many or as few programs as necessary, to utilize, wherever possible, mnemonics rather than numeric information for control purposes, to afford as effortless a handling of I/O as possible, and to allow a wide range of output formats.

Efficiency. Typical data bases in our current research involve files of approximately 25,000 words. Typical run configurations often run more than 20 separate program calls for successive manipulations of this data. A total run, then, can easily involve the computer in the manipulation of well over one million records. Thus, on a machine with the speed of the 7074, a high degree of program efficiency is a clear necessity.

[2] Throughout the development and programming of the WORDS System, the advice and assistance of Mrs. Barbara Rothe has been invaluable.

Protectiveness. The use of WORDS almost invariably demands repetitive runs on the computer with the input for any given run being based, at least in part, on output from prior runs; in such a case, some procedures are needed to protect prior data from possible destruction during a run. Additionally, any extensive processing by WORDS can generate a complicated calling sequence with massive I/O operations so that a software or hardware failure is always a possibility. WORDS is designed to fail-safe and to produce as much diagnostic information for the user as possible.

CURRENT RESEARCH

Methodologic Issues

The UHH Approach. Over the past several years, apart from the complete reprogramming of WORDS, our major research emphasis has been to investigate some of the methodological problems confronting this technique. One of the most important of these issues, both on a practical and theoretical level, derives from the technique used for the reduction of the number of different words found in the raw data base. The question that we have investigated was whether alternative methods for reduction of these words could be found that did not involve the extensive use of synonymization.

In our analysis of a typical data base—five psychotherapy interviews— we encounter about 1300 different words making up the total 25,000 word protocol. Since the maximum matrix with which we can work is 215 variables, we must make reductions comprising 83 percent of the total number of different words.

The method that we initially employed was based on a four-phase process. Utilizing the PARSE programs, all articles, prepositions, conjunctions, and the like were removed. The next phase used STRIP to change all words into root form. The third phase, heavily employing synonymization, combined words having the same basic meaning and being used in the same fashion. Finally, a list of remaining different words, sorted by frequency of occurrence, was generated; beginning with the word of highest frequency, this list was downcounted to reach 215 different words that were then subjected to matrix analysis. It is the synonymization phase that we have found most difficult in implementation and most dangerous in terms of objectivity. Synonymization requires two basic commitments from the user: (1) extensive amounts of time, and (2) the use of subjective and potentially unreliable judgments. In many respects, synonymization places the same demands on the user as does the typical content-analytic method of a priori categorization. Except for the fact that the data itself, rather than the initial interests of the investigator, generates the potential categories (generic word), we are faced in synonymization with the same degree of subjectivity and inefficiency that we would be faced with if we had begun word reduction with a set of categories into which the data was to be allocated.

With a synonymizing procedure, the time demands placed on us in reduction of the data in a typical set of five interviews was considerable. At least a month was required, from both investigators, with a heavy investment of 27 prefactor runs on WORDS being necessary before producing the final rotated factor structure representing the content-recognition portion of the analysis.

More important than time, however, was the constant requirement that we exercise our own judgment as to when two words were being used in a fashion and with a meaning such that they could be combined into one. While WORDS is implemented to make this task easier and more reliable than before, there is little question but that our ability to maintain a high degree of freedom from a priori needs and ideas in the selection of combinations decreased as the time wore on and the combinations became more and more difficult to locate.

Our experience, then, in the analysis of data using ad hoc synonymization procedures to carry a large bulk of the reduction process demanded that we investigate other techniques that were more efficient and less subjective. Accordingly, we began work with a different approach in which synonymization played a minimal role and in which major reductions were accomplished by deletion procedures.

This new technique, which we have euphemistically labeled UHH (Untouched by Human Hands) as opposed to SYN (Synonymization), operates according to a generalized set of rules. The application of these rules, rather than ad hoc decisions deriving from our own inspection of the data, clearly reduces both the time required and the subjectivity involved in the reduction process.

UHH rules currently fall into two phases: prefactoring and postfactoring. In the prefactor phase, we first parse and then subject the data to a common STRIP run for the purposes of deinflection and a change to root form of all comparatives. Following this, EDIT is applied. EDIT is used to make four kinds of change: (1) deletion by part of speech so that all articles, prepositions, conjunctions, and the like are removed; (2) deletion of certain words that carry very little meaning outside of context, for example, "sort," "still," "be," "thing," and "ago"; (3) deletion by the combination of word/speech categories so that, for example, "kind" (adjective) is retained while "kind" (noun) is deleted, or "like" (verb) is retained while all other forms of the word are dropped; and

(4) a low level of *predetermined* synonymization is applied in which generic words are created to subsume a set of other highly related high frequency words, for instance, "NO" is held as a generic word which will contain all occurrences of "neither," "never," "nobody," "none," "nor," "not," "nothing," and "nowhere."

It is important to the UHH approach to note that this kind of synonymization rule is applied to data prior to any analysis of the data and, where feasible, is applied prior to any inspection of the data itself.

After subjecting the data to this set of prefactor rules, a downcount is taken on a frequency ordered list and the 215 words with the highest frequencies are then subjected to factoring. Postfactoring rules serve a common goal: the improvement of the obtained factor structure. This improvement can come about in two major ways within the constraints of our methods and techniques; the first kind of improvement obtains factors that have a better statistical structure so that loadings are improved, the amount of variance extracted is increased, and factor independence is better. The second kind of improvement, obviously not independent of the first, is to improve the "meaningfulness" of the factors.

In our attempt to improve both structure and content, we have begun to investigate postfactor rules for the deletion and/or synonymization of words. There are basically two such rules. The first derives from clusters within the factors themselves. Thus, one factoring run yielded a factor with the days of the week heavily loaded within it; we utilized this information to produce a generic "TIME" term subsuming the days and thus opened the matrix size for the inclusion of seven additional words should this be indicated.

The second rule, which we make use of in postfactoring, derives from the fact that common usage holds loadings less than .30 as being fundamentally uninterpretable. Thus, we are also investigating the results from refactoring after having dropped all words that never obtain a loading greater than .29 anywhere in the obtained factor structure. Obviously, both of these rules result in a reduction of total matrix size; one of the questions, within a UHH approach, with which we are concerned is whether we better obtain our goal of improved structure by refactoring with a smaller size matrix or whether it is more fruitful to include additional words (formerly unincludable) now available because of the open slots in the matrix. Our initial results suggest that replacements, rather than a size reduction per se, is the more appropriate technique.

Using a UHH approach, the time for complete analysis of the same set of data mentioned earlier has changed to approximately four hours of investigators' time as opposed to almost a month using SYN and, as would be expected, the number of computer runs has sharply reduced.

Typically, four runs carry us through initial screening, parsing, deinflection, editing, factoring and refactoring. Depending on turnaround times and daily load requirements at the university computing center, we can reasonably expect to complete analyses in something less than a normal work week. With SYN, turnaround time and repetitive runs made six weeks a minimum.

The results, with UHH, have been quite encouraging. Before beginning the UHH factoring of interview 23–27 of subject P1, we had available the SYN results on that same data.[3] Accordingly, we used, as a partial criterion, the comparability of the two factor structures to make some judgment about the viability of a UHH approach. Although the factor structures were not identical, there was sufficient similarity between the two to make us believe that the method should be refined further.

Table 1 illustrates the kind of structure and the basic similarity between the two approaches.[4]

Factor Scoring. One of the more important uses for WORDS, in a postfactor environment, is for content analysis. It is of importance to us that we be able to investigate content changes over time, across speakers, and under different circumstances. Our first step for implementing this goal involves locating those portions of the data base from which specific content and/or thematic areas were being elicited. The SCORE program in WORDS is designed to accomplish this task.

With the final factor structure loadings as the prime data, SCORE will scan the data base, from which these loadings were obtained, and will assign to each of the observations (segments or combinations thereof) a numeric factor score. Using only factor loadings greater than .49, this score is obtained, for each factor, by using the loading of all words on that factor, as a multiplier for the frequency of occurrence of that word in the observation being scored; these separate word scores are then summed over all the selected words on that factor yielding a factor score. To afford comparability between factor scores, SCORE computes standard scores as well as raw scores for each factor on each observation.

Table 1 also illustrates the use of SCORE. The segment presented in Table 1 is the highest scoring segment for the SYN factor seen in

---

[3] This data consists of a set of 462 consecutive psychoanalytic treatment sessions which were tape recorded and made available to us by F. Gordon Pleune. We are grateful for his help and his cooperation in the analysis of this data.

[4] In this, and in all other analyses reported in this chapter, a combination factor of 5 has been used in preparing the data for correlation. Thus, if psychotherapy data is being analyzed, each successive set of five minutes is combined and analyzed as one observation; analogously, in analysis of the book data to be reported later, each successive set of five pages has been combined and analyzed as one observation.

Table 1. *Comparison of SYN and UHH factors* (Varimax rotated loadings truncated at < .30)*

Part 1

SYN Factor 3		UHH Factor 12	
OLD	95	OLD	94
CHANGE	94	CLOTHES	91
DRESS	85	HIGH	91
LOOK	83	SCHOOL	83
FRIEND	79	FRIEND	82
OKAY	77	DRESS	62
SCHOOL	77	LOOK	53
CLOTHES	75	ENJOY	50
SLOVEN	72	DEFINITE	47
ATTRACT	70	SEE	45
RELAX	63	LONG	43
KEEP	56	APOLOGIZE	41
APOLOGIZE	41	ALWAYS	34
GOOD	38	KEEP	34
SHAVE	38	LOT	34
MEET	36	ATTENTION	32
DIFFER	34	NORMAL	30
PECULIAR	33		
ATTENTION	32		
SEE	32		

Part 2

SYN FACTOR 3 HIGH SCORING SEGMENT

Friend of mine and I and every time I see this old high school friend, I am always dressed in old clothes. And one day, I sort of apologized for always seeing him this way and he said he never saw anybody look as good or as well in old clothes as I do. I don't know if I do it for, I know that I have done this, that I have gone to parties not shaven and dressed this way and would go weeks in high school, not weeks but a whole week, with dressing this way or slovenly. But I, I guess it, it would attract attention. I know if I see somebody dressed this way and unshaven for a whole week I would look at them myself.

---

* SYN refers to word reductions via synonymization as well as deletion; UHH data is reduced without synonymization.

that table. This is a typical result and there seems little question that SCORE can quite well locate that portion of the data base which is heavily saturated with the material that is helping to elicit the factor which is being scored and that the material located is consonant with the content of the factor.

Illustrative Results. As a part of our continuing research program, we have recently begun application of the system to data other than the series of over 400 continuous psychotherapeutic interviews which comprised the initial data base from which the system was developed. As a suitable vehicle, we chose a set of two psychotherapy interviews recorded over 15 years ago. Our choice of these two interviews was dictated by the fact that they form the nucleus of a book, *Comparative Psycholinguistic Analysis of Two Psychotherapeutic Interviews* (Gottschalk, 1961). The purpose of the symposium, from which this book was generated, was to bring together several workers in the area of content analysis and to bring their different approaches and skills to bear on the same set of two interviews. The results of these different analyses form the major part of the book; our hope was that analysis of these same two interviews by WORDS would yield data which would illustrate the utility of the system by allowing comparison of our results with those of some of the members of the symposium. Our purpose in presenting these results is not to offer or interpret further information concerning the particular case under analysis; instead, by showing some portion of our results, we hope to demonstrate the utility of WORDS as a method for content analysis.

The data incorporated in the two interviews analyzed in the symposium is based on two separate meetings (interviews number 8 and 18) of the patient under treatment. Following a description of the patient and the comments of the psychotherapist as to the content of the interviews, the book then details the interviews themselves, a set of physiological observations as to skin temperature and heart rate for both therapist and patient (on a minute-by-minute basis) and then presents papers by Strupp, Jaffe, Mahl, Gottschalk et al., and DiMascio. The papers by the last four authors present materials which are reported in tabular or graphic form in the text in a quantifiable fashion; thus, Jaffe uses the verbal diversification index (type-token ratio) and a percent present-tense index, Mahl defines a speech disturbance ratio and silence quotient, Gottschalk presents and scores categories for anxiety, hostility, and schizophrenic disorganization, and DiMascio makes use of the physiological indices listed above.

In analyzing the data of these interviews by WORDS, we used the UHH approach. Following the usual prefactor rules, we submitted a list of 190 different words for factoring. With these results as a baseline, we then included, as an additional set of 25 variables, the various indices derived from the papers presented by the members of the symposium; inclusion was done by representing the variables as though they were words with a frequency equivalent to their "score." Thus, for example, if the patient had had a heart rate of 75 in segment four of interview eight, a variable PHR was included 75 times within that same segment; following usual WORDS reduction and summarization procedures PHR would yield a combined frequency of 75 in segment four of interview eight. After analysis of the basic plus auxilliary data matrix, we compared this with the matrix of words only and found little basic difference between the two sets of factors. The substantive data factors were almost the same; that auxiliary data which had been submitted simply loaded *within* various of these factors.

Although we extracted 20 factors, we found, to our surprise (perhaps because we were dealing with a data base only 40 percent of our usual size), that almost 100 percent of the variance had been extracted by the first 19 factors.

The results of the analysis have been very provocative. The significant and frequent loadings of so much of the auxiliary data clearly indicate the extent to which content themes extracted by WORDS relate to indices extracted according to other widely different theoretical constructs. It is important, however, to notice that some of the relationships are probably artifacts. In Factor 13 we have a loading of .70 for "OUTWARD HOSTILITY" and a dominant loading of .96 for the word "kill"; this simply suggests that the word "kill" plays an important role in scoring the category. On the other hand, such indices as the type-token ratio, physiologic measures such as heart rate and skin temperature, and percent of present tense verbs cannot be reasonably explained in terms of content artifact.

The results of this analysis are too extensive to include here in their entirety. Instead, we shall show four factors of the second analysis (in which the auxilliary data was included) in order to illustrate the kind of materials produced.

In the beginning of the Gottschalk book, in a chapter by Kanter and DiMascio, a summarization of the content of the two interviews is furnished by the psychotherapist. Table 2 contains a portion of the therapist's description, the significant loadings on Factor 15 of the WORDS analysis, and the segments chosen by the SCORE program as the highest loaded in the data on that particular factor.

In a later paper, Mahl presents information as to his analysis of the data using the speech disturbance ratio and silence quotient. Mahl raises a question as to what causes the variations in the speech disturbance ratio; noting that his objective measures are not designed to answer this

Table 2. *Gottschalk data, Example 1*

Part 1. Therapist Statement. He continued to work at understanding his feelings. In the course of this, he told of blocking himself and hurting himself and handling the humiliation by clowning and playing the buffoon as his father had before him. With a feeling of horror, he told of his identification with being publicly humiliated before those who matter (Gottschalk, 1961).

Part 2. Factor 15 (Varimax Rotated Loadings Truncated at < .30).

ANXIETY	92	*THERAPIST HEART RATE	−46
HUMILIATE	89	OTHER	44
*EMOTIONAL DISCOMFORT	81	*INTRAPRSNL SCHIZ WITHDRWL	−38
*FREE ANXIETY	73	*BLOCKED RELATIONS	−36
SPECIAL	72	*PATIENT SKIN TEMPERATURE	−36
FAIL	64	*TOTAL SCHIZ WITHDRWL	36
UPSET	54	WIFE	35
CERTAIN	50	ALL	−34
WANT	50	EXPECT	−32
*% PRESENT TENSE VERBS	50	MANY	−31
INTELLECTUALIZE	−47	*GRATIFYING RELATIONSHIPS	31
*TYPE TOKEN RATIO	−46		

Part 3. High Scoring Segments 40–41

40. being the therapist to this group and then this woman on a program which I identified with. Of course I was really upset for this woman in front of her child. I remember a similar feeling of the greatness of the movie "Bicycle Thief," the humiliation of the father in front of his son when he was caught stealing the bicycle. I thought that was the greatest part of the movie, very much aroused. I am sure I cried at that part of the movie. Uh that really affected me but ah I don't know, and then yesterday I started talking about my father and his humiliation and then his handling the humiliation by clowning

41. and being buffoon and so do I, I clown and play the buffoon. Humiliation is a real issue to me, humiliation in front of people, I think of tarring and feathering someone. I think of it with horror. The humiliation with which they treated collaborators when they were stripped and had their heads shaved, especially the women. It really deeply affects me. I must identify with that—being humiliated. . . . Gee, I always talk about my anxiety, ha ha, I can talk freely to people, I'm very anxious, I'm very anxious over such and such, almost ready to have them say no, you weren't, or to show them that I wasn't really. . . .

---

* Nonverbal categories.

question, Mahl nevertheless attempts to pinpoint some of the variation by noting that "the therapist's increasingly prodding, insistent questions and comments on the patient's lateness . . . are associated with the progressive rise in speech disturbance level . . . ." Mahl identifies the 29th–32nd minute of interview 18 as being these points. Table 3 presents Factors 11 and 18 which contain the two highest loadings of SDR across all of the extracted factors. Factor scoring for Factor 11 selects segments (minutes) 26–30; scoring on Factor 18 analogously retrieves segments 31–35.

As a final illustration of the results, it is helpful to consider some of the physiological materials presented and analyzed by DiMascio in another chapter of the book. Because each of the participants in the symposium had utilized his own methods and skills for construction of the various

Table 3.   *Gottschalk data, Example 2 (Varimax rotated loadings truncated at < .30)*

Factor 11		Factor 18	
RETALIATE	97	FEAR	78
IDENTIFY	81	*STRUCTURAL SCHIZ WITHDRWL	−75
CONFIDENT	80	MUST	69
REASON	72	YES	58
*INWARD HOSTILITY	71	*SPEECH DIST. RATIO	53
CHANGE	70	NEW	50
YOU (Therapist)	68	RESIST	49
SPEAK	60	COURSE	42
*SPEECH DIST. RATIO	54	MANY	−42
*TYPE TOKEN RATIO	−54	CONCERN	−36
*GRATIFYING RLTNSHPS	53	EXPECT	−36
SEE	47	*TOTAL SCHIZ WITHDRWL	−33
REACT	46	MAYBE	−31
SAY	44	LESS	30
CHANCE	38		
FEEL	33		
TAKE	32		
ACTUAL	31		
TALK	−31		
*FREE ANXIETY	30		
*EMOTIONAL WELL BEING	−30		
*TOTAL SCHIZ WITHDRWL	−30		
High scoring segments or minutes	26–30		31–35

* Nonverbal categories

indices to be applied to the data, DiMascio's ability to relate the various physiologic indices to this other data was confined to a series of correlations. What WORDS allows, on the other hand, can be easily seen by inspection of Factor 4 presented in Table 4.

Again, we should note that this reanalysis of the data from the content analysis symposium is not an attempt to offer new information or conclusions about the data analyzed by that group, although it could indeed serve such a purpose. Rather, we cite this information and show these results to begin our attempts in making an assessment of the validational properties of WORDS and of the factors and factor structures that it produces.

We have been concerned about the validational properties of this method since its very inception. Although there are many validational criteria that might be applied, two major aspects of validity have seemed to us of primary importance. The first of these two criteria concerns the extent to which the factor "fits" the data. That is, considering each factor independently, how well does it identify its portion of the data (as defined by high factor score) and to what degree is that portion of the data selected consonant with the factor? The second validational criterion concerns the factor configuration derived; how well can the data base, or portions of the data base, be described in terms of the factors? Our attempts to answer these questions with the kinds of data for which the system was originally developed—psychotherapeutic protocols—are difficult. We used the Gottschalk data in the hope that it would offer enough ancillary information to help us assess these questions. While the data did, indeed, make it easier for us to assess our factors—by utilizing descriptions of the protocols from the book—it demonstrated that, once again, we would be forced to buttress these factors by judgmental statements made by others as to what actually was the content of the data base. Since it is precisely in order to avoid such dependence on judgmental techniques that we developed the system, we felt dissatisfied with the results of the Gottschalk analysis. It seemed evident that what we needed for analysis, was a data base that had clearly defined content that was

Table 4. *Gottschalk data, Example 3*

Part 1. Factor 4. (Varimax Rotated Loadings Truncated at < .30).

FLY	98	HOPE	54
BOY	95	REMEMBER	51
LET	94	*OUTWARD HOSTILITY	47
MUMPS	93	GOOD	44
AGGRESS	91	*INTRAPRSNL SCHIZ WITHDRWL	42
BACK	88	*SELF ESTEEM	40
*THERAPIST HEART RATE	−77	MAYBE	−39
GI	68	PRETTY	39
*OUTWARD HOSTILITY THEME	65	SHOULD	39
FEW	64	*SPEECH DIST. RATIO	−39
*PATIENT HEART RATE	−61	FAMILY	−32
*PATIENT SKIN TEMPERATURE	−58	CAN	31
*INTERPRSNL SCHIZ WITHDRWL	−56	MANY	−30

Part 2. High Scoring Segment 52

(Prior to this segment, patient describes a private beach used by his family and his discovering a group of soldiers there one day who refused to leave. He speaks of his maneuvers to get them to go, his hopes that they will contract his son's mumps, his wife's fear he will get into a fight; he talks of getting ready to flycast the beach area and remarks that if one is not skillful people behind the caster can sometimes get hurt. He states his inability to tell the soldiers:)

. . . would you mind moving I'd like to cast this area, I don't let my kids sit there, which I don't. Uh, I just didn't say anything. I let the fly fall a few times thinking I hope one of them gets the fly, and then being afraid though to really hook someone with a fly or whip them with it. Actually, it's a whipping, a good sharp slap. Being afraid I realized well here I'm going through all this indirect aggression and suffering it through and I can't really express it. Even if it were a physical fight I would have been proud of myself to have been able to do it and feeling that I could have carried it off. I was physically in wonderful shape. I'd been swimming and I'm usually in good shape anyway, thinking if it would just help establish a relationship between me and my son. I'd just seen the picture ———— in which . . . .

---

* Nonverbal categories.

known to large numbers of people. In short, we wanted a data base whose content was clear enough and public enough to make a "face validity" approach toward factor assessment a reasonably tenable procedure.

Accordingly, we turned our attention to famous children's books. These books are relatively short; they utilize somewhat restricted language, tend to have clearly defined content, and are usually known, in broad outline, to many people. Having examined a number of possibilities, we selected Frank Baum's *The Wizard of Oz* as satisfying all of the criteria mentioned above.

In the analysis of *Oz*, we felt that we were posing a fairly stringent but appropriate test for the WORDS System. The major themes of *Oz* are well known both from the book and the movie.[5] Certainly, if the method is viable, one must expect to see content themes and/or materials clustering around, for example, the Tin Woodman, Dorothy's flight in the cyclone to the land of OZ from her home in Kansas, the Cowardly Lion, the Scarecrow, the Wicked Witch, and the Wizard himself.

Oz was the largest single data base we have ever analyzed, numbering almost 42,000 words. The data was analyzed according to the UHH rules mentioned earlier. After assignment of parts of speech, and deinflection to root form, we were left with a data base of approximately 1400 different words. This list, in frequency order, was downcounted to obtain the 215 highest frequency words; these words constituted the UHH analysis. Twenty factors were extracted, rotated by varimax, and factor-scored for each chapter. The factors account for 80 percent of the variance represented by the initial 215×215 matrix submitted.

The two questions posed earlier were examined in the light of these results. The first of the questions, the validity of each factor for its eliciting content, may be examined by referring to the factors both in terms of their four highest loading words and in terms of a brief description of the content of the total factor. This is presented, for the first six factors, in Table 5. With the presentation of each factor will be found that chapter yielding the highest factor score for the factor and the title of the chapter.

---

[5] *Oz*, now in the public domain, is available in numerous editions. We checked several editions to confirm the fact that ours was standard in content. Two changes were made to the book in our analysis: (1) Chapter 20, "The Dainty China Country," was omitted, since it added many different words for a very small increment in total data; (2) Chapters 23 and 24 were combined, since Chapter 24 is but one-half page long. Notice that several differences exist between the movie and the book: the movie has ruby slippers, the book silver shoes; the movie pays much attention to Kansas and reproduces the Kansas characters in Oz while the book does neither; the movie has Oz as a "dream," in the book Oz is "real"; finally, the movie omits any reference to the Kalidahs, the Golden Cap, the Hammer Heads, and the Field Mice.

Table 5. *Identification of factors in Oz*

Factor and Four High-Loaded Words	Factor Content	Highest Loading Chapter and Title
1. AX OIL TIN WOODMAN TIN	The Woodman, his body, one time romance with Munchkin girl.	5. The Rescue of the Tin Woodman
2. OZ (HEAD) OZ (LADY) KILL SEND	Meetings with Oz in his various disguises. Oz's demand that they kill Wicked Witch of West in order to receive their requests.	11. The Emerald City of Oz
3. FARMER BRICK SCARECROW ROAD	The scarecrow, his creation, stupidity, clumsiness, need for a brain.	3. How Dorothy Saved the Scarecrow
4. MUNCHKINS WITCH EAST WOMAN	People of the East; freed by Dorothy whose house killed the Witch.	2. The Council with the Munchkins
5. UNCLE HENRY HOUSE AUNT EM BED	Dorothy's aunt and uncle, her home in Kansas, her trip to the land of Oz.	1. The Cyclone
6. WOLF LIE CROW DIE	Attacks by animals on one or more members of group during book; chief such attack is instigated by Wicked Witch.	12. The Search for the Wicked Witch

On inspection of the complete set of factors, 12 of the 20 factors were immediately verified by inspection of the key loadings, on the one hand, and the chapter title (in which they occur most heavily), on the other. The remaining 8 factors did not automatically link with the chapter titles; however, all related quite appropriately, as can be seen in Table 5 under the "content," which relates the factor content to the chapter content; for example, Factor 2, describing the various meetings of the group with the disguised Wizard, occurs in Chapter 11, "The Emerald City of Oz"; it is, however, in that chapter that all of these particular meetings take place.

Our reaction to these results, then, is that the factors are indeed relevant to the content areas that they identify. This approach has dealt only with the *highest* factor-loading score for each factor; factors, however, have a factor score for *each* of the chapters under analysis, and we therefore turned our attention to those areas in which factors were occurring at some significantly high level. The most effective way to present this kind of analysis is on a chapter-by-chapter basis; thus, we are raising the question as to how well the *chapters* are described by the factors as opposed to how well a particular factor dovetails with its highest scored segment. Table 6 illustrates this chapter-by-chapter analysis for Chapters 10 through 17. The chapter, its title, and a brief description of its content are furnished; for each chapter, the factor number, standard score for that factor, and a mnemonic based on the basic factor structure are listed. All factors with a standard score of $+2.00$ or greater are presented. Factor scores with asterisks indicate the highest score ever obtained by the factor.

Again, the results are very encouraging. In Chapter 1, which is devoted to Dorothy's home in Kansas and to her trip, the only factor scoring at 2.00 or more is Factor 5, "Home." In Chapter 2, which details her arrival in Oz, the meeting of the Munchkins, receipt of the Silver Shoes, and her plans to see the Wizard (Factors 4, 14, and 13) score at or above 2.00 thus identifying the "Munchkins," the "Silver Shoes," and the "Wizard."

Close inspection revealed that certain themes, were not being supported by appropriate factors and that one chapter (Chapter 21) had no factor scored at $+2.00$ or greater. This chapter is concerned with the cowardly lion's "election" to become king of beasts after he has killed a monster spider terrorizing the other animals in the forest. "Spider" and "monster," the two words most closely associated with the chapter's theme, did not obtain frequencies high enough to be included in the 215 word list for factoring. Whether enough other words, themselves associated with these two key words, are included in the 215 list and are potentially available in factors beyond number 20 is presently something we cannot ascertain. The issue of what words are included, and the consequences of missing words, is a topic that we shall discuss later. It is perhaps significant that the highest scoring factor in Chapter 21, with a standard score of $+1.29$, is Factor 7, "Cowardly Lion."

After concluding this initial analysis of *Oz*, we tried another approach which would yield information concerning the effects of word choice on factor extraction. In order to do this, we again started with the list of 1400 different words (used in the last analysis to yield the downcounted 215 list) but, on this occasion, we approached the list in a completely different fashion. Disregarding *any* attempt at objectivity, we carefully selected a set of 215 words corresponding to our knowledge of the book and our hopes as to what factors would be extracted. In short, we loaded

Table 6. *Relationship between factors 10–17 and chapters in Oz*

Chapter and Major Themes Presented	Factor and Mnemonic	Z-Score
10. *The Guardian of the Gates.* Lion awake, trip continues; spend night at cottage discussing hope for success with Oz; reach Emerald City, admitted by Guardian of Gates; all must wear spectacles to prevent blindness from brilliance of city.	11. Emerald City 13. Wizard 20. Needs	8.95* 2.52 2.20
11. *The Emerald City of Oz.* Enter city, reach palace, each assigned separate room pending their separate audiences with Oz; each sees Oz as a different figure; Oz refuses each pending death of Wicked Witch of West; they agree to kill her.	2. Audience 15. Palace 7. Cowardly Lion 20. Needs 3. Scarecrow	6.95* 6.62* 3.17 2.69 2.40
12. *The Search for the Wicked Witch.* Leave city, Guardian of Gates removes spectacles; In land of West seen by Wicked Witch who sends wolves, crows, etc. to kill; all fail; sends Winkies—slaves —also fail; uses Golden Cap and sends Winged Monkeys who destroy Woodman and Scarecrow; rest prisoners; Witch's greed for Silver Shoes angers Dorothy who tosses water on her and melts her.	6. Animal Attack 14. Silver Shoes 9. Winkies 8. Winged Monkeys 7. Cowardly Lion 11. Emerald City	8.42* 7.57* 4.57 3.00 2.40 2.39
13. *The Rescue.* Ask Winkies, freed from Witch, to rescue Woodman and Scarecrow; both saved; Winkies carefully repair Woodman; start for Emerald City; Dorothy takes pretty Golden Cap.	9. Winkies	9.97*
14. *The Winged Monkeys.* Lost; call field mice who suggest Golden Cap; call Winged Monkeys and begin flight to Emerald City; on way, Monkeys tell their story and explain charm behind Cap.	8. Winged Monkeys 10. Mice 13. Wizard 18. Pole	7.43* 3.22 2.49 2.29
15. *The Discovery of Oz the Terrible.* Back at Emerald City Oz delays seeing them; agrees at threat of Monkeys; discovery of Oz as humbug; he tells of trip via balloon from Omaha; they still believe he can grant their wishes.	20. Needs 13. Wizard 16. Balloon 11. Emerald City	8.38* 4.11* 2.95 2.07
16. *The Magic Art of the Great Humbug.* Oz puts pin and needles in Scarecrow to make him "sharp," gives the Woodman a heart inside his chest, feeds the Lion a dose of courage.	20. Needs	2.46
17. *How the Balloon Was Launched.* Oz and Dorothy try to leave via another balloon they have built. Balloon, with Oz, leaves without Dorothy who is chasing Toto.	16. Balloon	8.10*

* Highest score achieved by the factor anywhere in the book.

the matrix for analysis with the *best* set of 215 words that we could possibly choose. From that point on, analysis was conducted according to standard procedures, and 20 factors were extracted.

Space does not permit us to present this complete factoring run here. Inspection of the two factor structures, that from the "downcounted" data and that from the "chosen" data, was very encouraging; from our knowledge of the book we found no difficulty in matching 16 of the 20 downcounted factors with those in the chosen word results. Table 7 presents these matchings and indicates those factors that could not be matched from one analysis to the other. While it was clear to us that, for example, downcounted Factor 15 was the "same" factor as chosen Factor 16, it was also clear that this congruence might not be apparent to someone who was not intimately familiar with the book. We therefore searched for a way in which to demonstrate this similarity. Our technique

Table 7.   *A comparison between downcounted word factors and chosen word factors*

Factor Mnemonic	Downcount Factor	Chosen Factor	Overlap		Correlation
Tin Woodman	1	2	$7/14$	50%	.99
Audience	2	3	$5/11$	45	.97
Scarecrow	3	7, 19			
Munchkins	4	5	$5/9$	56	.97
Home	5	4	$4/10$	40	.98
Animal Attack	6	1	$4/8$	50	.86
Cowardly Lion	7	6	$4/5$	80	.98
Winged Monkeys	8	20	$3/8$	38	.79
Winkies	9	18	$2/7$	29	.97
Mice	10	9	$3/7$	47	.99
Emerald City	11	12	$4/5$	80	.99
Poppies	12	13	$4/9$	44	.98
Wizard	13	10	$4/8$	50	.69
Silver Shoes	14	14	$3/7$	43	.99
Palace	15	16	$1/6$	11	.97
Balloon	16	8	$1/7$	14	.49
Hammer Heads	17				
Pole	18				
Trees	19				
Needs	20				
King of Beasts		11			
Leaving Oz		15			
Kalidahs		17			

was to take the factor scores for Factor 15 across the entire book and correlate them with the factor scores for the (ostensibly) matched Factor 16. We did this for each of the 15 matched factors in the data and the results were startling. The last column of Table 7 presents these correlations; there is one correlation of .49, one of .79, one more at .86, and the remaining twelve correlations all have values equal to or greater than .97.

Because of the size of these coefficients, we were concerned that some artifact might be operating. We could think of only one: the number of words in common between each two potentially matched factors. Thus, despite our different methods of choice, if a pair of factors were yielding high correlations based on basically the same set of highly loaded words (loadings greater than .49), we would be building correlations based mainly on a common set of frequencies.

Table 7 also examines this possibility and demonstrates that it is untenable. Using the downcounted factors as the base, we established the number of downcounted factor-scoring words in common with the possibly matched chosen factor-scoring words. This data is presented both as a fraction and a percentage; inspection of the correlations clearly demonstrates the complete lack of effect of the "commonality" on the correlation.

The only other possibility for an artifact, of which we were aware, also hangs on the question of common words. Thus, if the total 215 matrix of downcounted data is composed of a high proportion of the 215 chosen word data, its similarity in total words might allow extraction of basically identical factors with the few different words holding onto the high loading areas. It is sufficient to note that only 98 words in the downcounted data and chosen word data are in common, that is, 46 percent.

DISCUSSION

The results presented in this chapter have led us to four major conclusions. We shall discuss each one in turn.

Factor Validity. We raised two questions concerning factor validity in our analysis of the *Oz* data. The first tested validity by asking the extent to which each factor "fit" the data: Were the segments for which a factor was most heavily scored good representations of that factor and vice versa? Second, we asked the extent to which the configuration of factors was able to describe the data base itself. Both of these questions were answered affirmatively in the *Oz* data and, although the second has never been tested on any other data base, the question of "fit" has been examined now over some widely differing sources of material. We assume, then, that the approach we have pursued is indeed a viable one and that the factors which it extracts are valid representations of the data which elicits them.

Data Base Description. While raised mainly as a validational criterion, the ability of the factors to describe the *Oz* data on a chapter-by-chapter basis has suggested the possibility of a configurational approach toward the description of major content. In such an approach, the information utilized would be the set of factors and their standardized scores operating configurationally over the various units of the data base under analysis; it might thus be feasible to describe changes in a data base by noting the configurational changes taking place. We have done no research in this area as yet, but there are several statistical techniques available for configurational analysis and we shall begin to investigate them soon.

Word Selection. The high degree of correlation between the *Oz* down-counted factors as contrasted with the chosen-word factors implies some degree of insensitivity, in the factor *structure,* to the words available for building these factors. We have no information, at present, as to the degree of that insensitivity other than that furnished by the analyses on *Oz.* Thus, we do not know whether the 46 percent overlap figure between the two sets of words analyzed represents a figure that is adequate because of the nature of the data; it is possible that a much greater overlap may be required when dealing with data whose interrelationships are more subtle and complex than is the case with *Oz.* Furthermore, our UHH rules, operating on the downcount analysis, fairly well restrict the data analyzed to nouns, adjectives, verbs, and adverbs. Whether the kind of concordance obtained with *Oz* would hold true when the data is analyzed with a heavy preponderance of articles, prepositions, and conjunctions, for instance, is something we cannot presently answer. Nevertheless, *some* degree of insensitivity is a clearly demonstrable finding and the fact that this robustness does exist has considerable implications for our future lines of research.

We have observed earlier in the chapter that the major critical problem we face in the operational procedures of WORDS is in the selection of what words to retain for analysis. We had tacitly assumed that the deletion of words would cause changes in the factors obtained and in the configurational relationships among these factors. Our first indication that this assumed sensitivity might be overstated came when we began our investigation of a UHH rather than an SYN approach. As noted in the chapter, both approaches yielded many factors that could be related to each other. Several of the factors, however, could not. The *Oz* data confirms this finding. Of the 20 factors extracted in both the downcounted and chosen-word analyses, four of the downcounted factors could not be matched to those in the chosen-word set while three of the chosen-word factors were not matchable (the discrepancy exists because one of the down-counted factors—the Scarecrow—separated into two factors in the chosen-word data). Both sets of unmatched factors, the three from the chosen-word data and the four from the downcounted data, were equally "good." Table 7 shows that the downcounted data extracted unmatched factors for the Hammer-Heads (Factor 17), The Pole (Factor 18), the Fighting Trees (Factor 19), and the Needs (Factor 20). Also, the chosen-word data allowed extraction of unmatched factors representing the Kalidahs (Factor 17), Dorothy's flight from the Land of OZ (Factor 15) and King of Beasts (Factor 11). This last factor is important because it will be remembered that no factor in the downcounted analysis obtained a standard score of over $+2.00$ in Chapter 21, "The Lion Becomes the King of Beasts"; scoring Factor 11 from the chosen-word analysis, how-ever, yields a factor score of $+8.00$ for Chapter 21. Clearly, then, as we have analyzed the data, a change in the set of words submitted for analysis *does* cause some change in the factors extracted. Possibly some of these "missing" factors might have been extracted if we had con-tinued factor extraction past our limit of 20, but this is problematic. Never-theless, a considerable change in submitted words still yielded a match on 16 of the 20 factors, a matched percentage of 80 percent.

The implication of this result seems clear: we have some margin of safety in our selection of what words will be submitted for analysis. This implication, coupled with the fact that the downcounted data furnished as good a description of the data as did the chosen-word analysis, strongly supports our feeling that a UHH approach, with its advantages of extreme speed and objectivity, is the correct way to pursue our future developments in the system. Later, we shall discuss more fully our plans for increasing the efficiency of the UHH approach.

Inclusion of Nonword Materials. It will be remembered that we did two analyses on the Gottschalk data presented earlier. In both analyses we submitted the same list of 190 different downcounted words for factor extraction but, in the first analysis, these words were examined by them-selves, whereas the second analysis added 25 nonverbal variables for analy-sis; these 25 variables were composed of various categories of content analysis, physiological data, and the like. The results indicated that the factor structure of both analyses was almost identical insofar as the words and their loadings were concerned. What happened was that the nonverbal data tended to appear within factors already established, in its absence, during the first analysis.

We feel that this finding offers a line of development for the use of WORDS that is quite interesting. We can envision at least two major uses for the inclusion of nonverbal data along with the submitted list of words. On the one hand, we believe it would be interesting to see what descriptive value could be furnished by such nonverbal data in order to add to the utility of the extracted factors and to clarify further the segments of the data base chosen for examination because of high scores on that factor. On the other hand, we can envision a use of WORDS in the developmental phases of a categorization system which would allow the developer or investigator of that content-analytic method to investigate the degree to which his content categories are intrinsically related to the various content materials uncovered by the factor structure itself.

PLANS FOR THE FUTURE

Methodologic Issues

There are three major research areas that we intend to pursue and that we shall discuss briefly.

Statistical Word Selection. The results presented here have clearly suggested that we have some flexibility in the choice of words to be submitted for analysis. We have long been interested in objective methods for such word selection, but we were troubled because objectivity seemed to demand a price in factor interpretability and meaningfulness. However, the UHH approach has given us sufficient encouragment to look into this issue further.

In the standard UHH approach as we had formulated it, the final selection of words for analysis was done by downcounting a frequency ordered list of remaining words; this technique, of course, guaranteed that the highest frequency words would be included for analysis with the low frequency words being deleted. There is nothing compelling, however, about such an approach. Rather than depending on frequency selection, we plan to pay extensive attention to that correlation matrix which precedes the factoring run as a method for making word choices. Our reasoning is as follows: An intercorrelation matrix computation is very much faster than a factoring run given the same size of matrix input. With correlations on a 215×215 matrix being computed across, say, 100 observations, we can reasonably expect the correlation program to run at least eight to ten times faster than the factoring run that will follow it. Furthermore, a factoring run demands more of the machine's available core capacity than does a correlational approach, and it is therefore feasible to run larger matrices through a correlation program than through a factor analysis program on a machine of a given size. Putting these facts together, we intend to allow correlational runs on word matrices of orders running to about 1000, a size that is usually capable of holding *all* different words left in a data base after deinflection to root form. We shall then utilize another program to inspect this matrix of intercorrelations and to choose from it the 215 words best meeting a set of criteria that will ensure the development of "good" factor structure if, indeed, such factor structure is inherent in the data. There are at least two criteria that make for "good" factors; one, which has been discussed extensively in this chapter, is the validity of each of the factors and of the factor configuration. Another, stemming from common factor analytic usage, is simply the loadings on each extracted factor—how much variance do they extract—and, as a result of summation across the factors, how much variance does the total extracted factor set remove from the input matrix. We do not believe that these criteria are independent; we have found, in prior research, that good statistical factors tend to be the more valid factors for our use.

The statistical criterion for factorial "goodness," then, is one approach that we can utilize. Since it is a fact that correlational matrices with very high overall correlations will yield better statistical factor structure than those with very low overall correlations, we should like to investigate the possibility that good factor structure can be obtained by eliminating words whose overall correlations are low in favor of those with high mean correlations. Another, nonindependent approach may lie with the variance of the correlations obtained between a given word and all other words in the matrix. Other things being equal, high variance is better than low variance for factor-analytic operations; such variance is obviously not independent of the mean correlational level associated with a word but may allow selection of words for retention from among other words with equal mean correlations.

If such an approach should prove productive, we would have a completely objective and very fast method for the selection of the "right" words to be included in a factoring run.

Measurement of Specific Words. We are interested in exploring a somewhat different approach toward the "measurement" of specific and key words in a data base. As is currently the case, all words are potentially admissable for analysis in a WORDS run. If a word (for example, "mother") is in the data base, then it stands a chance of admission for analysis that is independent of its meaning. We believe, however, that if the word "mother" is an important one for the user of the system, it might be fruitful to analyze the data base deliberately leaving out the word in any such analysis. We should then be interested to see what happens to factor scoring techniques as they are applied, for *all* factors, on those observational segments where "mother" does not appear versus those where it does. We have no evidence on what the effect of such an operation will be, but we think that the possibility of success is interesting enough to give it some priority in our future research efforts.

Reprogramming of WORDS

The University of Rochester has recently acquired an IBM 360 model 50 computer and will, within another year, update that machine to a model 65. WORDS will be reprogrammed to run on the 360. Programming on the IBM 7074, of necessity, had to be in assembler language because no higher level language existed capable of doing the job. PL/I has met that need, and reprogramming for WORDS will be in that language. Because the 360 is a very popular machine, we shall, for the first time, have the ability and opportunity to make the WORDS System available to others outside of the University.

While PL/I cannot come even close to matching the efficiency of assembler language coding, it allows us a high degree of programming efficiency and offers the distinct possibility, within the next two years, of being implemented on a number of other manufacturers' machines; this, of course, would allow even further dissemination of the WORDS System. Furthermore, with the increasing speed of third-generation machines, the overhead generated by PL/I should be more than compensated for by the increased operating efficiency of the target computer.

In this reprogramming, we shall begin investigation of a data flow logic which we hope to implement. As originally constructed, WORDS was based on the concept of repetitive runs on the computer for the purpose of data reduction with each run taking its input from the prior run's output. With the marked success we have obtained in a UHH approach, with much faster and larger machines available, and with the possibility of word selection being accomplished by a statistical criterion embodied in the correlation matrix, we believe it will be possible to reduce the complete analysis of a data base into two runs on the computer. The first (and trivial) of these two runs would be for purposes of correcting spelling and any other errors that have crept into the data base during punching and initial entry into the system. The second run would then take place in a fashion somewhat similar to the following: The data would have parts of speech determined, would go to an analytically oriented deinflection routine, would have words changed and/or deleted according to preset rules (for example, delete all nonverb forms of "like"), and would have all words whose frequency is equal to or less than some preset criterion deleted; the remaining words would then be readied for a complete intercorrelation matrix whose results, as mentioned earlier, would be used to select the N highest correlating words for submission to factoring. Results of the factor procedure would be automatically submitted for rotation and the rotated factors would be channeled through for factor scoring on the original data with results of the scoring being made available graphically (for plotting offline) as well as in their usual printed form.

Although an automatic procedure of this kind must await the results of our research concerning the effect of using the correlation matrix as the statistical criterion for selection of the factoring matrix, the programming and systems logic embodied in the preceding description are well within the state of the art of both hardware and software of present third-generation machines. Indeed, the entire second run we have described, assuming 1000 different words for initial screening, with final factoring on approximately a 200×200 matrix should run in somewhat less than two hours on the model 65 IBM 360 that will soon be available at the University of Rochester. Thus, the possibility of utilizing WORDS on an almost completely automatic, (and, therefore, almost completely objective), approach toward the analysis of major content clusters is potentially quite feasible.

23 A Microfilm and Computer System for Analyzing Comparative Politics Literature

Kenneth Janda

Political Science
Northwestern University

This chapter describes a microfilm and computer system in current use on a comparative study of hundreds of political parties across the world. The methodology employed in the study should be applicable to other topics in comparative politics and perhaps to topics outside the social sciences and humanities. The first section describes the information system of the International Comparative Political Parties Project and the code categories used in indexing the parties literature for inclusion in the information system. The next section discusses indexing instructions and indexing reliability. The chapter concludes with a content analysis of material already indexed for the first nine countries under study.

THE INFORMATION SYSTEM OF THE ICPP PROJECT

The International Comparative Political Parties Project was established in 1967 to conduct a comprehensive study of the world's political parties.[1] Its objective is a comparative analysis of the organization and activities of about 250 political parties which existed between 1950 and 1962 in about 90 foreign countries.[2] Data for this analysis will be gathered not through costly field research but through a systematic search of published and unpublished writings about party politics in these countries.

[1] This project is supported by the National Science Foundation Grant GS-1418. Northwestern University's Research Committee generously supported one year's work pretesting the methodology before application was made to the National Science Foundation. Northwestern's Council for Intersocietal Studies graciously provided some data processing equipment to facilitate our research.
[2] Conceptually, we limit our definition of a political party to organizations that nominate candidates for public office and contest elections. Operationally, we have defined a political party as any sponsoring organization whose candidates won at least 5 percent of the seats of the lower house of a national legislature in two successive elections in the time period, 1950 to 1962.

The presumption underlying the ICPP Project is that countless man-years of research have produced valuable information about foreign political parties which is captured in the pages of books, articles, government documents, newspapers, and unpublished theses. We propose to access this information through the use of a variety of modern information retrieval techniques, to analyze the data that we assemble, and to make the retrieved information available for research by other scholars. For a detailed account of project objectives and methodology, see Janda (1968a).

The information files created during the course of the project should prove to be the most extensive and most thoroughly indexed files in existence for the parties and period under study.[3] We do not pretend that our files will be exhaustive of the literature on political parties in countries that have been popular targets for study, such as the "major European powers," since we must conform to a limit of 2500 pages per country in keeping with our financial resources. Our experience to date, however, suggests that this limit imposes problems of choice in very few countries; in most cases we can easily accommodate all of the literature on party politics in the country under study.[4]

We plan to handle the massive amount of textual material gathered for the project with the use of Eastman Kodak's MIRACODE system for storage and retrieval of information on 16 mm microfilm (see Janda, 1968a, 1968b). The basic components of the MIRACODE system are a special microfilm camera and microfilm reader. The microfilm camera records the original pages along with corresponding machine-readable index codes, which can be sensed by the microfilm reader to retrieve any page tagged with any combination of index codes. Upon retrieval, the page

---

[3] Whenever the English language literature appears sufficiently well-developed on party politics in a given country, we limit our files to this material. When coverage in English is not extensive, we seek out material in other languages—most notably French and Spanish, which are needed for parts of Africa and most of Latin America. For East European and Asian countries, heavy use is made of English translations prepared by the U.S. Joint Publications Research Service.

[4] Our experience during the first year of the project consists of researching nine countries each sampled at random from nine geographical regions of the world. We selected our countries at random to provide an unbiased estimate of problems involved in working with literature on political parties in 90 countries. For the countries that turned up in our sample—Bulgaria, Congo-Brazzaville, Denmark, Dominican Republic, Ecuador, Greece, Guinea, Iran, and North Korea—we were able to identify and process only 7621 pages on political parties, for an average of 837 per country, with a high of 1191 pages for Denmark. Although our research on these countries is not yet finished, we do not expect to disclose enough additional material to raise our average above 1000 pages of parties literature per country in our sample. Because we selected our countries at random, we expect much the same situation for most of the remaining 80 countries in the study.

is projected for display at the reader, and a hard copy can be printed if desired. Depending on the average number of codes per page, several hundred pages of material can be stored on one 100 foot film magazine and searched for specified combinations of code numbers in ten seconds.

Material is prepared for the MIRACODE system by indexing the topics discussed on each page with reference to a set of coding categories, similar to the practice followed at the Human Relations Area Files (Murdock et al., 1961). These code numbers are recorded on coding forms, which are then given to keypunchers who record all code numbers for a given page on one card. As the original pages are being microfilmed, the corresponding punchcards pass the "read" station of a modified IBM 026 keypunch connected to the MIRACODE camera. Code numbers read by the keypunch are transmitted to the camera where they are translated into a binary pattern of clear and opaque rectangles recorded on the film next to the page image. The page image and the codes are produced on the film in accordance with the diagram in Figure 1.

The binary codes on the film are sensed by an optical scanning device, which reads the codes flashing by the scanning head at the normal film transport speed of ten feet per second. The retrieval station has the capability of testing for logical relationships among as many as fifteen different three-digit codes as the film passes the optical scanner. A code is involved in a search by pressing down the appropriate keys on a bank of buttons at the MIRACODE keyboard. The keyboard is modular in design, allowing from one to a maximum of fifteen banks of keys to operate a retrieval station. Figure 2 shows a keyboard configuration involving six banks of keys, which permit testing for logical relationships among six three-digit codes. At present, the available logic for MIRACODE searches consists of "and," "not," "or," "greater than," "less than," and "equal to."

A search command is communicated to the reader by pressing the SEARCH button, which starts the film transport. When the machine senses the appropriate relationship among the numbers entered on the keyboard, the film immediately comes to a halt and backs up several frames to display the image retrieved by the search command. The operator has the opportunity to examine the page for its relevance to his request. If a hard copy is desired, a black-on-white photographic print can be made from the projected image in twenty-five seconds.

If the retrieved image does not satisfy the user, the search can be continued by pressing the search button again. The film will advance and stop to project the next image on the film that satisfies the search command.

While seated at the MIRACODE reader-retrieval station, the user can interact with his data files by changing his search command to affect the character and amount of information retrieved. To increase the number of "hits," the user can relax the search command by turning off a small toggle switch associated with each bank of keys—thus removing code numbers from the search. To decrease the number of "hits" and make his search more selective, he can enter additional code numbers on remaining keys, depending on the number of keyboard banks in the system.

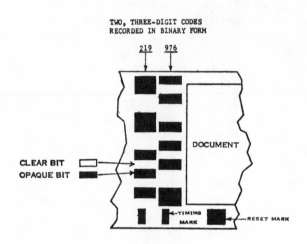

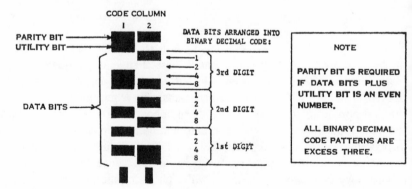

BINARY DECIMAL CODE FOR 1st COLUMN: 219

$$3\text{rd DIGIT } 8 + 4 - 3 = 9$$
$$2\text{nd DIGIT } 4 \qquad - 3 = 1 \Big\} = 219$$
$$1\text{st DIGIT } 4 + 1 - 3 = 2$$

BINARY DECIMAL CODE FOR 2nd COLUMN: 976

$$3\text{rd DIGIT } 8 + 1 - 3 = 6$$
$$2\text{nd DIGIT } \quad + 2 - 3 = 7 \Big\} = 976$$
$$1\text{st DIGIT } 8 + 4 - 3 = 9$$

Figure 1   MIRACODE format for 16 mm film.

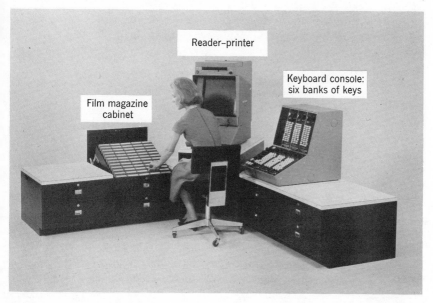

Reader-printer

Keyboard console: six banks of keys

Film magazine cabinet

Figure 2 MIRACODE retrieval station: file cabinets, reader-printer, and keyboard console.

The user can determine in advance of retrieval how many "hits" he will get for any given command through the operation of a "response monitor," which reads the film and tallies the number of satisfied conditions without actually stopping to display the retrieved images. This tally is instantaneously displayed as the film is read.

Two different sets of numbers are used in indexing material for the MIRACODE system. One set, consisting of three-digit numbers from 000 to 999, is used exclusively as *identification codes* for specific parties. The other set, which uses only the first two digits of the codes from 000 to 990, is used to code *substantive information* about parties. The two sets of codes can be differentiated in the MIRACODE system by means of a "utility bit" recorded on the film with every column of code. The MIRACODE retrieval station can decipher the utility bit code during the searching process so that a given number can be interpreted properly as an identification or substantive code.

Identification Codes

The party-identification codes are organized on the basis of ten broad cultural-geographical categories. The first digit of the three-digit code stands for each main division as follows:

Code	Cultural-geographical division
0—	Anglo-American political culture
1—	West Central and Southern Europe
2—	Scandinavia and the Benelux countries
3—	South America
4—	Central America and the Caribbean
5—	Asia and the Far East
6—	Eastern Europe
7—	Middle East and North Africa
8—	West Africa
9—	Central and East Africa

The second digit of the three-digit code stands for a particular country within each division. This scheme permits recording up to ten countries within each division, thus accommodating a maximum of 100 countries. Although there are more than 100 countries in the United Nations alone, the coding scheme is adequate for the ninety countries in the parties project. The third digit stands for a particular party within each country, providing for a maximum of ten parties within each country and 1000 parties overall. These ranges are quite adequate for the parties project, which includes only about 250 parties and not more than seven in any single country. Sample identification codes for Japanese political parties in the project are as follows:

541 Progressive (Kaishinto)
542 Left-Wing Socialist (Saha Shakaito)
543 Right-Wing Socialist (Uha Shakaito)
544 Liberal Democratic (Jiyu Minshuto)
545 Socialist (Shakaito, Social Democratic before 1955)
549 General and other parties

Party-identification codes are used to tag locations in texts where information about specific parties is presented. The substantive nature of the information is recorded by means of substantive codes.

Substantive Codes

On the basis of our pretest experience in coding literature on political parties, we decided to index only at the two-digit level of classification, which provides 100 coding categories for substantive information on political parties while retaining room for expansion of the code by activating the third digit.

The substantive codes have been organized in an attempt to answer several basic questions about political parties. Each of these questions encompasses up to ten coding categories. The first digit of the information codes stands for a given question.

Code	Questions about political parties
0—	What is a political party?—Definition, function, theory
1—	How do political parties begin?—The origin of parties
2—	What does a party do?—Party activities
3—	Who belongs to the party?—Party composition
4—	How is the party organized?—Party structure
5—	What does the party seek to accomplish?—Party goals
6—	Under what condition does the party operate?—Political environment
7—	Under what conditions does the party operate?—Social, economic, and geographical environment
8—	Are there any other parties in the country?—Party system

Each of the code divisions has been subdivided into a maximum of ten concept categories. The complete set of codes is presented in the *ICPP Codes and Indexing Manual* (available from the author). An outline of the codes is given in Figure 3.

ORGANIZATION OF MICROFILM FILES

After sufficient pages have been photographed and encoded on the film by the MIRACODE camera, the exposed reel of film is developed with conventional 16 mm processing. Because a reel may contain material on parties in different countries, the film must be edited and spliced together to form magazines with common information. This type of file organization facilitates research on party politics in given countries, which is the main way the files will be used. Because one 100-foot reel of film will accommodate about 1200 pages of coded material, most of our country files will probably fit on one magazine. If the literature indexed for any country exceeds 1200 pages, the material will be grouped on magazines in accordance with some basis of classification—perhaps having different reels for different parties in the country.

The ICPP film magazines are filed at the retrieval station and labeled according to the countries they cover. Each magazine carries a table of contents as the first frame on the film, which can be addressed by pressing the "image forward" button on the console. By including a detailed table

0— What is a political party—definition, functions, theory, method of studying
000 Definition of a political party
010 Typology of parties
020 Functions of political parties
030 Explicit propositions about parties
040 General theory about parties
050 Purpose of studying parties
060 Approaches to the study of parties
070 Methodology of studying parties

1— How does a political party begin—party origin
100 When was it formed
110 Who formed it and what was its base of electoral support
120 Why was it formed
130 How was it formed
140 Political history of party
150 Organizational history of party

2— What does a political party do—party activities
200 Selects candidates and party officials
210 Conducts election campaigns
220 Formulates party policy and builds party organization
230 Influences government policy
240 Propagandizes its goals and activities
250 Discipline—maintenance of group solidarity
260 Raises and disperses funds
270 Causes demonstrations, riots, assassinations, sabotage, etc.
280 Intercedes in government action on behalf of citizens (including members)
290 Social activities

3— Who belongs to the party—party membership
300 Party supporters
310 Party contributors
320 Party members
330 Party workers and activists
340 Party candidates
350 Party members in government posts
360 Party leaders and officials
370 Party factions
380 Organizational support
390 Independents

4— How is the party organized—party organization
400 Local party organization
410 Constituency party organization
420 Regional party organization
430 National party convention, conference or congress

440 National party committee
450 Legislative organization
460 Ancillary organizations
470 Functional/dysfunctional aspects of party structure
480 Articulation of party structure
490 Centralization of power

5— What does the party seek to accomplish— party goals
500 Gain control of the government
510 Engage in coalitions and constitute oppositions
520 Place members in government positions
530 Issue orientation
540 Ideological orientation
550 Subvert the government
560 Efficiency and effectiveness

6— Under what conditions does the party operate—political environment
600 National crises
610 Political issues of consensus or cleavage
620 Electoral system
630 Popular participation
640 Political norms and attitudes
650 Administrative bureaucracy
660 The executive
670 The legislature
680 Government structure and political history
690 Geographical allocation of authority

7— Under what conditions does the party operate—social, economic, geographic
700 Economic
710 Geographic
720 Social
730 Religious
740 Social norms and attitudes
750 Activities of the military
760 Activities of the students
770 Activities of the trade unions
780 Activities of voluntary associations and interest groups

8— Under what conditions does the party operate—party system
800 Number of parties
810 Election results
820 Stability of parties in system
830 Interparty competition
840 Interparty cooperation
850 Origin, support, and history of system
860 Status of party in party system
870 Typology of party systems
880 International party system

Figure 3 Outline of substantive information codes for the parties project.

414

of contents in the magazine, we eliminate the user's need for an external guide to the files. Indeed, the film itself contains virtually all the information necessary for effective use of the system, as can be seen by the example in Figure 4.

The table of contents indicates that a film magazine will be organized into three sections of material. Each of these sections—A, B, and C—will be discussed in turn.

Section A of each magazine copies a published bibliography on party politics in the country, authored by one of the research analysts on the ICPP staff. These bibliographies are intended to be the most comprehensive available on the parties in our study for the period 1950 to 1962. Each number in the series will follow a common format, commenting on the scholarly concern with party activities in the country, assessing the available literature in English and other languages, and dicussing the search strategy for locating relevant literature. The bibliography listings themselves will be prepared by a computer program, and each entry will be indexed by author and by the five most frequent coding categories. The essay portion of the bibliographies will conclude with the analyst's observations on the state of the parties literature, including substantive focus, quality of the writings, and scholarly needs.

Section B reproduces output from a computer program written to analyze the indexing process using the same punchcards employed as input to the MIRACODE camera. This program reads all of the codes used to index a given document and then produces the following data: the mean numbers of substantive and parties codes used per page, a frequency and percentage distribution of both substantive and parties codes for that document, a rank-ordering of both sets of codes according to frequency of use, and a frequency and percentage distribution of substantive codes by the nine major coding categories, 0 through 8.[5]

Section C contains the actual documents in the files, with the individual pages indexed for retrieval as described earlier in this chapter. By means of file organization and the inclusion of summary information about the material stored on the film, this basic capability for retrieving individual pages is supplemented by a macro-level retrieval capability which enables the user to identify and retrieve entire documents relevant to his interests. The user can identify these documents by consulting the bibliographic index (Section A) or the summary statistics on coding categories (Section B). By searching on the last three digits of the appropriate document numbers, the user can retrieve the first page of the document directly

---

[5] The computer program which produces this information is called SANUK, and was written in FORTRAN IV for the CDC 3400 by Dennis Goldenson. See the sample output from this program in Figure 5.

Film Magazine No. ICPP/429: DOMINICAN REPUBLIC

This magazine contains 1128 pages of literature indexed from 32 documents pertaining to political parties in the Dominican Republic; 69 percent of the pages are in English, the remainder are in Spanish (September, 1967).

TABLE OF CONTENTS, LISTED IN SEQUENCE WITHIN SECTIONS

Section A

Microfilm of Marcelino Miyares, "Bibliography of Party Politics in the Dominican Republic, 1950–1962," in Kenneth Janda (ed.), *ICPP Bibliography Series* (Evanston: International Comparative Political Parties Project, Northwestern University, 1967). This publication is a critical review of the state of literature on political parties in the Dominican Republic.

To learn the substantive coding categories used in indexing this literature and their frequency of usage, consult Table 1.

To locate specific documents of interest on the film, consult the computerized bibliography, which indexes all documents in two ways: by author and by the five most frequent substantive coding categories.

To obtain a statistical summary of the content indexed in any of the documents located in the bibliography, search on the last three digits of the document number, which will retrieve the corresponding computer output in Section B.

Section B

Output from the computer program summarizing the use of coding categories in indexing each document in the file. A summary distribution of codes is given for each document, providing a statistical profile of its content. The coding statistics for any document can be retrieved by searching on the last three digits of the document number, which is given with each bibliographic entry in Section A.

To retrieve the document corresponding to any statistical summary reported in Section B, search on the last three digits of the document number, which will advance the film to the first page of the document in Section C.

Section C

This section contains the actual documents with individual pages intended for retrieval. A suggested search strategy is as follows:

1. Identify the coding categories relevant to your inquiry by consulting Table 1 in Section A. (Be alert to alternative code categories.)
2. Note the frequency of usage for these categories to determine the number of pages that would be retrieved on a simple search.
3. If the number seems too large for retrieval, consider qualifying your search by adding another code number.
4. Turn on the response monitor and search for pages with both codes to determine the number jointly coded.
5. If the number of pages seems manageable, turn off the response monitor and retrieve the pages. Otherwise further qualify the search and count again.

Figure 4 Sample table of contents on ICPP film magazine.

from Section C. He can then advance the film manually, reading the material at his own pace.

INDEXING AND RELIABILITY

Indexing literature for the ICPP Project is the responsibility of a staff of research analysts, most of whom are graduate students employed full-time during the summers and part-time during the academic year. Usually, an analyst comes to his task with little knowledge of politics in the country which he has been assigned. But after reading hundreds of pages about party politics in his country, he becomes a well-informed observer of the political scene, capable of authoring a critical bibliography on parties in his country.[6]

In the interests of incorporating into the information files as much literature as possible with available funds, analysts are not expected to read material beforehand, and all code numbers are recorded during first reading. Because the page is the unit of retrieval in the MIRACODE system, the page serves as the indexing unit for the research analyst, who tags the text with one or more code numbers in order to index information that he decides is worth retrieving. The analyst makes his decision to index or not to index according to a "Rule of Usefulness," which states, "Any coded item of information should be defensible in terms of its usefulness after retrieval for at least one of three objectives: (1) describing parties for the purpose of operationalizing variables, (2) understanding the environment within which parties operate, and (3) inventorying explicit propositions about political parties." Additional rules and definitions to guide indexing are contained in the *ICPP Codes and Indexing Manual.*

After indexing a page (and before continuing to the next one), the analyst is instructed to review the codes while (a) checking for duplicate codes; (b) assessing the applicability of codes to the content in accordance with various rules in the *Indexing Manual,* especially the Rule of Usefulness; and (c) insuring that all useful information has been indexed. The impact of these instructions on the indexing process is systematically as-

---

[6] We have found that far more time is required to identify, locate, and obtain relevant literature for our project than to read, index, and process it for inclusion into our information retrieval system. Therefore, we established the *ICPP Bibliography Series* to make available the results of our wide-ranging search for information on political parties. The series will consist of about 90 numbers, each on party politics in a given country, and each number will be authored by the research analyst concentrating on that country. The first nine numbers in the series, covering the countries named in footnote 4, are in preparation and will be published by the International Comparative Political Parties Project.

sessed by having a second analyst re-index selected material without knowledge of the codes used by the first analyst. The results are assessed by calculating reliabilities between analysts for each document that has been re-indexed.

Our calculations of inter*indexer* reliabilities are analogous to the more familiar inter*coder* reliabilities reported for content analysis, but we use the different term to emphasize the important difference between "indexing" and "coding." Knowledge of intercoder reliabilities is important in content analysis because each coder is essentially *scoring* his material on some nominal or ordinal scales to produce variables for direct analysis in subsequent stages of the research. For example, once an answer to an open-ended interview question is coded a "3," the respondent's score on the variable is essentially fixed for analysis. To insure that variables are scaled accurately for research, it is esssential to obtain high levels of intercoder reliability, with 90 percent sometimes proposed as an "acceptable" level of agreement between coders.

In evaluating ICPP indexing reliabilities, one should understand that our codes serve a purpose that is different from codes in content analysis. In applying a code number to a given page, our analysts are *indexing* the text under that coding category rather than *scoring* the content on a given variable. Our coding categories support a method for retrieving information, which the user is expected to use in scaling his own variables. Hence, we use the term *indexing* the literature instead of *coding* it.

Because of different objectives between indexing and coding, it seems that a lower level of reliability would be "acceptable" for indexing than for coding. This seems true for three reasons: (1) disagreement between analysts sometimes occurs in the use of different but related codes for the same passage, which can be retrieved by using "see also" alternative codes; (2) disagreement between coders often occurs in indexing brief references or mentions, which are of marginal utility after retrieval; and (3) the researcher would not normally treat index codes as data for analysis, the way variable codes are treated in content analysis—although this will be done later in this chapter.

While agreement among indexers may not be as crucial in the research process as agreement among coders, it is still important to know how much agreement exists between two analysts asked to process the same material for inclusion in the files. The ICPP Project systematically evaluates indexing reliabilities by routine re-indexing of 10 percent of all the pages indexed for each country. Codes used by a second analyst for a given document are keypunched and read into the computer along with the punchcards carrying the first analyst's codes. After making a page-by-page comparison of the codes, the computer furnishes the following information: the mean number of substantive and party codes used per page by each indexer, the product-moment correlation between indexers for both substantive and party codes, and the familiar coefficient of reliability between indexers for both sets of codes. In addition, the program provides frequency distributions of substantive and party codes used by each indexer. A sample of computer output with this information is given in Figure 5, which reports results of re-indexing 21 pages from Kim Ch'ang-sun, "A Fifteen-Year History of North Korea," translated from the Korean by the U.S. Joint Publications Research Service.[7]

The re-indexing example in Figure 5 presents fairly typical reliabilities for the project to date. Interindexer agreement over the use of substantive codes, as represented in Figure 5 by a product-moment correlation of .78 and a coefficient of reliability of .52, is usually lower than that obtained in the use of parties codes, represented by a correlation of .91 and a coefficient of .56. Table 1 reports reliability data for 53 documents repre-

Table 1. *Mean interindexer reliabilities over 53 documents for first set of nine countries*

Codes	Parties	Substantive
Mean product-moment correlation	.73	.42
Mean coefficient of reliability	.74	.46

senting 924 pages of material re-indexed for the nine countries studied in the first phase of the project. We are now in the process of evaluating these results before processing parties literature for other countries.

The coefficient of reliability and the product-moment correlation are both calculated because they provide different information about the extent of agreement between indexers. The coefficient of reliability is calculated by the familiar formula, C.R. $= \Sigma 2M/N_1 + N_2$, where M is the number of codes on each page that "match" for each indexer, N_1 is the total number of codes used by the first indexer, and N_2 is the total number used by the second indexer. The product-moment correlation is calculated by treating the indexers as the variables, the frequency with which both

[7] The United States Joint Publications Research Service (JPRS) was established in 1957 to translate foreign language material into English for use by various agencies of the government. Approximately 1000 pages of foreign language material is translated daily by professionals under contract to JPRS. The *Monthly Catalog of U.S. Government Publications* lists many, but presumably not all, of the JPRS translations. Research and Microfilm Publications, Inc. in Washington, D.C., catalogs and indexes all current JPRS material.

DOCUMENT NO. = 560-025
THIS DOCUMENT HAS 21 PAGES.

--STATISTICAL SUMMARY--

	PARTIES	SUBSTANTIVE
THE MEAN NUMBER OF CODES PER PAGE FOR INDEXER NO. 16 ARE--	1.90	2.62
THE MEAN NUMBER OF CODES PER PAGE FOR INDEXER NO. 10 ARE--	1.48	3.81
PRODUCT MOMENT CORRELATIONS OF CODING BETWEEN INDEXERS ARE--	0.916	0.780
COEFFICIENTS OF INTER-INDEXER RELIABILITY ARE--	0.563	0.519

FREQUENCY DISTRIBUTIONS

SUBSTANTIVE

CODE	INDEXER NO. 16 FREQ.	PCT.	INDEXER NO. 10 FREQ.	PCT.
10	0	0.0	1	1.3
100	3	5.5	5	6.3
110	0	0.0	1	1.3
120	0	0.0	2	2.5
130	1	1.8	3	3.8
140	13	23.6	11	13.8
150	0	0.0	5	6.3
210	0	0.0	1	1.3
220	0	0.0	2	2.5
240	5	9.1	0	0.0
250	6	10.9	5	6.3
320	4	7.3	6	7.5
330	0	0.0	1	1.3
360	5	9.1	6	7.5
370	1	1.8	4	5.0
380	0	0.0	2	2.5
400	0	0.0	1	1.3
430	0	0.0	1	1.3
440	2	3.6	2	2.5
460	0	0.0	1	1.3
480	1	1.8	0	0.0
490	3	5.5	3	3.8
500	0	0.0	1	1.3
530	0	0.0	2	2.5
540	0	0.0	1	1.3
560	0	0.0	2	2.5
680	0	0.0	2	2.5
840	0	0.0	1	1.3
850	6	10.9	3	3.8
880	5	9.1	5	6.3

PARTIES

CODE	INDEXER NO. 1 FREQ.	PCT.	16 FREQ.	INDEXER NO. 10 PCT.
521	1	2.5	2	6.5
559	2	5.0	0	0.0
561	21	52.5	18	58.1
569	0	0.0	4	12.9
609	1	2.5	0	0.0
619	1	2.5	0	0.0
629	1	2.5	0	0.0
639	1	2.5	0	0.0
649	1	2.5	0	0.0
659	1	2.5	0	0.0
669	2	5.0	0	0.0
671	4	10.0	7	22.6
679	4	10.0	0	0.0

Figure 5. Results of re-indexing 21 pages from Kim Chiang-sun, A Fifteen-Year History of North Korea

use a given code as values of the variables, and the coding categories used by both as the number of cases. The scatter diagram in Figure 6 illustrates how the data are treated in calculating the correlation coefficient.

We refer to the product-moment correlation as our "macroscopic" measure of indexing reliability, since it measures agreement in use of codes over the entire document without being sensitive to the joint occurrence of codes on the same pages. Because of characteristics of the product-moment formula, the high correlation of .91 calculated for the scatter diagram in Figure 6 results largely from both analysts' heavy use of code 14 (political history of the party), which indexer number 10 used eleven times and indexer number 16 used thirteen times. While we have no assurance that the indexers used these codes on the same pages (indeed, we know that on two pages they must not have), we know that they found a similar number of references to party history throughout the text. High values obtained for our macroscopic measure of indexing re-

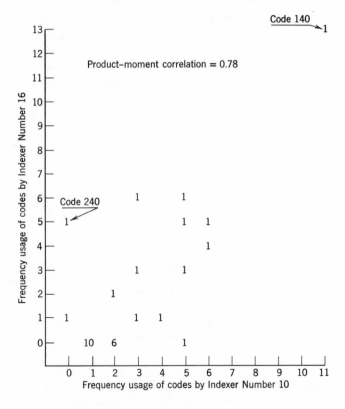

Figure 6 Joint distribution of 30 substantive codes assigned to Document 560-025 by Indexer Number 10 and Indexer Number 16.

liability indicate that two indexers agree in characterizing the document's focus, which is important to the researcher who wishes to retrieve entire documents on a given subject by reference to the bibliographic index in Section A of the film or the statistical summaries in Section B.

We refer to the coefficient of reliability as our "microscopic" measure of indexing reliability, since it is sensitive only to joint occurrences of codes on the same pages and ignores frequencies for the same codes over the entire document. Obviously, if the coefficient of reliability is 1.0, the product-moment correlation will also be 1.0—disregarding the trivial case when only one code is used and the variance and therefore the correlation coefficient are both 0. Once the coefficient of reliability drops below unity, however, the product-moment correlation can fluctuate widely—even taking on negative values if indexers systematically use different codes for the same theme.[8] It is even possible for the correlation to be unity while the reliability coefficient is 0.0, if the indexers use the same codes but on different pages.

Our two measures of reliability can be supplemented with other information from the SANUK program (Figure 5) to tell us something about the sources of disagreement between indexers. We see that indexer number 16 has used more parties codes per page (cpp) than indexer number 10 (1.90 cpp to 1.48), but that indexer 10 has used far more substantive codes (3.81 to 2.62). Referring first to the frequency distributions for the parties codes, we see that the main discrepancy between the analysts lies in number 16's use of codes 609 through 679, pertaining respectively to Albania, Bulgaria, Czechoslovakia, East Germany, Hungary, Poland, Rumania, and the USSR. Analyst 16 used these codes to index the countries mentioned in the third and fourth paragraphs of Figure 7; the other analyst apparently decided that the mentions were not sufficiently important to warrant indexing. Before evaluating this discrepancy, let us examine the situation for the substantive codes.

[8] Because it is calculated by the product-moment formula, our "macroscopic" measure of reliability has some well-known characteristics. It is very sensitive to disagreements when the number of "cases" is small, which means the number of coding categories for our purposes. It is also affected by the distribution of the data which, as coding frequencies, tend to be positively skewed. The data in Figure 6 are heavily skewed to the right for both variables (indexers), meaning that the correlation will be influenced by the outlying observation and will result in a high value. For the purpose of assessing interindexer reliability at the macroscopic level, this is a desirable attribute of the statistic, for a high value indicates that the two indexers agreed in their use of the most frequent coding category. The properties of the product-moment correlation make it a suitable measure for macroscopic reliability except when the number of pages coded is small (say less than 10), for this usually means that few codes will be used (low N) and those that are used will be used infrequently (low variance).

The third stage was a forced coalition period, in which the Communists established their dictatorship. During this period, those political parties which bannered socialistic slogans were amalgamated into a single party, and the party line was exclusively decided by the Communists. Nor was the existence of any opposition party tolerated in the legislative body (the people's assembly). Freedom of press, speech, and assembly to oppose Communism was totally ruled out. It was during the third stage that those socialist party leaders who were opposed to the amalgamation successively took political exiles in other countries, and that non-Communist elements were persecuted. It is needless to say that the second and third stages were carried out with the Soviet military and political support.

After World War II, East European nations where Communist or labor parties are now in power have gone through the above three stages. Depending upon individual conditions that existed, some countries experienced all of the three stages, while some started with the second stage, and some went through the last stage alone Some even experienced the second and third stages at one time after going through the first stage. These stages generally lasted from 1945 to 1949.

Countries which started with the first stage include Rumania, Bulgaria, Hungary, and Czech, while Poland and East Germany skipped over the first stage.

Countries that started from the third stage without going through the first two stages are Yugoslavia and Albania, where the Soviet military power had little things to do with government establishment. It is Czechoslovakia that went through the last two stages at one time after the first stage.

In North Korea there were no political parties before the Liberation in 1945. In this respect, NK was much different from East European nations. However, tactical stages up to the establishment of dictatorship were much the same as those in East Europe.

The NK Communist Party (actually, the Korean Communist Party NK Division), the New People's Party (also known as the Korea Independence League), the Korean Democratic Party, and the Religious Ch'ongu-dang Party were all organized after the Liberation of Korea, and they did go through the first stage of cooperation, second stage of camouflaged coalition, and third stage of Communist dictatorship, not exactly like those observed in East Europe, but with some modifications.

- 43 -

Analyst number 16 indexed country references in these paragraphs, while analyst number 10 did not.

Figure 7 Page from Kim Ch'ang-sun, *A Fifteen-Year History of North Korea* (translated by U.S. Joint Publications Research Service), which produced low inter-indexer reliability.

Analyst 10 tended to employ about 50 percent more substantive codes per page than analyst 16. This suggests either that analyst 10's threshold for deciding what constitutes useful information for retrieval is lower than analyst 16's or that analyst 16 is missing information through oversight. Although either factor would lower reliability by the same amount, "threshold" differences are less important to the retrieval system than "oversight" errors. If the user can be assured that analysts are likely to agree in indexing discussions of "substantial" length or importance, he may tolerate disagreements between analysts over decisions to index or not to index brief mentions and passing references—such as the country references in Figure 7. However, he is unlikely to be satisfied knowing that important discussions of a given topic may not be indexed for retrieval.

An examination of the frequency distribution of codes for both indexers given by the computer output (Figure 5) cannot establish the reason for the disagreement between the indexers, but it can point out differences in the use of codes, thereby serving as a basis for discussion and resolution in interindexer coding conferences.[9] Our experience thus far, and it is only impressionistic at present, indicates that most of the disagreements between indexers involve threshold decisions rather than genuine oversight. We intend to study the sources of disagreement in indexing as we seek to improve our indexing instructions, procedures, and reliabilities before we undertake to index our next group of forty countries in the ICCP project.

Analysis of Parties Literature for Nine Countries

In addition to providing a capability for information retrieval, systematic indexing of the parties literature provides a means for analyzing the content of that literature. By examining the frequency distributions of coding categories assigned to the literature for each country studied, we are able to evaluate the coverage of available information on party politics in that country, confirming or disproving impressionistic ideas about the state of the literature. We may further evaluate the *quality,* as opposed to the *coverage,* of the parties literature by reference to the data quality control codes that the research analyst applies to each document after it is indexed.

Although it would be possible to analyze the coverage of the parties literature for each country across all coding categories from 00—through 88—we will limit our comparison to percentage distributions across the nine major substantive categories (0—through 8—) prompted by the basic questions about parties listed earlier. Table 2 contains these major categories and their usage for each country, expressed as a percentage of the total codes used for that country.

One of the first things to be noted from Table 2 is the range in amount of material indexed, from 425 pages (Congo-Brazzaville) to 1,191 pages (Denmark). This reflects the obvious fact that the amount of schol-

---

[9] The frequency distribution of codes for both indexers provides essentially the same information as a cross-tabulation of codes by indexers, which is the method of presentation used by Funkhouser in evaluating the adequacy of the codes against the performance of coders. See G. Ray Funkhouser, "A Method of Analysing Coding Reliabilities: The Random-Systematic Error Coefficient." Stanford University, mimeograph, undated.

Table 2. *Percentage distribution of substantive codes used in indexing literature on party politics in nine countries*

Code Description	Bulgaria	Congo-Brazzaville	Denmark	Dominican Republic	Ecuador	Greece	Guinea	Iran	North Korea
0— Definition/theory	0	2	6	0	1	4	0	0	0
1— Origin of party	3	6	6	6	4	4	3	3	12
2— Party activities	18	8	6	18	11	4	12	10	20
3— Party composition	17	32	15	31	16	20	14	16	22
4— Party structure	13	2	6	1	6	1	18	5	15
5— Party goals	19	7	7	9	14	12	13	12	10
6— Political environment	9	18	22	15	20	38	14	27	8
7— Social environment	13	10	13	13	16	7	16	16	3
8— Party system	9	17	19	7	12	22	10	12	11
	100%								
Total pages indexed	1,183	425	1,191	1,128	936	509	699	901	649
Mean number of codes per page	2.69	2.37	2.19	1.77	1.96	2.55	2.06	1.99	2.17
Number of documents	104	25	78	32	54	45	34	67	31
Mean number of pages per document	11	17	15	35	17	11	21	13	21

arly attention given to political parties varies widely across countries. However, this variation does not always occur as expected. For example, we expected to find more material on party politics in Greece than in Bulgaria, while the results were diametrically opposite.

Newsome (1967), our analyst for Bulgaria, attributes the large number of pages she indexed to "the incorporation of small pieces of widely scattered source material" rather than the existence of a smaller number of more substantial writings. The data in Table 2 supports her explanation by indicating almost thirty additional documents (104) processed for Bulgaria compared to its nearest competitor, Denmark (78). For Greece, on the other hand, Antunes (1967) attributes the relative paucity of literature to the fact that, with the exception of the Communist party, "political parties *per se* have not been an object of scholarly investigation." Moreover, he contends, "While ancient Greece has been the object of a great deal of attention, scholars have evidenced little interest in contemporary Greek politics."

Antunes' evaluation of the parties literature in Greece is also supported by the distribution of coding categories. No other country has so little material indexed on party activities and party structure—the two major coding categories that embrace our "hardest" information about political parties. Only 5 percent of the codes used to index Greek literature dealt with one or the other of these two major coding categories, compared to 8 percent of the codes for Iran, the country with the next most "underdeveloped" parties literature in our sample of nine.

Using the same two categories to judge the specificity of information about political parties, one would have to rate North Korea, Bulgaria, and Guinea—in that order—as the countries with the most relevant literature on party organization and activities. For both North Korea and Bulgaria, this high rating undoubtedly results from large amounts of material translated from party documents, which tend to discuss organization and activities in great detail. Guinea seems to be the only country on our list which obtains a high rating on these categories by virtue of the scholarly literature written on political parties. In evaluating the Guinean literature, Skogan (1967) ascribes this literature in part to Western scholars' interest in Guinea "as an example of an at least theoretically nontotalitarian single-party state engaged in a thorough-going reconstruction of the social system."

Other information about the coverage of the literature is offered by the distribution of usage for code category 3—, "party composition." Both Congo-Brazzaville and the Dominican Republic score high on this category, which accounts for almost one-third of the total codes used for each. The relatively high usage of this major coding category for both countries is due to an especially heavy reliance on code category 36—, which stands for party leaders and officials—suggesting that the literature deals largely with political personalities. In the case of the Dominican Republic, as Miyares (1967) points out, "the literature focuses on the person of R. L. Trujillo," while Lauffer (1967) describes the focus of literature for Congo-Brazzaville as centering more broadly "around individuals as Youlou, Opangault, Massemba-Debat, and other prominent political figures."

It should be remembered that the coverage "profile" depicted by our coding categories reflects political life in the period we are studying (1950 to 1962) and does not necessarily portray the situation today. In discussing the literature that he indexed for Ecuador, Johnson (1967) remarks, "The period of the early 1950's, because of the then unique event of Galo Plaza's successful completion of his term as president of the republic, and the period from 1962 to 1965, because of the return of the coup d'etat (or *golpe de gobierno*) as an instrument of political selection with the return of the military as an active political force, are the periods of recent Ecuadorian political history receiving the greatest amount of attention from American scholars." As a result of our focus on the period from 1950 to 1962, the Ecuadorian material in the ICPP files will reflect the earlier period of stability rather than the more recent instability.

It is at least as important to evaluate the quality of the parties literature for given countries as its coverage. Immediately after indexing each document, our research analysts score it on the basis of 22 "data quality" variables, such as "place of publication," "original language of source," "position of author," "sources of data," "scope of study," "field research," and subjective judgments of the document's "quality," "ideological orientation," and "objectivity." A complete listing of the data quality control codes is contained in the Appendix to this chapter.

Each of the numbers in the *ICPP Bibliography Series* contains a table which reports the overall usage of these data quality codes in rating the documents on 17 of the 22 variables in the set. Figure 8 is a reproduction of this table for the 31 documents indexed for North Korea. Discussing this table, Schwestka (1967) observes:

Almost half of the documents were published either in North Korea or in that area of the world; almost half were translated from Korean; and more than half of the authors were either North Koreans or South Koreans. The distribution of authors' positions is deceptive, however, for it was impossible to determine the position of many North Korean authors. Consequently, authorship seems weighted toward academia rather than government/party officials.

One of our guides for assessing the "scholarly" nature of the material

DATA QUALITY CODES	MOST FREQUENT:	(N)	2nd MOST FREQUENT:	(N)	3rd MOST FREQUENT:	(N)	4th MOST FREQUENT:	(N)
Document Type	Journal article	13	Government documents	9	Book	9	Newspaper feature or magazine item	2
Place of publication	United States	17	In country studied	12	In area of world where country exists	2		
Original language of source	English	17	Language of country studied	14				
Position of author	Academic	16	Government official	2	Journalist	1	Not applicable/no information	12
National background	From country studied	10	United States	9	From area of world where country exists	4	Not applicable/no information	8
Language resources	Cites native language sources	12	Document itself translated	9	Uses native interviews to collect data	5	No information	2
Date of data	Post-World War II	16	1955–1959	9	Prior to World War II	2	1960–1964	2
Data source types	Government publication	10	Secondary sources	6	Election returns or ecological data	6	Sample survey	
Quantitative analysis	Raw data on percents reported in text	26	No quantification	5				
Theoretical treatment	No explicit propositions	29	One or more explicit propositions	2				
Traditional scholarship	No footnotes	15	Between 1 and 2 per page	6	More than 3 per page	5	Less than 1 per page	3
Nature of sources cited	Primary—party and government documents	14	Primary—personal records	1	Secondary—books, journal articles	1	Not applicable/no information	15
Scope of study	Case study of single country	16	Case study of single party	10	Comparison of government systems	5		
Field research	Author resident native of country	14	No evidence of work in country	10	Author nonresident native of country	4	Evidence of work in geographic area	1
Overall judgment of quality	High	24	Medium	6	Low	1		
Author's ideology	Leftist	13	Not classifiable on left-right scale	11	Rightist	5	Centrist	2
Author's objectivity	Values detectable	15	No reason to doubt objectivity	14	Objective/"scientific" analysis	2		

Figure 8 Data quality codes for 31 documents for North Korea.

that we index is the proportion of codes in category 0—, "Definitions, functions and theories" of political parties. Denmark, with only 6 percent of its index entries in this category, scores the highest of all nine countries on this category. Nevertheless, Billingsley (1967) reports in her data quality analysis for the 78 documents indexed on Denmark that "most documents are news features, only half of them are written by academics, the material is seldom footnoted, is generally considered (subjectively) to be of medium quality, and the data sources (when revealed) do not involve quantification."

The other analysts' assessments of the parties literature for their countries are much the same as Billingsley's: most of the literature is rated "nonscholarly" in character. Although this may result partly from uniqueness in our sample of nine countries, none of which have been common objects of study by political scientists, it is likely that much the same situation will be found for most of the other countries we study. Our search for material on party politics produces a great deal of nonscholarly material in the form of party documents, newspaper accounts, and government reports. Although lacking in theoretical character, this material contains basic information necessary for scoring parties on such variables as nature of party membership, ideological orientation, centralization of power, leadership selection, and cohesiveness—important variables for making cross-national comparisons.

When diverse sources disagree in statements about a party, we will seek to determine the basis of the disagreement by using our data quality codes as suggested by Naroll in *Data Quality Control* (1962). We will analyze the source of variance in coding a party on a given variable from information in the file. This analysis will be done automatically with a computer program which treats the data quality control codes as the independent variables and the codes for the party as the dependent variable. The program will try to identify the existence of systematic differences among data quality variables which account for variance in the dependent variable as we have coded it from information in the files.

For example, the MIRACODE system may retrieve a total of 25 documents discussing membership requirements in party X. Ten of these 25 documents may report that membership in the party does *not* require the payment of dues, while 15 other documents may state that payment of dues *is* a membership requirement. Through an analysis of variance in our coding of this variable, we may discover the discrepancy to be explained by a data quality variable, for example, "position of author"— with academics reporting no dues requirement and former party officials revealing that members are indeed required to pay dues to stay in good standing.

This example is only intended to illustrate the general procedure that will be employed in using our data quality codes for "quality control" of the information we generate. Although problems inherent in "library research" are not unique to the ICPP project, the scope of our activities is such that we must develop systematic procedures for evaluating the information that resides in and emerges from our files. Fortunately, the very technology that enables us to index and retrieve information from massive amounts of literature can also be utilized in a microfilm and computer system for analyzing that literature.

APPENDIX: DATA QUALITY CONTROL CODES

Columns	Variable
1–18	SENIOR AUTHOR'S LAST NAME AND INITIALS
19–20	YEAR OF ORIGINAL PUBLICATION
21–23	COUNTRY CODE
24–26	DOCUMENT CODE
27–29	INDEXER CODE
30	TYPE OF DOCUMENT

    0 not otherwise classified

    1 reference source—Facts-On-File, Keesings Archives, etc.

    2 newspaper or magazine item—popular periodical

    3 newspaper or magazine feature story—popular periodical

    4 party document—constitution, platform

    5 government documents—reports, statistical abstracts

    6 journal article

    7 article or chapter in book (used for reprints of journal article)

    8 thesis, monograph

    9 book

| 31–32 | PERIODICAL CODE—specific for each country |
| 33 | PLACE OF PUBLICATION |

    blank don't know (missing data)

    0 not otherwise classified (use also when not applicable)

    1 United States (except if 2 is applicable)

    2 in colonizing country (U.S., Britain, France, Germany, Spain, Portugal, Netherlands)

    3 in area of world where country exists—i.e.., Latin America, Africa, Europe, Asia

    4 in country studied

Columns	Variable

34 ORIGINAL LANGUAGE OF SOURCE
 0 not otherwise classified
 1 English
 2 French
 3 Spanish
 4 German
 5 language of country studied (if two apply, favor using this code)

35 AUTHORSHIP
 0 no author named
 1 one author
 2 two authors
 3 three or more authors
 4 corporate author (e.g., Bulgarian National Committee)

36 POSITION OF FIRST-NAMED AUTHOR (favor higher code if two apply)
 blank no information (missing data)
 0 not otherwise classified
 1 journalist
 2 government official in country studied
 3 ex-government official
 4 party official in country studied
 5 ex-party official
 6 academic

37 PRESUMED NATIONAL BACKGROUND—judged from last name and source of publication
 blank not applicable—no author given
 0 no judgment made/not otherwise classified
 1 United States (except if 2 is applicable)
 2 from colonizing country—U.S., Britain, France, Germany, Spain, Portugal, Netherlands
 3 from area of world where country exists—e.g., Latin America, Africa, Europe (use if in doubt of 4)
 4 from country studied

38 EVIDENCE OF USE OF LANGUAGE RESOURCES
 blank not applicable (use for general theory, not country studied)
 0 no information
 1 coder infers author has no ability in native language
 2 cites translated materials, worked with interpreter

Columns	Variable

38   EVIDENCE OF USE OF LANGUAGE RESOURCES (*Continued*)

    3   cites native language sources, uses native language phrases in text (excluding the native names of political parties)

    4   uses native interviewers to collect survey information

    5   document itself translated from native language or written in native language or written by native in English

39   DATE OF MAJOR PORTION OF DATA (code later period if other choice cannot be made)

    blank   not applicable (use for general theory)

    0   not otherwise classified

    1   prior to World War II (1939 or earlier)

    2   1940–1944

    3   1945–1949

    4   1950–1954

    5   1955–1959

    6   1960–1964

    7   1965–present

    8   post-World War II (give preference to above categories)

40   NOT USED

41–49   CODE FOR DATA SOURCES (entered in columns 41–49, ranked by importance)

    blank   not applicable (use for speeches, election reports, etc.)

    0   no data sources revealed

    1   not otherwise classified

    2   secondary sources—newspapers, books, journals, broadcasts

    3   government publications or party documents

    4   election returns or ecological data

    5   roll call votes

    6   sample survey of individuals

    7   interviews with party officials or leaders

    8   personal experience as participant observer

50   NUMBER OF DATA SOURCES USED

51   NOT USED

52   QUANTITATIVE ANALYSIS SCORE

    0   no quantification involved

    1   raw data or percents reported in text but not in tables

    2   one raw data or percentage table reported

    3   two or more raw data or percentage tables reported

    4   bivariate measures of association reported

Columns	Variable

52 QUANTITATIVE ANALYSIS SCORE (*Continued*)

  5 multivariate statistics reported

53 THEORETICAL TREATMENT SCORE

  0 no explicit propositions advanced or tested

  1 general theory that discusses "relevant" variables, but does not state relationships among them

  2 one or more explicit propositions advanced but not statistically tested

  3 one or more explicit propositions advanced and statistically tested

  4 enumeration of three or more propositions with common concepts into a body of theory

  5 incorporation of three or more propositions with common concepts into a body of theory

54 TRADITIONAL SCHOLARSHIP SCORE

  blank not applicable (speeches, election returns)

  0 no footnotes cited or attribution of sources

  1 less than 1 footnote per page

  2 between 1 and 2 footnotes per page

  3 between 2 and 3 footnotes per page

  4 more than 3 footnotes per page

55 NATURE OF SOURCES CITED IN FOOTNOTES (enter the highest when appropriate)

  blank not applicable—no footnotes

  0 not classified

  1 tertiary sources—encyclopedias, references only

  2 secondary sources—newspapers and magazines

  3 secondary sources—books, journal articles

  4 primary sources—party and government document

  5 primary sources—personal records, memoirs, interviews, data from unpublished sources

56 CITATION OF DUVERGER (enter highest applicable)

  blank not applicable—no footnotes in text

  0 footnotes, but none to Duverger

  1 one footnote to Duverger

  2 two or more footnotes to Duverger

  3 mentions Duverger in the text

  4 tests out Duverger's propositions or theory, modeled after Duverger's analysis, uses Duverger's concepts or "branch" and "caucus" parties, "majority bent" parties, etc.

Columns	Variable

57   SCOPE OF STUDY (use for whole document whether all is coded or not)

   0   not otherwise classified

   1   conceptual or theoretical, without emphasis on data and evidence

   2   survey of parties or politics in given area, e.g., Latin America

   3   compartive analysis of governmental systems

   4   comparative analysis of political parties

   5   study of a single country

   6   study of a single event

   7   news event

58–60   FOCUS OF STUDY—MOST FREQUENT SUBSTANTIVE CODING CATEGORY USED

61–63   NUMBER OF TIMES MOST FREQUENT SUBSTANTIVE CODING CATEGORY USED

64–66   FOCUS OF STUDY—SECOND MOST FREQUENT SUBSTANTIVE CODING CATEGORY USED

67–69   NUMBER OF TIMES SECOND MOST FREQUENT SUBSTANTIVE CODING CATEGORY USED

70   FIELD RESEARCH

   blank   not applicable or no information

   0   evidence of no work in country studied

   1   evidence of work in geographical area

   2   spent less than one year in country

   3   spent more than one year in country, or two trips of any length or author writing in country

   4   author a nonresident native of country

   5   author a resident of country

71   CODER'S SUBJECTIVE JUDGMENT OF QUALITY OF SOURCE

   1   low

   2   medium—code unless evidence points to low or high

   3   high

72   CODER'S SUBJECTIVE JUDGMENT OF IDEOLOGICAL ORIENTATION OF AUTHOR

   0   not classifiable on left-right demension

   1   leftist

   2   centrist—code unless evidence points to low or high

   3   rightist

Columns	Variable
73	CODER'S SUBJECTIVE JUDGMENT OF AUTHOR'S OBJECTIVITY
	1 antiseptically objective—e.g., "scientific" analysis, mainly tabular presentation of data
	2 no reason to doubt objectivity
	3 values detectable
	4 emotional language
74–76	NUMBER OF PAGES CODED
77–80	CODING TIME IN MINUTES

24   Analyzing Dyadic Interaction[1]

George Psathas

Sociology
Boston University

Verbal interaction between two persons differs from written text in ways which require that its specific characteristics be considered before a computer system of content analysis is utilized.[2] In this chapter, the analysis of interaction between therapist and patient in the therapy interview will be used to illustrate the problems involved and to suggest solutions within the framework of the General Inquirer (GI) system for content analysis. The presentation assumes a familiarity with the General Inquirer system (Stone, 1966).

In discussing two-person interaction, the particular kind of situation that will be analyzed will be one in which each person has a special role to play. For example, an interviewer and a respondent, an experimenter and a subject, a teacher and a student, a doctor and a patient. In these situations, each participant is involved in the performance of his own role and the support of the other's role. That is, he is aware that some aspects of his behavior are concerned with maintaining his role in the eyes of the other so that the other will regard him as the special person-in-role that he is. He also does the same for the other, that is, accords to him the recognition that the other is a special person-in-

[1] The research has been supported by a grant from the National Institute of Mental Health, MH 12889. Dennis J. Arp, who has served as Project Director, and J. Philip Miller, who has planned the programming of the 360 version of the General Inquirer, have contributed generously their ideas and suggestions at every phase of this research. The dictionaries described herein have been developed by Dennis J. Arp and, under his direction Diana Reed, Sandra Gold, Robert Miller, Edith Guyot, and Joel Achtenberg.
[2] The possibility that the analysis of interaction will contribute to the solution of many of the problems of content analysis has been noted by David G. Hays (Chapter 3, *infra*), who states that "the analysis of content will achieve its greatest successes by operating with a model of the conversationalist." The manner in which conversation is generated and understood by those participating in it needs to be better understood before substantial progress can be made on this task.

role and acknowledges that he knows that the other knows the same about him. When both parties interact in such a way, they can be said to be mutually aware of one another's role.

Before role performance can be achieved, some basic underlying conditions must be met. The two persons are physically and temporally co-present, that is, they share the same time and space. Furthermore, they are mutually aware of one another's presence. This means that each is aware of the other and aware that the other is aware of him. This mutual awareness is continual, that is, it goes on recurrently throughout the interaction. Explicit recognition is made of such continuity by the use of various indicators to show that they are attentive to one another. Because they are within close sensory range of one another, they are able to use a variety of senses. They can, for example, use eye contact or nonverbal gestures to indicate continued awareness as well as verbal indicators.

Their verbal interaction follows some patterning in regard to sequencing, although it is not absolutely essential that an alternation of talk (where one talks and is followed by the other) occurs. It is possible for one person to talk extensively while the other interacts only to indicate continued attention and awareness. Therefore, it is necessary to distinguish interaction from verbal interaction. Interaction can occur without verbal interaction but not the converse. Vocalizations may be the channel used, but any channel (vocal or nonvocal) can be represented by language symbols. For example, nonverbal gestures can be described in words or their meanings can be coded by using symbolic notation.

The interaction we refer to is symbolic, using the medium of language and shared cultural meanings for the nonverbal gestures. We are specifically concerned with the words generated by the participants, although it is possible to include other aspects of the interaction by using words or other symbols to describe them. We expect that they use a shared language system in interacting with each other, but the sharing of meanings is not necessarily perfect for each word or statement. We assume only that there is *some* sharing; otherwise, continuing interaction would be impossible.

Each participant intends to convey some meaning when he speaks, but we cannot assume that his intended meaning is identical to the interpretation made by the other participant. It is essential only that there is a giving and a receiving of meanings.

The giver, as he talks, is communicating not only with the other but with himself. He monitors his own statements and reflects on them so that he attempts to determine whether he is saying what he intends to say. He is also involved in monitoring the responses of the other, and this aids him in determining whether his intended meanings are being similarly interpreted by the other. Feedback *to* the self *from* both the self and from the other with reference to the meanings of one's own behavior is a continual process in interaction.

The use of an already developed shared symbolic system, such as language, facilitates the interaction considerably. It means that the two participants do not have to build a language. By using a language they both know, they can show each other very quickly that they understand each other. The language system has its own structure (syntax) and set of meanings (semantics). If we, as observers, share the same language, it is possible for us to adopt their same framework for interpreting meanings. We can proceed as though we "know" what they are talking about. However, in practice, this assumption is not always borne out. Our participants can be speaking in a special code, they can be developing a set of new meanings using the same words that we all know, or they can be acting as though they are communicating with one another when, in fact, they are having serious difficulty understanding each other. As observers, we cannot be completely certain of what is going on in their interaction. We need to be aware that we may jump to the conclusion that we understand what they are talking about merely because we speak the same langauge as they do and can assign similar meanings to what they say.

The determination of the special idiosyncratic meanings that each participant holds is a formidable problem. We recognize that making such determinations is an important task and one that is of great concern to the therapist, for example, in trying to understand the patient. In this chapter I shall not attempt to solve this problem nor suggest how it might be solved. Instead, I shall start at the level of shared language and operate in terms of the understandings that we have about the same language that our participants are using. We shall use all that we know about the situation to assist us in understanding their interaction. If, for example, they perform special roles and if certain aspects of their behavior can be understood by reference to the characteristics of these roles as they are defined in the culture, then we shall want to include this information in any interpretive schema we apply to the project of "making sense" of their interaction. The fact that they are a therapist and a patient, for example, provides us with considerable knowledge concerning some of the meanings that may enter into their interaction. The therapist is involved in accomplishing certain goals, a major one being the production of talk by the patient. At the same time, he is trying to understand the patient, to discover the meanings of events as the patient perceives them, to instruct and even subtly guide the patient in interpreting and understanding the meanings of these same events from a new perspective, to provide interpretations of his own, and to suggest the connections between events that the patient may not understand. He is simultaneously involved in a number of tasks while talking about persons, events, and the present situation with the patient. The content of their interaction (the *what*) is one of the concerns of both parties; another concern is their method or strategy (the *how*). We must give some attention to this distinction in order to understand interaction, since all meaning does not reside in the content of what is being said.

We wish to work with a computer system for analyzing interaction despite the fact that we are aware of its limitations in dealing with complex data of the kind described. We want to approximate, if possible, some solutions to the problem of making sense out of the interaction of two persons who are engaged in a face-to-face interaction. We can draw on existing knowledge concerning the analysis of language and also try to include procedures that will help us to solve the problems that are of special relevance to face-to-face interaction. We recognize that we must include instructions to the computer so that the program can make the same interpretations of the language used by the participants as they themselves make. At one level, this involves discovering and programming that set of rules for analyzing language which is common to users of the same language. At another level, it involves analyzing the interaction in terms of the distinctive set of meanings which the particular individuals may be engaged in creating and developing through their continuing conversation. The rules that are built into a dictionary for assigning meanings to words, phrases, or sentences represent a theory of the way in which these words and phrases are understandable to those who use them. In explicating these rules, we can draw on all that is known about the language in question (English). We can draw from the extensive knowledge that exists concerning grammatical and syntactic structure, for example, in developing sets of rules for interpreting whether a word is a subject, noun, or verb, whether a person is being talked about or talked to, whether an action is being described as having occurred or as about to occur, and the like. Explicating general meanings—those known in common by "most" users of the language—is perhaps easier (though nonetheless complex) than explicating the idosyncratic meanings that may be held by these and only these two persons.

The distinction here is one between the subjects' own world of meanings, which serve as a framework for their making sense out of their continuing conversation, and the general set of meanings that any one of us, as users of the same language, would share. If we want to enter into their world of meanings so that the same sense which they make of their conversation can be understood by us, then we must make some effort to understand their meaning structures and their rules for "making sense."

At the present time, this task seems too difficult for us to handle. We shall be satisfied if we can capture the "common cultural meanings" and, by specifying these as rules, enable the computer to make similar interpretations. The meanings that any one of us would make if we were in the same situation and in the roles being performed are the meanings that we shall focus on.

We want to add the considerable information that comes from our knowing that the two persons are a patient and a therapist. We do not view them as just two people who are sitting and talking. Instead, we recognize that we are dealing with special roles and these roles carry with them some set of meanings that are properly designated as constituent elements of the role. How would anyone know that the person talking is a therapist? If he is playing that role, then there must be some patterns in his talk which are distinct and different from those of the patient or from those of any other kind of role found in a two-person interaction. He may show some patterns that are the same as those used by any speaker of the language, since he is speaking the same language as others. However, we want to look for the patterns that are special or what might be termed the constituent elements of the role of, say, therapist. If we can find these, then we shall be able to classify some of his talk in terms of the characteristic patterns that represent the therapist role. Similarly, with reference to the patient, we want to be able to classify some of his statements in terms of the key patterns that represent the patient role. In order to do this, we want to learn as much as we can about these two roles so that we can improve our chances of capturing the meanings of the statements generated by both parties in the interaction. Aside from an examination of the literature to learn what has been written about these roles, we want to experience actual verbal interactions, transcripts of therapy interviews, to determine the actual patterns of interaction via language that may occur. Our task of developing a dictionary for these two roles can thus be facilitated by examination of a set of data. That is, the task begins with the examination of interaction by persons in the same situation that we are studying.

MULTIPLE DICTIONARIES AND THE GENERAL INQUIRER

Given the characteristics of two-person interaction referred to above and given further that each participant has a different role to perform, multiple dictionaries are required to classify the content of the interaction.

Multiple rather than single dictionaries are needed in order to make classifications of the content and tactics of interaction by using different levels of interpretation, different units for classification and, in short, multiple modes of interpretation. General content dictionaries, such as the Harvard III Psycho-Sociological Dictionary, could be applied to the same data for which special-purpose dictionaries are also being used. Dictionaries designed to analyze selected aspects of the role of therapist and patient are one example of such special dictionaries. Any number of dictionaries, some overlapping with others, could be developed to tap particular dimensions of the content and tactics of interaction. The manner in which these different dimensions were interrelated would be a matter for further study but empirical determinations could be made if the several dictionaries could be applied to the same data and if all tagging was available for use in subsequent retrievals and analysis.

Heretofore, in the several uses of the GI system, only one dictionary has been applied to the set of data being processed. The dictionary could be fairly complex or relatively simple, but the basic strategy of every dictionary was to assign tags either to single words, words and phrases (idioms), or sentences. Because of limitations of programs and hardware, it has not been possible to use multiple dictionaries, each of which might use a different unit as the unit for tagging, in processing data with the General Inquirer System. In addition, the GI system was oriented to written text. As it was initially developed, the GI system allowed only word look-up so that tags were either assigned or not assigned to a word, depending on whether the word was in the dictionary. A Quick Dictionary in which were listed many frequently used words such as articles, determiners, and prepositions, assigned no tags but by virtue of being included in the dictionary, the word would not appear on the leftover list. A major revision of the GI system made it possible to tag idioms, that is, words which when used with other words would take on a different meaning from that of each of the words when used separately. Conditional tests, either for particular words or for tags within a specified range around a key word, became possible thereby extending the tagging system. However, it was not possible to include in the conditional test an examination of the ID field. Thus, the assignment of a particular tag could not be made conditional on the code in the ID field which might contain some reference to the characteristics of the source. Nor was it possible to test for final punctuation in a sentence and use the type of punctuation as part of the conditional. Eventually, Sentence Summary Tagging (SST) routines were added which made possible the assignment of tags to a sentence, depending on occurrence of specified tags in a specified sequence.[3] Such tags could even be assigned depending on the pattern of tags occurring in sequential sentences.

[3] These are reported by Ogilvie in his description of the Harvard Need-Achievement Dictionary (See Stone et al., 1966:191–206). Thus far, only tag tests are possible.

These limitations were of special significance for the analysis of dyadic interaction and only an expanded and revised GI system could solve them all. Goldhammer (Chapter 20, *infra*) has incorporated many of these changes in a revised and expanded GI tagging system (GIT). This version differs substantially from that described in the *User's Manual for the General Inquirer* (Stone et al., 1968), but is still restricted to 100 tags. Furthermore, the IBM 7094 has a core load dictionary which makes the use of large (over 4000 words) dictionaries difficult to process. The arrival of the IBM 360 Sytem made possible new flexibilities, and our experience with earlier versions of the GI suggested the necessity of others. Reference to some of these changes and the 360 system[4] will be made in this discussion to show how the analysis of dyadic interaction can be facilitated. Generally, we have been trying to solve the multiple dictionary problem with existing 7094 programs, but our revision of the GI system for the 360 system will solve the problem more directly and simply. This new system is now called Inquirer II.

We have been proceeding with the development of several dictionaries in order to analyze the interaction occurring between therapist and patient. Three different dictionaries will be described and the kinds of results that may be expected from their application will be indicated.

INTERPERSONAL IDENTIFICATION DICTIONARY

An example of a person-identification dictionary is the Interpersonal Identification Dictionary (IID), which we have developed for the analysis of the Wolberg case.[5] This type of dictionary, designed primarily to eliminate costly hand coding previously used to identify persons, classifies persons according to their relationship to the speaker. However, it requires information concerning the person named by the speaker, since it does not know who "Mary" is when the name is mentioned. Personal pronouns such as "he" and "she" are more difficult to identify, since their referents can change in the course of the interaction, although at least a classification of these as to sex role can be made. Self-references, using personal pronouns such as I, me, my, are somewhat easier to classify, since a check of who is speaking can indicate whether it is the doctor or the patient that is being referred to, although even this is not always accurate since indirect references can be made. Because such distinctions are important, two separate IID's are needed, one for each speaker. Thus, "John" may

[4] A more complete description and outline of the system is presented in Miller et al. (1967).

[5] The Wolberg case consists of nine verbatim transcripts of a brief intensive psychotherapy of a female patient treated and reported by Wolberg (1964).

be tagged FAMILY-OF-PROCREATION + MALE when mentioned by the patient but tagged only MALE when mentioned by the doctor, since he is not a member of the doctor's family. The person taken as the point of reference in the IID determines how the classification is to be made.

In order to classify persons, it is necessary to have information concerning the identity of all persons named in the interview or series of interviews. Since all the data are available, a quick reading is sufficient to select all proper names and personal pronouns that occur in the data. Basically, the IID represents the construction of a table of equivalences such as:

$$JOHN = HUSBAND$$
$$SAM = BROTHER$$
$$SUSAN = SISTER, \text{ etc.}$$

Each subsequent mention of the name is looked up in the dictionary and assigned to the appropriate category. It may be necessary to build context searches to make some classifications unambiguous, for example, "my wife" is not to be classified the same as "his wife." A backtest for particular pronouns may achieve this clarification. It is obvious that in the reading of the data to construct the IID, it is necessary to look for such context indicators so that conditional tests can be specified. Tags used in the patient IID for the Wolberg case are listed in Figure 1.

The immediate context does not always provide the indicators that are sufficient to classify persons. Consider the following example from

Tag Number	
87	LOWER STATUS
88	EQUAL STATUS
89	HIGHER STATUS
90	MALE
91	FEMALE
92	FAMILY OF PROCREATION
93	FAMILY OF ORIENTATION
94	FRIENDS
95	LOVE OBJECTS
96	PERSONAL AUTHORITY FIGURES
97	SELF
98	THERAPIST
99	IMPERSONAL

Figure 1 Patient Interpersonal Identification Dictionary.

a Wolberg interview to see how a named person can be identified in terms of his relationship to the speaker.

123 PT.: And I was talking to *an old friend of mine. She's* the one that recommended you. *She* said you helped *her* a lot and *she* was sure you could help me.

124 DR.: You would really like to get rid of this trouble?

125 PT.: Doctor, there is nothing I wouldn't do to get rid of it. Life doesn't mean anything, you know, the way things are going.

126 DR.: How did you come to the conclusion that it was your nerves that were at fault?

127 PT.: Well, doctor, you know *Mrs. Henshaw* and I'm very fond of her, and I've seen how she's come along so nicely that I thought that maybe I could get something out of it, too.

In 123, the patient indicates the nature of the relationship (an old friend) but does not name the person until 127 (Mrs. Henshaw). For the purposes of an IID, Mrs. Henshaw can be classified as FRIEND, FEMALE. (When the therapist refers to Mrs. Henshaw, the same tags could be applied so long as it is clear that the relationship is defined with reference to the patient.)

If an IID were not available, the program would have no way of knowing that this word is the name of a person rather than just another word. Capitalization is a common way of indicating proper names in writing, but if capitals are not available or not used in inputting data, then this device is not possible. Even if capitals were used, how is Henshaw to be distinguished from Florida—both are names, but one of a person and the other of a place—unless all possible names were to be included in the dictionary? One might note the presence of "Mrs." in front of "Henshaw" as a clue to a person. Thus a backtest for titles of address conceivably could resolve the ambiguity of whether "Henshaw" is a word or a person. The problem would remain if a first name, "Mary", were used to refer to her instead of a last name. And what if the last name were used without a title preceding it?

One approach to solving the problem is to provide the computer with a way of distinguishing names of persons from places and then asking "Who is that?" or "What is that?" or "Where is that?"[6] In interacting with the content analyst, the computer could wait for this clarification

---

[*] *Editor's note.* The Casimir Borkowski paper, which was not available at the conference, is included herein as Chapter 28 and focuses explicitly on this problem.

before proceeding. Otherwise, it would put this word on the leftover list together with all others not found in the dictionaries.

An alternative would be to provide rules for searching the context, possibly extending back to the preceding statements, to reduce the ambiguity concerning who Mrs. Henshaw is.

In the example given, in 123, the patient's second statement refers to an old friend as "she." To classify the pronoun "she" in terms of more than the tag FEMALE, a backtest to the preceding sentence is necessary. When the word "friend" is found, the tags FEMALE and FRIEND could be applied. This procedure would not necessarily be correct if the sentences were:

> . . . *my mother's old friend. She was a great help to me . . .*

since it would not be clear from a backtest whether "she" referred to "mother" or to "mother's friend." The elaboration of the rules for making such disambiguations remains a major problem. We wish to point to the possibility of solutions for this problem if procedures similar to Stone's disambiguation rules were followed. The problem of defining relationships for personal pronouns may be approached in a manner similar to the clarification of word senses. An analysis of the context in which persons' names occur should yield a set of rules for distinguishing persons from places.[7]

It can therefore be seen that the construction of an Interpersonal Identification Dictionary (IID) involves not only the development of a set of tags defining the types of relationships that are of particular interest to the investigator but also the development of procedures for disambiguating whether a word refers to a person and what that person's relationship to the participant in the conversation is. The basic notion behind an IID is similar to that found in preliminary stages of interpersonal relationships: the identification of particular persons so that "we" (the persons involved in the dialogue) know who we are talking about. Persons are then known to "us" when subsequently referred to. The specific sense of a conversation involving named others depends on our sharing the same set of meanings about who these other persons are. Separate IID's involve, in addition, the notion that my view is different from your view and that others do not stand in the same relation to me as they do to you, although they may, for certain purposes, be the same to "us." The elaboration of these special distinctions is important. Also, the same problem is involved in developing special meanings for words that we use in a developing conversation, that is, the creation of a common culture. What words mean to "us" as we use them may be somewhat different from what they mean

---

[7] The procedure would be similar to the strategy reported by Philip J. Stone (Chapter 11, *infra*) on disambiguating different word senses.

to others. We may want to increment a general dictionary with the specific meanings that our words have for us. If so, the problem of incrementing and modifying a dictionary of words is similar to that of defining names for an IID, as outlined above. Names of persons are most similar to the kinds of words that, although they exist in the language, can be defined differently for each person, depending on his relationship to the person named. The general problem is similar to the problem of learning programs, that is, programs that can acquire a new concept and add it to what they already "know." Some information about the new name must be obtained before it can be assimilated into the set of meanings (dictionary) already in use or have a new meaning (tag) added to the dictionary.

THERAPIST TACTICS DICTIONARY (TTD)

Another type of dictionary is one that tries to classify the tactics of interaction rather than the content. A different unit (such as the sentence, utterance, or that burst of speech sandwiched between the other person's preceding and succeeding remarks) may be the unit to be classified. For example, one may wish to classify statements according to whether they are interrogative, exclamatory, or declarative. Such classifications may then be tabulated in order to describe some aspects of a person's interaction style. In the need achievement analysis, Ogilvie examined sequences of sentences in order to determine the presence of achievement imagery (in Stone, et al., 1966). Similarly, a therapist's statement can be examined in order to classify it in terms of interaction strategies or tactics such as the therapist's use of open-ended probes.

An example of such a dictionary is illustrated by our development of a Therapist Tactics Dictionary (TTD), which is designed to examine and classify the tactics used by the therapist. Content patterns are determined by the presence of combinations of words and/or tags, the sequence in which they occur in the sentence, and the presence or absence of other formal markers that designate whether the sentence is a question or statement, positive or negative.

It is also possible to define some tactics on the word level. For these, a tag is constructed which contains all words identified as belonging to that tactic. An example is the tag DIRECT-PRAISE which includes words and phrases such as fine, good, very well, and excellent.

This dictionary was developed out of our previous work (Psathas and Arp, 1966; Arp, 1967) that analyzed therapy-analog interviews by using the earlier (1962) version of the GI. Retrievals were made for subject of the sentence and the presence of particular words. These retrievals

Part I	Part II	Part III
Function Words (01–42)	*Tactic Relevant Words (43–81)*	*Sentence Summary Tags (84–93)*

Part I	Part II	Part III
01 Determiners (2–15)	43 Direct Praise	84 Direct Question
02 Articles		85 Statement
03 Demonstratives	44 Openers	86 Negative
04 Demon. I		87 Positive
05 Demon. II	45 Tentativity	88 Probing Reflection
		89 Prodding Suggestion
06 Possessives (7–10)	46 Question Triggers	91 Direct Praise
07 2nd Person		92 Agreement
08 1st Single	47 Special Verbs (48–51)(67)	93 Disagreement
09 1st Plural	48 Tell	
10 3rd Person	49 Remember	
	50 Think	
11 Numbers (12–13)	51 Feel	
12 Numbers Ordinal		
13 Numbers Cardinal	52 Prepositions	
14 Negative (no, none)	53 Conjunctions	
15 Prearticle		
	54 Not (NOT)	
16 Pronouns (17–31)		
17 Personal (18–28)	55 Space Reference	
18 Nonreflexive (19–23)		
19 You	56 Time Reference	
20 I, me		
21 We, us	57 Quantity Reference	
22 Others I		
23 Others II	58 Quality Reference	
24 Reflexive (25–28)		
25 Yourself	59 Emotional State	
26 Reflexive I		
27 Reflexive We	60 Continue	
28 Reflexive Other		
29 Impersonal (30–31)	61 Begin	
30 Nonreflex. Impersonal		
31 Reflex. Impersonal	62 Want	
32 Auxiliary Verbs (32–39)	63 Mean	
33 To be		
34 To do	64 Let	
35 To have		
36 To be able to	65 Mild Agreement	
37 Should (shall, should, ought)		
38 Volition (will, would)	66 Regular Agreement	
39 Must		
	67 Know	
40 Adverbs (41–42)		
41 Time	68 Summarize	
42 Positional-Spatial		
	69 Compare-Contrast	
	80 Ability Potential	
	81 Open-ended Modifier	

Figure 2   Therapist Tactics Dictionary.

448

were used to build new tags which could then be used in subsequent retrievals.

The strategy in the Therapist Tactics Dictionary (TTD) is more flexible since the 1966 GI is used including Sentence Summary Tagging (SST). A dictionary has been devised (see Figure 2) which includes the feature of tagging some words according to their grammatical function and others according to their relevance for therapist tactics. The first part of the dictionary serves a function similar to the marker words which Stone has described in his disambiguation project. In fact, many of our tags are similar, since we had exchanged ideas during the early stages of this work although we had arrived somewhat independently at a list of necessary markers.

As Figure 2 shows, auxiliary verbs are divided into seven subclasses (be, do, have, able, should, volition, and must). Each subclass may contain one or more verbs. It is thus possible to instruct the computer to distinguish between the statements "You should do X" and "You have done X" by referring to the appropriate subclass of auxiliary verbs.

To illustrate how the TTD may be used to classify a sentence, consider the following types of statements made by the therapist, which we call *probing*.

Probing

What did you think of that?
You mean you think that is necessary.
Then you are saying in all these ways you are different from him.
Or are you telling me that is what he thought?

A number of these sentences were collected from our earlier study and were examined to determine what patterns of words and/or tags, in what sequence, and within what range of one another could be found. Four basic types of PROBING statements were defined. These were defined as follows for Sentence Summary Tagging.

Probing Type

I. IF (OCCUR1(33,0).AND.OCCUR3(81,0,2))

II. IF   ((OCCUR3(19,0,4).OR.(OCCUR1)44,0).AND.OCCUR2 (19,0))).AND.OCCUR2(47,0))

III. IF   ((OCCUR3(19,0,4).OR.(OCCUR1(44,0).AND.OCCUR2 (19,0)).AND.OCCUR2(32,0).AND.OCCUR2(47,0))

IV. IF (OCCUR1(30,0).AND.OCCUR2(63,0).AND.OCCUR2 (19,0))

The sentence summary tagging is written in FORTRAN IV, and the instructions are defined in the *User's Manual for the General Inquirer.* Basically,

OCCUR1 (TAG, SYNTAX-CODE) starts the scan at the beginning of the sentence and tests for the tag indicated.

OCCUR2 (TAG, SYNTAX-CODE) continues the scan and tests for the tag indicated.

OCCUR3 (TAG, SYNTAX-CODE, RANGE) continues the scan for words within the range.

Other instructions of the SST are also available but are not listed here. Let us examine Type-I PROBING to see how it works. Type I: if tag 33 (an auxiliary verb, to be), regardless of its syntax code, is found and is followed by tag 81 (an open-ended modifier), one or two words later, the sentence is classified as PROBING. If this test fails, then the next one is attempted.

Is there anything else that you can remember?
33   81
Are there some other things you can recall?
33   81

Type-III PROBING would be found if [tag 19 (YOU) were found within the first four words of the sentence] or [if the sentence began with tag 44 (OPENER) and were followed by tag 19 (YOU)] and then tag 32 (any AUXILIARY-VERB) and tag 47 (any SPECIAL-VERB) were found.

Examples

Then you are saying in all these ways you are different from him.
44 19 32 47
You were telling about his episode.
19 32 47

The tag order and tag occurrence are considered. In examining the way the language is used, it often turns out that sequences determine certain word usages. For instance, the syntactic structure of the sentence is largely determined by the sequence. Thus, if "YOU" occurs in the above two sentences, in either the first or second word position, it is probable that it will be the subject of the sentence. By this kind of detailed analysis of sentence structure and the construction of a set of specifications, we begin to detect patterns of usage of the language that we had not noticed before, and some of our classification problems are thereby solved.

As the interaction proceeds, it is desirable not only to notice the number of probes generated by the therapist but also to notice the types of patient statements that follow these probes. To do this, it is necessary to make some classification of patient statements, either in terms of general content or of patient tactics. We are engaged in formulating a Patient Tactics Dictionary (PTD), which would classify the patient's statements into categories including many that have been of major theoretical concern in the study of psychotherapy, (for example, resistance, ambivalence, and intellectualizing). Although these categories are generally defined more broadly and take a larger context into account, we are looking for operational equivalents on the sentence level.

The TTD and the PTD are separate dictionaries which are looked up depending on which person is speaking. Prior tagging by a general-purpose dictionary is assumed, since some conditional tests using these dictionaries are based on tags that have previously been assigned. Thus, there is a sequence of tagging involving several dictionaries. One of the first would be a dictionary that assigns tags according to their grammatical function (see the first 42 tags in the TTD, Figure 2). Another would be a general psychological-content dictionary. Both of these dictionaries are general in scope with tags assigned by either or both dictionaries available to be used in conditionals in succeeding passes. The strategy for tagging would be to run those dictionaries last that are dependent on earlier-assigned tags. Such a multiple-pass processing of multiple dictionaries is another method for achieving what has long been sought in GI tagging, namely, forward tests. Heretofore, tagging conditional on tags or words that *followed* the key word was not possible. (Goldhamer has recently added this feature to the GI 7094 version by use of elaborate iterative procedures.)

THE PSYCHOLOGICAL CONTENT DICTIONARY (PSYCODIC)

PSYCODIC is still another dictionary involved in the analysis. The list of tags that it contains is given in Figure 3. Because this dictionary is similar in basic philosophy to the Harvard III Dictionary for Psycho-Sociological Content, less space will be devoted to its discussion.

This dictionary is designed to classify words and phrases occurring in the therapy interview situation according to general social psychological theory. The level of meaning is the more overt or denotative level but not necessarily that which the patient himself would adopt. It is closer to the meanings that the therapist would use as he interprets the psychological significance of the content. It was developed after the examination of Key-Word-In-Context printouts of many therapy interviews, and there-

Tag 01 Age and/or Time	Tag 46 Action Direction
Tag 03 Body Parts	Tag 47 Approach
Tag 04 Internal Body Parts	Tag 48 Avoid
Tag 05 External Body Parts	Tag 49 Action Achievement
Tag 06 Genital Body Parts	Tag 50 Success
Tag 07 Somatic Conditions	Tag 51 Failure
Tag 08 Health	Tag 52 Cognitive Processes
Tag 09 Illness	Tag 53 Contemplative
Tag 10 Death	Tag 54 Cognitive Awareness
Tag 11 Treatments	Tag 55 Uncertainty
Tag 12 Tests	Tag 56 Decisiveness
Tag 13 Nonspecific References	Tag 57 Regard
Tag 14 Object Orientation	Tag 58 Positive
Tag 15 Retaining	Tag 59 Negative
Tag 16 Expelling	Tag 60 Fortune
Tag 17 Attaining	Tag 61 Good
Tag 18 Gender	Tag 62 Misfortune
Tag 19 Male	Tag 63 Emotional Type
Tag 20 Female	Tag 64 Anger
Tag 21 Neuter	Tag 65 Affection Present
Tag 22 Authority Figures	Tag 66 Affection Absent
Tag 23 Treatment-Guidance	Tag 67 Fear and Apprehension
Tag 24 Legal	Tag 68 Happiness
Tag 25 Sensory Perceptions	Tag 69 Sadness
Tag 26 Visual	Tag 70 Distress and Arousal
Tag 27 Auditory	Tag 71 Positive Emotional Value
Tag 28 Gustatory	Tag 72 Negative Emotional Value
Tag 29 Olfactory	Tag 73 Undefined Need States
Tag 30 Dermal	Tag 74 Obstacles
Tag 31 Action Norm	Tag 75 Present
Tag 32 Passive	Tag 76 Struggle Against
Tag 33 Active	Tag 82 Self
Tag 34 Overt Sexual Acts	Tag 83 Specific Others
Tag 35 Sexual Action	Tag 99 Nonspecific Others
Tag 36 Fore-Play	
Tag 37 Pre-Fore-Play	
Tag 38 Social Action	
Tag 39 Aggressive	
Tag 40 Friendly	
Tag 41 Isolative	
Tag 42 Communicative	
Tag 43 Dominative	
Tag 44 Submissive	
Tag 45 Helping	

Figure 3   Tag categories of the Psychological Content Dictionary.

fore is able to classify the content of verbal interaction better than the dictionaries developed for the analysis of written text. It is designed to classify both the patient's and the therapist's verbal statements and to facilitate the development and subsequent testing of hypotheses concerning the content of interaction in psychotherapy. In subseqent studies, it would be possible to compare the results from the use of PSYCODIC with either general- or special-purpose dictionaries applied to the same data.

PSYCODIC incorporates the multiple dictionary principle by use of subsets of tags. A subset of tags consists of a header tag (called a supertag) and one or more subheadings (called minitags). An entry word (or phrase) may be assigned to one or more supertags and to one or more minitags on a list. For example, consider the two tag lists 38 SOCIAL ACTION and 34 OVERT SEXUAL ACTS.

Supertag	34 OVERT SEX	38 SOCIAL ACTION
Minitags	35 SEXUAL ACTION	39 AGGRESSIVE
	36 FORE-PLAY	40 FRIENDLY
	37 PRE-FORE-PLAY	41 ISOLATIVE
		42 COMMUNICATIVE
		43 DOMINATIVE
		44 SUBMISSIVE
		45 HELPING

The entry words are assigned as follows.

$$\text{hug} = 34, 37, 38, 40$$
$$\text{molest} = 34, 36, 38, 39$$
$$\text{date} = 34, 37, 38, 40$$
$$\text{embrace} = 34, 37, 38, 40$$

Each of these entry words is assigned the supertag (underlined) associated with the list. Each entry word is also assigned one or more minitags as necessary. The general principle, then, is that every word is assigned a supertag and only in instances where a word may not be clearly defined by one or more minitags will it be assigned no minitag at all. Entry words on one list do not necessarily have to appear on any other tag list.

In certain respects, each supertag list can be regarded as a separate dictionary. The fact that all are included in what is called one dictionary is an indication that they are designed to be used together and that some interrelationships exist among the tags. As an example, in the case of

PSYCODIC, we are interested in determining relationships between tags such as 38 SOCIAL ACTION, 52 COGNITIVE PROCESSES, and 63 EMOTIONAL TYPE. The frequency and patterning of co-occurrences can be examined for the set of data being analyzed. Since the same dictionary is being applied to both participants in the interaction (the therapist and the patient), it is possible to determine similarities and differences between them. We can try to determine the extent to which they are talking about the same things. That is, if patient statements include co-occurrences of ANGER and UNCERTAINTY, do the therapist's statements also show the same patterning? Do similar proportions of the sentences generated by each contain the same tags? Are co-occurrence patterns similar within the sentences generated by each participant? For example, does the therapist's pattern more frequently contain ANGER plus COGNITIVE AWARENESS? Does this indicate that he is trying to get the patient to think about and become more aware of his feeling of hostility? Validating interpretations of patterns will depend on retrievals done specifically for that purpose. PSYCODIC offers the possibility of interpretations relating to the psychological significance of the interaction and to the assessment of changes in the patient's functioning as these are reflected in the content of his talk.

PROCEDURES

Now let us examine some of the system requirements and specific pro-
described.
cedures involved in the kind of multiple dictionary look-up being

1. The source of a statement must be identified in order that the appropriate dictionary(ies) will be searched. For example, if the speaker is the therapist then the Therapist Tactics Dictionary rather than the Patient's will be searched. It is also possible for the assignment of tags within any dictionary to be conditional on the particular characteristics of the speaker that may be coded into the ID field, such as age, sex, social class, and demographic and psychological characteristics. For example, if the speaker is a young child, references to Family will more likely be Family of Orientation.

2. Some tags may be assigned conditional on words and/or tags in the previous sentence or on the utterance generated by the previous speaker. For example, the distinction between proaction and reaction made by Bales (1953) in scoring interaction was in terms of whether the previous statement was spoken by a different speaker (reaction) or by the same speaker (proaction). In analyzing the relation between therapist tac-

tics and succeeding patient statements in order to assess the effects of particular therapist tactics, a check for the source of the previous statement is necessary.

Depending on the content and the source of the previous statement, particular tags may be assigned. For example, if the previous utterance was by a different speaker, and if it included particular content references, then Tactic A may be assigned. However, if the previous utterance was by the same speaker on the same content topic, then Tactic B may be assigned. Thus, it becomes necessary to store, temporarily, the previous statement in order to allow a comparison to be made at the time the next statement is ready for classification. In this way the source and the content of the statement can be examined to determine whether conditional specifications have been met.

However, we are aware that, in interaction, the meaning of a statement may depend on a whole series of prior statements as well as on subsequent statements. Thus it would be ideal if several statements, and not just the preceding one, could be examined before the next one was tagged. Forward checks pose more difficult problems, since the statement must be stored until subsequent statements are examined. For example, a "How are you," spoken by the therapist, may be taken as a greeting or as a question about one's state of health. The manner in which it is taken by the responding other cannot be known until he responds. If his response is "Fine, how are you," then the original statement may be classified as a greeting. If he answers at length about his health, it may be taken as a probe concerning health. A more common solution in computer content analysis has been to classify the statement as having both meanings or, if that is not satisfactory, to select the more frequent meaning. In interaction, however, the crucial question is what sense is made of the statement by those who hear it and respond to it. Its meaning lies in its use, that is, the work that it does in the context of the interaction. This can be determined by observing its antecedents and its consequents. The response of others tells us how they are interpreting it and what it means to them in the context.

The prospective-retrospective nature of meaning cannot be handled to our satisfaction unless forward *and* backward conditionals are possible. If only retrospective conditionals are possible, then the intent of the speaker must be guessed and used as the major basis for classification. If prospective conditionals were possible, then the response of the other could be used together with the guessed intent of the speaker in deciding on the classification. A possible solution is what might be called "tentative tagging." That is, tags are assigned but are held subject to change after some specified sequence of next statements. In the above example, if the discussion of health and physical symptoms followed the "How are you," then the greeting could be retagged as a health probe. Obviously, the specification of which tags are tentative and for how long they are to be so regarded involves the investigator in the elaboration of his theory of meanings. In fact, the entire set of procedures being outlined here represent a direct confrontation of the issues involved in determining how humans actually do interact and how they themselves assign meanings to communications.

3. Because the number of tags assigned in such multiple dictionaries is enormous, some means for reducing these numbers in making summary tabulations is necessary. For example, supertags, which represent major content categories, can be used for summary purposes rather than minitags, which are subcategories. We have used these distinctions in TTD and PSYCODIC, for example, to be able to examine major category frequencies before deciding whether to look within the category to its various subclasses; for instance, the supertag PRONOUNS can be examined to determine what its frequency is before looking within it to subdistinctions between types of pronouns (PERSONAL, IMPERSONAL). In PSYCODIC, the supertag SOCIAL-ACTION can be tabulated without showing a breakdown for AGGRESSIVE, FRIENDLY, COMMUNICATIVE, and the like. For both supertags and minitags, it is possible to make comparisons with specified comparison groups such as base rates, previous sessions, or ideal norms. For example, it should be possible to determine what topics are being "avoided" as well as which ones are "high" in comparison with specified norms.

Contingencies and interrelationships between content categories can be calculated and reported. Thus, the association of particular content themes with each other within a specifiable unit, such as an interview or over several sessions, could be calculated. For example: Has there been any change in the reporting of symptoms, of relationships with particular other persons, or in the descriptions of past experiences? Indices of change can be reflected in the interrelationships between tags over time.

4. A comparison of the interaction of two speakers is necessary so that a matrix can report the kinds of statements (tactics or content) generated by one speaker which are followed or preceded by particular statements by the other. In keeping track of what is classified, it should be possible to indicate, for example, whether patient intellectualization follows particular therapist tactics, such as interpretation or open-ended probes more frequently. The requirements for making such a classification are different from those of an ordinary tag tally or sentence-retrieval system. In this instance, a matrix operation of some kind is needed so that, for every therapist tactic, a count is kept of what patient tactic follows. We

can call this an "interaction map." A similar notion was involved in Bales (1953) tables of proaction and reaction in which he tried to show which Interaction Process Analysis category followed another category. In this way, the probability that one type of category would follow another could be empirically described.

The same kind of interaction mapping should be possible for the general content of the interaction as classified by the PSYCODIC. The question here is whether certain content patterns go together. Are they "talking about the same thing" or are they diverging?

CONCLUSION

Considering the features of two-person interaction presented initially, the strategy of multiple dictionaries for special purposes and including different types of units for tagging represents an approach to the special problems posed by this kind of data. We do not feel that all issues have been satisfactorily solved. However, with the advent of new hardware, in the form of the IBM System 360, and the development of more flexible software that will allow such procedures as forward tests as well as back tests, larger dictionaries with a larger number of tags (as well as a larger number of dictionaries), and multiple passes of the same data so that dictionaries used in a second pass can include conditional tests for tags applied in a previous pass, some solutions have been achieved.[8] Contributions to the extension and development of the General Inquirer can be expected from the effort to analyze different kinds of data. A foremost consideration in any such development is the prior attention to the characteristics of the data. The next extension of the General Inquirer that can be anticipated is the analysis of interaction as it is generated in an interactive mode, on-line to computer. The interaction may be between two persons at remote in-put devices or between a person and a stored program in the computer. The aim of such a system would be to analyze

[8] Each of these requirements is being incorporated into the 360 system, Inquirer II, in order to facilitate the analysis of interaction. They will extend the capability of the system for handling conventional text materials as well. Inquirer II will run under IBM's Operating System (OS) with PL/1. Dictionaries are contained on a disk, drum, or core and a maximum of $256 \times 256 = 65,536$ tags (enough to accommodate any present user) can be used. Data tagged in one pass can be used as input in another tagging run. The context that can be checked in deciding on what tags to apply can include any or all of the following: backward and forward checks for words and tags; sequence of words and tags; terminal punctuation; ordinal position of the word within a sentence; characters in the ID field; and the syntax assigned to a word or tag. See the detailed description of the system in Miller et al. (1967).

interaction in-process, that is, as it occurred. Classifications of the content would be made according to various stored dictionaries, summary tables could be made, statistics could be computed, and feedback could be provided to one or both of the participants. The system would assume some of the characteristics found in teaching programs, (for example, computer aided instruction). To allow for increments to stored dictionaries, particularly dictionaries such as IID described here, some features of learning programs must be included. That is, the system would have to be able to interrogate the user in order to obtain information concerning how new words, not previously placed in a dictionary, could be tagged.

The classification and analysis of interaction, as it proceeds, presents a more challenging problem but one that can be solved as computers expand in capacity and as time sharing becomes more and more feasible. Solutions to the problems of analyzing interaction, as described in this chapter, can contribute to the further extension of the system so that data generated in on-going interaction can also be analyzed.

25 Automatic Content Analysis in Information Retrieval[1]

Gerard Salton

Computer Science
Cornell University

Information retrieval is a field that is concerned with the structure, analysis, organization, storage, searching, and retrieval of information. An information retrieval system operates, on the one hand, in conjunction with a stored collection of items and, on the other, with a user population desiring to obtain access to the stored items. The system is thus designed to extract from the files the items that most nearly correspond to existing user needs as reflected in requests submitted by the user population. A library that stores books and serves a population of customers is, then (among other things), an example of an information retrieval system.

Conceptually, it is possible to reduce the operations of a typical information retrieval system to two main types: *information analysis,* and *information search* and retrieval. Information analysis consists, normally, in identifying each stored item and each search request by assigning to it one or more *content indicators* designed to reflect the information content, or the property set, which characterizes the given information item. Information search and retrieval is mainly a matching operation between content indicators attached to stored items and indicators attached to search requests, followed by the retrieval of those items whose content indicators exhibit a sufficiently high degree of similarity with the query indicators. In a library environment, where the stored items are books or documents, the information analysis normally produces for each item one or more classification numbers or, alternatively, one or more keywords or index terms, and the retrieval operation is preceded by a comparison of these sets of classification numbers, or keywords, or terms.

In most operational situations, the content analysis of the stored items and search requests is manually conducted by using, for this purpose, trained cataloguers and indexers, or trained subject experts. The aim of the analysis is to pick, for each item, some set of identifiers that best reflects

[1] This study was supported in part by the National Science Foundation under Grant GN-495.

459

the interests of the expected user population. Obviously, several different types of *indexing strategies* can be picked: the content analysis may be quite exhaustive, resulting in a large set of quite specific content indicators or, alternatively, the analysis may be less detailed, resulting in a smaller set of more general indicators. In the former case, the corresponding retrieval system is likely to produce *high precision* (but low recall) in that most retrieved items will, in fact, be pertinent to the given query (but some pertinent ones may not be retrieved at all); in the latter case, *high recall* (but low precision) may result, since a search might then produce most everything that is relevant (together with many items that may not be). Compromises are generally made in picking an idexing strategy so as to obtain both a reasonably high recall while holding the precision to within tolerable limits.

Although the information analysis is generally performed manually, the information search (that is, the comparison between analyzed items and analyzed search requests) is often mechanized in that a computerized file of stored items is automatically searched and retrieved items are displayed without manual intervention.

The experimental SMART document-retrieval system differs from most presently operating systems in that both the analysis and the search and matching operations are performed automatically. Specifically, documents and search requests are stored as abstracts, paragraphs, or sentences in English, and automatic language analysis procedures are used to generate the content identifiers for each stored item. The search and retrieval operations are also conducted automatically by comparing the respective sets of content identifiers for stored documents and incoming search requests.

In the remainder of this chapter, the content analysis problem arising in information retrieval is briefly outlined. Thereafter, the principal analysis operations incorporated into the SMART system are examined, and their effectiveness in a retrieval environment is described. An attempt is made to contrast the automatic procedures with alternative methods used in manual systems.

THE CONTENT ANALYSIS PROBLEM

Before describing the operations of the SMART system, it is useful to introduce a distinction between two different types of automatic text processing systems: the *text inference* systems and the *text retrieval* systems. A text inference system is one where one or more written texts are studied, for their own sake, with the aim of confirming or denying a previously established hypothesis. For example, the hypothesis might be that a given text of unknown authorship was, in fact, written by author A or author

B; such a hypothesis might be confirmed by comparing the unknown text with texts known to have been written by A or by B. Alternatively, the hypothesis might be that the verbal utterances contained in a given written transcript might have been made by a schizophrenic person rather than a normal one; or, that a given political manifesto reflects the Republican party platform more closely than the Democratic one. In each case, an investigator has made some hypothetical guesses, and a study of the corresponding texts is used to supply evidence from which the truth or falsity of the guesses can be inferred.

In a *text retrieval* system, on the other hand, the texts are not normally studied for their own sake but, instead, they constitute a commodity that is to be distributed to a given user population on demand. No hypothesis is formulated in advance, and the texts are analyzed only to determine whether they fit the user's description of what he wants.

Superficially, the two types of systems are somewhat similar, since the same operations are used in both systems (as shown in the flow chart of Figure 1). Search requests, or hypothetical statements, are introduced; then they are transformed into components acceptable to the system, often by using authority lists or dictionaries of various kinds. The resulting sets of content indicators (termed "concept vectors" in Figure 1) are

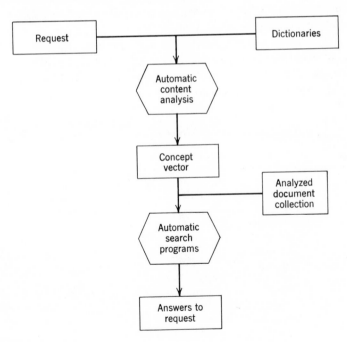

Figure 1 Simplified text processing system.

then compared with the content indicators of a given information store, and items are extracted from the store if the respective content indicators assigned to the stored items match the query indicators sufficiently well.

Actually, fundamental distinctions exist between text inference and text retrieval systems as outlined in Table 1. In a text inference system, the users of the system have a well-defined aim, which is generally known in advance; as a result, specialized procedures can be called into play which are specifically chosen to handle the particular problem at hand. In a text retrieval system, on the other hand, the user class is often much larger (and, in any case, much more heterogeneous), and its particular interests and concerns are not generally known. A text retrieval system must then be prepared to perform a content analysis which produces acceptable results for a wide class of users of diverse interests, whereas an inference system can attack the problem at hand much more directly.

As a result, the content analysis tools of the inference system, including dictionaries, tables, and thesauruses, can often be tailored to the specific problem in that they reflect the investigators' theories relating to the available verbal data (Stone et al., 1966). In the retrieval situation, no theories may be said to exist, other than a general knowledge of the language structure, and the dictionaries then take the form of general language processing tools, designed to recognize the regularities that exist over relatively wide ranges of texts in a given subject area. The analysis in the latter case may then be likened to a type of macroanalysis, where an attempt is made to recognize the more important synonymous elements, and the principal subject-verb-object construction of the text, as opposed to a microanalysis which would use each available word or particle.

Table 1. *Principal differences between text inference and text retrieval systems*

	Text Inference	Text Retrieval
Search request	Hypothesis made by one or more investigators	Requests for information made by a given user population
User population	Investigators interested in text study	Customer population desiring access to information store
Query type	Generally oriented in a specific direction	Often unknown in advance
Content analysis	Specialized toward solution of a given problem	General in order to fit heterogenous user population

The main content analysis operations incorporated into the SMART document retrieval system are outlined in the next few sections, and differences with a typical mechanized text inference system, such as the General Inquirer, are pointed out (Stone et al., 1966; Stone, 1963; Salton and Lesk, 1965a.; and Salton, 1965b.).

THE SMART SYSTEM

SMART is a fully automatic document retrieval system operating on the IBM 7094. Unlike other computer-based retrieval systems, the SMART system does not rely on manually assigned key words or index terms for the identification of documents and search requests, nor does it use primarily the frequency of occurrence of certain words or phrases included in the texts of documents. Instead, an attempt is made to go beyond simple word-matching procedures by using a variety of intellectual aids in the form of synonym dictionaries, hierarchial arrangements of subject identifiers, statistical and syntactic phrase generation methods, and the like in order to obtain the content identifications useful for the retrieval process.

Stored documents and search requests are then processed *without any prior manual analysis* by one of several hundred automatic content analysis methods, and the documents that most nearly match a given search request are extracted from the document file in answer to the request. The system may be controlled by the user, in that a search request can be processed first in a standard mode; the user can then analyze the output obtained and, depending on his further requirements, order a reprocessing of the request under new conditions. The new output can again be examined and the process iterated until the right kind and amount of information are retrieved (Salton, 1968a.).

SMART is thus designed as an experimental automatic retrieval system of the kind that may become current in operational environments some years hence. The following facilities, incorporated into the SMART system for purposes of document analysis, are of principal interest.

(a) A system for separating English words into *stems* and *affixes* (the so-called *suffix "s"* and *stem thesaurus* methods) which can be used to construct document identifications consisting of the stems of words contained in the documents.

(b) A synonym dictionary, or *thesaurus*, which can be used to recognize synonyms by replacing each word stem by one or more "concept" numbers; these concept numbers then serve as content identifiers instead of the original word stems.

(c)   A *hierarchical arrangement* of the concepts included in the thesaurus which makes it possible, given any concept number, to find its "parents" in the hierarchy, its "sons," its "brothers," and any of a set of possible cross references; the hierarchy can be used to obtain more general content identifiers than the ones originally given by going *up* in the hierarchy, more specific ones by going *down,* and a set of related ones by picking up brothers and cross-references.

(d)   *Statistical procedures* to compute similarity coefficients based on co-occurrences of concepts within the sentences of a given collection; the related concepts, determined by statistical association, can then be added to the originally available concepts to identify the various documents.

(e)   *Syntactic analysis* methods which make it possible to compare the syntactically analyzed sentences of documents and search requests with a precoded dictionary of syntactic structures ("criterion trees") in such a way that the same concept number is assigned to a large number of semantically equivalent, but syntactically quite different constructions.

(f)   *Statistical phrase* matching methods which operate like the preceding syntactic phrase procedures, that is, by using a pre-constructed dictionary to identify phrases used as content identifiers; however, no syntactic analysis is performed in this case, and phrases are defined as equivalent if the concept numbers of all components match, regardless of the syntactic relationships between components.

(g)   A *dictionary updating* system, designed to revise the several dictionaries included in the system:

(1)   Word stem dictionary.

(2)   Word suffix dictionary.

(3)   Common word dictionary (for words to be deleted during analysis).

(4)   Thesaurus (synonym dictionary).

(5)   Concept hierarchy.

(6)   Statistical phrase dictionary.

(7)   Syntactic ("criterion") phrase dictionary.

The operations of the system are built around a supervisory system which decodes the input instructions and arranges the processing sequence in accordance with the instructions received. The SMART systems organization makes it possible to evaluate the effectiveness of the various processing methods by comparing the outputs produced by a variety of different runs. This is achieved by processing the same search requests against the same document collections several times, and making judicious changes in the analysis procedures between runs. Illustrations are given of some of the evaluation results obtained with the system when the content analysis methods are covered in more detail in the next few sections (Salton, 1968b.).

THE STEM DICTIONARIES AND SUFFIX LIST

One of the earliest ideas in automatic information retrieval was the suggested use of words contained in documents and search requests for purposes of content identification. No elaborate content analysis is then required, and the similarity between different items can be measured simply by the amount of overlap between the respective vocabularies. Although such an analysis system is normally considered to be too crude to be of use in a standard text inference system, since no facilities are provided to recognize even the simplest kinds of synonymous constructions, it will be seen that vocabulary matching methods can produce completely satisfactory results for certain types of users of a document retrieval system.

Several different types of entities can be used in a word-matching system.

1. The complete English words originally present in documents and search requests can be matched.

2. A minimal amount of vocabulary normalization can be provided by cutting off final "s" endings, so as to confound singular and plural noun forms, and third-person verb endings characteristic of standard verb forms.

3. More extensive vocabulary normalization is available if the original text words are first converted to word-stem form by deleting standard suffixes and prefixes before matching.

Whichever of the three alternatives is used, the matching process can be applied to *all* the words in the original text or, alternatively, certain "common" words, deemed to be unimportant as content indicators, can be deleted. Furthermore, the individual text items (words, words with deleted final "s," or word stems) can be weighted in accordance with their presumed importance in a given text. Word frequency is often used as an indication of relative word importance, and a weight proportional to word frequency may then be attached to the text items.

In the SMART system, a decision was made to apply at least a minimal type of language normalization by using word stems instead of original words, deleting common words appearing on an exclusion list, and attaching to each word stem a weight proportional to its frequency in the text.

Stem and suffix dictionaries are first constructed by taking a sample document collection and using the words occurring in the sample as dictionary entries. New incoming documents and search requests are then processed by using a left-to-right letter-by-letter scan in the stem dictionary, and a right-to-left letter-by-letter scan in the suffix dictionary. The longest stem that leaves an acceptable suffix is taken as the correct decomposition of the word. For example, the left-to-right scan of a word like CODING generates potential stems COD (as in CODE), and CODI (as in CODIFY). The latter possibility produces the longer stem, but the remaining suffix NG is not found as an entry in the suffix dictionary. The next longest stem COD is then accepted as correct, since it leaves a proper

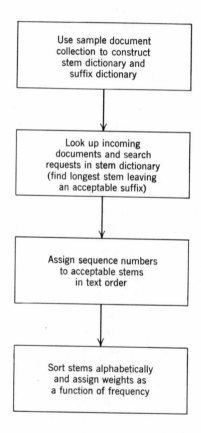

Figure 2   Simplified look-up in stem dictionary.

Table 2.   *Excerpt from word stem frequency list*

Fre-quency	Stem	Suffix	Sequence Number	Fre-quency	Stem	Suffix	Sequence Number
11	MODULE	S	2099	12	CONCEPT		2113
11	PLACE	S	2100	12	DECIS	ION	2114
11	RESPONSE		2101	12	DEPOSIT	ED	2115
11	RF		2102	12	DUE		2116
11	SOURCE		2103	12	ECONOM	ICAL	2117
11	THICK		2104	12	ESAKI		2118
11	TRUNC	ATION	2105	12	EXAMIN	ED	2119
11	WAVE		2106	12	FUNCTION	AL	2120
11	WHEREB	Y	2107	12	GRAPH		2121
11	WIR	ING	2108	12	HAV	ING	2122
12	ALPHABET	ICAL	2109	12	IMPROVE	MENT	2123
12	BASE		2110	12	IMPROV	ED	2124
12	CAP	ABLE	2111	12	INDIVIDU	AL	2125
12	CENT		2112	12	LEAST		2126

suffix ING. If a complete word is found in the stem dictionary, the search for the "remaining" suffix is always trivially successful.

A sequence number provided in the stem dictionary is assigned to each acceptable word stem. These sequence numbers are used during subsequent processing to represent the corresponding word stems. The stems pertaining to a given document are then sorted into alphabetic order, and weights are assigned as a function of the corresponding stem frequency. A simplified form of the stem look-up is shown in Figure 2, and a set of sample stem-suffix decompositions is included in Table 2 together with frequency indications and sequence numbers.

A number of English morphological rules are incorporated into the stem-suffix cut-off process to insure that correct stems are identified. Thus,

Table 3.   *Spelling rules incorporated in the stem look-up process*

Input Word	Corresponding Thesaurus Stem	Original Stem Detected	Modified Stem	+ Suffix
HOPPING	HOP	HOPP	HOPP	+ ING
HOPING	HOPE	HOP	HOP	+ ING
HANDING	HAND	HAND	HAND	+ ING
EASIER	EASY	EAS	EASI	+ ER
EASING	EASE	EAS	EAS	+ ING

```
ENGLISH TEXT PROVIDED FOR DOCUMENT DIFFERNTL EQ    SEPT. 28, 1964

GIVE ALGORITHMS USEFUL FOR THE NUMERICAL SOLUTION        1
OF ORDINARY DIFFERENTIAL EQUATIONS AND PARTIAL DIFFER-   1
ENTIAL EQUATIONS ON DIGITAL COMPUTERS. EVALUATE THE      1
VARIOUS INTEGRATION PROCEDURES (TRY RUNGE-KUTTA,         2
MILNE-S METHOD) WITH RESPECT TO ACCURACY, STABILITY,     2
AND SPEED.                                               2
```

Figure 3   Typical search request.

a check is made to identify doubled consonants preceding a suffix (as in HOPPING, which is decomposed into HOP+P+ING). Changes from Y to I are also taken into account (as in EASIER which is EASY+ER), as well as deletions of final E before a suffix (as in CODING which is CODE+ING). The spelling rules actually used during suffix look-up are summarized in Table 3.

A typical search request is shown in Figure 3 in the form normally used as input to the SMART system. The top part of Figure 4 shows the reduced form of the text of Figure 3 as it would appear after look-up in the stem dictionary. It may be seen that a number of common words have been deleted, and weights have been assigned to the remaining entries. (In Figure 4, a weight of 12 corresponds to an actual frequency of occurrence of 1, and only six characters of each stem are printed, although the complete stem is actually stored.)

In a simple retrieval system, sets of word stems extracted from documents and search requests can be used directly as an indication of subject similarity. The SMART system does, however, provide more sophisticated procedures to carry out the language analysis. The best known of these procedures is the standard thesaurus process described in the next section.

THE SYNONYM DICTIONARY OR THESAURUS

A thesaurus is a grouping of words, or word stems, into certain subject categories, hereafter called concept classes. A typical example is shown in Table 4, where the concept classes are represented by three-digit numbers, and the individual entries are shown under each concept number. In Table 5, a similar thesaurus arrangement is shown in the alphabetic order of the words included. The concept numbers appear in the middle column of Table 5 (concept numbers over 32,000 are attached to "common" words which are not accepted as information identifiers); the last column consists of one or more three-digit syntax codes attached to the words and used for purposes of syntactic analysis.

When constructing a thesaurus for vocabulary normalization, three types of problems must be faced: (1) What words should one include in the

OCCURRENCES OF CONCEPTS AND PHRASES IN DOCUMENTS

DOCUMENT   CONCEPT, OCCURS

DIFFERNTL EQ

ACCUR	12	ALGORI	12	COMPUT	12	DIFFER	24	DIGIT	12
EQU	24	EVALU	12	GIVE	12	INTEGR	12	METHOD	12
NUMER	12	ORDIN	12	PARTI	12	PROCED	12	RUNGE-	12
SOLUT	12	SPEED	12	STABIL	12	USE	12	VARIE	12

STEM DICTIONARY

DIFFERNTL EQ

4EXACT	12	8ALGOR	12	13CALC	18	71EVAL	6	92DIGI	12
110AUT	12	143UTI	12	176SOL	12	179STD	12	181QUA	24
269ELI	4	274DIF	36	356VEL	12	357YAW	4	384TEG	12
428STB	4	505APP	24						

REGULAR THESAURUS

DIFFERNTL EQ

4EXACT	12	8ALGOR	12	13CALC	18	71EVAL	6	92DIGT	12
110AUT	12	143UTI	12	176SOL	12	179STD	12	181QUA	24
269ELI	4	274DIF	36	356VEL	12	357YAW	4	375NUM	36
379DIF	72	384TEG	12	428STB	4	505APP	24		

STATISTICAL PHRASES LOOK-UP

Figure 4 Indexing products for "differential equations."

Table 4. *Thesaurus excerpt (concept class order)*

408	DISLOCATION JUNCTION MINORITY-CARRIER N-P-N P-N-P POINT-CONTACT RECOMBINE TRANSITION UNIJUNCTION	411	COERCIVE DEMAGNETIZE FLUX-LEAKAGE HYSTERESIS INDUCT INSENSITIVE MAGNETORESISTANCE SQUARE-LOOP THRESHOLD
409	BLAST-COOLED HEAT-FLOW HEAT-TRANSFER	412	LONGITUDINAL TRANSVERSE

Table 5. *Thesaurus excerpt in alphabetic order*

Text Words	Concept Numbers	Syntax Codes
BLOCK	663	070043040
BLUEPRINT	58	070043
BOMARC	324	070
BOMBARD	424 0343	043
BOMBER	346	070
BOND	105	070043
BOOKKEEPING	34	070
BOOLEAN	20	001
BORROW	28	043
BOTH	32178	008080012
BOUND	523 0105	070043134135
BOUNDARY	524	070
BRAIN	404 0235	070
BRANCH	48 0042	070042
BRANCHPOINT	23	070
BREAK	380	043040070
BREAKDOWN	689	070
BREAKPOINT	23	070
BRIDGE	105 0458 0048	070043
BRIEF	32232	001043071
BRITISH	437	001071
BROAD-BAND	312	001071

thesaurus? (2) What type of synonym categories should be used (that is, should one aim for broad, inclusive concept classes, or should the classes be narrow and specific)? (3) Where should each word appear in the thesaurus structure (that is, given a word, what are to be its assigned concept classes)?

Obviously, the answers to these questions depend on the use to be made of the thesaurus and on the environment within which the thesaurus is expected to operate. Experiments conducted with a variety of different types of thesauruses used with the SMART system show that some thenauruses are more effective in a retrieval environment than others. In particular, high-frequency common terms should either be eliminated or they should appear in concept classes of their own. Low-frequency terms should be grouped into classes with other low-frequency terms. Terms of little technical significance should be eliminated, and ambiguous terms should appear only in the classes that may be expected to be needed in practice. The thesaurus construction rules used with the SMART system are summarized in Table 6.

A comparison of a typical SMART thesaurus with a thesaurus used with the General Inquirer indicates that the SMART thesaurus classes often have a broader scope, and that many entries normally excluded from a SMART thesaurus would be used with the General Inquirer. This is true notably of particles expressing negation (which are not used with SMART), of personal pronouns and pronoun references, and of many

Table 6. *Sample thesaurus construction rules*

Type of Term	Thesaurus Rule
Very rare terms	Do not place into separate categories in the thesaurus, but combine if possible with other rare terms to form larger classes (low frequency categories provide few matches between stored items and search requests)
Very common terms	High-frequency terms should be either eliminated since they provide little discrimination, or should be placed into synonym classes of their own so as not to submerge other terms with which they might be grouped
Terms of no technical significance	Terms which have no special significance in a given technical area (such as "begin," "automatic," "system," etc. in the computer science area) should be excluded from the thesaurus
Ambiguous terms	Ambiguous terms should be entered into the thesaurus only in those senses likely to occur in the given subject area

terms expressing emphasis. However, the main aim of the two types of thesauruses is the same (the transformation of an input text into a set of normalized concepts expressing information content), and both types of thesauruses reflect, in one way or another, the investigators' theories concerning the language structure and the ways in which words are used to express information content.

In the SMART system, the main entries of the thesaurus are normally word stems, and a text is looked up in the thesaurus one word at a time, in each case replacing the input word by the corresponding thesaurus class or classes. Thus, search requests dealing with the "production of diodes" would normally be assigned the same classes as documents on the "manufacture of transistors." A given text is then transformed into a set of concept numbers with weights, as shown in the middle part of Figure 4 for the text of Figure 3.[2]

The weight of a concept is determined both by the number of words that map into the given concept class and by the particular thesaurus mapping used. Specifically, a given occurrence of a word is allowed to contribute, at most, a total weight of 1; the weight of ambiguous words, which map into more than one concept, is then divided by the number of applicable concept classes in such a way that a total weight of 1 results (that is, a weight of $1/n$ is assigned to each concept for a word mapping into n individual concepts). This strategy often results in an automatic resolution of the ambiguities inherent in the vocabulary, because the partial weights of the concepts which actually apply will tend to reinforce each other, whereas the weights of the other inapplicable concepts will be randomly assigned. An example of this phenomenon is shown in Table 7 where the "baseball" category is reinforced with a total weight of 1 and $\frac{5}{6}$ for four terms.

A comparison of the first two parts of Figure 4 shows that the transition from word-stem match to thesaurus results in a replacement of stems by concept numbers, and in alterations in the weight structure. For example, a weight of 24 attached to the stem "differen" (from "differential equations") is increased to 36 for the corresponding concept (number 274). The weight is further increased to 72 for phrase concept 379 when phrase assignments are made, as shown in the lower part of Figure 4.

The philosophy used in the SMART analysis may then be summarized by stating that no attempt is made to eliminate an occasional incorrect concept assignment, but that the automatic procedures are designed to

[2] Notice that the same dictionary look-up program serves for both the stem dictionary and the SMART thesaurus, since the sequence numbers used in the stem dictionary cannot be distinguished by the computer from the concept classes used in the SMART thesaurus.

Table 7. *Sample thesaurus mapping*

		Thesaurus Classes					Thesaurus Frequency
		Lamps	Games Baseball	Animals	Military Usage	Clothing	
Original terms	base	$\frac{1}{3}$	$\frac{1}{3}$		$\frac{1}{3}$		1
	bat		$\frac{1}{2}$	$\frac{1}{2}$			1
	glove		$\frac{1}{2}$			$\frac{1}{2}$	1
	hit		$\frac{1}{2}$		$\frac{1}{2}$		1
Frequency in document		$\frac{1}{3}$	$1\frac{5}{6}$	$\frac{1}{2}$	$\frac{5}{6}$	$\frac{1}{2}$	

assign a large number of concepts, many of which may be expected to be correctly applicable to the corresponding documents, while at the same time differentiating among individual concepts by the weighting procedure.

The effectiveness of the thesaurus procedure may be judged by the sample evaluation output of Figure 5 showing recall-precision curves averaged over 17 search requests. *Recall* is the proportion of relevant material actually retrieved, whereas *precision* is the proportion of retrieved material actually relevant. For a perfect system that retrieves everything of use to a given customer, and also rejects everything that is not useful, the recall-precision curve would shrink to a single point in the upper right hand corner of Figure 5 where both recall and precision are equal to 1. In general, the closer the curves are to the upper right-hand corner, the better will be the system performance. Figure 5, which was produced by the evaluation techniques incorporated into the SMART system (Salton, 1966b), shows that a word-stem matching process using only words from the title of documents is clearly inferior to the other methods shown. The word-stem match using complete document abstracts is quite effective at the low-recall high-precision end of the curve, where only a few relevant items are desired as output by the user. As more relevant items are wanted, and the recall needs increase, the thesauruses (termed "Harris Two" and "Harris Three" in Figure 5) become increasingly useful. This shows that *different* types of analysis procedures may be needed to satisfy different types of search requirements. The Harris Three Thesaurus is a recent version of a thesaurus constructed for the field of computer science in accordance with the thesaurus construction principles summarized in Table 6.

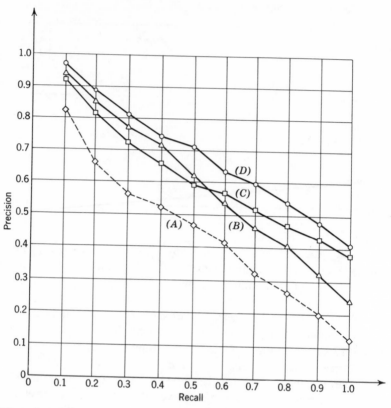

Figure 5   Comparison based on thesauruses (averages over 17 search requests).

THE STATISTICAL AND SYNTACTIC PHRASE DICTIONARIES

Both the thesaurus and the stem dictionary are based on entries corresponding either to single words or to single word stems. In attempting to perform a subject analysis of written text, it is possible, however, to go further by trying to locate "phrases" consisting of sets of words that are judged to be important in a given subject area. For example, in the field of computer science, the concepts of "analysis" and "language" may mean many things to many people. On the other hand, the phrase concept that results from a combination of these individual words (that is, "language analysis") has a much more specific connotation. Such phrases can be used for subject identification by building phrase dictionaries to be used in locating combinations of concepts, rather than individual concepts alone. Such phrase dictionaries would then normally include pairs, triples, or quadruples of words or concepts, corresponding in written texts to the more likely noun and prepositional phrases which may be expected to be indicative of subject content in a given topic area.

Many different strategies can be used in the construction of phrase dictionaries. For example, it is possible to base phrase dictionaries on combinations of high-frequency words or word stems occurring in documents and search requests; alternatively, one may want to use a thesaurus before appeal is made to a phrase dictionary. Furthermore, given the availability of a phrase dictionary, one can recognize the presence of phrases in a given text under a variety of circumstances: for example, the existence of a phrase may be recognized whenever the phrase components are present within a given document, or within a sentence of a given document regardless of any actual syntactic relation between the components; alternatively, phrases can be accepted only after verifying that a preestablished syntactic relation actually exists between the phrase components in the document under consideration.

In the SMART system, the phrase dictionaries are based on co-occurrences of thesaurus concepts, rather than text words, in order to profit from the greater degree of language normalization inherent in the use of the concepts. Two principal strategies are used for phrase detection.

1. The so-called *statistical phrase* dictionary is based on a phrase detection algorithm which takes into account only the statistical co-occurrence characteristics of the phrase components; specifically a statistical phrase is recognized, if all of the components are present within a given document, and no attempt is made to detect any particular syntactic relation between the components.

2. On the other hand, the *syntactic phrase* dictionary includes not only the specification of the particular phrase components which are to be detected but also information about the permissible syntactic dependency relations which must obtain if the phrase is to be recognized.

Thus, if it were desired to recognize the relationship between the concept "program" and the concept "language," then any possible combination of these two concepts (such as, for example, "programming language," "languages and programs", and "linguistic programs") would be recognized as proper phrases in the statistical phrase dictionary. In the syntactic dictionary, on the other hand, an additional restriction would consist in requiring that the concept corresponding to "program" be syntactically dependent on the concept "language." This eliminates phrases such as "linguistic programs," and "languages and programs," but would permit the phrases "programming languages" or "programmed languages."

A typical excerpt from a statistical phrase dictionary, used in connection

Phrase Concept	Component Concepts					
543	544	608	-0	-0	-0	
282	280	281	-0	-0	-0	
282	306	281	-0	-0	-0	
280	69	648	-0	-0	-0	
280	69	215	-0	-0	-0	
694	1285	1284	-0	-0	-0	
291	265	290	-0	-0	-0	
291	265	496	-0	-0	-0	
422	646	185	-0	-0	-0	
640	309	290	-0	-0	-0	
294	21	293	-0	-0	-0	
393	21	635	-0	-0	-0	
393	635	106	-0	-0	-0	
294	21	245	-0	-0	-0	
695	44	150	-0	-0	-0	
78	572	565	-0	-0	-0	
411	370	328	-0	-0	-0	
411	370	389	-0	-0	-0	
411	370	476	-0	-0	-0	
666	46	601	-0	-0	-0	
666	330	53	601	-0	-0	-0
666	347	46	-0	-0	-0	

Figure 6 Excerpt from Statistical Phrase Concept Dictionary.

with the SMART system, is shown in Figure 6. It may be observed that up to six phrase components are permitted in a given phrase, but that the usual phrase specification consists of two (or, at most, three) components. With each phrase included in Figure 6 is listed a phrase concept number which replaces the individual component concepts in a given document specification whenever the corresponding phrase is detected by the phrase processing algorithm in use. For example, the first line of Figure 6 shows that a phrase with concept number 543 is detected whenever the concepts 544 and 608 are jointly present in the document under consideration. Whenever such a phrase concept is attached to a given document specification, the weight of the phrase concept can be increased over and above the original weight of the component concepts to give the phrase specification added importance. This is illustrated in the lower portion of Figure 4 where the phrase concept 379, representing the concept "differential equations," and obtained by juxtaposing concepts 274 ("differential") and 181 ("equation"), receives a weight of 72 instead of the original component weights of 36 and 24, respectively.

Since the phrase components used in the SMART system represent concept numbers rather than individual words, a given phrase concept number does then, in fact, represent many different types of English word combinations depending on the number of word stems assigned to each component concept by the original thesaurus mapping.

The syntactic phrase dictionary has a more complicated structure, as shown by the excerpt reproduced as Figure 7. Here, each syntactic phrase (also known as a "criterion tree" or "criterion phrase") consists not only of a specification of the component concepts but also of syntactic indicators, as well as of syntactic relations which may obtain between the included concepts. For example, the first phrase shown in Figure 7 carries the concept number 422, and the mnemonic indicator MAGSWI to indicate that this phrase deals, in one way or another, with magnetic switches. Figure 7 also shows that the first component of the phrase must consist either of concepts 185 or 624, while the second phrase component must represent concept 225. The indicators after the dollar sign in the output of Figure 7 carry the syntactic information. In particular, the information given for the phrase MAGSWI indicates that this particular phrase must be either of syntactic types 7, 15, or 16.

The automatic process used to perform the syntactic analysis of the original texts and to assign syntactic indicators to the concepts, as well as the matching process between syntactic phrases occurring in documents and search requests have previously been described in the literature (Salton, 1966a). An evaluation of the phrase techniques shows that the statistical phrase process is often more effective than a simple thesaurus look-up. On the other hand, the automatic syntactic procedures do not appear

```
Name  Output  First  Second Type 7 Type 15 Type 16
  of   Con-    Node   Node   Serial Serial  Serial
Tree   cept    Concepts      143    143     399

MAGSWI=422(185,624)/(225)$7/143,15/398,16+
MANMCH=517(600)/(516)$7/144,15/400
MANROL=286(290)/(113)$7/145,5+,15/401,16+,19+
MATHOP=594(615)/(7,116,376)$7/147
MCHBKD=69(689)/(600)$1/148
MCHCOD=304(102,281)/(14,41,600,601)$1/149,15/404
MCHOPE=93(615)/(600)$7/150
MCHORI=41(513)/(600,601)$7/151,15/405
MCHTIM=691(617)/(52,600,601,605,1281)$7/152
MCHTIM=691(617)/(72,615)$1/153
MCHTRA=303(98)/(119,600)$1/154,4+,5+,6+,10+,15/406,16+,19+
MEMACC=593(672)/(121)$1/159,15/409
MEMCOR=557(669)/(121)$7/137,15/395
MEMEFF=284(64)/(121)$1/160,6+,15/410
MEMSPA=552(212)/(121)$1/162,13+,15/411
```

Figure 7 Excerpt from Syntactic Criterion Phrase Dictionary.

to be substantially superior to the statistical methods, even though they are far more expensive to perform on the computer. The reasons for this unexpected result may be due, in part, to the relative inadequacy of presently existing programs for automatic syntactic analysis and, in part, to the fact that the syntactic procedures appear to be too refined for the document retrieval environment in which they are used. Thus, in the sentence "for people who need a great deal of information, effective retrieval is vital," the phrase "information retrieval" would not be recognized by the syntactic procedures in use, since "information" and "retrieval" do not exhibit the appropriate syntactic relationships. The sentence does, however, deal with information retrieval—a fact that is properly recognized by the statistical phrase methods used. This example demonstrates again that a content analysis method which is too sophisticated is not more useful than one which is not sophisticated enough. The difficulty lies in recognizing the appropriate depth of the analysis to be used in each given case.

THE CONCEPT HIERARCHY

Hierarchical arrangements of subject headings have been used for many years in library science and related documentation activities. In general, such arrangements make it possible to classify more specific topics under more general ones, and to formulate a search request by starting with a general formulation, and progressively narrowing the specification down to those areas that appear to be of principal interest.

In a content analysis system, a hierarchical arrangement of words or word stems can be used both for information identification and for retrieval purposes. Thus, if a given search request is formulated in terms of "syntactic dependency trees," and it is found that not enough useful material is actually obtained, it is possible to "expand" this request to include all "tree structures" or indeed all "abstract graphs," by using a hierarchical subject classification.

A hierarchy of concept numbers rather than text words is included in the SMART system, and it is assumed that a thesaurus look-up operation precedes any hierarchical expansion operation. A typical example from the SMART concept hierarchy is shown in Figure 8. The broad, more general concepts appear on the left side of the figure, corresponding to the "roots" of the hierarchical tree; and the more specific concepts appear further to the right. For example, concept 270 is the root of a subtree; this concept has four sons on the next lower level, namely, concepts 224, 471, 472, and 488. Concept 224, in turn, has two sons, labeled 261 and 331; similarly, concept 471 has four sons, including 338, 371,

```
053        350        625              Concept   Sequence
   584                                 Number    Number
130                                      53         1
   074     192                          584         2
   114     725        101                -0         3
   494     725        101               130         4
195                                      74         5
   246     120                          114         6
   374     120                          494         7
   468                                   -0         8
   469                                  195         9
   491                                  246        10
260                                     374        11
   485     435                          468        12
270                                     469        13
   224                                  491        14
      261----------130                  -0        15
      331                               260        16
   471----------641                     485        17
      338                                -0        18
      371                               270        19
      458                               224        20
      470                               261        21
   472----------641-----------200       331        22
      034----------641                  471        23
   488                                  338        24
309        597        321               371        25
   551     341        335               458        26
   628     659        597      630      470        27
   642     341                          472        28
   643     659                           34        29
                                        488        30
                                         -0        31
                                        309        32
                                        551        33
                                        628        34
                                        642        35
                                        643        36
```

———— SONS

- - - - - CROSS-REFERENCES

Figure 8   Hierarchy excerpt.

458, and 470. It may be seen from Figure 8 that the sons of a concept, representing more specific terms, are shown below their parents and further to the right.

The hierarchy of Figure 8 also provides for the inclusion of cross-references from one concept to another, connected to the original concept by broken lines. Such cross references represent general, unspecified types of relations between the corresponding concepts, and receive in general a different interpretation than the generic inclusion relations normally represented by the hierarchy.

It would be nice if it were possible to give some generally applicable algorithm for constructing hierarchical subject arrangements. This is, in fact, a topic that has preoccupied many people including mathematicians, philosophers, and librarians for many years. In general, one might expect that broad concepts should be near the top of tree (close to the root), whereas specific concepts should be near the bottom (close to the leaves); furthermore, there appears to be some relationship between the frequency of occurrence of a given concept in a document collection and its place in the hierarchy. More specifically, the concepts that exhibit the highest frequency of occurrence in a given document collection, and that by this very fact appear to be reasonably common, should be placed on a higher level than other concepts whose frequency of occurrence is lower.

Concerning the specific place of a given concept with the hierarchy, this should be made to depend on the user population and on the type of expansion that is most often requested. Thus, a concept corresponding to "syntactic dependency tree" would most reasonably appear under the broader category of "syntax," which in turn could appear under the general class of "language," assuming that the user population consists of linguists or grammarians; on the other hand, if the users were to be mathematicians or algebraists, then the "syntactic dependency trees" should probably appear under "abstract trees," which in turn would come under "graph theory," a branch of algebra. It is unreasonable to expect that a hierarchical arrangement of concepts will serve equally well for all uses under all circumstances. Instead, any hierarchy will serve its function if it can be counted on to suggest ways of broadening or narrowing a given search request or a given interpretation of the subject matter under most of the circumstances likely to arise in practice.

STATISTICAL TERM ASSOCIATIONS

The content analysis procedures previously described either do not take into account any kind of relationships between individual content identifiers or, alternatively, the relationships that exist are specified by the dictionaries used in the analysis. The phrase dictionaries, for example, specify a type of association between individual concepts within a phrase, and the hierarchical expansion operations make use of generic inclusion relations between concepts.

However, it is also possible in a retrieval environment to take into account various kinds of associations between concepts that are inherent in the query and document texts, instead of being specified by a dictionary

	Terms
Document 1	A - - D - -
Document 2	A B - D - -
Document 3	- - C D E F
Document 4	- B C - - F
Document 5	A - - D E -
Document 6	- - C - E -
Document 7	- B - D - F
Document 8	A B C - - -

Figure 9   Original term assignment for eight documents.

or thesaurus. Specifically, if it is assumed that two document identifiers are related whenever they are found to co-occur frequently in the same context (for example, in the same sentences of a document or in the same documents of a collection), then it is possible to compute an index of similarity between each pair of concepts based on these co-occurrence characteristics. Thereafter, each given concept vector representing a document or search request can be expanded by addition of all the associated concepts whose similarity coefficients with some original concept are sufficiently high.

Consider, as an example, a typical set of concept vectors such as those shown in Figure 9, for eight documents. The terms assigned to the eight documents are labeled A to F, and no weights are used in the example of Figure 9. A similarity coefficient can now be computed between each pair of terms, based on joint assignment of the corresponding terms to the documents of the collection, by comparing the corresponding two columns of the matrix of Figure 9. If the similarity coefficient between two terms is computed by a formula such as

$$\frac{\text{Number of joint occurrences of terms i and j}}{\text{Number of i's} + \text{Number of j's} - \text{Number of joint occurrences}},$$

then the similarity matrix of Figure 10 results for the original specification of Figure 9. To compute, for example, the similarity between terms A and B, a comparison of the first two columns of Figure 9 shows that there exist two joint assignments (to documents 2 and 8), four individual occurrences of A (documents 1, 2, 5, and 8), and four occurrences of B (documents 2, 4, 7, and 8). The similarity coefficient is then

$$\text{Similarity (A,B)} = \frac{2}{4 + 4 - 2} = 2/6$$

	A	B	C	D	E	F
A	.	2/6	1/7	③/6	1/6	0
B		.	2/6	2/7	0	②/5
C			.	1/8	②/5	②/5
D				.	2/6	2/6
E					.	1/5
F						.

Figure 10   Term-term similarity matrix.

If the further assumption is now made that a similarity coefficient of at least $2/5$ is to be indicative of a statistical association between the corresponding terms, then the four pairs (A,D), (B,F), (C,E), and (C,F) would be accepted as associated, according to the statistical criterion used. Consequently, to a document specification consisting of terms A, B, and C, one might then add the associated terms D, E, and F, thus ensuring, hopefully, that a query dealing with "airplanes" would also retrieve documents about "aircraft."

Tests were made to determine to what extent the automatically generated term association methods incorporated into the SMART system could be considered to be equivalent to the manually or semiautomatically constructed thesauruses (Salton, 1968b; Lesk, 1967). The results indicate that while a retrieval system using term associations provides greater effectiveness than one based on simple word matching alone, the normal thesaurus process is much more effective as a language normalization device than the statistical word associations. Furthermore, the associations that are automatically determined are not related to those specified in the thesaurus, and do not approximate normal synonym relations between words. Associative methods are therefore most effective in situations where a thesaurus is not available, and where the time and effort needed to generate one cannot be expended.

USER-CONTROLLED INFORMATION SEARCH

In the SMART system, document retrieval takes place following the information analysis. Specifically, the concept vectors which are generated for the individual documents during the analysis phase are compared with the concept vectors assigned to the search requests, and those documents which are found to be most similar to the queries are retrieved for the user's attention. A typical output form is shown in Figure 11 in the format

```
          CURRENT REQUEST - *LIST DIFFERNTL EQ NUMERICAL DIGITAL SOLN OF DIFFERENTIAL EQUATIONS

REQUEST   *LIST DIFFERNTL EQ NUMERICAL DIGITAL SOLN OF DIFFERENTIAL EQUATIONS
-------

          GIVE ALGORITHMS USEFUL FOR THE NUMERICAL SOLUTION OF ORDINARY
          DIFFERENTIAL EQUATIONS AND PARTIAL DIFFERENTIAL EQUATIONS ON DIGITAL
          COMPUTERS . EVALUATE THE VARIOUS INTEGRATION PROCEDURES (E.G. RUNGE--
          KUTTA, MILNE-S METHOD) WITH RESPECT TO ACCURACY, STABILITY, AND SPEED .


ANSWER          CORRELATION          IDENTIFICATION
------          -----------          --------------
384STABILITY      0.6675             STABILITY OF NUMERICAL SOLUTION OF DIFFERENTIAL EQUATIONS
                                     W. E. MILNE AND R. R. REYNOLDS (OREGON STATE COLLEGE)
                                     J. ASSOC. FOR COMPU ING MACH. VOL 6 PP 196-203 (APRIL, 1959)


ANSWER          CORRELATION          IDENTIFICATION
------          -----------          --------------
360SIMULATIN      0.5758             SIMULATING SECOND-ORDER EQUATIONS
                                     D. G. CHADWICK (UTAH STATE UNIV.)
                                     ELECTRONICS VOL 32 P 64 (MARCH 6, 1959)


ANSWER          CORRELATION          IDENTIFICATION
------          -----------          --------------
200SOLUTION       0.5663             SOLUTION OF ALGEBRAIC AND TRANSCENDENTAL EQUATIONS ON AN AUTOMATIC
                                     DIGITAL COMPUTER
                                     G.N. LANCE (UNIV. OF SOUTHAMPTON)
                                     J. ASSOC. FOR COMPUTING MACH., VOL 6, PP .97-101, JAN., 1959


ANSWER          CORRELATION          IDENTIFICATION
------          -----------          --------------
392ON COMPUT      0.5508             ON COMPUTING RADIATION INTEGRALS
                                     R. C. HANSEN (HUGHES AIRCRAFT CO.), L. L. BAILIN (UNIV. OF SOUTHERN
                                     CALIFORNIA, AND R. W. RUTISHAUSER (LITTON INDUSTRIES, INC.)
                                     COMMUN. ASSOC) FOR COMPUTING MACH. VOL 2 PP 28-31 (FEBRUARY, 1959)


ANSWER          CORRELATION          IDENTIFICATION
------          -----------          --------------
386ELIMINATI      0.5483             ELIMINATION OF SPECIAL FUNCTIONS FROM DIFFERENTIAL EQUATIONS
                                     J. E. PCWERS (UNIV. OF OKLAHOMA)
                                     COMMUN. ASSOC. FOR COMPTING MACH. VOL 2 PP 3-4 (MARCH, 1959)
```

Figure 11 Answers to search requests.

in which it is transmitted to the user. The original query (already shown in Figure 3) is reproduced at the top of the figure, followed by an itemization of the first few documents in decreasing correlation order with the search request. The user now has the option to quit or to request that additional items be displayed for his attention.

Although the SMART system includes a variety of content analysis procedures, which produce different types of results for different users—some stressing high recall and some high precision—it is unreasonable to expect wholly satisfactory service to all users under all circumstances, particularly if only a single search is made of the stored collection. Attempts to meet the user problem usually take the form of multiple rather than single searches. Thus, instead of submitting a search request and obtaining in return a final set of relevant items, a partial search is made first and, based on the preliminary output obtained, the search parameters are adjusted before attempting a second, more refined search. The adjustments made may then be different from user to user, depending on individual needs, and the search process may be repeated as often as desired. A typical user feedback system is shown in simplified form in Figure 12.

Several strategies are available for improving the results of a search, as summarized in Table 8. The first is simply a *mechanized dictionary* print-out routine in which a set of potential search terms, related to those initially used by the requestor, are extracted from the stored dictionary and presented to the user. The user is then asked to reformulate the original query after selecting the new associated terms that appear to him to be most helpful in improving the search results. Usually the statistical term associations previously discussed can be used to obtain the set of related terms, or the sets of associated thesaurus classes can be taken from the thesaurus. This search optimization procedure is straightforward, but it leaves the burden of rephrasing the query in the user's hands.

A second strategy consists in automatically modifying a search request by using the partial results from a previous search. Specifically, the user is asked to examine the documents retrieved by an initial search, and to designate some of them as either relevant (R) or irrelevant (N) to his purpose. Concepts from the documents termed relevant can then be added to the original search request if not present already, or their importance can be increased by a suitable adjustment of weights; conversely, terms from documents designated as irrelevant can be deleted or demoted. A great deal of work has been done to optimize this kind of *relevance feedback* operation, and evaluation results indicate that the process produces considerable improvements in search effectiveness (Salton, 1968a.).

The third possibility for search optimization leaves the search request

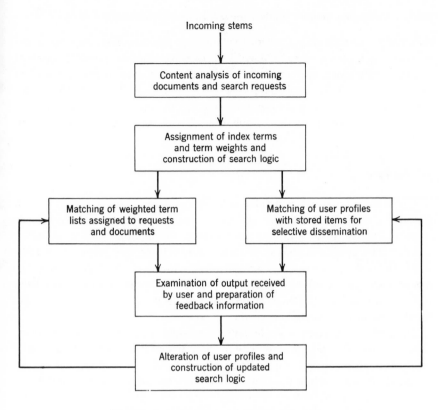

Figure 12 Simplified user feedback process.

Table 8. *Methods for search optimization*

Type of System Alteration	User Function
Display of related terms from stored dictionary or generation of term associations	User adds to search request related terms suggested to him by the system
Automatic query change by promoting terms from relevant documents and demoting those from irrelevant documents	User identifies some previously retrieved items as either relevant or irrelevant to his purposes
Automatic change of search process, using additional dictionaries, hierarchies, or statistical and syntactic analysis methods	User criticizes result of an initial search by pointing out insufficiency of output (narrow or broad subject interpretation, theme recognition, and so on)

effectively unchanged but alters the analysis process. This requires a retrieval organization, like SMART, providing several possible content analysis techniques and an iterative search procedure which can utilize the various analysis methods for retrieval purposes. User feedback can also serve here as a basis for choosing, from among the large number of available analysis methods, the one that seems most appropriate in each given case.

SUMMARY

The SMART system is a fully automatic text-processing system, which includes a variety of content analysis methods designed to transform incoming English texts into sets of concept vectors reflecting information content. The programs consist of about 150,000 program steps on an IBM 7094/II, and fourteen tapes are required on-line if the full facilities of the system are called into play. Various parts of the system have been reprogrammed for an IBM 360/65, but the full system is not yet available for the 360 at the time of this writing.

The SMART system is implemented as a text retrieval system; however, given appropriate inputs and dictionaries, it could operate just as easily as a text inference system. In fact, all of the facilities provided by the programs that constitute the General Inquirer are also present in SMART, including dictionary look-up programs, "tag tally" programs, and syntactic analysis facilities. The SMART programs, in addition, permit a fully automatic text analysis without manual operations at the input side, and also include sophisticated search and retrieval evaluation facilities. It is to be hoped that sooner or later the SMART programs may find application in the social sciences for content analysis and other related research endeavors.

26 Categories and Procedures for Content Analysis in the Humanities[1]

Sally Yeates Sedelow

English and Information Science

Walter A. Sedelow, Jr.

Sociology and Information Science
University of North Carolina

As part of an exploration of style in language, we[2] have been concerned for several years with content analysis—not for the humanities alone but also for the social sciences. Humanistically, we have been interested, among other things, in the specification and location of literary themes; in other texts, we have been concerned with what are sometimes called structuring ideas. We undertook content analysis in this rather generalized way because we suspected that the distinctions between themes and ideas were more minimal than is sometimes argued or suggested. It is true that literature (and we are assuming throughout this chapter that the aspect of the humanities most relevant for content analysis is literature, although paintings, musical scores, and the like, also may be content analyzed) or, more properly, the analysis of literature, does differ in part from the study of texts in some other disciplines. The use made of ambiguity is probably a good example of a major distinguishing characteristic, where the variance has repercussions as to the appropriate analyses: for much literature revels in the kinds of ambiguity implied by puns and other word play, and such a use of language runs counter, for example, to that strain toward explicit or implicit operational definition which is criti-

[1] The research described in this chapter has been supported, in part, by the Office of Naval Research, Information Systems Branch.

[2] Other people who have been associated with this project include Terry Ruggles of the System Development Corporation, Joan Bardez, William Hickok, and William Buttelmann of the Information Science Department at the University of North Carolina (Chapel Hill), and Joan Peters of Washington University (St. Louis). For further elaboration, and relevant readings, see Sedelow (1964, 1965a, 1965b, 1966a, 1966b, 1967a, 1967b).

cally significant for much social analysis prose. But, then, humanistically one also enjoys and exploits the kind of ambiguous connotations which psychologists, too, may study when, for example, they are engaged in clinical analyses. And, insofar as an interest in using the language of motive, intention, and attitude as applied to verbal material is shared in other disciplines, such as political science and sociology, content analysis which is desirable for the humanities is also content analysis appropriate to social science. Thus, the categories and procedures that we shall discuss in this chapter are not, in fact, restricted to the humanities; and we have used them for such varied texts as *Hamlet,*[3] *Soviet Military Strategy,*[4] and very long strings from Hume's *History of England.*[5]

As is the case with much content analysis, the major question we faced was how to set up grouping procedures, the categories which would contain words forming the thematic or conceptual patterns in the texts; since, initially, we were not testing particular theories or looking for specific syndromes, but rather were searching—with an effort to avoid premature closure—for whatever patterns the text might reveal itself to exemplify, we did not want to begin with categories already set up for their relevance to a particular theory or concept scheme. Therefore, our content analysis program (really a series of computer programs grouped under the general title VIA, for Verbally-Indexed-Associations) begins simply by indexing the text, grouping the content words in the text together by root, and counting the occurrences of the words within the root group. Our procedure was next to assume that we might want to sort on any nonfunction word root and form subgroups around it, that is, that *any* nonfunction word or group of words with a common root might serve as a category key with which other words would eventually be grouped. The word or root group serving as a key we designated by the word, primary, and the words ultimately placed in that category we designated as associated words. This designation could be misunderstood, because the associated words may be no less valuable, no less critical, for the delineation of a theme than the primary word or root group. We used the designation simply to indicate which word or root group served as the key for the construction of a category because we needed to make such distinctions

---

[3] William Shakespeare, *Hamlet,* George Lyman Kittridge, ed., Ginn and Company 1939.
[4] We used two translations of V. D. Sokolovsky's *Soviet Military Strategy:* I. Dinerstein D., Goure and Wolff, Prentice-Hall, Inc., 1963; II. Translation Services Branch, Foreign Technology Division, Wright-Patterson AFB, Frederick A. Praeger, Inc., 1963. Customarily we refer to the former as the RAND translation, and the latter as the Praeger translation.
[5] David Hume, *The History of England.* 6 Volumes, London, 1841.

in order to talk about our programming procedure. The selection of such a category key or root group was based upon frequency. In most cases we used high frequency, although in one instance when we were interested in comparing two translations of the same work we used any frequency, from one up, for words that occurred in one translation and not in the other. The researcher may, of course, choose any frequency level that he likes, high or low, for keying his categories. An important characteristic of this procedure thus far is that the words serving as keys to the categories are words which occur in the text with any frequency, n, of interest to the researcher.

The next and crucial step in our content analysis procedure has been to select the words which, if they occurred in the text, would be appropriate to one of the categories designated by the key word. Up to the present, the selection of these words has been made manually. We have consulted various thesauri, synonym dictionaries, and the context of the primary words in order to draw up lists of possible associated words. As a consequence of this use of various sources for the input lists of possible associated words, we call these lists the computer's thesaurus—and because of the way the program operates, we have been constructing clusters of words which might be used in a new thesaurus if one were building such a thesaurus from scratch. Such clusters differ from those in any available thesaurus not only because of the varied sources for the words in the input thesaurus but, much more essentially, because the program links words down through five levels although the researcher provides just the first level links. The links may be spoken of as implicit in the material the researcher supplies to the computer, but the computer program pulls them together into new clusters of semantically associated words. It systematically explores for the network of transitivity implications in sets of particular associations. For example, in Figure 1, the words HEAVEN, LAND, NATURE, and WORLD were all first level links to the word EARTH. On the other hand, the words LIFE and UNNATURAL did not appear on any list linked directly to EARTH; LIFE and UNNATURAL were on a list linked to NATURE and the operation of the computer program in turn links them to EARTH. As was the case with LIFE and UNNATURAL, the program links STARS to EARTH because STARS has appeared on a list linked with HEAVEN. Also in the list with STARS is a recurrence of EARTH, exemplifying the indication of cross-referencing often provided by the content analysis program. A new version of the content analysis program will permit the researcher to suppress the second occurrence of EARTH if he so desires.

It is very important to remember, of course, that these thesauri are text-specific; that is, we have an output consisting of groups of associated

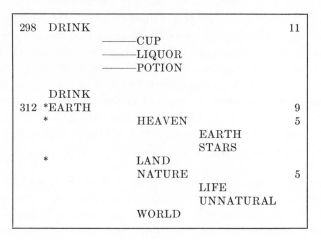

Figure 1   A sample of VIA's output for *Hamlet.*

words for *Hamlet* as well as separate outputs for both translations of *Soviet Military Strategy* and for Hume's *History of England.* A good deal of cross-referencing, as well as much additional use of the VIA program on extensive bodies of text, would be required if one were thinking of using the text-specific thesauri as bases for a new general thesaurus. As our research has progressed, the selection of words which, if they occur in the text, will form the categories for that text has become less eclectic and more "automatic." For example, initially, when looking at *Hamlet,* the tendency was not to include words appearing in the various thesauri or synonym dictionaries if it seemed reasonably certain that Shakespeare did not use such words. The reason for this selectivity was the desire to eliminate a good deal of manual work as well as computer processing time. Despite these considerations, it has seemed increasingly important to list *all* words in the appropriate categories found in thesauri and synonym dictionaries for two reasons: (1) the researcher probably does not know his author's vocabulary as thoroughly as he thinks he does, and (2) we began to think it would be desirable to automate this selection of possible associated words and wanted to see what the inclusion of all words in a category would do to our output. That is, we wanted to see if, by listing all words, our text-specific thesauri became overly swollen with extraneous words; and, if so, to begin thinking about controlling the excess by rule.

Since we do want to automate this manual section of our VIA procedure, and because we would like to utilize in some way an already existing thesaurus rather than construct a new subjectively structured group of semantic categories, we conducted some experiments using *Webster's Dictionary of Synonyms, Roget's University Thesaurus,* and *Roget's International Thesaurus* to see whether, if the researcher were restricted to one of those thesaurus texts as the base for the computer thesaurus, one of them alone would prove satisfactory. We should quickly state that we do not envision our input thesaurus as being restricted to any one of these thesaurus texts. Instead, we were interested in seeing whether one of them looked promising enough so that it would be worthwhile to devise methods of amplification, or other modification, for its use. Our procedure was to choose a restricted number of words in the RAND translation of *Soviet Military Strategy,* and use *Webster's Dictionary of Synonyms, Roget's University Thesaurus,* and *Roget's International Thesaurus,* respectively, for the input thesaurus for each of three computer runs on chapter two. The number of words used for this experiment was restricted because the quantity of data involved turned out to be enormous, especially for the run using *Roget's University Thesaurus.* We were interested in trying the *University Thesaurus* because it does not subdivide categories as does the *International Thesaurus.* For example, the index for the word DEATH in the *University Thesaurus* refers to a category which includes both nouns and verbs in a great range of meanings. The index for DEATH in the *International Thesaurus* subdivides on the basis of meaning and syntax; the indexed section for DEATH as a noun in the *International Thesaurus* contains 26 entries as opposed to the single all-inclusive category of about 221 entries in the *University Thesaurus.* Our thought was that the *University Thesaurus,* because its entries were not subdivided, might provide a richer, more useful output than the *International Thesaurus.* In part this thought was confirmed, since the *University Thesaurus* produced a much more extensive text-specific thesaurus than did the *International Thesaurus.* Unfortunately, many of the words suggested by the *University Thesaurus* seemed extraneous to a given category. That was much less the case for the *International Thesaurus.* Extensive examination of the results[6] has convinced us that the greater richness of the results produced by the *University Thesaurus* is far outweighed by the extremely tangential nature of many of the words resulting in the output categories.

For example, when we were working with the word DEAD the number of words in our list based upon *Roget's International Thesaurus* was 268; the number of words from *Roget's University Thesaurus* was 2452. Given these numerically disparate lists as input, VIA's output, of course, reflected the disparity. The total number of words in the output list for the computer run using the *International Thesaurus* was 39; the computer run using

---

[6] Joan Peters has given us much valuable assistance in this phase of the project.

the *University Thesaurus* generated 229. Although the output produced by the use of the *University Thesaurus* was much more extensive, a great many words in that output seemed inappropriate in a list of words clustered around the word DEAD. Examples of such words are GO, METRIC, ANALYSIS, PRACTICE, PROPORTION, INDEX, LINE, LINES, and ESTIMATE. In our judgment—and the judgments used at this early stage of research are not based upon explicit, weighted criteria— four of the words in the output list based on an input from the *International Thesaurus* seemed irrelevant and two seemed only marginally relevant. By contrast, in our judgment, 110 words in the output produced by the *University Thesaurus* seemed irrelevant to some degree. So that, for the *University Thesaurus,* just under half of the total number of entries seemed questionable.

We have made similar comparisons using thirteen other words: DE-CLINE, DECREE, DEFLECT, DELIBERATE, DELUSION, DE-VELOP, DEVISE, DISARRAY, DISASTER, DISTRICT, DOUBLE, and DRILL. These other comparisons amplify the comments based upon the research using DEAD. Our conclusion was that the output based upon *Roget's International Thesaurus* is perhaps a little spare, but relatively free of irrelevant terms. The disadvantage of that slight spareness is obviated, in large measure, by VIA's operating procedure. Since VIA cross-links lists of words, the enrichment otherwise given by a bigger indexing net (such as that in the *University Thesaurus*) is available while, at the same time, the provenance of the enrichment is clearly shown. Our next step, if we were to pursue further the possible use of the *International Thesaurus* would be the very interesting project of exploring in some detail the biases of its indexing and internal structure. To accomplish this task without prohibitive cost, we will need a machine-readable version of the *International Thesaurus.*

Webster's Dictionary of Synonyms, per se, produced too little input and consequently too little output to be of interest for our purposes. However, if that dictionary were available in computer accessible form, it might be possible to move around within the dictionary and collect a good number of acccurately linked words for any given category. It may be that a large dictionary also would be usable as a base for thesaurus construction, and we have begun to think along those lines as well.

In addition to the comparison of thesauri, we have begun to think how we might enlarge any given thesaurus and, on something of another tack, how we might use the structure of a thesaurus to help resolve semantic ambiguities. Our work in enlarging a thesaurus is still in the thinking stage. But, in general, we are curious to see whether a word that does not appear in the thesaurus might, when appropriate, be added to the thesaurus through an examination of the categories into which fall words near it in the text that do appear in the thesaurus. For example, if the word "ICBM" occurred a great many times followed by the word missile, and if "ICBM" did not appear in the thesaurus but missile did, one might feel safe in letting the computer program add "ICBM" to a category including missile; or, perhaps better, one might put "ICBM" in the output list containing missile with a notation that "ICBM's" assignment to this category is tentative, letting the researcher decide whether it should be entered permanently in that category in the thesaurus. If this sort of procedure is indeed helpful, there is still the problem of automating the initial selection of possible categories upon which the researcher would base his final allocation of words to specific categories.

Regarding the use of a thesaurus or a thesauruslike set of categories to resolve ambiguities, we are largely concerned with semantic rather than syntactic ambiguity. It is obvious that semantic and syntactic ambiguities do not always coincide. The word CONTROL, for example, does not differ significantly in meaning when its syntactic usage shifts from nominal to verbal, but the word STATE does. On the other hand, the word STATE has several different meanings even when used as a noun. One of the tacks that we have taken is to see whether thesaurus categories for words modifying, for example, STATE helped to clear STATE's ambiguity. This lead looks interesting enough to follow further and, if it continues to look fruitful, once again we shall begin to think about ways of automating such a procedure. In conjunction with this clarifying of ambiguity, we also think we may learn much from studies of intratextual semantic and syntactic stability—probabilities for consistencies in the opted uses of terms within any given strings.

Currently, we are considerably enlarging VIA's options as to the kinds of categories or word groupings it produces. We are conceptualizing this output in terms of ring structures which not only will show rings of words which are semantically associated but will show the ring of concepts associated with any given word. This part of the program system is being designed by William Buttelmann; in it, searches may be keyed on an individual word or root group, on an individual category, or on all of the categories in which a given word appears. Furthermore, by working back and forth between a thesaurus and the text, this program is going to have the power to show what words within a category an author avoids, or even what categories an author avoids as well as those he chooses. This power means that the researcher, if he chooses, will be able to key searches on words not appearing in the text as well an on those appearing in the text. Or, in fact, he could key a search entirely on words not appearing in the text.

The current version of VIA is being retained with some minor modifications. To indicate its adequacy for use in content analysis, we shall describe and briefly compare the text specific thesauri for *Hamlet* and the RAND translation of *Soviet Military Strategy.*

For *Hamlet,* our "cut-off" point for designation of primary root groups was 10 or more occurrences; this figure resulted in 37 primary root groups in ACT I, 35 in Act II, 48 in Act III, and 24 in each of Acts IV and V. To give these figures relative meaning, it should be noted that there are approximately 1450 content word types in Act I; remember that 37 content word root groups occur 10 or more times. There was a great deal of overlap from one act to the next; with 10 as the threshold, the number of primary root groups for all of *Hamlet* totaled 65. Even some of these words, such as the quantifiers MUCH, MANY, and MOST, can be considered content words only marginally.

A detailed study of output would be beneficial both to the individual who has never read *Hamlet* and to the scholar who knew *Hamlet* very well. For the person *unacquainted* with *Hamlet,* a glance at the primary root groups for Act V would suggest, for example, that a drink or the act of drinking was of some importance in this act. The presence of the word POTION on the list linked to DRINK might imply something unusual about the drink. The researcher would guess that a KING had an important role in this act and would note that the words associated with KING have connotations of a king's court and of his kingdom. Among proper names used in this act, he would find that the names of Hamlet, Horatio, and Laertes qualify as primary words, with Hamlet having the highest frequency. The researcher would notice that the more generic word, MAN, occurs with some frequency and that some of the words associated with it imply familial relationships. If he were to glance at those words in the output which had qualified as primary words in earlier acts, the researcher would discover some of the familial terms: FATHER, DAUGHTER, and MOTHER. He would take note of the fact that these familial terms no longer had primacy in the final act (in fact, DAUGHTER does not occur at all) but that the more general, more impersonal terms KING and MAN did. If the word POTION associated with DRINK had overtones of the unusual, the presence of MADNESS as a primary word amplifies them. The word ILL linked to MADNESS may suggest disease, as does the linking of ILL to WELL.[7]

---

[7] WELL is an example of a word that qualifies as a primary word because it is multifaceted as to function and meaning. In *Hamlet,* WELL is used, among other ways, as an interjection (as in "Well, again"), as an idiom implying some sort of assent or agreement ("Very well"), and as a descriptor of health or condition. Thus, if this primary word group appeared in isolation its implications as to content

Another primary word of possible interest in this act is the word TELL. The researcher would notice that a number of words associated with TELL suggest an emphasis upon speaking or talking. He would note, in fact, that the word SAY also qualified as a primary word in this act and that the word SPEAK has had primacy in an earlier act or acts, as had the word WORDS. There would seem to be an interest in language, especially the spoken language (the word WRITE appears for the first time, and only once, in this final act), as well as perhaps an interest in reporting or relaying something. The latter interest seems especially important in this last act, with the emphasis upon TELL (a glance at the output from earlier acts would show the researcher that TELL had not qualified as a primary word in those acts). The researcher would also notice a premium upon knowledge; the words KNOW, KNOWS, KNOWN, and KNOWING all occur as well as the words LEARNING and UNDERSTAND which are associated with them. The contrasting word IGNORANCE is also present. Although the word DEATH does not quite qualify as a primary word in this act (it occurs eight times), 14 of the words on the computer's thesaurus list which might be associated with death occur in this act. An examination of this list reveals words which definitely imply violence: BLEED, MURD'ROUS, MURTHER, and SLAIN. The word PLOT, which also appears on this list, may provide some insight into the importance of knowledge, of KNOWING. In keeping with the theme of violence, it may be of interest that three of the words associated with LOVE, which does not quite qualify as a primary word, imply violence rather than tenderness. The fourth word, DOTE, also suggests a lack of restraint, although not quite of the same sort as that connoted by DESIRE, HOT, and PASSION. Other words among those which do not qualify as primary in this act but did qualify earlier—and which catch the eye because of the relatively large numbers of words linked to them—include SLEEP, SOUL, HEAVEN, EARTH, HEARERS, and ACT. In this act, SLEEP occurs just once but, even so, there is nothing of restfulness or soothingness in the words associated with it. Instead, there is the violence associated with DEATH which is linked to SLEEP. The presence of words clustered around SOUL, HEAVEN, and EARTH, indicates that *Hamlet* is not simply a description of derring-do for the sake of derring-do. The words FEELING, CONSCIENCE, and HEART are associated with

---

would have to be investigated thoroughly by examination of context. However, because of the presence of MADNESS as a primary word, and the high incidence of words associated with DEATH in this chapter, the presence of ILL as an antonym to WELL would not seem too misleading insofar as a general assessment of content (or "theme" or "tone") was concerned.

SOUL. Words associated with both HEAVEN and EARTH include NA-
TURE, WORLD, STARS, LIFE, and UNNATURAL. When, bearing
these groups in mind, the researcher sees that GOD, THINK, and
THOUGHT have also qualified as primary words in earlier acts, and
that in this act the words BELIEVE and REASON are linked to THINK,
he might suspect that there is some emphasis upon abstract speculation
and upon speculation about the abstract in this play. Considering the
already noted emphasis upon saying and speaking, the presence of
HEARERS as a sometime primary word will not surprise the researcher.
He might also suspect that ACT, another earlier primary word, has some
connection with SPEAK; the word STAGE, which is linked to ACT, would
strengthen this suspicion.

High-frequency words which seem unequivocally to be verbs—words
such as COME, DO, and GO—would present more difficulty. The researcher might conclude that there is a good deal of coming and going
but he would not be able to attach these actions to individuals. If he
knew anything about Shakespeare, he would realize that many of the
verbal references to coming and going are simply a part of Shakespeare's
staging technique. These verbs provide stage directions in the text itself,
and also they help to fill intervals during which characters are making
entrances and exits. Lacking this information, the researcher would need
to turn to the context of the occurrences of the verbs in order to determine
who was coming and going and the reasons for the activity.

Even after this quick initial glance at VIA's output from Act V, the
researcher would have a good notion of important content, as to both
plot and theme, of the fifth act of *Hamlet*. It is in this act that the King
(Claudius) successfully plots to kill Hamlet. The murder will occur during
a duel, which Hamlet supposes to be a friendly sporting match between
Hamlet and Laertes. The tip of Laertes' foil will have been coated with
a poison. Although Laertes is an excellent fencer, the King takes the
additional precaution of preparing a poison potion (if the researcher's
suspicions had been aroused by POTION he could have consulted the
complete output for Act V and could have discovered that both POI-
SON'D and POISON occur) in the event that Hamlet should have occasion to drink a toast in victory. In the general carnage at the end of
the play, Hamlet, Laertes, and the King are all dispatched by the poisoned
foil, and the Queen, in an effort to drink to Hamlet's early success in
the duel, dies of the poisoned potion. The final act's emphasis on TELL
is clearly pointed out when Hamlet, dying, urges Horatio to "Absent
thee from felicity awhile,/ And in this harsh world draw thy breath in
pain,/ To tell my story."

A separate chapter would be required to delineate the aspects of VIA's output on *Hamlet* that would be of interest to the Shakespearean scholar. Suffice it to say that there are shifts in thematic emphasis—such as the decline in familial reference and the increase in more general impersonal reference at the end of the play—which the traditional scholar may not have noticed and may find illuminating or strengthening for this interpretation of *Hamlet.*

As might be supposed, VIA's output for the translation of *Soviet Military Strategy* differs both in kind and detail from that for *Hamlet.* For example, it was possible to use a cut-off point of 50 or more for primary word designations in the first chapter of the Praeger translation of *Soviet Military Strategy.* Unlike *Hamlet,* there were root groups with very high frequency. For example, the root group containing WAR has 293 occurrences; the root group containing MILITARY has 285 occurrences; and the root group containing STRATEGY has 283 occurrences. In Act V of *Hamlet* the two root groups with the highest frequency (containing GO and KNOW) have only 32 and 30 occurrences, respectively. Because of the very high occurrence of certain root groups in *Soviet Military Strategy,* a reading of the chapter from which they are taken would make the information they convey seem, for the most part, obvious. Thus, VIA's output, using a high cut-off point, for *Soviet Military Strategy* would be of value to the information analyst or content analyst who had no knowledge of the book. Nevertheless, even though the high cut-off point was used, the information conveyed by VIA is more subtle than one might at first suppose. For example, the sublists under WAR include the word AVIATION as well as the word BALLISTICS. The latter might bring missiles to mind, and a glance at the sublist under ARMS would reveal the presence of MISSILE, ROCKET, and NUCLEAR. The information analyst should also notice that FIREARM and GUN appear on that list and that GUNPOWDER is on the list linked to WAR. The terms cited in the above two sentences might imply two kinds of strategy: that involving nuclear missiles and that involving conventional weapons. Pursuing this lead further, the investigator could check the complete output and discover that words associated with NUCLEAR occur 30 times and the terms MISSILES and ROCKETS a total of 7 times. On the other hand, words associated with FIREARMS and GUNS occur a total of 14 times, and the word ARMED occurs in the phrase ARMED FORCES 47 times (the latter information can be obtained from a perusal of the indexes for ARMED and FORCES, or from a MAPTEXT[8] printout, or by going directly from the index entries for ARMED to the indicated context). A further investigation of the contexts for the occurrences of

---

[8] A separate program that provides abstract representation, or graphs, of the text.

ARMED FORCES would show that the phrase seems most often to refer to conventional warfare. Thus insofar as frequency is concerned, conventional warfare receives a greater emphasis than nuclear warfare (approximately 61 to 47), although the latter is by no means ignored. A complete reading of Chapter One shows this picture to be accurate; there is, in fact, an ambivalence toward nuclear warfare, revealed in such passages as the following:

> The country that finds itself in a catastrophic situation as the result of mass nuclear-missile strikes may be forced to surrender even before its armed forces have suffered any decisive defeat. But we must remember that such results can be accomplished only by means of force, by means of armed conflict.[9]

Or, again, having earlier noted that nuclear warfare had completely changed military strategy, this statement is made: "Modern war involves mass armies . . ."[10]

Hamlet and Sokolovsky are certainly very different types of text, and the researcher's interest is not necessarily the same in both cases. For example, no one is likely to use VIA on *Hamlet* to determine whether he wants to read *Hamlet*. Instead, VIA might be used to provide a more detailed basis for interpretation or to make a more general study of the genre of tragedy. With respect to documents like Sokolovsky's, VIA could be used both for gross information retrieval purposes (that is: Should the document be designated for close examination?) and for close analysis. The man-machine interaction which VIA provides can be used both to guide close reading to important sections of a document and to enrich comprehension of that reading so as, for example, to speed effective response to emergency diplomatic communications from other states. For this range of purposes, VIA seems to show considerable promise.

It is through the revelation of content detail and its interconnections within a work that VIA achieves something of a fusion of thematic analysis with idea analysis. The elaboration of an associational structure for terms provides us with some of the conceptual understanding of a work which otherwise would depend on a detailed, human reading. That is, we seem to be finding some of the meaning that eludes nonassociational content analysis by developing through VIA, a structure of intratextual content term relationships somewhat to replace syntactical structures, which content analysis does not reflect. An enriching of theme detail analysis begins to give us some of the understanding of a text which we generally have

---

[9] Praeger, translation, p. 107 (see footnote 4).
[10] Praeger, translation, p. 36 (see footnote 4).

expected to find only when we had, in a traditional way, dealt with concepts by examining themes within their syntactic structures.

In conclusion, then, we are sufficiently encouraged by our content analysis procedures to develop VIA further, along the lines described, including the ring structure analysis option, as well as to continue work on the sizable ancillary research project—thesaurus analysis and construction—necessary to make our content analysis procedure more completely automatic.

27 Pilot: A System for Programmed Inquiry, Learning or Teaching

John A. Starkweather

Medical Psychology
University of California
San Francisco

There is little question that computers can be more useful to people if there is a natural way to communicate with them. Interactive communication appears to be the most natural, since the computer can then develop characteristics of a guide and tutor as well as those of a servant. As a tutor, the computer can then be the means to instruction which meets the individual needs of students. It can provide aids to learning that are more than a drill of new facts; they are exercises in the application of problem-solving methods. For example, the computer can be the means of building repeatable laboratory excercises for students who are learning clinical skills which involved interviewing (Starkweather, 1967a,b,c). Such exercises might take the form of a graded series of pseudopatients or of diagnostic games. With conversational capability, the computer may also develop the capacity to engage in a process of inquiry and testing, gathering information about characteristics of its user which allow it better to match his needs.

There are a number of areas in which the computer is already acting as an assistant, but an individual user of the computer may be hampered by inadequate communication. Conversational ability would allow the computer to consult with a potential user, letting him proceed rapidly if he knows what is required, but shifting into instructional and guiding activity if this is more useful. One can imagine this as a useful introduction for new users of the computer, for assistance to those who wish to use the computer for calculation, or for assistance in framing a question for information retrieval. Conversational mechanisms can provide a route to computer control of file handling and program execution while avoiding much of the pain which users must currently experience.

Here, we are imagining a rapid form of content analysis, with automatic preprogrammed computer methods capable of appropriate reply to human

501

responses. Such immediate and conversational processing suggests the use of available information about the context in which a response occurs. A program can then make reference to a miniature dictionary which has particular relevance to that context. It need not embark on a time-consuming search of a large dictionary and face the concurrent problems of multiple word meanings, such as those discussed by Stone in Chapter 11 of this volume.

To realize goals that require conversational capability by computer, we must have methods for describing recognition strategies, and methods that protect an author of instructional or inquiry programs from direct machine complexity as much as possible.

PILOT, an acronym for *Programmed Inquiry, Learning Or Teaching*, is designed to make this description of recognition strategies easy by providing natural facilities for specifying a conversational dialog to take place between a computer and a person. Machine-assisted learning (computer-aided instruction), specialized inquiry systems, simulated diagnostic interviews, and similar endeavors are a few of the ways in which the system may be used.

PILOT allows the specialist in a noncomputer field to take advantage of the power and versatility of a computer by interacting with conversational programs written in PILOT. He need not have a knowledge of technicalities of the machine if the author of the PILOT program has done his job well. He may be a student, responding to an instructional sequence, or he may be a user of other computer assistance.

A typical conversation with a computer, using a previously written PILOT program, might have the following form:

1. Information or a question is presented by the computer.
2. The user types a reply.
3. Recognition techniques permit the computer to make decisions based on this reply.
4. The computer may make one of several comments, present new information, or ask another question based on its previous decisions.
5. The conversation continues from (2).

PILOT permits a program author to describe to the computer, in a natural way, how to make these decisions and what to do about them. PILOT can also keep a record of user responses. This and many other features of the language are optional so that the author may use only what he needs.

The system is designed to be as machine independent as possible so that its use is not restricted to a particular manufacturer's equipment. PILOT is general enough so that it may be used at different levels of program complexity on a range of machines from a small computer with a typewriter to a large system with many typewriters and visual displays, using one or many programs simultaneously. Particularly in the situation where PILOT is used to converse with remote users of a large computer system, we expect that programs written in PILOT will become capable of teaching a novice user of the computer how to benefit from its services. As more students, teachers, and investigators make use of the computer by this means, we believe that the system will adapt to their needs and become an increasingly valuable assistant.

Athough we expect PILOT to develop truly adaptive program elements, capable of modifying its pattern recognition capacity in response to user activity, this is not a part of its current mechanisms. PILOT programs now improve through active intervention by their authors, who rely on a review of program operation to improve the strategy of content analysis employed at each point in a conversation. This may entail additions to dictionary lists which are relevant in the immediate context. On the other hand, improvement may entail a change in content analysis strategy. For example, a question may need to be reworded so that context is redefined in order to make the recognition of meaning more likely. It sometimes becomes necessary to restrict reponse possibilities in order to handle a recognition problem with limited analysis tools.

A programmer attempting this kind of conversational activity faces problems similar to a tourist who knows only a small portion of the local language in a foreign country. Such a tourist may find that this response to an open-ended question fits with none of his previously stored phrases. Assuming that he can recognize the responses *yes* and *no,* however, he can formulate a question which restricts response even to this extreme degree if necessary.

Appendix A gives an example of a rudimentary PILOT program and the interaction of a student with this program, followed by an explanation. The content was adapted from a program written by third-grade pupils. The numbers at the beginning of each line are for reference only. They are not part of the program.

Appendix B presents a concise description of PILOT definitions and operations.

APPENDIX A

1. Example

A Program to Test Third Grade Students	Program Interaction with a Student
(1) T: HELLO, I AM THE FRIENDLY COMPUTER. WOULD YOU LIKE TO TALK TO ME? TYPE YES OR NO, THEN PRESS THE RETURN KEY TWICE.;	HELLO, I AM THE FRIENDLY COMPUTER. WOULD YOU LIKE TO TALK TO ME? TYPE YES OR NO, THEN PRESS THE RETURN KEY TWICE.
(2) A: ;	.YES.
(3) R: YES;	
(4) G: GOOD. I AM GLAD YOU UNDERSTAND WHAT I SAID.;	GOOD. I AM GLAD YOU UNDERSTAND WHAT I SAID.
(5) C: GJUMP TO QUESTIONS;	
(6) T: PLEASE TRY TO TYPE YES, THEN PRESS THE RETURN KEY TWICE.;	
(7) A: ;	
(8) R: YES;	
(9) G: THAT'S BETTER.;	
(10) B: TRY AGAIN LATER. GET HELP.;	
(11) C: BJUMP TO END;	
(12) T: QUESTIONS: I AM GLAD TO MEET YOU. PLEASE TYPE YOUR NAME SO I WILL KNOW YOU.;	I AM GLAD TO MEET YOU. PLEASE TYPE YOUR NAME SO I WILL KNOW YOU.
(13) A: NAME;;	.MARTY.
(14) T: I HAVE SOME QUESTIONS FOR YOU. HERE IS THE FIRST ONE. DOES ELECTRICITY GO THROUGH WOOD EASILY?;	I HAVE SOME QUESTIONS FOR YOU. HERE IS THE FIRST ONE. DOES ELECTRICITY GO THROUGH WOOD EASILY?
(15) A: ;	.NO.
(16) R: NO, NOT, WET;	
(17) G: YOU SMARTY, HOW DID YOU GUESS IT.;	YOU SMARTY, HOW DID YOU GUESS IT.
(18) B: YOU OUGHT TO STUDY IT .	

HOW LONG DOES A FLY LIVE?
.ABOUT FOUR MONTHS.

YOU DON'T STUDY HARD ENOUGH ABOUT FLIES.
WHAT IS A BABY FROG CALLED?
.A POLLYWOG.

GOOD.

IN BASEBALL, HOW MANY BALLS WALK THE BATTER?
.FOUR.

YOU MUST KNOW HOW TO PLAY BASEBALL.

CONGRATULATIONS MARTY, YOU HAVE REACHED
THE END OF THE TEST.

(19) T: HOW LONG DOES A FLY LIVE?;
(20) A: ;
(21) R: 24 HOURS, ONE DAY, 1 DAY, TWENTY FOUR HOURS;
(22) G: YOU MUST BE SMART TO KNOW THAT.;
(23) B: YOU DON"T STUDY HARD ENOUGH ABOUT FLIES.;
(24) T: WHAT IS A BABY FROG CALLED?;
(25) A: ;
(26) R: TADPOLE, POL*WOG;
(27) G: GOOD.;
(28) B: YOU NEED A GOOD BOOK ON FROGS.;
(29) THIS QUESTION ILLUSTRATES SOME OF THE MORE AD-
VANCED FACILITIES OF PILOT;
(30) T: IN BASEBALL, HOW MANY BALLS WALK THE BATTER?;
(31) A: ANSWER:;
(32) R: 4, FOUR;
(33) G: YOU MUST KNOW HOW TO PLAY BASEBALL.;
(34) C: GJUMP TO NEXT, IF ALPHA THEN JUMP TO ENDQ,
MARK ALPHA;
(35) ALPHA INDICATES WHETHER THE QUESTION WAS NOT
ANSWERED CORRECTLY;
(36) B: THAT'S WRONG. HERE'S A HINT. IT'S 3 OR 4. TRY
AGAIN;
(37) C: JUMP TO ANSWER;
(38) B: ENDQ: I GUESS YOU DON'T KNOW HOW TO PLAY
BASEBALL.;
(39) T: NEXT: CONGRATULATIONS = NAME:, YOU HAVE
REACHED THE END OF THE TEST.;
(40) E: END:;

2. Explanation of Examples

The basic unit of PILOT is the statement, which is terminated by a semicolon. The general form of a statement is:

Statement type: (LABEL: . . . .) body of statement;

The statement type is a single letter code that begins the statement. This must be followed by a colon. The optional label is the next element. Its use and form will be described later. The body of the statement may contain text or control information.

1. The body of a T(EXT) statement is displayed to the subject immediately when the statement is encountered in the program.
2. A(CCEPT) statements instruct the computer to accept an answer from the subject. If the statement body is blank, the computer accepts input from the typewriter after a period is typed, which indicates the machine is ready.
3. The body of a R(ECOGNIZE) statement is a list of elements to be recognized in a subject's response. In this case the list has only one element.
4. G(OOD) statements contain text that is presented to the subject if the previous R statement is satisfied by an answer. In this case the text would be displayed if the subject's response was 'YES'.
5. C(ONTROL) statements contain logical control information for the program. 'GJUMP TO QUESTIONS' (G for good) will cause the statement labeled QUESTIONS (12) to be the next one used in the program only if the previous R statement (3) was satisfied. If it was not satisfied, then the control element is ignored and the following statement is used as the next statement in the program.
6. If (3) is not satisfied, then (4) and (5) are ignored and this statement (6) is the next one used in the program.
7. (7), (8), and (9) are familiar.
10. The text of a (BAD) statement is used only if the previous R statement (8) is not satisfied.
11. 'BJUMP TO END' is used if (8) is not satisfied, otherwise it is ignored.
12. This statement has the label 'QUESTIONS'. This allows (5) to refer to this statement (12). The label is ignored when (12) is encountered in the normal sequence of the program.
13. This statement accepts the subject's name from the typewriter. The label 'NAME' allows the name of the subject to be used by the program by using the label 'NAME'.

14. Statement (14) asks the first question and (15) accepts the answer.

16. This statement is satisfied if any of the elements of the list are recognized in the subject's response.

17. Statements (17) through (22) introduce no new ideas.

23. The PILOT language requires the text that contains quotes (') use two single quote marks (") in the program. This is demonstrated in (23).

24. (24) and (25) are familiar.

26. The second element in the list in this statement will recognize a response containing: POL(anything)WOG. For example, the following responses would be recognized by 'POL*WOG'; pollywog, polywog, polliwog, poliwog, polwog, pol3wog, polxwog.

27. (27) and (28) are familiar.

29. This statement has no (or a null) operation code. It serves as documentary comment for the programmer. The computer will not display the text to the subject.

30. This is the next question.

31. (31), (32), and (33) are familiar.

34. The elements in a list of controls in a 'C' statement are used in the order in which they appear. If a JUMP transfers control out of a 'C' statement, the elements following it will be ignored. The first element (GJUMP TO NEXT) transfers to 'NEXT' (the following T statement). The next element means "If the number that has the label ALPHA is greater than zero then JUMP to the statement labeled ENDQ. Otherwise, ignore this control element." ALPHA is always set to zero initially. In the next element, (MARK ALPHA), MARK means "set the value of alpha to 1."

35. This is a comment explaining the use of ALPHA.

36. The reply if the answer is wrong.

37. This statement asks the question again.

38. This reply is used only if the second answer is wrong. (30) asks the question and (31) accepts an answer. If (32) recognizes the answer (33) replies and (34) jumps to the next question or statement. If the answer is not recognized then (33) is skipped and the 'GJUMP' in (34) is skipped. The next element in (34) tests ALPHA to see if its is greater than zero. Since it was initialized to zero automatically, and hasn't been changed yet, the 'JUMP TO ENDQ' is ignored. 'MARK ALPHA' sets ALPHA to 1. (36) gives a hint and says try again. (37) jumps to (31) to accept an answer. If (31) is recognized by (32) then (33) is typed and (34) jumps to NEXT. The answer is not recognized then (33) is skipped and 'GJUMP TO

NEXT' in (34) is ignored. Since ALPHA was set to one previously, (34) causes a jump to (38) (ENDQ). Here's the interaction with the student for various responses.

First answer correct
IN BASEBALL, HOW MANY BALLS WALK THE BATTER?
.4.
    YOU MUST KNOW HOW TO PLAY BASEBALL.

First answer wrong, second correct
IN BASEBALL, HOW MANY BALLS WALK THE BATTER?
.THREE.
    THAT'S WRONG. HERE'S A HINT. IT'S 3 OR 4. TRY AGAIN
.4.
    YOU MUST KNOW HOW TO PLAY BASEBALL.

Fist and second answers wrong
IN BASEBALL, HOW MANY BALLS WALK THE BATTER?
.FIVE.
    THAT'S WRONG. HERE'S A HINT. IT'S 3 OR 4. TRY AGAIN.
.3.
    I GUESS YOU DON'T KNOW HOW TO PLAY BASEBALL.

39. In this statement, '= NAME:' will be replaced with the input text received by the statement labeled 'NAME' (2).
40. E indicates the end of the program. The label 'END' is referred to by (11).

APPENDIX B. CONCISE DESCRIPTION OF PILOT MECHANISMS, VERSION I

Definitions

The following four symbols are used in this description, but have no special meaning in the PILOT language.
    [   ] Encloses optional material
    .... Last element may be repeated indefinitely
    | Indicates alternative choices
    — Indicates blank
The following terms will be used in describing the language.

Alphameric Characters. The characters A through Z (upper and lower case) and the numbers 0 through 9.

String. A sequence of characters from the set specified, but no characters not in that set.

Word. A string of any number of alphameric characters.

Label. A string of alphameric characters from 1 to 20 characters in length, beginning with a letter. A label may refer to a statement (program location), a string of text, or to a numeric value.

Text. A string of any length and any characters except : ; ' / which are represented by ':' ';' ' ' '/' respectively. Note: ' ' (2 single quotes is not " (1 double quote). The occurrence of = label: will cause the referenced string to be inserted in its place.

List. A series of elements separated by commas, and enclosed in parentheses in certain contexts.

Opcode. One of the following characters; T A R G B C E F N — (Blank).

Author. A person who writes a PILOT program.

Special Character. Any non-alphameric character. The following have special meaning in PILOT:

   ; Terminates a statement.

   : Follows an opcode or label.

  ( ) Encloses lists in certain contexts.

   , Separates elements of a list

   / Starts a new line on the terminal when it occurs in text that is being typed.

Special characters may have special meaning in an 'R' statement.

Expression. The form of an expression is:

$$[+ \ -] \text{ number } | \text{ label}$$

The value of an expression is the value of the number or label. An expression is true if its value is > 0, and false if the value is $< = 0$.

Statement. A statement has the following general form:

$$[\text{label:}] \ . \ . \ . \text{ opcode: } [\text{text}] \ | \ [\text{list}];$$

Statements differ in form according to the opcode involved. The following section describes these different forms. If no opcode is present, the statement is ignored, but may be useful for program comments.

PILOT Operation Codes

Type	T(EXT) or (T(YPE)
Form	[label:] . . . T:[text];
Function	The text will be displayed to the subject when the statement is executed.
Rules	The text will start on a new line at the left margin and continue for as many lines as necessary, except that occurrence of '/' in the text will cause continuation on a new line.
Type	A(CCEPT)
Form	[label:] . . . A:[text];

Function   Accepts a response, ordinarily from the typewriter.

Rules
1. If there is no text the typewriter will type a period on a new line to indicate to the subject that the PILOT program is ready to accept a response.
2. A response is terminated by two successive carriage returns by the subject.
3. If the statement contains text, the text will be used in place of a new response.
4. If the statement is labeled, the label(s) may be used to retrieve the last response accepted by the labeled statement.

Type   R(ECOGNIZE)

Form   [label:] . . . R:[$match expression [OF:]] word [,word] . . . ;

Where each word consists of one or more of the following:
Alphameric strings
Special characters enclosed in quotes
—(BLANKS)
* (ASTERISKS)

Function   Recognition of 'A' text (response).

Rules
1. The conditions for matching an 'R' word are as follows:

Component of 'R' word	Component of 'A' text
A. Alphameric String	Corresponding upper or lower case letters
B. Special characters (including blank) in quotes	Corresponding special characters
C. —(blanks)	One or more blanks or special characters
D. (*asterisks)	Any exclusively alphameric string or no characters

2. The matching process is as follows:
A. The first character of the first 'R' word is compared to the first alphameric character of the 'A' text. If they are the same, the next character of each is compared. This process is continued until the characters differ or until the 'R' word is exhausted.
B. If a character comparison fails the process is repeated, using the next alphameric character of the 'A' text, and the same 'R' word.

Note   If the first character of an 'R' word is a special character, the matching process may start with a non-alphameric character.

C. If the 'A' text is exhausted and the 'R' word is not matched, the matching process if repeated starting at the beginning of the 'A' text, using the next 'R' word.

D. If an 'R' word is matched, the total number of matched 'R' words is compared to the value of the expression in the $MATCH option. (A value of 1 is assumed if the option is missing). If the value of the comparison is positive, the 'R' statement is satisfied. If the value is zero or negative, matching continues with the next 'R' word.

E. Matching stops when the 'R' statement is satisfied (Good), or when the list of 'R' words is exhaused (Bad). Control then passes to the next statement in the program.

Type   G(OOD)

Form   [label:] . . . G:[text];

Function   The text is displayed to the subject if the previous 'R' or 'F' statement was satisfied.

Rules   1. Let N be the number of 'G' statements between the preceding 'R' or 'F' statement and the following 'R', 'A' or 'F' statement. Let L be the number of times the preceding 'R' or 'F' statement has been executed in the program. Then the "M-th" 'G' statements will be used if $M = L$ or $M = N$ and $L > = N$.

2. If there is only 1 'G' statement, it will always be used.

3. In all other respects, the 'G' statement is the same as the 'T' statement.

Note   If there are 3 'G' statements #1 will be used the first time, #2 the second time, and #3 everafter.

Type   B(AD)

Form   [label:] . . . B:[text];

Function   The text is displayed to the subject if the preceding 'R' or 'F' statement was not satisfied.

Rule   In all other respects the 'B' statement is the same as the 'G' statement.

Type   C(ONTROL)

Form   [label;] . . . C:[list];

Function   Control of the logical branching, scoring, and other forms of program maintenance.

Rules   1. The form of list is [prefix] option [,[prefix] option] . . .
          2. Whether an option is used or ignored, the following option is used next. (except for 'IF' and 'JUMP', which see.)

The following are available within a C statement:

Prefix   G(OOD)
Form   The character 'G' as a prefix to any option
Function   The option to which it is prefixed will be executed only if the preceding 'R' or 'F' statement was satisfied.

Prefix   B(AD)
Form   The character 'B' as a prefix to any option
Function   The option to which it is prefixed will be executed only if the preceding 'R' or 'F' statement was not satisfied.

Option   JUMP
Form   JUMP[TO] label list [ON expression]
Function   Conditional transfer of control
Rules   1. Let 'N' be the value of 'expression.' (If on 'expression' is not present N is set to 1.) the statement labeled with the n-th label is used as the next statement in the program.
           2. If N < = 0 or if N > the number of labels in the list, the option is ignored.

Option   CALL
Form   CALL label list [ON expression]
Function   Conditional tranfer of control with automatic return.
Rules   1. If 'ON' expression' is not present then control passes to the statement referenced by the first label in the list. The program continues normally from that statement until an 'E' statement is encountered, which automatically returns control to the first of:
           a. The next label in the list of the CALL option.
           b. The next option in the 'C' statement.
           c. The next statement.
           2. If 'ON expression' is present, the "N-th" label is called (N = value of 'expression'). When an 'E' statement is encountered control passes to the next option in the 'C' statement (*not* the next label in the list), or to the next statement.

Option   ADD
Form   ADD expression [INTO] label list [ON expression]
Function   Addition of a value to a label

Rules 1. The value of the first expression is added to the "N-th" label in the list, where N is value of the second expression.

    2. If the second expression is missing, the value of the first expression is added to all the labels in the list.

Option PUT

Form PUT expression [INTO] label list [ON expression]

Function Assigning a value to a label

Rules 1. The value of the first expression is assigned to the "N-th" label in the list, where N is the value of the second expression.

    2. If the second expression is missing, the value of the first expression is assigned to all the labels in the list.

Option CLEAR

Form CLEAR label list [ON expression]

Function Assigning a value of 0 to a label

Rules 1. The value 0 is assigned to the "N-th label in the list, where N is the value of 'EXPRESSION'.

    2. If 'ON expression' is missing, 0 is assigned to all labels.

Option IF

Form IF expression [THEN] option

Function Conditional use of a 'C' statement option.

Rules 1. If the value of expression is > 0, the option following THEN is used. If the value is $< = 0$, the option is ignored.

    2. "IF's" may be used to any level.

Option MARK

Form MARK label list [ON expression]

Function Assigning a value of 1 to a label

Rules 1. The value of 1 is assigned to the "N-th" label in the list, where N is the value of expression.

    2. If 'ON' expression is missing, 1 is assigned to all lables.

Type E(ND)

Form [label:] . . . E:[text];

Function End programs or subroutines

Rules 1. The 'E' statement generates a return from the last call in effect.

    2. If no calls are in effect, the program is terminated.

    3. Any text on the statement is ignored.

Type F(RAME)

Form [label:] . . . F:[REQUIRE expression];

Function   Defines the conditions necessary to score a frame.

Rules   1. Let N be the value of 'expression'. If the number of 'R' statements that have been satisfied since the last 'A' statement is $> = N$, then the 'F' statement is satisfied; if it is $< N$, the statement is not satisfied.

2. If the require option is missing, a value of 1 is used for expression.

Type   N(OTE)

Form   [label:] . . . N:[text];

Function   Filling strings

Rules   1. The label on the 'N' statement may be used to reference the text in the statement.

2. The 'N' statement has no other effect.

28 Some Principles and Techniques of Automatic Assignment of Words and Word Strings in Texts to Special-Purpose Sublanguages[1]

Casimir Borkowski

Knowledge Availability Systems Center
University of Pittsburgh

A MODULAR VIEW OF THE ENGLISH LANGUAGE

It may be useful to view the English language as containing various special-purpose subsystems—let us call them *sublanguages* or *microlanguages*—each with its own structure which, relative to the *total* structure of the English language, is quite simple.

For example, our rules for naming people can be viewed as the rules of an autonomous linguistic system, that is, as the rules of a microlanguage within the total English language. In other words, our rules for assigning names to people can be viewed as the rules of a language whose permissible utterances are personal names.

Similarly, the rules for assigning names to various points in time—for example, "July 27, 1967"—can be viewed as the rules of a special-purpose microlanguage. Stated another way, the rules of the calendar can be viewed as the grammar of a special-purpose sublanguage whose sentences are dates. The rules of the calendar-language enable us to assign names to each day, month, and year of one century or of five billion years. The rules of the clock and of the calendar are like meters for indexing points in the continuum of time. Of course, they are *linguistic* meters, little linguistic counters—each with its own set of rules which, relative to the *total* set of linguistic rules, is quite simple.

Among the many denotative and connotative sublanguages within the English language, some of the most familiar are the following ones.

1. The sublanguage whose permissible utterances are addresses (for example, "1600 Pennsylvania Avenue," "530 South State Street"):

[1] This chapter was written while I was a Research Staff Member of Thomas J. Watson IBM Research Center, Yorktown Heights, N.Y. For related information, see also Borkowski (1966, 1967), Matthews (1962), and Oettinger (1961).

2. The sublanguage whose permissible utterances are personal titles (for instance, "the First Executive Vice President pro tempore," "Specialist 4").

3. The sublanguage whose permissible utterances are names of organizations (for example, "John Diebold Associates," "Lafayette Radio Store").

4. The sublanguage whose permissible utterances are kinship terms (for instance, "a great maternal uncle," " a second cousin").

5. The sublanguage whose permissible utterances are personal names and so forth.

An important common feature of the sublanguages listed above is their PRODUCTIVITY. Each sublanguage has its own set of words plus a small set of rules for combining its words into infinitely many legitimate phrases. Thus, the sublanguage of personal names possesses a vocabulary and the rules of combination for forming infinitely many full personal names; the sublanguage of names of organizations possesses a vocabulary and the rules of combination for coining infinitely many names of organizations; the sublanguage of names of numbers possesses a vocabulary and the rules of combination for forming infinitely many numbers, and so on.

Perhaps it would be useful to view English as containing both *productive* linguistic subsystems, such as the ones listed above, and *unproductive* linguistic subsystems. A productive sublanguage differs from an unproductive one in that the list of legitimate utterances of an *unproductive* sublanguage is closed, whereas the list of the legitimate utterances of a *productive* sublanguage is open. For instance, the *vocabulary* of the productive sublanguage of personal names (that is, the list of given names and surnames) can be viewed as an *unproductive sublanguage.* Similarly, the list of the names of trees, the list of the names of insects, and so forth, are closed lists, and it may be useful to view them as unproductive sublanguages which are included in the vocabularies of various productive sublanguages.[2]

Notice that productive sublanguages can be used to form utterances that are included in the vocabulary of higher-level productive sublanguages. For instance, the productive sublanguage of names of numbers forms utterances that are part of the vocabulary of such productive sublanguages as the sublanguage for forming dates, the sublanguage for forming street addresses, and the like.

[2] The boundary between productive and unproductive sublanguages is not clearly drawn—instead, productivity and unproductivity should be viewed as the opposite ends of a *continuum.* (It may be possible to classify special-purpose sublanguages according to their degree and type of productivity.)

It seems that if we accept the hypothesis that the English language contains various special-purpose sublanguages, we can isolate and describe many of them quite acccurately and exhaustively. Furthermore, it seems that such descriptions require, for the most part, only a limited expenditure of time and effort on the part of the investigator. This may result from the fact that the structures of many special-purpose sublanguages are rather simple.

The rules of various productive special-purpose microlanguages within English can generally be expressed either in terms of a pattern-and-substitution grammar or in terms of a phrase-structure rewriting grammar. Either formalism (or related formalisms, for instance, Yngve's (1961)), provides an adequate descriptive device for a large number of productive sublanguages.

Unproductive sublanguages can be described simply by listing all their legitimate utterances. Some unproductive microlanguages, such as the language of telephone numbers and the Dewey decimal system, can be easily (1) listed and (2) generated by means of a list of legitimate words and of a simple set of rules for combining these words. (The boundary between artificial and natural microlanguages is not clearly drawn; artificial microlanguages shade into natural ones. An interesting aspect of linguistic change is the phasing of microlanguages into and out of the total natural language.)

The pay-off of (1) hypothesizing the existence of special-purpose sublanguages within total language and then (2) isolating and describing them accurately and exhaustively may be considerable because such descriptions would probably provide valuable data for documentation specialists attempting to classify automatically words and word strings in computer-legible texts.

Personal names, personal titles, dates, place names, number names, measures, and many other words and word strings which can be viewed as belonging to special-purpose sublanguages of English play an important role in indexing and cataloguing documents and also in various systems for extracting and distributing information. Consequently, an accurate, exhaustive, and explicit linguistic description of names, titles, dates, and the like may be useful in developing procedures for automatic identification of various types of words and word strings in computer-legible texts.

SOME TECHNIQUES OF AUTOMATIC ASSIGNMENT OF WORDS AND WORD STRINGS IN TEXTS TO SPECIAL-PURPOSE SUBLANGUAGES

Let us now describe very briefly three broad and overlapping experimental techniques for automatic identification in texts of words and word strings belonging to two important special-purpose sublanguages: personal names and personal titles. But, first, a word of caution: our present set of identification techniques is intended as a first approximation and as a frame of reference in a *series* of investigations aiming at automatic assignment of words and word strings in texts to appropriate special-purpose sublanguages. Various refinements of identification techniques as well as changes in basic methodology can be brought in later as required.

Because many personal titles and names have simple structure, (namely an "immediate-constituent" structure), they can generally be identified with a reasonable degree of accuracy by means of an identification technique known variously as "predictive analysis," "recognition by synthesis," and so on. This identification technique consists in scanning a text from left to right and assigning a word or a string of words in that text to a special-purpose sublanguage whenever it matches a word or a string of words produced by the rules and the vocabulary of a special-purpose sublanguage.

Thus, for example, our "recognition by synthesis" technique for identifying personal titles consists in having an automaton scan a text from left to right and label a word or a word string in that text as a personal title

either

(1)   if it matches a word or a string of words on a list of titles (for example, "Mayor," "President")

or

(2)   if it matches a word or a string of words which is on a list of words and phrases which commonly combine with titles (for instance, "Acting," "Assistant," "Vice") and is followed by a personal title, as in "Acting Mayor," "Acting Assistant Vice President"

or

(3)   if it is a personal title followed by a word or a string of words which is on a list of words which commonly combine with titles (for example, "-elect," "at Large," "pro tempore") as in "Senator-elect," "Ambassador at Large," and "President pro tempore."

Our second mechanism for automatic assignment of words and word strings in texts to appropriate special-purpose sublanguages is called the *pattern-matching mechanism*. It consists in scanning a text from left to right and assigning a word or a string of words in that text to a special-purpose microlanguage if it matches some given pattern of upper- and lower-case letters, numbers, punctuation marks, and so on.

Thus, an automaton is made to scan a text from left to right and label as the name of a person any word beginning with the capital letter "O" followed by an apostrophe, and followed in turn by a word beginning with any capital letter (for example, "O'Brian"). The automaton is kept informed of the exceptions to this rule and to similar rules (for instance, "5 O'Clock").

Similarly, an automaton is made to scan a text and label as the name of a person any string of words of the pattern

$$\$\cent \ldots \#\$.\#\$\cent \ldots Pc$$

where "$\$$" stands for any capital letter, "$\cent$" for any lower-case letter, ". . ." indicates that the preceding character may be repeated, where "$\#$" stands for a space between words, where "." is a period, and "Pc" stands either for a space or for any punctuation mark other than a hyphen.

Our third mechanism for automatic assignment of words and word strings in a text to appropriate sublanguages is called the *decision-table mechanism*. It consists in having an automaton scan a text from left to right and base its decision as to whether a word or word string in that text is to be assigned to a special-purpose sublanguage on sets of decision tables constructed along the lines of Table 1.

Table 1.

Is this string of letters an English word?	Can this string of letters be a personal name?	Is this string of letters the name of a person?
Yes	Yes	Probably yes
Yes	Unknown	It's unlikely
No	Yes	Yes
No	Unknown	It's likely

The question "Is this string of letters an English word?" can be answered by means of (1) a look-up in a dictionary based on some desk dictionary and (2) simple rules for identifying affixes of the plural, the past tense, the gerund, the negation, and so on.

The question "Can this string of letters be a personal name?" can be answered by means of (1) a look-up in a dictionary based on a large telephone directory, and (2) simple rules for identifying the plural (for instance, "es" and "s" as in "the Joneses" and "the Weinbergs") and other affixes.

Since our identification procedures were embodied in dictionary entries and flow charts that were sufficiently detailed to permit an accurate manual execution of identification procedures, it was decided that our identification system would be tested out by hand on a sample of *The New York Times* texts.

Our 40,000-word sample contained approximately 800 occurrences of names of persons. Of the 800 occurrences of names of persons, 46 (or approximately 6 percent) of the total were missed. In addition, about 50 words and word strings were mistakenly identified as personal names or personal titles.

Figure of merit *F* for the results of our identification system was computed by means of the following formula of A. R. Meetham (1963):

$$F = \frac{C^2}{(C + M) \times T}$$

where *C* is the number of correct identifications, *M* is the number of mistaken identifications, and *T* is the number of names of persons in the sample.

For $T = 806$, $C = 746$, and $M = 47$

$$F = \frac{746^2}{(746 + 47) \times 806} = .87$$

Note. Because of our scoring rules, the number of correct identifications and misses does not add up to the number of names of persons in the sample.

SOME POSSIBLE APPLICATIONS OF AUTOMATIC ASSIGNMENT OF WORDS AND WORD STRINGS IN TEXTS TO SPECIAL-PURPOSE SUBLANGUAGES

In our present state of knowledge, the subject of the applications of computer programs capable of recognizing personal titles and names in texts must remain in the domain of speculation. We would conjecture that if the speed of computation was high and its price could be kept low, and if the figure of merit could be raised to .95 or higher, then a computer program for identifying personal titles and names in texts would be worth incorporating into existing information retrieval systems of very large newspapers and periodicals.

It is not clear whether a program with a figure of merit lower than .95 would be useful in information retrieval. We would surmise that it might be adequate for some purposes, provided that it is sufficiently fast and cheap.

Several uses suggest themselves immediately for computer programs capable of identifying cheaply, rapidly, accurately, and exhaustively the names and titles of persons in computer-legible texts. They fall into five broad and overlapping categories: (1) automatic indexing, (2) determining how the names of persons cluster with one another and with other words, (3) establishing frequency counts of names of persons, (4) tracing associations between names of persons, and (5) answering questions of the "Who-Whose-Whom" type within an automatic or semiautomatic system capable of providing answers to "Who?", "Whose?", "Whom?", "When?", and "Where?" types of questions addressed to a file of computer-legible texts.

Systems for (1) automatic classification of words and word strings in texts and (2) subsequent automatic extraction of data from texts may be useful to many groups. Among these groups are:

1. Political scientists, sociologists, lexicographers, onomasticians, and literary scholars concerned with the occurrence of names, titles, and other words in texts.

2. Editors, documentalists, librarians, and others concerned with automation of editing and of literature searching.

3. Opinion survey and market research statisticians concerned with the occurrence of names in texts, celebrity ratings, measurement of opinion trends, and the like.

29 Confrontation of Issues: Excerpts from the Discussion Session at the Conference

Philip J. Stone

Center for Advanced Study in the Behavioral Sciences
Palo Alto, California

A discussion session could only touch on a few of the many issues raised in the articles. Between the time the articles were available to the editor and the conference, four sets of questions were circulated to the participants for consideration, each relevant to several of the articles. The themes of these question sets were threaded through the discussion:

1. What needs to be added to present content analysis procedures to make them approximate the "understanding" that occurs in communication between humans? Is this an appropriate goal of content analysis? Can this be done by a computer?

2. In what ways can we go beyond the sentence as a unit of context for content analysis? By so doing, what kinds of information can be produced? What special problems are posed by conversational data? Are any guidelines suggested by linguistic theory?

3. Can there be a generalization of computer procedures for content analysis? At what level (from the user's point of view) should this generalization take place? What kinds of pitfalls of built-in limitation shoud be avoided in designing general systems?

4. What is the relation between the tasks of leading one to information (Janda's "indexing") and evaluating information ("coding")? How are they best combined?

Throughout the discussions, the point was emphasized that the procedures used in content analysis depend on the purposes of the investigator. Basic differences in purpose, of course, could easily be distinguished. The investigator inferring authorship of documents looks at idiosyncratic and regional language characteristics. A person cataloging topics focuses on noun words, making the task an information retrieval problem. The investigator inferring motivations and life styles of the speaker focuses on

523

other clues. A person recreating the process of conversation, as Starkweather outlined, has still different concerns. Although the existence of such different purposes was clear, it nevertheless was difficult to keep them separated in the discussion.

About 75 people attended the discussion, including many participants from other sections. In the text below, persons are identified by their last names. If they have not authored a chapter in this volume, a footnote gives their full name and institutional affiliation. Two participants (one a professor who looked on himself as a potential user of content analysis and one a University of Pennsylvania graduate student who raised questions about linguistics) are unfortunately unidentified. The linguistics question was raised only a few minutes before we had to disband.

As editor, I have taken slight liberties in the name of readable English and have attempted to condense what proved, on careful listening, to be repetition. A draft of these excerpts was circulated with the option for each person (except, of course, our unidentified participants) to make revisions, which all of them did. The reader can assume, therefore, that the comments here represent the participants' views.

As the contributed papers made evident, one major procedural issue is whether to test for the presence of categories made up in advance, or whether to call upon the computer to somehow formulate "natural" categories. While different measures of association might be used, in fact, the main technique for deriving categories from data has been factor analysis (such as used by Iker and Harway in Chapter 22). Several persons present called this second approach, in general, into question and challenged the use of factor analysis, in particular. The discussion session opened on this point with a comment by Gerard Salton.

SALTON: I'd like to say something about factor analysis.

STONE: Well, we all have our prejudices on factor analysis . . .

SALTON: No, no, no, I have results, not prejudices. We have a great many results where we compare, for example, an automatically produced dictionary which effectively consists of word groups generated by a process similar to factor analysis with an ordinary manually produced thesaurus. We, unfortunately, find that the automatically produced groupings do not at all approximate in effectiveness the regular thesaurus. In other words, to make it slightly more specific, suppose we take a document collection and cut it in half arbitrarily, and then construct our word groups from the first half using automatic term-term correlation and clustering procedures, while using the resulting groupings to analyze the other half of the same collection. After evaluation, we find that the automatic dictionary is not able to approximate the work that a human being puts into an ordinary synonym dictionary. I wish it weren't so, but it is so, at least in our results.

Now let me mention one additional point about factor analysis, and this is in response to Phil [Stone's] remark that we all have prejudices. If I were to construct an automatic dictionary, I would never use factor analysis. I think factor analysis is one of the most complicated, cumbersome, inefficient, and costly methods for that task that is available. Some very pretty ones suggested by Roger Needham and by Loren Doyle (1966) use the order NlogN operations instead of N^2. This method does not require a matching of each term with each other term. The only justification for factor analysis would occur if some statistical interpretation were needed which requires the autocorrelation function. The other reason is that you might already happen to have a program package that does include factor analysis [general laughter].

GOLDHAMER: I think Dr. Krippendorff's paper of last night, in which he described three types of messages, is very relevant. The comment was made that we need to distinguish the approaches (and their depths) that we want to use. I thought it was relevant that he set out to answer the question of what the *structure* of the information is that enables the analyst to make content inferences about a source. Of the three models presented, I think the association model is relevant to the idiosyncratic-nomothetic distinction we are making here. Association models realize content in the *statistical correlation* between observational variables. Discourse models of messages realize content as *linguistic referents* on denotations and connotations. Communication models of messages realize content as the manifestation of *processes of control* within dynamic systems of interaction. The present description of where association analysis stops being useful and other approaches are needed seems to be very close to the limitations that Dr. Krippendorff described.

STONE: A number of us over time have discussed building a synonym dictionary automatically from word context information in the data. I've often wondered why no one has programmed a distributional structure analysis procedure such as outlined by Harris (1954). Certainly approaches are needed other than those relying on word-word matrices, which get to be of immense size. As the analysis becomes more elaborate and concerned with the idiosyncratic context of each document, doesn't this mean then, in addition, a turn to Krippendorff's discourse and communication models?

KRIPPENDORFF: Harris' distributional analysis aims at semantic structures that are internal to a body of text. It does not get at what a discourse is about. Discourse models indicate a set of procedures that process a body of text in terms of their linguistic references to objects that are external to it. Communication models suggest viewing documents as instances of linguistic exchanges in particular communication situations. For example, it is quite obvious that a purely linguistic interpretation of diplomatic documents would not suffice to understand the political situation from which they are sampled. Such documents are almost always viewed by politicians in the light of their possible consequences. The level of formalization regarding communication models has not progressed far enough so as to allow computer implementations.

Factor analysis has a built-in assumption about correlations. When this computational device is used in content analysis, it is implicitly assumed that the semantic structures which a communicator conveys in a text can be represented adequately by the statistical procedures that go into this technique. This assumption is not warranted in all situations. For example, the kind of content analysis that David Hays talked about presupposes analytical procedures that in fact would amount to an operationalization of English language usage, with discourse specific dictionaries, etc. Factor analysis has neither been developed for such analyses nor could it possibly account for how a conversationalist makes use of linguistic utterances. Analytical procedures must be formally compatible with the object of analysis.

PARKER[1]: I would like to direct this question to Gerard Salton. Do you have any data or any opinions with respect to the question of clustering on the basis of term-term associations as distinguished from context associations? For example, there is the problem that one term may be a synonym for another but not correlated because they are substitutable. Therefore, we need terms that correlate with the same terms, but not necessarily with each other as the basis for an automatic dictionary.

SALTON: We have performed term-term associations on all our collections. The conjecture has been made that term-term associations, using, say the sentences of documents as a context, will identify so-called contiguity relations. When you take second order relations, that is when you group terms A and C because A co-occurs with B and B co-occurs with C, then you get synonymous relations. From our results, this conjecture appears to be false, that is, the second order correlations are not equivalent to synonymy relations any more than single-link associations. At least this has been the case in our work. Is this what you are asking?

PARKER: That was the question I was asking, whether you had data on this point. You have answered very nicely.

IKER: Content analysis is that analysis of a data base which yields the kind of information relevant to the needs with which you began. Ole [Holsti] had three sentences in a recent paper that had exactly the same words, involving Russian-American relations. If it is important in your analytic system to know who has what attitude toward whom or to know who started it, then a correlation approach is going to die. If, on the other hand, it is of sufficient import to know there is an area or domain internal to your data base that talks about "Russians," "Americans," and "irritation" and that allows you to go back to that segment and find out who did it, then the correlational analysis does the job to

---

[1] Edwin Parker, Department of Communications, Stanford University.

this point. I can't really see that there is a disagreement here.

PSATHAS: I think there is a disagreement here because a correlational approach often means that you bring in interpretation at some point, either prior to or after the analysis. The implicit set of rules that you are using to make an interpretation of a correlation may be explicit in the other approach, which describes how to infer from subject, object and verb a certain kind of action orientation between the subject and object.

IKER: Yes, but look at what is going to happen if someone disagrees with you. Now we are going to start talking about which one is the safest approach. At some point or other, you are always going to have to introduce some kind of abstraction. You have to do it. If you deal with a classical content analysis system, then you make that abstraction before you begin by setting up categories. You then finish up your data analysis and, if you like it, you're home free. But if I read it and I don't particularly like your categorizational system, I have lost everything you have done because I can't use it. Now if you use a factor analytic technique, you make no assumptions about that data other than the basic theoretical one of the associational structure, which you either buy or you don't buy. When we get done, we will give you a set of factors and we will give you what we think are a good set of names. If you don't like our set of names, apply your own. You do not have to reanalyze. The data is there as it was and nothing you can do will change it. You may interpret it differently; that is your privilege. But you may not ever come along and reinterpret a classical content analytic system, because to do so instantly takes you back to starting all over again since the categories are not the same any more.

PSATHAS: I am arguing for the explication of the rules you are using to make your interpretation. I'm saying that a correlational model doesn't provide these. You may bring them in later, you may bring them in earlier, but often not explicated are the criteria and the structure of those rules which are operative.

STONE: Maybe Dr. Hays will get us out of this quickest [general laughter].

HAYS: The argument about whether to establish categories by direct analysis from material from one person is different from the question of whether to get the categories out of the material or to have them in advance. The question is whether individuals have structures which at the level of these categories (like earth, air, fire, and water) are different from individual to individual. That is a point I was trying to make last night. People don't all speak the same language. And so there is a substantive issue here which is not just technical. On the other hand, I strongly disagree with the implication of the last remark that if there is structure in your data factor analysis will bring it out. It may be that the guy who rejects your factor analysis will come to exactly the same data with a set of categories established in advance which by his analysis shows him something new about the same original data base. He may find himself in the same position as you were ascribing to the rejector of the pre-categorized analysis.

IKER: Earlier, I mentioned to somebody that it was perfectly possible, but I suspect accidental, that you could come out with exactly the same analyses, starting with a present categorizational system and starting with a factor analytic, if you will, atheoretical, utilization. I am not arguing this point. I think it is possible. I don't think it probable.

HAYS: That is not my point. I understood your argument to be that if an analyst comes to the data with preestablished categories, and a second analyst doesn't like the results because he thinks the categories were mischosen, he has to redo the job. Whereas, if you do a factor analysis, then whatever categories you bring out are the sole categories that could result and therefore no second analyst can ever have to throw away your results, although he might throw away your names for the results. I say that is just statistically not a corect point.

IKER: Why?

HAYS: Because by having categories in advance, he is able to use more sensitive techniques and therefore may find structures in the data that the weaker methods of factor analysis just can't bring out.

[A number of people start talking at once.]

HOLSTI: It doesn't seem in any way to differ from the point that there are different kinds of purposes to content analysis and the kind of thing I think you [Hays] are pointing out that cannot be borne out through factor analysis is exactly the kind of point that you [Iker] were trying to illustrate with those three sentences of mine.

IKER: Yes.

STONE: The gentleman in the back.

FIRST UNIDENTIFIED PERSON: I come to these meetings as a possible purchaser of the techniques of content analysis [general laughter] . . . but I think that maybe it ought to be called "discontent analysis" [more laughter] . . . I am wondering to what extent in that Oz study [Chapter 22 by Iker and Harway, *infra*] are the cards stacked by virtue of the fact that you already have let yourself in for a frequency count of the most frequent words. To what extent does that already affect the categories? My second question is to what extent are the General Inquirer and your technique [Iker's] the inverse of one another. Is it because the General Inquirer is so heavily loaded and has to be stripped of its loadings? Is the reverse true in your case?

IKER: To the first question concerning frequency, the answer is no, there was no loading. The reason is very straightforward. We did two analyses on the Oz data. One of them was a strict countdown on the top 215 high frequency words which yielded the twenty factors which I presented this afternoon. The other analysis was to pick the best set of 215 words. We specifically chose that set of 215 words which we knew very well were the right words. I know that book; I'm an expert on the Wizard of Oz [laughter]. In each analysis, 215 words went in, both of them from the same basic 1400 word list. There were only 98 of those 215 words in common. We had nearly perfect content matches on 16 of the 20 factors, that is, 80 percent matching.

To the second question I would say no, I don't think the General Inquirer and the WORDS system are the inverse of each other. I think they are simply basically different approaches to content analysis.

STONE: I don't know what "inverse" means in this case.

IKER: That they are on opposite ends of a continuum.

STONE: But what is the continuum?

OGILVIE: I am a little disturbed about the implication, whether it was intended or not, that once you have a dictionary you know what your results will be. That's both true and not true. Of course, a dictionary automatically imposes some restrictions on what you can look at, but if the categories are chosen sensibly, with enough flexibility, some of them based on intuition, some on theory, some on hypotheses, some on guesses, then you can at least allow some of the patterns that are in the data to emerge and still be centrally involved in that process of discovery. In fact, once you have a dictionary, you don't know what results are going to be unless you have two or three variables and it is a simple study.

[The recording tape was changed at this point and a part of the discussion was lost.]

SALTON: Could it be that the text of Oz is made up of a series
(to IKER): of relatively homogeneous stories? The factors that you presented this afternoon looked reasonable but is that a result of a fact that your text is not representative of sets of non-homogeneous documents?

IKER: Yes and no. The neatness and, in a sense, the elegance of this was indeed in part a fact of the way Oz is made up. But we have also done 50 analyses of this type on direct tape-recorded transcriptions and psycho-therapeutic interviews. There isn't anything more messy. Yet, we come out with the same kinds of things. One reason we went to Oz was as a kind of stringent test of the system to see if it could do this, the other was for public presentation. There is, in a sense, face validity of Oz and this is the reason we used it.

NAMENWIRTH: I would like to direct myself to a central question: What is the generality of the interpretive scheme which is used in the assessment of meaning? In making these assessments, one or another interpretive scheme is always introduced. One of these interpretive schemes is the scheme of the communicator himself, but in the assessment of meaning the communicator's scheme is surely not the only possible one and among these possible schemes it is one of rather low generality.

In choosing among possible interpretive schemes the purpose of the analysis is a most important consideration. Most of us do not try merely to assess some meaning attribute of a document or communication. We try to relate this attribute to something else, for instance, a characteristic of the communicator, or a characteristic of the audience. Whatever these characteristics, we try to do that in increasingly comprehensive and systematic terminology. One of the advantages of the computer in this process was that it suggested more universal procedures for the interpretation of meaning. These procedures in turn would lead to cumulative knowledge in this respect.

The suggestions that have been discussed too long already are, of course, directly opposed to cumulative knowledge. If it is maintained that the meanings of words are determined by their empirical associations to other words and that, furthermore, these associations are likely to vary from communicator to communicator, then we need a new dictionary for each new case. And, with these unique dictionaries cumulative knowledge becomes utterly impossible. On the other hand, we are forced to realize that there is no general scheme of interpretation possible for all situations, that there is no general dictionary possible for all situations.

What can the computer offer in the resolution of these issues? Can it help us to determine at what level of abstraction optimum universality exists in word interpretation and meaning assessment or can't it do such things at all? If the latter is the case, I respectfully submit that the computer is a very interesting bookkeeping tool, but not really a creative instrument at all for resolving the central problems of content analysis.

HAYS: I had wanted to say that factor analysis is not content analysis and the problems of doing it are not the computer problems of content analysis. One of the interesting questions from the computer side is why doesn't somebody (1) take a pretty good-sized dictionary of English and really dress it up with a tremendous variety of tags very reliably assigned by clever psychological, psychometric techniques and use that as the dictionary for any content analysis that needs this technique in general and (2) get hold of some of the very high-speed dictionary lookup procedures that have been developed in the course of the last decade, then make a utility package consisting of high-speed dictionary lookup and a dictionary of English with a mass of tags in it? Making that available as a utility package, it seems to me, would satisfy Ogilvie because he says that if you put a wide enough variety of tags in in the first place that you are really doing the job in a serious way.

GOLDHAMER: With regard to the second point of preparing a utility package of dictionary storage and look-up, I don't think it is a good idea because I don't think we have arrived at a manner of storing semantic information, that is, meanings of words, which is satisfactory for reasons given. I don't think it would be a wise idea to pin people down to the lousy procedures we now have for storing information and retrieving it, even though they are fast and technically very efficient. I don't think the procedures are realistic in terms of giving one freedom to develop them in the way the human mind might try to; that is, to develop them in parallels to human processing.

MILLER[2]: I think sometimes we get into the bind of trying to make the machine operate the same way we operate. Machines operate differently. A student who is learning programming may decide that to find the log of a number he should look it up in a table and, therefore,

[2] J. Philip Miller, Washington University, St. Louis.

writes a program to read in a table of logs and do lookup every time he needs one, extrapolating as needed between the values given. That is ridiculous. There are techniques which are suited to the machine much better and structured very differently from the way a human goes about solving a problem.

GOLDHAMER: But they are not functionally incompatible, that is, they do not prevent you from doing in the machine something that the mind can do. Maybe people do it in an entirely different way, that doesn't matter to me at all, but our procedure must be functionally compatible, not similar, but compatible. In this regard, to give an example, you must be able to relate one word to another as having something in common. There have to be linkages. You must be able to indicate that one word is a subset in some respect of another word, that is, hierarchies of generality. You must be able to include these possibilities within a dictionary; otherwise you hang yourself; and, in fact, as Quillian (1965) argued (since I think he has shown it to be possible within a limited range), you must be able to implement something like psychological set or a predisposition to choose one path of meaning rather than another. Given, we have gotten into this far enough to know what other things we "must" do, why hand somebody a package which has a closed-end on it?

SALTON: I think there is no disagreement between what you say and what they have said.

HAYS: We're just a generation apart, that's all [general laughter and clapping]. Oh, thank you.

SALTON: I think what Dave [Hays] was saying, and he is perfectly right, I think, is that there exist now very fast hashing schemes for looking up words in dictionaries. The techniques are reasonably well-known, and if you have available a program package that you can use with any dictionary, assuming a certain basic kind of a format—it doesn't prevent you from adding in other things later on. You certainly use it. I can tell you what happened to us. We had a very fast lookup scheme implemented at Harvard some years back on the [IBM] 7094. Instead of reprogramming it at Cornell, it was just so much easier to keep using the old scheme on the 7094. The fact that you have a utility program to use, even though some of your dictionary coding may not be optimum for what you want to do two years from now doesn't prevent you from . . . .

GOLDHAMER: I would only hypothesize that when you carry that package from Harvard back to Cornell, you carry with it the restrictions from going into new areas and new possibilities that you had back at Harvard. For example, the difference between an active memory and a passive memory is just too large to be included within a package. That is, freedom to modify things within the dictionary as you go along—temporary modifications, temporary paths of information and so on within a dictionary—is not really within a package. Frankly, I agree it would be nice to have a utility package, but not one that would be so nice that people would hesitate to look into it. I would hate to see it as a closed box.

SECOND UNIDENTIFIED: PERSON: I just want to inject a completely different note into the proceedings. Listening to the discussions over the past two days, there seems to me a notable lack by the workers in the field of using some of the modern techniques of current linguistics to try and help them with their problems. There has been hardly any discussion about this, apart from David Hays' paper (Chapter 3, *infra*) yesterday. So can I ask the panel and the audience at large why they are not using them, what they would like to see, and what they would project their use to be in the next few years?

GOLDHAMER: At a technical level, that is what I tried to do in my paper.

NAMENWIRTH: But there is a difference here; you (Goldhamer) want to do it in two years and Mr. Hays in 15.

STONE: [To unidentified person] What in particular do you have in mind?

SECOND UNIDENTIFIED   Well, let me put it another way. Are there any linguists in the audience who would like to say how they would

PERSON: foresee their current grammars being built being applicable to this kind of content analysis?
[short pause]

STONE: We have been following what people like Kuno and Jane Robinson have been doing. I would be glad to discuss what in particular we might implement. The possibilities of applying certain aspects of this work have been rather appealing, but our group has not done any major reconceptualization of our programming in several years.

SALTON: I am afraid you are going to have to be more specific than that. What do you think the linguists have to offer to us?

SECOND UNIDENTIFIED PERSON: I thought part of the linguist's job was to put forward certain criteria by which they could isolate meaningful parts of the sentence and relate these things to each other, and this is exactly the kind of thing you want to do.

STARKWEATHER: I am not sure that is really true. It seems to me that one of the few things people seem to agree about tonight was the notion that what is meant by content analysis, or you might say what is meant by the meaningful part of the sentence, differs a great deal according to the purpose. Thus, we have differences between retrieval and content analysis and various approaches to content analysis. For example, in one kind of context it makes sense, within the corpus of word usage of one individual, to look at an individual's usage in a statistical fashion and to develop factor or cluster scores. We may, however, be concerned with working up groups of synonyms that are useful in a different way. Other people would not be happy with that because for their particular needs they would have to develop some kinds of logical clusters that make sense in another way but that you can't really tag as synonyms per se. This hasn't been discussed tonight at all.

The direction that I think content analysis is going within my meaning of content analysis, is toward finding ways to handle immediate interactional response and immediate conversational recognition methods. In that situation one has to be in a very flexible position to be able to change one's strategy from one moment to the next. This is true because the purposes of analysis change as one carries on a conversation. One has to be in a position to track those changes with changes in strategy and method. Ways that you make up lists that you use, and ways that you reference this dictionary or that one, or that subsection or that other subsection, or clues that you get from what is going on, lead you to do things one way versus another. At this moment, it seems to me, people haven't begun to see that need yet. They are separated out with each person's having a special main purpose and, therefore, developing methods along one line. I think before we get through we will all be doing content analysis by many different strategies.

STONE: I think that is a realistic prediction and hope on which to end this session. Thank you all very much.

Editor's conclusion. As the papers and discussion in this section reflect, computer-aided content analysis has gone from being only an idea, less than ten years ago, to an active field that includes several quite different approaches. The discussion was pointed toward the future, but was based on experience from a number of completed studies. I hope that the workers in this field will convene again before another decade elapses. It will be of interest to see how the issues presented here become resolved with time. This editor believes that while computer-aided content analysis has had considerable success in attaining an initial plateau, further sophistication will require much more cumulative effort than has been put in to date. A key question is whether there will continue to be qualified people willing to invest the necessary energies and talents.

Appendix: Education in Content Analysis: A Survey

F. Earle Barcus

School of Public Communication
Boston University

The future development of content analysis as a research approach in the social sciences and humanities will be determined largely by the quantity and quality of instruction given in institutions of higher learning. To our present knowledge, no one has attempted to investigate the extent of content analysis teaching or to study systematically the evaluation of content analysis by teachers and researchers. The study reported here, therefore, has attempted to gain a limited insight into these questions by means of a mail questionnaire survey.[1]

The primary purpose of this study was to gain information about the type and extent of formal training in content analysis offered students in United States colleges and universities. Two questionnaires were mailed to a sample of departments in these colleges and universities. The initial mailing was to gather data on the nature and extent of content analysis teaching and to provide a list of institutions for a second mailing.

Colleges and universities, included in the universe from which the sample was drawn, were from those listed in the *Directory of Higher Education* (1965–1966), published by the U.S. Office of Education. Eliminated from the universe were colleges that offered less than four years of work beyond the 12th grade (that is, primarily junior colleges); institutions offering only terminal occupational programs, teacher preparatory programs, and only professional programs in law, medicine, science, or engineering; and a few schools in the "miscellaneous" classification. Included were institutions offering a liberal arts program and the bachelor's and/or the first professional degree; master's and/or several professional degrees; and the doctor of philosophy or equivalent degree.

[1] The research reported here was supported by a grant from The Annenberg School Content Analysis Conference Committee. I thank William Paisley for valuable advice in the planning stage. I also acknowledge the encouragement and support of the Boston University Communication Research Center, and thank Mrs. Carolyn Teich, Graduate Assistant in the Center, for her help with the analysis.

This procedure yielded a universe of 1181 institutions of higher learning in the United States, enrolling approximately 4 million students. From this universe, a sample of 100 institutions was drawn proportionate to enrollment.

After selecting the sample of institutions, the *College Blue Book* (11th Ed., Vol. I, 1965) was utlized to locate names and addresses of heads of the departments considered relevant to the study. Thus, any of the following departments listed was selected for mailing:

1. Anthropology
2. Business, Commerce, Business Education, Marketing, Business Administration, Business and Public Administration
3. Communication, Telecommunication, Journalism and Communication
4. Communication Arts, Radio-TV
5. Communication Research
6. Education, Educational Research and Service, Educational Psychology
7. English
8. Government, Government Research, Government and Politics
9. History (also History and Political Science)
10. Journalism, Agricultural Journalism, Journalism and Public Relations
11. Language and Literature, Comparative Literature
12. Library School, Library Science
13. Linguistics
14. Political Science
15. Psychology
16. Social Psychology
17. Sociology, Sociology and Anthropology, Rural Sociology
18. Speech, Speech and Dramatic Arts, Theatre Arts, Speech Communication
19. Information Science, Computer Science

Where no specific department was listed, the request was mailed to the dean of the school or college.

The initial sample consisted of 501 mailings, primarily to departments. The mailing consisted of a covering letter explaining the purpose of the study, a three-page questionnaire, and return envelope. The procedures yielded a total of 199 returns and 175 usable questionnaires.

The second questionnaire was designed to obtain more detailed "qualitative" data from the instructors who were involved in teaching content analysis, as reported on the questionnaires received from the first mailing.

Also, additional questionnaires were sent on the basis of information gained from the first mailing. Although the total first mailing was 501, a few questionnaires were photocopied by the institutions, distributed, and returned from other departments or divisions. For simplification, these were treated as mailings and a base of 509 is used for tabulation purposes.

RATE OF RETURN

The highest rates of return were from the departments of Communication and Journalism (70 percent), and Sociology and Anthropology (64 percent). The top five departmental groupings, representing one-third of all mailings, accounted for one-half of the total returns, as can be seen on Table 1.

Since the questionnaires were ultimately intended for individual departments, about 100 mailings addressed to schools, academic deans, or directors of studies could be eliminated from tabulations of deparmental response. It is evident from the low response to these mailings that they were not generally forwarded to the appropriate departments for reply.

Table 1. *Rate of return by department (listed in rank order by rate of return)*

Department or School	Mailings	Usable Returns	Return Rate (Percent)
Communication and Journalism	30	21	70
Sociology and Anthropology	39	25	64
Speech, Theatre Arts, and Radio-TV	38	18	47
Library School, Library Science	23	10	43
History	31	13	42
Education	75	30	40
Linguistics and Information Science	5	2	40
Psychology	26	9	35
English: Language and Literature	44	14	32
Political Science and Government	22	7	32
Business Administration, Commerce	73	20	27
Other (College of Liberal Arts, College of Arts and Sciences, College Deans, etc.)	103	6	6
Total	509	175	34
Departmental Inquiries (excluding the "other" category above)	406	169	42

Thus, including only those addressed to department heads, a return rate of 42 percent accurately reflects the response. That is, an estimated 42 percent of all departments *reached* responded to the questionnaire.

AVENUES OF EXPOSURE

There are several avenues by which the student may be exposed to content analysis. Six of these were explored in the questionnaire.

1. The first and most obvious means of exposure is the course designed specifically for teaching theories and methodologies of content analysis—the course or seminar devoted to content analysis teaching.

2. A second method is through those courses in various departments which are devoted to analysis of documentary materials—although traditionally these courses have not been dubbed with the content analysis rubric.

3. There are also the general introductory research methods courses given by a majority of departments in which exposure to content analysis studies or techniques is included as an integral part of the methods course. The extent of exposure may vary from a brief lecture or reading to extended consideration of the subject, including projects involving the technique.

4. In other cases, the department may not offer content analysis training in any of the above forms, but may refer students to other departments known to offer such training.

Table 2. *Extent of potential student exposure to content analysis education*

Item	Number of Departments	Percent of Responding Departments
1. Offer specialized course in content analysis	10	6
2. Offer related course in documentary research	57	33
3. Offer general or introductory research methods course in which content analysis is included	101	58
4. Know of content analysis course in another department	20	11
5. Member(s) of departmental faculty currently engaged in research utilizing content analysis	58	33
6. Have had graduate student theses or dissertation in content analysis in past year	22	13
7. Reported none of the above	54	31
(Total responding departments)	(175)	(100)

Table 3. *Availability of formal content analysis training*

Departmental Title	N =	Number of Departments that Listed Content Analysis Course Training[a]	Percent
Library Science (also Library and Information Science)	11	10	91
Communication and Journalism	21	17	81
Sociology and/Anthropology	25	18	72
Education	30	21	70
Political Science and Government	7	4	57
Other (for example, Social Science, etc.)	6	3	50
History	13	6	46
Business, etc.	20	9	45
Speech, Speech and Radio-TV	18	7	39
English, Language, Literature	14	5	36
Psychology	9	1	11
Linguistics	1	—	0
Total	175	101	58

[a] As defined by categories 1 and 3 only in Table 2.

5. Students may also be exposed to such methodologies through the work of faculty. Thus, departments with faculty engaged in content analysis research offer another avenue of exposure, even though an informal one.

6. Finally, departments which allow (or encourage) theses and/or dissertations utilizing content analysis techniques provide another means of exposure.

Table 2 illustrates the extent of potential exposure of students to content analysis as measured by these six criteria.

Because of the response bias evident in the return rates, it is estimated that the figures in Table 2 are considerably inflated. For example, if one were to generalize to the total population, it is assumed that students in the nonresponding departments had considerably less opportunity for exposure to content analysis than students in responding departments. The 10 out of 175 departments (6 percent) offering content analysis seminars could thus be considered a high estimate. The low estimate would be 10 out of 501, or 2 percent of departments in the total sample (or by extension, in the universe).

The departments most likely to offer courses in or to list research courses that include content analysis are indicated in Table 3.

SPECIALIZED COURSES IN CONTENT ANALYSIS AND RELATED AREAS

Students may be exposed to content analysis in a variety of settings, disciplines, and with varying approaches or emphases. Respondents listed, for example, the following as "content analysis" courses.

Communication/Tele-communications:
Theory and Analysis of Message Content
Content Analysis and Scaling
Analysis of Documentary Evidence
Analysis of Broadcasts
Measurement of Audiences and Messages
Seminar in Message System Analysis
Seminar in Content Analysis

Sociology and/or Anthropology:
Structures and Functions of Oral Literatures
Analysis of Oral Literatures
Content Analysis of Oral Literatures
Methods of Content Analysis
Seminar in Social Psychology/ Group Dynamics

Library Science:
Information Systems Analysis
Information Sciences and Data Processing
Seminar in Information Science

Information Science:
Computational Stylistics
Language Processing

Government:
The Analysis of Political Propaganda

Speech and Theatre/Drama:
Seminar in Techniques of Content Analysis
Rhetorical Criticism
Film as Art and Communication

Educational Communication:
Seminar in Media Research and Demonstration Development

History:
Historiography

Social Science:
News Interpretation

Agricultural Journalism:
Seminar in Writing Style

Inspection of the above titles demonstrates the major problem of definition and also discloses some dimensions that can be used to talk more intelligently about the area.

1. Analysis of these titles, along with additional information received (follow-up questionnaires, course outlines, reading lists, and instructors' comments), points up differences between the courses with a methodological versus a theoretical emphasis.

2. What may be called a utilization approach versus a didactic one can be seen.

3. A focus on stylistic versus content elements of messages constitutes another dimension.

4. A frequency versus nonfrequency perspective (quantitative versus qualitative) is implicit.

5. Computerized versus noncomputerized methods may help distinguish some of the courses listed.

6. Finally, there is the added dimension of disciplinary emphasis.

To include all of the above dimensions to describe a single grouping of "content analysis" courses would seem so all-inclusive as to be virtually meaningless. The use of some of the dimensions described above, however, does provide clues that help to communicate about "content analysis" education.

1. Orientation and Techniques Courses (Examples: "Measurement of Audiences and Messages," "Methods of Content Analysis," "Seminar in Techniques of Content Analysis," and "Seminar in Message Systems Analysis").

This classification includes the courses that attempt to orient the student to the traditional written literature of content analysis methodology as well as to empirical studies utilizing the technique. The major purpose of the courses seems to be that of acquainting the students with the basic techniques, often utilizing projects or exercises to illustrate and gain practice in content analysis.

These purposes are illustrated by instructors' comments such as: "During the content analysis section, I try to stress the problem of definition, and hope that they learn to count." Another instructor comments: "The major concern of the course is with the use of certain computerized techniques for the analysis of content data from both written and oral communication. . . . We discuss . . . such things as Cloze Procedure testing, Cue-word Motive and Fear Appeals, Interaction Process Analysis. . . ." Another of the methods courses is described as a ". . . seminar-lab involving completion of individual content analysis projects devised by participants."

The basic reading lists for these courses usually include such materials as Berelson (1952), Lasswell (1952), North et al. (1963), Pool (1959a), Stone et al. (1966), and Budd et al. (1967).

2. Disciplinary/Utilization Courses. A second group of courses focuses on certain media or subject-matter areas utilizing content analysis techniques that seem applicable. (Examples: "Seminar in Social Psychology/Group Dynamics," "Analysis of Broadcasts," "News Interpretation," "Content Analysis of Oral Literatures," and "Film as Art and Communication.")

Depending somewhat on disciplinary orientation, these courses range from informal or nonquantitative analyses to systematic and quantitative approaches. Illustrative of the less formal approach is a course devoted to analysis of the elements of documentary or avant-garde film, or another involving critical analyses of purpose, content, structure, or video/audio design of such materials as disk-jockey programs, newscasts, comedy, and the like. The more quantitative approach is represented by the analysis of communication content in small group interaction or the systematized study of "corpuses of myths, from one or another non-Western society where myth texts have been collected."

Reading material varies greatly in this group. The procedures for instruction often emphasize projects, with students actually involved in, rather than reading about, the analysis of messages. They are viewing, listening, or reading with a systematic approach or explicit set of categories in mind.

3. Theoretical Approaches. (Example: "Theory and Analysis of Message Content"). Only one course was found to illustrate this type of approach. Although this course does serve to familiarize the student with techniques, the major thrust seems to be that of theory relevant to the analysis of content—such concerns as frameworks for the study of symbolic behavior, reference and meaning, semantics and semiotics, as well as problems of inference and validity.

In addition to standard readings for orientation, this approach also used readings by Bertrand Russell (1963); B. F. Skinner (1961); Irving Janis (1943a; 1943b) and Abraham Kaplan (1943).

4. Stylistics (Examples: "Computational Stylistics," "Rhetorical Criticism," and "Seminar in Writing Style"). This approach includes courses designed primarily to study language patterns (for instance, structure, style, and form). Again, the rigor or degree of systemization varies, as does the theoretical or applied focus of the studies. "Rhetorical Criticism" may utilize categories for modes of speech presentation dating from Aristotle to recent empirical linguistic studies. On the other hand, "Computational Stylistics" is described as "The use of the computer in the specification and discrimination of stylistic patterns in literature, musical composition, paintings and other aesthetic artifacts. . . ."

5. *Information Science* (Examples: "Seminar in Information Science," "Information Systems Analysis," "Processing of 'Natural' and Artificial Language"). It is difficult to determine which of these courses should be included and to what extent such information science courses are concerned with content analysis. I believe that they can best be described as specialized research courses utilizing content analysis at various phases (for example, dictionary and concordance design, choice of descriptors).

6. *Psycholinguistics*. This represents another area in which certain principles or procedures of content analysis are often utilized. Psycholinguistics, defined by Fodor et al. (1967:161) as "the study of those psychological processes that contribute to the acquisition, production, and comprehension of language" would seem to have an identity of its own, and need not confuse the issue of approaches to content analysis education. However, one major concern of psycholinguistics could be described as the making of inferences about individual sources from a study of their messages, bringing this aspect into the realm of content analysis.

In reality, all of the specialized courses discussed above provide only a small fraction of total student exposure to content analysis. Another avenue of student exposure is through the general research methods courses offered in various social and behavioral science departments.

GENERAL RESEARCH METHODS COURSES

Of the 175 departments responding to the first mailing, 90 percent listed at least one research methods course given by the department. Of these, 58 percent claimed to include instruction in content analysis as a part of those courses. The inclusion of content analysis as part of general research methods training is more common at the graduate level than at the undergraduate level. Whereas 69 percent of those listing only graduate research courses included content analysis, 53 percent of those listing only undergraduate research courses included it.

From the second mailing (designed to get more detailed course information, as compared to the first mailing which simply listed course titles), data were received on 91 general research methods courses. In 30 of these, the subject of content analysis was indicated to be either by-passed or treated in a cursory manner. Sixty-one other responses, however, offer a substantial amount of data on the nature of such courses, the varying degrees of emphasis to content analysis within the body of research methodologies available, and the procedures and readings utilized.

The departments that give the greatest emphasis to content analysis in general research courses are Communications and Sociology. Other methods courses giving some emphasis to content analysis were those in Speech, Library Science, and Political Science.

Communication and Journalism. Although a wide range of treatment and emphasis on content analysis exists in Journalism and Communication courses in research methodology, a large proportion of such courses focus attention specifically on content analysis. There is also the greatest amount of specialized reading of traditional and current literature in the area. In addition, a frequent mode of training involves student projects analyzing media of communication.

Sociology. The general emphasis on content analysis in research methods courses in Sociology was on the analysis of available data. To a large degree, content analysis meant the classification and coding of open-ended questionnaire data, or was simply discussed briefly as one of several methods of social research. The most frequent comments from instructors of such courses were "Content analysis is one topic among many covered in the course."

The major exceptions are more specialized courses represented by such titles as "Cross Cultural Methods," described as "comparative analysis based on available data," utilizing some specialized content analysis programs such as The General Inquirer (Stone et al., 1966).

Other Areas. Library Science research courses involving content analysis are either (1) traditional—that is, oriented toward research in librarianship and the application that might be termed "statistical bibliography"— or (2) computer-oriented information systems approaches to library science, with the use of content analysis in portions dealing with the development of categories and representation of materials.

Speech communication courses include general introductions to research methods, and two more specialized contexts in which content analysis methods seem relevant. These are (1) analysis of methods of argumentation, debate, persuasion, and propaganda, and (2) analysis of message systems.

Political Science and Government courses yielded three of four listings that could be classified as general orientations to research with some emphasis on political propaganda materials. The exception was the course

"Structure and Sources of Ideologies," which included specialized readings about methods for the analysis of ideologies.

"Historical Methodology" included a section on quantitative analysis in history, and "Bibliography and Methods of Research" in an English department included analysis of essays as relevant to a content analysis approach.

In general, it is evident that the emphasis devoted to content analysis is partly a function of the instructor's particular approach to his discipline. This somewhat idiosyncratic factor may determine whether content analysis will be given the "once-over-lightly" treatment or will constitute a major unit in the course.

VIEWS AND COMMENTS ON CONTENT ANALYSIS

Comments on various aspects of content analysis were received from 75 instructors. The following is a summary of these comments with representative quotations given.

The only definition of content analysis used in this survey was purposefully broad in nature in order to elicit responses from a variety of fields in which work or teaching in the area might take place. (The covering letter in the first mailing, for example, defined content analysis simply as a research method for "the systematic study of communications messages.") Although this definition served to elicit the desired responses, comments from a number of departments illustrate the problem of traditional disciplinary usage as well as certain inherent ambiguities of the term:

> Effectively, all courses in this department involve content analysis. (Anthropology.)

> I am so old-fashioned that I haven't any idea what you mean by content analysis. If it means to you what it means to me, then every course I have ever taught involves analysis of content. (English.)

> Content analysis [is utilized]—not statistical or rigorous in method. Rather, symbolic content (mythic, archetypal Jungian approach). (Speech and Theatre Arts.)

> The term "content analysis" is somewhat ambiguous due to a lack of context and elaboration. (Education.)

The above comments reflect patterns of usage applicable to those disciplines. This is a somewhat different problem from two respondents who explicitly recognized the different possibilities of definition:

> . . . my colleagues and I are unsure of what is to be included . . . [respondent continues with examples of studies of 5-minute verbal samples, story completions, and psychodiagnostic protocols] . . . Do any of these types of activity represent content analysis to you? (Psychology.)

> I wonder if you and I are talking about the same sort of "content analysis?" To us, the term is one involved in the production of abstracting and indexing tools for use in literature searching. You speak of the use of content analysis as a research method. Somehow this doesn't jibe with our connotation, except perhaps as the abstracts and indexes are used as tools in discovering what has been written in a given area of knowledge. (Library and Information Science.)

One might expect such different usages in certain traditionally oriented English and Humanities departments as well as the explicit recognition of specific usages by such fields as Psychology or Information Science. However, I was a little surprised to receive the following note from an instructor in a Department of Linguistics at a major university:

> None of the members of this department have heard of content analysis and I suspect that this is true of most linguistics departments in this country.

What was of specific concern to respondents as difficulties and issues in content analysis?

First, a general skepticism was demonstrated by a number of respondents. This skepticism was often related to long-recognized problems of reliability and validity.

> We do not emphasize it as a research methodology, primarily because we consider its reliability and validity to be suspect. (Communication.)

> I would like to see an objective and honest appraisal of content analysis. The more I see of it the more skeptical I am of it. (Library Science.)

> I wish that the standards of Content Analysis were more clearly stated. The usual validity and reliability measures can be applied when doing simple counts, but sometimes are forgotten by people who claim they are doing an analysis when all they are doing is "describing from their guts." (Communication.)

> The greatest difficulties I see are:
> (a) The problem of reliability in coding . . . .
> (b) The problem of adequately sampling the universe when the universe is not known and cannot be encompassed.
> (c) The problem of missing data . . . (Sociology.)

> Validity . . . is often clouded by content analysts who ignore the interaction of given syntactical and contextual elements with the selected context units, i.e. too much "context" is lifted out of context. (Speech Communication.)

A second frequently mentioned "pragmatic" difficulty was the "tedium and boredom" associated with content analysis:

The major drawbacks are in the inevitable tedium of the method. (Journalism.)

. . . Beating the frightful boredom of the operation itself. (Journalism.)

Its use up to the present has been handicapped by the extreme tediousness of this technique. (Sociology.)

A third major issue revolves around certain fundamental theoretical questions, the nature of inferences, and the importance of results:

> Clearly, the bigger part of content analysis is of very little, if any, theoretical importance, providing lots of information, trivial and otherwise, which doesn't add up to much. The increasing application of computer procedures is not likely to improve this aspect of content analysis. Therefore, in my view, the problems are as follows:
>
> What is the relationship between the counting of words and the decoding of meaning?
>
> What kind of theories and procedures could specify the former relationship?
>
> How can the theories of traditional linguistics, especially grammatical theory, be integrated in existing procedures of content analysis? (Sociology.)
>
> Our faculty tends to feel there is a lack of theoretical background. (Sociology.)
>
> The greatest problem with content analysis is finding a theoretical base for it. It is not as much a matter of this not being possible as that it is not being done. (Journalism.)
>
> A key challenge facing content analysts concerns the model of meaning/communication from which we make inferences . . . should we assume a representational or instrumental model? (Speech Communication.)

These statements reflect an implicit recognition of, and concern about, the relationship between content analysis and theories of symbolic processes. This problem is stated explicitly in the following comment:

> 1. I believe that the knowledge of symbolic processes is one of the most important prerequisites for insights in the social sciences and humanities.
>
> 2. I suggest that the current state of content analysis is underdeveloped. It cannot provide these prerequisites.
>
> 3. This is in my opinion only partly due to methodological insufficiencies. The greatest problem I see is the lack of theories of symbolic processes that: (a) provide the logical basis for analytic procedures, (b) are integrated in theories of social communication processes.
>
> 4. Consequently, results of content analysis bring only isolated results. Much of the aimless counts are wasted efforts and are bound to be insignificant.
>
> 5. One of the sources of this insignificance is the preoccupation with statistical rather than algebraic procedures. (Communication.)

The use of the computer was cited by some respondents as a hope for the solution of various problems in content analysis. However, the majority view was that computer applications, although useful, will not solve the basic problems which face the field.

In discussing content analysis, instructors in various disciplines have pointed out a wide variety of uses. In Speech, for example, it was described as having "a great deal to offer," especially in analysis of persuasive communication. A teacher of history predicts a shifting from the "older, traditional techniques" as "the cross-fertilization process continues to develop between history and the social sciences."

Content analysis was viewed by one Journalism instructor as "the only behavioral science research method whose origin was principally in the field of journalism." Journalism researchers seem to have a special interest in the method for applications to problems of mass media output and as a "barometric check on the content of the media (and consequently their performance)."

Content analysis was viewed by many respondents as of particular value in studying problems difficult to approach via other research methods—for example, the analysis of closed societies or historical materials. In addition, a major feature noted was that it is "nonreactive in nature, and is one of those 'unobtrusive measures.' "

CONTENT ANALYSIS IN THE CURRICULUM

Three points were evident in comments relevant to content analysis as part of departmental curricula. First, the area is seen as a highly specialized one. It was variously described as "for research specialists" (in Education); "not really the sort of thing one would ordinarily offer an entire course in" (Sociology); and "not of sufficient *general* use in library science research" (Library School). Several respondents felt that its specialized nature made it appropriate only at the graduate level. One reason given in several instances for not including such training was that small departments simply could not support specialized courses.

A second major theme was concerned with the lack of adequately trained or interested faculty to offer such a course. Respondents who otherwise felt that such training would be highly relevant for their students said that there was simply no one on the staff who could handle it.

A final theme relates to the benefits that students derive from employing content analysis. Content analysis problems are often chosen as topics for individual and class research projects. Respondents cited the need for rigorous training which content analysis projects can provide. It is thus viewed as useful in teaching to focus student attention on the necessity for systematic and analytic thinking in evaluating such materials as broadcast programs, literary text, and historical documents, among others.

CONCLUSIONS

Education in content analysis is not in a highly developed state. The results of this study indicate that the most likely exposure students have to content analysis consists of a simple orientation to the technique. There is little sophisticated teaching in the area—that is, teaching that would produce future scholars specializing in content analysis.

The reasons for this state are perhaps to be found in three basic conditions. First, the theoretical bases for content analysis have yet to be fully developed. In one sense, this is part of a larger problem of the underdeveloped state of communication theory generally, and of theories of symbolic behavior specifically. In another sense, however, it is not strictly the problem of an underdeveloped state of theory, but simply that no one has yet brought the relevant theoretical formulations to bear on message analysis as a part of the study of communication processes.

A second reason for the state of education in content analysis lies in the technical or methodological problems associated with it. It is a specialized endeavor among research methodologies. It also involves detailed and laborious procedures in translating data into proper form for analysis. Upon closer inspection, however, one finds that most of the problems, both theoretical and methodological, are not peculiar to content analysis. They are general problems of social science.

A third reason for the state of content analysis education stems from the first two reasons. Here I am referring to the attitude component that this study has revealed. Future scholars will be influenced by the research preferences of current teachers. Until the general practice of content analysis gains the degree of theoretical sophistication that is reflected in this book, some negative attitudes no doubt will continue.

The final problem is one of definition. It is tempting to suggest that the term "content analysis" should simply be abandoned. One has the feeling sometimes that the term is more of an obstacle than an aid to communication. But one cannot so easily dismiss such a broadly used term around which a good deal of traditional literature has been written and to which so many different meanings are attached. Content analysis has been described as the scientific study of message content. This should be no more difficult (nor any easier) to understand than the scientific study of anything. All social science labors under the problems of reliability of observations and measurement and the validity of inferences made.

Content analysis must then first be viewed as an interdisciplinary approach. Although, in the past, certain disciplines may have found the approach more fruitful than others, there is currently little reason to assume that it need be more useful in one area than another.

Content analysis has a distinct advantage in social research as one of those "unobtrusive" or "nonreactive" measures described by Webb et al. (1966). A document, once recorded, does not react to the researcher who is studying it and, therefore, produce the kind of artifact often noted in laboratory and field studies of human behavior.

As to the future of education in content analysis, we need not assume that it must be taught as separate and distinct subject matter, requiring full course treatment in most departments. It may well be integrated with general research courses as a phase or approach basic to many studies. We should expect, however, that instructors in research methodology become familiar with more current and sophisticated theories and procedures and that such approaches be introduced into the basic research courses.

Bibliography

Allen, Layman E. "Automation: Substitute and Supplement in Legal Practice," *The American Behavioral Scientist* (**7**:39–44, 1963).

Allport, Gordon W., and Philip E. Vernon. *Studies in Expressive Movement.* New York: Macmillan, 1933.

Allport, Gordon W. *The Use of Personal Documents in Psychological Science.* New York: Social Science Research Council, 1942.

Allport, Gordon W. "Anonymous Letters from Jenny," *Journal of Abnormal and Social Psychology* (**41**:315–350, 1946).

Allport, Gordon W., Jerome S. Bruner, and E. M. Jandorf. "Personality and Social Catastrophe: Ninety Life Histories of the Nazi Revolution," in C. Kluckhohn, H. Murray, and D. Schneider (eds.), *Personality in Nature, Culture, and Society.* New York: Knopf. Revised Edition, 1953.

Allport, Gordon W. *Letters From Jenny.* New York: Harcourt, Brace and World, 1965.

Alpert, Murray, Richard L. Kurtzberg, and Arnold F. Friedhoff. "Transient Voice Changes Associated with Emotional Stimuli," *Gen. Psychiat.* (**8**:362–365, 1963).

Angell, Robert C., Vera S. Dunham, and J. David Singer. "Social Values and Foreign Policy Attitudes of Soviet and American Elites," *Journal of Conflict Resolution* (**8**:329–491, 1964).

Antal, László. *Content, Meaning, and Understanding.* The Hague: Mouton & Co., 1964.

Antunes, George. "Party Politics in Greece, 1950–1962," in Kenneth Janda (ed.), *ICPP Bibliography Series.* Evanston: International Comparative Political Parties Project, Northwestern University, 1967.

Arieti, Silvano. *Interpretation of Schizophrenia.* New York: Robert Brunner, 1955.

Arnold, Magda B. *Story Sequence Analysis: A New Method of Measuring Motivation and Predicting Achievement.* New York: Columbia University Press, 1962.

Arp, Dennis J. "Verification and Replication of a Thematic Analysis of Interviewer's Statements in Therapy Analogue Interviews," paper presented at the meetings of the Midwest Psychological Association, 1967.

Asersinsky, E., and Nathaniel Kleitman. "Regularly Occurring Periods of Eye Motility and Concomitant Phenomena During Sleep," *Science* (**118**:273–274, 1953).

Ashby, W. Ross. *An Introduction to Cybernetics.* London: Chapman & Hall, 1958.

Ashby, W. Ross. "Computers and Decision Making," *New Scientist* (**7**:746, 1960).

Atkinson, John W. (ed.) *Motives in Fantasy, Action, and Society: A Method of Assessment and Study.* Princeton, N.J.: Van Nostrand, 1958.

Auld, Frank W., and Edward J. Murray. "Content Analysis Studies of Psychotherapy," *Psychological Bulletin* (**52**:377–395, 1955).

Auster, Donald A. "A Content Analysis of 'Little Orphan Annie,'" *Social Problems* (**2**:26–33, 1954).

Austin, John. *How To Do Things with Words.* London: Oxford University Press, 1962.

Aydelotte, William O. "Quantification in History," *American Historical Review* (**LXXI**:803–825, 1966).

Babbitt, Milton. "Use of Computers in Musicological Research," *Perspectives of New Music* (74–83, 1965).

Bales, Robert F. *Interaction Process Analysis: A Method for the Study of Small Groups.* Cambridge: Addison-Wesley, 1950.

Bales, Robert F. "The Equilibrium Problem in Small Groups," in T. Parsons, R. F. Bales, and E. A. Shils, *Working Papers in the Theory of Action,* Glencoe, Illinois: The Free Press, 1953.

Barad, Martin, Kenneth Z. Althshuler, and Alvin I. Goldfarb. "A Survey of Dreams in Aged Persons," *Archives of General Psychiatry* (**4**:419–424, 1961).

Barcus, F. Earle. "Communications Content: Analysis of the Research, 1900–1958 (A Content Analysis of Content Analysis)" Ph. D. dissertation, University of Illinois, Ann Arbor, Mich.: University Microfilms, Inc., 1959.

Barron, Milton L. "A Content Analysis of Intergroup Humor," *American Sociological Review* (**15**:88–94, 1950).

Barzun, Jacques. *Computer for the Humanities.* New Haven: Yale University Press, 1965.

Bateson, Gregory. "Cybernetic Explanation," *American Behavioral Scientist* (**10**,8:29–32, 1967).

Bellman, Richard, Merrill B. Friend, and Leonard Kurland. *A Simulation of the Initial Psychiatric Interview.* Santa Monica: The Rand Corporation, 1966.

Bengtsson, Ingmar. "Studies of Performed Music with the Aid of Computers." Paper read at the 10th Congress of the International Musicological Society in Ljubljana, 1967.

Berelson, Bernard, and Paul F. Lazarsfeld. *The Analysis of Communications Content.* Chicago and New York: University of Chicago and Columbia University, Preliminary Draft, 1948.

Berelson, Bernard. *Content Analysis in Communication Research.* Glencoe, Ill.: The Free Press, 1952.

Berelson, Bernard. "Content Analysis," in G. Lindzey, (ed.), *Handbook of Social Psychology.* Cambridge: Addison-Wesley Publishing Co. (**1**:488–522, 1954).

Bessinger, Jess B., and Stephen M. Parrish (eds.). *Proceedings of the IBM Literary Data Processing Conference.* Yorktown Heights, New York: IBM, 1964.

Billingsley, Carolyn. "Party Politics in Denmark, 1950–1962," in Kenneth Janda (ed.), *ICPP Bibliography Series.* Evanston: International Comparative Political Parties Project, Northwestern University, 1967.

Blalock, Hubert M. *Social Statistics.* New York: McGraw Hill, 1960.

Blalock, Hubert M. *Causal Inferences in Non-Experimental Research.* Chapel Hill, N.C.: University of North Carolina Press, 1961.

Blankenship, Jane. "A Linguistic Analysis of Oral and Written Style," *Quarterly Journal of Speech* (**XLVIII**:4, 419–422, 1962).

Bobrow, Daniel G. "Syntactic Analysis of Language by Computer—a Survey," *Proceedings of the Fall Joint Computer Conference* (**24**:365–387, 1963).

Borkowski, Casimir. *A System for Automatic Recognition of Personal Names in Newspaper Texts.* Report RC-1563, Yorktown Heights, N.Y.: Watson IBM Research Center, 1966.

Borkowski, Casimir. "An Experimental System for Automatic Identification of Personal Names and Personal Titles in Newspaper Texts," *American Documentation* (**18**:131–138, No. 3, 1967).

Bousfield, W. A. "The Occurrence of Clusters in the Recall of Randomly Arranged Associates," *Journal of General Psychology* (**49**:229–240, 1953).

Brodie, Bernard. *Strategy in the Missile Age.* Princeton, N.J.: Princeton University Press, 1959.

Brodie, Bernard. *Escalation and the Nuclear Option.* Princeton, N.J.: Princeton University Press, 1966.

Brook, Barry S., and Murray Gould. "Notating Music with Ordinary Typewriter Characters (A Plaine and Easie Code System for Musicke)," *Fontes Artis Musicae* (**XI/3:**142–159, 1964). Also published as a pamphlet, N.Y. Queens College, 1964.

Brook, Barry S. "The Simplified 'Plaine and Easie Code System' for Notating Music —A Proposal for International Adoption," *Fontes Artis Musicae* (**XII/2–3:** 112–122, 1965).

Bruner, Jerome S., and Cecile D. Goodman. "Value and Need as Organizing Factors in Perception," *Journal of Abnormal and Social Psychology* (**42:**33–44, 1947).

Budd, Richard W., Robert K. Thorpe, and Lewis Donahew. *Content Analysis of Communications.* New York: The MacMillan Company, 1967.

Burks, Arthur W. "Icon, Index and Symbol," *Philosophy and Phenomenological Research* (**9:**673–689, 1949).

Byrne, Donn, Gerald L. Clore, and Philip Worchel, "Effect of Economic Similarity-Dissimilarity on Interpersonal Attraction," *Journal of Personality and Social Psychology* (**4:**220–224, 1966).

Byrne, Donn, Don Nelson, and Keith Reeves. "Effect of Consensual Validation and Invalidation on Attraction as a Function of Verifiability," *Journal of Experimental Social Psychology* (**2:**98–107, 1966).

Campbell, Donald T. "Systematic Error on the Part of Human Links in Communication Systems," *Information and Control* (**1:**334–369, 1958).

Capote, Truman. *In Cold Blood.* New York: Random House, 1965.

Carroll, John B. "Vectors of Prose Style," in T. Sebeok, (ed.), *Style in Language.* Cambridge, Mass.: MIT Press, 1960.

Carroll, John B., Paul M. Kjeldergaard, and Aaron S. Carton. "Number of Opposites Versus Number of Primaries As a Response Measure in Free-Association Tests," *Journal of Verbal Learning and Verbal Behavior* (**1:**22–30, 1962).

Casagrande, Joseph B., and K. L. Hale. "Semantic Relationships in Papago Folk-Definitions," *Studies in Southwestern Linguistics.* The Hague: Mouton, 1967.

Cattell, Raymond B. *Personality.* New York: McGraw Hill, 1950.

Cattell, Raymond B., and John R. Nesselroade. "Likeness and Completeness Theories Examined by Sixteen Personality Factor Measures on Stably and Unstably Married Couples," *Journal of Personality and Social Psychology* (**7:**351–361, 1967).

Chagall, Marc. *My Life.* New York: Grossman, 1960.

Chambers, Edmund K. *William Shakespeare: A Study of Facts and Problems.* Oxford: Clarendon Press, 1930.

Chomsky, Noam. *Syntactic Structures.* The Hague: Mouton & Company, 1957.

Chomsky, Noam. "Review of B. F. Skinner, 'Verbal Behavior'" *Language* (**35:** 26–58, 1959).

Chomsky, Noam. *Current Issues in Linguistic Theory.* The Hague: Mouton, 1964.

Chomsky, Noam. *Aspects of the Theory of Syntax.* Cambridge, Mass.: M.I.T. Press, 1965.

Ciarlo, James A. "Ascensionism in Fantasy and Action." Unpublished Doctoral thesis, Department of Social Relations, Harvard University (1964).

Cliff, Norman. "Adverbs as Multipliers," *Psychological Review* (**66:**27–44, 1959).

558   Bibliography

Cochran, Thomas, C. *Railroad Leaders, 1845–1890: The Business Mind in Action.* Cambridge, Mass.: Harvard University Press, 1953.

Coddington, Alan. "Policies Advocated in Conflict Situations by British Newspapers," *Journal of Peace Research* (2:398–404, 1965).

Cofer, Charles N. "Some Evidence for Coding Processes Derived from Clustering in Free Recall," *Journal of Verbal Learning and Verbal Behavior* (5:188–192, 1966).

Cohen, Joel E. "Information Theory and Music," *Behavioral Science* (VII/2:137–163, 1962).

Colby, Benjamin N. "The Analysis of Culture Content and Patterning of Narrative Concern in Tests," *American Anthropologist* (68:374–388, 1966a).

Colby, Benjamin N. "Culture Patterns in Narrative," *Science* (151, No. 3712: 793–798, 1966b).

Colby, Benjamin N. "Development and Applications of an Anthropological Dictionary," in P. J. Stone, D. Dunphy, M. Smith, and D. Ogilvie, *The General Inquirer.* Cambridge, Mass.: M.I.T. Press, 1966c.

Colby, Benjamin N., G. A Collier, and Susan K. Postal. "Comparison of Themes in Folktales by the General Inquirer System," *Journal of American Folklore,* (76:318–323, 1963).

Colby, Kenneth M. "Sex Differences in Dreams: A Contribution to the Masculinity-Femininity Problem," in *A Skeptical Psychoanalyst,* New York: Ronald Press, (107–145, 1958).

Colby, Kenneth M. "Computer Simulation of Change in Personal Belief Systems," *Behavioral Science* (12:248–253, 1967).

Colby, Kenneth M., James Watt, and John P. Gilbert. "A Computer Model of Psychotherapy," *Journal of Nervous and Mental Disease* (142:148–152, 1966).

Conklin, Harold C. "Hanunoo Color Categories," *Southwestern Journal of Anthropology* (11:339–344, 1955).

Couch, Arthur S. "Data-Text System," Preliminary Manual. Department of Social Relations, Harvard University, 1966.

Craddick, Ray A. "Size of Santa Claus Drawings as a Function of Time Before and After Christmas," *Journal of Psychological Studies* (12:121–125, 1961).

Craddick, Ray A. "Size of Witch Drawings as a Function of Time Before, On, and After Halloween," *American Psychologist* (17:307, 1962).

Cronbach, Lee. *Essentials of Psychological Testing* (Second Ed.) New York: Harper & Row, 1960.

Danielson, Wayne A. "Content Analysis in Communication Research," in R. Nafziger, and D. White (eds.), *Introduction to Mass Communications Research.* Louisiana State University Press (180–206, 1963).

DeCharms, Richard, and Gerald H. Moeller. "Values Expressed in American Children's Readers: 1800–1950," *Journal of Abnormal and Social Psychology* (64:136–142, 1962).

Deese, James E. *The Structure of Associations in Language and Thought.* Baltimore, Md.: The Johns Hopkins Press, 1965.

De Saussure, Ferdinand. *Cours de Linguistique Genérale.* Paris: Payot, 1931, third edition.

DeSoto, Clinton B. "The Predilection for Single Ordering," *Journal of Abnormal Psychology* (62:16–23, 1961).

Dibble, Vernon K. "Four Types of Inferences from Documents to Events," *History and Theory* (3:2, 203–221, 1963).

Dollard, John, and O. Hobart Mowrer. "A Method of Measuring Tension in Written Documents," *Journal of Abnormal and Social Psychology* (**42**:3–32, 1947).

Dovring, Karen, "Quantitative Semantics in 18th Century Sweden," *Public Opinion Quarterly* (**18**:4, 389–394, 1954–1955).

Dunnette, Marvin D. "Fads, Fashions, and Folderol in Psychology," *American Psychologist* (**21**:343–352, 1966).

Dunphy, Dexter C., Philip J. Stone, and Marshall S. Smith. "The General Inquirer: Further Developments in a Computer System for Content Analysis of Verbal Data in the Social Sciences," *Behavioral Science* (**10**:468–480, 1965).

Eckhardt, William. "War Propaganda, Welfare Values, and Political Ideologies," *Journal of Conflict Resolution* (**9**:3, 345–358, 1965).

Economic Almanac. New York: National Industrial Conference Board, 1964.

Eggan, Dorothy, "The Manifest Content of Dreams: A Challenge to Social Science," *American Anthropologist* (**54**:469–485, 1952).

Ekman, Paul. "Personality, Pathology, Affect and Nonverbal Behavior." Paper presented at Western Psychological Association Convention, Honolulu, Hawaii, 1965.

Ekman, Paul, and Wallace V. Friesen. "Origin, Usage, and Coding: The Basis for Five Categories of Nonverbal Behavior." Paper presented at the Symposium: Communication Theory and Linguistic Models in the Social Sciences. Buenos Aires, Argentina, 1967.

Ekman, Paul, and Wallace V. Friesen. "Nonverbal Behavior in Psychotherapy Research," in J. Shlien, (ed.), *Research on Psychotherapy.* Vol. III. Washington, D.C.: American Psychological Association, 1968.

Feigl, Herbert. "Validation and Vindication: An Analysis of the Nature and the Limits of Ethical Arguments," in Wilfrid Sellars and John Hospers (eds.), *Readings in Ethical Theory.* New York: Appleton-Century-Crofts, Inc., (667–680, 1952).

Fenichel, Otto. *The Psychoanalytic Theory of Neurosis.* New York: Norton, 1945.

Fermin, M. H. J. *Le Vocabulaire de Bifrun dans sa Traduction des Quatre Evangiles.* Amsterdam: L. J. Veen's Uitgevers Mij. N.V., 1954.

Fillmore, Chalres J. "Toward a Modern Theory of Case." Report No. 13, Project on Linguistic Analysis, the Ohio State University, 1966.

Finlay, David J., Ole R. Holsti, and Richard R. Fagen. *Enemies in Politics.* Chicago: Rand McNally, 1967.

Fischer, Ronald A. *The Genetical Theory of Natural Selection.* Oxford: Clarendon Press, 1930.

Flesch, Rudolf. *How to Test Readability.* New York: Harper & Brothers, 1951.

Fodor, Jerry A., and Jerrold L. Katz. *The Structure of Language: Readings in the Philosophy of Language.* Englewood Cliffs, N.J.: Prentice-Hall, 1964.

Fodor, Jerry A., James J. Jenkins, and Sol Saporta. "Psycholinguistics and Communication Theory," in Frank E. X. Dance (ed.), *Human Communication Theory.* New York: Holt, Rinehart & Winston (160–201, 1967).

Forte, Allen. "The Domain and Relations of Set-Complex Theory," *Journal of Music Theory* (**IX/1**:173–180, 1965).

Forte, Allen. "The Structure of Atonal Music—Practical Aspects of a Computer-Oriented Research Project," in B. Brook (ed.), *Musicology and the Computer.* New York: Queens College Press, in press.

Foster, H. Schuyler, Jr. "How America Became Belligerent: A Quantitative Study of War News," *American Journal of Sociology* (**40**:464–475, 1935).

Francis, W. Nelson. "A Standard Corpus of Edited Present-day American English for Computer Use," in J. Bessinger and S. M. Parrish (eds.), *Proceedings of the IBM Literary Data Processing Conference*. Yorktown Heights, New York: IBM (79–89, 1964).

Freud, Sigmund. *Psychopathology of Everyday Life*. (Trans. A. A. Brill.) New York: Random House, 1938.

Freud, Sigmund. *On Aphasia (1891)*. New York: International Universities Press, 1953a.

Freud, Sigmund. "Psycho-analytic Notes Upon an Autobiographical Account of a Case of Paranoia (Dementia Paranoides) (1911)," Vol. XIII. *Standard Edition of the Complete Psychological Works of Sigmund Freud*. London: Hogarth Press, 1953b.

Freud, Sigmund. "The Unconscious (1915). Vol. XIV of *Standard Edition of the Complete Psychological Works of Sigmund Freud*. London: Hogarth Press, 1953c.

Frye, Northrup. *The Well-Tempered Critic*. Bloomington, Indiana: Indiana University Press, 1963.

Fucks, Wilhelm. "Gibt es Mathematische Gesetze in Sprache und Musik," *Umschau* (**LVII/2**:33–37, 1957).

Fucks, Wilhelm. "Mathematical Analysis of Formal Structure of Music," *IRE Transactions on Information Theory* (**IT-VIII/5**:225–228, 1962a).

Fucks, Wilhelm. "Musical Analysis by Mathematics—Random Sequences, Music and Accident," *Gravesaner Blätter* (**VI/23–24**:146–155, 1962b).

Fucks, Wilhelm. "Uber Mathematische Musikanalyse," *Nachrichtentechnische Zeitschrift* (**XVII/1**:41–47, 1964).

Fucks, Wilhelm and Josef Lauter. *Exaktwissenschaftliche Musikanalyse*. Westdeutscher Verlag: Köln und Opladen, 1965.

Galtung, Johan, and Mari Holmboe Ruge. "The Structure of Foreign News: The Presentation of the Congo, Cuba and Cyprus Crisis in Four Norwegian Newspapers," *Journal of Peace Research* (**2**:64–91, 1965).

Garraty, John A. "The Application of Content Analysis to Biography and History," in Ithiel de Sola Pool (ed.), *Trends in Content Analysis*. Urbana, Ill.: University of Illinois Press, 1959.

Garth, Thomas R. "A Statistical Study of the Content of Newspapers," in *School and Society* (**3**:140–144, 1916).

Garver, Richard A. "Polite Propaganda: USSR and America Illustrated," *Journalism Quarterly* (**38**:480–484, 1961).

Garvin, Paul L. *Natural Language and the Computer*. New York: McGraw-Hill, 1963.

Geller, A., D. Kaplan, and Harold D. Lasswell. "An Experimental Comparison of Four Ways of Coding Editorial Content," *Journalism Quarterly* (**19**:362–370, 1942).

George, Alexander L. *Propaganda Analysis*. Evanston, Ill.: Row, Peterson & Co. 1959a.

George, Alexander L. "Quantitative and Qualitative Approaches to Content Analysis," in Ithiel de Sola Pool (ed.), *Trends in Content Analysis*. Urbana, Ill.: University of Illinois Press (7–32, 1959b).

Gerbner, George. "On Content Analysis and Critical Research in Mass Communication," *AV Communication Review* (**6**, 2:85–108, 1958a).

Gerbner, George. "The Social Role of the Confession Magazine," *Social Problems* (**6**:29–40, 1958b).

Gerbner, George. "The Social Anatomy of the Romance-Confession Cover Girl," *Journalism Quarterly* (**35**:3, 299–306, 1958c).

Gerbner, George. "Psychology, Psychiatry and Mental Illness in the Mass Media: A Study of Trends 1900–1959," *Mental Hygiene* (**45**:89–93, 1961a).

Gerbner, George. "Press Perspectives in World Communications: A Pilot Study," *Journalism Quarterly* (**38**:313–322, 1961b).

Gerbner, George. "Mass Communications and Popular Conceptions of Education; a Cross-Cultural Study," Cooperative Research Project No. 876, U.S. Office of Education (1964a).

Gerbner, George. "Ideological Perspectives and Political Tendencies in News Reporting," *Journalism Quarterly* (**41**:495–509, 1964b).

Gerbner, George. "Content Analysis and Critical Research in Mass Communication," *AV Communication Review* (**6**:85–108, 1958). Reprinted in *People, Society, and Mass Communications,* L. A. Dexter and D. M. White (eds.). Glencoe, Ill.: The Free Press, 1964c.

Gerbner, George. "An Institutional Approach to Mass Communications Research," in Lee Thayer (ed.), *Communication: Theory and Research.* Springfield: Charles C. Thomas, 1966a.

Gerbner, George. "Education About Education by Mass Media," *The Educational Forum* (**31**:7–15, 1966b).

Gerbner, George. "Images Across Cultures: Teachers and Mass Media Fiction and Drama," *The School Review* (**74**:212–229, 1966c).

Gerbner, George. "Mass Communication and Human Communication Theory," in *Human Communication Theory: Original Essays,* edited by Frank E. X. Dance. New York: Holt, Rinehart and Winston, 1967a.

Gerbner, George. "The Press and the Dialogue in Education; A Case Study of a National Educational Convention and Its Depiction in America's Daily Newspapers," *Journalism Monograph No. 5,* 1967b.

Goffman, Erving. *The Presentation of Self in Everyday Life.* Garden City, N.Y.: Doubleday, 1959.

Gottschalk, Louis A. (ed.). *Comparative Psycholinguistic Analysis of Two Psychotherapeutic Interviews.* New York: International Universities Press, 1961.

Gould, Murray. "A Keypunchable Notation for the Liber Usualis," in H. Heckmann (ed.), *Elektronische Datenverarbeitung in der Musikwissenschaft.* Regensburg, 1967.

Gould, Murray, and George W. Logemann. "Alma: Alphameric Language for Music in Analysis," in B. Brook (ed.), *Musicology and the Computer.* New York: Queens College Press, in press.

Grey, Alan, David Kaplan, and Harold D. Lasswell. "Recording and Context Units— Four Ways of Coding Editorial Content," in Harold D. Lasswell, Nathan Leites and associates, *Language of Politics: Studies in Quantitative Semantics.* Revised Edition. Cambridge, Mass.: The M.I.T. Press, 1965.

Guptill, Lloyd H. "A Study of the Icarus Complex: The Dynamics of Doing Nothing at All." Unpublished Honor's Thesis, Department of Social Relations, Harvard University, 1965.

Haggard, Ernest A., and Kenneth S. Isaacs. "Micromomentary Facial Expressions as Indicators of Ego Mechanisms in Psychotherapy," in L. S. Gottschalk, and A. H. Auerbach (eds.), *Methods of Research in Psychotherapy.* New York: Appleton-Century-Crofts, 1966.

Haldane, John B. S. *The Biochemistry of Genetics.* London: Allen & Unwin, 1954.

Hall, Calvin S. "A Comparison of the Dreams of Four Groups of Hospitalized

Mental Patients with Each Other and with a Normal Population," *Journal of Nervous Mental Disease* (**143:**135–139, 1966).

Hall, Calvin S. and William Domhoff. "A Ubiquitous Sex Difference in Dreams," *Journal of Abnormal Social Psychology* (**66:**278–280, 1963).

Hall, Calvin S., and Robert L. Van de Castle. *The Content Analysis of Dreams.* New York: Appleton-Century-Crofts, 1966a.

Hall, Calvin S., and Robert L. Van de Castle. "Studies of Dreams Reported in the Laboratory and at Home," *Institute of Dream Research Monograph Series* (No. 1: 1–55, 1966b).

Hall, Calvin S. "Experimente zur Telepathischen Beeinflussung von Traumen," *Zeitschrift für Parapsychologie und Grenzgebiete der Psychologie* (**10:**18–47, 1967).

Hall, Edward T. *The Silent Language.* Garden City, N.Y.: Doubleday, 1959.

Hallig, Rudolf, and Walther Von Wartburg. *Begriffssystem als Grundlage für die Lexikographie. Versuch eines Ordnungsschemas.* Berlin: Akademie-verlag, 1963 (2nd ed.).

Hamilton, Thomas. "Social Optimism and Pessimism in American Protestantism," *Public Opinion Quarterly* (**6:**280–283, 1942).

Hammel, Eugene A. (ed.). "Formal Semantic Analysis," *American Anthropologist* (67, 5, Part 2, 1965).

Hardy, Godfrey H. "Mendelian Proportions in a Mixed Population," *Science* (**28:** 49–50, 1908).

Hargreaves, William A., and John A. Starkweather. "Recognition of Speaker Identity," *Language and Speech* (**6:**63–67, 1963).

Harlow, Harry F. "The Nature of Love," *American Psychologist* (**13:**673–685, 1958).

Harlow, Harry F. "Primary Affectional Patterns in Primates," *American Journal of Orthopsychiatry* (**30:**676–684, 1960).

Harris, Zellig S. "Discourse Analysis," *Language* (**28:**1–30, 1952).

Harris, Zellig S. "Distributional Structure," *Word* (10, 2–3: 146–162, 1954).

Hart, Jim A. "Election Campaign Coverage in English and U.S. Daily Newspapers," *Journalism Quarterly* (**42:**2, 213–218, 1965).

Hart, Jim A. "Foreign News in U.S. and English Daily Newspapers: A Comparison," *Journalism Quarterly* (**43:**3, 443–448, 1966).

Hartman, John J. "Sunshine and Shadows: A View of Negro Lower-Class Culture and Personality." Unpublished Honor's Thesis, Department of Social Relations, Harvard University, 1964.

Harway, Norman I., and Howard P. Iker. "Computer Analysis of Content in Psychotherapy," *Psychological Reports* (**14:**720–722, 1964).

Harway, Norman I., and Howard P. Iker. "Objective Content Analysis of Psychotherapy by Computer," in K. Enslein (ed.), *Data Acquisition and Processing in Biology and Medicine,* Vol. 4, New York: Pergamon Press, 1966.

Hayakawa, Samuel I. "Popular Songs vs. the Facts of Life," in B. Rosenberg and D. M. White (eds.), *Mass Culture.* London: Collier-Macmillan Ltd., 1964 (393–403).

Hays, David G. *Automatic Content Analysis.* Santa Monica, Calif.: Rand Corporation Publication, 1960.

Hays, David G. "Automatic Language and Data Processing," in H. Borko (ed.), *Computer Applications in the Behavioral Sciences.* Englewood Cliffs, N.J.: Prentice-Hall, 1962.

Hays, David G. *Introduction to Computational Linguistics.* New York: American Elsevier, 1967a.

Hays, David G. *Linguistic Problems of Denotation.* Santa Monica, Calif.: The Rand Corporation, P-3645, 1967b.

Hempel, Carl G. *Philosophy of Natural Science.* Englewood Cliffs, N.J.: Prentice Hall, 1966.

Henley, Nancy M. "The Semantics of Common Animal Names." Baltimore, Md.: Ph.D. dissertation, The Johns Hopkins University, 1968.

Herdan, Gustav. *Type-Token Mathematics.* 'S-Gravenhage: Mouton and Company, 1960.

Hermann, Charles F., and Margaret C. Hermann. "An Attempt to Simulate the Outbreak of World War I," *American Political Science Review* (**61**:400–416, 1967).

Higgins, Trumbull. *Korea and the Fall of MacArthur: A Precis in Limited War.* New York: Oxford University Press, 1960.

Hilsman, Roger. *To Move A Nation.* Garden City, N.Y.: Doubleday, 1967.

Hirsch, Walter. "The Image of the Scientist in Science Fiction: A Content Analysis," *American Journal of Sociology* (**63**:5, 506–512, 1958).

Historical Statistics of the United States, Colonial Times to 1957, and Its Continuation to 1962 and Revisions. Washington, D.C.: U.S. Bureau of Census, 1960; 1965.

Holsti, Ole R. "The Belief System and National Images: A Case Study," *Journal of Conflict Resolution* (**6**:244–252, 1962).

Holsti, Ole R. "An Adaptation of the 'General Inquirer' for the Systematic Study of Political Documents," *Behavioral Science* (**9**:4, 382–388, 1964a).

Holsti, Ole R., Richard A. Brody, and Robert C. North. "Theory and Measurement of Interstate Relations: An Application of Automated Content Analysis," Stanford University, Stanford, Calif. 1964b (mimeo).

Holsti, Ole R., Richard A. Brody, and Robert C. North. "Measuring Affect and Action in International Reaction Models: Empirical Material from the 1962 Cuban Crisis," *Peace Research Society, Papers, II* (170–190, 1965a).

Holsti, Ole R., and Robert C. North. "The History of Human Conflict," Elton B. McNeil (ed.), *The Nature of Human Conflict.* Englewood Cliffs, N.J.: Prentice Hall, (155–171, 1965b).

Holsti, Ole R. "East-West Conflict and Sino-Soviet Relations," *Journal of Applied Behavioral Science* (**1**:115–130, 1965c).

Holsti, Ole R. "The 1914 Case," *American Political Science Review* (**59**:365–378, 1965d).

Holsti, Ole R. "Perceptions of Time, Perceptions of Alternatives, and Patterns of Communication as Factors in Crisis Decision-Making." *Peace Research Society (International) Papers* (**3**:79–120, 1965e).

Holsti, Ole R. "External Conflict and Internal Consensus," in Philip J. Stone, D. Dunphy, M. Smith, and D. Ogilvie, *The General Inquirer.* Cambridge, Mass.: M.I.T. Press, 1966a.

Holsti, Ole R., and Robert C. North. "Comparative Data from Content Analysis: Perceptions of Hostility and Economic Variables in the 1914 Crisis," in Richard L. Merritt and Stein Rokkan (eds.), *Comparing Nations: The Use of Quantitative Data in Cross-National Research.* New Haven, Conn.: Yale University Press, 1966b.

Holsti, Ole R. "Computer Content Analysis in International Relations Research," in Edmund A. Bowles (ed.), *Computers in Humanistic Research.* Englewood Cliffs, N.J.: Prentice-Hall (108–117, 1967a).

Holsti, Ole R. "Cognitive Dynamics and Images of the Enemy," *Journal of International Affairs* (**21:**16–39, 1967b).

Holsti, Ole R., with the collaboration of Joanne K. Loomba and Robert C. North "Content Analysis," in Gardner Lindzey and Elliot Aronson (eds.), *The Handbook of Social Psychology.* Cambridge, Mass.: Addison-Wesley, second edition, 1968a.

Holsti, Ole R., Robert C. North, and Richard A. Brody. "Perception and Action in the 1914 Crisis," in J. David Singer (ed.), *Quantitative International Politics: Insights and Evidence.* New York: The Free Press, 1968b.

Holsti, Ole R. *Content Analysis for the Social Sciences and Humanities.* Reading, Mass.: Addison-Wesley, 1969.

Horton, David. "The Dialogue of Courtship in Popular Songs," *American Journal of Sociology* (**62:**569–578, 1957).

Howe, Edmund S. "The Associative Structure of Quantifiers," *Journal of Verbal Learning and Verbal Behavior* (**5:**156–162, 1966).

Hunt, Earl B., Janet Marin, and Philip J. Stone. *Experiments in Induction.* New York: Academic Press, 1966.

Hymes, Dell (ed.). *The Use of Computers in Anthropology.* London: Mouton, 1965.

Iker, Howard P., and Norman I. Harway. "A Computer Approach Towards the Analysis of Content," *Behavioral Science* (**10:**173–183, 1965).

Jackson, Roland, and Philip Bernzoyt. "A Musical Input Language and a Sample Program for Musical Analysis," in B. Brook (ed.), *Musicology and the Computer.* New York: Queens College Press, in press.

Jacob, Philip E., and James J. Flink. "Values and Their Function in Decision Making," *The American Behavioral Scientist* (5, 9, Supplement, 1962).

Jacobson, Roman. "Boas' Views of Grammatical Meaning," in Walter Goldschmidt (ed.), *The Anthropology of Franz Boas* (139–145). *The American Anthropologist,* Memoir No. 89, 1959.

Janda, Kenneth. "Retrieving Information for a Comparative Study of Political Parties," in William J. Crotty (ed.), *Approaches to the Study of Party Organization.* Boston: Allyn and Bacon, 159–215, 1968a.

Janda, Kenneth. "Political Research with Miracode: A 16mm. Microfilm Information Retrieval System," *Social Science Information* (6, 1967). This article is reprinted in Kenneth Janda, *Information Retrieval: Applications in Political Science.* Indianapolis: Bobbs-Merrill, 1968b.

Janes, Robert W. "A Technique for Describing Community Structure Through Newspaper Analysis," *Social Forces* (**37:**2, 102–109, 1958).

Janis, Irving. "Meaning and the Study of Symbolic Behavior," *Psychiatry* (**6:**4, 425–439, 1943a).

Janis, Irving, Raymond N. Fadner, and Morris Janowitz. "Reliability of a Content Analysis Technique," *Public Opinion Quarterly* (**7:**293–296, 1943b).

Janis, Irving. "The Problem of Validating Content Analysis," in Harold D. Lasswell, Nathan Leites and Associates, *Language of Politics: Studies in Quantitative Semantics.* Cambridge, Mass.: The M.I.T. Press (55–82, 1965).

Johnson, James B. "Party Politics in Ecuador, 1950–1962," in Kenneth Janda (ed.), *ICPP Bibliography Series.* Evanston, Ill.: International Comparative Political Parties Project, Northwestern University, 1967.

Johnson, Michael G. "The Distributional Aspects of Meaning Interaction in Agrammatical Verbal Contexts," Ph.D. Dissertation, Johns Hopkins University, 1968.

Johnson, Wendell. "Studies in Language Behavior," *Psychological Monographs* (56, 1944).

Johnstone, John, and Elihu Katz. "Youth and Popular Music: A Study in the Sociology of Taste," *American Journal of Sociology* (**62**:563–568, 1957).

Jones, Dorothy B. "Quantitative Analysis of Motion Picture Content," *Public Opinion Quarterly* (**16**:3, 411–428, 1952).

Jones, Edward E. *Ingratiation*. New York: Appleton-Century-Crofts, 1964.

Jones, Edward E. "Conformity as a Tactic of Ingratiation," *Science* (149, 144–150, 1965).

Jones, Robert L. with Verling C. Troldahl and J. K. Hvistendahl. "News Selection Patterns from a State TTS Wire," *Journalism Quarterly* (**38**:3, 303–312, 1961).

Kalin, Rudolf, William N. Davis, and David C. McClelland. "The Relationship Between Use of Alcohol and Thematic Content in Folktales in Primitive Societies," in P. J. Stone, D. C. Dunphy, M. S. Smith, and D. M. Ogilvie, *The General Inquirer*. Cambridge, Mass.: M.I.T. Press, 1967.

Kaplan, Abraham. "Content Analysis and the Theory of Signs," *Philosophy of Science* (**10**:4, 230–247, 1943).

Kassebaum, Gene G., Arthur S. Couch, and Philip E. Slater. "The Factorial Dimensions of the M.M.P.I.," *Journal of Consulting Psychology,* (**23**:226–236, 1959).

Katz, Elihu, Michael Gurewitch, Brenda Danet, and Tsiyona Peled. "Petitions and Prayers: A Content Analysis of Persuasive Appeals." Chicago, Ill.: University of Chicago, 1967 (mimeo).

Katz, Jerrold J., and Jerry A. Fodor. "The Structure of a Semantic Theory," *Language* (**39**:170–210, 1963).

Katz, Jerrold J. and Paul M. Postal. *An Integrated Theory of Linguistic Descriptions*. Cambridge, Mass.: M.I.T. Press, 1964a.

Katz, Jerrold J., and Jerry A. Fodor. "The Structure of a Semantic Theory," in J. A. Fodor and J. J. Katz (eds.), *Structure of Language: Readings in the Philosophy of Language*. Englewood Cliffs, N.J.: Prentice-Hall, 1964b.

Kautsky, Karl (ed.). *German Documents Relating to the Outbreak of the War*. New York: Oxford University Press, 1924.

Kay, Martin. *Experiments with a Powerful Parser*. Santa Monica, Calif.: The Rand Corporation (RM-5452), 1967.

Kehl, William (ed.). *Fall Joint Computer Conference Proceedings (1965)*. Baltimore, Md.: Spartan Books.

Keller, Hans E. *Étude Descriptive sur le Vocabulaire de Wace*. Berlin: Akademie-Verlag, 1953.

Kelly, E. Lowell. "Marital Compatibility as Related to Personality Traits of Husbands and Wives as Rated by Self and Spouse," *Journal of Social Psychology* (**31**:193–198, 1941).

Kelly, George. *The Psychology of Personal Constructs*. Two volumes. New York: Norton, 1955.

Kendall, Maurice G. *Rank Correlation Methods*. Second Revised Edition. New York: Hafner, 1955.

Kluckhohn, Clyde, Henry A. Murray, and David Schneider. *Personality in Nature, Society and Culture*. Second Edition. New York: Alfred A. Knopf, 1953.

Kracauer, Siegfried. "The Challenge of Qualitative Content Analysis," *Public Opinion Quarterly* (**16**:4, 631–642, 1952–53).

Kramer, Ernest. "Judgment of Personal Characteristics and Emotions From Non-verbal Properties of Speech," *Psychological Bulletin* (**60**:408–420, 1963).

Krippendorff, Klaus. "A Coefficient of Agreement for Situations in which Qualitative Data are Categorized by Many Judges." Philadelphia: University of Pennsylvania, Annenberg School of Communications, 1966a (mimeo).

Krippendorff, Klaus. "A Preliminary Inquiry Into the Expression of Values in Political Documents." Report to the International Studies of Values in Politics, Philadelphia: University of Pennsylvania, 1966b, (mimeo).

Krippendorff, Klaus. "An Examination of Content Analysis; A Proposal for a General Framework and an Information Calculus for Message Analytic Situations." Ph.D. Dissertation. Urbana: University of Illinois, 1967.

Kris, Ernst, and Nathan Leites. "Trends in 20th Century Propaganda," in B. Berelson and M. Janowitz (eds.), *Reader in Public Opinion and Communication*. Second Edition. New York: Free Press (278–288, 1966).

Kuhn, Thomas S. *The Structure of Scientific Revolutions*. Chicago: University of Chicago Press, 1962.

Kuno, Susumu. "The Augmented Predictive Analyzer for Context-Free Languages—Its Relative Efficiency," *Communications of the ACM* (**9**:810–823, 1966).

Kuno, Susumu. "The Predictive Analyzer and a Path Elimination Technique," *Communications of the ACM* (**8**:453–462, 1965). Reprinted in David G. Hays, *Readings in Automatic Language Processing*. New York: Elsevier, 1967.

Kyburg, Jr., E. Henry, and Ernest Nagel (eds.). *Induction: Some Current Issues*. Middletown, Conn.: Wesleyan University Press, 1963.

Laffal, Julius. "The Contextual Associates of Sun and God in Schreber's Auto-biography," *Journal of Abnormal and Social Psychology* (**61**:474–479, 1960).

Laffal, Julius. "Freud's Theory of Language," *Psychoanalytic Quarterly* (**33**:157–175, 1964a).

Laffal, Julius. "Psycholinguistics and the Psychology of Language: Comments," *American Psychologist* (**19**:813–815, 1964b).

Laffal, Julius. *Pathological and Normal Language*. New York: Atherton Press, 1965.

Laffal, Julius. "Characteristics of the Three-Person Conversation," *Journal of Verbal Learning and Verbal Behavior* (**6**:555–559, 1967a).

Laffal, Julius. "Language, Consciousness and Experience," *Psychoanalytic Quarterly* (**36**:61–66, 1967b).

Laffal, Julius. "An Approach to the Total Content Analysis of Speech in Psychotherapy," in John M. Shlien (ed.), *Research in Psychotherapy*. Washington, D.C.: American Psychological Association, 1968.

Lamb, Sydney M. "The Nature of the Machine Translation Problem," *Journal of Verbal Learning and Verbal Behavior* (**4**:196–210, 1965).

Lane, Robert E. *Political Ideology*. Glencoe, Ill.: The Free Press, 1962.

Lang, Kurt, and Gladys Lang. "The Unique Perspective of Television," *American Sociological Review* (**18**:3–12, 1953).

Lang, Kurt, and Gladys Lang. "The Inferential Structure of Political Communications: A Study in Unwitting Bias," *Public Opinion Quarterly* (**19**:163–183, 1955).

LaRue, Jan. "Two Problems in Musical Analysis: The Computer Lends a Hand," in E. A. Bowles (ed.), *Computers in Humanistic Research*. Englewood Cliffs, N.J.: Prentice Hall, 1967.

Lasswell, Harold D. *Propaganda Technique in the World War,* New York: Knopf, 1927.

Lasswell, Harold D. "The World Attention Survey: An Exploration of the Possibilities of Studying the Attention Being Given to the United States by Newspapers Abroad," *Public Opinion Quarterly* (**5**:3, 456–462, 1941).

Lasswell, Harold D. "Describing the Contents of Communications," in B. Smith, H. D. Lasswell, and R. Casey (eds.), *Propaganda, Communication, and Public Opinion.* Princeton: Princeton University Press (74–94, 1946).

Lasswell, Harold D., and Abraham Kaplan. *Power and Society.* New Haven: Yale University Press, 1950.

Lasswell, Harold D., Daniel Lerner, and Ithiel de Sola Pool. *The Comparative Study of Symbols.* Hoover Institute Studies, Series C: No. 1. Stanford, Calif.: Stanford University Press, 1952.

Lasswell, Harold D., Nathan Leites, and associates. *Language of Politics: Studies in Quantitative Semantics.* Revised Edition. Cambridge, Mass.: The M.I.T. Press, 1965.

Lasswell, Harold D. "Why Be Quantitative?" in B. Berelson and M. Janowitz (eds.), *Reader in Public Opinion and Communication* (Second Edition). New York: Free Press (247–260, 1966).

Lauffer, Susan. "Party Politics in Congo-Brazzaville, 1950–1962," in Kenneth Janda (ed.), *ICPP Bibliography Series.* Evanston, Ill.: International Comparative Political Parties Project, Northwestern University, 1967.

Lazarsfeld, Paul F. "Remarks on Administrative and Critical Communications Research," *Studies in Philosophy and Social Science* (**9**:1, 2–16, 1941).

Leed, Jacob (ed.). *The Computer and Literary Style.* Kent, Ohio: Kent State University Press, 1966.

Leites, Nathan, Elsa Bernaut, and Raymond L. Garthoff. "Politburo Images of Stalin," *World Politics* (**3**:317–339, 1951).

Leites, Nathan. "Trends in Affectlessness," in C. Kluckhohn, H. Murray, and D. Schneider (eds.), *Personality in Nature, Society, and Culture.* Revised Edition. New York: Knopf, 1964.

Lesk, Michael E. "Word-Word Associations in Document Retrieval Systems," Report No. ISR-13 to the National Science Foundation, Section IX, Department of Computer Science, Cornell University, December, 1967.

Lewin, H. S. "Hilter Youth and the Boy Scouts of America," *Human Relations* (**1**:206–227, 1947).

Lewis, Oscar. *The Children of Sanchez.* New York: Random House, 1961.

Lewis, Oscar. *La Vida.* New York: Random House, 1966.

Lindsay, Robert K. "Inferential Memory as the Basis of Machines which Understand Natural Language," in Edward A. Feigenbaum and Julian Feldman (eds.), *Computers and Thought.* New York: McGraw-Hill (217–233, 1963).

Lockwood, Lewis. "A Stylistic Investigation of the Masses of Josquin Desprez with the Aid of Computer: A Progress Report," in B. Brook (ed.), *Musicology and the Computer.* New York: Queens College Press, in press.

Lockwood, Lewis. "Computer Assistance in the Investigation of Accidentals in Renaissance Music." Paper read at 10th I.M.S. Congress, to be published in its Congress Report.

Lord, Joseph P. "Psychological Correlates of Nocturnal Enuresis in Male Children." Unpublished Doctoral Thesis, Department of Social Relations, Harvard University, 1952.

Lowenthal, Leo. "Biographies in Popular Magazines," in W. Petersen (ed.), *American Social Patterns*. New York: Doubleday-Anchor (63–118, 1956).

Lowenthal, Leo (ed.). "The Triumph of Mass Idols," in *Literature, Popular Culture and Society*. Englewoods Cliffs, N.J.: Prentice-Hall (Chapter 4, 109–136, 1961).

Lyon, H. "The Sailing Charts of the Marshall Islanders," *Geographical Journal* (**72:**325–328, 1928).

Macalpine, Ida, and Richard A. Hunter. "Discussion of the Schreber Case," in *Daniel Paul Schreber: Memoirs of My Nervous Illness*. Ida Macalpine, and R. A. Hunter (trans.). Cambridge, Mass.: Robert Bentley, 1955.

MacVaugh, Gilbert S. "Structural Analysis of the Sermons of Harry Emerson Fosdick," *Quarterly Journal of Speech* (**18:**4, 531–546, 1932).

Mahl, George F. "Exploring Emotional States by Content Analysis," in Ithiel de Sola Pool (ed.), *Trends in Content Analysis*. Urbana, Ill.: University of Illinois Press (89–130, 1959).

Mahl, George F. "Some Observations About Research on Vocal Behavior," in D. M. Rioch (ed.), *Disorders of Communication*. Proceedings of ARNMD, Vol. 42, Baltimore: Williams and Wilkins Co., 1964a.

Mahl, George F., and Gene Schulze. "Psychological Research in the Extralinguistic Area," in Thomas Sebeok, A. S. Haynes, and M. C. Bateson (eds.), *Approaches to Semiotics*. The Hague: Mouton & Co. (50–124, 1964b).

Mala, Hana. "Statisticka Srovnavaci Analyza Sboru Leose Janacka a Moravskych Lidovych Pisni" in *Hudebni Veda* (IV/4, 1967).

Mandelbrot, Benoit. "An Informational Theory of the Statistical Structure of Language," in Willis Jackson (ed.), *Communication Theory*. London: Butterworth, 1953.

Marsden, Gerald. "Content Analysis Studies of Therapeutic Interviews: 1954–1964," *Psychological Bulletin* (**63**, No. 5, 298–321, 1965).

Martel, Martin U., and George J. McCall, "Reality-Orientation and the Pleasure Principle: A Study of American Mass-Periodical Fiction (1890–1955)," in L. A. Dexter and D. M. White (eds.), *People, Society and Mass Communication*. New York: The Free Press of Glencoe (283–333, 1964).

Martin, Helen. "Nationalism and Children's Literature," *Library Quarterly* (Vol. 6, 1936).

Matarazzo, Joseph D., Morris Weitman, George Saslow, and Arthur N. Weins. "Interviewer Influence on Duration of Interviewee Speech," *Journal of Verbal Learning and Verbal Behavior* (**1:**451–458, 1963).

Matarazzo, Joseph D., Arthur N. Wiens, George Saslow, Richard M. Dunham, and Robert B. Voas. "Speech Durations of Astronaut and Ground Communicator," *Science* (**143:**148–150, 1964).

Matthews, G. Herbert. "Analysis by Synthesis of Natural Languages," Proceedings of the 1961 International Conference on Machine Translation of Languages and Applied Language Analysis. London: Her Majesty's Stationary Office, 1962.

McClelland, Charles A. "Action Structures and Communication in Two International Crises: Quemoy and Berlin," *Background* (**7,**4:201–215, 1964).

McClelland, David C., William N. Davis, H. Eric Wanner, and Rudolf Kalin. "A Cross-Cultural Study of Folktale Content and Drinking." Unpublished Manuscript, Department of Social Relations, Harvard University, 1966.

McGranahan, Donald, and Ivor Wayne. "German and American Traits Reflected in Popular Drama," *Human Relations* (**1:**429–455, 1948).

Meetham, Andrew R. "Preliminary Studies for Machine Generated Vocabularies," *Language and Speech* (**6,** Part 1: 22–36, 1963).

Meggitt, M. J. "Dream Interpretation Among the Mae Enga of New Guinea," *Southwestern Journal of Anthropology* (**18:**216–229, 1962).

Mendel, Gregor. *Experiments on Plant Hybridization.* Cambridge, Mass.: Harvard University Press, 1924.

Mendenhall, Thomas C. "The Characteristic Curve of Composition," *Science* (**9:**237–249, 1887).

Merritt, Richard L. *Symbols of American Community, 1735–1775.* New Haven: Yale University Press, 1966.

Merton, Robert K., and Paul F. Lazarsfeld. "Studies in Radio and Film Propaganda," in R. K. Merton, *Social Theory and Social Structure.* New York: Free Press of Glencoe (509–528, 1957).

Meyer, Leonard B. "Meaning in Music and Information Theory," *Journal of Aesthetics and Art Criticism* (**XV/4:**412–424, 1957).

Milic, Louis T. "Some Risks of Technological Overindulgence for the Humanities," in J. B. Bessinger and S. M. Parrish (eds.), *Proceedings of the IBM Literary Data Processing Conference.* Yorktown Heights, N.Y.: IBM, 55–63, 1964.

Milic, Louis T. "Unconscious Ordering in the Prose of Swift," in J. Leed (ed.), *The Computer and Literary Style.* Kent, Ohio: Kent State University Press, (79–106, 1966).

Miller, J. Philip, Dennis J. Arp, and George Psathas. "Description of the 360 General Inquirer System," 1967 (mimeo).

Miller, J. Philip (ed.). *Inquirer II Programmer's Guide.* St. Louis, Mo.: Washington University, 1969.

Mitchell, Robert E. "The Use of Content Analysis for Explanatory Studies," *Public Opinion Quarterly* (**31:**230–241, 1967).

Miyares, Marcelino. "Party Politics in the Dominican Republic, 1950–1962," in Kenneth Janda (ed.), *ICPP Bibliography Series.* Evanston, Ill.: International Comparative Political Parties Project, Northwestern University, November, 1967.

Moles, Abraham. *Theorie de l'information et Perception Esthetique.* Paris: Flammarion, 1958.

Moles, Abraham. *Information Theory and Aesthetic Perception.* A revised edition, translated into English by J. E. Cohen. Urbana, Ill.: University of Illinois Press, 1965.

Morris, Charles. *Signs, Language and Behavior.* New York: Prentice-Hall, 1946.

Morris, Charles. *Signification and Significance: A Study of the Relations of Signs and Values.* Cambridge, Mass.: The M.I.T. Press, 1964.

Morton, Andrew Q. "A Computer Challenges the Church," *The Observer,* 1963.

Morton, Andrew Q., and Michael Levison. "Some Indications of Authorship in Greek Prose," in J. Leed (ed.), *The Computer and Literary Style.* Kent, Ohio: Kent State University Press (141–179, 1966).

Mosteller, Fredrick, and David L. Wallace. "Inference in an Authorship Problem," *Journal of American Statistical Association* (**58:**275–309, 1963).

Mosteller, Fredrick, and David L. Wallace. *Inference and Disputed Authorship: The Federalist.* Reading, Mass.: Addison-Wesley, 1964.

Murdock, George P. *Outline of Cultural Materials.* New Haven, Conn.: Human Relations Area Files, 1961.

Murdock, George P. (ed.). "Ethnographic Atlas," *Ethnology* (Vols. I–IV, 1962–1965).

Murray, Henry A. "The American Icarus," in A. Burton and R. E. Harris (eds.), *Clinical Studies of Personality.* New York: Harper & Bros. (Vol. II, 1955).

Murray, Henry A. "Note on the Icarus Syndrome," *Fol Psychiat. Neurol. Neurochirurg.* Neirland. (**61:**204–208, 1958).

Nakamura, Hajime. *The Ways of Thinking of Eastern Peoples.* Tokyo: Japanese Government Printing Bureau, 1960 (available from Charles E. Tuttle Co., Rutland, Vermont).

Namenwirth, J. Zvi, and Thomas L. Brewer. "Elite Editorial Comment on the European and Atlantic Communities in Four Continents," in Philip J. Stone D. C. Dunphy, M. S. Smith, and D. M. Ogilvie, *The General Inquirer: A Computer Approach to Content Analysis.* Cambridge, Mass.: The M.I.T. Press, 1966.

Namenwirth, J. Zvi, and Harold D. Lasswell, "Culture vs. Social Action in the Explanation of Social Change," in *Changing Language in American Party Platforms: A Computer Analysis of Political Values* (forthcoming).

Naroll, Raoul. *Data Quality Control: A New Research Technique.* New York: The Free Press of Glencoe, 1962.

Needham, Roger and Loren B. Doyle. "Breaking the Cost Barrier in Automatic Classification." Report SP-2516, Santa Monica: Systems Development, 1966.

Newsome, Judith A. "Party Politics in Bulgaria, 1905–1962," in Kenneth Janda (ed.), *ICPP Bibliography Series.* Evanston, Ill.: International Comparative Political Parties Project, Northwestern University, 1967.

North, Robert C., and Ithiel de Sola Pool. "Kuomintang and Chinese Communist Elites," Hoover Institute Studies, Series B: Elite Studies No. 8. Stanford, Calif.: Stanford University Press, 1952.

North, Robert C., Ole R. Holsti, M. George Zaninovich, and Dina A. Zinnes. *Content Analysis: A Handbook with Applications for the Study of International Crisis.* Evanston, Ill.: Northwestern University, 1963.

North, Robert C., Richard A. Brody, and Ole R. Holsti. "Some Empirical Data on the Conflict Spiral," *Peace Research Society (International) Papers* (**1:**1–4, 1964).

North, Robert C. "Perception and Action in the 1914 Crisis," *Journal of International Affairs* (**21:**103–122, 1967).

Nowak, Leopold. "Das Autograph von Haydns Cellokonzert D-Dur op. 101," in *Osterreichische Musikzeitschrift* (Vol. IX, 1954).

O'Donnell, Bernard. "The O'Ruddy: A Problem in Authorship Discrimination," in J. Leed (ed.), *The Computer and Literary Style.* Kent, Ohio: Kent State University Press, (107–115, 1966).

Oettinger, Anthony G. "Automatic Syntactic Analysis and the Pushdown Store," *Proceedings of Symposia on Applied Mathematics, Vol. XII: Structure of Language and Its Mathematical Aspects,* American Mathematical Society (104–129, 1961).

Ogilvie, Daniel M. "Some Psychological Implications of Matriarchal Residence Patterns." Unpublished Manuscript, Department of Social Relations, Harvard University, 1962.

Ogilvie, Daniel M. "The Second Icarus Dictionary." Unpublished Manuscript, Department of Social Relations, Harvard, June 1967.

Ohlstrom, Bo. "Information and Propaganda: A Content Analysis of Editorials in Four Swedish Daily Newspapers," *Journal of Peace Research* (**3**:75–88, 1966).

Osgood, Charles E., and Thomas A. Sebeok (eds.). "Psycholinguistics: A Survey of Theory and Research Problems," *Journal of Abnormal and Social Psychology* (Supplement) (Vol. 49, No. 4, Part II, 1954).

Osgood, Charles E., Sol Saporta, and Jim C. Nunnally. "Evaluative Assertion Analysis," *Litera* (**3**:47–102, 1956).

Osgood, Charles E., George J. Suci, and Percy H. Tannenbaum. *The Measurement of Meaning*. Urbana, Ill.: University of Illinois Press, 1957.

Osgood, Charles E. "The Representation Model and Relevant Research Methods," in Ithiel de Sola Pool (ed.), *Trends in Content Analysis*. Urbana, Ill.: University of Illinois (33–88, 1959a).

Osgood, Charles E., and Evelyn Walker. "Motivation and Language Behavior: A Content Analysis of Suicide Notes," *Journal of Abnormal and Social Psychology* (**59**:58–67, 1959b).

Osgood, Charles E. "Some Effects of Motivation on Style of Encoding," in T. A. Sebeok (ed.), *Style in Language*. Cambridge, Mass.: The M.I.T. Press (293–306, 1960).

Osgood, Charles E. "Studies on the Generality of Affective Meaning Systems," *American Psychologist* (**17**:10–28, 1962).

Osgood, Charles E., and Thomas A. Sebeok (eds.). "Psycholinguistics: A Survey of Theory and Research Problems," with Richard Diebold, *A Survey of Psycholinguistic Research* **1954–1964.** Bloomington, Ind.: Indiana University Press, 1965.

Paisley, William J. "Identifying the Unknown Communicator in Painting, Literature and Music: The Significance of Minor Encoding Habits," *Journal of Communication* (**14**:219–237, 1964).

Paisley, William J. "The Effects of Authorship, Topic, Structure, and Time of Composition on Letter Redundancy in English Texts," *Journal of Verbal Learning and Verbal Behavior* (**5**:28–34, 1966).

Paisley, William J. "Minor Encoding Habits II: The Case of Extemporaneous Speech in the Kennedy-Nixon Debates." Stanford, Calif.: Institute for Communication Research, 1967 (mimeo).

Paisley, William J. "The Analysis of Communication Content," in W. Schramm and Ithiel de Sola Pool (eds.), *The Handbook of Communication*. Chicago: Rand McNally, in press.

Palermo, David S., and James J. Jenkins. "Sex Differences in word association," *Journal of General Psychology* (**72**:77–84, 1965).

Palermo, David S., and James J. Jenkins. "Oral Word Association Norms for Children in Grades One Through Four," *Research Bulletin No. 60*. Department of Psychology, Pennsylvania State University, University Park, Pa., 1966.

Parsons, Talcott, Edward A. Shils, and James Olds. "Values, Motives, and Systems of Action," in Talcott Parsons and E. A. Shils, *Toward a General Theory of Action*. Cambridge, Mass.: Harvard University Press (1952).

Perry, Campbell. "A Manual of Procedures for Analyzing Manifest Dream Content into Narrative Elements and for Classifying such Elements with Respect to Distortion from Reality." Department of Psychology, the University of Sydney, 1964 (mimeo).

Piault, Colette. "A Methodological Investigation of Content Analysis Using Electronic Computers for Data Processing," in Dell Hymes (ed.), *The Use of Computers in Anthropology.* The Hague: Mouton (273–293, 1965).

Pitcher, Evelyn G., and Ernst Prelinger. *Children Tell Stories.* New York: International Universities Press, 1963.

Pittenger, Robert E., Charles F. Hockett, and John J. Danehy. *The First Five Minutes: A Sample of Microscopic Interviews Analysis.* Ithaca, N.Y.: Paul Martineau, 1960.

Polanyi, Michael. "Sense-Giving and Sense-Reading of Language," *Philosophy,* (42:301–325, 1967).

Pool, Ithiel de Sola, Harold D. Lasswell, and Daniel Lerner. "Symbols of Internationalism," Hoover Institute Studies, Series C, Symbols: No. 3. Stanford, Calif.: Stanford University Press, 1951.

Pool, Ithiel de Sola, Harold D. Lasswell, and Daniel Lerner. "Symbols of Democracy." Hoover Institute Studies, Series C, Symbols: No. 4. Stanford, Calif.: Stanford University Press 1952a.

Pool, Ithiel de Sola, Harold D. Lasswell, and Daniel Lerner. "The Prestige Papers: A Survey of Their Editorials," Hoover Institute Studies, Series C, Symbols: No. 2. Stanford, Calif.: Stanford University Press, 1952b.

Pool, Ithiel de Sola (ed.). *Trends in Content Analysis.* Urbana, Ill.: University of Illinois Press, 1959a.

Pool, Ithiel de Sola. "Trends in Content Analysis Today: A Summary," in Ithiel de Sola Pool (ed.), *Trends in Content Analysis.* Urbana: University of Illinois Press, 1959b.

Porter, Kirk, and Donald B. Johnson, *National Party Platforms, 1840–1960.* Urbana: University of Illinois Press, 1961.

Propp, Vladimir I. *Morphology of the Folktale.* Laurence Scott (trans.), Bloomington, Ind.: Indiana University Research Center in Anthropology, Folklore, and Linguistics, Publication 10, 1958.

Psathas, George and Denis J. Arp. "A Thematic Analysis of Interviewer's Statements in Therapy Analogue Interviews," in Philip J. Stone, D. C. Dunphy, M. S. Smith, and D. M. Ogilvie, *The General Inquirer: A Computer Approach to Content Analysis.* Cambridge, Mass.: M.I.T. Press 1966.

Quillian, Ross. "Word Concepts: A Theory and Simulation of Some Basic Semantic Capabilities," Report SP 2199. Santa Monica, Calif.: System Development Corporation, 1965.

Quillian, Ross. "Semantic Memory." Report AD 641 671, Clearinghouse for Federal Scientific and Technical Information, U.S. Department of Commerce, 1966.

Ramallo, Luis I. "The Integration of Subject and Object in the Context of Action: A Study of Reports Written by Successful and Unsuccessful Volunteers in Field Work in Africa," in Philip J. Stone, D. C. Dunphy, M. S. Smith, and D. M. Ogilvie, *The General Inquirer.* Cambridge, Mass.: The M.I.T. Press, 1966.

Ray, Michael L. "Cross-Cultural Analysis: Its Promise and Its Problems." Unpublished Paper, Northwestern University, 1966a.

Ray, Michael L. and Eugene J. Webb. "Speech Duration Effects in the Kennedy News Conferences," *Science* (153:899–901, 1966b).

Rechtschaffen, Allan, Paul Verdone, and Joy Wheaton. "Reports of Mental Activity During Sleep," *Canadian Psychiatric Association Journal* (8:409–414, 1963).

Regener, Eric. "A Multiple-Pass Transcription and a System for Music Analysis by Computer," in H. Heckmann (ed.), *Elektronische Datenverarbeitung in der Musikwissenschaft,* Regenburg, 1967.

Reinecke, Hans-Peter. "Anwendung Informationstheoretischer und Korrelationsstatistischer Verfahren fur de Analyse musikalischer Strukturen." Paper read at the 10th Congress of the International Musicological Society in Ljubljana, 1967, and to be published in its forthcoming Congress Report.

Reitman, Walter. "Computer Simulation Models: How to Invent What You Need to Know." Paper presented at the University of Chicago (1967).

Revesz, Geza (ed.). *Thinking and Speaking: A Symposium.* Amsterdam: North Holland Company, 1954.

Richardson, Lewis F. *Arms and Insecurity.* N. Rashevsky and E. Trucco (eds.), Chicago: Quadrangle Press; and Pittsburgh: Boxwood Press, 1960.

Rimberg, J. D. "Social Problems as Depicted in Soviet Film—A Research Note," *Social Problems* (**7:**351–353, 1960).

Robertson, John M. *The Shakespeare Canon.* Oxford: Oxford University Press, 1920–1930.

Robinson, Jane. "Parse: a System for Automatic Syntactic Analysis of English Text." RM-4654-RR. Santa Monica, Calif.: Rand Corporation, 1965.

Rosi, Eugene J. "How 50 Periodicals and the *Times* Interpreted the Test Ban Controversy," *Journalism Quarterly* (**41:**545–556, 1964).

Ruesch, Jurgen, and Weldon Kees. *Non-Verbal Communication: Notes on the Visual Perception of Human Relations.* Berkeley, Calif.: University of California, 1956.

Russell, Bertrand. *An Inquiry into Meaning and Truth.* New York: Humanities Press, 1963.

Salton, Gerard, and Michael E. Lesk. "The SMART Automatic Document Retrieval System—An Illustration," *Communications of the ACM* (**8:**6, 391–398, 1965a).

Salton, Gerard. "Progress in Automatic Information Retrieval," *IEEE Spectrum* (**2:**8, 90–103, 1965b).

Salton, Gerard. "Automatic Phrase Matching," in D. Hays (ed.), *Readings in Automatic Language Processing.* New York: American Elsevier Publishing Co., 1966a.

Salton, Gerard. "Evaluation of Computer-Based Information Retrieval Systems," *Proceedings of the FID Congress 1965,* Washington, D.C.: Spartan Books, 1966b.

Salton, Gerard. "Search Strategy and Optimization of Retrieval Effectiveness," In K. Samuelson (ed.), *Mechanized Information, Storage, Retrieval and Dissemination.* Amsterdam: North Holland Publishing Co., 1968a.

Salton, Gerard, and Michael E. Lesk. "Computer Evaluation of Indexing and Text Processing," *Journal of the ACM,* (**15:**1, 8–36, 1968a).

Sanders, Luther W. "A Content Analysis of President Kennedy's First Six Press Conferences," *Journalism Quarterly* (**42:**1, 114–115, 1965).

Sapir, Edward. *Culture, Language and Personality.* David G. Mandelbaum (ed.), Berkeley and Los Angeles: University of California Press, 1956.

Schachter, Stanley, and Jerome E. Singer. "Cognitive, Social and Physiological Determinants of Emotional State," *Psychological Review* (**69:**379–399, 1962).

Schelling, Thomas. *The Strategy of Conflict.* New York: Oxford University Press, 1963.

Schelling, Thomas. *Arms and Insecurity.* New Haven: Yale University Press, 1966.

Scheuch, Erwin K., and Philip J. Stone. "The General Inquirer Approach to an International Retrieval System for Survey Archives," *American Behavioral Scientist* (7:23–28, 1964).

Schiødt, Nanna, and Bjarner Sveygaard. "Application of Computer Techniques to the Analysis of Byzantine Sticherarion Melodies," in H. Heckmann (ed.), *Elektronische Datenverarbeitung in der Musikwissenschaft*, Regensburg, 1967.

Schlesinger, L. E. "Prediction of Newspaper Bias," *Journal of Social Psychology* (42:35–42, 1955).

Schneider, Louis, and Sanford M. Dornbusch. *Popular Religion: Inspirational Books in America*. Chicago: University of Chicago Press, 1958.

Schreber, Daniel P. *Memoirs of My Nervous Illness (1903)*. Cambridge, Mass.: Robert Bentley, 1955.

Schutz, William C. "On Categorizing Qualitative Data in Content Analysis," *Public Opinion Quarterly* (22:4, 503–515, 1958).

Schwestka, Jon O. "Party Politics in North Korea, 1950–1962," in Kenneth Janda (ed.), ICPP Bibliography Series. Evanston, Ill.: International Comparative Political Parties Project, Northwestern University, 1967.

Sebald, Hans. "Studying National Character Through Comparative Content Analysis," *Social Forces* (40:318–322, 1962).

Sebeok, Thomas A., and Valdis J. Zeps. "An Analysis of Structured Content, with Application of Electronic Computer Research in Psycholinguistics," *Language and Speech* (1:181–193, 1958).

Sebeok, Thomas A. *Style in Language*. Cambridge, Mass.: The M.I.T. Press, 1960.

Sebeok, Thomas A., Alfred S. Hayes, and Mary C. Bateson (eds.) *Approaches to Semiotics*. The Hague: Mouton, 1964.

Sebeok, Thomas, A. "The Structure and Content of Cheremis Charms." *Anthropos: International Review of Ethnology and Linguistics*. (48:369–388, 1953). Summarized in *Style and Language*, Cambridge, Mass.: The M.I.T. Press, 1966.

Sechrest, Lee, and John Wallace. "Figure Drawing and Naturally Occurring Events: Elimination of the Expansive Euphoria Hypothesis," *Journal of Educational Psychology* (55:42–44, 1964).

Sedelow, Sally Yeates, Walter A. Sedelow Jr., and Terry Ruggles. "Some Parameters for Computational Stylistics: A Computer Aid to the Use of Traditional Categories in Stylistic Analysis." *Literary Data Processing Conference Proceedings*, in Jess B. Bessinger Jr., Stephen M. Parrish and Harry F. Arader (eds.). New York: IBM, 1964.

Sedelow, Sally Yeates. "Form Recognition in Literature." *Proceedings of IFIP Congress 1965*. Washington, D.C.: Spartan Books (II:626–627, 1965a).

Sedelow, Sally Yeates. "Stylistic Analysis, Report on the First Year of Research, TM-1908/100/00." Santa Monica, Calif.: System Development Corporation, 1965b.

Sedelow, Sally Yeates. "Stylistic Analysis, Report on the Second Year of Research, TM-1908/200/00." Santa Monica, Calif.: System Development Corporation, 1966a.

Sedelow, Sally Yeates and Walter A. Sedelow Jr. "A Preface to Computational Stylistics." Jacob Leed (ed.). *The Computer and Literary Style*, Kent, Ohio: Kent State University Press, 1966b.

Sedelow, Sally Yeates and Walter A. Sedelow Jr. "Stylistic Analysis." Harold Barko (ed.). *Automated Language Analysis*, New York: John Wiley and Sons, Inc., 1967a.

Sedelow, Sally Yeates. "Stylistic Analysis, Report on the Third Year of Research TM-1908/300/00." Santa Monica, Calif.: System Development Corporation, 1967b.

Shaw, Donald L. "News Bias and the Telegraph: A Study of Historical Change," *Journalism Quarterly* (**44:**1, 3–12, 1967).

Shepard, David W. "Henry J. Taylor's Radio Talks: A Content Analysis," *Journalism Quarterly* (**33:**15–22, 1956).

Shneidman, Edwin S. "The Logic of Suicide" in E. Shneidman and N. L. Farberow (eds.). *Clues to Suicide.* N.Y.: McGraw Hill, 1957.

Shneidman, Edwin S. "Psycho-Logic: A Personality Approach to Patterns of Thinking," in Jerome Kagan and Gerald Lesser (eds.), *Contemporary Issues in Thematic Apperceptive Methods.* Springfield, Ill.: Charles C. Thomas, (153–189, 1961a).

Shneidman, Edwin S. "The Logic of El: A Psychological Approach to the Analysis of Test Data," *Journal of Projective Techniques* (**25:**390–403, 1961b).

Shneidman, Edwin S. "The Logic of Politics," in Leon Arons and Mark A. May (eds.), *Television and Human Behavior.* New York: Appleton-Century-Crofts (178–179, 1963).

Shneidman, Edwin S. *The Logics of Communication: A Manual for Analysis.* China Lake, Calif.: U.S. Naval Ordinance Test Station, 1966.

Shneidman, Edwin S. "Psycho-Logic: The Explication of Argument," in Henry A. Murray (ed.), *Aspects of Personality,* in press.

Sikorski, Linda, Donald F. Roberts, and William J. Paisley. "Analyzing Letters in Mass Magazines as 'Outcroppings' of Public Concern." Institute for Communication Research, Stanford University, 1967 (mimeo).

Simmons, Robert. "Answering English Questions by Computer: A Survey," *Communication of the Association for Computing Machinery* (**8:**53–70, 1965).

Simon, Herbert A. "On a Class of Skew Distribution Functions." *Biometrika* (**42:**425–440, 1955).

Singer, J. David. "Media Analysis in Inspection for Disarmament," *The Journal of Arms Control* (**1,3:**248–260, 1963).

Skinner, Burrhus F. "The Problem of Reference," in Sol Saporta (ed.), *Psycholinguistics,* New York: Holt, Rinehart and Winston, 1961.

Skogan, Wesley. "Party Politics in Guinea, 1950–1962," in Kenneth Janda (ed.), *ICPP Bibliography Series.* Evanston, Ill.: International Comparative Political Parties Project, Northwestern University, 1967.

Smith, M. E., and Calvin S. Hall. "An Investigation of Regression in a Long Dream Series," *Journal of Gerontology* (**19:**66–71, 1964).

Solley, Charles M., and Gerard A. Haigh. "A Note to Santa Claus." *Topeka Research Papers,* The Menniger Foundation (**19:**4–5, 1957).

Sorenson, E. Richard, and Carlton Gajdusek. "The Fore of New Guinea. A Continuing Film Study of the Kuru Afflicted People's Changing Environment, Culture and Behavior." *Oceania,* 1967.

Speed, Gilmer J. "Do Newspapers Now Give the News?" *The Forum* (**15:**705–711, 1893).

Spiegelman, Marvin, Carl Terwilliger, and Franklin Fearing. "The Content of Comics: Goals and Means to Goals of Comic Strip Characters," *Journal of Social Psychology* (**37:**189–203, 1953).

Spurgeon, Caroline. *Shakespeare's Imagery and What it Tells Us* (*1935*). Cambridge, England: University Press, 1958.

Starkweather, John A. "Vocal Communication of Personality and Human Feelings," *Journal of Communications* (**11**:63–72, 1961).

Starkweather, John A. "Variations in Vocal Behavior," in D. Rioch (ed.), *Disorders of Communication.* Proceedings of ARNMD. Baltimore: Williams & Wilkins Co. (Vol. 42, 1964a).

Starkweather, John A., and J. Barry Decker. "Computer Analysis of Interview Content," *Psychological Reports* (**15**:875–882, 1964b).

Starkweather, John A. "Computest: A Computer Language for Individual Testing, Instruction, and Interviewing," *Psychological Reports* (**17**:227–237, 1965).

Starkweather, John A. "Computer-Assisted Learning in Medical Education," *Canadian Medical Association Journal* (**97**:733–738, 1967a).

Starkweather, John A. "Computer Methods for the Study of Psychiatric Interviews," *Comprehensive Psychiatry,* 1967b.

Starkweather, John A. "Psychiatric Interview Simulation by Computer," *Methods of Information in Psychiatry* (**6**:15–23, 1967c).

Starkweather, John A. "Vocal Behavior as an Information Channel of Speaker Status," in K. Salzinger and S. Salzinger (eds.), *Research in Verbal Behavior and Some Neurophysiological Implications.* New York: Academic Press, 1967d.

Stayton, Samuel E., and Morton Weiner. "Value, Magnitude and Accentuation," *Journal of Abnormal and Social Psychology* (**62**:145–147, 1961).

Stempel, Guido H. III. "The Prestige Press Covers the 1960 Presidential Campaign," *Journalism Quarterly* (**38**:157–163, 1961).

Stempel, Guido H. III. "Content Patterns of Small and Metropolitan Dailies," *Journalism Quarterly* (**39**:1, 88–90, 1962).

Stempel, Guido H. III. "How Newspapers Use the Associated Press Afternoon A-Wire," *Journalism Quarterly* (**41**:3, 380–384, 1964).

Stern, Richard G. *Golk.* New York: Criterion, 1960.

Stewart, Janice S. "Content and Readership of Teen Magazines," *Journalism Quarterly* (**41**:4, 580–583, 1964).

Stoltz, Walter, Percy H. Tannenbaum, and Frederick Carstensen. "A Stochastic Approach to the Grammatical Coding of English." Unpublished paper, Center for Cognitive Studies, Harvard University, 1964.

Stone, Philip J., Robert F. Bales, J. Zvi Namenwirth, and Daniel M. Ogilvie. "The General Inquirer: A Computer System for Content Analysis and Retrieval Based on the Sentence as Unit of Information," *Behavioral Science* (**7**, No. 4, 484–498, 1962).

Stone, Philip J., and Earl B. Hunt. "A Computer Approach to Content Analysis: Studies Using the General Inquirer System," *Proceedings of the Spring Joint Computer Conference.* Washington, D.C.: Spartan Books (241–256, 1963).

Stone, Philip J., Dexter C. Dunphy, Marshall S. Smith, and Daniel M. Ogilvie. *The General Inquirer: A Computer Approach to Content Analysis.* Cambridge, Mass.: M.I.T. Press, 1966.

Stone, Philip J., and Cambridge Computer Associates, Inc. J. Kirsch, Technical Editor. *User's Manual for the General Inquirer.* Cambridge, Mass.: M.I.T. Press, 1968.

Suci, George, and Theodore Husek. "A Content Analysis of 70 Messages with 55 Variables and Subsequent Effect Studies." Urbana, Ill.: Institute for Communication Research, University of Illinois, 1957 (mimeo).

Tannenbaum, Percy H., and Mervin D. Lynch. "Sensationalism: The Concept and Its Measurement," *Journalism Quarterly* (**37**:381–392, 1960).

Tasman, Paul. "Literary Data Processing," *IBM Journal of Research and Development* (**1**:3, 249–250, 1957).

Tenney, Alvin A. "The Scientific Analysis of the Press," *The Independent* (**73**:895–898, 1912).

Thayer, Lee (ed.). "Communication Theory and Research," *Proceedings of the First International Symposium on Communication Theory Research.* Springfield, Ill.: Charles C Thomas, 1967.

Tomkins, Silvan S. *Affect, Imagery, Consciousness, The Positive Affects.* New York: Springer, 1962.

Tuchman, Barbara W. *The Guns of August.* New York: Dell, 1962.

Tulving, Endel. "Subjective Organization in Free Recall of 'Unrelated' Words," *Psycholigical Review* (**69**:344–354, 1962).

Ullmann, Stephen. *Semantics, An Introduction to the Science of Meaning.* New York: Barnes & Noble, 1962.

Van de Castle, R. L. "Animal Figures in Dreams: Age, Sex, and Cultural Differences." Paper presented at the Convention of the American Psychological Association, 1966.

Von Domarus, E. "The Specific Law of Logic in Schizophrenia," in J. S. Kasanin, (ed.), *Language and Thought in Schizophrenia.* Berkeley and Los Angeles: University of California Press, 1944.

Von Grunebaum, Gustave E., and Roger Caillois (eds.). *The Dream and Human Societies.* Berkeley: University of California Press, 1966.

Warchol, Philip. "Stamp Illustrations and Militarism in Nazi Germany." Unpublished Paper, Stanford University, 1967.

Watson, John B. *Behaviorism* (*1924*). New York: W. W. Norton, Revised 1930.

Watzlawick, Paul, Janet Helmiek Beavin, and Don D. Jackson. *Pragmatics of Human Communication; A Study of Interactional Patterns, Pathologies, and Paradoxes.* New York: Norton, 1967.

Wayne, Ivor. "American and Soviet Themes and Values: A Content Analysis of Pictures in Popular Magazines," in *Public Opinion Quarterly* (**20**:1, 314–320, 1956).

Webb, Eugene J., Donald T. Campbell, Richard D. Schwartz, and Lee Sechrest. *Unobtrusive Measures: Non-Reactive Research in the Social Sciences.* Chicago: Rand McNally and Company, 1966.

Weinreich, Urial. "Explorations in Semantic Theory," in T. A. Sebeok (ed.), *Current Trends in Linguistics,* Vol. 3, Theoretical Foundations, The Hague: Mouton and Company, 1966.

Weizenbaum, Joseph. "Eliza-A Computer Program for the Study of Natural Language Communication Between Man and Machine," *Communications of the ACM* (**9**:36–45, 1966).

Weizenbaum, Joseph. "Contextual Understanding by Computers," *Communications of the ACM* (**10**:474–480, 1967).

White, Ralph K. "Value-Analysis: A Quantitative Method for Describing Qualitative Data," *Journal of Social Psychology* (**19**:351–358, 1944).

White, Ralph K. "Black Boy: A Value Analysis," *Journal of Abnormal and Social Psychology* (**42**:440–461, 1947).

White, Ralph K. "Hitler, Roosevelt, and the Nature of War Propaganda," *Journal of Abnormal and Social Psychology* (**44**:157–174, 1949).

Whorf, Benjamin L. (edited by J. B. Carroll). *Language, Thought and Reality.* New York: John Wiley and Sons, Inc., 1956.

Willey, Malcolm K. *The Country Newspapers.* Chapel Hill, N.C.: University of North Carolina Press, 1926.

Willner, A. E., and Willard E. Reitz. "Association, Abstraction, and the Conceptual Organization of Recall: Implications for Clinical Tests," *Journal of Abnormal Psychology* (**71:**315–327, 1966).

Wohlstetter, Roberta. *Pearl Harbor: Warning and Decision.* Stanford, Calif.: Stanford University Press, 1962.

Wolberg, Lewis R. *The Technique of Psychotherapy.* New York: Grune and Stratton, 1964.

Wolfenstein, Martha, and Nathan C. Leites. "An Analysis of Themes and Plots," *Annals of The American Academy of Political and Social Science* (**254:**41–48, 1947).

Wolfenstein, Martha, and Nathan Leites. *Movies: A Psychological Study.* Glencoe, Ill.: The Free Press, 1950.

The World Almanac, 1965

Wright, Charles R. "Cultural Content of American Mass Communications," in Charles R. Wright, *Mass Communications: A Sociological Perspective,* Chapter Four. New York: Random House (75–89, 1959).

Wright, Quincy, and Carl J. Nelson. "American Attitudes Toward Japan and China," *Public Opinion Quarterly* (**3:**46–62, 1939).

Wright, Sewell. "The Roles of Mutation, Inbreeding, Crossbreeding and Selection in Evolution." *Proceedings VI International Congress on Genetics* (**1:**356–366, 1932).

Yule, G. Udny. *The Statistical Study of Literary Vocabulary.* London: Cambridge University Press, 1944.

Yngve, Victor. "A Model and an Hypothesis for Language Structure," *Proceedings of American Philosophical Society* (No. 104, 444–466, 1961).

Zaninovich, M. George. "Pattern Analysis of Variables Within the International System: The Sino-Soviet Example," *Journal of Conflict Resolution* (**6:**253–268, 1962).

Zinnes, Dina A., Robert C. North, and Howard E. Koch, Jr., "Capability, Threat, and Outbreak of War," in James N. Rosenau (ed.), *International Politics and Foreign Policy.* New York: The Free Press of Glencoe, 1961.

Zinnes, Dina A. "Hostility in International Decision-Making," *Journal of Conflict Resolution* (**9:**236–243, 1962).

Zinnes, Dina A. "A Comparison of Hostile Behavior of Decision-Makers in Simulate and Historical Data," *World Politics,* 1966.

Zipf, George K. *Human Behavior and the Principle of Least Effort.* Cambridge, Mass.: Addison-Wesley, 1949.

Zwicky, Arnold W., Joyce Friedman, Barbara C. Hall, and Donald E. Walker. "The MITRE Syntactic Analysis of Transformational Grammars." *AFIPS Conference Proceedings* (**27, 1:**317–326, 1965).

Name Index

Names in brackets refer to author listed first in references.

Subject Index